S0-BOB-810

SELECTED WRITINGS OF LEWIS HANKE ON THE HISTORY OF LATIN AMERICA

In Memoriam

Isaac Joslin Cox

(1873-1956)

Clarence Henry Haring

(1885-1960)

PRELIMINARY REMARKS

More than fifty years have passed since I first started to study Spanish in Piqua High School, in a small Ohio town, and to fall under the spell of Spain and Latin America. Later in my undergraduate days at Northwestern University and at Harvard University Graduate School I was fortunate enough to study with two of our pioneer scholars who helped to build solid foundations for the development of Latin American history in the United States. I dedicate this volume to Isaac Joslin Cox and Clarence Henry Haring in recognition of how much we owe to these precursors, whose quiet work over the years helped to make possible the present relatively developed state of the field.

My aim in selecting studies for inclusion here has been to provide a representative collection of my writings. No one will be surprised to find material on the struggle for justice, Las Casas, or the Villa Imperial de Potosí. More general themes are included also: Brazilian history, how to teach Latin American history, microfilm developments, historical films, mestizaje, and the relationship of our field to European history. Those of my colleagues and students who think of me as a "colonialist" will perhaps be amused--I was, myself--to find a large section on "Contemporary Affairs." But this simply illustrates the fact that sometimes the past is also contemporary, especially in Latin America.

The footnotes, sometimes originally rather extensive, have been omitted, and those who wish to examine the underpinnings of my work should consult the original publications. In a few cases, articles have been shortened. Although some duplication still remains, this is inevitable when one treats large themes. Within each section the material is presented chronologically, so that readers may see how my interpretations evolved, although I am not aware of having made any dramatic changes through the years.

Finally, I am grateful to the various publishers who have authorized the reprinting of this material, and to all the editors and others who have helped to make possible this volume--especially my wife Kate, Pauline Collins, and Drucilla Jaffe.

L.H.

University of Massachusetts, Amherst
February, 1977

CONTENTS

PART I

THE STRUGGLE FOR JUSTICE IN THE CONQUEST OF AMERICA

CHAPTER 1.

THE REQUIREMENT AND ITS INTERPRETERS

Las Casas confessed that he could not decide whether to laugh or to weep as he read the terms of the Requirement, that document which Spain used during the early years of the conquest to justify waging war against the Indians, nor is it easy today to interpret it.

This article was published by Silvio Zavala, the Mexican historian, who had just obtained authorization to establish the Revista de historia de América under the auspices of the Pan American Institute of Geography and History. Eager to get the enterprise under way, he decided to bring out issue No. 1 as soon as possible and asked me to send him something by return mail. I happened to have this little study ready, so it was included in the first slim number of the Revista, along with contributions by Rafael Altamira and Zavala.

At the beginning of the article stood the following quotation (from Henri Berr and Lucien Febvre, "History and Historiography," Encyclopedia of the Social Sciences, VII 367), an appropriate warning for everyone concerned with the many controversial topics in Latin American history included in this volume:

> The study of human societies is not only of an almost inconceivable diversity and multiplication of aspects but is of such a nature that no man, however balanced he may be, however determined to maintain himself on the line of strict impartiality, can ever escape from the thousand biases created in him by the many particular acquired or inherited traits of his personal nature. Nor can he avoid the influence of his own theoretical ideas concerning the relative value and the comparative role of the various factors economic or religious in the evolution of societies; or the secret influence exercised upon him without his knowing it by his nationality, his religion, his social position, his avowed or unconscious affinities with, for example, the bourgeoise or the working class; not to mention the subtle and profound influences emanating from his historical environment, each one of them reflecting on to him in its way the general life of his time.

If these distinguished historians were writing today, would they not hasten to explain that man is a generic term (and so accepted even by some theologians), since women as well as men are writing history?

Revista de historia de América, No. 1 (Mexico City, 1938), 25-34.
Reprinted by permission.

The Requirement and Its Interpreters

The good faith of a nation is bound to be questioned when it invokes moral sanctions for its actions, whether the question involved is a world war debt, the status of the Japanese army marching against China under the official label "The Jehol Pacification Expeditionary Force," or a "just war" waged by Spaniards in sixteenth century America. It was not to be expected that foreign nations would interpret sympathetically the Requerimiento, that curious document by which Spain justified to herself the wars waged against the natives during the early years of the conquest of America.

This was the manifesto which the conquistadores were ordered by the crown to have read to the Indians by an escribano (notary) before hostilities could be legally opened:

> On the part of the King, Don Fernando, and of Doña Juana, his daughter, Queen of Castille and León, subduers of the barbarous nations, we their servants notify and make known to you, as best we can, that the Lord our God, Living and Eternal, created the Heaven and the Earth, and one man and one woman, of whom you and I, and all the men of the world, were and are descendants, and all those who come after us. But, on account of the multitude which has sprung from this man and woman in the five thousand years since the world was created, it was necessary that some men should go one way and some another, and that they should be divided into many kingdoms and provinces, for in one alone they could not be sustained.
>
> Of all these nations God our Lord gave charge to one man, called St. Peter, that he should be Lord and Superior of all the men in the world, that all should obey him, and that he should be head of the whole human race, wherever men should live, and under whatever law, sect, or belief they should be; and he gave him the world for his kingdom and jurisdiction.
>
> And he commanded him to place his seat in Rome, as the spot most fitting to rule the world from; but also he permitted him to have his seat in any other part of the world, and to judge and govern all Christians, Moors, Jews, Gentiles, and all other sects. This man was called Pope, as if to say, Admirable Great Father and Governor of men. The men who lived in that time obeyed that St. Peter, and took him for Lord, King, and Superior of the universe; so also have they regarded the others who after him have been elected to the Pontificate, and so it has been continued even until now, and will continue until the end of the world.
>
> One of these Pontiffs, who succeeded that St. Peter as Lord of the world, in the dignity and seat which I have before mentioned, made donation of these isles and Terra-firme to the aforesaid King and Queen and to their successors, our lords, with all that there are in these territories, as is contained in certain writings which passed upon the subject as aforesaid, which you can see if you wish.
>
> So their Highnesses are kings and lords of these islands and land of Terra-firme by virtue of this donation; and some islands, and indeed almost all those to whom this has been notified, have received and served their Highnesses, as lords and kings, in the

way that subjects ought to do, with good will, without any resistance, immediately, without delay, when they were informed of the aforesaid facts. And also they received and obeyed the priests whom their Highnesses sent to preach to them and to teach them our Holy Faith; and all these, of their own free will, without any reward or condition, have become Christians, and are so, and their Highnesses have joyfully and benignantly received them, and also have commanded them to be treated as their subjects and vassals; and you too are held and obliged to do the same. Therefore as best we can, we ask and require you that you consider what we have said to you, and that you take the time that shall be necessary to understand and deliberate upon it, and that you acknowledge the Church as the Ruler and Superior of the whole world and the high priest called Pope, and in his name the King and Queen Doña Juana our lords, in his place, as superiors and lords and kings of these islands and this Terra-firme by virtue of the said donation, and that you consent and give place that these religious fathers should declare and preach to you the aforesaid.

If you do so, you will do well, and that which you are obliged to do to their Highnesses, and we in their name shall receive you in all love and charity, and shall leave you your wives, and your children, and your lands, free without servitude, that you may do with them and with yourselves freely that which you like and think best, and they shall not compel you to turn Christians, unless you yourselves, when informed of the truth, should wish to be converted to our Holy Catholic Faith, as almost all the inhabitants of the rest of the islands have done. And besides this, their Highnesses award you many privileges and exceptions and will grant you many benefits.

But if you do not do this, and wickedly and intentionally delay to do so, I certify to you that, with the help of God, we shall forcibly enter into your country and shall make war against you in all ways and manners that we can, and shall subject you to the yoke and obedience of the Church and of their Highnesses; we shall take you and your wives and your children, and shall make slaves of them, and as such shall sell and dispose of them as their Highnesses may command; and we shall take away your goods, and shall do all the harm and damage that we can, as to vassals who do not obey, and refuse to receive their lord, and resist and contradict him; and we protest that the deaths and losses which shall accrue from this are your fault, and not that of their Highnesses, or ours, nor of these cavaliers who come with us. And that we have said this to you and made this Requisition, we request the notary here present to give us his testimony in writing, and we ask the rest who are present that they should be witnesses of this Requisition.

Having promulgated the Requerimiento in due form the Spanish captain sent the official report back to Spain with the necessary signatures and his conscience was clear. Certainly this remarkable proclamation offers many vulnerable spots to the barbs of cynics, and the use made of it by the Spaniards affords consummate proof of the hypocritical religiosity in the Spanish character to persons who already see it there.

The Requerimiento has naturally attracted the attention of most students of the Spanish conquest of America, and has been interpreted by many persons during the four centuries since it was first read to the wondering Indians of the new world. Sir Walter Raleigh, eager to see England supplant Spain in America, treats of it in an interesting passage in his History of the World (1600) where he seriously considers, controverts and, to his own satisfaction, refutes its theological assumptions. Raleigh even contemplated sending broadcast through the Inca empire a sort of counter-Requerimiento, for he suggested that, in his own words,

> The Bartol: de las Casas booke of the Spanish crueltyes with fayr pictures or at least a large table of pictures expressing the particularityes of the crueltyes there specified (neatly wrought for the better credite of our workmanship, and their easier understanding) would be sent to the Inga, and his Cassiques by some interpreters, that they may publish them among their vassals, and to all the estates of the confining countryes rounde about that thei may bee all (as much as is possible) conjoyntly linked, and exasperated against the Spaniards. And by informing them that the Spaniards doe holde their religion of the Pope, the great inchantor or cousner, and troubler of the world, who sent them first to invade those countryes, who teacheth them to breake all fayth, promises, oathes, covenantes with all such as bee not of their owne religion, so farr forth as may serve his and their turne, who giveth his followers dispensacions to steale, robb, rebell and murthers; and likewise pardoneth for many whatsoever wrongs or villanyes are by them committed.

In the eighteenth century rationalist philosophers seized upon the Requerimiento with enthusiasm, citing it as evidence of the all-pervading folly of human nature. As Corneille de Pauw stated, "the discovery of a new world which changed the face of the universe, which plucked astronomy, geography, and physics out of the profound darkness which enveloped them, was accompanied by circumstances extremely bizarre and ridiculous as a result of the fatality attached to the action of man". The Scottish historian William Robertson, however, far from ridiculing the Requerimiento, treated it seriously and translated it for the benefit of his readers because he considered it "so extraordinary in its nature and [because it] gives us such an idea of the proceedings of the Spaniards, and the principles upon which they founded the right to the extensive dominion which they acquired in the new world". The Italian priest, Giovanni Nuix, who composed one of the most interesting and most erroneous apologetics on the España defendida theme entitled "Riflessioni imparziali sopra l'umanità degli Spagnuoli nell' India . . .per servire di lume alle Storie de . . .Raynal e Robertson," solved the problem of the Requerimiento very easily. He declared it to have been drawn up by an obscure jurist who did not represent truly the theories prevailing at the time of the conquest and furthermore asserted that it had never received the approbation of the king or council, and that it was never actually proclaimed in America.

Modern historians, too, have usually interpreted this theological document in a derisive or ironical spirit. Even Sir Arthur Helps described the Requerimiento as "an illustration of how long foolish conceits linger in the halls of learning and among professions, even when they are beginning to be banished from the world at large," and, he confessed, "the comicality of the document has often cheered me in the midst of the tedious research or endless details of small battles. The logic, the history, even the grammatical construction are all, it seems to me, alike in error". To Hubert Howe Bancroft, indefatigable compiler of valuable historical materials, the Requerimiento "was no less void in practice than absurd in theory". A contemporary student of the Spanish Empire, Mr. Philip A. Means, has delivered a more sarcastic judgment.

Spaniards themselves, when describing this document, have often become confused and evidently find themselves in the same dilemma as did Las Casas, who confessed that on reading the Requerimiento, he could not decide whether to laugh or to weep. After devoting a whole chapter of his Historia de las Indias to a thoroughgoing criticism of the Requerimiento on practical as well as on theoretical grounds, he concluded by roundly condemning it as "injusto, impío, escandaloso, irracional y absurdo". The Argentinian, Juan B. Terán, one of the many modern students who have attempted to present the ideology of the Spanish conquest, believes that the Requerimiento was a fundamentals ordinance of the conquest, but considers its application an expressive example of the impractical idealism of the laws of the Indies.

Heretofore, students of the Requerimiento have almost invariably condemned it, for one reason or another and substantially agreed with Louis Bertrand and Sir Charles Petrie, authors of the latest attempt to compress the history of Spain into one volume, who state that "the invaders brandished Bulls and theological texts, a whole rubbish heap of documents, by way of justifying their invasion." But the examination of all the material available today, published and unpublished, leads one to the definite conclusion that something still remains to be said for the sixteenth century Spanish viewpoint, not as justification, but as explanation. The amusing picture conjured up by Mr. Means of a shuffling friar giving off a "long winded theological discourse" full of "the more absurd sacerdotal dogmas of his day" must be supplemented by a glimpse of the men in Spain whose minds devised this extraordinary document.

The student who would fully comprehend the Requerimiento must consider the controversy in Spain which led to its formulation and must review the many interesting situations which arose when the Indians were confronted with a Spanish notary or friar, mumbling his long sentences full of medieval theology. Moreover, as the conquest proceeded, the Requerimiento was supplanted by other regulations, less bizarre, but likewise fashioned in the same general mould. A study of these subsequent rules for "just war" will reveal how universal was the desire of the sixteenth century Spaniards to open up the new continent by methods derived from their religious and cultural heritage and which would be justifiable to their own consciences. If studied in this way, the Requerimiento becomes more than a ridiculous collection of outworn dogmas, and its history illumines one important facet of that many-sided problem--the Spanish conquest of America.

CHAPTER 2.

THE DEVELOPMENT OF REGULATIONS FOR CONQUISTADORES

During my first visit to Buenos Aires in 1935 I met Emilio Ravignani, the Director of the Instituto de Investigaciones Históricas of the Universidad de Buenos Aires. His rigorous editing of the Boletín of the Instituto, his leadership in establishing history as a respected discipline in Argentine university circles, and his own solid historical publications had made him one of the truly outstanding figures among Latin American historians of the twentieth century. I have always been grateful to him for the encouragement he gave me to continue work on Las Casas, and for his other wise advice over a period of years.

Thus when his Argentine colleagues decided to honor him by a volume of essays, I was pleased to be invited to participate. My contribution was the following study of the regulations devised to govern conquistadores, a story closely connected with the previous article on the Requerimiento. The following quotation prefaced the article:

> Por justas causas y consideraciones conviene, que en todas las capitulaciones que se hicieren para nuevos descubrimientos, se escuse esta palabra conquista, y en su lugar se use de las de pacificación y población, pues haviendose de hacer con toda paz y caridad, es nuestra voluntad que aun este nombre, interpretado contra nuestra intención no ocasione ni de color a lo capitulado para que se pueda hacer fuerza ni agravio a los Indios.

(Item 29 of Law on Discoveries and Pacification dated July 13, 1573, Recopilación de leyes de los reynos de las Indias, lib. IV, tít. I, ley VI)

Homenaje al Doctor Emilio Ravignani. Contribuciones para el estudio de la historia de América (Buenos Aires: Editorial Peuser, 1941), 71-88. Reprinted by permission.

The Development of Regulations for Conquistadores

No more curious document pertaining to the Spanish conquest of the New World has ever been found than the Requerimiento, that theological proclamation by which Spain justified to herself the wars waged against the natives during the early years of the conquest. Having promulgated the Requerimiento in due form, the Spanish captain sent the official report back to Spain with the necessary signatures and his conscience was clear.

The ordinance of November 17, 1526, by which the Requerimiento became at last mandatory for all conquistadores to read before warring on the Indians was devised only after a strenuous battle before the newly organized Council of the Indies. President García de Loaisa, moved by the clamors of those who thought the conquest was not proceeding according to Christian principles, ordered the council to hold a special session in the Alhambra over which the Emperor himself presided.

The lawyer Martín Fernández de Enciso, ever ready to defend what he considered royal rights, drew up a memorial embodying all the arguments presented earlier before the San Pablo friars in 1513. As for the opinion of "a doctor" who wrote that lands possessed by infidels cannot be taken from them without cause because they held their lands by the ius gentium, Enciso controverted him with the following line of reasoning. When God created the earth and everything upon it, he made man a rational being with the knowledge of the distinction between good and evil. Therefore, if these Indians in the new world are idolators, that alone constitutes sufficient cause to conquer them, for they are adoring many gods and do not know the true God who created them.

Enciso's arguments triumphed. For the "Ordinances on discoveries and good treatment of the Indians" which were speedily promulgated on November 17, 1526, ordered that when captains of the King discover or conquer a territory they are to proclaim immediately to its "Indians or inhabitants that they have been sent to teach them good customs, to dissuade them from vices such as the practice of eating human flesh, and to instruct them in the holy faith and preach it to them for their salvation." This decree further ordered that every leader of an expedition officially licensed to make discoveries in the Indies must take along a copy of the Requerimiento and have it read by interpreters "as many times as might be necessary." Furthermore, every expedition must carry at least two ecclesiastics approved by the Council of the Indies, as a regular part of their equipment. These ecclesiastics were to instruct the Indians in religious matters, protect the natives "from the rapacity and cruelty of the Spaniards" and in general to ensure that the conquest be carried out justly. The contract of any conquistador who waged a war which was unjust, in the opinion of the ecclesiastics attached to his expedition, was to be revoked. War was to be waged only after the ecclesiastics had given their consent in writing. Their sanction could only be given when the war was to be waged according to the method permitted by "the law, our Holy Faith and Christian religion".

Throughout the long wars by which Spain had slowly recovered herself from the Moslems, ecclesiastics had naturally come to assume a prominent and important position. In the camp, in the council chamber, their voices were heard and obeyed; for as the war aimed at the Christianization of Spain, it was proper that the ministers of the church should play a conspicuous part in matters which particularly concerned it. Hence it is not surprising to find prominent colonists taking the right of ecclesiastics to exert authority over soldiers so much for granted that they wrote from Mexico to the King early in 1526 to advise him not to permit any new conquests to be made unless friars accompanied and blessed the expedition. The royal ordinance which put this policy into effect remained as a standard for a generation and was never officially superseded by any other general law until Philip II issued his 1573 ordinance. Fortunate indeed for historians was the passage of the 1526 law. The ecclesiastics were intelligent observers and recorded their adventures and observations. Whether the occasion was the discovery of the Amazon, or a perilous descent into a smoking volcano of Central America, there was a friar and he often left to posterity interesting and well-nigh priceless descriptions of his experience.

It will be noticed that this 1526 law did not include any new and startling provisions but standardized previous theory and practice. Ecclesiastics had accompanied most of the previous expeditions and Bernal Díaz records that he and his companions in 1517 specifically requested that a priest be carried on their voyage to Yucatán in order that "it should proceed on just principles". Dominicans were ordered to accompany Diego Cavallero on the trading expedition he proposed to make in 1525 to Cabo de la Vela; they were to make sure that the Indians were well treated and not cheated in their business dealings with the Spaniards. This first important law governing conquests was made an integral part of every important capitulation for over twenty years and was even included in the contract Charles V signed in 1528 with the Welsers of Germany for the exploitation of the Santa Marta region.

The Emperor ordered by the New Laws of 1542, "that henceforth for no cause of war or any other cause whatsoever though it be under title of rebellion, nor by ransom nor in any other manner can an Indian be enslaved, and we will that the Indians be treated as our own vassals of the Crown of Castile, for such they are."

By this time the Requerimiento seems to have disappeared from the lawbooks, and the subsequent development of regulations for the exploration and settlement of America reveals a steady démarche from the arrogant demands of the Requerimiento. The "Royal letter to the kings and republics of the mid-way and western lands" dated May 1, 1543 breathes a conciliatory spirit entirely alien to that of the Requerimiento. The dubious papal history outlined in the Requerimiento was omitted and great stress was laid upon the spiritual duties of the kings of Spain resulting from their temporal overlordship. To fulfill these obligations, says the letter, the King is sending Bishop Juan de Zumárraga and other ecclesiastics to the mid-way and western lands. Perhaps because of the influence of Las Casas and other Indian champions then present at the Court of Spain, no mention is made of dire punishments to follow if the native kings do not receive the missionaries properly. Indeed, the whole message is couched in such brotherly and friendly language that the possibility of a refusal is not even touched upon.

Likewise, President Pedro de la Gasca omitted the Requerimiento in his 1548 instructions to Captain Diego Centeno on conquests in the Río de la Plata region and those given June 18, 1549 to Captain Juan Nuñez de Prado for the pacification of Tucumán. Ecclesiastics were to accompany both expeditions and were to be consulted on all important matters. The captains were particularly ordered to explain to the Indians that the Spaniards' chief aim was to teach them Christianity and good habits.

Although the letter to the "kings of the mid-way and western lands" and the La Gasca instructions exhibit a wholly new spirit, Las

Casas and other reformers were pressing for a wholesale revision of the 1526 law. The respectful attention given to the venerable Bishop of Chiapa by the Council of the Indies during 1549-1551 is formidable testimony to the power of his mind and person. Fresh from triumphant spiritual conquests in the land known as Vera Paz (True Peace) where the Dominicans had won over a province of fierce Indians in Guatemala by using peaceful methods alone, Las Casas argued before the Council of the Indies that no more conquests should be authorized until a junta of theologians could determine whether such conquests were just and could devise a law for the guidance of future conquistadores which would better protect the Indians against ill treatment. On July 3, 1549, the Council of the Indies formally advised the King that such action be taken, and in December of the same year a royal order made known this remarkable decision to officials in the Indies.

Probably in no other colonizing nation but Spain could such an order ever have been given, or been followed in all seriousness by a long, involved discussion in which some of the foremost contemporary jurists and theologians of the land challenged or defended the justice of their own national conquests. Critics of national policy are to be found in every country, but rarely, if ever, are they given the respectful hearing accorded Las Casas in the Valladolid juntas of 1550 and 1551. Although the theologians wrangled long and hard, no general law resulted. . .

It may be said at once, however, that the ideas of the Requerimiento did not triumph. No such theology or uncompromising legalism appears in the capitulation made with Jaime Rasquín on December 30, 1557 concerning the La Plata region, or in the royal instruction to the New Granada Audiencia regulating new settlements dated July 15, 1559. According to this instruction, the Indians were to be favored and assisted in all possible ways, but Spaniards might use force to defend themselves or to punish Indians who impeded the preaching of Christianity. A reward of ten years' exemption from tribute was held out to those natives who should peacefully accept Christianity and the sovereignty of the King of Spain.

Requerimiento ideas did not die out entirely, for in 1557, Dr. Pedro de Santander declared:

> Florida is the land promised by the Eternal Father to the faithful, and we are commanded by God in the Holy Scriptures to take it from them, and by reason of their idolatry and sin to put them all to the knife, leaving no living thing save maidens and children, their cities robbed and sacked, their houses and walls levelled to the earth.

Philip II, however, ordered the colonization to be carried out in a far different spirit and, after much deliberation, entrusted the supervision of the settlement of Florida to the Viceroy of Mexico, Luis de Velasco. This great Viceroy, whose rule deserves more careful investigation than has been given it, was able to satisfy even the Dominicans, for, as Friar Pedro de Feria stated, Velasco

> treated this matter in a most Christian way, with much wisdom and counsel, insisting strenuously on their understanding that they did not go to conquer those nations, nor to do what has been done in the discovery of the Indies, but to settle and by good example, with good works and with presents, to bring the natives to a knowledge of our Holy Faith and Catholic truth.

The Viceroy Conde de Nieva in Peru went even further in his instructions of 1561 to discoverers and colonizers. Besides showing the friendly attitude prescribed above, the Spaniards were instructed to take along "mirrors, knives, combs, needles, and bonnets to give to the Indians if it be convenient".

Nor was this "truly Christian spirit" to be reserved for use in Florida alone. Essentially the same motives appear to have directed Philip, when he issued on August 16, 1563 to President Ramírez de Quiñones of the Audiencia of La Plata the "Order which is to be observed in making new discoveries and settlements". As in the New Granada law of 1549, colonists were to make every effort to settle peacefully. Indians accepting Christianity and Spanish rule in a like spirit were to be granted a ten-year exemption from tribute. Natives who sought to impede the preaching of the Faith could be punished. However,

> If the natives attempt to prevent the Spaniards settling, they are to be made to understand that the colonists come there with no intention of harming them or taking their farms, but rather to gain their friendship and to teach them to live politically and to know God, explaining to them the law of Jesus Christ by which they will be saved. And this admonition is to be made three times in accordance with the opinion of the ecclesiastics who were named to accompany the expedition. If the natives still maintain their opposition, the Spaniards are to proceed to make the settlement, doing no more harm to the Indians than may be necessary. . .
>
> If, after being required many times to allow the ecclesiastics to enter and declare the word of God, the natives refuse to allow the missionaries to enter their province, the Spaniards may enter the province by the force of arms, in order to compel them to do so and to subject them and bring them to our obedience.

The various laws described above were all superseded by a general ordinance promulgated by Philip II on July 13, 1573, which was designed to regulate all future discoveries and pacifications by land or by sea. A detailed study of the provisions of this ordinance indicated how the King had departed from the <u>Requerimiento</u> policy for the Spaniards are to explain the obligation resting upon the crown of Spain and the wonderful advantages bestowed upon those natives who have already submitted --a sort of justification by works. The Spaniards are charged with emphasizing particularly:

> that the king has sent ecclesiastics who have taught the Indians the Christian doctrine and faith by which they could be saved. Moreover, the king has established justice in such a way that no one may aggravate another. The king has maintained the peace so that there are no killings or sacrifices, as was the custom in some parts. He has made it possible for the Indians to go safely be all roads and to peacefully carry on their civil pursuits. He has freed them from burdens and servitude; he has made known to them the use of bread, wine, oil and many other foods, woolen cloth, silk, linen, horses, cows, tools, arms and many other things from Spain; he has instructed them in crafts and trades by which they live excellently. All these advantages will those Indians enjoy who embrace our Holy Faith and render obedience to our king.

To avoid all possibility of misunderstanding, the law decreed particularly that the word "conquest" should no longer be used but the term "pacification". The vices of the Indians were to be dealt with very gently at first so as not to scandalize them or prejudice them against Christianity. If, after all the explanations, natives still opposed a Spanish settlement and the preaching of Christianity, the Spaniards might use force, but must do as little harm as possible. No license was given to enslave the captives. This general order governed conquests until the end of the colonial period.

A few years later, Philip II dispatched a group of Augustinian friars to call upon the pagan king of China. In a letter dated June 11, 1580, Philip addressed the Emperor Wan-li as "poderoso y muy estimado Rey de la China" and said that he had heard much from his governors and friars concerning the prudence and justice with which the Emperor was governing his great kingdom. The friars who carried the letter had come to explain to him their Holy Faith and the true path by which all souls might be saved. Philip "very affectionately" requested the Emperor to hear them and to believe their message. In choosing this policy of peace, Philip had flatly rejected the enthusiatic proposal made by Dr. Sande on June 7, 1576 to wage just war against the Chinese, whom he described as "vile people, heathens, tyrants and sodomites". Moreover, Dr. Sande continued,

> War with this nation would be most just, for it would give freedom to poor, wretched people whose children are ravished by strangers, and whom judges, rulers and king treat with unheard-of tyranny. . . Moreover, a war could be waged against them because they prohibit people from entering their country. Besides, I do not know, nor have I heard of, any wickedness that they do not practice; for they are idolators, sodomites, robbers and pirates, both by land and sea. And in fact the sea, which ought to be free according to the law of nations, is not so, as far as the Chinese are concerned; for whosoever navigates within their reach is killed and robbed, if they can do it.

Yet Philip rejected this proposal and replied that Spaniards should treat the people of China in a friendly fashion.

Nor did Philip's amiability exhaust itself in polite and diplomatic phrases. Four oil paintings, especially made by the court painter, Alonso Sánchez Coello, accompanied the friars to China as testimony of the esteem in which the Christian King of Spain held the Buddhist Emperor of China. Appropriately enough, one of the paintings represented "Nuestra Señora de la Concepción," another showed Charles V in his imperial glory and two were of Philip himself, afoot and on horseback. Besides these paintings, a vast array of costly presents was collected from all parts of Spain and Mexico and despatched to the Emperor of China, as may be seen in the following sections from the official inventories:

> Watches, large and small, for the King and his Governors.
> Beds of diverse colors, one of crimson with a brocaded canopy, another of green and gold, candles of green and gold and the third orange with turquoise blue trimmings.
> Half a dozen coats of armor with designs engraved thereon.
> A picture of the Queen.
> A pair of the king's suits for the King of China.
> Four pipes of good wine.
> Bonnets and hats (two dozen of each).
> Laced buskins of various colors.
> A box of Venetian glass ware.

Unfortunately, no reply has come to light describing the impression this varied assortment of gifts made upon the Emperor of China and whether they facilitated the preaching of the Faith. But it is possible that these solid proofs of the complete abandonment of the Spanish Requerimiento policy may even now be gathering dust in some Chinese palace as yet untouched by the ravages of the Japanese "Army of Pacification". . .

CHAPTER 3.

THE DAWN OF CONSCIENCE IN AMERICA: SPANISH EXPERIMENTS AND EXPERIENCES WITH INDIANS IN THE NEW WORLD

Comparative history has become very popular in recent years, and one of the most discussed subjects is racial relations. A vigorous movement is under way to re-study and re-evaluate the attitudes of the various European peoples to Negroes and Indians in America. The American Philosophical Society, in its 1962 annual meeting, cast an even wider net in its Symposium on "Our Contacts with American Indians, Polynesians, and Africans." Spanish experience of course was involved, which gave me an opportunity to look at the subject in a broad, comparative way.

Proceedings of the American Philosophical Society, Vol. 107, No. 2 (Philadelphia, 1963), 83-92. Reprinted by permission.

The Dawn of Conscience in America: Spanish Experiments and Experiences with Indians in the New World

The image many English-speaking people have of Spanish action in America is one of almost unrelieved cruelty to the Indians, and many unfavorable judgments have been made on Spanish action in the New World in comparison with English colonization. Spaniards naturally resented these judgments and a "war of the myths" has resulted. One myth makes the Spaniards the heroes, the English the villains, and the Indians the victims and the opposing myth makes the Spaniards into villains, the English into heroes, but still casts the Indians in the role of victims. My aim is to present some relatively little-known aspects of Spanish-Indian relations, not to present a well-rounded comparison of European colonial practices, and certainly not to engage in the war of the myths.

All European explorers and colonists who came to the New World encountered native peoples. But only the Spaniards met so many millions of natives, whom they called Indians, in the vast stretches of their empire which eventually reached from California to Patagonia. The very fact of large numbers of natives settled under the control of the Aztec, Inca, and Maya empires required the Spaniards to devise a different method of treating them from that worked out by the English, French, and Portuguese for the largely nomadic and much smaller number of natives they found sparsely scattered in their territories.

The enormous area in which contacts occurred between Spaniards and Indians was another circumstance peculiar to the Spanish empire. The English and the Portuguese, for at least a hundred years after their first settlements, clung to narrow coastal strips. Though the French roamed far and wide in Canada they established few towns of any size. Spaniards, on the other hand, were not only in the forefront of the explosive geographical expansion following Columbus, when Europeans discovered "more territory in seventy-five years than in the previous thousand" but they also organized urban centers in many parts of their great domain. In less than a century after 1492 the Spanish urban tradition had been so successfully implanted in America that many organized towns flourished: the viceregal capitals at Mexico City and Lima, mining centers such as Guanajuato in Mexico and Potosí in upper Peru, Asunción in the middle of South America, Buenos Aires, Santiago de Chile, Quito, Bogotá, Caracas, Havana, Guatemala City, and far across the Pacific, Manila in the Philippine Islands. In Mexico alone, in the fifty years after the landing of Ferdinand Cortez in 1519, "a territory that could contain thirty or forty Iberian peninsulas had been claimed, and much of it settled, by a few thousand men."

In the effort to govern the mass of Indians in their great empire the Spaniards adapted some institutions from their own medieval experience of long fighting against the Moslems and created others to meet the needs of New World conditions. The determination of the crown and the church to Christianize the Indians, the imperious demand of Spaniards for labor forces to exploit the new lands for revenue for the Crown and for themselves, and the attempts of some Spaniards to protect the Indians resulted in a very remarkable complex of relations, laws, and institutions which even today leads historians to contradictory conclusions on the reality of Spanish rule in America. The encomienda system, by which groups of Indians were assigned to Spaniards, a device to provide both labor and goods to the Spaniard and protection and religious instruction for the Indians, was both stoutly defended as necessary and bitterly attacked as un-Christian throughout the sixteenth century by Spaniards themselves. The Spanish imperial policy of attempting to civilize the Indians by urbanizing them led to many curious experiments and experiences, and in the end was fatal for large numbers of natives. George Kubler has pointed out in his substantial work on Mexican architecture:

> No building could be achieved without the prior urbanization of the participants. To urbanize the Indian populations was to dislocate and destroy the patterns of indigenous culture. Such cultural extirpation brought about, in turn, the biological decrease of the Indian race. . . Each building, and each colonial artifact, was nourished by the destruction of a culture and the decline of a race.

Spain made many efforts to mitigate the lot of the Indians by appointing official "Protectors," setting up special courts to try cases involving them, and sending out numerous investigating groups to discover what might be done to help them. She tried many stratagems in the sixteenth century particularly to ensure that Indians would be brought under Spanish rule by peaceful means alone, and be persuaded to accept Christianity by reason instead of by force. To achieve this end the Dominican Bartolomé de Las Casas and his brother Dominicans attempted to preach the faith without the backing of the sword in Chiapas, and Vasco de Quiroga established his Utopian communities in Michoacán. In many places a system of Indian segregation was worked out by friars and royal officials to protect them from other Spaniards who would exploit them, and this practice was followed throughout the colonial period, culminating in the famous Jesuit missions in eighteenth-century Paraguay. The difficult, indeed impossible, double purpose of the crown to secure revenue and also to Christianize the Indians inevitably led in fact to a series of angry disputes, evil compromises, and some glorious episodes throughout the more than three centuries of Spanish rule in America.

Today, as we look back on the total encounter of Spaniards and Indians, two developments hold special interest for us, living as we do in a world society whose multiplicity and variety of cultures become daily more evident and more significant. For the first time in history one people--the Spaniards--paid serious attention to the nature of the culture of the peoples they met; and, perhaps most striking of all, the controversies which developed in sixteenth-century Spain and America over the just method of treating the Indians led to a fundamental consideration of the nature of man himself. This "dawn of conscience in America" was only a faint daybreak; indeed, who can say that in the twentieth century we have reached high noon? The fact that we are still struggling ourselves to discover how to live justly in a world of many races and many cultures gives the Spanish struggles of the sixteenth century a poignant and familiar ring.

Why did Spaniards, expecially friars, desire so intensely to learn Indian languages and study Indian cultures? The most compelling reason, of course, was that only by speaking the languages of the Indians could the friars speak to their hearts to acquaint them with Christian doctrine. This linguistic effort severely challenged the Spaniards, because they had to deal with a large variety of Indian tribes of widely differing speech in their onward rush through the New World. As Norman McQuown has recently stated:

> This area is in all probability unmatched, anywhere in the world, in its linguistic multiplicity and diversity. A couple of thousand languages and dialects, at present divided into 17 large families and 38 small ones, with several hundred unclassified single languages, are on record. In one small portion of the area, in Mexico just north of the Isthmus of Tehuántepec, one finds a diversity of linguistic types hard to match on an entire continent in the Old World.

Despite this variety Spaniards made real progress in mastering the Indian languages, and compiled so many dictionaries and grammars that simply to record them bibliographically requires a large volume. The Library of the American Philosophical Society, as befits an institution that has long maintained scholarly relations with Latin America, possesses an excellent collection of these linguistic works. The friars largely responsible for preparing them as instruments for their work of Indian conversion had as their guide the famous Gramática castellana of Antonio de Nebrija, who had published this first grammar of any modern European language in the year Columbus set sail. When Queen Isabella bluntly enquired: "What is it for?" the reply was: "Language, Your Majesty, is the perfect instrument of empire." With this Gramática in hand friars of several different orders set forth for America and used its rules in their attempt, sometimes in vain, to adapt the rules of a neo-Latin grammar to the intricacies of the Indian languages they knew they must master. Anthropologists and philologists today consider that the many grammars thus produced in the sixteenth century have only limited use for philological study. But the fervor with which friars tackled Indian languages, inspired by their master Nebrija, reminds one of the conviction of some machine-linguisticians today that language analysis and automation hold the golden key to our future communications.

Another reason for the intense dedication to the study of the Indian languages was the burning desire many felt to establish a New Jerusalem in America. Protestantism had shattered the unity of Christendom in Europe but many Spaniards yearned to accomplish in the New World a bright and shining spiritual conquest; many writers then and later pointed out that Luther and Cortez had been born in the same year, one to destroy Christian unity in Europe and the other to make possible a New World free from the religious dissensions which were splitting the Old World asunder. To achieve this dream the souls of the Indians must be won; this could be realized, they were convinced, since they believed Indians had souls like soft wax which could be molded so as to form true Christians, provided that the friars knew their languages, were familiar with their culture, and kept zealously to their work.

When doubts on the rationality of the Indians began to disturb the Spaniards, grammar played a part in the widespread debates on the nature of the Indians. In early years of the conquest Spanish officials conducted experiments in Cuba and in Hispaniola to determine whether the Indians could "live like Christian laborers in Castile." These first social experiments in America did not settle the question of the nature of the Indians. It was the Dominican Domingo de Santo Tomás who anannounced in his Gramática, o arte de la lengua general de los indios del Perú that his principal intention in offering the King his account of the beauty and intricacies of the Indian languages was that "Your Majesty might see how very false is the idea--as many would persuade Your Majesty--that the natives of Peru are barbarians." As Professor of Theology in the University of St. Mark in Lima, Friar Domingo continued to defend the rationality of the Indians against all comers.

In addition to languages, sixteenth-century Spaniards also studied Indian cultures and produced a copious literature which remains valuable for anthropological study today. Some of the conquistadores displayed the perfectly simple attitude of the English gentleman who, about 1900, spent some time among wild tribes in a foreign land and allegedly wrote a book about them on his return home. One chapter headed "Customs and Manners," consisted solely of these words: "Customs, beastly; manners, none." Benjamin Franklin perfectly described the ethnocentrism that has characterized the attitude of many people when he said: "Savages we call them, because their Manners differ from ours, which we think the Perfection of Civility: they think the same of ours."

Speculations on the origins of these newly discovered peoples gave rise to some curious theories: more than one grave Spanish historian considered them descendants of the lost tribes of Israel; that Quetzalcóatl, the Indian god who appears in the preconquest history of Mexico as a great civilizer, was actually Thomas Aquinas. Quetzalcóatl fascinated other writers too, for an eminent nineteenth-century anthropologist, Edward Tylor, who also held the theory that the lost tribes of Israel had somehow wandered to Mexico, believed as firmly that the Mexican god was a real man, and hinted that he may have been an Irishman.

It was the friars, looking for souls to win, rather than the conquistadores, who first began to study Indian customs, history, and religion. The missionaries needed to know the names and attributes of Indian gods, the sacrifices made to them, and as accurately as possible the mentality of the Indians in order to lead them away from their pagan rites toward Christianity. The founder of American anthropology was Friar Ramón Pané, who accompanied Columbus on his second voyage for the express purpose of observing the natives and reporting on their ways and who was the first European to learn an Indian language.

The Crown encouraged ecclesiastics throughout the sixteenth century to study the Indians, and numerous volumes on their cultures were in fact prepared. Administration officials such as Alonso de Zurita also compiled reports, and the questionnaires sent out regularly to all Spanish governors in the New World by the Council of the Indies included a number of items on Indians. The result of all this enquiry is a magnificent body of linguistic, archaeological, and ethnographical material which is both contradictory at times and difficult to assess because so much remains in manuscript and even the printed editions available are often poor, lacking indexes and proper notes.

A few samples of the well-prepared editions may be described briefly. Toribio de Motolinía's <u>History of the Indians of New Spain</u> was written at the order of the Franciscan chapter in Mexico which desired an account of the life and beliefs of the pre-Cortesian Indians and the missionary labors of the Franciscans since their arrival in 1524. Completed in 1541, this work includes not only the material requested by the Chapter but also information on rivalry between Dominicans, Augustinians, and Franciscans, some frank reports on oppression of the Indians by Spaniards, descriptions of Mexico City, and the condemnation of the avarice of the Spaniards. Though he was a declared enemy of Bartolomé de Las Casas who was notorious for his denunciations of Spanish cruelty to the Indians, Motolinía did not hesitate to condemn his fellow countrymen as bitterly as Las Casas and stated that Spaniards had killed so many Indians in and about the mines in Mexico that "for half a league around and for a great part of the way one could scarcely walk, except over dead bodies or over bones, and so numerous were the birds and the crows that came to feast on the dead bodies that they greatly obscured the sun."

Las Casas was another anthropologist and remarkable in that he did not assume that the Indians should be measured by a Spanish yardstick but must rather be understood within the framework of their own culture. He looked at all peoples, ancient Greeks and sixteenth-century Spaniards as well as the newly discovered New World natives, as human beings in different stages of development. He began to write his Apologetic History, in which he set forth his views in great detail, in 1527 while he was in a monastery in Hispaniola, deeply dejected by the failure of his project to colonize Venezuela by peaceful means. He completed it in time to use it in 1550 as a weapon against the Spanish Renaissance scholar Juan Ginés de Sepúlveda, who maintained that the Indians were "natural slaves" according to the dictum of Aristotle, so that their property and services could be commandeered by Spaniards and war could be justly waged against them. Las Casas opposed this doctrine as un-Christian, and advanced the idea, so astonishing to many Spaniards of his day, that the Indians compared very favorably with the peoples of ancient times, were eminently rational beings, and in fact fulfilled every one of Aristotle's own requirements for the good life. Throughout the Apologetic History, a wonderful mixture of fact and fantasy, Las Casas even advanced the thought that the Greeks and Romans were in several respects inferior to the Indians. The Indians were clearly more religious, for instance, because they offered more and better sacrifices to their gods than did any of the ancient peoples. The Mexican Indians were superior to the ancient peoples in rearing and educating their children. Their marriage arrangements were reasonable and conformed to natural law and the law of nations. Indian women were devout workers, even laboring with their hands if necessary to comply fully with divine law, a trait which Las Casas felt many Spanish matrons might well adopt. The Apologetic History thus had a political purpose, just as the Domingo de Santo Tomás Gramática was intended to demonstrate the rationality of the Indians, but it also contained much material on Indian culture. Despite the obvious defects and prejudices of Las Casas' work, anthropologists of our own time need be neither surprised nor embarrassed to find him in the company of their distinguished forerunners.

Another substantial work is the Franciscan Diego de Landa's Account of the Things of Yucatan, prepared about 1566. Though Landa tortured Indians in an effort to eradicate idolatry, and burned a large number of Indian books, his study contains information on "practically every phase of the social anthropology of the ancient Mayas" including the first accurate knowledge of their hieroglyphic writing and is especially complete on Indian religion. Landa obtained much help from a native informant, Juan Cocom, a practice used by most anthropologists today. He felt a strong desire to set down everything he could find out about Maya culture, even though he condemned some of the practices. He described the tropical storms that swept over Yucatan and gave a detailed account of the Maya's baptismal ceremonies, their plants, their impressive buildings, and their fear of death. He firmly believed that the Spanish conquest had highly benefited the Indians by bringing them Christianity and many material advantages but he also greatly admired certain parts of their culture--their calendar, food, architecture, some of their moral ideas and the beauty of their women.

The most complete and objective study of Indian culture made by a Spaniard was the General History of the Things of New Spain, by the Franciscan Bernardino de Sahagún, now being made available to English readers for the first time through the translation from the Aztec language being made by Charles E. Dibble and Arthur J. O. Anderson.

Sahagún was an able and attractive friar--in his early years in Mexico his superior kept him out of the pulpit because women had their minds distracted from religious matters when he preached--who began to collect materials on Aztec culture in 1547. Ten years later his provincial ordered him to prepare a history of Indian culture and he devoted the years 1558-1560 to the systematic questioning of a dozen of the oldest and most knowledgeable Indians he could find. They spent this period in the village of Tepepulco, with Sahagún conferring with the wise men through young Indian interpreters who had learned Latin and Spanish. He used a carefully prepared list of culture elements as the basis for his investigation, and the Indians drew many pictures to explain their history. During 1560-1561 he moved to Santiago Tlatelolco and checked his data by using a fresh set of informants. Then for three years he examined and re-examined his material, revised the complete manuscript, organized the mass of material into twelve books, each book into chapters, and each chapter into paragraphs. The result was a methodically arranged mass of carefully verified information on the gods worshiped by the Indians, their fiestas, ideas on immortality and death ceremonies, astrology, witch doctors, rhetoric and philosophy, lords and government, merchants and mechanical arts, vices and virtues, animals, birds, fishes, herbs, trees, fruits, and flowers, and on the conquest of Mexico as the Indians saw it.

Sahagún completed this enormous task in 1569, half a century after Cortez invaded Mexico, so that the Indian life he described had already been somewhat modified by Spanish influence. The work remains, however, the most important and indispensable single source for the study of Aztec culture. His technical methods, his sympathetic and yet realistic scrutiny of a culture so alien to his own, and his determination to find out exactly what the Indians thought set his study apart from all the other anthropological writings of sixteenth-century Spaniards.

Sahagún's investigations were opposed by some Franciscans who evidently considered them too expensive for a friar to undertake--even in the sixteenth century scholarship was expensive--or perhaps found it inappropriate for a Franciscan to spend time delving into the seamy aspects of Aztec life such as the numerous ways in which the Indians became ceremonially drunk. Sahagún defended his research by attacking Motolinía and others for their lack of "serpentine wisdom" in avoiding too deep a study of Indian culture lest it strengthen Indian loyalties to their ancient customs. Sahagún insisted that missionaries needed to know all the sins of the Indians in order to cure them, just as doctors must study diseases.

Anthropologists and historians today are becoming aware that the study of culture itself has a history, and that the way people look at cultures different from their own is itself an important subject for research. Ethnohistory is more and more accepted as a field of special importance to the understanding of the history of the Americas while they were under the domination of various European nations. When comparative studies of the institutions and ideas developed by Europeans in the Americas are more fully elaborated--through the stimulus and activities of such institutions as the John Carter Brown Library--it will be established, I believe, that the broadly based anthropological investigations made by Spaniards showed a valuable, even unique, approach to conquered peoples. For not only did many Spaniards scrutinize Indian cultures with a sympathetic and often realistic eye, but they also viewed them in the round, including data on disease and death, art and cooking, linguistic matters, child-bearing, and indeed practically all the significant elements that anthropologists identify today.

Closely linked with these anthropological studies and with Spain's struggle to work out a just Indian policy was the much disputed question of the nature of the Indians. The first twinge of official conscience was expressed by Ferdinand and Isabella in 1495 when they learned that a shipload of Indians Columbus had sent back from Hispaniola had been sold as slaves because they had been taken in rebellion. The monarchs thereupon instructed Bishop Fonseca, who managed Indian affairs, that the money from this sale should not be accepted until their Highnesses could inform themselves from men learned in law whether these Indians could be sold with good conscience. No document that I know of has recorded the answer the sovereigns requested. A dramatic public protest in America against Indian slavery was made by a Dominican friar named Antonio de Montesinos who in a revolutionary sermon preached in 1511 on the island of Hispaniola thundered: "Tell me, by what right or justice do you keep these Indians in cruel servitude? On what authority have you waged a detestable war against these people, who dwelt quietly and peacefully on their own land?. . . Are these not men? Have they not rational souls?" This sermon led to serious disputes and discussions in Spain, out of which came the 1512 Laws of Burgos to govern relations between Spaniards and Indians as well as juridical treatises on the basis for Spanish dominion in the New World.

The legalistic and religious nature of the Spaniards led both to their intense preoccupation with the just basis for their newly discovered overseas territory and with the nature of the Indians whom they were attempting to draw into the Christian world. Francisco de Vitoria, a Dominican professor at the University of Salamanca, discussed these matters with great vision and clarity in his lectures and many of his students later went to America with their attitudes determined by his teachings. Vitoria remarked in one treatise, De Indis: "The Indians are stupid only because they are uneducated and, if they live like beasts, so for the same reason do many Spanish peasants." He also asserted that discovery alone gave Spaniards no more right to American territory than the Indians would have acquired had they "discovered" Spain. Vitoria and other Spanish political theorists of the time addressed themselves to the fundamental legal questions raised when Europe invaded America and, long before Grotius, laid down an enduring basis for international law.

Most significant of all, the Spanish inquiry into the nature of the Indians and their capacity for entering into the Christian commonwealth led Spaniards to grapple with that ultimate problem--the nature of man himself. Of all the ideas churned up during the early tumultuous years of American history, none had more dramatic implications than the attempts made to apply to the natives there the Aristotelian doctrine of natural slavery: that one part of mankind is set aside by nature to be slaves in the service of masters born for a life of virtue free of manual labor. Learned authorities such as the Spanish scholar Sepúlveda not only sustained this view with great tenacity and erudition but also concluded, without having visited America, that the Indians were in fact such rude and brutal beings that war against them to make possible their forcible Christianization was not only expedient but lawful. Many ecclesiastics, especially Las Casas, opposed this idea scornfully, with appeals to divine and natural law as well as to their own experience in America. The controversy became so heated and the emperor's conscience so troubled over the question of how to carry on the conquest of the Indies in a Christian way that Charles V actually ordered the suspension of all expeditions to America while a junta of foremost theologians, jurists, and officials was convoked in the royal capital of Valladolid to listen to the arguments of Las Casas and Sepúlveda. All this occurred in 1550, after Cortez had conquered Mexico, Francisco Pizarro had shattered the Inca empire, and many other lesser-known captains had carried the Spanish banners to far corners of the New World.

Las Casas and Sepúlveda duly fought their great battle of ideas before the junta in Valladolid. The details of their arguments cannot be indicated here. The foundation on which Las Casas based his argument was that the Indians were truly men capable of becoming Christians. Drawing upon the information he had brought together in his massive anthropological work the Apologetic History, he documented his contention that the Indians had many skills and accomplishments and in fact possessed a culture worthy of respect. He cited their agricultural methods as well as their irrigation systems; illustrated their ingenuity by the way they derived twenty-two products from the maguey tree, contrived delicate ornamental collars of fish bones, and created remarkable gold jewelry. He drew special attention to their extraordinary capacity to learn the Old World crafts which the Spaniards had brought with them, giving a careful account of the way the Indians made knives and rubber balls. He also described the cleverness of their painters, their feather work, their silver making with few tools, and, after little training, their competence in fashioning musical instruments, their work as carpenters, and their hand lettering so fine that it could sometimes not be distinguished from printing. The only thing he found an Indian could not do as well as a Spaniard was to shoe a horse. He described the Indian mining methods and included an account of their ball games. Above all, however, he claimed, the Indians excelled in the dramatic arts and demonstrated this with various illustrations. He described the military organization of both the Mexican Indians and the Incas of Peru, a topic on which relatively few data are provided by other works, and gave much information on their coca chewing and tobacco smoking, together with an excellent description of the great teeming market in Mexico City.

He devoted many pages to the religion of the Indians, and the most striking aspect of this section is his attitude toward Indian sacrifices. He considered that the most religious peoples were those which offered to God the most magnificent sacrifice, and those who offered human beings had--in his opinion--a very noble concept indeed of their God. The Indian fasts, mortifications of the body, sacrifices of animals and men, were clearly superior to the sacrifices of the ancient peoples. Under the horrible and bloody aspects of these rites Las Casas discerned a commendable spirit of religious devotion which could be directed to higher ends and enlisted in the service of the only true God.

Las Casas was deeply convinced of the importance of education and therefore was particularly impressed by the meticulous attention paid by the Mexican Indians to the education of their children in the ways of chastity, honesty, fortitude, obedience, and sobriety. He cried:

> Did Plato, Socrates, Pythagoras, or even Aristotle leave us better or more natural or more necessary exhortations to the virtuous life than these barbarians delivered to their children? Does the Christian religion teach us more, save the faith and what it teaches us of invisible and supernatural matters? Therefore, no one may deny that these people are fully capable of governing themselves and of living like men of good intelligence and that they are more than others well ordered, sensible, prudent, and rational.

Las Casas believed firmly in the capacity of all people for civilization; he emphatically rejected a static and hopeless barbarism. "All the peoples of the world are men," he insisted, and declared that God would not allow any nation to exist, "no matter how barbarous, fierce, or depraved its customs" which might not be "persuaded and brought to a good order and way of life" provided the persuasion was peaceful. To practical conquistadores and administrators, men aiming at immediate worldly goals and faced with different kinds of Indians, and perhaps to the crown as well, jealous of all royal prerogatives, Las Casas' reiteration that the only justification for the presence of Spaniards in the New World was the Christianization of Indians by peaceful means alone must have seemed dangerous nonsense. One can imagine with what contempt and horror his announcement was received that Spain ought to abandon America, with all its Indians un-Christianized, rather than to bring them into the fold by forcible and--to him--profoundly un-Christian methods. The important fact to us today is that Sepúlveda's doctrine did not triumph at Valladolid in 1550 and that his treatise was not approved for publication until late in the eighteenth century.

Since the Valladolid debate the problem of how to treat peoples unlike ourselves in color, race, religion, or customs has given rise in every century to the most diverse and inflammatory opinions. In general the idea of the inferiority of natives to Europeans appeared in whatever far corners of the world Europeans reached. In the English colonies, for example, only Roger Williams had any respect for Indian culture and small attention was given the theories about Indians.

The battle waged by Las Casas and all the other Spaniards of his opinion to win recognition of the humanity of the Indians and to understand their culture is far from won. But today those who believe that "all the peoples of the world are men" have powerful allies. Anthropologists have gone on record that "the basic principles of opportunity and equality before the law are compatible with all that is known of human biology. All races possess the abilities needed to participate fully in the democratic way of life and in modern technological civilization." The United Nations Universal Declaration of Human Rights, adopted four centuries after the Valladolid controversy, announced: "All human beings are born free and equal in dignity and rights. They are endowed with reason and conscience and should act towards one another in a spirit of brotherhood." The Ecumenical Council, now in session at the Vatican, with members "from every nation under heaven" expressed the thought even more succinctly in its Message to Humanity: "We proclaim that all men are brothers, irrespective of the race or nation to which they belong."

Only a partisan in the "war of the myths" would dare to claim that the ideals announced by the Spanish crown were generally followed in the American territory under Spanish rule. Nor should anyone claim that the Spaniards fully accomplished their purpose: to incorporate the mass of New World Indians into a Christian and a European world.

For we know in the twentieth century that the Spaniards faced impossible problems: the clash of cultures complicated by the great area in which they operated, the tremendous diversity of the Indians encountered, and the small number of Spaniards available for conversion and education of the millions of Indians. One important doctrinal question remains. Why did Negroes never receive the same solicitous attention as Indians, and why did the conscience of Spaniards twinge so much more easily for Indians than for Negroes?

The Jesuit Alonso de Sandoval did indeed write a treatise in the seventeenth century on the culture of the different tribes of Negroes brought to Cartagena and may therefore be called the first Africanist in America. But neither Sandoval nor his disciple Pedro Claver ever denounced Negro slavery as an un-Christian institution, and the moral conscience of Europe was first roused in modern times by the plight of the Indian of America. The difference between the Spanish attitude toward Indians and Negroes has not yet been satisfactorily explained, and remains an important problem for investigation.

Is it not remarkable enough, however, that some sixteenth-century Spaniards studied Indian cultures and that a whole school of powerful and articulate members of this intensely nationalistic people fought stoutly for the rights of the Indians? During the early years of expansion which eventually carried European ideas and goods to almost every corner of the earth, Spain produced, it is true, an aggressive advocate of Aristotle's doctrine of natural slavery. But she also produced the powerful champion of Indians as men whose voice along with many other Spanish voices proclaimed the dawn of conscience in America. No matter how far rockets may reach into outer space, will any more significant problems be discovered than those which agitated many Spaniards during the conquest of America? When the story is told of man's attempts in history to grapple with this most difficult problem--how to relate to other men of unfamiliar cultures--will not this become clear: that when the Spanish Crown and Council of the Indies refrained from stigmatizing the natives of the New World as natural slaves they placed an important milestone on the long road, still under construction, which winds all too slowly toward civilizations which respect the dignity of man, that is to say of all men?

CHAPTER 4.

MORE HEAT AND SOME LIGHT ON THE SPANISH STRUGGLE FOR JUSTICE IN THE CONQUEST OF AMERICA

It is as difficult for a historian who has once studied Las Casas in depth to leave this absorbing subject as it was for Madame Ernestine Schumann-Heink to renounce the concert stage. The first time I took formal leave of Fray Bartolomé was in 1954 when Manuel Giménez Fernández of Sevilla and I published our bibliography on Las Casas in Santiago, Chile, and dedicated it to Eligio de la Puente of Havana. Copies of this volume, sponsored by the Fondo Histórico y Bibliográfico José Toribio Medina, were sent to a number of colleagues with this message:

> May this volume, dedicated to a Cuban, prepared in collaboration with an Andalusian and with the assistance of numerous other persons in various countries, testify to the widespread interest, today as in the past, in the ideas and battles of Las Casas on behalf of the American Indians.
>
> Through study of the many publications by and about this passionate sixteenth-century friar may the world come to understand better his eloquent books, his errors, his exaggerations, his glorious defeats, his struggles to make his concept of justice prevail.
>
> Las Casas died 389 years ago in Madrid, full of years and accomplishments, but his influence lives on in many hearts, in many lands.

Thereafter my research was concentrated on the history of the Villa Imperial de Potosí. But when Ramón Menéndez Pidal, the veteran Spanish scholar, published a vigorous attack on Fray Bartolomé, *El padre Las Casas. Su doble personalidad* (1963), I was moved to respond. My purpose was to place his interpretation in the context of the long succession of writers who have treated the subject since the sixteenth century.

The last word has not, of course, been said on either side, but the voluminous footnotes in the original article and the smoke rising from my text indicate the flavor and nature of the polemic today.

The Hispanic American Historical Review, XLIV (1964), 293-340. Reprinted by permission.

More Heat and Some Light on the Spanish Struggle for Justice in the Conquest of America

Was There a Struggle for Justice?

Has the Spanish conquest of America been the event of Latin American history most bitterly and most continuously discussed during the last 450 years? No one familiar with the hundreds of items recorded in the first 25 volumes of the Handbook of Latin American Studies would deny the statement of the Swedish scholar Sverker Arnoldsson that this is so, and the entrance of the Soviet and Soviet-oriented publications into the field indicates that the flood of polemical articles and monographs will not abate in the foreseeable future. No one who has even sampled the mountain of writings which sets forth the many conflicting interpretations of the conquest is likely to question Arnoldsson's explanation of the uproar as not at all an ivory tower controversy among academics but rather a "part of life itself. . . the economic, social, and racial problems which were created by the conquest of the New World still exist. The conquest, thus, is in the highest possible degree a living past." Arnoldsson concluded his essay on the contradictory attitudes assumed toward the conquest since the sixteenth century by quoting Manuel Gamio, Luis Valcárcel, and José Vasconcelos, noting that no more disparate views could be held than these thinkers expressed, "three of the best-known and most widely read authors in the continent."

The key question on the conquest for many historians is how Spanish action in America affected the Indians, and the most frequently cited author on this basic question is Bartolomé de Las Casas, the Dominican monk who became the most articulate and most formidable defender of the Indians. As the Spanish-speaking world prepares to commemorate in 1966 the four hundredth anniversary of the death of this bold and controversial Spaniard, his ideas and influence have rightly become the focus of ever-widening interest. A bibliography on Las Casas up to 1954 included 849 items; today Professor Raymond Marcus of Paris has in preparation a supplemental work which will list many additional items published during the last 10 years. The quality of the material has improved as more of Las Casas' writings became available, and in better editions; and the arguments are usually presented with vigor and learning.

Looking back to 1932 when I first began to search in Spanish archives for manuscripts on Las Casas, I am still surprised at the reactions of two eminent scholars to my proposal to study his work and influence. Karl Vossler, the outstanding German authority on Hispanic culture, believed that "all sources for his history are accessible in print," and Earl J. Hamilton, who had already begun to produce his fundamental contributions on the rise of prices resulting from the conquest, hoped that I would get Las Casas out of my system as soon as possible and turn to more significant topics.

Today the whole range of Las Casas' moral convictions and intellectual interests is being taken seriously, not only his allegations of the millions of Indians killed, and several hitherto ignored topics are being explored. A Yugoslav Dominican Antoninus Zaninović of Dubrovnik has been studying the ideas of Vicente Palatino de Curzola of Dalmatia, the only Dominican who opposed Las Casas in his lifetime, and the Instituto Peruano de Altos Estudios Islámicos has begun to investigate his position on Islam. General Cândido Rondon told me a few months before he died in 1954 at over 90 years of age that his work as pacifier of the Brazilian Indians and as the director of the earliest national agency in Latin America to protect Indians had been inspired by the example of Las Casas. Other hitherto unknown aspects of the life and influence of Friar Bartolomé may be brought to light by the Marcus bibliography.

Despite the increasing quantity of sources and increasing complexity of interpretation, the fundamental convictions of Las Casas are found to remain the same as when he enunciated them in the sixteenth century. He believed that Indians were rational human beings, who could be converted to the faith by peaceful means alone; conversion should involve a real understanding of Christian doctrine and not simply lead to superficial baptism of the uninstructed. The only real justification for Spanish rule in the New World, he insisted repeatedly, was the fulfillment of this mission. His experiences since he first went to Hispaniola in 1502 and the documents sent to him from many parts of the Indies until his death in 1566 convinced him that the years of Spanish dominion there constituted a betrayal of that mission. The conquest of America, in his eyes, was one of the darkest pages in the annals of mankind; his own countrymen, he contended, carried away by blind lust for gold and good living, had displayed the most wanton and fiendish barbarity toward the meek and defenseless natives, to whom they were supposed to bring the knowledge of Christ.

A full account of recent literature on the conquest would require at least an entire issue of the HAHR. This review article must therefore be limited to examining two of the principal authors who have lately concerned themselves with the Spanish struggle for justice in the conquest of America: Juan Friede of Colombia, who doubts at times that any struggle for justice to the Indians took place at all, and Ramón Menéndez Pidal of Spain, whose volume on Las Casas spreads far and wide his passionate conviction that the Dominican was a pathological personality, an abnormal person, in fact a paranoic. In considering the works of these writers who have little in common, one should bear in mind the conclusions of Juan Pérez de Tudela Bueso who has done much in the thorny field of Las Casas studies. He regards Las Casas as "a gigantic and indispensable protagonist in the formation of Hispanic America" and argues that the Las Casas theme offers "one of the most significant subjects for meditation on the nature of history."

For one whose mother tongue is not Spanish, the fire and smoke generated by the controversy over the true nature of the Spanish conquest has special meaning. The tremendous and continuing divergence of opinion on the life and work of Bartolomé de Las Casas seems to point to a fundamental fact of Spanish culture: that the struggle on behalf of the Indians has had a profound effect on the writing of the history of Spain in America. We may learn much about Spanish history and about the convictions of Spanish-speaking scholars today in an analysis of the bitter and four-century long debate over the true significance of the discovery of America, which the sixteenth-century historian Francisco López de Gómara characterized as the greatest event since the coming of Christ.

It was this same historian who set the stage for the battle of charges and counter-charges on the conquest by thus extolling the benefits of Spanish rule:

Loor de españoles

Tanta tierra como dicho tengo han descubierto, andado y convertido nuestros españoles en sesenta años de conquista. Nunca

> jamás rey ni gente anduvo y sujectó tanto en tan breve tiempo como la nuestra, ni ha hecho ni merescido lo que ella, así en armas y navegación como en la predicación del santo Evangelio y conversión de idólatras; por lo cual son españoles digníssimos de alabanza en todas las partes del mundo. ¡Bendito Dios, que les dió tal gracia y poder! Buena loa y gloria es de nuestros reyes y hombres de España que hayan hecho a los indios tomar y tener un Dios, una fe y un baptismo, y quitándoles la idolatría, los sacrificios de hombres, el comer carne humana, la sodomía y otros grandes y malos pecados, que nuestro buen Dios mucho aborresce y castiga. Hanles también quitado la muchedumbre de mujeres, envejecida costumbre y deleite entre todos aquellos hombres carnales; hanles mostrado letras, que sin ellas son los hombres como animales, y el uso del hierro, que tan necesario es a hombre; asimismo les han mostrado muchas buenas costumbres, artes y policia para mejor pasar la vida; lo cual todo, y aun cada cosa por sí, vale, sin duda ninguna, mucho más que la pluma ni las perlas ni la plata ni el oro que les han tomado.

López de Gómara did not bother to justify the conquest on theoretical grounds but recommended that his readers consult "Sepúlveda, the Emperor's chronicler, who wrote most elegantly in Latin on this topic, and thus you will be completely satisfied in this matter." Some Spaniards, however, were not "completely satisfied," nor were non-Spaniards, and the battle of words has continued to this day on the nature of the Spanish conquest of America. . .

Ramón Menéndez Pidal Versus Bartolomé de Las Casas

Beside the great cathedral in Mexico City visitors observe a large statue of a friar and an Indian, with these words below:

> Stranger if you love virtue,
> Pause and venerate this man
> This is Friar Bartolomé de Las Casas,
> Father of the Indians.

Other monuments of respect for this sixteenth-century Dominican stand in most Spanish American countries. But the visitor will find no monument to Las Casas in Madrid, where the most venerable and highly respected Spanish scholar, Don Ramón Menéndez Pidal, published in 1963 a large book attacking the Dominican and recording his passionate conviction that Las Casas was unworthy of such devotion, being instead a megalomaniac, an egotist, whose true villainy no one has until now fully plumbed despite the hundreds of publications written about him. Don Ramón has assumed the task of writing the "true history" of Las Casas as a patriotic duty and in so doing has produced, at the age of 93, probably the most remarkable, most complete, and most carefully-planned of all the many assaults on the Dominican made in the last 450 years; that is, since 1514 when Las Casas first determined to defend the original inhabitants of the New World from what he considered to be the un-Christian despoliation and destruction of the Indians by his fellow countrymen.

Let us review briefly who this Dominican was. Las Casas first appears on the stage of history, so far as documents about him are concerned, as he prepared to leave the island of Hispaniola in 1515 and return to Spain to begin his battle in court circles on behalf of the Indians. The letter of recommendation he carried from a group of Dominicans and Franciscans described him as "a person of truth and virtue, a special servant and friend of God and zealous in observing His law." The friars urged that "much reliance be placed in him, because he merits such, for he is moved by no other desire in the affairs of the Indians except the desire to serve God and Your Highness."

The last glimpse we have of him comes through the eyes of Friar Gabriel de Cepeda, historian of the convent of Atocha in Madrid, as Las Casas lay dying there in the month of July, 1566, at the age of 92. His numerous manuscripts had been left to the monastery of San Gregorio in Valladolid, to which he had bequeathed what money he had as an endowment for fellowships for poor students. Las Casas urged all who were with him during his last moments to continue to defend the Indians. He regretted that he had been able to accomplish so little on their behalf, and "with candle in hand, ready to depart from this world, he publicly affirmed his conviction that everything he had done in this cause he believed to be right."

In the centuries since Las Casas on his deathbed summed up his life's work, he has seldom been taken at his own valuation as a modest defender of the Indians who, though he had accomplished little, had always been right in his action on their behalf. Disputes began during his own lifetime, and the Franciscan Toribio de Motolinía probably represented a large body of opinion in the Indies when he complained to the Emperor Charles V in 1555: "Truly, for the few canons Las Casas has studied he presumes a great deal, and his disorder seems very great and his humility small; he thinks everyone is wrong and he alone is right."

Time has not wrought its usual softening influence; on the contrary, until today his memory has been kept fresh by keen and active disputation. The Dominican scholar Venancio D. Carro, who has done so much to elucidate the theological background of the conquest, goes so far as to say that the struggle for justice in America not only did not originate with Las Casas but that the controversy "developed and would have continued its course even though Las Casas had never lived." Another eminent Spanish scholar, Américo Castro, attributes such influence to the Dominican that he declares that his "anarchical doctrines" were largely responsible for the Spanish American revolutions that began in 1810; one "need not search for foreign ideas and influences to explain the independence of the Hispanoamerican colonies." Another writer asks whether Las Casas was not a _converso_, and the Soviet historian D. E. Michnevich looks upon him as merely a kind of _rara avis (mirlo blanco)_ among the Spanish clergy in America. And always there are writers who contemplate the many problems present in Latin America today and conclude, as does Paul Johnson in the London _New Statesman_, that "The origins of the continental _malaise_ can be traced back to the Spanish conquistadores. It is impossible to be too critical of this mindless bunch of ruffians." Nor is this opinion confined to non-Hispanic writers. The Venezuelan Francisco J. Herrera Luque argues in a recent volume that the pressing social problems of his country may be traced back to the actions of sixteenth century Spaniards and treats the _criminalidad_, the _patología_, and the _sintomatología psiquiátrica_ of the conquistadores, and has a special chapter on _Pizarro el esquizoide_. Now that Don Ramon is stigmatizing Las Casas as a paranoic, perhaps we are on the verge of a psychiatric interpretation of the conquest.

Significantly enough, no official or religious group has come forward to claim ownership of Las Casas and exploit him for its own purposes, except for such indigenistas as exalt Indian virtues at the expense of the Spaniard. His own Dominican Order has paid little attention to him. Nor has the Order ever published any of his treatises or a single major work about him. Spain itself has been bitterly divided on his true worth. While America has on the whole considered him a noble figure, one of the most forthright denunciations in recent years was made by an Argentine historian. But the most sustained and the most uncompromising attack has been the recent volume by Don Ramón Menéndez Pidal.

It is a difficult work to review; indeed, a proper treatment of all the many topics included in it might require another volume of similar size. It is likely that no other life of Las Casas will be so widely discussed in this generation. The battle lines are already forming, and ten years hence there will doubtless be so many items in print that another supplementary volume will be needed to bring the standard bibliography up to date. Many of these writers will enthusiastically support Don Ramón and his conviction, frequently stated, that previous biographers of Las Casas have obscured him by burning too much incense to his memory. Similarly one can see those who support Don Ramón already beginning to produce a powerful and pungent cloud of smoke offered to him, the great detractor. Those who oppose him, and there must be many even in Spain though they do not all see fit to publish their conviction, are doubtless preparing their broadsides. For Don Ramón reiterates over and over again that Las Casas was a hopelessly biased writer who simply could not tell the truth in describing Spanish action in America or the nature of the Indians. Although in some few respects a normal person, he was a propagandist rather than a thinker who incorporated in his works some Christian ideas, though at times incorrectly. Essentially, however, Las Casas was abnormal, declares Don Ramón, who employs his rich Castilian vocabulary in attempting to convey to the reader an idea of Las Casas' defects. Here is some of the language used, which surely must merit some kind of prize for variety and expressiveness:

> Anticristiano, austero y vehemente exagerador, egotismo vanidoso, presuntuosa vanidad, vanagloria megalómana, le faltaba una mínima partecilla de la fuerza moral de un San Francisco de Asís o de un Savonarola, pueril vanidad, delirio de grandeza, inexactitudes tendenciosas, genialidades excéntricas, bullicioso, injuriador, delirio sistematizado, imtemperamente vehemencia, hinchada truculencia, deleite descriptivo de bestialidades, lenguaje sañudo, chocante imprudencia de lenguaje, una irresistible propensión patológica, el vértigo de la enormización, exageración enormizante habitual irreprimible, maniática preocupación, una víctima inconciente de su delirio incriminatorio, prejuicio totalitario, canonista medieval, un rezagado, ataca con sus lanzallamas y con sus gases venenosos la ciudadela de los encomenderos, patológica certidumbre, confusionista, infantiles fantasías nobiliarias, no es posible imaginar un egotismo más puerilmente vanidoso, tono jactancioso, tenía arte natural para paliar su autoelogio con actitudes piadosas y altruistas, infantil jactancia, manía protagonista, inteligencia debil, infatuación vanagloriosa, vanidad fantástica de un niño imaginativo, vanidosa altanería, su irrefrenable desfiguración de los hechos, ultrarigorismo moral, un ciego para la realidad como un delirante en planes quiméricos, su providencialismo egocéntrico, sus arbitrismos, ilusionista extravagante, impetuoso, sus obsesionantes ideas

antiencomenderas, regocijo vanidoso, febril delirio, sobre-arrogante alegato, contradicciones irrazonables, prurito egoista, dominico tardío, vehemente rigorismo, su total ensimismamiento, siempre extraido del mundo real, iluminado, alabancioso fatalmente irreflexivo, vanidoso engreimiento, iracundo, el hombre más admirado de sí mismo que ha existido.

These representative samples of Don Ramón's rich prose indicate that his biography of Las Casas will be an excellent manual for students interested in the vituperative possibilities of the Spanish language. Even his vast and expert vocabulary proved insufficient to convey an adequate idea of Las Casas' exaggeration; he has found it necessary to invent a word: enormización (p. 321). Don Ramón occasionally allows a kind word to escape his pen on Las Casas: "De la buena fe y pura intención del Clérigo es imposible dudar, pero sí debemos desconfiar totalmente de su fantasía, de su ilusionismo, y de su poca discreción. . . ni era santo, ni era impostor, ni malévolo, ni loco; era sencillamente paranoico."

Few new documents are offered to substantiate all these charges; the volume is rather a massive and carefully organized collection of what the opponents of Las Casas have been saying these past 450 years. The result is a magnificent example of tendentious writing by a practiced hand. Before examining in detail some of the more important propositions of the book, it would be well to consider briefly the spirit in which Don Ramón has written his study:

It was a disagreeable task, reluctantly undertaken, but it was his duty to perform it. After 400 pages devoted almost wholly to blasting Las Casas, he concludes: "I have nothing more to say. I have fulfilled an unpleasant duty demanded by historical criticism." One feels that Don Ramón has acted with the supreme confidence of an Inquisitor who has performed dutifully in the torture chamber.

Underneath the meticulous prose, the many footnote citations, the extensive quotations from Las Casas, and the frequent protestations of the most rigid and scientific impartiality one can see boiling an intense and unquenchable passion. One wonders whether Don Ramón did not perhaps absorb this passion from Las Casas himself. One Spanish biographer of Las Casas, Manuel José Quintana, emphasized the "electric nature" of the great Dominican's spirit and stated that it was almost impossible for anyone to consider his opinions and activities, even centuries after his death, without becoming affected by the passions they aroused.

Don Ramón exhibits at times the same "pathological dogmatism" which he discovers so basic in Las Casas. He has never done any original research in the field, but uses extensively the contributions of Marcel Bataillon, Manuel Giménez Fernández, Juan Pérez de Tudela, and others, although on many individual points differing from them, even dissenting at times from Bataillon who is by no means an uncritical admirer of Las Casas. Don Ramón blandly gives his own opinions on many complicated institutions and events without troubling to explain how he has arrived at his conclusions. Sometimes facts and interpretations inconvenient to Don Ramón's thesis are not mentioned, either by design or ignorance. Indeed, on some questions one might apply to him the description Motolinía gave of Las Casas: "He thinks everyone is wrong and he alone is right." Some readers, unaware of the extensive literature on the history of Spain in America and eager to dispose of such an irritating figure as Las Casas, may be led astray by Don Ramón's assumption of omniscience when he asserts his opinion as gospel truth on all these highly controversial and sometimes still unresolved problems. Others will penetrate the veil of Don Ramón's apparent objectivity to see clearly the unmistakable prejudices of this cleverly written diatribe.

In presenting his version of Las Casas, Don Ramón reminds one both of a Royal Canadian mounted policeman stalking a criminal in the wastelands of the north and of a prosecuting attorney rather than of a historian at work. The tendentious and unhistorical nature of Don Ramón's brief against Las Casas discloses itself in several ways:

1. His use of sources

When a writer praises Las Casas, as Antonio de Remesal does on the Vera Paz attempt to preach the faith peacefully in Guatemala, Don Ramón denounces him. When the same writer disagrees with Las Casas, Remesal becomes a "mente sana." Even when there is no documentary proof of the charge that Las Casas abandoned his bishopric--and Bataillon doubts the veracity of Remesal on this point--Don Ramón accepts the story and even criticizes Fabié and Pérez de Tudela because they do not follow Remesal. His attitude is a simple one: "No veo motivo de duda, toda vez que presenta aspectos no glorificadores."

Don Ramón inveighs against biographers of Las Casas who do not question Remesal's account of Vera Paz or do not analyze the way he reaches his many favorable comments on Las Casas. Yet he himself uncritically accepts the Franciscan Toribio de Motolinía, one of his stellar witnesses because of Motolinía's famous letter of 1555 to Charles V against the Dominican. He does not mention that Motolinía was possibly biased, due to his resentment that Las Casas worked actively and successfully against his appointment as bishop, which Manuel María Martínez, O.P., sets forth in an article not cited though easily available. The reader is told that Motolinía describes the number of Indians killed in the conquest and condemned Spanish actions "a veces con exageración lascasiana," but pro-Indian remarks by Motolinía do not disturb Don Ramón's confidence in him.

The well-known scandal of 1539 when Las Casas refused to baptize an insufficiently prepared Indian at Motolinía's request is described in considerable detail. Don Ramón does not disclose that Las Casas was upheld, in his insistence that Indians be instructed in the faith before baptism, by a commission of Salamanca theologians headed by Francisco de Vitoria, for whom Don Ramón shows great respect in other sections of the volume.

At times it appears that Don Ramón favors the Franciscans over the Dominicans because he devotes so much attention to Motolinía and the great differences between his ideas and actions and those of Las Casas, and extols the splendid work of the Franciscans in Nueva Granada in the middle of the sixteenth century:

> Luchaban tenaz pero pacientemente con oidores y encomenderos sin la violenta ruptura de relaciones practicada por Las Casas; véase. . . la carta de Fray Juan de San Filiberto al Emperador (Bogotá, 3 febrero 1553) donde en las págs. 197-199 se ve cómo funcionaban las restituciones de los tributos mal cobrados por los encomenderos que no cumplían sus deberes de tener en justicia, en buena policía y en doctrina a los indios; en Panamá y otras partes muchos vecinos tenían sus indios para el servicio doméstico muy regalados y doctrinados, y, hasta vestidos de seda.

This idyllic picture of Spanish action in the New World suggests that Don Ramón's primary objective may be the establishment of a leyenda blanca; that he attempts to destroy Las Casas as an indispensable step toward this larger purpose. If so, he will encounter much skepticism among those familiar with the "reality in America," as Professor Friede makes clear. For example, Don Ramón has great confidence in the Franciscans, and one wonders how he would explain away the following descriptions of Spanish cruelty in New Granada by Fray Jerónimo de San Miguel, first custodio of the Franciscans, about the time the Indians were reputed to be wearing silks:

> En este Reino, aunque es poca tierra, se han hecho tantas y tan grandes crueldades que, si yo no las supiera de raiz y tan verazmente, no pudiera creer que en corazón cristiano cupieran tan crueles y fieras inhumanidades. Porque no hay tormento tan cruel ni pena tan horrible que de éstos, que de muy servidores de Vuestra Alteza se precian, no hayan experimentado estos tristes y pobrecitos naturales. Porque unos los han quemado vivos, otros les han, con muy grande crueldad, cortado manos, narices, lenguas y otros miembros; otros, es cierto haber ahorcado gran número de ellos, así hombres como mujeres; otros, se dice, han aperreado indios y destetado mujeres y hecho otras crueldades, que en sólo pensarlo tiemblan las carnes a los que algo de cristiano tienen. Estos son los servicios que acá a Vuestra Alteza, se hacen y por los cuales piensan ser remunerados. . .
>
> De los cuales vi yo muchos--cuenta--altados y con colleras y otras prisiones, llorando y dando gritos, aunque les aprovechaba poco, y, como acá aún tenemos muy poco favor, no lo pude remediar. Y ya que en el pueblo no hallaron tantos ladinos como era menestar, salían a saltear por los caminos y tomar por fuerza los indios que iban a sus labranzas y mercados, y así llegaban atados y presos . . . Tenga por cierto Vuestra Real Alteza que de seiscientos indios que habrán llevado, sin los ladinos, que ninguno ha de volver, antes quedarán por allí muertos, porque son gente que en sacándoles de su natural se mueren, como ya se sabe por muy cierto. Si Vuestra Alteza permite esta manera de poblar, yo no lo sé. Lo que sé es que para poblar cincuenta casas de españoles, se despueblan quinientos o más de indios. . .

There are no well-treated Indians dressed in silks in the pages of Friede's well-documented Vida y luchas de Don Juan del Valle, primer obispo de Popayán y protector de indios, a monograph not cited by Don Ramón. In fact, he refers to none of the many Friede publications which would have been pertinent. Why is no article from the HAHR cited, why are so few references made even to the Revista de Indias published in Madrid, the Estudios Americanos of Sevilla, The Americas of the Academy of American Franciscan History in Washington, or to the historical reviews and publications of Spanish America? Some gaps in the documentation may be due to the weakness of Madrid libraries, but cannot some of the strange omissions be due to Don Ramón's determination to draw up the strongest indictment possible against Las Casas, and thus he did not search for or cite evidence that did not support his thesis?

The most flagrant abuse by Don Ramón of the accepted canons of the historian may be seen in his account of the incident of the pacification of Enriquillo in Hispaniola. This famous cacique, educated and Christianized by the Franciscans, had rebelled in 1519 because his wife was wronged by a Spaniard. For many years war ensued until Charles V appointed Captain Francisco de Barrionuevo on July 4, 1532, to offer the cacique peace or suffer the consequences of war by fire and sword.

Barrionuevo finally located Enriquillo in August, 1533, in the mountain fastnesses at Baoruco and in two days convinced him that he should renew peaceful relations with the Spaniards. During the negotiations Enriquillo never ate any food the Spaniards offered for fear of poisoning, but Don Ramón records that in this brief period Enriquillo was tremendously influenced by the action of the Emperor and by being referred to as Don:

> . . . su triunfo es espléndido, al verse honrado y solicitado a la paz por el gran Emperador Carlos V. No tiende a la vida selvática. No odia la sociedad en cuyo seno se producen las injusticias que le agraviaron; admira la organización estatal poderosa, profesa la divina religión de ese Estado. Una vez reivindicado su honor individual, no siente un parcial nacionalismo indio, sino que, como el inca Garcilaso, presiente que las dos razas deben formar una unidad histórica, y acepta con estoica o resignada conformidad las consecuencias de la inferioridad cultural de los indios, así que, respondiendo a su educación franciscana, apoya la encomienda y se siente satisfecho cooperando al mantenimiento de tal institución.

No footnote is provided to support this astonishing assertion.

Don Ramón reports that Las Casas was making a nuisance of himself at the time by opposing the encomienda, and even refused absolution to a dying encomendero until he agreed to leave his goods to the Indians instead of his heirs. The Audiencia sent strong representations to Spain against this difficult friar, whom they termed "escandaloso, desasosegado, estorbador de la real justicia."

Las Casas now feared that the peace arranged by Captain Barrionuevo would not be kept, and in a later letter explained how in August, 1533, he persuaded his Dominican superiors to allow him to go to Baoruco, "without authorization of the Audiencia." There he exhorted Enriquillo for about a month to remain faithful to the Emperor and assured him that the peace would be respected by the Spaniards. Las Casas also celebrated mass daily, and instructed Enriquillo and his band in matters of the faith.

This account comes from the historian Gonzalo Fernández de Oviedo y Valdés, and Don Ramón qualifies it as "notoriamente fantástico," based on obviously erroneous Dominican reports given to Oviedo, though no evidence is given to support this assertion. Don Ramón then goes on to term Las Casas' description of his participation in the letter of April 30, 1534, as another prime example of his "delirio de grandeza," and Don Ramón is firmly convinced that "el recio viento documental disipe las nubes del incienso lascasiano y nos permita ver la verdad."

Let us examine briefly the documents now available. Las Casas' own account of April 30, 1534, might appropriately be questioned as that of an interested party, but no evidence is given by Don Ramón to support his brushing aside Oviedo's account; and it should be remarked that he accepts Oviedo as a good and reliable witness when the material is not favorable to Las Casas. The case against Las Casas, as Don Ramón presents it, rests entirely upon a letter signed by Enriquillo in 1534, in which Las Casas' share in his pacification is not mentioned, and upon a number of letters by the Audiencia. But would a historian not analyze the circumstances under which Enriquillo wrote the letter (or rather signed the letter, which appears to have been written by a Spanish scribe). Did the Indian know what he was signing? Does the fact that there is no mention of Las Casas in the letter necessarily mean that he had no role in the pacification of Enriquillo? More important still, would not the Audiencia be classified as a hostile witness? A historian would be expected to evaluate all the documents now known, and at least to suspend judgment in the face of doubt and disagreement among the witnesses.

Perhaps enough has been said to indicate that Don Ramón draws upon the great quantity of sources on the Spanish conquest captiously and in the spirit of a lawyer determined to win a case. Such a use of sources may be permissible or at least expected in the courtroom, but can one who aims at discovering historical truth employ such a questionable method?

2. His attitude toward Indians

One wonders whether Don Ramón has ever seen an Indian, or been moved by the great drama of the confrontation in a New World of Spaniards with the many kinds of Indians ranging from almost Stone Age folk to highly cultured groups. Certainly he has an exalted opinion of European culture, for he exclaims at one point that:

> Todos los pueblos del mundo están, poco o mucho, penetrados de unos principios de civilización bastante uniformes, cuyas raices y recursos principales están en Europa, esa Europa colonizadora genial, que desde los tiempos más remotos viene irradiando su alta cultura y su bienestar sobre toda la redondez de la tierra. Hoy día, los indúes, los chinos, los árabes, todos los imperios que más brillante papel desempeñaron en lo antiguo, se unen a los pueblos de Africa y de Oceanía en el universal referéndum con que hoy tácitamente aprueban el multisecular colonialismo del Occidente como principal unificador de la humanidad; ellos dan su voto aprobatorio en su mismo traje, en esa corbata que quieren vestir los principales dirigentes de todas las razas; quieren dejar sus ropas nacionales para vestir su cuerpo al uso occidental, lo mismo que ellos van revistiendo su espíritu con ideas occidentalistas de libertad que ellos no engendraron.

Don Ramón betrays almost as much indifference to the Indians as he accuses Las Casas of showing. Las Casas, he asserts without citing his source, never worked with the Indians as a missionary, and showed a marked repugnance toward them; his motive was not love for Indians but hatred toward the Spaniards: "legista a palo seco, no ama a los indios." Don Ramón, looking back several hundred years through rose-tinted spectacles, sees few dead Indians, though his much respected authority Motolinía declared that so many had died in the mines that the birds and crows that came to feast on their dead bodies greatly obscured the sun. He sees, rather, a scene of contentment and cultural advance:

> Para descrédito de la utopía lascasiana, florecía una Nueva España, donde gobernantes y misioneros practicaban y depuraban la encomienda, donde los indios habían salido de una edad prehistórica, de la edad de piedra, con antropofagía y sacrificios humanos, para entrar en una vida civilizada, enriquecida ya con los mejores vegetales y animales útiles del mundo viejo y con las instituciones creadas por la vieja cultura, comenzando por la encomienda y llegando hasta la imprenta y los colegios mayores; una España Nueva donde gobernantes, obispos y misioneros sembraban catequesis, colegios, talleres y hospitales para los indios.

Where did Don Ramón obtain his knowledge of Indian culture? He ignores such principal sixteenth-century writers as Diego de Landa and José de Acosta, and does not refer to the greatest of them all, the Franciscan Bernardino de Sahagún, except to quote him on the superiority of the natives of Asia to the Indians. The two witnesses he calls to testify on the nature of the Indians were carefully selected to prove his point, for both witnesses sang the same tune. He quotes the Dominican Tomás Ortiz who held in 1519 that "nunca crió Dios tan cocida gente en vicios y bestialidades, sin mezcla de bondad o policía," and the Franciscan bishop Francisco Ruiz who reported that "aunque es gente maliciosa para concebir ruindad en daño de los cristianos, no es gente capaz ni de juicio natural para recibir la fe ni las otras virtudes de crianza necesarias a su conversión."

His bibliography is equally meager on modern studies of Indian cultures. He cites none of the numerous learned publications of the Carnegie Institution of Washington on the Mayas or the copious contributions of Mexican anthropologists, he ignores the _Handbook of South American Indians_, uses no articles from the _Journal de la Société des Américanistes_ of Paris, the _American Anthropologist_, or the many volumes produced by the Congreso de Americanistas, although these volumes are full of descriptions and analyses of Indian cultures.

Some congresses have concerned themselves with the work of Las Casas. The last one held in Spain, in 1935, was marked by sharp controversies which followed Rómulo Carbia's paper accusing Las Casas of forging documents to further his own ends. This single paper, of all the many items on Indian affairs published by the congresses, is the only one given much attention by Don Ramón. The Argentine employed more than sixty times in this paper such words and concepts to describe Las Casas as make him a spiritual precursor of Don Ramón: "loco, falsario, ladrón, mendaz, embaucador, vengativo, frenético y pintoresco." Don Ramón appears to accept these charges, though the Congress did not: instead it unanimously recommended that a critical edition of Las Casas' works be published and almost unanimously resolved that the men who criticized the colonial practices of Spain--Montesinos, Las Casas, and Vitoria--should be considered "como auténticos representativos de la conciencia española del Nuevo Mundo."

Neither these resolutions nor the fact that before and after 1935 Carbia was challenged by Rinaldi Caddeo and others are mentioned by Don Ramón, although their publications are listed in the standard Las Casas bibliography which he used intensively in the preparation of his volume. At times it appears that he has climbed into an ivory tower with the books and articles favorable to his thesis, pulled up the ladder behind him, and then proceeded to write his version of history. In addition Don Ramón never stops to recognize that attacks on his position, which he first enunciated in a speech in Cuba in 1937, have appeared over the years. Some of them are listed in the standard bibliography, but these too he gives the silent treatment.

Don Ramón gives no evidence that he has ever heard of Justino Fernández's _Coatlicue_, a study and defense of the aesthetic qualities of Aztec art, or of the publications of Father Angel María Garibay G. in which he both asserts the values of Aztec poetry and raises his voice against prejudices against Indian culture. Nor is there any recognition of Inca contributions to music.

Don Ramón's only excursion into the rich and diversified modern literature on the Indians is his mention of a George Montandon, whom he identifies merely as "a Swiss ethnologist" and then goes on to state: "Bien piensan muchos. . . Montandon por ejemplo. . . que la cultura mejicano-andina, la de Moctezuma y Atahualpa no se encontraba en una vía normal de evolución; no podía llegar a un natural empalme con la civilización del Occidente y estaba condenada a desaparecer, al ponerse al lado de esa civilización inmensamente más adelantada." How little the subject of Indians interests Don Ramón is evident from his omission of any bibliographic information on the one modern work he uses to give an unfavorable description of the Indians, and his reliance on "a Swiss ethnologist" without reputation in the field of American anthropology is a curious lapse by such an experienced scholar. This cavalier treatment of a subject so basic to any serious consideration of the conquest can be understood, in part at least, as a reflection of the rudimentary development of the study in Spain of Indian cultures. Few Spaniards have made field studies in Spanish America since the time of Sahagún in the sixteenth century.

Don Ramón here illustrates the attitude against which Juan Friede has written so sharply. The true role of the Indian in the history of America has never been adequately described by historians, Friede feels, because some of them hold to the false idea that Indian culture was of no importance and few scholars have investigated the enormous amount of material in archives available for a study of the past played by Indians in the formation of America.

3. His inconsistencies, exaggerations, and dogmatisms

It may seem strange to apply these words to Don Ramón, for they are precisely the charges he makes against Las Casas.

The first inconsistency one notes is his attitude toward the writings of Las Casas. He naturally deplores above all the Brevísima relación de la destrucción de las Indias. It is the "único fundamento de la fama mundial" of Las Casas which he describes and condemns at great length, for the horrifying material in this denunciation of Spanish cruelty to the Indians fascinates Spaniards, who have done a great deal to spread the leyenda negra through their fulsome refutations. One feels at times that Don Ramón believes that, except for this work by Las Casas, Spain and the world would have been convinced that on the whole the Conquest was a noble effort marked mainly by the glorious deeds of conquistadores or the kindly acts to Indians of encomenderos. He sees Cortez defended by Vitoria, praised by Motolinía, favorable to Friar Martín de Valencia's peaceful preaching projects, a "genial and courteous" gentleman even in his meeting with the rancorous Las Casas. He admits cruelties on some occasions and some oppressive encomenderos in the early days, but generally seems to agree with the first important apologia for the conquest written by Francisco López de Gómara, and referred to earlier. Nowhere does he consider the position of such a historian as the Mexican scholar Genaro García, and makes no reference to the latter's well-known study Carácter de la conquista española en América y en México según los textos de los historiadores primitivos, in which he states:

> Para dar mayor fuerza á mis estudios, no sólo me refiero continuamente á los conquistadores é historiadores más autorizados, sino que transcribo sus palabras literalmente; y para que no se me objete que doy por probado lo que trato de demostrar, no cito á nuestro irreprochable don fray Bartolomé de Las Casas en cuento tiendo á determinar el carácter de la conquista.

Nor does he consider that the natural jealousy of other European nations would have in any case tempered their enthusiasm for the expansion of Europe by Spaniards.

Don Ramón at first praises other writings of Las Casas, such as the Historia de las Indias and the Apologética historia, but later attacks both works, so that his opinions fluctuate according to his mood of the moment.

Another inconsistency appears in his treatment of relations between the Dominican Domingo de Betanzos and Las Casas. He tells how Betanzos influenced Las Casas to enter the order, but later became his decided enemy. We do not learn that these two fiery figures were linked together for many years by their common devotion to the ideal of peaceful persuasion. Why did these two men fall out? One of the reasons probably was their divergent convictions on the nature of the Indians. These were the years when the subject was being fiercely debated, and when Pope Paul III issued in 1537 his bull Sublimis Deus, proclaiming that "the Indians are truly men. . . capable of understanding the Catholic faith. . . are by no means to be deprived of their liberty or the possession of their property, even though they be outside the faith of Jesus Christ." Don Ramón pays slight attention to this bull, though it is central to Las Casas' doctrine in his treatise on The Only Method of Attracting All People to the True Faith. Nor does Don Ramón emphasize that Betanzos' view on Indian affairs was so worrisome to some of his brother Dominicans that in 1549 they apparently prevailed upon him to renounce on his deathbed in Valladolid the anti-Indian memorial he had presented to the Council of the Indies long before.

Other inconsistencies, discrepancies, and doubtful judgments occur throughout El Padre Las Casas. Su doble personalidad, but they cannot all be considered here. Don Ramón manifests an equivocal attitude on the Las Casas-Sepúlveda dispute by labelling both contestants "Aristotelian" without explaining what he means, the New Laws are treated summarily, and his use of argument from silence does not inspire confidence in the validity of his opinions. One particularly noticeable lack of balance is the treatment of Las Casas' idea of peaceful preaching of the faith and the Vera Paz experiment. The idea is nothing new, merely an old Christian doctrine, we are told, and the experiment was greatly exaggerated in importance by Las Casas and by Antonio de Remesal, the 17th-century Dominican historian. Don Ramón follows Marcel Bataillon's analysis and that of the Jesuit Carmelo de Sáenz Santa María, the latter presenting a very derogatory picture, but makes no reference to the valuable study by Benno M. Biermann, O.P. Peaceful conversion itself seems to be a dubious enterprise from Don Ramón's narrative of Vera Paz, though when Martín de Valencia, Juan de Zumárraga, and Domingo de Betanzos favor it the idea is given warm approval. The Emperor Charles V backed the policy of peaceful conquests, according to one writer today, but Las Casas' exposition of this doctrine and his attempt to put it into effect in Guatemala are treated as fantastic and farcical aberrations of a paranoic.

One further discrepancy should be mentioned: the proportion of space devoted to the two aspects of the doble personalidad of Las Casas. From the book's title, one might hope for a judicious weighing of Las Casas' faults and virtues, but in fact, since the diagnosis is unfavorable, the proportions are distorted. On occasion some dubiously favorable comment is made, such as: "la grave inequidad. . . no era una falta moral, sino intelectual"; "es en general un escritor razonable," "no tiene intención de falsear los hechos, sino que los ve falsamente." On Las Casas' four statements in the thorny case of Archbishop Domingo de Carranza before the Inquisition Don Ramón is even almost lyrical in recounting Las Casas' courageous declarations on behalf of his friend in trouble: "nos revelan a Las Casas libre de su idea fija, bajo un aspecto altamente simpático y noble, defendiendo a Carranza con la mayor entereza en medio de la turbación causada por el apasionante proceso del Arzobispo. . . Esas cuatro declaraciones son la comprueba más clara de la enfermedad de Las Casas. El paranoico, cuando sale del tema de sus delirios, es un hombre enteramente normal en el ejercicio de sus facultades grandes y chicas."

But the reader who would see in full detail the approach Don Ramón uses in his delineation of the _doble carácter_ of Las Casas should consult the carefully compiled _Sumario sinóptico_. Under the rubric _El carácter. Las Ideas_ is a brief section on _El Las Casas normal, sus dotes positivas_ which includes nevertheless such items as _no es un pensador, sino un propagandista; maneja ideas cristianos corrientes, a veces deformadas_ and ends on this note: _todos los datos que poseemos, salvo raras excepciones, son referentes al Las Casas anormal_. Then follow sections on _Hombre defectuoso, Idea fija, arbitrista, Enfermedad mental, Vocación anormal_, and _Delirio de grandeza_.

Don Ramón is ironical and denunciatory when considering Las Casas' exaggerations on the number of Indians killed by Spaniards in the conquest. In this large section he brings forward no new arguments or facts, mostly confining himself to employing a number of examples previously set forth in the eloquent attack by the Catalan Jesuit Juan Nuix upon Las Casas in 1780. Don Ramón classifies Las Casas as a "mente medieval," but does not indicate that this might involve exaggeration of the kind described by Steven Runciman:

> Every medieval historian, whatever his race, invariably indulges in wild and picturesque exaggeration whenever he has to estimate numbers that cannot easily be counted. It is therefore impossible for us today to establish the actual size of the Crusading armies. When Fulcher of Chartres and Albert of Aix tell us that the fighting men of the First Crusade numbered 600,000 while Ekkehard gives 300,000 and Raymond of Aguilers a modest 100,000, or when Anna Commena declares that Godfrey of Lorraine brought with him 10,000 knights and 70,000 infantrymen, it is clear that the figures are only meant to denote a very large number indeed.

Nor does Don Ramón appear familiar with the many wild and fantastic exaggerations of other Spaniards brought together in one of the many Spanish American publications he does not cite. We should never forget, also, that Las Casas' own doubtful statistics were in turn blown up by foreign translators to make them appear still more damning.

Don Ramón is himself on shaky ground when he denounces Las Casas' description of the Guatemala earthquake of 1541. In one of his earlier publications he criticized Las Casas' statement but, having later learned that he himself had exaggerated what Las Casas had said, he does not make it quite clear in _El Padre Las Casas. Su doble personalidad_ that he has retreated somewhat toward Las Casas' position which, however, he still feels so wrong that he concludes:

> Los admiradores a ciegas de Las Casas sólo le tachan de _cándida credulidad_ y de _exageración_; dirán sencillamente que el clérigo sevillano propende a la andaluzada. Sí; pero es una andaluzada en grado patológico, porque la emplea en una obra de acusación histórica, y deforma, no una noticia oral, volandera, sino el

> testimonio escribanil o notarial, que, aunque ya abultado, le deja insatisfecho, por lo que tiende irresistiblemente a abultarlo más. Esta exageración, extendida sistemáticamente a todos los relatos acusatorios, tiene una gravedad psicológica que no tiene la fugaz andaluzada conversacional.

The last word has probably not been said on the Guatemalan earthquake, and in due course we may have a more exact view of precisely how many _bueyes_ were carried along by the earthquake. Meanwhile, we should suspend judgment on whether the report of the incident demonstrates the "pathological deformation" of Las Casas.

Dogmatism is another characteristic of Las Casas shared by Don Ramón, since both men believed in the absolute validity of their convictions. Neither considers it necessary at times to do more than state them, and just as Las Casas sometimes delivered himself of broad generalizations without producing evidence, so does Don Ramón. He qualified Las Casas as "pathological" because he asserts that everything the _encomenderos_ did was wrong; Don Ramón is just as absolute in his own way for, though the encomienda was a highly controversial institution, he maintains:

> Todas ven que la convivencia tutelar con el español es el único medio para que los indios abandonen inhumanas y salvajes costumbres somo los sacrificios de hombres o niños y la antropofagía, y para que se habituasen a la vida en poblados, al trabajo regular, al matrimonio, etc.; la encomienda era, pues, benéfica; y para dominicos y franciscanos, la encomienda parecía, además, hacia 1530, el único medio posible de contener la rápida desaparición de los indios amenazada por la vida selvática y por espantosas epidemias.

Don Ramón endeavors to show that Las Casas was not taken seriously in his own time: "en general los contemporáneos lo miraban como una excentricidad o manía disculpable, cuyas extremosidades por violentas que fuesen no había que tomarlas en consideración." No evidence is adduced to document this generalization; considerable material could be cited to show that in fact Las Casas received much support for his ideas throughout his life and that his powerful political influence was recognized by many different kinds of sixteenth-century Spaniards. Friars wrote to him from many parts of the Indies to report atrocities and the needs of the Indians, oidor Cristóbal Lebrón appealed to Las Casas for help in his difficulties with the audiencia of Nueva Galicia, the ancient conquistador Bernal Díaz del Castillo even had the audacity to ask Las Casas for assistance in keeping his _encomienda_ and offered a bribe, the conquistador-chronicler Pedro Cieza de León willed his manuscripts to him, the Council of the Indies used him on confidential missions when he was 90 years of age, and he was active as a witness on Indian affairs until a few weeks before his death.

There were few more respected Indian "experts" in his time, and the influence of his doctrine and his example during his lifetime and in later years may be shown in many ways. Ciriaco Pérez Bustamante has demonstrated how close was Alonso de Ercilla to the doctrine of Las Casas and that the epic poet exalted in _La Araucana_ (1569) "la radical originalidad y el eterno descontento del alma española, que al mismo tiempo que conquista gigantescos continentes vive obsesionada con los justos títulos y con el derecho de gentes, niega el poder temporal del Papa sobre los infieles y la jurisdicción universal del emperador y condena esta misma conquista que realiza." Even Spanish captains were affected by Las Casas' ideas according to F. J. Sánchez Cantón:

> Un Capitán dezia que si la Isla Española fuera bien governada, rentara más que todas las Yndias juntas aora; estos era haziendo varionias, dando a cada varionia tantos mil Indios y tanta tierra, assí curaran de los yndios como de cosa propia, y poblaran la tierra, y no los mataran como los mataron por los Repartimientos que de ellos hizieron, y a personas que residían en Castilla y no los vían ni los oyan; y unos muertos pedían otros, y luego se los davan, y assí murieron en sola aquella isla millón y tantos mil yndios.

A recent documented study by Rev. Stafford Poole, C. M., of Cardinal Glennon College, demonstrates that the Third Mexican Council of 1585, "a gathering of all the bishops of the Mexican province, legislated in a vast number of areas in favor of the Indian population" in the spirit of Las Casas, and states that the Council "shows us that there was a powerful and articulate body of men in the New World who condemned the system of repartimientos as intrinsically evil, theoretically unjustifiable, and in practice inseparable from the most atrocious abuses." Those who follow Don Ramón in believing that the ecclesiastics supported the Indian labor system in the Indies and looked upon it as the best possible solution for Spanish-Indian relations, should study the documentation of Rev. Poole which led him to the following conclusion:

> Even though some churchmen may have defended the repartimientos as theoretically licit and many more--the precise percentage we shall never know--profited by the exploitation of the Indian worker, the leaders of the Church in sixteenth-century Mexico condemned the repartimiento as an infringement of the liberty of men created free by God and secured in their freedom by pope and king.

The Jesuit José de Acosta, one of the foremost authorities on sixteenth-century Peru, not mentioned by Don Ramón, manifests in his De procuranda indorum salute (1580) a marked Las Casas influence, which visibly pains his present-day editor, and it would be easy to cite other examples which have occurred from that day to this. One could with equal ease list the many powerful and articulate opponents of Las Casas who have flourished from Motolinía until Don Ramón, a fact insisted upon above in connection with the examination of the interpretations of Professor Friede. A study of these opponents would be an interesting exercise, but cannot be attempted here. Las Casas was never brought before the Inquisition, despite his habit of free-speaking. In a recently discovered document in the Archivo General de la Nación in Mexico we see his nephew Pedro Suárez de Peralta testifying in Guatemala on June 28, 1568, that he had come to the New World about 24 years previously with his uncle and proudly stating that none of his family had ever been sentenced by the Holy Office.

Another way to assess the dogmatism of Don Ramón is to see how he meets criticism of his cherished opinions. He scores Manuel Giménez Fernández roundly for holding fast to certain expressions after they were described as "erroneous," but he does much the same thing himself. Don Ramón wishes to be as "scientific" as possible in his analysis of paranoia, a word he uses freely throughout the book, and his personal interpretation of this central concept explains much about his methodology and the temper of his mind. To him, the only explanation of Las Casas' life is that he was a paranoico, and Don Ramón unconsciously reveals in his approach to psychiatry how he obstinately clings to his own preconceived ideas no matter what the specialists say:

> En mi trabajo de 1957. . ., Una norma anormal del Padre Las Casas, expuse algunos indicios que yo percibía de esa anormalidad enfermiza, y a pesar de mi total ignorancia de la psiquiatría, me arrojé calificar tal anormalidad de delirio paranoico, calificación que yo entregaba a la corrección de los especialistas. Según el concepto vulgar, que utilizo como profano (y que tendrá, bien lo sé, mucha imprecisión técnica), el paranoico no es un loco, no es un demente, privado de normal raciocinio; todos su juicios son normales, salvo los relacionados con una idea fija preconcebida, los cuales son fatalmente falseados, sistematizados para conformarlos con el preconcepto. . . .
>
> Toda la vida pública y todos los innumerables escritos de Las Casas tocan a los indios, y los escritos, completamente deformados por la anormal idea fija, los que han tenido resonancia mundial, son los que han determinado la única acción destacada de Las Casas, mientras que los otros escritos, en que la anormalidad aparece sólo de tarde en tarde, apenas nos dan notas biográficas sobre la actividad lascasiana libre del falso prejuicio, así que el Las Casas normal casi nunca aparece ante nuestros ojos.
>
> Para este total cambio de perspectiva que expongo, espero disculpa por parte de los psicólogos. Cuando ya esta mi biografía estaba completamente preparada para la imprenta, varias conversaciones con los profesores J. Germain y R. Alberca me tranquilizaron bastante respecto a mi antiguo trabajo de 1957 y a la publicación del presente libro; ellos leyeron estas páginas en pruebas tipográficas, sobre las cuales me hicieron varias observaciones muy orientadores para retocar mi lenguaje tan profano. Sin embargo, algunas frases y expresiones dejé sin corregir, intencionadamente, queriendo quedase manifiesta mi calidad de lego en en la materia. Conste aquí mi muy cordial gratitud a los profesores Germain y Alberca.

Another example of how Don Ramón uses expert opinion as it suits his purpose involves a question of theology--the action of Las Casas in refusing absolution to conquistadores unless they restored to the Indians the goods he felt had been taken unjustly from them. For a judgment on this issue he requested the advice of his colleague in the Academia Española, Dr. Eijo Garay, Bishop of Madrid, who condemned Las Casas' ideas in his Confesionario as "absurdo." One notes that Don Ramón did not call for an opinion from the one theologian in Madrid who had devoted most attention to questions of theology in the conquest, Friar Venancio D. Carro, O.P., who probably would have delivered a more subtle and more theologically informed opinion than the Bishop of Madrid.

A pointed example of the intuitive rather than historical approach is Don Ramón's handling of the possible connection between Francisco de Vitoria and Charles V on the question whether Spain should abandon Peru. Marcel Bataillon, whose authority Don Ramón usually respects, doubts that Vitoria intervened on this issue. Don Ramón, giving us no shred of evidence, asserts that it is "inconceivable" that Charles V would not have consulted the famous Salamanca Dominican, and then gravely concludes: "En este caso concreto, como en otros varios, creo comprobado que fue Vitoria, en oposición a Las Casas, quien contribuyó eficientemente a soluciones definitivas."

Enough has been said to illustrate how this veteran scholar, who indignantly denies that he is an antilascasista, exhibits in this extraordinary book some of the worse defects he attributes to Las Casas: inconsistency, exaggeration, and dogmatism. This curious book, which reveals Don Ramón's tendency to transform conjecture into certainty, does make one important contribution; it helps us to understand--as did the work of Don Ramón's spiritual ancestor Marcelino Menéndez Pelayo--those "dos Españas que desde hace mucho tiempo han coexistido o luchado en la Península." Will future students reach the same conclusion on Don Ramón as the following on Menéndez Pelayo? "Viene a ser, así, una especie de símbolo a través del cual podemos ver la pugna y la tragedia de la historia de España; es él mismo un problema histórico."

The Significance of Don Ramón's Attack on Las Casas

How can Don Ramón's dedication to his objective of demolishing Las Casas be explained? Is it merely a strange aberration? I cannot believe this. The volume is rather an astonishing _tour de force_ which required great energy and acumen in marshalling data. Some have interpreted his campaign as a political effort, but this seems unlikely, although it is true that his first publication against Las Casas appeared at the end of the Spanish Civil War in the Falangist periodical _Escorial_. The many lectures and articles against Las Casas, between his first lecture in Cuba in 1937 and the climax reached with this book of 1963 constitute a personal crusade, I believe, sustained by his own passionate and very Spanish convictions.

Why did he write this book at an age when he could justifiably have devoted himself to being honorary president of literary congresses and to travelling about in the world? Incidentally he does this too! Recently he went to Israel, and in June, 1963, he told me he hoped to visit Russia, where a translation of some of his _Romancero_ studies is being done, and he plans to go by air as he finds train travel boring. The Mexican writer Antonio Castro Leal has made some acute observations on what he considers to be the true explanation of the attack. In reporting on Don Ramón's address in Oxford in 1962 to a group of Hispanists, Castro Leal wrote:

> En esta ocasión dió España--ante una asamblea internacional de hispanistas--un espectáculo que confirma sus más arraigadas tradiciones. Porque un viejo de noventa años, respetado y admirado internacionalmente, se puso a hablar mal de otro viejo, respetable también y todavía más admirado de propios y estraños. Desde hace unos años Menéndez Pidal se ha dedicado a destruir, con tenacidad muy española, a Fray Bartolomé de las Casas. Es una obra sistemática, llevada a cabo con un método científico, y en aparencia, con gran objetividad.
>
> Sorprende que el gran erudito español, que con tanta sabiduría y poder de adivinación ha descubierto y fijado aquellas hazañas a las que los héroes españoles de la historia y la leyenda deben su renombre y culto populares, no sea capaz ver y aquilatar que la acción y el anhelo constante de Fray Bartolomé por defender y salvar a los indios, se sobreponen a todos los cargos de inexactitud histórica, de exageración y aun de lo que pueda haber de difamación en la crítica de las violencias españolas en

América. Y a este apóstol tan emprendedor y activo, a este polemista tan furibundo y consciente de los males de su época ¿porqué se le va a juzgar simplemente como historiador? Es un héroe que ganó una causa justa y noble. Es un héroe y ha echado raíces en la conciencia popular tanto como el Cid Campeador.

Another scholar, the Bolivian historian Gunnar Mendoza, has also considered the meaning of Don Ramón's attack and has reached this thought-provoking conclusion:

A menos que ocurra un milagro, no se puede esperar todavía un juicio español ecuánime sobre las Casas porque eso es psicológicamente imposible, a si se quiere psiquiátricamente imposible ya que se ha traído a cuento la psiquiatría. Y, desde luego, no es que los españoles desde este punto de vista sean enfermos mentales, como muchos de ellos piensan de las Casas, pero lo que está fuera de toda discusión es que se enferman mentalmente apenas se les pone delante las Casas. No soy malicioso ni Menéndez lo es, pero estoy dispuesto a apostar que en su biografía de las Casas va a hacer algo parecido a lo que ha hecho Madariaga en su biografía de Bolívar. . . .Hay además de por medio un complejo de desquite o represalia, desquite y represalia con quien--las Casas--siendo español se dice que infamó a España. Lo mismo ocurre con Bolívar. Nadie pretende que Bolívar fue un santo ni que las Casas no exageró, pero Bolívar con sus flaquezas y todo fue el Libertador, y las Casas con sus exageraciones y todo dijo esencialmente la verdad. Con las Casas, aparte del complejo del desquite o la represalia, hay el complejo de la conciencia atormentada. Pero cuando los españoles se serenen en sus transportes anti-lascasianos, acabarán por ver lo que ahora es obvio para los demás: que las Casas salvó la conciencia de España, o, aún más, que las Casas fue la voz de la conciencia atormentada de España por la contradicción dramática implícita, para el caso del indio, en la famosa fórmula "se obedece pero no se cumple." Las Casas fue en América el verdadero Quijote (antes de que naciera don Quijote) contra los conquistadores andantes. Esta trilogía explica muchas cosas, y si Dios quiere para la commemoración de las Casas en 1966 trataré de escribir un papel para el que ya tengo (sublime progreso) el título: "De las Casas a don Quijote, y de don Quijote a Bolívar."

Another powerful and expressive voice, that of Agustín Yáñez, Mexican novelist and former Governor of the State of Jalisco, helps us to understand that attitude toward Las Casas in Spanish America:

Se habla de Fray Bartolomé de las Casas tan familiarmente como si fuese un personaje de nuestro tiempo. . . Y cuando Las Casas muere. . . América tiene ya por siempre la fisonomía que su Padre y Doctor le trabajó; fisonomía y estilo que retratan perdurablemente a Fray Bartolomé. Como éste, América es intransigencia, tenacidad, coraje; su clima es clima de lucha; su aspiración a la libertad, irreductible; América es dialéctica inacabable de abuso y derecho, de tropelía y verbo insumiso, de tiranía y democracia. Bien puede triunfar la violencia y vencer las argucias de los detentadores; América no se conformará, no se rendirá, como en jamás, ni en la hora de la muerte, pese a la adversa realidad y a lo aparentemente inútil del esfuerzo vital,

> se doblegaron el ánimo y las convicciones del fraile. Cuántos entre los americanos eminentes copian el temple de Las Casas; perseguidores de una idea, no les interesa que se les venga encima el mundo, que se les tache de soñadores, fanáticos o dementes; los ahogan ultrajes, calumnias, desprecios; enfrentan la muerte y más aún: el ridículo; por el resultado de sus empresas parecerá que los desmiente la realidad; ni su voz, ni su doctrina cejarán; les asiste la certidumbre de que si es preciso, del sepulcro mismo surgirán sus ideas perseverantes hasta el triunfo final.
>
> Por todo ello queda dicho que Fray Bartolomé de las Casas es uno de los sumos Padres y Doctores de América.

Is it any wonder that in Spanish America, except for some discordant voices such as Rómulo D. Carbia and the venerable Chilean historian Francisco A. Encina, many persons of different orientations have come to feel a special affection for Las Casas? The conservative historian of Argentina, Ricardo Levene, noted for his respect for Spanish traditions in America, has written some of the most acute and laudatory observations on Las Casas in recent times, and the Mexican Communist painter Diego Rivera recognized the contribution of Las Casas by including him in the famous mural in the Cortez palace in Cuernavaca, and characteristically placed on the opposite panel the fires of the Inquisition. The battles waged by Las Casas have also found their way into modern Spanish-American literature, for one hears in the Uruguayan poet Juan Zorrilla de San Martín's _Tabaré_ the echoes of the Las Casas-Sepúlveda controversy of 1550, and the Colombian dramatist Enrique Buenaventura presents in his "Requiem por el Padre Las Casas"--a play which, as is sometimes the case with historical dramas, includes little history--roused the usual polemical discussions when presented in Cali Colombia, in June, 1963. Such incidents reveal the truth of Professor Castro Leal's remark that Las Casas has become a symbol, a folk-hero like the Cid Campeador.

One might describe this Spanish preoccupation with Las Casas as the Nessus-shirt of Spanish American history, to borrow a phrase Professor Peter Russell of Oxford employed about the history of Spain. But this figure of speech from Greek mythology is not wholly exact for America, since the shirt that Nessus gave to Deianira and which eventually pricked her husband Hercules was a burden thrust upon Hercules. The burden some writers on the conquest assume is more like a hair shirt, as voluntarily and as eagerly put on as the real hair shirts were by medieval monks.

However one describes the fatal fascination that draws Spaniards toward the conquest, one non-Spaniard at least believes that by attempting to diminish Las Casas they are thereby diminishing Spain itself. Let everyone freely admit that Las Casas not only exaggerated the statistics of Indian deaths, but that he also failed to give a well-balanced or full account of Spanish accomplishments overseas. But should Spaniards not be proud of the fact that the King and his councilors listened sympathetically to him no matter how horrible a tale he had to tell or how radical a solution he proposed for Indian problems? They allowed him to print and circulate his ideas widely while his opponents were not allowed to publish, and he received many marks of royal favor in his lifetime. But he could not stop the forcible conquest of the Indies, nor prevent the Indians from being exploited.

Don Ramón winces when he looks back at the life and reputation of Las Casas. How is it that some Spaniards from the sixteenth century onward have tolerated, even praised him, when such men as Motolinía opposed him? And when Captain Bernardo de Vargas Machuca composed such a convincing Apologías y discursos de las conquistas occidentales? Don Ramón laments the blindness and pusillanimity of some of his ancestors, and condemns their timidity and error. For the Captain's apologia was never allowed to be published, despite the fact that it was prefaced by laudatory sonnets by four Dominicans. The Captain had a different experience with theologians, for when he drowned an Indian child he was absolved in the confessional. His modern biographer comments: "Perhaps, perhaps Padre Las Casas would have condemned him to Hell."

Let us hope that the four-hundredth anniversary of the death of Las Casas--which falls in July, 1966--will be the occasion for less heat and more light on the life and work of this great Spaniard. We may at least agree with Don Ramón Menéndez Pidal that the story of the Spanish conquest of America should be approached in the spirit of impartial historical criticism even if he himself has not led the way.

Now let us return to the great plaza in Mexico City where the monument to Las Casas as the apostle to the Indians stands so firmly. Will we ever see there a monument to Cortez, the conqueror of Mexico whose life and achievements are as integral a part of her history as those of Las Casas?

Cortez has long been a problem in Spain as well as in Spanish America, as Professor Marcel Bataillon reminds us in another of his acute studies, and it is not surprising that thus far Mexicans have emphatically refused to raise a monument to him just as Spaniards have never erected a statue to Las Casas in Madrid. Don Ramón at Oxford in conversation with Castro Leal expressed astonishment that Mexicans still cherished such feeling against Cortez and were not yet ready to forget the cruelties of the conquest. Why did they not remember instead the cultural contributions of Spain to Mexico, he asked with that curious naïveté that marks the attitude of some Spaniards toward Spanish-America.

The Mexicans' usual reply to this question is that their nation is not yet racially unified enough to permit any public recognition of the conquistador who symbolizes the action of the sixteenth-century imperialist invaders. Samuel Ramos, the Mexican philosopher, quotes Rubén Darío's cry that his soul was the object of contention "between the Cathedral and the pagan ruins," and then asks:

> Isn't this, perhaps, a valid image of the drama of America? Today very serious problems persist because of the schism between the culture inspired in our cathedrals, and the other, which emanates from our ruins. When the two heritages met they could not be combined in the creation of a new synthesis.

But is it not possible that Mexico, despite her important Indian heritage, is still so profoundly Spanish that Mexicans also share the burden of Spanish American history and will no more tolerate compromise than the Spaniards? If we ever see a statue to Las Casas in Madrid and a monument to Cortez in Mexico we can be sure that a new day has dawned, that mature acceptance has at least been reached, on both sides of the Ocean Sea, of the strange but strong relationship which always existed between the soldier and the priest whom the Spanish sovereigns sent together to the New World to conquer and to Christianize that world. Men will then see the long struggle for justice as a vital part of Spanish American history. They will see how many kinds of fighters participated and will understand how strongly the struggle has influenced historical writing on the Spanish empire.

The day of serene historical judgment has not yet arrived. Thus the views of the conquest held by the Colombian Juan Friede and the Spaniard Ramón Menéndez Pidal underline the truth of Sverker Arnoldsson's statement: that the conquest has been so vigorously discussed for over four centuries because this great period of history created the still-smoking problems of today.

The conquest is the "living part" of both Spain and Spanish America. How long ago it all happened! And yet how persistently the historical consequences remain as part of our world, our time, our problems.

DE HABILITATE ET CA-
PACITATE GENTIVM SIVE IN-
dorum noui mundi nũcupati ad fidem Chri-
sti capessendam, & quã libenter suscipiãt.

ROMAE Anno M. D. XXXVII.

CHAPTER 5.

INDIANS AND SPANIARDS IN THE NEW WORLD: A PERSONAL VIEW

When Charles Gibson enquired whether I would present a general statement on the attitudes toward Indians in the Spanish Empire in America as a part of a lecture series on comparative colonial history at the University of Michigan, I considered the task far too difficult. So much had been thought and written on that subject during the almost five centuries since Columbus reached the New World! The approach that seemed useful and possible to me was to recount how I discovered the significance of Indians in history, and how my ideas had developed through the years on this great and still much disputed subject.

Professor Gibson was courageous enough to encourage me in this endeavor, and the following personal essay resulted. Graduate students may be astonished at my remarks on job opportunities available, until they note that the lecture was delivered in 1968.

In Attitudes of Colonial Powers Toward the American Indian, Charles Gibson and Howard Peckham, eds. (Salt Lake City: University of Utah Press, 1969), 1-18. Reprinted by permission.

Indians and Spaniards in the New World: A Personal View

Since I am neither an Indian nor a Spaniard, I owe the reader an explanation for describing my remarks as "a personal view." Historians rarely write or talk much about themselves or their methods. They have grander subjects to discuss, larger canvases to paint. Occasionally an Edward Gibbon tells of his moment of inspiration while contemplating the ruins of ancient Rome when he determines that his lifework will be the study of the fall of its far-flung empire, or a William H. Prescott records in his diary the long search he undertook to find a suitable subject before he decided upon the Spanish conquest of Mexico and Peru. Historians are not noted for devotion to methodology, though Hubert Howe Bancroft defended himself and his historical methods in that remarkable final volume, Number 39, which he correctly and perhaps impishly entitled Literary Industries. In our own time, Halvdan Koht has narrated his role in Norwegian history because he was an important part of it; J. H. Hexter has given us a blow-by-blow account of how he spends his days as a prelude to explaining why history is constantly being rewritten. But these are exceptions. Others, like Henri Pirenne and Marc Bloch, even while in prison, wrote not about themselves, but about history.

Perhaps I have been influenced in this presentation by Carl Becker and his views on Everyman His Own Historian. Forty years ago, as the most junior member of the faculty of the American University of Beirut in Lebanon, I had the audacity to write him on the subject of historical interpretations, and he had the generosity to reply wittily and at length. Afterward, I followed his writings with special interest. At a time when graduate students in history are being urged to "get with it" and learn the mysteries of the computer in order to portray the past more quantitatively, it may seem downright exhibitionistic to write about how I discovered the Indians and what an impact their relations with the Spaniards made on me, but I hope this paper will demonstrate that the subject can be approached meaningfully in this personal way; indeed, there are so many parallels between the days of the Spanish empire and our own time that new insights, or at least new approaches, are possible if we analyze those parallels.

The first contact I had with the Indians was an exhibit of arrowheads in the public library in Piqua, Ohio--a small town which I grew up in and where I began to study Spanish under a lively teacher who first roused in me a curiosity about all things connected with Spain and the Spanish language. But neither then nor in my undergraduate years did Indians of any part of the Americas particularly interest me. They were part of the scenery as the Spanish conquistadors performed their great exploits; their ancient civilizations were for archaeologists to dig up for exhibition in museums, of purely antiquarian interest. Indians were buried for me under a mass of particular facts about innumerable tribes.

Then followed my first teaching experiences at the University of Hawaii and the American University of Beirut. Let us kindly draw a veil over this four-year period--I am sure that I learned much more than my students--but these years gave me some firsthand contact with other peoples, with different cultures than that of the United States under Calvin Coolidge. Following this apprenticeship in teaching, I returned to undertake graduate work. By chance a brief but suggestive study by a Spanish scholar, Fernando de los Ríos, in the field of law and political science came to my attention and brought out the fact that many theories of government were involved in the Spanish conquest of America. When it became necessary to prepare a term paper for a course on the history of political theory from Aristotle to Rousseau, I discovered that the writings of the sixteenth-century Spanish Dominican, Bartolomé de Las Casas, were full of ideas, and I worked out a monograph on this subject which was limited largely to theoretical and legal aspects of Spain's attempt to rule the Indies by just methods. This approach emphasized the juridical treatises by those who preceded Las Casas (such as Matías de Paz and Juan López Palacios Rubios), his own views, and those of his great contemporaries of the first half of the sixteenth century, Francisco de Vitoria and Juan Ginés de Sepúlveda. But, as I studied more deeply the great legacy of law and political theory that has come down to us from the sixteenth century, I began to be aware of some of the larger problems in the interpretation of the history of Spain in America.

The laws devised by Spain to govern her vast American dominions also formed a part of this juridical approach, for many of the ordinances were drawn up to protect the Indians by regulating the behavior of the Spaniards toward them. As political enemies of Spain and others have been quick to point out, these thousands of laws could not all be enforced throughout an empire that extended from California to Patagonia. The phrase with which royal officials in the New World received a new law which they did not intend to put into effect--"Let this law be formally obeyed, but not enforced"--has become embedded in all the textbooks as a clear case of Spanish hypocrisy. More correctly, it could be interpreted as a means by which the execution of an unpopular or unsuitable law could be suspended until an appeal could be made across the seas to authorities in Spain. Of course laws were broken throughout the enormous Spanish empire, and one of the best ways to find out what evils the Spanish crown was attempting to abolish is by analyzing the laws themselves. Some of the most telling descriptions of Spanish cruelty to Indians, for example, are found in the texts of royal orders --so much so that the seventeenth-century jurist Juan Solórzano y Pereira was ordered to remove from the manuscript of his fundamental work, Política indiana, some of the ordinances designed to prevent mistreatment of Indians so that notice of these incidents would not reach foreigners.

Laws also reflect attitudes and practices of society. Consider the significance of No. 24 of the Laws of Burgos, the first formal and detailed regulations drawn up to govern relations between Spaniards and Indians on the Caribbean island of Hispaniola only twenty years after Columbus landed: "We order and command that no person or persons shall dare to beat any Indian with sticks, or whip him, or call him dog, or address him by any name other than his proper name alone." I have long suspected that some Spaniards, given their legalistic nature, must have had an Indian or so baptized with the name of perro (dog) so that they could call them by this name with entire legality! The laws of many peoples of course contain similar revelations. For example, the 1967 state legislature of California passed the following law: "It is unlawful to drive an automobile under the influence of glue fumes or other chemicals classed as poisons." How useful historians in future years will find this ordinance as a clue to the mores of California today!

Las Casas knew his people and their veneration for legal principles, and once said, "For forty-eight years I have been engaged in studying and inquiring into the law. I believe, if I am not mistaken, I have penetrated into the heart of this subject until I have arrived at the fundamental principles involved." These fundamental principles Las Casas expounded in great, and at times painful, detail in the many treatises that I read as preparation for my study of his political theories. For this apostle, who burned with a fierce zeal on behalf of the newly discovered Indians, the true title of Spain and the only possible justification for Spain's actions lay in the donation by the pope, which was made in order to bring the Indians to a knowledge of Christ. Las Casas was bitterly scornful of the justifications which some people brought forward. To those who suggested that Spain's proximity to the Indies gave her a superior right, Las Casas pointed out that Portugal really lies closer to the New World. To those who urged the greater wisdom and understanding of Spaniards as justifying their lordship over the Indians, he replied that many other nations were wiser and of greater genius than Spain--witness the Greeks, the Africans, the Asians. To those who cited the opinion of the medieval thinker Ostiensis to the effect that all infidels are unworthy of exercising jurisdiction, he retorted that these persons do not really understand the true meaning of Ostiensis. As for those who established Spain's title because the Indians were idolatrous or committed unnatural crimes, they did not seem to realize that the Indians live for the most part an orderly political life in towns and in some respects are superior to Spaniards. And the worst reason of all was that advanced by those who justified Spain's title by her mere superiority in arms, which was an ". . . absurd, nefarious argument unworthy of being advanced by reasonable and Christian men."

Francisco de Vitoria, the Dominican professor at the University of Salamanca, never went to America, but he was also confronted with the problem of how to establish relations between Spain and the Indies. His was a more academic mind than that of Las Casas, though on many fundamental points their views coincided; in addition, he had a sense of humor, for he once remarked that if a canoe full of Indians had somehow reached Spain and "discovered" it, this fact would by no means justify Indian sovereignty over Spain. Today Vitoria is honored as one of the first and most important founders of international law, the development of which in modern times we owe to the many political theorists who sprang up in sixteenth-century Spain to argue over the true nature of her rule over the Indies.

But the legal approach is never wholly satisfactory; besides, even after the course on political theory was over, I was faced with the necessity of making "an original contribution to knowledge" in the shape of a doctoral dissertation. So in the fall of 1932, I took my wife and two small sons to Sevilla, after a summer in Germany where Adolf Hitler was beginning to reach for power with the help of his doctrine of racial superiority. In Spain I hoped to find the papers of Bartolomé de Las Casas, and, with ample documentation, to treat adequately the life of this passionate and determined friar whose influence in history has been so marked. But the papers of Las Casas--which were so voluminous during the last few years of his life that it was difficult for visitors to get in and out of his cell in San Gregorio monastery in Valladolid--simply could not be found. After some months of desperation, I came to realize that the story I wanted to tell did not depend upon finding more Las Casas papers. His essential doctrines and ideas, for the most part, had been published. My real discovery was that he was only one, the most aggressive and articulate to be sure, of those Spaniards who sought to have the conquest follow Christian and just principles.

Therefore, during nearly two years of work in Spanish and other collections, I abandoned the plan to write about one man, Las Casas, and decided that my aim would be to demonstrate that the Spanish conquest of America was far more than a remarkable military and political exploit, that it was also one of the greatest attempts the world had seen to make Christian precepts prevail in the relations between peoples.

Since those days in the Spanish archives, my life has consisted of more study, followed by observation in the field. Sometimes these essential activities of the historian were combined. In the summer of 1935, a grant enabled me to visit Latin America for the first time to consult some original Las Casas documents in the Convento de San Felipe in Sucre, Bolivia. The Chaco War between Bolivia and her neighbor, Paraguay, was still raging, and the young German pilots in my hotel in Sucre constituted a convincing illustration of the way in which outside forces and foreign nations have so often influenced or tried to influence the course of events in Latin America. As is frequently the case, I found a manuscript I was not looking for in the convent archive. Besides the Las Casas material, there was a copy of a formal record made in Spain of the deathbed statement made by Dominican friar Domingo de Betanzos, which was related by a notary public as follows:

> In the very noble city of Valladolid on September 13, in the year of Our Lord 1549, before me, Antonio Conseco, notary public of Your Majesties, being in the monastery of San Pablo of the Order of Preachers, in a room in that monastery there was an old man with head and beard shaven, lying in bed apparently ill but in his right mind, called Friar Domingo de Betanzos. And he handed over to me, the aforesaid notary public, a sheet of paper on which he had written and declared certain matters, which concerned his conscience, and which related especially to the affairs of the Indies, which manuscript and declaration he delivered to me.

This declaration referred to a written memorial Betanzos had presented to the Council of the Indies some years before in which he had declared that the Indians were beasts (<u>bestias</u>), that they had sinned, that God had condemned them, and that all of them would perish. Now on his deathbed the friar believed that he had erred ". . . through not knowing their language or because of some other ignorance," and formally retracted the statements in the memorial.

As I walked through the streets of Sucre after the archive closed for the day, I realized that for those of us interested in Latin American history the archive is not a sepulchre of dead information, but living documentation of a society much like the present. For, on my way home after my archival work had ended, I visited the ancient silver mining center of Potosí and there observed a Bolivian army officer viciously kicking Indian recruits brought together in the great Casa de Moneda for dispatch to the front. This officer also called the Indians "dogs" and other unplesant names. Later, when philosophically-minded historians eager to split hairs denied that any Spaniard had ever called Indians "beasts" in the full scientific and philosophic sense of the word, I found it difficult to follow their subtle reasoning. I had seen with my own eyes both the retraction of Domingo de Betanzos of 1549 on his deathbed and the treatment meted out to Indians in Bolivia in 1935.

On my return to the United States, plunging into the final struggle to organize in some meaningful way the material dug out of the solid historical rock in the archives, I completed my dissertation, which had the kind of dull title too often given to academic exercises --"Theoretical Aspects of the Spanish Conquest of America."

Then in the next year I observed living Indians closely in Mexico, Guatemala, and Brazil while studying anthropology and geography after emerging from the long process of graduate study as a "depression doctorate." No jobs were available since Latin American history was still considered a kind of fringe subject, and besides our universities were not expanding. Today, of course, the situation is reversed. Our newly-minted Ph.D.s kindly allow chairmen of departments and deans to compete eagerly for their services. Young scholars inquire into the fringe benefits offered and summer research grants available before they decide which position to accept. But in 1937, faced with the prospect of no job, I applied for a Social Science Research Council Postdoctoral Fellowship, and for eighteen months my family was supported while I studied cultural anthropology under the aegis of Robert Redfield and human geography with Preston James. The purpose was to broaden my interests and I was able to do so with the aid of this fellowship. Besides library study, I studied Redfield in the field as he studied the villagers in Agua Escondida above Lake Atitlán in Guatemala--a kind of parasitical existence! I discovered that this experience, brief as it was, deepened my concern for the native peoples and enlarged my understanding of the problems which the Spaniards met in their explorations. Because, in the written records of this now-distant time, Spanish voices spoke so much more loudly than those of the Indians, the historian in the Latin American field must never fail to try to hold in mind the Indian realities that were so meagerly documented, and sometimes only reflected, in Spanish records.

I had an opportunity to see how Indians and Indian problems were still of enormous concern to a number of Latin American countries, and also that present-day attitudes often influenced interpretations of the work of Spain in the New World, particularly its actions toward Indians and Indian civilization. This feeling was deepened during the twelve years I served in the Hispanic Foundation of the Library of Congress, 1939-51, a position which enabled me to travel widely in Spanish- and Portuguese-speaking lands and to discuss historical problems with their scholars. I published rather regularly in Latin American reviews and received valuable suggestions for the improvement of my work from my colleagues. My 1949 volume on The Spanish Struggle for Justice in the Conquest of America was based upon my doctoral dissertation, but also reflected my experiences and discussions over a dozen years or more.

These were the days before the phrase "publish or perish" came to have such sordid connotations. Spanish-speaking historians taught me that publication was the way to express one's personality, to engage in discussion and argument with other historians in the world and thus to learn from your peers. The most regrettable result of the present "publish or perish" syndrome is not that the world has to suffer some articles and books that are too green for human consumption, but that our younger colleagues, and some older ones too, have not come to realize that unless they do let the world know what they are thinking, they will not only have no evidence to be weighed on the scales outside the dean's office, but they will cease to grow intellectually. Reluctance to write, though, is no new phenomenon. The official Spanish chroniclers of the Indies were not paid the last quarter of their annual salary until they had handed in some writing to the Council of the Indies.

My experience in the Library of Congress not only gave me an opportunity to travel widely in the Hispanic world and discuss with many scholars their ideas and their preoccupations, but also to experience the changes going on in Washington, D.C., between 1939 and 1951; many significant things occurred during this time in the nation's capital, especially concerning racial matters. One of my secretaries for a time was a young Negro whose husband was a lieutenant in the army. The Library cafeteria was opened to Negroes, and I still remember my sense of adventure when the late Professor E. Franklin Frazier of Howard University had lunch with me there. One day I noticed that a Negro was eating in the Methodist Cafeteria, opposite the Supreme Court, and discovered that this excellent eating place had been desegregated without fanfare. So I invited my old friend from graduate school days, Professor Rayford W. Logan, then Chairman of the History Department at Howard University, to lunch with me there. He had not heard of the quiet revolution at the Methodist Cafeteria, but characteristically accepted, remarking that if any difficulty arose he would speak French so that he could pass as a Haitian diplomat.

All these experiences naturally affected the way I looked at the Spanish struggle for justice in America. Now this struggle on behalf of justice for the Indians appeared to have a more universal significance than before. This feeling was reinforced on our removal to Texas in 1951 to re-enter the academic world. Those were the days when the United States government and foundations alike had apparently forgotten Latin American and poured millions of dollars into the study of other areas of the world. There was some advantage in this poverty for one had an opportunity to think.

Texas, moreover, was a stimulating place to be in the decade 1951-61. This southwestern state was searching its soul on the question of justice for Negroes, and the regents of the University of Texas admitted Negroes before the Supreme Court required them to do so. But the power and the rigidity of the social structure, which had for so long maintained segregation, helped me to understand the bitter battles Las Casas fought. His intemperance alienated many in his own time and later too. His vehemence, his exaggeration, his unwillingness to sugar-coat the pill of his continuous and unpalatable criticism, and his incorrigible habit of speaking his mind freely to king, courtier, or conquistador, roused much resentment. His central idea was itself shocking to many of his contemporaries.

As I observed the events of the ever increasing battle over civil rights in Texas--for those of Mexican origin as well as for Negroes--the sixteenth century seemed to me to be drawing steadily closer to our own time. It was no superficial notion, but a fact that the social turbulence aroused then by the question of justice for the Indians had an important connection with the world situation today. In particular, I saw this with respect to the confrontation at Valladolid in 1550 and 1551 between Las Casas and Sepúlveda over the application of Aristotle's doctrine of natural slavery to the Indians.

Some controversies over men and ideas of the past are no more relevant to men today than the famous medieval disputes over the number of angels that can be accommodated on the head of a pin. But the struggle for justice between men of different races and cultures, which Las Casas and other Spaniards of the sixteenth century waged, was of a different order; it concerned the fundamental challenge that Europeans had to meet when they first encountered men of different cultures and different religions on American soil in that tremendous chapter of history known as the expansion of Europe. Viewed in this perspective, the Valladolid dispute lives on principally because of the universality of the ideas on the nature of man which Las Casas enunciated. He set forth, in dramatic and compelling fashion, his doctrine that ". . . all the peoples of the world are men," and his faith that God would not allow any nation to exist, ". . . no matter how barbarous, fierce, or depraved its customs," which might not be ". . . persuaded and brought to a good order and way of life, and made domestic, mild, and tractable, provided the method that is proper and natural to men is used; namely, love, gentleness, and kindness."

One of the finest passages in the Valladolid argument of Las Casas serves to illustrate the simple grandeur of which he was capable at his best:

> Thus mankind is one, and all men are alike in that which concerns their creation and all natural things, and no one is born enlightened. From this it follows that all of us must be guided and aided at first by those who were born before us. And the savage peoples of the earth my be compared to uncultivated soil that readily brings forth weeds and useless thorns, but has within itself such natural virtue that by labor and cultivation it may be made to yield sound and beneficial fruits.

Las Casas was here arguing against Aristotle, but he was also stating a proposition which has rallied men in many parts of the world. He was basing his argument on the belief that the way to civilize any people was to bring religion and education to them rather than just accustoming them to the material goods they had previously not known. The recommendation of Bernardo de Gálvez in eighteenth-century Mexico that Indians were to be given ". . . horses, cattle, mules, guns, ammunition, and knives," and were to be encouraged to ". . . become greedy for the possession of land," would have been an anathema to Las Casas.

Las Casas may have been wrong in his bold declaration that ". . . all peoples of the world are men," if this is taken to mean equality in all things. Recent scientific investigations demonstrate that, on the contrary, men vary greatly in many of their physical and psychological characteristics. But few today can be unmoved by his affirmation that ". . . the law of nations and natural law apply to Christian and gentile alike, and to all people of any sect, law, condition, or color without any distinction whatsoever," or by the words in which he set forth the sixth reason for the composition of his <u>History of the Indies</u>:

> To liberate my own Spanish nation from the error and very grave and very pernicious illusion, in which it now lives and has always lived, of considering these people to lack the essential characteristics of men, judging them brute beasts incapable of virtue and religion, depreciating their good qualities and exaggerating the bad which is in them. These peoples have been hidden away and forgotten for many centuries, and [it has been my purpose] to stretch out our hands to them in some way, so that they would not remain oppressed as at present because of this very false opinion of them, and kept permanently down in the darkness.

At a time when the conquistadors were bringing to the notice of the European world a whole new continent inhabited by strange races, it was Las Casas, rejecting Sepúlveda's view that the Indians were an inferior type of humanity condemned to serve the Spaniard, who "stretched out his hand" to the American Indians with faith in the capacity for civilization of all peoples. This conviction, in Las Casas and other Spaniards, and the action which flowed from it, gives a unique distinction to the Spanish effort in America. Las Casas represents both that "authentic Spanish fury" with which Spaniards confront human and divine matters, and the typical attitude of the Salamanca school of sixteenth-century theologians, who believed that thought and action must be so intimately fused that they cannot be separated and that spiritual truth must be made manifest in the world about us. Las Casas thought that the end of the world might not be far off--indeed, he wrote his History of the Indies in order to explain God's action in the event that He decided to destroy Spain for her misdeeds in America--but meanwhile there was work to be done in the world. He would have agreed perfectly with the seventeenth-century Puritan, Matthew Henry, who declared: "The sons and daughters of heaven, while they are here in the world, have something to do about this earth, which must have its share of their time and thoughts." He would also have considered as one of his followers Thomas Jefferson, who wrote a few days before he died on July 4, 1826, ". . that the mass of mankind has not been born with saddles on their backs, nor a favored few booted and spurred, ready to ride them legitimately, by the grace of God."

In an attempt to put the sixteenth-century struggle between Las Casas and Sepúlveda in perspective, I wrote a small book, Aristotle and the American Indians. In it I tried to show the relevance of this struggle to the present travail of our epoch of history, which might be called the expansion of the world, resulting, paradoxically, from the contraction of the world because of improved transportation and communication.

The passion aroused in Spain and America more than four centuries ago over the establishing of proper relations between peoples of different colors, cultures, religions, and technical knowledge, has a contemporary and poignant ring. Sepúlveda and Las Casas still represent two basic, contradictory responses to the culture clash resulting from the encounter between peoples who differ in important respects from one another, particularly in the power they hold. The hostility of those who have power toward those who can be called inferior because they are different--because they are others, the strangers--has been a historical constant. Indeed, at times it seems to be the dominant theme in human history. The challenge in our time is not only geopolitical and ideological on the international front, but touches us closely within our own society, where the cry for justice is uttered by embattled minorities who are articulate as the Indians of Latin America never were--or at least never were so far as we know from the records of history.

Today, because we North Americans hold so much power, we are beset by its consequences. The restlessness in many societies of the dispossessed, the disadvantaged--and our attitudes toward strangers, the ones who are different--has stirred in us an uneasiness because of those who now question our behavior. Sepúlveda has many followers who do not know that they follow him in believing that differences mean inferiority. So does Las Casas have followers who are deeply troubled because they believe that all the peoples of the world are men, with the rights and just claims of men, and that they must work to forward justice at home and internationally.

In November 1967, I attended the III Latin American Conference on Political and Social Sciences at the University of Santo Domingo.

Of all the troubled lands of Latin America, Santo Domingo is perhaps in the most difficult situation; it suffered for thirty years under the dictatorship of Generalissimo Trujillo, and, in April, 1965, was invaded by United States troops. The marks of those tragic events are still to be seen in Santo Domingo, in the minds of men as well as in the bullet holes which scar buildings there. The hostility of most conference delegates and of apparently all the student body to practically everything from the United States and to the vestiges of Spanish colonial rule was very marked. Many of the university buildings were festooned with "Go Home, Yankee" and "Down with American Imperialism" signs. Speakers at the afternoon session of November 27 could scarcely be heard, even with the aid of loudspeakers. Just outside the meeting hall, students kept up a steady barrage of slogans and rhythmic hand clapping, broken only by the ceremony of burning the United States flag and by periods of reading passages from the writings of Mao Tse-tung and Lenin.

As a historian, I could not forget that on the Sunday before Christman in 1511, a Dominican friar named Antonio de Montesinos preached a revolutionary sermon in a thatched-roof church on the island of Hispaniola, now called the Dominican Republic. Speaking on the text, "I am a voice crying in the wilderness," Montesinos delivered the first important and deliberate public protest against the kind of treatment being accorded the Indians by his Spanish countrymen. This first cry on behalf of human liberty in the New World was a turning point in the history of America, and, as Pedro Henríquez Ureña termed it, one of the great events in the spiritual history of mankind. . . .

The struggle that began in Santo Domingo continues today in that same troubled land, in all America, and throughout the world. The confusion over what constitutes justice and how to achieve it is also still with us, and historians still disagree sharply over their interpretations of the work of Spain in America. I still remember vividly the challenge hurled at me by a Spanish priest as I concluded a series of lectures on Las Casas in Havana in 1950--a verbal challenge, for he wanted to arrange a three-day debate between us, with secretaries present, on Spanish-Indian relations. And I also remember the tremendous denunciation of Las Casas by the ninety-five-year-old Spanish scholar, Ramón Menéndez Pidal, in 1963.

A totally different view was recently expressed by students in an undergraduate course at the University of Minnesota on "Man's View of his World, 1400-1800, and Now," conducted by John Parker, who reports thus on one part of their readings:

> We read *The Spanish Struggle for Justice in the Conquest of America*, and we talked about the world as a field for Christian mission as it appeared to men of faith in earlier centuries. We discovered how much has been forgotten about the debate that went on as to the Christian's duty to the American Indian, that in the sixteenth century men like Bartolomé de Las Casas, bishop of Chiapa, saw the civil rights problem then as one which related to both law and religion. After all, it was asked, weren't these missionary champions of the Indians showing their feeling of superiority to the Indians just as much as the enslavers of Indians, but tempering their admission of inequality with benevolence?

Were the friars and the other Spaniards who sought to defend the Indians basically paternalistic? Some--indeed, many--undoubtedly were firmly convinced of the immense superiority of their religion and their culture over the Indian way of life. But Las Casas and some of the other missionaries were not bigoted superpatriots. He respected many Indian customs and composed a remarkable treatise on their culture in which he did not assume that the Indians should be measured by a Spanish yardstick, but must rather be understood within the framework of their own culture. He looked at all peoples--ancient Greeks and sixteenth-century Spaniards as well as the newly discovered New World natives--as human beings in different stages of development.

Las Casas was deeply convinced of the importance of education and therefore was particularly impressed by the meticulous attention paid by the Mexican Indians to the education of their children in the ways of chastity, honesty, fortitude, obedience, and sobriety. . . .

To practical conquistadors and administrators, men aiming at immediate worldly goals and faced with different kinds of Indians--and perhaps to the crown as well, jealous of all royal prerogatives--Las Casas' reiteration that the only justification for the presence of Spaniards in the New World was the Christianization of Indians by peaceful means alone must have seemed dangerous nonsense. One can imagine with what contempt and horror his announcement was received that Spain ought to abandon America, with all its Indians unchristianized, rather than to bring them into the fold by forcible and, to him, profoundly unchristian methods.

As historians, we must recognize that, no matter what conclusion one reaches on Las Casas or on Spanish efforts in America, the struggles for justice--though they often failed--have endowed the history of Spain in America with a unique quality which powerfully influences the researches and the teachings of all who are concerned with Latin-American affairs, whether of the past or of the present. Cannot the undergraduates in our classes, aware as never before of the imperfections of our own society, now better understand the turbulent events of the history of Spain in America? Will they not see that the aspect of Latin-American history most bitterly discussed during all the years since 1492 has been the relations between Indians and Spaniards? The Spanish conquest has been so passionately discussed for so long because it created new societies whose old problems continue to haunt them today.

Thus the conquest is the still-living past of both Spain and Spanish America. Can we North Americans, engaged in world relations and our greatest social revolution, not learn something about Latin America's tragic problems and our own by recalling the events and protagonists of the first struggle for justice in the New World?

In the almost fifty years that have passed since, as a high school boy, I saw those Indian arrowheads in the Schmidlapp Free Public Library in Piqua, Ohio, I have come to see in my studies on the Spanish empire in America the significance of the view that all history is contemporary history.

CHAPTER 6.

THE THEOLOGICAL SIGNIFICANCE OF THE DISCOVERY OF AMERICA

James Cummins of the University of London, long-time friend and colleague in Las Casas studies, called to my attention several years ago the fact that an English encyclopedia on Catholic theology had included a brief article on "America: theological significance of" and the phrase struck my attention. Browsing around in the bibliography I found that remarkably little had been written in English on the subject. At the same time, I was completing an analysis of Las Casas' large treatise Defense of the Indians Against the Persecutors and Slanderers of the People of the New World Discovered Across the Seas. I also discovered that the John Carter Brown Library had recently acquired what appears to be the only known printed copy of the famous letter by Bishop Julián Garcés of Tlaxcala to Pope Paul III on the capacity of American Indians for Christianity.

So when Fredi Chiappelli, Director of the Center for Medieval and Renaissance Studies of the University of California, Los Angeles, organized in February, 1975, a conference focussing on the impact of the New World on the Old, there was my subject ready for elaboration. This article appeared in the proceedings of the conference, with appropriate footnotes and a facsimile of the letter by Bishop Garcés.

First Images of America: The Impact of the New World on the Old. 2 v., Edited by Fredi Chiappelli. Co-editors: Michael J.B. Allen and Robert L. Benson (University of California Press, 1976), I, 363-372. Reprinted by permission.

The Theological Significance of the Discovery of America

In reading the historical literature on the Renaissance and the Reformation, one gets the impression that Spain and Portugal had relatively little to offer, and that theology particularly was a learned enterprise that flourished only in certain soils, particularly those near Rome. American experience and American problems received almost no attention at the Council of Trent (1545-63), that great ecumenical gathering of bishops which was probably the most thoroughgoing reform in the history of the Roman Catholic Church. The Council was principally concerned with launching a theological attack on the Protestants, and the powerful Jesuits and other ecclesiastical authorities in Europe had not yet developed much interest in New World problems.

However we may explain the fact that most European thinkers in the sixteenth century paid little or no attention to the Iberian scholastic renaissance, this neglect continued for three centuries. Standard histories of philosophy and theology and general histories of the Church rarely made any reference to America or to the disputes which its discovery provoked among Spaniards of the Conquest period. Even such a generally conscientious and competent scholar as the nineteenth-century historian of the papacy, Ludwig von Pastor, included little on America in his massive opus, and not until Robert Streit began in 1916 to publish his monumental Bibliotheca missionum did the scholarly world have any solid bibliographical and documentary basis for the study of the history of the Roman Catholic Church in America. For this and other reasons, during the last half century the world of American and European scholarship has become more generally aware of the doctrines and disputes of the Dominicans Francisco de Vitoria, Bartolomé de Las Casas, and other Spanish theologians who concerned themselves with the ecclesiastical problems raised during the years between 1492 and the Council of Trent. But even now much remains to be discovered in this field, though what has been learned is not always recognized. The most detailed study on the salvation of pagans, by the Spanish Jesuit Angel Santos Hernández, for example, devotes little attention to America, although some substantial contributions on the subject have been published in Spanish and in other languages.

Throughout the Middle Ages Christian theologians debated whether pagans could be saved. The Catalan Raymond Lull declared in the thirteenth century: "God has such love for His people that almost all men in the world shall be saved; since, if more were damned than saved, Christ's mercy would be without great love." This assertion, however, was solemnly condemned as heretical by Pope Gregory XI, and the question whether force should be used to promote conversion to Christianity also produced deep disagreements. In the early fifteenth century the Order of Crucifers (Teutonic Knights) claimed that papal and imperial privileges authorized them to conquer the lands of pagans on Poland's frontiers by force of arms, a position which was strongly opposed by Paul Wladimiri, rector of Cracow University, at the time of the Council of Constance (1414-18). The Knights cited Aristotle's "natural slave" theory to justify their actions against the pagans.

Theologians paid considerable attention to what they called "God's virtuous heathen," but they achieved no consensus in the centuries preceding Columbus. Many believed that only a few could be saved. Thomas Aquinas, however, had a more generous position than that of the Augustinians, for example, for he held that God would employ extraordinary means to bring the conscientious pagan into the Christian fold, according to the axiom of the scholastics, Facienti quod in se est, Deus non denegat gratiam: "God does not refuse grace to one who does his best." But this was a theoretical attitude, rarely put to the test of reality, for few Europeans actually saw or had meaningful relations with many heathens (virtuous or not), inasmuch as their missionary activities had taken place largely on the periphery of the medieval world. Thus the first time Christians confronted millions of people unaware of their religion and were faced with the many practical and theoretical problems of converting them was when America was discovered. One student has explained in this way the inability of the medieval thinkers to cope with American problems:

> Medieval philosophers, including the Thomists, were generally under the influence of Aristotelian and Ptolemaic natural science and geography. Hence from a philosophical and theological point of view they were unequipped at first to deal with the new and astonishing problem of a New World. A fairly good parallel would be if, in our age, we should suddenly discover that intelligent life exists on a nearby planet. The theologians would be running all over the place trying to explain, and we would probably end up discussing many of the same questions that the Spaniards of the sixteenth century did.

As Richard M. Morse has concisely explained:

> Initially Spanish jurists and theologians were at a loss in characterizing the Indian. Certainly he was not a Christian. Neither could he rightly be considered an infidel or a heretic, categories amply defined in such sources as Las siete partidas. Was he an innocent child of nature with a human mind and soul, amenable to life in a Christian community? Or did his idols and human sacrifice show him to be inherently bestial and nonrational, a creature of Satan, an Aristotelian "natural slave?"

Missionaries who attempted to "get inside" the alien culture of the Indians became the first "cultural relativists," and many wavered "curiously between the dogmatic zeal of proselytizing and the pluralistic, freely inquiring temper of the Renaissance."

Spaniards were not only in the forefront of those who explored the vast reaches of the New World--Marcel Bataillon has pointed out that they roamed over as much territory in the 70 years after 1492 as had been explored in the previous thousand years by other Europeans--but they were pioneers too in tackling the theoretical and theological issues involved. Spanish efforts to Christianize the Indians have been characterized by Robert Ricard as a "spiritual conquest" of no less significance than the astounding military conquests of Hernando Cortés, Francisco Pizarro, and the other conquistadores who carried the banners of Spain to the far corners of her empire in America. As Enrique Tierno Galván says, in the discovery of America "the present and the past came together in a collision without precedent."

Europeans did not entirely ignore American developments, despite their preoccupation with the Turkish peril and the Protestant revolt. Bartolomé Sybilla in his Speculum peregrinarum quaestionum (1516) made one of the first attempts to understand the implications for Christians of the existence of masses of Indians in the New World who had had no previous contact with Christianity. Then Emperor Maximilian (1459-1519) became interested in the souls of the Indians and requested an opinion from Juan de Heindenburg, better known as Trithemio, who replied in his _Curiositas regia_ (1521) that "those infidels who had led innocent lives would suffer no positive punishment whatsoever, though they would be excluded from supernatural felicity or divine vision." Here Trithemio was applying the concept of limbo, which medieval theologians had developed to explain what happened to the patriarchs of the Old Testament and also to explain what happened to infants who died without baptism. About the same time as Trithemio, the archbishop of Turin, Claude Seyssel, elaborated the doctrine that ordinary pagans would be consigned to limbo, the intermediate stage between heaven and hell. None of the Spanish thinkers who wrestled with the theological problems created by the discovery of America seems to have followed the example of Trithemio and Seyssel in trying to apply the medieval limbo idea to the American Indians; indeed, the concept of limbo has never been and is not now an official teaching of the Church.

There seems to have been no sustained interest in Rome during the early years concerning America and the Indians, as John W. O'Malley makes clear: "Although representatives of the missions in the New World were present at the Fifth Lateran Council which met in Rome from 1512 until 1517, there is not a single mention of the New World in its acts and orations which have survived." An individual authority, however, such as Cajetan (Tommaso de Vio), cardinal and former Master General of the Dominican order, showed good sense and concern when he replied in 1532-33 to various pastoral questions sent him by Dominican missionaries in America. Cajetan had earlier argued strongly that conversions could not be forced and could be effected only by good preaching and good instruction by holy missionaries. He naturally denounced as unjust and immoral the wars of conquest in America.

Early in the history of America a new element entered into the problem--the idea that all Spaniards, laymen and priests alike, had an obligation to Christianize the Indians. During the long centuries of the _Reconquista_, when Spain was slowly recovering her lands from the Moslems, there had developed no doctrine that the Spanish _people_ had an obligation to help convert the Jews or Moslems. There was little effort by anyone in Spain to Christianize the Moslems, though there were some concerted attempts to convert Jews, especially by St. Vincent Ferrer. One of the methods used was compulsory attendance at sermons, but there seems to have been little or no theological doctrine behind these attempts, and certainly there was no feeling that lay Spaniards had a special responsibility to bring Jews or anyone else into the Christian fold. As Harold B. Johnson, Jr. has stated in a thoughtful analysis of missionary efforts in medieval Spain, even the Crown "had not been especially eager to convert Jews and Moors until the late fifteenth century, and then only for reasons of Castilian internal politics."

With the opening up of the New World with its millions of pagans, however, the idea emerged that all Spaniards should look upon the Indians as potential brothers and attempt to Christianize them. The Spaniards who enjoyed tribute and labor from Indians were expressly charged to aid in their conversion, a commitment never imposed on the _encomenderos_ in medieval Spain. Most important of all, the Spanish crown regarded the conversion of the Indians as establishing the "justness" of Spanish rule.

The missionaries were fired with a burning zeal to convert the Indians, and many of the hundreds of missionaries who hurried to America were determined to reestablish in the New World the foundations of Christendom which had been so severely shaken in Europe by the Protestant revolt. Their harvest was impressive. As Alonso de Zorita pointed out in an eloquent statement to the Council of the Indies in 1584, if Spaniards had made very little headway in converting the Moors in Granada during a 70-year period, in America they had achieved much: "Usually the missionaries taught the Indians to read, write, and observe good customs. Many have been taught how to play musical instruments so that they can play in church, while others have been taught grammar and rhetoric. Some have become excellent Latinists and have composed very elegant orations and poetry." Some six million Indians were baptized by 1540 according to one estimate.

But the success in America had not been accomplished easily. From the earliest years of the conquest there had been sharp differences of opinion, among lay and religious figures alike, on the capacity of the New World natives for Christianity and European civilization. The archives of the Council of the Indies, from the time it was established in 1524, began to fill with divergent testimony on the nature of the Indians, and occasionally Europeans who stayed at home had an opportunity to see a few Indians or their handiwork. Thus Albrecht Dürer in 1520 marvelled at the artistic ability shown by the Indian jewelry and featherwork sent by Cortés to Charles V for exhibition in Brussels. And when Cortés was engaged in getting several of his natural children legitimized he sent a group of Aztec jugglers to Rome to assist in obtaining papal approval. Charles V also once spent a pleasant afternoon in Valladolid watching Indian dancers and listening to their exotic music. But the first time that theological and ideological questions originating in America were reflected in a publication in Europe occurred in 1537 when the Latin letter written in 1535 by the Dominican Julián Garcés, the bishop of Tlaxcala in Mexico, was printed in Rome. This rare item, whose only known copy, well preserved, is in the John Carter Brown Library, was part of the campaign to convince Pope Paul III that the Indians could and should be Christianized, and their bodies and property protected from rapacious _conquistadores_.

The Council of the Indies, which considered that it had the principal authority and responsibility in the matter, had sought advice in many quarters, and a flood of sharply contradictory opinions resulted. One Dominican, Domingo de Betanzos, submitted such an unfavorable response that other ecclesiastics concluded that he considered Indians incapable of Christianity. Therefore they carried the dispute not only to the Council of the Indies but to Rome itself, where in 1537 Pope Paul III was prevailed upon to issue the famous bull _Sublimis Deus_ which declared Indians "truly men" and capable of the faith, in notable words. The first two paragraphs read as follows:

> The sublime God so loved the human race that He not only created man in such wise that he might participate in the good that other creatures enjoy, but endowed him with capacity to attain to the inaccessible and invisible Supreme Good and behold it face to face; and since man, according to the testimony of the sacred scriptures, has been created to enjoy eternal life and happiness, which none may obtain save through faith in our Lord Jesus Christ, it is necessary that he should possess the nature and faculties enabling him to receive that faith, and that whoever is thus endowed should be capable of receiving that same faith. Nor is it credible that any one should possess so little understanding as to desire the faith and yet be destitute of the most necessary

> faculty to enable him to receive it. Hence Christ, who is the Truth itself, that has never failed and can never fail, said to the preachers of the faith whom He chose for that office "Go ye and teach all nations." He said all, without exception, for all are capable of receiving the doctrines of the faith.
>
> The enemy of the human race, who opposes all good deeds in order to bring men to destruction, beholding and envying this, invented a means never before heard of, by which he might hinder the preaching of God's word of Salvation to the people; he inspired his satellites who, to please him, have not hesitated to publish abroad that the Indians of the West and South, and other people of whom We have recent knowledge should be treated as dumb brutes created for our service, pretending that they are incapable of receiving the Catholic faith.

By this time Las Casas had re-entered the fight on behalf of the Indians, after a long period of silence in the Dominican convent on the island of Hispaniola. He emphasized the need to educate the Indians and to persuade them individually of the truth of Christian doctrine. He entered into conflict with those missionaries--especially certain Franciscans--who favored rapid and wholesale baptism of the natives, without too many questions asked or catechisms learned. So hot did this argument become in America that it was referred to Spain, where the Emperor Charles V called upon a distinguished committee of theologians at the University of Salamanca, headed by the Dominican Francisco de Vitoria, which in 1541 decided in favor of those who insisted on proper doctrinal instruction. In this instance the Dominicans of Salamanca supported this position, while some of their old competitors the Franciscans took the opposite one. Yet there were larger issues involved, and adherents of both positions were to be found in all the missionary orders. It is even clearer that the theological problems posed by the discovery of America puzzled and profoundly disturbed Spanish ecclesiastics, no matter which order they belonged to.

Could the Indians really be educated? The Franciscan school for Indians at Tlatelolco in Mexico was opposed, particularly if the objective was to get them ready to be ordained for the priesthood; and in this instance the Dominican Betanzos was among those who opposed. As usual, the dispute was carried back to Spain for further discussion, and we find one prominent Franciscan, Alfonso de Castro, who supported the education theory in his treatise (1542) <u>Whether the Natives of the New World Should be Instructed in the Mysteries of Theology and the Liberal Arts</u>.

Castro had taught for 30 years in the Franciscan convent in Salamanca and had become famous for his treatise against Protestantism, <u>Adversus omnes haereses</u> (Paris 1534). With Francisco de Vitoria, he was considered one of the outstanding theologians of the time. His 1542 opinion in favor of instruction for the Indians is also of value in understanding the arguments against instructing them, which were:

1. The Indians are inconstant in the Christian faith;
2. They live obscene lives. Because they are like swine, Christians should not throw pearls before them;
3. The sacred texts of the Bible should not be shown to the people.

On the last point, Castro argued that the "mysteries of the Christian faith have value in themselves"; thus the Bible should not be hidden from the people. In this Castro's doctrine coincided with that of Bishop Juan de Zumárraga of Mexico, who in his "Conclusion exortatoria" favored translating the Bible into the popular languages so that it might be read by everyone: "I do not understand why our doctrine should be hidden away from all but those few called theologians. No one can be called a Platonist unless he has read Plato. Likewise, no one may be called a Christian who has not read the doctrine of Jesus Christ." Castro's argument that Scripture should be made widely available to the people must have surprised some of his contemporaries and perhaps explains why he buttressed his own views with the written support of five other established theologians, including the already famous Dominican Francisco de Vitoria. They not only approved Castro's doctrine, but explained in detail why they did so. They had never been to the New World, and they may never have seen the Indians brought to Spain by missionaries or _conquistadores_. But they perceived the deep issues involved in Castro's treatise, and their formal opinions, as drawn up at the time Castro presented his treatise to Charles V, are a notable part of the documentation available on the theological aspects of early American history. Vitoria had this to say:

> Everything that has been said by the Reverend Father Fray Alfonso de Castro seems to me to have been said in a way that is learned, pious, and religious. I am all the more amazed that anyone should have been the author or inventor of such dangerous (or better, deadly) advice for keeping those barbarians from learning and instruction, both human and divine. Certainly not even the devil could have thought up a more effective means than this for instilling in those peoples a perpetual hatred for the Christian religion. Many have abandoned Christ the Lord and the apostles after they had received the faith in different places. But it has not been thought for that reason that Christian doctrine should not be taught to others or that anyone should be kept from instruction.

Four other theologians also approved Castro's doctrine, including Luis de Carvajal who stated:

> I think that care should be taken that the peoples of the Indies be instructed with the liberal arts and the knowledge of Sacred Scripture. For who are we that we should show the partiality that Christ himself did not have? On the contrary, if these new peoples should see that they are carefully kept from our mysteries, we would give them the opportunity to form a most deadly suspicion. Further, it is ridiculous to admit them to baptism, to the Eucharist, and to the absolution and forgiveness of sins, but not to the knowledge of Scripture. Now it is indeed true that when the unworthy are admitted to a participation in the sacraments that which is holy is thrown to dogs. But whoever are by right admitted to these are for that reason worthy to share in the mysteries.

But the opponents of Indian education triumphed. In the year after Castro's treatise appeared, Betanzos and the Dominican Provincial Diego de la Cruz sent the Emperor Charles V a letter in which they declared strongly against Indian education:

> Indians should not study because no benefit may be expected from their education, first because they will not be able to preach for a long time inasmuch as this requires an authority over the people which they do not have; moreover, those who do study are worse than those who do not.

> In the second place, Indians are not stable persons to whom one should entrust the preaching of the Gospel. Finally, they do not have the ability to understand correctly and fully the Christian faith, nor is their language sufficient or copious enough as to be able to express our faith without great improprieties, which could lead easily to serious errors.

The Mexican ecclesiastical council in 1555 forbade the creation of an Indian priesthood, which meant that the Tlatelolco school lost one of its principal reasons for existence and the seminary withered away, even though some missionaries continued to fight for what they considered Christian treatment of the Indians. The policy and practice that led Tlatelolco to failure and that made it difficult if not impossible for the Indians to enter the clergy had grave consequences for both Mexico and the Church. As Robert Ricard, whose book on the "spiritual conquest" of Mexico is one of the best brief treatments we have of the early ecclesiastical history of Mexico, explains, the Church came to be considered a largely foreign institution whose fortunes were dependent upon the favor of the governing power at the capital, the ruling white Spanish group. Indians began to enter the priesthood in the seventeenth century, it is true, but in a sporadic fashion, and they were relegated to humble positions in rural parishes. There came into being, says Ricard, two groups of clergy who knew very little of each other, who loved each other hardly at all, and whose mutual antagonism may be symbolized by the rivalry between the two Virgins: that of the Indians, the _Virgen de Guadalupe_, and that of the Spaniards, the _Virgen de los Remedios_, the _Gachupina_. The Indians were served by a poor and miserable clergy, but the Spaniards had a white clergy that belonged to the ruling class and enjoyed enormous revenues. Ricard concludes that "if the _colegio_ at Tlatelolco had trained only one bishop for the country, the whole history of the Mexican Church would have been far different."

The controversy over the nature of the Indians and also the related question of whether force should be used in their conversion to the Christian faith came to a head--at least so far as Las Casas is concerned--in 1550 at Valladolid, where he attacked the ideas of an outstanding Spanish scholar, Juan Ginés de Sepúlveda, who held that Indians were definitely inferior to Spaniards, and that force was necessary to make them Christians. The Emperor Charles V and his advisers were sufficiently impressed by the problems created by this dispute to order conquests in the New World stopped until it could be determined whether they were just, and to set up in Valladolid a council of theologians and jurists to listen to the arguments of Las Casas and Sepúlveda.

We know a great deal about this dispute, thanks to the treatises written by the contestants. We find detailed arguments against Sepúlveda expressed with a singular force and richness in Las Casas' _Defense Against the Persecutors and Slanderers of the Peoples of the New World Discovered Across the Seas_. In this polemical volume, Las Casas sets forth in tremendous detail his passionate conviction that "all peoples of the world are human" and consequently can become Christians--if only they are properly educated by peaceful means in the true faith. This remarkable doctrine was the first enunciation and detailed theological justification in the modern world that all mankind is one, that all may be saved--a fundamental doctrine of "open admission" to the celestial world. When the full story of the theological significance of the discovery of America is known, surely the _Defense_ will be recognized as one of the fundamental documents in the history of those great disputes which shook the Iberian world in the sixteenth century. No more vigorous attack was made, at least in the Christian world, on "discrimination against men or harassment of them because of their race, color, condition of life, or religion" until the issuance by Vatican II of its Declaration on the Relationship of the Church to Non-Christians.

PART II

BARTOLOME DE LAS CASAS

CHAPTER 7.

THE ONLY WAY TO ATTRACT ALL PEOPLE TO THE TRUE RELIGION

Thirty five years ago it was an audacious move for a publisher to bring out a treatise by Bartolomé de Las Casas, and the influence of Silvio Zavala with the pioneering Mexican Fondo de Cultura Económica was needed to achieve the first publication of De único vocationis modo. For this relatively unknown work of the Indian defender was neither complete nor what readers expected. For it was not a fiery attack on the cruelty of conquistadores, but a reasoned and powerful plea for peaceful preaching. The publisher was pleasantly surprised; the edition was sold within a year, and recently another edition was issued.

My introduction for the treatise has never appeared in English, and was written on shipboard enroute to Brazil. During the voyage conversations with the anthropologist Melville Herskovits provided much information and perspective on the way in which peoples of different cultures have treated each other, conversations which were continued in Rio de Janeiro with Gilberto Freyre. It was easy to see that though De único vocationis modo referred to Indians and Spaniards in America in the sixteenth century, the problem Las Casas treated is of universal significance to all people everywhere and in all centuries.

For a more complete and up to date account of the remarkable Vera Paz experiment, see the model monograph by André Saint-Lu, La Vera Paz. Esprit évangelique et colonisation (Paris, 1968).

Fr. Bartolomé de Las Casas. Del único modo de atraer a todos los pueblos a la verdadera religión. Advertencia preliminar de Agustín Millares Carlo. Introducción de Lewis Hanke (Fondo de Cultura Económica, México, 1975), 21-60. Reprinted by permission. Trans. by Antenógenes Santamaría.

The Only Way to Attract All People to the True Religion

I. El Manuscrito y Su Autor

El tratado que ahora se imprime por primera vez es considerado como una de las tres grandes obras de Fr. Bartolomé de Las Casas, y dará gloria a su nombre mientras se estudie la conquista de América por los españoles. Las ideas principales de esta disertación sobre el único método verdadero para la predicación de la fe han sido conocidas hace mucho tiempo a través del excelente resumen hecho por Antonio de Remesal en la segunda década del siglo XVII, pero el manuscrito mismo se creía perdido. Así lo pensaba don Joaquín García Icazbalceta, y tan sólo gracias a los esfuerzos de otro gran erudito mexicano del siglo pasado, Nicolás León, fue descubierto este fragmento del trabajo y salvado para la posteridad.

Aunque el manuscrito así rescatado del olvido parece incluir todos los conceptos esenciales del tratado original, hay que subrayar que la obra aquí publicada contiene tan sólo los capítulos 5, 6 y 7 del Libro primero. Nadie sabe si el resto de la obra aparecerá alguna vez. Tenemos que contentarnos con la porción que se ha podido conservar, y tratar de comprender su importancia teórica y su influencia en la conquista.

No hay indicación precisa en el tratado de cuándo ni de dónde fue escrito. Es probable que fuera compuesto en Guatemala durante los años 1536 y 1537. Remesal indica que fue a comienzos de 1537 cuando Las Casas hizo a los españoles que allí residían, su famoso ofrecimiento de poner en práctica en Guatemala los principios contenidos en este tratado. Pero como Las Casas hace referencia en el presente manuscrito a la bula Sublimis Deus de Paulo III, fechada en junio de 1537, resulta que la obra, tal como ha llegado hasta nosotros, debe de ser una revisión posterior del primer tratado, porque la bula difícilmente pudo llegar a Guatemala hasta fines de 1537.

Pocos escritos han tenido en la historia del mundo un efecto tan inmediato como este denso tratado, recargado con cientos de citas, puesto que condujo al famoso experimento de la Vera Paz en Guatemala, del que hablaremos más adelante. Las Casas nunca imprimió este compendioso volumen, aunque empleó con frecuencia sus ideas en otros tratados, y poco antes de su muerte en 1566 parece haber estado gestionando que el Papa Pío V lo aprobara y lo publicase. En esto no tuvo éxito, pero la obra continuó siendo citada y era tenida en tanta estima que se sabe de cuatro copias que estuvieron en circulación en los primeros años del siglo XVII. Ignoramos por qué raros medios el presente fragmento ha sido conservado a través de los siglos; pero aquí está, ofreciéndose al examen de todo el que quiera tratar de comprender los vigorosos trabajos de Fr. Bartolomé de Las Casas, obispo de Chiapas, una de las figuras más grandes y más descutidas de la conquista de América por los españoles.

En la época en que Las Casas compuso este tratado era ya uno de los hombres más experimentados en los asuntos del Nuevo Mundo. Habiendo llegado a La Española en 1502 formando parte de la primera gran emigración de españoles a las tierras recién conquistadas, había tenido indios en encomienda, había renunciado a ella en 1514 porque consideraba el sistema injusto, y en 1515 había comenzado su carrera como protector de los indios, que continuó hasta su muerte en 1566. Uno de sus primeros experimentos había sido el infructuoso intento en 1519 y 1520 de fundar una colonia en la costa de Paria con honrados labradores españoles que enseñaran a aceptar a los indios las creencias y las costumbres españolas por medios pacíficos. El fracaso de estos proyectos--debido en no pequeña parte a las acciones de otros españoles menos humanitarios --sumió a Las Casas en profundo abatimiento. Se retiró al convento de dominicos de la ciudad de Santo Domingo, Española, en 1521, y entró en la orden dos años más tarde. Durante varios años parece haberse dedicado a las obras de religión y al estudio. En 1529 pudo someter a la autoridad de los españoles al cacique indio Enriquillo, muy notorio por su rebeldía, mediante procedimientos pacíficos y amistosos. Durante los cinco años siguientes visitó a México, Nicaragua, Honduras y otras partes del imperio español en el área del Mar Caribe. Así pues, pocos funcionarios, colonos o eclesiásticos habían disfrutado de una experiencia más amplia en las nuevas tierras que Las Casas, cuando en 1536 comenzó a escribir este tratado.

II. Antecedentes de la Situación

La doctrina enunciada por Las Casas en esta obra, la primera de una larga serie de sus escritos polémicos, era bien sencilla. Citaba, como lo hizo el Papa Paulo III en la bula Sublimis Deus, las palabras de Cristo, "id y predicad a todas las criaturas", y los dos hombres estaban acordes en que los indios americanos quedan incluidos. Las guerras contra ellos eran injustas y tiránicas, declaraba Las Casas; por lo tanto, el oro, plata, perlas, joyas y tierras que se les habían arrebatado tenían que serles devueltos. No sólo era ilegal emplear la fuerza para dominarlos y convertirlos, sino que era innecesario.

Este era el argumento, y antes de examinar la doctrina en detalle, será útil subrayar que el punto central de discusión, si la fuerza debería o no ser empleada para convertir a los indios, era un viejo problema que había surgido durante los primeros años de la conquista. A Colón le fue ordenado que tratara "amorosamente" a los indios, en las instrucciones reales relativas a su segundo viaje, fechadas el 29 de mayo de 1493, pero siempre ocurrían "incidentes" que algunos españoles creían que debían ser castigados por la fuerza. Los sacerdotes enviados en este segundo viaje para evangelizar a los indios y enseñarles "paz y buena voluntad" pronto quisieron dar un ejemplo, castigando a sangre y fuego a la tribu que había destruido la guarnición que había dejado el Almirante en su primer viaje.

Las instrucciones reales, no obstante, ordenaban que a los indios se les instruyera en la fe por medios pacíficos. Pero, ¿qué iba a hacerse cuando había eclesiásticos como el fraile jerónimo Fr. Bernardino de Manzanedo, que informaba en 1518 que los indios de La Española y de San Juan parecían no tener amor por la doctrina cristiana y no la aceptarían a menos que se les forzara a hacerlo? Siempre que los monarcas españoles trataban de los asuntos de Indias este problema era el principal. En 1524, por ejemplo, el rey aprobó la liberación de ciertos indios, a despecho de que habían confesado ser caníbales, porque pensaba que la mejor manera de atraerlos a la fe y de apartarlos de sus usos abominables era mediante la benevolencia.

A pesar de esta actitud de los reyes, opiniones de índole contraria seguían siendo remitidas desde el Nuevo Mundo. El 1º de mayo de 1532 el Presidente y la Audiencia de la Nueva España, junto con los prelados y los frailes, dieron al rey el parecer unánime de que los indios eran tan belicosos que se hacía muy necesario que sintieran la fuerza del brazo real, no sólo para la seguridad de los españoles, sino también para que los indios fueran con ello adoctrinados en la fe.

En la respuesta real no se aprobaba esta política, recomendándose, en cambio, que los indios de la Nueva España fueran atraídos a la fe y a las costumbres de los españoles haciéndoles vivir entre éstos. Durante la junta de 1533, celebrada en España para discutir lo que había de hacerse con los indígenas de La Trinidad, se decidió que deberían ser llevados al conocimiento de la fe tan sólo por la gracia de Dios, y no por la fuerza, pero que si se resistían o impedían la predicación, la fuerza podría ser empleada.

De un modo análogo, los teólogos y juristas de la época se ocuparon del problema y escribieron disquisiciones que conocemos tan sólo por sus títulos. Juan López de Palacios Rubios, que compuso el primer tratado sobre el Nuevo Mundo, el De Insulis, escribió un Tratado esforzando a los Indios a la Fe católica. Isolanis de Milán compuso De Imperio militante Eccesiae (1515), y Nikolaus Herborn De Insulis noviter inventis (1532).

Pero cuando Las Casas se puso a examinar los escritos sagrados y profanos existentes sobre la manera adecuada de tratar a los infieles y de atraerles a la fe, tenía la idea no sólo de corregir los errores de los funcionarios reales y de los autores de tratados eruditos, sino también los de los colonos y conquistadores españoles. Algunos de éstos estaban tan seguros de que los indios eran bestias o casi bestias, y que no había que tenerles consideración ni darles cuartel, que otro dominico, Bernardino de Minaya, tuvo que ir hasta Roma para obtener de Paulo III en 1537 la bula Sublimis Deus, que afirmaba que los indios eran seres racionales, cuyas vidas y propiedades tenían que ser respetadas. Oviedo, a quien Las Casas consideraba como uno de sus principales enemigos, representaba bien la actitud de estos españoles cuando afirmaba rotundamente: "Ya se desterró Sathanás desta isla [la Española]: ya cesó todo con cesar y acabarse la vida a los más de los indios."

Otros colonizadores, tales como Espinosa y Zuazo, pensaban que "parece que es Dios Nuestro Señor servido de que estas gentes de indios se acaben totalmente, o por los pecados de sus pasados o suyos, o por otra causa a nosotros oculta, e que pase e quede el señorío e población en Vuestra Magestad e sus sucesores y pobladas de gente cristiana."

Como Oviedo decía: "¿Quién puede dudar que la pólvora contra los infieles es incienso para el Señor?". Las Casas compuso su De Unico Vocationis modo contra este estado de cosas de media centuria de conquista violenta, de odio acumulado y de vejación de los indios.

III. La Doctrina

Para quienes hayan leído las vigorosas fulminaciones y los tremendos epítetos de Las Casas en su Brevísima Relación de la Destrucción de las Indias o en la Historia de las Indias, el moderado lenguaje y las exhortaciones elocuentes del presente tratado serán una sorpresa agradable. Podría parecer que aquí está haciendo un esfuerzo especial para practicar lo que ha predicado. Rara vez menciona las Indias, y desarrolla su argumento en un plano elevado en el que sólo se consideran las verdades universales. Es digno de observarse también que Las Casas nunca parece haber invocado ningunas autoridades contemporáneas, tales como la de Tomás Moro, cosa que hacía Vasco de Quiroga.

Los cuatro primeros capítulos del tratado, que no figuran en el presente manuscrito, los dedicaba Las Casas a explicar la sencilla verdad de que todas las gentes sobre la faz de la tierra han sido llamadas por Dios a recibir la fe como un beneficio de la liberalidad divina. Aunque es cierto que los hombres difieren unos de otros en todas partes, es sencillamente imposible que toda una raza o nación--por estúpida o idiota que sea--, carezca en absoluto de capacidad para recibir la fe. Es evidente que esta afirmación incluía a los indígenas del Nuevo Mundo, en particular cuando se aprecia que los indios son en su mayoría seres inteligentes, y que en una proporción elevada están dotados de un entendimiento excepcional, como puede verse por lo que hacen en las artes mecánicas y liberales.

Las Casas entra aquí en el meollo de la cuestión, afirmando:

> La Providencia divina estableció, para todo el mundo y para todos los tiempos, un solo, mismo y único modo de enseñarles a los hombres la verdadera religión, a saber: la persuasión del entendimiento por medio de razones, y la invitación y suave moción de la voluntad. Se trata, indudablemente, de un modo que debe ser común a todos los hombres del mundo, sin ninguna distinción de sectas, errores, o corrupción de costumbres.

Las Casas demuestra esta proposición de una manera muy erudita, en treinta y seis largos apartados, mediante citas y ejemplos del Antiguo y del Nuevo Testamento, con referencia a las enseñanzas y a la conducta de Cristo y sus Apóstoles, mediante la solemne autoridad de los santos doctores de la Iglesia y de su antigua tradición, y con una multitud de decretos de los distintos Papas. Aunque el espacio no nos permite una exposición detallada de estos treinta y seis apartados, algunos de los argumentos empleados por Las Casas son dignos de especial atención.

La única manera de influir sobre los seres racionales, explica, es mediante "la persuasión de su entendimiento", según lo dijo Aristóteles. Además, siguiendo a San Agustín, la fe depende de la creencia, la cual presupone el entendimiento. Por lo tanto "el modo de enseñar, de encaminar o de atraer al seno de la fe y de la religión cristiana a los hombres que se encuentran fuera de él, debe ser un modo que persuada al entendimiento y que mueva, exhorte o atraiga suavemente la voluntad."

A fin de creer las verdades del cristianismo, quienes las escuchen deberán estar con ánimo tranquilo, tener tiempo suficiente, que les permita apreciar y darse cuenta de la verdad, y no habrán de sufrir violencia que pueda inspirarles aversión a las nuevas ideas. Es indudable que Las Casas, aunque no lo menciona, no aprobaría el Requerimiento, aquel largo documento jurídico que era leído a los indios por los capitanes españoles, por el cual se justificaba la conquista por las armas si los indios no reconocían desde luego la autoridad de los monarcas españoles y no consentían la predicación de la fe. En opinión de Las Casas, la precipitación o el empleo de la fuerza repelen más que atraen a los que todavía no son cristianos. A decir verdad, la predicación a los infieles es un arte que tiene que ser estudiado. Sobre todo, los ánimos de los oyentes no han de estar dominados por la pena o la cólera si han de aceptar la verdad. Las Casas demuestra conocer las leyes naturales que los psicólogos están ahora pregonando ante el mundo, cuando afirma:

> Pero la costumbre es un hábito, o engendra un hábito con la repetición de actos adquiridos; el cual, si no es una naturaleza propiamente dicha, es indudablemente una forma de naturaleza, ya que la costumbre hace que las operaciones acostumbradas sean fáciles, prontas y desembarazadas, como si la misma naturaleza les hubiera dado principio.
>
> Es necesario que quien se propone atraer a los hombres al conocimiento de la fe y de la religión verdaderas, que no pueden alcanzarse con las fuerzas de la naturaleza, use de los recursos de

este arte. Es decir, que frecuentemente, que con la mayor frecuencia posible, proponga, explique, distinga, determine y repita las verdades que miran a la fe y a la religión; que induzca, persuada, ruegue, suplique, imite, atraiga y lleve de la mano a los individuos que han de abrazar la fe y la religión. Y que prosiga por este camino hasta que, con la frecuente presentación, manifestación, predicación y distinción de la doctrina; con la explicación de las verdades creíbles; con el ruego, la súplica, la inducción, la invitación, la suave atracción, la conducción fácil y segura; con la frecuente repetición de estos actos, se engendre paulatinamente en el corazón de los oyentes una fuerza, una disposición, una costumbre o un hábito agradable que dé origen, finalmente, a una inclinación casi natural a las verdades de la fe y de la religión. El ánimo del hombre entonces, fortalecido y dispuesto con esta inclinación, escuchará con mayor placer las verdades mencionadas que, por estar acostumbrado a oírlas, le serán ya agradables; se alegrará de ver proporción para el conocimiento de las verdades de la fe que oye o se le proponen, y las aceptará con más facilidad; y las verá, no como extrañas a la razón, sino como conformes y ajustadas a ella en cuanto a la verdad. Y de consiguiente, a los hombres, aun a los idólatras e infieles, no les será tan difícil abandonar los ritos de la infidelidad y las supersticiones de su depravada religión; y si han recibido ya la fe y religión verdaderas, pero tal vez con simulación o tibieza, mudarán sinceramente de ánimo, comenzando a vivir con fervor y adelantándose hasta conseguir un verdadero provecho.

El argumento deriva ahora hacia otro punto. Las Casas principia con Adán y muestra que desde el comienzo del tiempo los santos patriarcas han dado muestras de un espíritu paternal al tratar con los demás hombres. Los libros de profecías dan abundantes testimonios sobre este punto, porque indican que la fe era enseñada--y aquí vemos un buen ejemplo de la suavidad de expresión de Las Casas en este tratado: "Así como la lluvia y la nieve bajan del cielo, no impetuosa, no violenta, no repentinamente, con suavidad y blandura, y empapando la tierra con su caída."

Este método fue instituido por Cristo, quien ordenó que fuera observado por sus Apóstoles. Aunque el método era usualmente eficaz, si los medios pacíficos no daban resultado, lo único que tenían que hacer era abandonar semejantes lugares. Así Cristo concedió a los Apóstoles licencia y autoridad para predicar la fe tan sólo a aquellos que voluntariamente desearan escucharla. No habían de forzar ni molestar a quienes no quisieran hacerlo. Ni habían de castigar a quienes expulsaban a los Apóstoles de sus ciudades. Según declaraba, "Os envío como ovejas en medios de lobos".

Expone luego Las Casas las cinco condiciones que deben existir si la predicación a los infieles ha de tener éxito. Son las siguientes:

1. Los oyentes deben comprender que los predicadores no tienen intención de adquirir dominio sobre ellos.

2. Los oyentes deben estar convencidos de que ninguna ambición de riquezas mueve a los predicadores.

3. Los predicadores deben ser tan "dulces y humildes, afables y apacibles, amables y benévolos al hablar y conversar con sus oyentes, y principalmente con los infieles, que hagan nacer en ellos la voluntad de oírlos gustosamente y de tener su doctrina en mayor reverencia".

4. Los predicadores deben sentir el mismo amor y caridad por la

humanidad que los que movieron a San Pablo, permitiéndole llevar a cabo tan enormes trabajos.

5. Los predicadores deben llevar vidas tan ejemplares que sea claro para todos que su predicación es santa y justa.

Para cada uno de estos cinco puntos, Las Casas acumula una multitud de autoridades y ejemplos, en particular de los escritos de San Juan Crisóstomo, a quien caracterizaba como "el brillantísimo San Juan Crisóstomo, quien habló más espléndida y copiosamente que los demás doctores de la santa Iglesia".

El razonamiento se hace ahora histórico. Las Casas muestra que la persuasión pacífica fue el método primitivo de la Iglesia, y se refiere en particular a la conquista espiritual de España y de Inglaterra. Aquí aparece una de las pocas referencias específicas a las Indias que Las Casas se permite en todo el tratado: Cuán diferente de estas conquistas fue la manera como los españoles llevaron a Moctezuma y Atahualpa el conocimiento de Cristo. Esto es lo único que dice Las Casas sobre un tema que más tarde había de desencadenar todos los torrentes de sus ásperas recriminaciones.

Por último, los decretos de la Iglesia, y en especial la bula Sublimis Deus de Paulo III--que reproduce en su totalidad--son citados para reforzar el argumento, y Las Casas llega a rematar triunfalmente los treinta y seis apartados con un detallado resumen de todo lo que ha dicha antes. Así termina el capítulo quinto.

El capítulo sexto es mucho más breve y está dedicado a exponer, para demolerlo inmediatamente, el método guerrero de predicar la fe. A aquellos que sostienen que los infieles han de ser sometidos primeramente, quiéranlo o no, para predicarles luego, Las Casas les replica que eso significa la guerra. Y la guerra lleva consigo los siguientes males:

> El estrépito de las armas; las acometidas e invasiones repentinas, impetuosas y furiosas; las violencias y las graves perturbaciones; los escándalos, las muertes y las carnicerías; los estragos, las rapiñas y los despojos; el privar a los padres de sus hijos, y a los hijos de sus padres; los cautiverios; el quitarles a los reyes y señores naturales sus estados y dominios; la devastación a la desolación de ciudades, lugares y pueblos innumerables. Y todos estos males llenan los reinos, las regiones y los lugares todos de copioso llanto, de gemidos, de tristes lamentos y de todo género de luctuosas calamidades.

Además, este sistema es contrario a la manera pacífica favorecida por los sabios filósofos, por el ejemplo de los patriarcas anteriores a la venida de Cristo y por Cristo mismo. Por lo tanto, todos los que emprenden semejantes guerras están privados del amor de Dios, y en realidad odian a Dios. No son cristianos, sino auténticos imitadores de aquel "notable y asquerosísimo seudoprofeta y seductor de los hombres, de aquel hombre que mancilló todo el mundo, de Mahoma, queremos decir".

Quienes emprenden guerra semejante, pero dicen que no están forzando a los infieles a aceptar la fe y que se limitan a apartar los obstáculos que impiden a los predicadores enseñar la fe, hablan--afirma Las Casas--de una manera absurda y disparatada, pues bajo tales condiciones lo único que resulta es un resentimiento perdurable y una fingida conversión por temor a males peores. Semejantes personas no sólo son precursores del Anticristo, sino también secuaces de Mahoma en su método de conversión a sangre y fuego. Así termina el capítulo seis.

El capítulo siete consta de un sumario y de los ejemplos finales de la conclusión alcanzada en los dos capítulos anteriores. La primera, y la única, conclusión de Las Casas, es ésta:

La guerra contra los infieles de la tercera categoría (es decir, aquellos que nunca han sabido nada de la fe ni de la Igleisa, y que nunca han ofendido a ninguna de las dos), es "temeraria, injusta, inicua y tiránica", aunque pueda alegarse que la guerra se emprende tan sólo para preparar a los infieles a recibir la fe o parà desplazar impedimentos a su predicación. Semejante guerra está claramente contra la ley natural, la ley divina y la ley humana.

A continuación Las Casas enuncia varios corolarios audaces, que deben haber motivado que más de ún conquistador lo denunciara como un hombre peligroso, que trataba de destruir la sociedad del Nuevo Mundo. Porque en una tierra en la que probablemente todos los españoles, en un momento o en otro, habían combatido a los indios, Las Casas se atreve a hacer las afirmaciones siguientes:

1. Todos los que emprenden semejantes guerras o que contribuyen a ellas de cualquier modo pecan mortalmente. Se extiende con gran detalle sobre la naturaleza exacta, la cualidad y los grados del pecado así cometido.

2. Todos los que son o hayan sido causantes de tales guerras están obligados, como requisito previo para su salvación, a hacer restitución a los infieles de todo lo que éstos hayan perdido en las guerras y--aquí hay una orden muy tajante--"a satisfacerles solidariamente por todos los daños que les hayan hecho". Sobre la extensión del daño a pagar Las Casas no deja duda, pues explica que, si bien parte de la angustia y del sufrimiento causados por la guerra nunca puede ser reparada, el español que hubiese matado a un infiel debería ciertamente estar obligado a mantener a la mujer e hijos del indio muerto durante todo el tiempo que éste pudiera haber vivido.

3. Como una especia de corolario suplementario, Las Casas declara que los eclesiásticos erraban grandemente--aun en caso de tener el poder y la autoridad episcopales--si, estando dedicados a la predicación e instrucción de los indios, los castigaban por cualquier pecado que pudieran haber cometido antes o después de su conversión, con azotes terribles, el encarcelamiento u otros castigos, bien aplicados por sus propias manos o bien por mandato suyo.

Cierra Las Casas el primer libro de su tratado con una exhortación tomada de San Próspero a ganar las almas por medios suaves y por una comprensión tierna con preferencia a la fuerza imperiosa.

IV. El Experimento de la Vera Paz

Si el De Unico Vocationis Modo fuera tan sólo uno más de los muchos tratados de naturaleza teórica escritos sobre América, apenas si estaría hoy justificada su publicación, aun tratándose de una obra de Fr. Bartolomé de Las Casas. Pero este extenso manuscrito, con su rico acopio de citas cuidadosamente reunidas de una multitud de escritos--que, por cierto, revelan la abundancia de libros que Las Casas pudo tener a su disposición en algún monasterio--es importante por dos razones:

1. Las Casas fue retado inmediatamente por los españoles seglares para que tratara de llevar a la práctica sus ideas, y

2. El experimento resultante, llevado a cabo en Vera Paz, Guatemala, es una ilustración excelente del hecho de que la conquista española de América fue mucho más que una empresa militar notable en la que un puñado de españoles sometió a todo un continente en un tiempo sorprendentemente corto. Fue también probablemente el esfuerzo mayor que

jamás haya visto el mundo para hacer prevalecer la justicia y los preceptos cristianos en una época brutal y sanguinaria. Este concepto es tan importante que requiere alguna explicación antes de describir la entrada de Las Casas en Vera Paz.

El concepto no es nuevo, porque investigadores como Rafael Altamira, José María Chacón y Calvo, Ricardo Levene, Ernest Nys, Fernando de los Ríos, Silvio Zavala, y algunos otros, han aportado contribuciones de importancia a este tema. Pero en general puede decirse que la historia de la conquista española de América ha sido escrita--al menos en los Estados Unidos--a la manera heroica de William Hickling Prescott, en el tono irónico de Philip A. Means, o en fragmentos monográficos destinados a servir de tesis doctorales en las universidades. Nadie ha estudiado todavía en conjunto los teóricos de la conquista española que estuvieron decididos a que la dominación española en América siguiera principios justos y cristianos.

Esta lucha comenzó casi con la conquista misma, pues surgió una disputa sobre el primer cargamento de indios que fueron llevados a España para ser vendidos como esclavos. El 12 de abril de 1495 el obispo Fonseca recibió orden de la corona para que vendiera dichos indios, y al día siguiente otro documento le ordenaba que guardase el dinero recibido de la venta hasta que los teólogos pudieran dar satisfacción a la conciencia real con respecto a la moralidad del acto. Conforme la conquista avanzó de las islas del Caribe a México, Perú, Chile y las islas Filipinas, surgió un torrente de libros y tratados polémicos escritos por misioneros y funcionarios de la corona en el Nuevo Mundo y por teóricos académicos y juristas profesionales de España, que hacen recordar las polémicas enconadas y eruditas que se produjeron durante la controversia medieval de las investiduras.

Fue una lucha quijotesca, podemos decir hoy, pero ha de recordarse que Don Quijote fue una auténtica expresión del genio español en la época de la grandeza de España. Era un hombre de ideales, inspirado por la pasión de corregir los defectos del mundo, y con este fin se lanzó sobre el mundo que veía. No es exagerado decir que en la conquista la corriente quijotesca del carácter español aparece en su forma mejor, y la sanchopancesca en la peor, hasta que la batalla llega en ocasiones a convertirse en una lucha abierta entre los aspectos más elevado y más bajo de la naturaleza humana.

Incluso cuando se ha hecho mención de las teorías españolas relativas a sus problemas coloniales, ha sido por lo general con un propósito despectivo, señalando cuán lejos estaba la conducta española en América de la teoría hispana. A veces la preocupación de los españoles por elaborar una política que pudieran justificar ante su propia conciencia se ha desechado como hipócrita religiosidad, algo así como el espíritu de la foca de Alicia en el país de las maravillas, que derramaba lágrimas tan amargas mientras se apresuraba a ayudar al carpintero a comerse las ostras. Fue su sed de oro la que llevó a Cortés a México y a Pizarro al Perú, dice Adam Smith, y Thorstein Veblen es todavía más explícito: "La empresa española de colonización fue una empresa de pillaje, inflamada e inflada por el fanatismo religioso y la vanidad guerrera." Los "revisionistas" españoles, deseosos de justificar los procedimientos de sus antepasados y de combatir la "leyenda negra" de España en América, han replicado a estas críticas citando largos extractos de la colección oficial de las humanitarias leyes de Indias, con la intención de demostrar la naturaleza justa de la conquista española y del sistema colonial.

Sin alistarse uno mismo en ninguno de los dos bandos, deberá confirmar la verdad que el historiador escocés William Robertson proclamó hace tiempo, al escribir que "los monarcas españoles, habiendo adquirido una especie de dominio antes desconocido, formaron un plan para ejecutarlo, al que no se encuentra nada parecido en la historia de los hechos humanos". Esto fue, desde luego, debido al hecho importantísimo de que las bulas de donación de Alejandro VI y las subsiguientes de Julio II, conferían a la corona de España el poder de dirigir tanto los asuntos de la Iglesia como los del Estado en América. Los eclesiásticos, que siempre habían tenido papel destacado en los consejos reales españoles, se convirtieron así en asesores de confianza del monarca y del Consejo de Indias, principal órgano administrativo para el gobierno de las colonias, y su influencia, que se dejó sentir en todas partes, aseguró que cada paso de la conquista fuera examinado desde el punto de vista de la moral cristiana.

Esta combinación única de poderes explica también la preocupación del Consejo con todo género de problemas religiosos. En una ocasión, por ejemplo, el Consejo llegó a discutir solemnemente la cuestion, acaloradamente disputada en las Filipinas, de si los chinos convertidos al cristianismo en Manila, deberían ser forzados a cortarse las coletas como muestra visible de haberse librado de sus anteriores creencias paganas. Incluso entre los simples soldados había una curiosa preocupación por observar las formas jurídicas correctas, y hasta un conquistador tan feroz como Lope de Aguirre se tomó la molestia de rebelarse en forma legal, redactando en plena selva del Amazonas un manifiesto en que anunciaba a la corona española que había dejado de estar sometido a las leyes de España.

La gran masa de material referente a este asunto que existe en el Archivo de Indias de Sevilla atestigua en silencio hoy hasta qué punto extraordinario las personas interesadas de todas clases, a ambos lados del Atlántico, se lanzaron en el conflicto.

La tendencia teológica y legalista de la mentalidad española del siglo XVI contribuye también a explicar la multitud de teorías ocasionadas por la conquista.

Cierto es que el solo examen de las teorías y de los teóricos de la conquista española de América nos llevaría a una árida e infructuosa enumeración de disputas teológicas, a no ser por el hecho de que algunas de las varias teorías derivadas de los confusos campos de la filosofía y la doctrina religiosa medieval influyeron de hecho, en ocasiones de un modo decisivo, en el curso de los acontecimientos en el Nuevo Mundo.

Uno de los ejemplos más dramáticos de la influencia de una teoría fue el experimento de la Vera Paz llevado a cabo en Guatemala durante los años 1537-1550 por Las Casas y sus compañeros dominicos. Cuando este fraile atrevido expuso en el púlpito la doctrina sustentada en el tratado De Unico Vocationis Modo, los colonizadores españoles que residían en Santiago de Guatemala lo tomaron a broma. Según lo describe un cronista, "aunque el libro estaba escrito en un latín elegante", los colonizadores se rieron de él y de su autor. El Señor había puesto a aquel tipo tan impertinente en sus manos, o al menos así lo creían ellos, y su regocijado desprecio tuvo la fuerza de estimular a Las Casas para que pusiera en práctica su proposición de convertir a los indios por medios pacíficos solamente. Estaban muy seguros de que aunque Las Casas escapase con vida, su fracaso sería tan estrepitoso que en adelante se verían libres de sus absurdos y molestos sermones.

Al ser así desafiado, Las Casas eligió la única tierra que quedaba por conquistar en aquella región, la provincia de Tuzutlán, un país de montañas, lluvioso, tropical, lleno de tigres, leones, serpientes, grandes monos y, por añadidura, falto de sal. Los indígenas que allí vivían eran feroces, bárbaros e imposibles de someter, o al menos así lo creían los españoles, porque tres veces lo habían intentado y otras tantas habían vuelto "con las manos en la cabeza" de aquella provincia que en el acto denominaron "Tierra de Guerra".

A esta provincia y a estas gentes se ofreció a ir Las Casas para inducirles voluntariamente a que se declararan vasallos del rey de España y le pagaran tributo de acuerdo con sus posibilidades; para predicarles y enseñarles la fe cristiana; y todo esto sin armas ni soldados. Sus únicas armas serían la palabra de Dios y las "razones del Santo Evangelio".

Las peticiones que Las Casas hizo fueron moderadas, y el gobernador Alonso Maldonado las aceptó sin dilación: Que los indios sometidos por medios pacíficos no habrían de ser repartidos entre los españoles, sino que dependerían directamente de la corona, debiendo pagar tan sólo un tributo reducido, y que durante cinco años no se permitiera a los españoles la entrada en la provincia, salvo a Las Casas y a los dominicos, a fin de que los españoles seglares no alteraran a los indios ni provocaran escándalo.

Habiendo concluido este acuerdo con el gobernador, Las Casas y sus compañeros--los frailes Rodrigo de Ladrada, Pedro de Angulo y Luis Cáncer--pasaron varios días dedicados a la oración, al ayuno y a otras disciplinas y mortificaciones espirituales. Luego planearon con cuidado su programa, y comenzaron por componer algunos romances en la lengua india de la Tierra de Guerra. Estos romances eran virtualmente una historia del cristianismo, porque describían la creación del mundo y la caída del hombre, su expulsión del Paraíso, y la vida y milagros de Jesucristo. Después Las Casas buscó y encontró a cuatro mercaderes indios cristianos habituados a traficar en la Tierra de Guerra, y con gran paciencia les enseñó de memoria todos los versos y, además, a que los contaran de una manera agradable.

Por fin, en agosto de 1537, los indios partieron solos con sus mercancías, a las que Las Casas había añadido algunas baratijas españolas, tales como tijeras, cuchillos, espejos y cascabeles, que eran muy preciadas por los indígenas. Los mercaderes se encaminaron directamente al gran cacique de las tribus de la Tierra de Guerra, un personaje belicoso, grandemente respetado y temido por todos. Después de comerciar todo el día, uno de los mercaderes pidió un _teplanastle_, instrumento indio, y el grupo se puso a cantar todos los versos que habían aprendido. La novedad de la situación, la armonía del instrumento y de las voces, y la nueva doctrina--en especial la afirmación de que los ídolos que adoraban eran demonios y de que sus sacrificios humanos eran malos --produjeron gran admiración e interés entre los indios.

Durante las ocho noches siguientes los mercaderes repitieron sus recitales, accediendo gustosos a las demandas del auditorio para que repitieran algunas partes preferidas una y otra vez. Cuando los indios quisieron saber más, les replicaron que sólo los frailes podían enseñarles. Pero ¿qué eran frailes? Entonces los mercaderes los describieron: hombres vestidos con trajes blancos y negros, solteros, que llevaban el pelo cortado de una manera especial; hombres que no querían ni oro, ni plumas, ni piedras preciosas, y que día y noche cantaban las alabanzas de su Señor ante bellas imágenes en las iglesias. Tan sólo estos santos varones--ni siquiera los grandes señores de España--podían instruir a los indios, y los frailes vendrían muy gustosos si se les invitaba. El cacique quedó contento con todo lo que le habían dicho y envió a su hermano menor para rogar a los frailes que vinieran y les enseñaran. Su emisario, no obstante, debería observar en secreto si los frailes se conducían como habían dicho los mercaderes.

Podemos estar seguros de que Las Casas y sus compañeros pasarían algunos días de ansiedad antes de que volvieran los mercaderes llevando consigo al emisario y su cortejo. Aceptaron gozosos los presentes enviados por el cacique y, mientras el emisario estaba visitando la ciudad, conferenciaron y decidieron enviar únicamente a Fr. Luis Cáncer, un misionero devoto y experimentado que conocía bien las lenguas indígenas. Así pues, los indios, cargados con las baratijas españolas, regresaron a su Tierra de Guerra llevando con ellos al padre Cáncer. Al entrar en el territorio del cacique encontró levantados arcos triunfales de flores, y grandes fiestas preparadas para darle la bienvenida. El propio jefe recibió a Cáncer con el mayor respeto y veneración y ordenó que se construyera en seguida una iglesia. Asistió con interés a la primera misa que se celebró allí, y le impresionaron particularmente las vestiduras y la limpieza del fraile, porque sus propios sacerdotes andaban con vestidos sucios, los cabellos pegados con sangre, y sus templos no eran más que chozas llenas de hollín y de basura. Asegurado por su hermano de que el fraile llevaba realmente el género de vida descrito por los mercaderes, y calmado su temor de una invasión armada por las noticias de la orden del gobernador Maldonado, el jefe decidió hacerse cristiano y ordenó a todo su pueblo que hiciera lo mismo. Fue el primero en derribar y en quemar sus antiguos ídolos. Así se ganó la primera alma en la Tierra de Guerra.

Cáncer se apresuró a volver a Santiago, donde Las Casas y los otros frailes se regocijaron al saber las nuevas del éxito de su sistema pacífico. Al cesar las lluvias, en octubre de 1537, Las Casas y Pedro Angulo fueron a la Tierra de Guerra y allí contemplaron un ejemplo de la firmeza de su cacique en la fe: no quiso permitir los habituales sacrificios de papagayos y otras aves y animales en la ceremonia nupcial de su hermano el emisario, a despecho de la oposición que hubo en Cobán, cuyo cacique era el padre de la novia. El fiel cacique también reedificó la iglesia, que algunos de sus vasallos desafectos habían quemado, y arregló el que los frailes visitaran otras partes de su territorio, donde hicieron numerosas conversiones.

Es natural que todo esto fuera una bomba para los colonizadores españoles de Guatemala, quienes habían esperado un desastre tan completo que Las Casas nunca se hubiera atrevido a escribir ni a decir palabra sobre el tema de la conversión pacífica ni de la restitución a los indios de sus propiedades. No cabe duda de que buscaron los medios para desbaratar el éxito de los dominicos, a pesar de la orden del gobernador Maldonado. Los documentos no arrojaron luz sobre los acontecimientos del año 1538 en la Tierra de Guerra--y he podido consultar todos los manuscritos existentes en el Archivo de Indias de Sevilla--pero es evidente que en noviembre de 1539 Las Casas era todavía más fuerte que sus detractores, porque Pedro de Alvarado, el conquistador más importante, y luego gobernador de Guatemala, escribía en aquel mes al rey que Las Casas estaba a punto de salir para España para traer más eclesiásticos, y elogiaba cálidamente su obra, como también lo hizo el obispo.

Este apoyo oficial, unido a la elocuencia y a la mucha experiencia de Las Casas, hizo su efecto. Durante el año de 1540 salió un verdadero torrente de decretos reales destinados a fomentar la conversión pacífica de los indios. Solamente el 17 de octubre se promulgaron doce de estos decretos. Los franciscanos debían proporcionar a Las Casas indios que estuvieran a su cuidado, y que, como los mercaderes, tuvieran talento musical; se encargó a los oficiales reales de que castigaran a todos los españoles que burlaran la orden del gobernador de no entrar en la Tierra de Guerra; y el acuerdo de Maldonado con Las Casas fue confirmado solemnemente. También se concedió dinero; y el rey concluyó por solicitar varios caciques indios--don Juan, el primer convertido, don Gaspar, del pueblo de Chequicizten, don Miguel de Chicicastenango, y don Jorge de Terpanatitan--para continuar ayudando en la conversión de los indios vecinos. Más tarde don Miguel, don Gaspar y otros, reciben escudos de armas por este importante trabajo.

Sería grato para quienes creen en el triunfo definitivo de la justicia en este mundo poder decir que en adelante las cosas siguieron bien en Guatemala; pero no ocurrió así. Durante diez años los colonizadores y los eclesiásticos, disputaron como perros y gatos sobre la predicación pacífica de la fe. En el curso de la lucha el concejo de Santiago informá al rey que Las Casas era un frailes iletrado, un tipo envidioso, apasionado, turbulento y nada santo, que tenía la tierra revuelta, y que podría destruir, si no se le ponía obstáculo, la dominación española en el Nuevo Mundo; además, que los llamados indios "pacíficos" se rebelaban cada día y mataban a muchos españoles. Pero de España siguieron saliendo reales órdenes en apoyo de Las Casas y de sus compañeros dominicos. Ya la Tierra de Guerra fue designada oficialmente Tierra de la Vera Paz, a despecho de la risa burlona de los colonizadores.

Las Casas volvió a Guatemala en 1544 como obispo de Chiapas, región que incluía la Tierra de la Vera Paz. La batalla fue emprendida con tanta violencia por los colonizadores que la corona tuvo que enviar un emisario especial a Guatemala en 1547 para que investigara los supuestos malos tratos a los dominicos, el cual informó que podían encontrarse muchas pruebas en apoyo de la acusación. Durante algún tiempo el obispo Las Casas tuvo que huir a Nicaragua para escapar a las iras de sus feligreses, a los que había excomulgado a diestro y siniestro, incluso a los jueces. La lucha para predicar la fe pacíficamente continuó, incluso hasta después de la renuncia de Las Casas como obispo en 1550, cuando tenía setenta y seis años.

El final del experimento se narra en una triste carta enviada por los frailes al Consejo de Indias el 14 de mayo de 1556. La escribían, dice el informe, para que el rey pudiera saber con claridad lo que había pasado. Durante años los frailes habían trabajado con energía a despecho del gran calor y de la "aspereza" de la tierra, habían destruido ídolos, edificado iglesias y ganado almas. Pero siempre "el demonio estaba vigilante" y por último, había espoleado a los sacerdotes paganos, que apelaron a ciertos indios infieles vecinos para fomentar la rebeldía. Los frailes y sus acólitos fueron expulsados de sus casas, a las que se prendió fuego, y unos treinta fueron muertos a flechazos. Dos de los frailes fueron asesinados en la iglesia, y uno fue sacrificado ante un ídolo. Uno de los que murieron fue Fr. Domingo de Vico, misionero celoso y sabio, que sabía predicar en siete lenguas indias diferentes. Cuando los frailes pidieron auxilio a los españoles de Santiago para castigar a los indios infieles, lo rehusaron suavemente, citando la disposición real que les prohibía tener trato con los indios o entrar en el territorio. Con posterioridad el rey ordenó el castigo de los indios revelados, la Tierra de la Vera Paz se empobreció todavía más, y se desvaneció la posibilidad de ganar a los indios por medios exclusivamente pacíficos.

V. Acontecimientos Posteriores

Es instructivo hacer notar que los promotores originales del experimento de la Vera Paz nunca cejaron en su convicción de que todas las gentes--incluso los indios--podían y debían ser llevados al conocimiento de la fe por medios cristianos y pacíficos. Pedro de Angulo, que formaba parte del grupo de frailes que hicieron la primera entrada, aceptó el obispado de la Tierra de la Vera Paz en 1561--aunque sabía todo lo que allí había pasado--y, cuando la muerte le sorprendió poco después, todavía estaba trabajando en pro de su ideal. Luis Cáncer, el fraile que primero había entrado en la tierra, informaba en una carta a Las Casas de que iba camino de la Florida, para conquistar allí pacíficamente, a despecho de algunas murmuraciones de que iba "al matadero". Así ocurrió, porque poco después de desembarcar en la Florida, indios hostiles atacaron a Cáncer y a los suyos, aniquilándolos. En cuanto a Las Casas, hasta que murió en 1566, a la edad de 92 años, continuó fiel a la idea de que los indios eran seres humanos que debían ser evangelizados pacíficamente, y no asesinados; protegidos, y no despojados. Para concluir esta introducción convendrá, por lo tanto, citar ejemplos posteriores de la práctica de las doctrinas expuestas en este tratado.

Tal vez debería afirmarse previamente que Las Casas no tenía la exclusiva de la idea. Asoka, el santo de la India, la había tenido ya algunas centurias antes de Cristo. Erasmo defendía la misma política en su Ecclesiastes sive contionator evangelicus (1535) casi por la misma fecha en que Las Casas escribía su tratado. Otros frailes, como el franciscano Jacobo de Testera, que estuvo en Yucatán en 1533, habían intentado llevar a la práctica esta política, al principio con bastante éxito. Es sabido que el arzobispo Zumárraga favoreció también la idea. Algunos oficiales españoles, tales como el virrey Antonio de Mendoza, fueron partidarios de la misma idea, pues Mendoza envió a Fr. Marcos de Niza a la conquista de Culiacán con órdenes de emplear la persuasión y no la fuerza. El fraile Hernando de Arbolancha, de la orden de la Merced, evangelizó pacíficamente a los indios de la provincia de Amatlán en Guatemala en 1550 y en el mismo año Fr. Rodrigo de la Cruz informaba al Emperador desde Ahuacatlán en Nueva Galicia de que uno de sus compañeros, llamado Bernardino, había evangelizado pacíficamente a los indios en un gran territorio de cuarenta leguas de largo. Informes análogos fueron enviados en 1561 por Fr. Jacinto y sin duda muchos otros ejemplos podrán descubrirse.

El significado de la obra de Las Casas está en el hecho de que solamente él elaboró de antemano una justificación completa y teórica de su política, y de que, al ser desafiado, puso en práctica su idea de un modo dramático, y durante cierto tiempo, con éxito. El imposible demostrar que todos los numerosos intentos posteriores de predicación pacífica de la fe, después de la Vera Paz, estuvieran inspirados por Las Casas y por sus compañeros dominicos. En ocasiones la influencia de Las Casas fue explícitamente reconocida, como en el caso del obispo Miguel de Benavides y Domingo de Salazar, quienes a fines del siglo XVI se opusieron en las islas Filipinas a la doctrina del jesuita Alonso Sánchez, partidario de la sumisión a sangre y fuego. Fr. Antonio de la Ascensión también invocó en 1602 las teorías de Las Casas en la conquista de California.

Pero, por los general, no había referencia específica a la influencia de Las Casas. El jesuita Juan Bautista de Segura intentó en 1570 convertir a los indios rappahanock sin la ayuda de la fuerza, pero la expedición de ocho misioneros fue asesinada al año siguiente. La real orden de 1573 que daba la pauta para la manera de hacer descubrimientos y conquistas proclamó una vez más la doctrina de la bondad y de la persuasión, expresada por primera vez en la instrucciones a Colón.

Otra ratificación importante de los aspectos esenciales de la doctrina de Las Casas se encuentra en el primer intento español para dar una exposición completa y coherente sobre la teoría y la práctica de las misiones en América, el De promulgando evangelio apud barbaros (1584?) de José Acosta. Se encuentra mucho material sobre intentos posteriores del jesuita Juan Font en Perú hacia 1600, y en la llamada guerra defensiva que emprendió en Chile hacia la misma época. Es de notar también que cuando los jesuitas fueron a fundar sus famosas reducciones del Paraguay, existió una analogía considerable entre la práctica de los jesuitas y la teoría de Las Casas.

Las disputas continuaron. En 1617 el Consejo de Indias se negó a permitir a un capitán español la conversión por fuerza de los indios de Talamanca en Costa Rica, aunque algunos españoles todavía seguían pensando que "la vox del Evangelio se escucha únicamente allí donde los indios han escuchado también el sonido de las armas de fuego". Otros seguían la opinión siguiente:

> Tratarles con blandura, mientras las maneras blandas se encuentre que sirven, será lo mejor sin comparación; pero si el blando pulimento no sirviere, entonces no dejaremos de pedir martilladores y albañiles bastantes--quiero decir nuestros soldados veteranos entrenados en los Países Bajos--para que los desbasten y los preparen para las manos de nuestros predicadores.

Contra estas actitudes Las Casas combatió durante toda su vida. A pesar de toda oposición, su ideal de conducir pacíficamente a la fe a los indígenas del maravilloso mundo nuevo descubierto por los españoles siguió viviendo después de él. Las doctrinas tan cuidadosamente sostenidas por multitudes de citas en su De unico vocationis modo nunca fueron totalmente olvidadas, no obstante el fracaso en la Tierra de la Vera Paz, porque otros frailes en distintas partes del imperio español del Nuevo Mundo se inspiraron en el tratado ahora impreso por primera vez y en el experimento de la Vera Paz para seguir el mismo ideal en su propio territorio.

Podremos no aceptar como verdad evangélica todas las cifras de Las Casas sobre la destrucción de los indios y encontrar imposibles de creer todos los duros cargos que hizo contra sus compatriotas españoles. Pero, ¿podrá nadie que conozca este tratado y el experimento de la Vera Paz dejar de simpatizar con la actitud del Consejo de Indias, que, al serle presentado para su aprobación un libro que atacaba a Las Casas, opinó "que al Obispo don Fray Bartolomé de Las Casas no se había de contradecir, sino comentarle y defenderle"?

CHAPTER 8.

BARTOLOME DE LAS CASAS: AN ESSAY IN HAGIOGRAPHY AND HISTORIOGRAPHY

A certain _furor lascasista_ characterizes the work of a number of writers concerned with the life of Bartolomé de Las Casas, the sixteenth-century Dominican defender of the American Indians. For some years now the Mexican historian Edmundo O'Gorman and I have disagreed in our philosophical and personal interpretations of the doctrines and achievements of Las Casas. Here is an example of my own _furor_, and those interested in polemics of this kind should complete their education by reading Professor O'Gorman's replies.* The article reproduced here is my _riposte_ to earlier statements by him.**

* See his "El método histórico de Lewis Hanke. Réplica a una sorpresa," _Cuadernos Americanos_ (mayo-junio, 1953) No. 3, and various notes in his edition of Las Casas' _Apologética historia sumaria_, 2 vols. (México: Instituto de Investigaciones Históricas, Universidad Nacional Autónoma de México, 1967). For my observations on this latter item see "A Note on Dr. Edmundo O'Gorman's Views on the _Apologétic historia_ of Las Casas," in my _All Mankind Is One_ (DeKalb: Northern Illinois University Press, 1974), 173-176.

** Edmundo O'Gorman, "Sobre la naturaleza bestial del indio americano", _Filosofía y letras_ (1941, Universidad Nacional Autónoma de México), No. 1, pp. 141-158; No. 2, pp. 305-315; "Lewis Hanke on the Spanish Struggle for Justice in the Conquest of America", _The Hispanic American Historical Review_, XXIX (1949), 563-571.

The Hispanic American Historical Review, XXXIII (1953), 131-151. Reprinted by permission.

Bartolomé de Las Casas: An Essay in Hagiography and Historiography

Some controversies over figures of the past have no more urgency for modern men than the famous medieval disputes concerning the number of angels that could be accommodated on the point of a pin. Consideration of the questions raised below falls into a different category and is therefore worth making today, for upon the reply rests our conception of the permanent value of Las Casas, one of the greatest men Spain sent to America.

Disputes over Las Casas have an astonishingly perennial quality. So persistent have been the misunderstandings of some of his actions, for example his supposed connection with the establishment of the Negro slave trade from Africa to America, that Fernando Ortiz has recently produced a long and carefully wrought defense of Las Casas entitled "La leyenda negra contra Fray Bartolomé." Indeed, such tremendous differences of interpretation are now current that it is difficult to believe that some historians, for example Edmundo O'Gorman of Mexico, are not talking about another person in history who happened to have the same name.

Temperamentally and philosophically Las Casas and Edmundo O'Gorman probably would have misunderstood each other had they lived at the same time; and even had they enjoyed the opportunity of discussing their disagreements face to face it is doubtful that they would have been able to resolve them on any fundamental aspect of the Spanish conquest of America. With four centuries of time between them, it is not surprising that O'Gorman has worked out theories of the doctrine of Las Casas which appear strange to some other students of Las Casas; if Fray Bartolomé were with us today it is quite possible that he would be puzzled and, given his impetuous temperament, indignant over some of the views attributed to him by O'Gorman. Let us examine the principal and more challenging allegations of O'Gorman, to see how far they can be substantiated. The interpretation is made by one who is a friend and admirer of both the sixteenth-century Spanish Dominican and the contemporary Mexican philosopher of history.

Did Las Casas Have the Experimental Spirit of a Physical Scientist?

One of O'Gorman's most doubtful interpretations is that Las Casas had the spirit of an experimental scientist. In commenting on the attempt by Las Casas and other Dominicans to preach the faith peacefully in Guatemala, O'Gorman observes that "when Las Casas accepts the challenge [of the Spaniards] and embarks on the Vera Paz experiment his attitude in no essential respect differs from that of the physicist who, armed with a hypothesis, interrogates nature. . . [the attempt] is, in the most precise terms, an experiment." Surely this is either a misunderstanding of Las Casas or of the nature of an experiment. The physical scientist develops a hypothesis which may or may not be proved correct when put to the test of experiment. He may or may not believe that the hypothesis is correct, and he certainly does not consider whether the hypothesis is in accordance with Christian justice or precepts; whatever the result of the experiment, he accepts the decision rendered by nature. The hypothesis for him is an instrument to be used to explore or verify nature and not a religious truth to be defended or demonstrated.

How different was the approach of Las Casas! He was convinced, profoundly and passionately, that the peaceful method of preaching the faith was the only true and just method for a Christian to practice. He was eager for an opportunity to demonstrate this conviction by putting the idea into practice in Guatemala, but his spirit in so doing seems to me to have nothing in common with that of a physical scientist in conducting his experiments. We do not have to look far for an explanation of Las Casas' decision to act in Guatemala, and in particular we do not need to consider his spirit one of premature modernity "lurking beneath his monk's habit and his scholastic loquacity."

The Spanish colonists living in Guatemala were hugely amused, we are told, when the troublesome Las Casas proposed, in a documented treatise, the peaceful method of preaching to the fierce Indians in the territory called Land of War. As one chronicler describes it, "even though the book was written in elegant Latin," the colonists laughed at it and at its author. The Lord had delivered this troublesome fellow into their hands, or so the colonists believed, and their contempt took the form of urging Las Casas to put into practice his proposal to convert the Indians by peaceful means alone. They were very certain that even if he should escape with his life, his failure would be so resounding that they would henceforth be spared his absurd and annoying sermons.

The Spanish authorities provided an opportunity for the theory put forward by Las Casas to be tested and may be said to have approached the problem in an experimental mood. But neither Las Casas nor the colonists in Guatemala felt any doubt whatsoever of the outcome. Certainly Las Casas did not consider the proposal to be an experiment at all, but a demonstration of God's truth. He strongly emphasized the fact that Christ did not rest content with uttering His truths, but insisted on putting them into practice in the world about Him. As one of Las Casas' favorite authorities, John Chrysostom, had declared: "Men do not consider what we say but what we do--we may philosophize interminably, but if, when the occasion arises we do not demonstrate with our actions the truth of what we have been saying, our words will have done more harm than good."

The above account assumes that the story of the Vera Paz experiment of 1537 is true. In a recent and penetrating analysis of this episode by Marcel Bataillon it appears that many of us have been too quick to accept the romantic version of the seventeenth-century Dominican chronicler Antonio de Remesal, upon whose sole testimony the story rests. Bataillon concludes, after a spirited and ironical recapitulation of the colorful story as told by Remesal--the dramatic challenge of the Guatemalan colonists to Las Casas and his acceptance of the gauge of battle, the Indian merchants with their ballads and their sweet music which helped to convert the Indians, the strategic marriage of a chieftain--was hagiography rather than history and was concocted by the Dominican chronicler to exalt his order in general and Las Casas in particular. Arguing partly from silence and partly from documents--with much common sense mixed in--Bataillon sets forth the idea that the peaceful preaching effort was in reality a slow, secret undertaking, at least in the early stages, until Las Casas was named Bishop of Chiapa in 1543 and could use his powerful influence at court on behalf of the missionary effort.

But this combination of careful research, imaginative interpretation, and effective presentation of the problem by Bataillon was not available at the time O'Gorman wrote and we must consider his views in the light of the situation as it was then accepted. It would still be interesting to know how O'Gorman, using the Vera Paz story as then generally accepted, elaborated the extreme and, it seems to me, unproved supposition that the missionary effort in Guatemala had all the characteristics of a physical experiment.

A much more likely example for his purpose of showing the sixteenth-century transition from scholasticism to pre-Cartesianism would have been the sociological experiments carried on in the islands in the years immediately before the peaceful preaching episode in Guatemala. Here we see Spanish administrative officials actually trying to discover, by experiments more akin in spirit to those of the physicist than the Las Casas missionary attempt, whether the Indians could "live like Christian laborers of Castile." They even had a control village in somewhat the same way modern sociologists would carry on their work to find out what would happen under certain conditions. But even here we should be cautious and not assert that these administrative attempts were, "in the most precise terms," experiments.

Las Casas would certainly be surprised to find himself likened to a physical experimentalist, and doubtless if he were here today would write a well-documented treatise entitled "Fifty-seven Reasons To Prove How Dr. Edmundo O'Gorman Has Misunderstood My Doctrine on the Only Way to Preach the True Faith to All Peoples."

What Was the Only True Method of Preaching the Faith?

Las Casas wrote an enormous treatise on this subject and, though only a portion has been preserved and printed, that remnant is a large volume. Nevertheless, we are still arguing what the true method was. O'Gorman, reacting against what he describes as the "consecrated interpretation" of Las Casas as a humanitarian and pacifist, has elaborated a distinctly original answer. For him "the central idea of Las Casas is not evangelization by peaceful means, as has traditionally been asserted; it is evangelization by means of reason, which is not the same thing."

This exegesis seems to me a shaky one, dependent upon a questionable emphasis for whatever appearance of truth it presents. The idea that infidels should be persuaded by reason to accept the faith was indeed put forward by Las Casas, as safely grounded in Christian example and doctrine. Las Casas takes this idea for granted and never argues the point in that part of his treatise which has come down to us. It is quite possible, of course, and even probable that he did explain and defend the idea, with numerous citations of authorities, in one of the chapters now lost. He fought stoutly, indeed, to make sure that the Indians understood the new faith before being baptized.

Many missionaries, eager to ring up an imposing number of souls saved, were willing to baptize hundreds or even thousands of Indians in one day without any emphasis on previous instruction and catechism. Against such attitude and action Las Casas protested so vigorously that the crown on March 31, 1541, referred the matter to one of the ablest theologians of the realm, Francisco de Vitoria. As the royal order explained it, "Las Casas has just come from the Indies and requests that no one there be baptized, whether Indians or Negroes or other infidels, until they are thoroughly indoctrinated in the faith. He says that it is the custom in the Indies to baptize these people even though they understand nothing of the faith." And the crown requested that Vitoria and other theologians of the University of Salamanca send their signed opinions on the subject to the Council of the Indies.

On July 1, 1541, a decision was handed down, duly signed by Vitoria, Domingo de Soto, and several other theologians, which supported Las Casas' viewpoint, and they cited the ancient authorities and usages of the church. If this emphasis on understanding is an evidence of pre-Cartesian thought, as O'Gorman believes, there were a number of embryonic rationalists in both Spain and the Indies, and their intellectual roots go back to Augustine and Aquinas. As Sergio Méndez Arceo has pointed out, some of the passages cited by O'Gorman to illustrate his view on this matter are passages not from Las Casas himself but quotations from treatises by Aquinas. The ideas in which O'Gorman sees a pre-Cartesian spirit were ideas common to both Aquinas and Las Casas.

The second idea, that the faith should be preached peacefully, was much more important in Las Casas' mind. Perhaps he took the evangelization by means of reason for granted, as something clearly "enjoined by Jesus and His apostles, by the custom of the church and its decrees, and by the holy doctors." Las Casas always asserted that infidels must be taught the faith by a method both _pacífica y razonable_, but he devoted most attention to establishing his contention that the faith should be preached by unwarlike methods.

His insistence upon a rational _and_ peaceful method was not a brand-new thought of Las Casas. He probably learned about this doctrine and became convinced of its truth as the result of the example of the Dominican, Pedro de Córdoba, whom he knew well, and he was familiar with the first attempt to use "the only true method" which Córdoba conducted in 1516 on the coast of northern South America near Cumaná. After Las Casas entered the Dominican Order in 1522 and spent eight years quietly studying in a convent on the island of Hispaniola he knew well the theological and juridical bases for the peaceful and rational approach, as was made clear in the _Del único modo_ treatise. During these years of meditation, he may have run across St. Bernard of Clairvaux's famous treatise on the peaceful rather than the forcible conversion of the Jews at the time of the Second Crusade in the twelfth century. At any rate, he became convinced of the truth of peaceful preaching in these years and never wavered in allegiance to it throughout the remainder of his long life.

In conclusion on this point, Las Casas did not "hit upon the idea that the only method to spread the faith was by reason in order to escape from the embarrassing implications of the doctrine of just war." Rather he worked out his theory of rational _and_ peaceful method of preaching the faith because his study of church doctrine, church law, and church fathers convinced him that this method was the correct Christian way to win over infidels. And in his approach to the baptism of the Indians, Las Casas supported the idea that the Indians should fully know about the faith before embracing it, and his view was approved by Vitoria and other theologians of Salamanca.

The next astonishing statement by O'Gorman on the thought of Las Casas is that: "for Las Casas, war is not evil, but good, inasmuch as it is a way to bring about justice. What happens is that there are unjust wars and he considers those made for the purpose of preaching the faith unjust, not because the intention is not praiseworthy _but because the method is not effective_."

This brings O'Gorman close to making Las Casas a pragmatist. It is true that Las Casas believed that peaceful preaching is more effective than warlike means, but this statement is made casually and the basic argument he makes rests upon the example and teachings of Jesus, the apostles, Chrysostom, Augustine, and other Christian authorities as he comprehended their doctrine. If anyone has any doubt on this point, he should stop reading glosses by O'Gorman or Hanke and consult Las Casas' own words in Del único modo, especially pp. 221-235. One of the advantages of such discussions as we are now having is that Las Casas' works will be more widely and intensively read than ever before.

Those who consult the writings of Las Casas will find that he exalts peace and condemns war. According to him war is irrational, unnatural and not in consonance with human nature. Moreover, it is against Christ's instructions and intentions as well as those of the apostles. War violates the commandment which charges every man to love his neighbor as himself, is an indecent and infamous act which at most can affect material things and not the spirit, and of all methods "the most miserable and criminal, full of every kind of evil and cruelty, a method adopted by robbers and the most impious of men. It will lead infidels to depreciate religion and avoid those who are preaching the faith." Clearly, therefore, warlike methods to establish a kingdom or to propagate Christianity "are incompatible with either the goodness of Christ or the royal dignity." Instead there must be used "the sweetness of His doctrine, the sacraments of the church, and mercy which will bestow many benefits with graciousness, gentleness, charity, and peace."

Of course Las Casas, in common with practically all Spaniards of his time (Luis Vives was an exception who condemned all war), believed that war could under certain conditions be just. In the Del único modo treatise he refers once, in passing, to the fact that "no war is just unless there is a just cause for declaring it," and he clearly followed Augustine on what constituted just war.

What distinguished Las Casas, however, was not that he agreed with most of his contemporaries on the theory of just war but that he declared the wars against the New World natives to be unjust, particularly as a prelude to their conversion. He condemned the use of force, not merely because the clamor and horror of armed conflict provided an unsuitable background against which Indians might listen to and consider the new doctrine of love and salvation, but also--and here is a point O'Gorman does not mention and apparently does not consider worth mentioning--because warlike methods had been condemned by Christ, by the apostles, and by the fathers of the church and other authorities. The practice of using force and war to advance Christianity was directly contrary to the faith that was being preached, Las Casas held, and therefore he advocated peaceful persuasion in its stead.

Were the Ideas of Las Casas Fundamentally Aristotelian or Fundamentally Christian?

It may be surprising to some that this question is raised at all. We know that Las Casas stated before King Charles in 1519 at Barcelona that "Aristotle was a Gentile, and is now burning in Hell, and we are only to make use of his doctrine as far as it is consistent with our Holy Faith and Christian customs." At that time he was opposing the first full-fledged presentation of the argument that the newly discovered Indians should be considered slaves "by nature," according to the Aristotelian doctrine that certain rude persons of limited understanding are inferior a natura and that it is only just and natural that prudent and wise men have dominion over them for their own welfare as well as for the service of their superiors. Las Casas replied in 1519 that Indians were not inferior beings and that Aristotle's dictum obviously did not apply to them.

The question was raised with much greater insistence during the great dispute which took place in 1550 and 1551 at Valladolid between

Las Casas and Juan Ginés de Sepúlveda. The contestants were both doctrinally opposed and emotionally upset by the discussion, and its true meaning has been and still is in doubt in some quarters. Despite the great attention paid to the argument the full story is not yet known, partly because the record of the proceedings of the encounter have not been found and also because the lengthy Apología presented by Las Casas for five straight days still remains in manuscript. It is concerning this dispute that O'Gorman brings up another of his startling paradoxes, for he states categorically that "all of Las Casas' thought is fundamentally Aristotelian, while Sepúlveda is just as much of a Christian as Las Casas." Without attempting to measure the exact Christianity displayed by Sepúlveda, an interesting point in itself but not necessary to the present discussion, let us examine the alleged Aristotelianism of Las Casas' thought.

It is true that Las Casas in his arguments both at Barcelona in 1519 and at Valladolid in 1550-1551 appears to accept the theory of Aristotle that some men are by nature slaves. It is also true that there are numerous references to various works of Aristotle in the Del único modo treatise, and that his compendious Apologética historia was put together by Las Casas to prove that the American Indians fulfilled, and in a most satisfactory manner, all the conditions listed by Aristotle as being necessary for the good life. But does this add up to making "all his thought fundamentally Aristotelian"?

It must be realized that though Las Casas never attempts to break down Aristotle's concept of natural slavery, neither does he defend it or seek to extend its scope. Rather he tries to confine the operation of the theory to the smallest area possible. He not only denies vigorously that the Indians fall into the category of natural slaves but his argument tends to lead to the conclusion that no nation of mankind should be condemned, as a nation, to such a life. . . .

How therefore should we look upon O'Gorman's latest pronouncement that

> Father Las Casas endeavored to be as good an Aristotelian as his formidable opponent, and therefore he was obliged to concede the existence of slaves by nature, so that the polemic resulted in favor of Sepúlveda in the theoretical plane of the discussion. But at the decisive moment Las Casas, with a gesture worthy of one devil-possessed, abandons reasons to go over to faith, and thus rejects the authority of the philosopher who so greatly disturbs him, asserting as a final argument that Aristotle was a Gentile and burning in Hell.

Both fact and interpretative emphasis are questionable in this passage. For Las Casas never abandoned Aristotle entirely, so far as the documents now available show; the statement about the burning occurred in 1519, thirty years before in Barcelona, and not, so far as I know, at Valladolid, and, most serious of all, O'Gorman neglects to consider the other three main divisions of the basic argument carried on at Valladolid. Sepúlveda declared it lawful and necessary to wage war against the Indians for these four reasons:

1. For the gravity of the sins which the Indians had committed, especially their idolatries and their sins against nature.

2. On account of the rudeness of their natures, which obliged them to serve persons having a more refined nature, such as the Spaniards.

3. In order to spread the faith which would be more readily accomplished by the prior subjugation of the natives.

4. To protect the weak among the natives themselves.

Only in point two does Aristotle's theory of natural slavery enter the picture and, even there, Las Casas accepted but did not defend it.

Why did he accept it at all, even in a limited and restricted sense? My own interpretation is that Las Casas here manifested that realistic and legalistic spirit which characterized a considerable part of his action. Part of his opponent's attack rested upon the allegation that the American Indians were slaves by nature. The defense of Las Casas was not to attack Aristotle frontally but to show that the doctrine should not be applied to the Indians. At the same time his explanation of what kind of person might fall into the Aristotelian category of natural slavery shows how faintly applicable it was in his opinion to the world at large. One might well conclude, therefore, that Las Casas paid lip-service to Aristotle for the purpose of refuting the application of his doctrine to the Indians.

One may sympathize with O'Gorman's annoyance at the uncritical attitude of the nineteenth century on the dispute with Sepúlveda, but the charge that Las Casas' thought was "all fundamentally Aristotelian" remains to be proved, in my opinion. When Agustín Millares Carlo produces his long-expected and much-needed index to the authorities and writings cited by Las Casas in his voluminous works it will then be clearly seen, I believe, that the body of his thought was thoroughly, even monotonously, Christian. As Las Casas remarked in that forceful letter written to the ecclesiastics of Guatemala at the age of almost ninety, he had studied the law assiduously for forty-eight years, and everything he had advocated with respect to the Indians, "no matter how rigorous or hard," he had substantiated with principles taken from St. Thomas Aquinas.

Did Las Casas Falsify History?

O'Gorman has devoted some attention to the enmity between Las Casas and Gonzalo Fernández de Oviedo y Valdés, particularly as shown in the different versions given in their respective histories of the colonization attempt made in 1521 by Las Casas on the coast of Venezuela. In discussing the matter O'Gorman asserts that one of the citations Las Casas gives from the text of Oviedo is false and that in another case Las Casas omits pertinent information. Thus, O'Gorman observes, Las Casas "does not show evidence of the intellectual honesty that one would like to see." This is a grave charge, which requires proof.

The charge that Las Casas was a prejudiced historian is not new. Since the first publication of his *Brevísima relación de la destrucción de las Indias* in 1552, Las Casas has been attacked for the exaggerated statements he made on the number of Indians killed by Spaniards, and it has also been charged that he was more propagandist than historian. But it is only in recent years that he has been accused of deliberately falsifying documents for his own purposes. The Argentine historian Rómulo D. Carbia, beginning about 1930, entered upon a vigorous campaign to convince the world that Las Casas in some instances forged documents and in others deliberately lied. Carbia maintained, for example, that Las Casas manufactured the 1498 Columbus letter as well as his *Journal*, the Toscanelli letter, the life of Columbus by his son Ferdinand, and other documents. For years Carbia published such accusations and strongly denounced Las Casas in lecture halls and at conference tables.

He never presented proof for his charges, though always promising to do so soon, and died without documenting his bill of indictment. Today it would be difficult and perhaps impossible to find a single historian in Europe or America who would repeat Carbia's charges.

If Las Casas did falsify history, O'Gorman has chosen a doubtful terrain on which to fight--the Venezuela colonization attempt. Indeed, the recent and revealing study by Marcel Bataillon shows rather conclusively that on this particular episode in the life of Las Casas Oviedo was the offender and not Las Casas. In the light of this recent article by the French scholar, it will be necessary for O'Gorman to document his charges before they will be accepted by historians.

Conclusion

Every allegation by O'Gorman, if established, would tend to diminish the stature of Las Casas. For to O'Gorman, Las Casas was not a man of intellectual honesty, but a falsifier of history; not a Christian missionary who favored the peaceful preaching of his faith because that faith required its message to be promulgated peacefully, but one who would resort even to war to achieve his ends if that method were successful; not fundamentally a Christian thinker, but an Aristotelian, who also had affinities with Descartes. To this bundle of paradoxes may be added O'Gorman's latest pronouncement on Las Casas:

> His head was confused, his learning as diffuse as it was undigested, his passion great, his intention good, his style extremely digressive. . . . Las Casas proceeded through life illuminated by an ideal, a curious and difficult mixture of heroic piety and systematic rationalism. . . the most credulous person that ever lived. . . to expect a bit of coherence from him is to ask an elm tree to produce pears.

Students of the Spanish conquest of America in the future may find it strange that so much controversy existed today--four hundred years after his first treatises were printed in Sevilla--on the true doctrine of Las Casas. They may conclude that all of us who are now attempting to grasp his significance have sought to relate him and his ideas too closely and too arbitrarily to the present world. Standing today on the top of a mountain of controversial writings about Las Casas through the centuries, perhaps we are all inclined to forget that he lived in the sixteenth century and must be judged ultimately as a man of his time.

The fact that Las Casas cherished ideas on various subjects which seem laughable now is brought forward to ridicule him by O'Gorman who also believes that scholars today "mutilate" Las Casas, and thereby give a false view of his work, by omitting reference to his views on magic and other beliefs considered absurd today. "Let anyone who wishes to get easily an intellectual profile of Las Casas," exclaims O'Gorman, "examine the Apologética historia of Las Casas, his most 'scientific' work. Here he will see discussed various problems of magic, such as whether witches may be converted into animals, and other things like this."

Is it not more sensible to see in these instances the inevitable complexity of sixteenth-century man which can so delight twentieth-century readers? Sir Francis Bacon is generally believed to have had a firm comprehension of scientific method and has been described as the father of modern science; does it invalidate his claim to respect as an outstanding thinker of his time to know that he also believed--we are told--that the strong breath of lions caused them to lose their teeth, and that gun powder taken with water just before battle would make soldiers and sailors brave? Or, to cite illustrations from Spanish history, take the case of Oviedo who is still considered a substantial historian. Though a much more sophisticated writer than Las Casas, Oviedo included a number of chapters in his work which seem ludicrous to us today. He discoursed on such subjects as the crowing of roosters and the caterwauling of cats in the New World (they made less noise, thus permitting Oviedo to study more concentratedly than in Spain), and pointed out that birth-pains of women were different in the New World (Oviedo cited the experiences of his own wife). Even such a wise and learned fellow as the seventeenth-century polygraph Antonio de León Pinelo was firmly convinced that Paradise was located in the New World and that Noah's Ark sallied forth on its famous voyage from some spot in America. At least one sixteenth-century writer was convinced that the Indian god Quetzalcoatl was in reality Thomas Aquinas. Legends relating to the Mexican Indians continued to fascinate other students in later years. The nineteenth-century English anthropologist Edward Tylor supported the theory that the ten lost tribes of Israel had somehow wandered to Mexico, and he also believed that Quetzalcóatl was not only a real man but suggested that he might have been an Irishman.

Can Las Casas be dismissed as scatter-brained because he held some ideas now known to be far-fetched, any more than we dismiss Bacon, Oviedo, León Pinelo, or Tylor as unworthy of serious consideration? It is in the basic doctrine of Las Casas that we find his permanent contribution.

Yet even on his fundamental thought disagreement continues to flourish as may be seen from the various paradoxes of O'Gorman. Other points of disagreement could be mentioned, but the reader must be spared further elaboration; we should leave something for future Lascasistas to do, particularly in the field of his theology. Perhaps some theologian will arise to study the precise nature of Las Casas' doctrine of grace and will show that all previous interpretations require revision.

Let us hope that by 2052, historians at least will be able to agree on what the real doctrine of Las Casas was. For it is clear that they do not agree today and it is also clear that in dealing with a figure as important in the work of Spain in America as was Las Casas, paradoxes--no matter how brilliant--are not enough.

CHAPTER 9.

THE MEANING TODAY OF THE LAS CASAS TREATISES PUBLISHED IN 1552

The role of Las Casas on the stage of history invites, even requires, an attempt at generalization. Most of the Europeans who participated in the great expansion of the world which occurred in the sixteenth century were willing and even eager, as he expressed it, to keep the peoples of the New World who had been hidden away and forgotten for centuries "kept permanently down in the darkness." His words and his actions, all tending "to stretch out our hands to them in some way" led to controversy in his own day and throughout the succeeding centuries.

One forward step in the study of Las Casas has been the publication in easily available form of his fundamental writings. Juan Pérez de Tudela has brought out through the Biblioteca de Autores Españoles in Madrid an excellent edition of all his Spanish works, and Edmundo O'Gorman has been responsible for the issuance by the Universidad Nacional Autónoma de México of a splendid version of the Apologética historia. Bruno Pagliai, who had previously demonstrated his concern for historical classics by establishing the Fondo Pagliai for the republication of rare works, was partly responsible for a new edition of all the 1552-1553 treatises by Las Casas, brought out by the Fondo de Cultura Económica of Mexico City, which had already done much through its editions of the Historia de las Indias and the Del único modo de atraer todos los pueblos a la verdadera religión.

Mr. Pagliai was also moved by the convictions of Las Casas, and published separately his own views in English together with the English version of my part of the introduction for the new edition of the treatises, in which the reader will see one of my latest attempts at generalization on this great theme.

Privately printed by Bruno Pagliai in Mexico City in 1965. Reprinted by permission.

The Meaning Today of the Las Casas Treatises Published in 1552

The present edition of the Treatises of El Obispo de Chiapa, made possible by the imaginative cooperation of the Fondo Pagliai and the Fondo de Cultura Económica, represents an important landmark in Las Casas studies. I am particularly happy to be a part of this enterprise, because once more I am privileged to be associated with my long-time colleagues in this field--Manuel Giménez Fernández and Agustín Millares Carlo.

The treatises themselves are old friends, too. I still remember the thrill of discovering the doctrine of Las Casas in the facsimile edition of the treatises brought out in Buenos Aires by the late Emilio Ravignani, that remarkable Argentine historian to whom I shall always be indebted because he encouraged me many years ago to persevere in my studies on Las Casas. It was while first reading these treatises in Widener Library in 1930 that I stumbled upon that brief but illuminating work of Fernando de los Ríos, Religión y estado en la España del siglo XVI, which led me to embark upon my investigations relating to the Spanish struggle for justice in the conquest of America. My ideal has been to follow his wise counsel: "Let us judge the Spanish colonial activities, not as Catholics or Protestants, but as observers with the great objectivity necessary to one who proposes to study a problem of great significance in history."

The treatises here printed demonstrate, among other things, that Las Casas was a powerful and skillful propagandist. His first weapons were memorials to the crown, for he felt that once the King and his councilors knew what cruelties his fellow Spaniards had been inflicting on the defenseless Indians, the crown would take the necessary action.

He often declared that the problems of the New World would be easily solved if only the King were unoccupied with wars and ready to listen to the truth. He spent his life composing memorials expatiating on the advantages of planned colonization, on the peaceful method of preaching the faith to the Indians, on the need to abolish the system of granting Indians to Spaniards, on the moral and economic responsibility of the Spaniards in their relations with the Indians, on the importance of insisting that the Indians really understand Christianity before baptism, on the value of Indian culture and the possibility of Indians learning to be civilized, and on the injustice of practically all Spanish action in America. These memorials were designed for the King's eye and for confidential consideration by his councilors who governed the great regions of the New World conquered by Spain.

Yet in the early days of 1552, after almost forty years of privately admonishing the crown, Las Casas went to Seville and had printed there nine inflammatory treatises by which he is principally known to the world today. Why this long delay in using the printed word to carry his message? Why had he fought almost forty years before King and council and before ecclesiastical convocations without once using the book as an instrument of his propaganda?

A simple answer, with considerable truth in it, would be that Las Casas had been too busy to publish books. It requires time to see a volume through the press, and he had traveled too constantly, had been embroiled in too many hot disputes, had been too much the man of action, and had tried to influence too many kings, to have had the leisure and solitude required to get a composition into print. But by 1552 Las

Casas had perhaps come to feel that his work was in danger of failing and that the printing press would help him to convince many Spaniards whom he could not otherwise reach. Also he had resigned his bishopric, and never crossed the ocean again after his return to Spain in 1547, at the age of seventy-three.

Surely Las Casas would have had good reason to be discouraged with his efforts up to 1552. His attempt to colonize Venezuela in 1520 had ended in resounding failure; the experiment in Guatemala of preaching the faith by peaceful means alone from 1537 on had come a cropper by 1552; the New Laws of 1542 in favor of the Indians, which had been pushed through by the implacable efforts of Las Casas against tremendous opposition, had been partially revoked in 1545; and Las Casas' experience as a bishop in Chiapa during six months of 1545 had been one long struggle with his parishioners, whom he thoroughly alienated and ultimately excommunicated. Finally, the bitter, scholastic battle Las Casas waged in 1550 and 1551 against Juan Ginés de Sepúlveda, in an attempt to show that Aristotle's dictum that some men were by nature slaves should not be applied to the Indians, had ended in a drawn decision. Now that the conquest of the New World was going forward again after the King had suspended it while Las Casas and Sepúlveda wrangled about Aristotle, Spaniards continued to hold Indians and wage war against them, despite the fulminations of the Bishop of Chiapa. Perhaps he was convinced that the time had arrived to give his ideas more permanent form and have them reach a wider audience. However the act may be explained, Las Casas did spend the year 1552 in Seville seeing his nine famous treatises through the press. All except one appeared in the popular Spanish language and not in the more universal and scholarly Latin. These treatises in black Gothic type, some with handsome title pages and interesting initials, are the works by which Las Casas has largely been known to collectors and bibliophiles.

The _Very Brief Account of the Destruction of the Indies_ was originally drawn up in 1542 at the time of the battle over the New Laws, and was a province-by-province description of the bloody deeds of the Spaniards during the conquest, in which Las Casas claimed that some fifteen or twenty millions of Indians had perished. More learned, though not less controversial, was the _Treatise Concerning the Imperial Sovereignty and Universal Pre-eminence which the Kings of Castile and Leon Enjoy over the Indies_. In this juridical writing Las Casas maintained that the only possible justification for the Spanish title lay in the donation by the Pope, made in order to bring the Indians to a knowledge of Christ. The Spaniards held their lands and mines in the New World against the will of native kings, and Spaniards must make restitution of what they have stolen from the Indians "to the penny". The _Advice and Regulations for Confessors_ was designed to withhold the sacraments of the church from all persons who held Indians and did not properly compensate them for their labor. The other six treatises all contain similar ideas, and a reading of them will illustrate what Antonio María Fabié meant when he said that all the writings of Las Casas are like peas in a pod.

The publication of these treatises demonstrated, if such was necessary even then, the tremendous power of the press. What had previously been private memorials to the crown now became world property, for the treatises were quickly shipped to America and almost as quickly found their way to other countries of Europe beyond the Pyrenees. These printed tracts constituted a public and solemn reply to the many enemies of Las Casas, and at the same time a deliberate provocation to the conquistadores and the other Spaniards in America.

The counterattacks were not long delayed in their launching. Juan Ginés de Sepúlveda, the most formidable opponent Las Casas ever had in doctrinal matters, almost immediately composed a hot blast entitled Rash, Scandalous and Heretical Propositions which Dr. Sepúlveda Noted in the Book on the Conquest of the Indies, which Friar Bartolomé de Las Casas Printed Without a License. The revered Franciscan Motolinía sent his famous letter from Mexico to Charles V in 1555, which constituted such a severe indictment of Las Casas that one nineteenth-century editor suspected that some disaffected Spaniards in America might have concocted it, and the arrival of the printed treatises stirred up the animosity of many Spaniards trying to make a living in the Indies.

The greatest opposition to the treatises developed in Mexico, even though Las Casas always said conditions were "less noxious" there than in other parts of the Indies. The Town Council of Mexico City, the richest and most important city in all America, gratefully recognized what Sepúlveda had done on their behalf, and as a token of their appreciation and "to encourage him in the future" voted on February 8, 1554, to present him with Mexican jewels and clothing to the value of two hundred pesos. The royal officials and burghers of Mexico were alarmed because in the same year that Las Casas published his treatises in Seville certain Indians of the pueblo of Texcuco presented a petition to the Town Council in which it was claimed that a large part of Mexico was still owned by the Indians, a point of view by no means congenial to the town fathers.

The questioning did not abate, for on January 24, 1558, the Town Council of Mexico City again took cognizance of the problem by voting a salary to Francisco Cervantes de Salazar, one of the most learned men in the land, who had started to write a book "in which is established the just title of the king to New Spain, and a general history of this New World", and continued to pay his salary for at least five years. In 1562, this same Town Council informed the King that Las Casas' writings had caused so much trouble and discontent in Mexico that it had arranged for the town attorneys and two theologians to prepare a formal statement to be sent to the Council of the Indies against "this audacious friar and his doctrine". It appears from the records of the Town Council that many persons in Mexico City had been busily writing on the subject in refutation of Las Casas ever since his printed works had arrived there, and the Town Council had requested several times that the King reprove Las Casas and prohibit the printing of his books.

On April 10, 1562, the council decided to aid the Franciscan Alonso de Santiago, who had already written on "the sound title that His Majesty holds to these parts of the Indies", for which opinions the friar had been badly treated by his Franciscan superiors so that he lacked the necessary funds to enable him to proceed to Spain. Because it was considered only just to aid the friar on account of his sufferings for "the common good", the Town Council decided to pay Santiago's travel expenses to Spain.

Nor were Las Casas and the propositions set forth in the treatises any more popular in the great viceroyalty of Peru. Viceroy Francisco de Toledo, wise lawgiver, energetic administrator, and the greatest ruler Spain ever sent to Peru (1569-82), found the ecclesiastics so difficult that at one time he determined to use the Inquisition to keep them in line. Of all the ecclesiastics the most troublesome was Las Casas, for his doctrines lived on after his death in 1566 to agitate some Spaniards as violently as during lifetime. The printed word continued to carry his ideas and, as Viceroy Toledo expressed it, "the books of the fanatic and virulent Bishop of Chiapa served as the spearhead of the attack on Spanish rule in America". The Viceroy felt so keenly that the writings of Las Casas should be suppressed that he collected as many copies as he could find, thus retiring them from circulation, and urged the King to allow no more to be shipped from Spain.

Toward the end of the sixteenth century another Spaniard, this time Bernardo de Vargas Machuca, Governor and Captain-General of the island of Margarita, became so incensed by a French translation of the Very Brief Account of the Destruction of the Indies that he indignantly worked up a full-length and passionate reply. To this book-length manuscript he prefaced four highly commendatory sonnets, all written by Dominicans, presumably to show that some of Las Casas' brothers did not agree with him, as well a special prologue, a legal defense of the justice of Spanish conquest which rested fundamentally on the doctrine elaborated half a century previously by the "elocuente y docto Sepúlveda". Despite all this, the Defense of the Western Conquests by the valorous Captain Vargas Machuca did not see the light of day, and quietly rested in the Royal Library in Madrid until Antonio María Fabié printed it in 1879.

Indeed none of these attacks on the books by Las Casas were published until the nineteenth century. The bitter denunciations of the Franciscan Motolinía, the hot and jurisprudential arguments of the scholar Sepúlveda, and the legal treatise written in the valley of Yucay in Peru at the time of Viceroy Toledo were not given the dignity of print. Neither the assaults of his contemporaries nor the outbursts against him in the latter part of the sixteenth century seem to have shaken the confidence of the crown of Spain in Las Casas. Moreover, the nine treatises apparently were printed in 1552 without any previous royal scrutiny and not one of them carried any indication that it had been approved for publication by the Council of the Indies.

How did Las Casas get away with this? In the years immediately previous to his unauthorized printing in 1552 there was considerable discussion in Spain on what kind of book should be permitted for publication and distribution in America. The writings of his enemy Sepúlveda were in 1550 forbidden to be sent to America. Colonial officials were instructed to collect all copies there and send them to the Council of the Indies. Even the Advice and Regulations for Confessors which Las Casas had worked out under twelve points during his tumultuous six months as bishop in Chiapa had earlier been prohibited. Copies had been circulating in manuscript form, but in 1548 instructions were sent widely throughout the Indies to collect and send them all to Spain "because it was not convenient that such things be printed without their first being seen by the Council of the Indies". At the same time, Las Casas had sufficient influence in 1548 at the Court to keep his opponent Oviedo from bringing out his history, and "lying histories" were to be kept out of America, according to an order of September 1550. In 1553, just after Las Casas had completed the printing in what must have been large editions of his nine treatises, we find the Council of the Indies ordering that the works of Francisco López de Gomara shall not go to the Indies, a prohibition generally attributed to the influence of Las Casas. And in 1560 a manuscript treatise in Latin justifying the Spanish conquest in contradiction to the theories of Las Casas, which curiously enough was written by a Dominican from Dalmatia named Vicente Palatino de Curzola, was also ordered to be picked up in America and sent to Spain.

The freedom with which Las Casas printed his tracts, even the previously prohibited Advice and Regulations for Confessors, remains an interesting and not wholly explained phenomenon. Perhaps the strong instruction of September 21, 1556, against any book being printed on Indian affairs without authorization was one result of this furious publication program of Las Casas during the years 1552-53.

The treatises Las Casas was able to publish have had a long history: they helped greatly to increase Spanish tenderness to foreign criticism, many translations into English were brought out for political purposes in the years 1588-1898, French translations had a considerable vogue in eighteenth-century France, and some of the treatises were used for propaganda purposes during the Spanish American revolutions, 1810-1826. In the subsequent history of Spanish relations with the American nations once under her rule Las Casas' writings played a significant role. This long and sometimes painful story cannot be given here, but when told will illuminate one more facet of the influence of Las Casas as propagandist. By the magic of the printing press his flaming declarations, designed to influence directly the decisions of his King in the sixteenth century, lived on to serve for centuries the political purposes of many nations. The reaction to Las Casas today, such as the recent attacks by Don Ramón Menéndez Pidal, indicate that this friar and his writings have had a profound influence on the writing of the history of Spanish America.

The four-hundredth anniversary of the death of Las Casas affords the world an opportunity to re-examine his ideas and appraise his influence. Anniversaries often follow a fairly regular and familiar pattern. Pious eulogies, sleep-producing banquets, heavy volumes of *discursos*, official pronouncements, and other types of academic Bacchanalia are organized for the gratification of those celebrating an event far removed in time. It would be most unfortunate, however, if the commemoration were to become a tame or perfunctory affair, for the ideas and principles for which Las Casas fought in the sixteenth century are living issues today.

During the last fifty years scholars have been increasingly pointing out that Las Casas was much more than a propagandist. He was also a historian, whose *History of the Indies* remains one of the basic documents of the discovery and early conquest of America. He has come to be recognized as a political theorist of importance, and as one of the first anthropologists of America. Likewise his contributions in the fields of geography, philosophy, and theology are being studied today. Although sixteenth-century Spain was a land of eminent scholars and bold thinkers, few of his contemporaries were more independent in their judgments, more learned in upholding their opinions, or more universal in their range of interests than Las Casas.

Today as the world gropes to find some honest basis for an enduring peace among peoples of diverse cultures, it is not the multiplicity of his intellectual interests nor the single-minded devotion of this friar to the Indians which excites our respect and sympathy as much as his attitude toward non-Spaniards and non-Christians. For Las Casas rejected the popular view that the Indians discovered in Spain's onward rush through the lands of the New World were beasts, nor did he subscribe to the theory that they were slaves by nature, according to the Aristotelian view, or childlike creatures with such limited understanding that they were to be treated as perpetual minors. . . .

Las Casas pitted all of his enormous vitality, wide learning, and skill in debate against these views. He passionately urged that the Indians, though different from Spaniards in color, customs, and religion, were human beings capable of becoming Christians, with the right to enjoy their property, political liberty, and human dignity, and that they should be incorporated into the Spanish and Christian civilization rather than enslaved or destroyed. One more step was thus taken along the road of justice for all races in a world of many races. For though Las Casas started out as a defender of Indians only, he came to oppose Negro slavery as well "for the same reasons", and to work for "the liberty of all the people of the world".

CHAPTER 10.

PARANOIA, POLEMICS, AND POLARIZATION: SOME COMMENTS ON THE FOUR-HUNDREDTH ANNIVERSARY OF THE DEATH OF LAS CASAS

The commemoration of the death of Las Casas in 1566 naturally stimulated many attempts to assess the historical and contemporary significance of his life and writings. Here is mine, prepared at the invitation of Josef Polisensky, Director of the Center for Ibero-American Studies at Charles University in Prague.

Ibero-Americana Pragensia, 5 (Prague, 1971), 83-92. Reprinted by permission.

Paranoia, Polemics, and Polarization.
Some Comments on the Four-Hundredth Anniversary of the Death of Las Casas

Doubts and disagreements concerning the actions of Spain in America will probably always be present, especially when Bartolomé de Las Casas enters upon the scene. For example, the most dramatic event of all the many commemorations associated with the four-hundredth anniversary of his death was the biography of Ramón Menéndez Pidal entitle El Padre Las Casas. Su doble personalidad. In this notable work Don Ramón, the oldest and most distinguished Hispanist of his time, considered that Las Casas, although in some respects a normal person, was a propagandist rather than a thinker, who incorporated in his work, though at times incorrectly, some Christian ideas. Menéndez Pidal employed his rich Castilian vocabulary in an attempt to convey to the reader an idea of Las Casas' defects. . . .

"Paranoic", of all the terms applied by Don Ramón in his characterization of Fray Bartolomé, is the one which has caused the most repercussion. Students concerned with the 500th commemoration in 2066 who look through the 1966 literature will be puzzled by this term as well as by the variety and the nature of opinions today on Las Casas. They will read the judgment on Las Casas by that remarkable French scholar Marcel Bataillon: "En cet apôtre authentique, mieux encore que dans le professeur Francisco de Vitoria, s'incarne l'âme généreuse de L'Espagne colonisatrice 'a lo divino'." And they will note that the German theologian Josef Cardinal Höffner, in one of the solid works of scholarship of our times on Spanish culture in the sixteenth century, has declared that "among all the Spaniards, it was the noble Las Casas who most profoundly understood the spirit of the Christian gospel." He was referring specifically to the question most at issue at Valladolid --whether force should be used by Christians in converting infidels. Dr. Höffner concluded that Las Casas had "without doubt, interpreted ably the true sense of the gospels."

Students in 2066 will also see that Juan Pérez de Tudela Bueso, one of the outstanding Americanists in Spain today, concluded the excellent Estudio preliminar to his five volume edition of the writings of Las Casas thus: "Fue un protagonista gigantesco e indispensable de la forjación de Hispanoamérica." Another Spaniard, the Dominican theologian Venancio Diego Carro, who has examined more minutely than anyone else the theological doctrines of Las Casas, has rendered a very favorable judgment in general. He concludes that Las Casas' ideas "coinciden fundamentalmente con las de los grandes téologos-juristas españoles", and that "no hizo más que aplicar los principios cristianos y el concepto cristiano."

The present-day Mexican scholar Teresa Silva Tena admires the universal quality of Las Casas' views, and points out that his interpretation of Aztec human sacrifice reveals the fact that he was the only one of his time who had the imagination to understand this much-discussed rite from the Indian point of view. Still another Mexican, in his analysis of the information on Indian art in Las Casas' works, concluded that he exhibited a most "modern" attitude in his attempt to discern and understand what the Indian arts were trying to express.

Las Casas has become a more universal figure than ever before: Soviet Latin Americanists have participated strongly in the 1966 commemoration activities. Perhaps the most impressive proof of the present widespread interest in the life of Fray Bartolomé may be seen in the many editions of his writings and the extraordinary number of high quality of studies about him in various languages. One of these studies was prepared by Father Lino Gómez Canedo, the well-known Franciscan historian, showing that many Franciscans from Fray Juan de la Deula (1502) to Fray Francisco de Morales (1564) were warm friends of Las Casas who shared his fundamental views on Indian problems. This is not a new idea, but is well worth stating again.

One of the outstanding new editions is the impressive version of one of Las Casas' most significant works, the Apologética historia, which not only contains the most complete and accurate text and a preliminary study of Edmundo O'Gorman raising fundamental questions of interpretation, but also has a most perceptive introductory essay by Miguel León-Portilla on the relevance of the Apologética historia today to Spanish America and to the world at large. León-Portilla considers the treatise the best possible reply to those who have accused Las Casas of demencia (probably a reference to Ramón Menéndez Pidal, though he does not say so), and emphasized that his doctrine--along with the contributions of José de Acosta, Vasco de Quiroga, and Bernardino de Sahagún--have made possible a reconciliation between Spain and Spanish America. These sixteenth-century friars censored Spanish violence in the conquest, but they also made possible, "en un plano de dignidad humana, el nacimiento de la que es nuestra fisonomía mestiza." For the rest of the world, the ideas and attitudes in the Apologética historia constitute an "aportación valiosa en el ámbito de la cultura universal como la primera y bien fundada afirmación de eso, que tanto se repite y no siempre se practica, la impostergable salvaguarda de los derechos humanos." Menéndez Pidal incorrectly asserted, incidentally, that Las Casas had no understanding of the role of mestizaje in America. On the contrary, as Manuel Giménez Fernández pointed out, mestizaje "es una idea clave en todos los planes del Defensor de los Indios." It was his great hope, as he explained in his April, 1516, Memorial de los remedios to Cisneros, that Spanish laborers and Indians "se mezclaran casándose los hijos de los unos con las hijas de los otros." The result would be highly beneficial: "multiplicarse ha la tierra de gente y de fructo."

Historians in 2066 will wonder whether anyone in 1966, during the four-hundredth commemoration of Las Casas' death, besides Don Ramón, considered Las Casas to be a paranoiac. They will indeed find some who seem to agree. Father Lino Gómez Canedo, in reviewing the biography, writes: "The central conclusion of the author, that Las Casas was a paranoiac, will appear excessive to many, but perhaps it might offer us one of the most plausible explanations of a personality which is certainly strange. What other [interpretation] is possible?"

Let us put ourselves in place of the student in 2066. Should he conclude that Gómez Canedo believes with Menéndez Pidal that Las Casas was, in fact, a paranoiac in the technical medical sense of the term? In the same review he seems to support Don Ramón's interpretation of Las Casas in general, for he refers to the "even temperament of Don Ramón" and says that the book is "written soberly in prose which is at once simple and beautiful." Don Ramón included "certain small errors of fact" and "an excess of polemic commentaries and remarks", but "the author always dissents in measured language without adopting extremist positions." May readers in 2066 not reasonably conclude, therefore, that Gómez Canedo does not consider calling Las Casas a paranoiac an extremist position?

But now comes the real problem. Today some historians debate whether any sixteenth-century Spaniards ever meant to call Indians "animals" or "beasts" in the full anthropological or philosophical sense of these terms. How, then, can historians in the 21st century determine whether Menéndez Pidal and Lino Canedo really intended to classify Las Casas as a paranoiac, in the full and rigorous scientific sense of this psychiatric term? Don Ramón did indeed consult with certain medical specialists in Madrid before applying "paranoiac" to Las Casas, though he did not consider it necessary to accept their definitions. In an interview with an enthusiastic admirer of his interpretation he maintained his position, and the interviewer quoted approvingly Don Ramón's words from the biography: "Las Casas es un paranoico, no un demente o un loco en estado de inconsciencia. Su lucidez habitual hace que su anormalidad sea caso difícil de establecer y graduar, como es muy difícil, respecto a algunos enfermos mentales, el decidir si reducirlos, o no, a un sanitorio. . . la única manera de comprender al Obispo es suponerle un enfermo mental."

Don Ramón's view has been challenged by such writers as the late Benno M. Biermann, O.P., who, after discussing the subject with medical experts, questioned sharply Don Ramón's use of "paranoiac", as scientifically applicable. We do not know whether Gómez Canedo consulted with psychiatrists before writing his review of _El Padre Las Casas. Su doble personalidad_ in which he seems to follow Don Ramón's view that Las Casas was indeed a paranoiac and ended up by asking the question: "What other [interpretation] is possible?"

Perhaps enough has been said to indicate that when passions run high Spaniards applied the words "brute animals", "beasts", "semi-beasts", "dogs", "incapable", "irrational", "little men", "natural slaves", and other pejorative terms to describe the Indians they met during the hectic early days of the conquest of America, but it does not satisfy the modern reader to dismiss all this by saying that of course they did not mean that the Indians were not men in the full anthropological or philosophical sense.

Would it not be more historically correct and meaningful to describe the doubts and disputes on Indian capacity, ventilated during the conquest, especially in the first half century, as leading to a kind of polarization of Spanish reactions to the strange beings they found in the New World? Between an Oviedo who declared that gunpowder used against Indians should be considered as incense to the Lord and a Las Casas who believed passionately that all people could be civilized through education and Christianization, there was no possible compromise. This polarization produced a wide spectrum of opinions ranging from the "dirty dog" to the "noble savage" schools of thought, which never fully disappeared, though these easy generalizations began to have less force by the later years of the sixteenth century. The real question for many Spaniards in the sixteenth century was the capacity of the natives of the newly discovered lands for Christianity and for civilization, not whether they were "animals" or "beasts" in the full philosophical or anthropological sense.

Students of Las Casas in 2066 will surely be pleased to discover that his detailed argument at Valladolid in 1550-1551 against Juan Ginés de Sepúlveda is finally about to be made available by publication in Rome. The main points set forth by both contestants have long been known through the summary Las Casas published in 1552. But the complete text contains much detailed information and some surprises. Thus this _Defense Against the Persecutors and Slanderers of the Peoples of the New World Discovered Across the Sea_ will be a prime historical source.

Indeed, one of the positive results of the commemoration of the four-hundredth anniversary of the death of Las Casas has been the publication of most of his writings in editions easily accessible to the public. Though predictions are dangerous in this field, it seems likely that no great treatise of his remains unpublished. Even if the second part of his argument at Valladolid turns up, the Apología in Spanish, even if the dialogue of the interlocutors Senior e Juvenis on the title of Spain to the Indies is discovered in some library, and even if the book he submitted to the pope at the end of his long life is located in the archives in Rome, it is reasonable to suppose that no startling new aspects of his doctrine will be revealed. And if Las Casas' tremendous collection of letters from correspondents throughout the Indies should somehow miraculously appear, much new detail on his life and on Indian affairs would undoubtedly be available, but the principles which guided his actions for half a century are all to be found in scattered and repetitious fashion on the works we now know: the treatises of 1552-1553, the Historia de las Indias, the Historia apologética, the De único vocationis modo, De thesauris, and his Defense Against the Doctrine of Sepúlveda.

Further analysis of these writings will doubtless yield valuable insights and facts. His views on economic matters will perhaps be clarified; he was one of the first to notice and comment on the inflation caused by the influx of New World treasure into Europe. Las Casas might have become an archeologist, for he apparently divined some of the practices of this field of knowledge. His observations of plants and animals in America has recently been characterized by Víctor Manuel Patiño as of "gran valor científico, superior en muchos casos al revelado por el historiador Oviedo y Valdés." What is now needed, continued this Colombian scholar, is a careful scrutiny of Las Casas' writings for his competence in cultural and social anthropology: "Y se patentizaría entonces que Las Casas no fue un desorbitado maniático, sino uno de los más sagaces y fieles observadores de la sociedad americana."

The Defense, because it includes so many of the essential parts of Las Casas' doctrine, will probably become the favorite treatise of those who wish to get a general appreciation of his theoretical labors. It was prepared as a part of the most solemn and bitter argumentation in an immensely long career marked by lively disputes. As background music, or noise, through all these disputes we hear the discussions on the nature of the Indians and their capacity for civilization. Questions of Indian capacity have a direct relationship to mestizo capacity. As one Mexican writer has emphasized, "the problem of the incapacity of the Indian is not a merely academic interest. For Mexico it is a vital matter; to accept Indian incapacity is the same as admitting our social inferiority." A Peruvian historian has suggested that Spaniards cultivated in the Indians "a tremendous complex of inferiority" which still influences the course of events.

The universal element in Las Casas' thought gives his writings a special relevance today: "No nation exists today, nor could exist, no matter how barbarous, fierce, or depraved its customs may be, which may not be attracted and converted to all political virtues and to all the humanity of domestic, political, and rational man." Las Casas thus expressed in other words the ancient Christian view: "He hath made of one blood all nations of men, for to dwell on all the face of the earth."

The issues struggled over by Spaniards as they opened up the New World face us today. Thus one Spaniard links Pope Paul III's 1537 bull

Sublimis Deus with the deliberations of the recent Vatican Council, and another Spaniard has this to say:

> Guerras santas, luchas de redención social y religiosa, Gott mit uns, destinos manifiestos y bombas atómicas arrojadas en homenaje a la causa de la dignidad humana, tienen ese obscuro fondo de común con la iniquidad de las Indias.
>
> Nuestro tiempo, testigo de quiebras generales del sentido ético, que todavía no han recibido adecuada sentencia, debe estar excepcionalimente capacitado para valorar la gesta de aquellos pocos osados que emprendieron la tarea de enderezar el magno entuerto de las Indias. Está claro, después de lo expuesto, que se trataba no simplemente de suscitar una reacción sentimentalista, sino de revisar un basamento espiritual--que arrastaba desde siglos atrás su simplicidad de premisas y de discurso--para ascender por la vía fatigosa en que el hombre vuelve críticamente sobre sí mismo. Tamaña empresa, que por distintos caminos llega a trascender a resultados permanentes, es así una de las capitales en el desenvolvimiento histórico del espíritu.

The Renaissance and Reformation period in which Las Casas lived has usually been considered an age in which the horizons of men were lifted: "New vistas of the world were being opened up by the voyagers; new types of men, of modes of life, of societies and states, were being discovered and described. . . and new questions, which were nevertheless as old as the hills, made eddies and rapids in the swift current of thought, and cried out for an answer."

Today, despite the voyages to the moon, we live in an "Age of Diminished Man", according to the poet Archibald Macleish, speaking at the Charter Day ceremonies of the University of California in May, 1969. However we may explain the "paradoxical diminishment in our own eyes at the moment of our greatest technological triumphs", Macleish maintained that a "belief in man--a return to a belief in man--is the reality on which a new age can be built." Was not Las Casas addressing himself at Valladolid essentially to this same question?

Did he really expect to win the argument?, one may ask. From his earliest years as an Indian defender he had been a resourceful and determined political strategist in the world of the Emperor Charles V. Yet at Valladolid, with many years of struggle in Spain and in America behind him, he proposed formally that all conquests be stopped. Did he think that at that late date, more than half a century after Columbus, the clock could be turned back, that the whole machinery of empire from which so many politically powerful Spaniards both lay and ecclesiastical profited could be dismantled?. . .

Whatever may be the correct answers to these questions, the historian in looking back on the conflict over the nature of the American Indians can see why the late José Almoina characterized it as "perhaps the most transcendental controversy that took place at the threshold of the Modern Age." And cannot we also see that, inasmuch as Las Casas' argumentation against Sepúlveda focussed on one of the overriding themes of the modern world--the relations between peoples of different customs, capability, colors, religions, and values--the Defense stands out as one of the fundamental positions taken on the bitter and continuing conflicts that divide mankind. If this be true will not both the "American reality" of the sixteenth century and the clashing ideas of Las Casas and Sepúlveda be of unquestioned meaning to our troubled age, and can we see in the Valladolid dispute yet another illustration of the fact that all history is contemporary history?

It is a pity that those of us concerned with the 400th anniversary will not be present in 2066. For it would be instructive to learn how our successors will confront the great historical questions involved in the interpretation of the Spanish conquest of America. In what way will the circumstances of their time affect their perception of the issues at stake in that sixteenth-century disputation at Valladolid?

CHAPTER 11.

COMMEMORATIVE STATEMENTS ON THE WORK OF BARTOLOME DE LAS CASAS

Commemorations of the work of Las Casas during the last few years have come thick and fast. In 1952 there was the anniversary of the publication of his famous treatises; in 1966 his death 400 years earlier brought forth many writings and meetings; and there were even more occasions in 1974 marking the 500th anniversary of his birth.

The following short pieces were all produced as a part of the latter event. The first and third talks were delivered in San Cristóbal de Las Casas in the state of Chiapas, Mexico, where he had served for a short time as bishop, while the second formed a part of the round table discussion organized by the Academia Nacional de Historia in Caracas.

There will be undoubtedly more commemorations! For recently there was discovered in Sevilla a document which indicates that Las Casas was born there not in 1474, the date heretofore accepted, but in 1484, so that we may confidently look forward to more conferences and more publications in 1984.

Will someone find another unpublished manuscript of a hitherto unknown treatise? Will there be elaborated new perspectives or old controversies? Will those who are now promoting his canonization by the Roman Catholic Church prevail?

Cuadernos americanos, año XXXIII, núm. 3 (México, 1974), 131-142, passim; Memoria del Segundo Congreso Venezolano de Historia, III (Caracas, 1975), 485-486; Fray Bartolomé de Las Casas en Hispanoamérica (San Cristóbal de Las Casas, 1976), 263-270. Reprinted by permission. Translations by Celso Rodríguez.

Commemorative Statements on the Work of Bartolomé de Las Casas

Cómo Deberíamos Conmemorar en 1974 La Vida de Bartolomé de Las Casas?

El Patronato Fray Bartolomé de las Casas, organizado por la Sra. Gertrude Duby Blom y el Lic. Angel Robles, has avanzado mucho en sus propósitos de establecer cuáles son los medios más apropiados para honrar y recordar los merecimientos de esa extraordinaria figura en la historia de la expansión de Europa--Fray Bartolomé de las Casas, el Obispo de Chiapa. Las variadas y numerosas celebraciones organizadas por este activo Patronato son una acabada demostración no sólo de la imaginación del progresista grupo de ciudadanos de San Cristóbal de las Casas que dirigen el Patronato, sino también de la asombrosa riqueza de las posibilidades inherentes en la vida de este controvertido dominico del siglo XVI, cuyas actividades y escritos son todavía relevantes en la era atómica que vivimos. Los conceptos que expresaré aquí, en ocasión en que el Patronato hace la apertura de un año dedicado a reconocer las contribuciones de Fray Bartolomé, tienen tembién la intención de servir como sugerencias adicionales sobre los eventos planeados por el Patronato en Chiapas y por grupos en España y otros lugares.

Comencemos expresando una verdad obvia: las conmemoraciones de 1974 darán la oportunidad para leer cuidadosamente los escritos de Las Casas, pues todos sus trabajos principales están publicados y son de fácil alcance. No era así cuando yo comencé a estudiar cuarenta años atrás, sus teorías políticas, siendo estudiante de posgrado en la Universidad de Harvard. Aunque el tratado sobre el único modo de atraer a los pueblos a la fe verdadera fue finalmente publicado en el latín original con una traducción al castellano hace treinta años, todavía había tantos escritos suyos sin publicar que escribí un artículo hace más de veinte años sobre "Lo que todavía necesita hacerse sobre la vida y los escritos de Bartolomé de las Casas".

Hoy me complace informar: misión cumplida. Han sido publicados todos los trabajos propuestos en ese artículo y además la Biblioteca de Autores Españoles ha lanzado una excelente colección de los escritos de Las Casas en cinco tomos, bajo la dirección del distinguido historiador español Dr. Juan Pérez de Tudela.

Los análisis e interpretaciones de las acciones e ideas de Las Casas incrementaron tanto en número como en sofisticación, como lo demostrará claramente la copiosa bibliografía del estudioso francés Raymond Marcus, próxima a aparecer. Pero la controversia no ha disminuido, pues Las Casas fue un revolucionario en sus tiempos y mientras el mundo se halle preocupado por las relaciones entre pueblos de diferente color, costumbre y religión, es inevitable que sus doctrinas han de provocar juicios contradictorios. Debemos estar preparados para estas diferencias de opinión y tratar de entenderlas. Para apreciar por qué esto es así, sólo tenemos que mirar a nuestro mundo y leer los escritos de Las Casas.

Existen antologías en castellano, francés e inglés, pero es de confiar que estas muestras han de alentar lecturas más extensas y profundas de las muchas páginas de los trabajos históricos y los tratados de Las Casas. Esta lectura a fondo conducirá al examen de los muchos estudios especializados y las interpretaciones que existen, y eventualmente deben dar lugar a la meditación sobre los principios fundamentales expuestos por Las Casas relacionados con apremiantes problemas de su tiempo, pero que también tienen su paralelo en nuestro mundo de hoy. . .

Por lo tanto, la lectura, el estudio y la meditación han de ser ampliamente estimuladas por los eventos conmemorativos de 1974. En realidad, si consumimos nuestro tiempo y nuestra inventiva meramente llevando a cabo intrascendentes ceremonias, y no hacemos hincapié en la necesidad de comprender a Las Casas a través de un estudio sereno de sus escritos y contemplando los profundos problemas sobre los que escribió, los esfuerzos conmemorativos del Patronato y todos los demás, habrán fracasado.

Otro beneficio que es posible lograr tal vez no pueda explicarse con facilidad: la organización y habilitación de los archivos eclesiásticos sobre los cuales la historia de España en América depende en gran medida. Alguien podría preguntar aún ¿no tenemos ahora acceso a más manuscritos en el Archivo General de Indias y otros repositorios en España y en América que pueden ser consultados adecuadamente por los historiadores? Nadie que haya trabajado en esos archivos, o que haya examinado cuidadosamente una obra de referencia como los múltiples tomos de la Bibliotheca missionum, puede dejar de impresionarse, y a veces hasta sentirse abrumado por los manuscritos y las otras fuentes que existen para documentar la acción de la iglesia católica en la América española. Las guías en preparación sobre los manuscritos eclesiásticos en archivos no religiosos son también impresionantes, pero pocas de ellas existen sobre materiales no publicados que se encuentran en los archivos eclesiásticos.

Con todo, si los historiadores han de comprender la verdadera contribución de Las Casas en relación a la realizada por otros dominicos, o franciscanos, jesuitas, en suma, por todos los eclesiásticos, debemos tener un acceso más abierto a los archivos locales en la América hispana donde se hallen preservados los trabajos de los curas de parroquia, obispos y arzobispos. Algunas veces estos registros han sido destruidos por el fuego, o por la negligencia o los estragos del tiempo, así como ha ocurrido también con archivos que no están bajo la jurisdicción de la iglesia. Pero aun los archivos eclesiásticos que han sido preservados, se hallan a veces organizados pobremente. Y cuando están bien organizados y con buenos índices, como ocurre con los de la catedral y los del Arzobispado de La Paz, en Bolivia, no están regularmente habilitados ni siquiera para los investigadores calificados.

¿Por qué son estos archivos tan importantes y hasta indispensables para comprender a Las Casas? Este es el nudo del problema. Poseemos un extenso conocimiento sobre el Obispo de Chiapa, pero sabemos mucho menos sobre las ideas y actuación de otros exlesiásticos en el mismo campo, cuya contribución, por supuesto, fue importante. Algunos no compartieron sus puntos de vista, otros sí, pero casi todos estuvieron influenciados de alguna manera por sus escritos. Deben existir documentos en muchas partes de Hispanoamérica, así como posiblemente en España, sobre los esfuerzos llevados a cabo por frailes y sacerdotes todavía desconocidos, para proteger a los indios y trabajar por lo que ellos consideraban que era lo que major servía los intereses de los naturales de América. Pero hasta que sus vidas y sus acciones también sean conocidas, tendremos solamente una visión parcial de lo sucedido en el largo historial de las complejas relaciones entre los indios y los españoles. Confiemos entonces que el año 1974 promoverá un renovado interés entre los historiadores por conocer todos los esfuerzos de la iglesia católica en América, como un paso adelante para lograr una certera dimensión de la estatura de Las Casas como una de las figuras más prominentes en la lucha por la justicia en la conquista española. Los historiadores no podrán ampliar y completar este conocimiento a menos que los archivos eclesiásticos estén organizados y habilitados a todos los historiadores. . . .

Contemplando los grandes esfuerzos de Las Casas y otros españoles del siglo XVI para comprender las culturas de los nativos del Nuevo Mundo cuyas almas aspiraban a ganar, y para convencer a sus coetáneos que esas culturas merecían ser estudiadas, ¿no encontramos un claro paralelo con los tiempos que vivimos? Hoy, más aún que en el siglo XVI, existe una enorme y creciente movilidad humana hacia los cuatro rincones del globo. Los aviones de colosal tamaño que han transformado en un hecho de rutina los viajes a lugares remotos para miles y miles de seres, darán un poderoso impulso a la movilización que hoy contemplamos. Con todo, habrá hoy muy pocas familias en los Estados Unidos en que alguno de sus miembros no haya viajado a tierras distintas, donde las costumbres y la cultura de la gente son profundamente diferentes a las nuestras.

Hoy, cuando el mundo busca como a tientas hallar algunas bases firmes para lograr una paz duradera entre los pueblos de distintas culturas, no es solamente la diversidad de sus inquietudes intelectuales y la devoción exclusiva por los indios de este fraile lo que provoca nuestro mayor respeto y simpatía, sino su actitud hacia los que no eran ni españoles ni cristianos. Pues Las Casas rechazó la noción de que los indios descubiertos por los españoles en su intrépida conquista del Nuevo Mundo eran bestias, ni tampoco compartió la teoría de que eran esclavos por naturaleza, de acuerdo al punto de vista aristotélico, o criaturas semejantes a los niños, con una capacidad de entendimiento tan limitada que debían ser tratadas como si estuvieran en permanente minoría de edad. Las Casas, por el contrario, insistió que la civilización de esos seres extraños que el mundo conoció a través del descubrimiento no sólo merecía ser estudiada sino también respetada. . . .

Los ideales de Las Casas no han prevalecido siempre, un hecho evidente a cualquiera que estudia los testimonios de las acciones de los españoles en América. Pero esta verdad ¿no nos revela una honda significación? Su vida, a pesar de unos pocos momentos de gloria, fue básicamente una tragedia, pues fracasó en muchos de sus objetivos inmediatos. No puede ignorar uno la oposición manifestada por respetables hombres de su tiempo hacia algunas de sus doctrinas y acciones, una oposición que no ha desaparecido con el correr de los años. Pero su percepción de la validez de la cultura de otras gentes, su fe en la humanidad, cualquiera fueran sus costumbres, color de la piel o religión, estas audaces afirmaciones ¿no provocan hoy una reacción solidaria?

Para estudiar a Las Casas honesta y adecuadamente uno debe incluir la historia de sus luchas, sus frustraciones, sus fracasos. Estos han sido una parte integral de su vida y nos han dejado su significación para el presente. Pero lo que aparece más saliente en nuestro tiempo cuando miramos hacia atrás a través de los años es su objetivo, que una vez describió de esta manera:

> Para liberar mi propia nación española del error muy grave y de la ilusión muy perniciosa en que ahora vive y ha vivido siempre, de considerar estos pueblos faltos de las características esenciales del hombre, juzgándolas bestias brutas incapaces de virtudes y religión, despreciando sus buenas cualidades y exagerando las malas que hay en ellos. Estos pueblos han estado escondidos y olvidados por muchos siglos y (ha sido mi propósito) extenderles nuestras manos de alguna manera, de modo que no permanezcan

oprimidos como al presente debido a esa falsa opinión sobre ellos, y mantenidos permanentemente en la penumbra.

¿De qué mejor manera podríamos hoy conmemorar a Las Casas sino esforzándonos por lograr que sea una realidad la vivencia de su doctrina fundamental sobre la naturaleza del hombre? No será una tarea fácil, porque en los Estados Unidos, y en realidad en muchos otros países americanos, hay tanto todavía por hacer. Pero por lo menos se ha logrado comenzar, los gobiernos están organizando sus propias fuerzas y algún progreso se ha obtenido. Proclamemos en 1974, el año de la conmemoración, las profundas verdades que Las Casas comprendió tan bien en el siglo XVI, pero no olvidemos nunca que la lucha que él comenzó en América no ha terminado aún y nunca terminará a menos que todos, hombres y mujeres, trabajemos para hacer efectiva la doctrina fundamental de Las Casas. . .

En el año conmemorativo 1974 este principio fundamental de Las Casas ocupará el lugar más destacado en nuestros pensamientos, porque las tensiones que existen en muchos lugares del mundo se han producido a causa de las diferencias entre los pueblso. Aunque hoy casi nadie apoyaría a Sepúlveda, tenemos una actitud neo-Sepulvediana, expresada por personas tales como el Dr. William B. Shockley, laureado con el Premio Nobel de Física, que ha entrado en el campo de la genética y ha causado una aguda controversia con su aserto de que los negros son genéticamente de una categoría más baja. Recientemente ha expresado: "Mi investigación me lleva a afirmar concluyentemente la opinión de que la causa principal de la inferioridad intelectual y social es. . . racialmente genética en su origen". El Dr. Shockley ha provodado una vigorosa oposición y tanto sus métodos como sus conclusiones han sido rebatidas. Pero su presencia hoy día en las universidades de los Estados Unidos demuestra que la lucha continúa existiendo para lograr paz en un mundo poblado por razas diversas. La actitud de Las Casas en Valladolid, encarnada en su tratado sobre la _Defensa contra los perseguidores y difamadores de los pueblos del Nuevo Mundo descubierto a través de los mares_ debería ayudarnos a comprender los problemas que hoy se presentan.

El debate sobre este tópico altamente controvertido bien puede llevar a nuevas y emocionales confrontaciones. Aquí también podemos aprender de Las Casas. A menudo fue sarcástico, incriminante y hasta inflamatorio en muchos de sus escritos. Pero cuando trataba de persuadir, como en _Del único modo de atraer a todos los pueblos a la verdadera religión_ su tono fue moderado y sereno. Confiaba en convencer a su audiencia de la verdad de su mensaje escribiendo en forma calma y juiciosa. Así debemos hacerlo nosotros, en nuestro examen de la suprema idea de Las Casas, que es hoy para todos uno de sus legados más significantes.

Las Casas, Un Hombre de Espiritu Lento, Gradual, Tardio

Algunos activistas hoy miran a Las Casas como co-religionario, y es verdad que el abogaba para cambios fundamentales en la vida americana. Pero nunca llegó a sus convicciones sin gastar mucho tiempo y no tenía fe en cambios rápidos. Vale la pena insistir en este aspecto de su vida, y podemos entenderle mirando algunas de las etapas de su larga y agitada actuación en la historia de España en América:

1502-1514

Doce años de experiencia en la isla de Española. Vio la realidad cruda de los primeros años de la conquista, y seguramente había oído del sermón famoso de Montesinos en el año de 1511. Defendía la encomienda en discusiones con su confesor dominico, y solamente en 1514 a la edad de 40 años el vio la luz.

1514-1522

Ocho años de protestas, proyectos y fracasos, culminando en su derrota en Venezuela.

1522-1530

Ocho años de estudio y silencio en el convento dominico de Española.

1552-1553

Solamente a la edad de casi 70 años mandó sus varios tratados a la imprenta después de más de 20 años de agitación ante el Consejo de Indias.

Podemos ver claramente que hablaba con vehemencia pero actuaba solamente después de mucha meditación. Nunca creyó en cambios bruscos; particularmente no pensaba que ningún pueblo puede cambiar sus creencias religiosas ligeramente. Siempre insistía en la necesidad absoluta de educación antes de bautismo. En 1538 argüía fuertemente con Motolinía contra bautismo superficial de los indios sin la debida doctrina. Esta lucha llegó a España, y en el año 1541 Fray Francisco de Vitoria y otros teólogos notables de la Universidad de Salamanca dieron su parecer formal en favor de la posición de Las Casas, apoyando bautismo solamente después de instrucción adecuada.

Podemos también ver hoy que el mundo tardaría en reconocer a Las Casas. No hubo conmemoraciones en 1674, 1774 o 1874. Pero hoy día Fray Bartolomé y sus esfuerzos en pro de los indios son el objeto de muchos actos y publicaciones de las muchas instituciones y personas en su deseo de honrarle en el quinientos aniversario de su nacimiento.

¿Por qué? ¿Por qué ahora ejerce una atracción grande en muchos países, incluso países que no pertenecen al mundo de habla española y entre historiadores no católicos? ¿No está suficientemente claro ahora que el creciente interés en el mundo por Las Casas se ha expandido debido a que él no pertenece a una sola tribu ni habla por las inquietudes de una sola nación? Sus escritos pueden concentrarse en América y en la situación de los indios que la habitaban, pero él realmente pertenece a una tribu que es toda la humanidad. Esto explica por qué ha de ser estudiado más y más, tanto por los eruditos como por los no especialistas, y la perspectiva que tengan de este paradigma de la América española del siglo XVI enriquecerá aún más nuestro conocimiento de su obra. Por eso es que hoy me animo a decir: "Las Casas es demasiado significativo para ser dejado a los Lascasistas". Ni a España que tan difícilmente ha aceptado a Las Casas como buen español--ni a América--aun ni a Chiapas!

La disputa de Valladolid es todavía otro ejemplo de que toda la historia es de alguna manera historia contemporánea. ¿Puede alguien dudar que el comentario del obispo Antonio Agustín, en abril de 1550, en la víspera de la confrontación entre Las Casas y Sepúlveda, es hoy tan válido como cuando declaró que el dilema en el cual se debatían era "una cuestión que merece ser considerada en el escenario de toda la humanidad"?. . .

Una Palabra Más

Quiero empezar con una confesión. He cambiado el título de mi ponencia. Nuestro tópico hoy, según el programa oficial es "Indigenismo y Colonialismo: una perspectiva contemporánea a partir de la obra de Las Casas". Y el título oficial de mi charla es "Mi vida con Fray Bartolomé de Las Casas: comentarios personales sobre nuestra relación durante más de 40 años". ¡Un poco pomposo!--por eso he cambiado, he cortado, mis recuerdos. Ni es dos palabras. Es una palabra, que podrá sorprender y tal vez asombrar a algunos de mis buenos amigos que por muchos años se han esforzado para que Fray Bartolomé sea mejor conocido. Mi tesis es muy sencilla: "Las Casas es demasiado importante para ser dejado a los Lascasistas--demasiado universal para ser confinado dentro de una cultura, aun una cultura tan variada y rica como es la cultura hispánica".

Permítanme agregar sin demora que no me atrevería a hablar así de este tópico si dedicados historiadores no hubieran hecho conocer los trabajos fundamentales de Las Casas en ediciones fácilmente accesibles, y si muchos estudiosos no hubieran publicado valiosos análisis e interpretaciones de su vida y su obra. Nuestro conocimiento de Las Casas es hoy mucho más vasto que cuando yo lo descubrí en la Biblioteca Widener en la Universidad de Harvard en 1930. Quizás algun día escribiré unas notas detalladas sobre "Mi vida con Fray Bartolomé"--tal vez el año próximo cuando me retire de mis actividades en la enseñanza, pero no hay tiempo ahora para relatar esta historia, excepto consignar las reacciones de varias personas a quienes consulté durante 1932 y 1933 sobre si Las Casas podría ser un tema apropiado para una tesis doctoral. El excepcional especialista alemán en la Edad de Oro y la literatura española, Karl Vossler, opinó que no. Conocíamos ya lo suficiente sobre Las Casas, escribió Vossler, y no esperaba que aparecieran nuevos elementos a manuscritos que justificaran realizar una investigación sobre Las Casas. El historiador económico norteamericano Earl J. Hamilton, que estaba es España en aquellos años abstraído en su fundamental trabajo sobre la historia de los precios en España en relación de la inflación debido al oro americano, tuvo una opinión distinta pero igualmente negativa. El quería que cambiara mi tópico por uno realmente importante: ¡tal como el de los precios! El Jesuita Pedro Leturia desde Roma fue más alentador y Emilio Ravignani, director del entonces floreciente Instituto de Investigaciones Históricas de Buenos Aires, hasta se mostró entusiasmado. El influyó en mí considerablemente con su convencimiento de que todavía había mucha que hacer acerca de la vida del controvertido andaluz. Ravignani demostró su confianza de manera muy gratificante para un joven estudiante, pues patrocinó mi primera publicación en 1935.

En las cuatro décadas desde entonces las publicaciones de y acerca de Las Casas se han sucedido con tanta rapidez que el registro bibliográfico de las mismas ha pasado a ser un problema serio. Por fortuna, Raymond Marcus está por finalizar su prolija y completa bibliografía, lo que hará posible trabajar en este campo con más facilidad que hasta ahora. En los últimos años han sido publicados trabajos sobre Las Casas en lugares tan distantes como Japón y la Unión Sovietica y tan alejados entre sí como De Kalb y la ciudad de México, para mencionar solo unos pocos. En Aix-en-Provence tendrá lugar en octubre próximo una conferencia de tres días sobre las ideas de Las Casas y los derechos del hombre. La obra de Las Casas, por lo tanto, ya no es sólo de interés para los estudiosos del mundo de habla hispana. Este es un hecho notable, en especial porque relativamente pocos historiadores han estudiado otra cosa excepto su propia historia. . . .

¿Por qué, entonces, es que Las Casas ha ejercido siempre una atracción grande en los historiadores que no pertenecen al mundo de habla española? Contestar satisfactoriamente a esta pregunta requeriría un tomo tan grande y tan sofisticado como el brillante trabajo de Benjamin Keen The Aztec Image in Western Thought. Janusz Tazbir en 1973 publicó en Polonia una interesante artículo sobre la forma en que los escritos de Las Casas eran recibidos en Polonia. Cada nación, cada grupo dentro de una nación de su interpretación a la luz de su historia, su ser. La cultura azteca pintada por los europeos, con la excepción del gran antropólogo franciscano Bernardino de Sahagún, era una reflexión de la cultura europea como Keen ha mostrado con mucho detalle.

¿No está suficientemente claro ahora que el creciente interés en el mundo por Las Casas se ha expandido debido a que él no pertenece a una sola tribu ni habla por las inquietudes de una sola nación? Sus escritos pueden concentrarse en América y en la situación de los indios que la habitaban, pero él realmente pertenece a una tribu que es toda la humanidad. Esto explica porque ha de ser estudiado más y más, tanto por los eruditos como por los no especialistas, y la perspectiva que tengan de este paradigma de la América española del siglo diez y seis enriquecerá aún más nuestro conocimiento de su obra. . . .

La perspectiva de dejar a otros estudiosos, tal vez todavía desconocidos, la responsabilidad de interpretar a Las Casas en el siglo anterior al seiscientos aniversario de su nacimiento, es de mi agrado. Ha llegado la hora de que otros investigadores se prodiguen en este campo. Confío en que algunos de ellos se dedicarán a lo que ha sido llamado en un artículo de una obra sobre teología católica "La significación teológica del descubrimiento de América". Aquellos en búsqueda de una exposición minuciosa de este importante tópico deberán consultar las publicaciones del dominico neo-tomista Venancio D. Carro. Y me alegro en saber que el padre Enrique Ruíz Maldonado ya está estudiando este gran tema. . .

En muchas partes del mundo las mujeres están luchando para ocupar una posición en el mundo igual a los hombres. La mayoría de las mujeres viven hoy día en un tipo de colonialismo de que no hablamos mucho. Tampoco hablamos mucho de la discriminación, el sistema económico feudal, la inferioridad legal que afectan a mujeres en muchos países. Aunque un historiador no debe actuar como profeta, yo creo que durante los próximos cien años la lucha en pro de las mujeres va crecer más cada día--en los Estador Unidos, en México, y en todos los países.

¿Puede Las Casas, o mejor dicho, puede el pensamiento de Fray Bartolomé ayudar al mundo aceptar la idea de que cuando hablamos de "los derechos del hombre" estamos naturalmente incluyendo mujeres? Dudo si durante los tres día en Aix-en-Provence cuando tendrá lugar en el octubre próximo una reunión sobre "Las Casas y los derechos del hombre", los derechos de las mujeres recibirán mucha atención.

Pero seguramente podemos esperar que cuando el mundo conmemore el sexto aniversario del nacimiento de Las Casas, mujeres ocuparán una posición mucho mejor en el mundo, que hoy--especialmente si las mujeres de México y de otros países estudian la obra de Las Casas. Porque Fray Bartolomé siempre negaba que existía un grupo o raza inferior. El siempre exaltaba la personalidad humana.

Es aun posible que habrá en 2074 una obra teológica sobre Las Casas escrita por una mujer. ¿Si teología incluye las relaciones entre el hombre y Dios, y si "hombre" incluye mujer, no sería provechosa la perspectiva de las mujeres? Naturalmente, este supone que los seminarios donde se estudia teología están dispuestos a recibir mujeres como estudiantes de teología. ¿Y sacerdotes? ¿Habrá mujeres como sacerdotes en 2074?

De todos modos, sabemos que se necesita hoy un ejército erudito para estudiar debidamente la obra de Las Casas, porque actuaba como historiador, pensador, político, misionólogo, antropólogo, teólogo, psicólogo, economista, literato, político práctico, etc. Ya es muy claro que historia escrita solamente por hombres en un sentido masculino, debe ser una historia parcial e incompleta. Recordemos que Sor. Juana Inés de la Cruz ha dicho que si Aristóteles hubiera pasado más tiempo en la cocina su filosofía hubiera sido más amplia.

En nuestras discusiones ayer, en un momento de exaltación indiscreta, pregunté si las mujeres están incluidas en los derechos del hombre. Recibí una lección de grámatica y una referencia a la Constitución Mexicana, del Lic. González Calzada. Pero no habló de la realidad de la situación de la mujer hoy en el gobierno, la economía, la iglesia, la universidad, y la vida social.

Y tengo que confesar que yo daría más fe a una mujer hablando sobre tal tema que a un hombre.

En mi país el problema ha llegado a tal punto que hay una enmienda constitucional propuesta para asegurar igualdad a las mujeres ante la ley. Es un problema complicado y difícil dada la historia de las relaciones entre hombres y mujeres desde hace muchos siglos. Hasta el siglo pasado hubo una división clara en muchas culturas entre los trabajos de las mujeres y de los hombres. Hoy este sistema, por varias razones y circunstancias, está cambiando o a lo menos está en transición. Va a ser una jornada larga, porque cambiar las relaciones fundamentales entre hombres y mujeres es casi tan difícil como cambiar su religión. Y todos nosotros sabemos que en este proceso Las Casas era un gradualista. El insistía en la dificultad de tales cambios de una religión a otra y proclamaba la necesidad de paciencia y persistencia de los misioneros.

¿Tendrá lugar la conmemoración en 2074 en China, que todavía--que yo sepa--no ha hecho ninguna aportación a la literatura lascasista? ¿O tal vez en una capital africana? No importa. Seguramente se reunirá en un centro donde esta tribu grande--la tribu que podemos llamar la humanidad--estará honrada. Pero nunca nadie olvidará que era España la que produjo este fenómeno llamado Bartolomé de Las Casas o que en tierras americanas--especialmente en México--Fray Bartolomé pasaba los días más gloriosos y los días más trágicos de su larga y fecunda vida.

PART III

THE VILLA IMPERIAL DE POTOSI

CHAPTER 12.

LUIS CAPOCHE AND THE VILLA IMPERIAL DE POTOSI

During my studies on Las Casas in Spain in 1932-1934, I found in the Biblioteca de Palacio in Madrid an enormous manuscript history of the Villa Imperial de Potosí, the famous silver mine in colonial Peru. Ever afterward I continued to be drawn to the tumultuous and gaudy annals of this treasure center and eventually published, with Gunnar Mendoza, the manuscript history. And in the years following 1932, though I was principally occupied in writing on various aspects of the struggle for justice in the conquest of Spanish America, material on Potosí turned up almost wherever I happened to look.

I went down the mine, still being worked but now for tin, in 1935 on my first visit to Bolivia. The sight of almost naked miners laboring in the deep shafts of this great mountain of Potosí at some 15,000 feet above sea level was a memorable experience. When a manuscript history of the early years of Potosí by a miner, Luis Capoche, came to my attention, I decided to enlarge my knowledge of Potosí by editing it. The following is an English version of the introduction for the Relación when the complete text was included in the Biblioteca de Autores Españoles.

Inter-American Economic Affairs, XII (Washington, D.C., 1958), 19-51.
Reprinted by permission.

Luis Capoche and the Villa Imperial de Potosí

The account prepared in 1585 by Luis Capoche on the history of the silver mining center in Upper Peru called the Villa Imperial de Potosí can best be understood against a background of the development among Spaniards of a keen interest in the history of the New World. Columbus started the practice of writing about America, and many followed his example. The conquest so excited the imagination of Spaniards that they came to look upon it as the greatest event since the coming of Christ. Even as the conquistadores roamed over vast areas of land and sea and missionaries attempted to Christianize millions of Indians, they collected historical materials and composed histories on a monumental scale.

Many of these documents reflect the character of sixteenth-century Spaniards. The youthful Diego de Ordaz yearned to find out what lay beneath the outpouring smoke of a Mexican volcano and finally wrung a reluctant approval for the ascent of the crater from his chief Ferdinand Cortez, who authorized the dangerous enterprise only "in order that the Indians might see that nothing is impossible for a Spaniard." Another bold deed was done by Governor Pedro de Valdivia's mistress who sought to discourage the Indians laying siege to Santiago in Chile by personally cutting off the heads of half a dozen chieftains held as hostages and rolling them down into the ranks of the invaders. An unusual kind of courage was displayed by the Dominican friar Luis Cáncer as he set forth stubbornly to convert the Indians of Florida despite the prediction, later fulfilled, that he would only be butchered by the natives. Many such tales of heroism, cruelty, and piety are imbedded in the thousands of depositions made by individual Spaniards on their exploits which still await the investigator in archives; for, despite advances in recent years, Spanish American historiography is a relatively uncultivated field.

As the conquest proceeded and as Spain developed a stable organization for governing the New World, a demand arose for an adequate history of Spanish accomplishments. Ecclesiastics early felt the need for a record of their contributions, and later disputes over the justice of Spanish rule led the town fathers of Mexico to commission histories. A decisive epoch for historiography began about 1570 when the president of the Council of the Indies, Juan de Ovando, decided that good administration required an archive containing organized information on previous laws and past events, adequate machinery for obtaining current reports, and an official historian-cosmographer. A detailed questionnaire was drawn up which required from every governor in America specific data on the history, people, products, climate, and geography of the territory he administered. Begun as a brief enquiry in 1569, this questionnaire soon grew to fifty items, and eventually became a printed volume of three hundred and fifty-five separate questions. The first royal "cosmographer and historiographer" was appointed in 1573 to make use of the material collected by this method, and later on also had available the documents sent to Spain as a result of the order of June 25, 1578, which instructed the principal royal representatives in America to search their archives for historical manuscripts and to despatch the originals or authentic copies to the Council of the Indies so that a true, general history of the Indies could be written.

Besides this official documentation, religious chronicles, and the personal narratives of great deeds done, another type of history was produced as individual Spaniards began to contemplate the conquest and to devote themselves to telling the story of particular aspects, events, or geographical areas. The classic Verdadera historia de la conquista de Nueva España by Bernal Díaz del Castillo, the polemic Historia de las Indias by Bartolomé de Las Casas, and the description of Peru by the youthful soldier Pedro Cieza de León are well-known examples of such works.

Except for the momentous discovery itself and the dramatic conquests by Cortez and Francisco Pizarro, few themes have so continuously aroused the wonder and interest of successive generations as the fabulous story of the Potosí mine. For almost four hundred years loyal Potosinos, and others too, composed poems, novels, plays, and histories relating to the tumultuous and romantic past of this mountain of silver located high in the Andes in one of the most desolate and inaccessible parts of South America.

The early years of Potosí since its discovery in 1545 were given over to such frenzied exploitation of the easily available and rich silver deposits that history writing did not flourish. Not until the rule of Viceroy Francisco de Toledo (1569-1581) was life at the roaring mining camp sufficiently stabilized for her inhabitants to be able to concern themselves with the past. When Toledo first visited Potosí in December, 1572, an Indian approached with a petition requesting that he be granted a pension as a son of the discoverer of the mine which even then had become the dominant element in the economy of the viceroyalty. The methodical viceroy appointed Rodrigo de la Fuente to enquire into the matter and ascertain the facts. His report forms a part of the large and contradictory literature on the way Indians stumbled onto the mine and then made known its existence to their conquerors. Toledo also stimulated the Florentine Nicolás del Benino, a member of the Medici family who had left his native city because of political difficulties about 1550 to begin a long and agitated career as a Potosí mine owner, to compose in 1573 a valuable geological description of the mountain.

Another veteran miner, Diego Rodríguez Enríquez de Figueroa, informed Viceroy Martín Enríquez in 1582 that he had been preparing, "as a relaxation from his other activities," an account of Inca culture as well as a history of the first Spaniards in Peru including Potosí, and had completed a painting showing all the mines and shafts in the mountain to accompany his story. He had a definite objective, too, for he warned Toledo that unless the twelve Indians taken away from his mine were restored he would be ruined. Many of the reports that today constitute a valuable part of the history of Potosí were designed to influence decisions at the viceregal capital in Lima or at the court in Spain, but rarely have they or the more formal histories also written in abundance been printed.

Among the Spaniards who drew up long reports for governmental authorities in the hope of determining their action was an operator of a mill for reducing the silver ore named Luis Capoche, who prepared a description of the discovery of the mine and its subsequent enormous development, as well as the story of its social and economic life up to 1585. On August 10 of that year he completed his manuscript, dedicated it to the incoming Viceroy Hernando de Torres y Portugal, the Conde del Villar, and transmitted it to Lima so that the viceroy could read it as soon as he reached his new post. The original report appears to be lost, as well as the "retrato" which Capoche attached to give some idea of how Potosí looked, but a usable contemporary copy is available in the Archive of the Indies in Seville of Capoche's *Relación general del asiento y Villa Imperial de Potosí y de las cosas más importantes a su gobierno*. The "*Relación*" has circulated in manuscript to some extent during the years since it was written and has been quoted occasionally, but never studied seriously nor in relation to other documentation of the first forty, critical years of the existence of Potosí. This essay will attempt to bring together what is known about the author and endeavor to explain the value of the "*Relación*" to an understanding of Potosí and to the story of Spanish America.

I

The name of Luis Capoche appears seldom in the manuscripts on Potosí, and not at all in the voluminous printed correspondence of the Audiencia de La Plata with the viceroys and the Crown. Probably he was born in Seville; he tells us that as a youth he saw there, and wondered at, a curious device painted on the walls of the home of one Juan de Marroquí, who had become rich at Potosí and had adopted the guaira or Indian ore furnace as his coat of arms. It was Capoche's first knowledge of the mine, though Seville must have exhibited many evidences in those days of the riches brought from the New World. As one of her proud historians asserted at about the time Capoche was writing, enough treasure had been brought to Seville from America "to pave her streets with gold and silver." Capoche also states that the wood brought to Potosí for the construction of the mining mills was transported great distances on the backs of Indians "just like the *alhameles* [porters] of Seville." So it is likely that he was a Sevillano, perhaps a member of one of those numerous Italian commercial families, or their descendants, that exercised such influence in the ports of southern Spain from the thirteenth century onward.

Capoche knew Castile and may have served in the Spanish army abroad; he declares that it was even colder in Potosí than in Flanders. He speaks of Africa and Tierra Firme in such a way as to suggest that he may have visited these parts. Before settling down in Potosí as a fairly young man, he had evidently visited other parts of Peru. His remarks on the stability that encomenderos, the well-to-do Spaniards who held Indians, give to a community by building substantial homes, by bringing wives to establish families, and by their distinction in dress and bearing, indicate that he had probably lived for a while at Lima. It is possible that he had passed through Mexico; he remarks that is was far easier to govern there than in Peru, "a much more complicated land." He became a mill operator and investor in mines at Potosí, possibly soon after Viceroy Toledo's visit in 1572, which he remembered, and by the time he was writing his "*Relación*" in 1585 he owned two mills and was a man of some substance. A lawsuit instituted against him in 1593 to recover certain sums he owed demonstrates the up and down nature of the economic life of Potosinos, for this formerly prosperous operator could no longer pay his bills. The court proceedings also reveal his noteworthy tenacity, for he fought his creditor every step of the way through a long legal process. On January 25, 1596, Captain Alonso Vázquez Dávila Arze made an inspection visit to Capoche's mill at Potosí and reported that it was "grinding and refining a great amount of metal." His other mill, at Tarapaya, was being repaired.

Capoche was thirty-eight years of age at the time he wrote the Relación" in 1585 and he lived on until about 1613, according to a document in the Potosí archive. He seems to have pursued a quiet life, if the relative absence of documentation is a true indication; he held no municipal or royal office, paid his taxes, and apparently participated little in the legalistic and governmental quarrels of the day. Capoche did testify, once, against a rapacious corregidor who had oppressed the Indians and was addicted to gambling. Scant information has come to light on Capoche's life, and we must depend almost wholly on his "Relación" to tell us what kind of man he was and why he brought together his curious and valuable report on Potosí.

Why did he prepare the work? Not to write "curiosidades" or with any literary pretensions, he exclaims at one point. In the introduction dedicating the study to the viceroy, he explains that his principal intention has been to make possible a better understanding of the difficulties of the affairs of the mine. He considers Potosí's problems the most complex the new viceroy will have to face and so labyrinthine that they can easily be seen in a false light unless presented by someone with experience there. He has therefore drawn up the "Relación" to be laid before the Conde del Villar, who was still engaged at that time in the long and arduous journey from Spain to Peru. The aged and infirm viceroy was to struggle during his rule (1585-1589) against English corsairs eager to prey on the rich treasure fleets in the Pacific, and to combat the Chiriguanes Indians, smallpox epidemics, earthquakes, and corruption among ecclesiastics and officials alike but Potosí proved to be indeed a peculiar and constant care.

The viceroy had been apprised of the swirling economic and social forces at Potosí even before leaving Spain and had commissioned a trusted friend and relative, Pedro de Córdoba Mesía, to spy out conditions at the mine so that on reaching Peru there would be a first-hand report available. Córdoba Mesía went to Potosí, came to know Capoche, probably arranged for him to have access to the royal records there, and not only encouraged him to prepare the "Relación" but also urged him to include a chapter on the taxation of Indians. Later Córdoba Mesía served as corregidor in Potosí, and what notices about him are to be found in the document suggest that he was an experienced, able administrator who enjoyed over a considerable span of time the confidence of high officials of the king.

Also readying a report for the viceroy's eye were the official agents (procuradores) of Potosí representing the miners, who were known by Capoche to be painting a dark picture of the desperate state of the mine as a justification for lower mercury prices and more Indians. All this rouses Capoche to comment ironically that these gentlemen will have to explain the connection between their sad account of destitute Potosinos with the actual facts. "For the royal revenues have been increasing steadily each year, the consumption of coca and mercury is great, and Potosí displays a notable luxury, abundance of goods, numerous fiestas, and generous donations to charity and churches."

The "Relación" may be classified, therefore, as one of the numerous documents in the "Pretensiones de Potosí" literature, compiled to exert an influence on or to extract concessions of various kinds from a reluctant but necessitous Crown. It may not be dismissed, however, as merely a lawyer's brief. Capoche also feels that deep-seated desire manifested by many Spaniards to give a "true account" of the history and affairs of the New World as they saw them. The preservation and economic welfare of the whole kingdom of Peru depends upon the mine, he exclaims in exuberant Potosino fashion; therefore he undertakes to describe the cerro and affairs of the mine in order to explain its situation in 1585 and what must be done to assure Potosí, and consequently the realm as a whole, of a bright future.

Capoche modestly states his own inadequacies for the task of telling the story of "the greatest seat of wealth the world has ever known." The author is, however, no ordinary person; his report could only have been put together by one who was unusually alert and informed. He may have received assistance--perhaps from the Mercedarian friar Nicolás Venegas de los Ríos who copied out the version of the manuscript upon which this account is based--and certain passages are obscure to the modern reader, but the "Relación" remains an impressive document. On the whole Capoche sets forth his story in a direct and expressive style which occasionally reaches eloquence. He writes succinctly, too. The tone of the "Relación" is consistently sober, rather than sensational, which gives weight to his remarks. He indulges in neither the idle chit-chat nor the stories dripping with crime, corruption, passion, and miracles which are so liberally strewn throughout the massive chronicle of Bartolomé Arsans de Orsúa y Vela and many of the other histories of the Villa Imperial.

In the first few pages he gives a brief description of the great mountain "shaped like a sugar cone," and of Potosí's harsh climate and bleak surroundings. Capoche gives precise figures which reveal the mind and habits of an engineer. Potosí is 8,652 varas in circumference, and is 430 leagues from Buenos Aires "by a good road." At one time there were 6,497 furnaces (guairas) burning at night on the slopes of Potosí, "a cheerful and pleasant sight all together." By 1574, when mercury was first used, 76,000,000 pesos of silver had been produced, and from then until St. John's Day in 1585, 34,715,215 pesos. He explains the round figure for the early period by remarking that everyone was so rich in those days that no one bothered to keep a detailed record. And his account of the disaster in which the Londoner Enrique Sandi [Henry Sandys?] lost his life conveys to the reader a sense of the heroism of the miners and their Indian workers, and of the perpetual fear of accidents which hung over those who descended into the dangerous depths. The exactness and fullness of Capoche's description recalls the judgment of Ramón Carande that Spaniards in the Indies were excellent observers whose writings reveal a wealth of information "comparable to the riches they extracted there."

Although the "Relación" supplies a mass of economic and statistical data, Capoche manages to preserve a familiar tone in telling his story. Never the pompous "official" historian, he praises the good Castilian wines that reached Potosí, "very purified" after the long journey across the sea, and the "good fruit brought from the valley of Chuquisaca" nearby. He knows the location of a warm spring "where one may swim pleasantly"--quoting "the philosophers" on the explanation of this phenomenon--and another whose medicinal waters benefit the sick. He mentions, in his minute listing of the socavones (mining shafts), that one owner, Cristóbal López, is the oldest person in all the province, who at the age of 120 "is still so well-preserved that he reads without spectacles, and occasionally climbs up to the top of the mountain." Here we have, incidentally, the only reference to reading in all the "Relación"; presumably Potosinos had little time or taste for the pallid pleasures of the library.

Capoche is independent, too, and criticizes the exploitation of the mercury mine at Huancavelica by royal officers; he has greater faith in individual initiative. He exhibits a balanced mind and does not rush into rash declarations refusing, for example, to say whether the rumors of great discoveries of new mines near Los Lipes are true: "I neither affirm nor further describe this because I have not seen it." Nor does he present his readers with black and white explanations of events.

The manuscript is roughly organized into two principal parts, and each part is divided into chapters. Potosí receives major attention but some information is given on mines in nearby Porco, Los Lipes, Berenguela, and Challacollo, in the district of Charcas. Capoche must have had access to official reports and other documents in Potosí archives, for he includes much factual information on seams, refineries, tunnels, shafts, and excavations which could only have been obtained by consulting the records. He knows which is the most dangerous mine, which mines have struck water, which are poor, which are virgin, and which produce heavily. When mines are jointly owned, he indicates the share each partner possesses, and provides raw material for the study of partnership in Spanish America.

The "Relación" is not a formal history developed on strictly chronological lines, or a tightly organized story. During the course of his account, however, Capoche gives much information of historical interest. He has talked with those who were in Potosí at the discovery or shortly after, and has diligently used what must have been confidential records on ownership and production. His own experience in Potosí enables him to give valuable glimpses into the life of this thriving mining camp. The houses are small and mean, thrown up quickly out of poor though expensive materials, and erected without any regard for the public welfare or future growth of the city. There is no public clock, yet Potosinos are affluent enough to spend tremendous sums on female finery. And there is a note of unconscious pride in Capoche's remark about this expensively dressed society: "Such is the luxury of women's dress, that they could compete with those in Spain itself." In the midst of all this wealth, however, Potosí could not boast a single hotel or even inn where strangers attracted by the fame of the mine could live. The traditional Spanish hospitality then came into play, and places were made for friends and countrymen in private homes, which became permanent lodgings where guests were shown "great liberality."

The markets of Potosí were the most animated in all Peru, and the "Relación" has much to say on this subject. Capoche sets down in rich detail the quantities, qualities, and prices of merchandise, food, and drink eagerly consumed by the Potosinos. Profits are so lush that even Spanish gentlemen deign to engage in commerce; 1,200,000 pesos are expended in one year for Castilian clothes alone. Another million pesos are spend on the coca leaves which the Indians chew as they work the mines. Capoche calls this habit a "superstitious vice" and urges that it be stopped. He reports the earlier efforts of Viceroy Toledo to end this nefarious traffic when his investigation showed that many of the Indians who harvest coca in the hot valleys of the eastern Andes contract "an incurable disease." Moreover, its sale at Potosí proved to be a constant drain of money Indians should be spending on food. The merchants of Cuzco, heavily engaged in the traffic, took umbrage at these investigations, explaining to the viceroy that four hundred Spaniards in Cuzco alone were dependent on the coca trade, that the transportation of coca across Peru was itself a business of considerable proportion, that even the Church's income was dependent on coca, and that "Potosí would exist only so long as the Indian workers there have coca." Toledo's efforts to curb the traffic by his famous laws failed, Capoche reports; the Indians continue to chew the comforting coca as they toil in the deep recesses of the mine. In the twentieth century, moreover, they still do.

The "Relación" does not provide much light on the gloriously diverse human types found at Potosí. We must go to other sources to learn about them--the conquistadores (including one who enjoyed the fame of being both a relative of Ignatius Loyola and the husband of an Inca princess), noblemen, musicians, druggists, pastry cooks, friars, a Negro town-crier mounted on a fine horse, merchants, tailors, carpenters, mechanics, and technicians needed to run the mills, vagabonds, mariners, and strangers from many lands, including one disguised Turk. Some of the Indians, too, were as colorful and as independent as the Spaniards. Don Juan Colqueguarache, the principle chieftain of the Quillacas, expressed a desire to have his five natural sons legitimized and in true Potosí spirit also wanted three of them to be educated in Spain, reported Judge Juan de Matienzo to the king, "so that they may know the Court and become acquainted with your Majesty." Matienzo recommended favorable action on this request, for without Don Juan's example and influence "the Indians would never work in the mines."

Miners kept expensive mistresses and gamblers flourished; Potosinos indulged in gaudy knightly tournaments, processions, and other pleasures with a medieval flavor; bull-fights were popular; scandals and murders occurred daily. Little of this familiar side of Potosí's life can be found in the "Relación." Nor does it relate at all the bloody battles that raged, from the earliest years, between the various "nations" of different provinces of Spain that stained so much of the history of Potosí. Nor does Capoche describe the political government of this mining camp in which the cabildo or municipal council of powerful and sometimes arrogant miners played such a prominent part.

The "Relación" proves particularly helpful to the modern student on certain fundamental aspects of Potosí during the formative period 1545-1585: technological development, Indian life and labor, and the growth of the acquisitive spirit in that significant epoch of the expansion of capitalism in Europe--the sixteenth century. Capoche's contribution to our understanding of each of these will be treated.

II

The history of science and technological change will find much of interest in the "Relación." Capoche shows no great respect for Indian techniques but gives a detailed description of their ancient method of working mines and of refining metals by the guaira process, involving small furnaces erected on the slopes or the tops of mountains which burned brightly when the Andean winds blew sharply.

The veins of silver were so rich in the early years that Spaniards believed the mine inexhaustible; an Indian legend later grew up that a mythical hermaphrodite being named Coquena had carried all the silver in the Andes to Potosí. The guaira process was efficient enough to enable the first miners to extract prodigious quantities of silver from the rich ore, the Spaniards were generous in their labor arrangements with the Indians, and everyone made money. Then mines became deeper, the ore was poorer, and the ancient refining methods no longer sufficed. Silver production declined sharply, adversely affecting Peru's economy as a whole; Indians returned to their old system of barter, and everyone connected with Potosí became greatly disheartened.

Francisco Toledo changed all this, and Capoche states that the renaissance of Potosí was largely the result of the actions of this vigorous viceroy. Even before reaching the mine, during the course of his methodical inspection of the viceroyalty, Toledo arranged at Cuzco for experiments in his presence in the use of mercury for refining silver ore brought from Potosí for that purpose. On reaching the Villa Imperial in December, 1572, Toledo energetically tackled the numerous problems of the mine. He ordered that Huancavelica mercury should not be sent to Mexico, but reserved for Potosí, allotted more Indians to work the mines according to the _mita_ system--against the stout opposition of non-mining Spaniards who wanted to use them on farms--and stimulated the construction of a series of large lakes above Potosí to impound the water necessary for the working of the many mills (_ingenios_) built to refine the ore. Carpenters, iron-workers, and masons named their own salaries; prices of iron and other materials for construction rose rapidly. Wood was brought at heavy expense to treeless Potosí from considerable distances, and some beams for the mills were so large that they required sixty Indians to move them. For a hundred leagues about the mine most of the produce of the surrounding regions moved toward Potosí which acted as a powerful magnet, and a wide range of luxury items was imported even from Mexico, Europe, and the East. The boom was on again; silver production spurted up so rapidly that the port for Potosí, established amidst the sandy wastes of Arica on the Pacific coast of Peru, became so well known that Francis Drake and many other foreign interlopers sought it out with "certidumbre y precisión."

Toledo took a census, which is supposed to have indicated the unbelievable total of 120,000 Spaniards and Indians, but this report has not turned up in any archive. He descended into the mine to observe operations, caused to be erected at the very top of the mountain a cross which he described with true Potosino eloquence as resting on "the richest pedestal in the world"; he initiated a housing program and, to assure the permanence of his work, drew up numerous laws for the protection of Indians, for the efficient extraction of silver and, in fact, for practically every kind of activity at Potosí. A period of such prosperity followed these improvements, above all the introduction of mercury, that for many years the miners and the Crown alike hearkened back to "the good old days" of Viceroy Toledo. His influence on Potosí--though still not fully studied--remained a vital one for generations. And when the viceroy died in 1582 he remembered the Indians of Potosí in his will by assigning 500 ducados for the upkeep of their hospital.

In spite of these improvements, important technical problems remained unsolved as the shafts and tunnels penetrated deeper into the mountain. Some mines struck water and had to be drained before operation could be resumed. In the period 1583-1585, there was not sufficient water power to run all the mills. The richer veins were exhausted rapidly, and new explorations had constantly to be made, as well as attempts to increase the percentage of silver extracted from the ore by improving methods of treatment. Many inventors rushed to Potosí with new ideas on such problems. Few of them were encouraged, however, or allowed to test the machines and processes they devised, though some innovations were introduced in spite of opposition. The apathy of the miners and their unwillingness to experiment or even permit others to do so provoked the wrath of Capoche, who manifests a forward-looking spirit, constantly on the watch for new methods to make the exploitation of Potosí easier and more productive. Another obstacle to technical progress, not mentioned by Capoche, was the decision of the Conde del Villar to maintain a high level consumption of mercury instead of fostering the method requiring much less mercury developed by Carlos Corso de Leca.

Capoche recommends highly the maintenance and extension of the socavones, or shafts cut vertically into the lower part of the mountain which connect with the principal veins (vetas) which start on the upper slopes and run horizontally. The socavones constitute one of the most important inventions, he declares, and are of such general utility in making it easier to get the ore out that any withdrawal of aid to their owners will be bad for Potosí as a whole. It becomes clear that one of his important objectives in preparing the "Relación" has been the defense of the socavones and their owners. He gives a list of them with specific information on each one--its present conditions, how far the shaft has penetrated the mountain, how many Indians had been requested to dig it and to keep it clear, and how many were actually granted. Capoche shows himself to be almost as familiar with the particular characteristics of each individual shaft and mine honeycombing the cerro as was Bernal Díaz with each horse that Cortez brought to Mexico.

Other chapters give much detail on the amalgamation process itself, and on the technical operation of the mills as they refined the ore. These matters need not be treated here, but it may be remarked that whoever compiles a dictionary of Peruvian mining terms will find the "Relación" useful. The metallurgists at Potosí were workmen, at best craftsmen, who were no more interested in writing about their processes than were metallurgists in Europe at the time. On both sides of the Atlantic formal treatises were produced only after generations of practical experimentation. Capoche wrote long before the appearance of the standard work by the priest Alonso Alvaro Barba, Arte de los metales (1640). The material available for writing this unknown and important chapter in the scientific history of America is voluminous, and a careful study of it may some day revise our conception of the Spanish contribution to mining.

III

The nature of the Indians, their conversion, their labor in the mine, and the treatment accorded them occupy an important place in the "Relación." No one familiar with the bitter and widespread struggle for justice that went on in sixteenth-century Spain and America will be surprised to see that Capoche earnestly worked for the Christianization of the Indians and stoutly opposed their enslavement by fellow Spaniards. His earliest references to Indians reveal compassion for them and frequently in the "Relación" he makes clear his deep concern for their welfare. He knows something of their religion, which he deplores as idolatrous and barbarous, describes their method of recording time and historical events by knotted strings (quipus), distinguishes clearly between the history and characteristics of the various tribes and in general, reveals an intimate understanding of their ways. He lauds Inca rule; his careful description of the distribution of the Aymara and Quechua Indians of the region and their customs make a contribution to our scanty knowledge on the subject.

He judges the Indians to be on the whole "of little talent and lacking in imagination," but recognizes distinctions among them and admits that there are some outstanding individuals, such as Don Hernando Ayaviri, an "Indian of much ability, who can read and write well." The interaction of Spanish and Indian cultures produces some strange fruits; Capoche mentions Don Juan Collqui the Younger, who "has studied grammar in the Jesuit colegio and goes about dressed like a Spaniard in much silk." The other Indians dislike Don Juan, however, because of his alien dress and because he robs them.

Capoche knows the Spanish system devised to govern the Indians and criticizes it in the typical free-speaking manner of many Spaniards of his time. The Indian officers (alcaldes) of each parish in Potosí do not keep their charges from getting drunk, as they are supposed to do, but are themselves the first to get intoxicated! Indian men and women frequently indulge in lengthy public drinking bouts in which ancient ceremonies and dances are performed. Toledo tried to remedy this evil by establishing taverns where Indians were encouraged to drink moderately and only at certain times, but the problem remains and their religious instruction is greatly hindered thereby. Capoche closes this section devoted to grave and religious matters with a most practical and earthy recommendation: the capitanes de mita are so fat that they should be given mules or horses so that they can daily visit their Indians to attempt to prevent their getting drunk and also to aid them to quickly round up on Monday mornings those mitayos whose turn it is to work that week in the mines or mills.

He devotes a long chapter to the history of the tasa or head tax levied on each male Indian from 18 to 50. He cries out against the shocking excesses committed in its collection by their own chieftains as well as by priests and other Spaniards, insists on a fixed tax, opposes the abolition of the office of protector of the Indians, and praises the works of the protector of Potosí, Francisco de Vera. There was need to defend the Indians, as Spanish administrators and friars constantly pointed out to the Crown. Fray Rodrigo de Loaysa reported in his graphic style: "These miserable Indians are like the sardines that are to be found in the sea. Just as all the other fish follow behind the sardines to pounce upon them and to eat them, so everyone in these lands follows these miserable Indians and, unless they obtain some support and protection, they will be finished, too, like the sardines."

Capoche turns an equally jaundiced eye on arrangements for the spiritual health of the Indians. The priests assigned to their villages often cannot communicate with the Indians in their own language, corruption is widespread, with the doctrineros using the most beautiful daughters of chieftains for immoral purposes; much improvement is needed. One bright spot is the work of the Jesuit professor Alonso de Barzana, who has demonstrated his vigor as a preacher and as a teacher of Indian languages.

The "Relación" includes much information on the problem that has plagued Potosí from its discovery in 1545 until today--labor. At first the ore was so rich that Indians contracted voluntarily with owners of mines, because the Spaniards were generous in the division of their bonanza wealth. When the ores ran poorer and the veins of silver became more difficult of access; a radical change began. Miners had to use Indians rounded up by Spanish authorities or they employed Indians called mingados, but the numbers decreased and production declined until Viceroy Toledo revolutionized the situation by establishing the mita by which Indians were forced to work on a regular basis. Capoche carefully describes the history of this forced labor system, by which approximately one-seventh of the tasa or tax-paying Indians in a large region around Potosí were levied annually to labor at the mine, though at a salary. No longer do mounted Spaniards casually divide up the natives by counting them with lance in hand while surveying the mass of Indians in each town. Now everything is so organized and on such a business-like basis that the mita must have impressed even that methodical monarch Philip II.

Under Viceroy Toledo some 13,340 Indians were required annually to leave their homes and make the exhausting and sometimes dangerous journey to Potosí. These *mitayos* were accompanied by their wives and children, so that more than forty thousand Indians were en route to the mine each year "which so filled the roads that it seemed the whole kingdom was on the march." Once arrived at Potosí the *mitayos* were divided up into three parts, with each group serving for a week in the mines or mills and at less exhausting labor during the other two weeks. Capoche knows the names of all the Indian leaders designated to keep this complicated labor machinery in action and how many *mitayos* owe obedience to each leader; he also provides exact figures on how many are apportioned for the necessary public works during their "so-called rest period," how many are needed for salt extraction and to repair the lakes, and how many are assigned to Dr. Franco, the surgeon brought to Potosí by Viceroy Toledo. This doctor, incidentally, found it extremely difficult to persuade injured Indians to enter the hospital. They fear it almost more than death itself, Capoche reports.

Many Indians came to Potosí on their own account, and worked for wages as *mingados*. Capoche considers them much less trustworthy than the *mitayos* and bitterly denounces them for their inconstancy. They have to be paid a higher wage than the *mitayos* and sometimes coca has to be provided as an additional inducement. In a brief but pungent chapter on "*De los indios mingados y de la desorden que hay con ellos*," Capoche appears to be speaking as a mill owner whose operations are frustrated by unreliable workmen, rather than in his usual tone of kindness toward the Indians.

One long chapter is taken up with the battle between the royal authorities, who wanted to permit Indians to obtain and sell silver ore on their own account, and the miners, who sternly opposed such actions on the ground that the ore was illegally obtained. But the Crown insisted, even more strenuously, that silver had become the only means of exchange in traffic with Indians on the slopes of the great mountain. The Indian workers paid in silver for the "food, fruit and other refreshments" they enjoyed as they emerged from the mine. Indian mothers even brought their daughters up the mountain slopes for the use of the workers and these services, too, had to be paid for in silver.

The Crown naturally wished to continue a system by which Indians were stimulated to obtain ore and to refine it by their *guaira* method in order to help meet the ever-present and ever-increasing deficit of the royal treasury. When Viceroy Toledo issued an order approving the *rescate*, the Jesuit Diego de Vaena preached publicly against the order, proclaiming all who permitted the Indians to sell silver in mortal sin. A first-class scandal resulted. Capoche related the story in detail and makes it clear that he looks upon Indians as free vassals of the Crown who should be allowed to profit from all the ore they could obtain. He believes emphatically in private enterprise and that "the Indians are not slaves." After all, they originally owned the land, their labor in the mine is both dangerous and fatiguing so that it is only right, concludes Capoche in a rousing peroration, that Indians should have the same opportunity to profit as other vassals. He condemns, too, in a separate chapter, the widespread practice of Indian slavery in Potosí.

Capoche displays some familiarity with the fine theoretical points at issue; he quotes verbatim the formal opinions of certain jurists and theologians who were inevitably dragged into the dispute, and disagrees with part of the opinion by the famous Jesuit José de Acosta, which he includes in the "Relación." He also quotes canon law on this matter of conscience, and indeed shows so much learning in this part of the "Relación" that one wonders whether it may not have been prepared by another hand. Or Capoche's knowledge of these subjects may be just another piece of evidence for the claim that every Spaniard in the sixteenth century was something of a theologian. It is clear that Capoche's bringing such matter in as an integral part of his story, whether he composed it or not, confirms what has long been understood: discussions on theology and political theory were inseparable from political action during the Spanish conquest of America.

At almost every point in the "Relación" where Indians are involved, Capoche's concern for their welfare is eloquently expressed, and his account of their sufferings in the mines bears the ring of truth. Some of his most colorful passages are descriptions of their anguish at being torn away from their fields, families and friends to labor in distant Potosí, their hatred of the unfamiliar work of digging in the mines, and their indifference to the prospect of gaining personal wealth, a concept utterly foreign to their way of life. Capoche gives an unforgettable picture of perspiring Indians climbing up and down on rickety ladders in the bowels of the mines and risking their lives in carrying heavy burdens. Their health suffers from the violent changes in temperature between the hot mines and the glacial winds outside, and their usual reward for all this: abuse from their Spanish masters who call them "dogs." Four months ago, says Capoche, one Indian was so fearful of the punishment his master would inflict that he fled into the mine and, in his terror and confusion, fell and "was smashed into a hundred thousand bits." Capoche coins a phrase which later historians have used: "The travail these Indians have to undergo and the labor required are such that more blood than ore is needed to produce silver." These are the words of a mill operator, keenly aware of the constant royal pressure to produce revenue and ever more revenue, but also insistent upon the obligation of Spain to Christianize and to protect the Indians from oppression. The "Relación" exemplifies Spain's main dilemma in the New World--how to profit from her American possessions without oppressing the Indians or hindering their conversion. Capoche does not attempt to ignore or to disguise this problem. He lets us see the Indians sweating and dying in the tunnels of Potosí, he exposes the difficulties to their effective conversion, and he also quotes ecclesiastical authorities in his passionate defense of their right to live as free vassals of the Crown and not to be exploited as slaves.

IV

The early history of Potosí holds a special importance for those who attempt to discover the spirit of the age, particularly the growth of the acquisitive urge in modern society. The powerful pull exerted by the news of the discovery of the first Peruvian mines led to a dramatic depopulation of the Caribbean islands. "Dios mío, al Perú," exclaimed many a Spaniard as he hurried toward the Andes. The discovery of Potosí increased the flow, until the Villa Imperial became known as the "Babylon of Peru," where everything was judged by the Potosinos to be larger, gaudier, and more splendorous than anywhere else. No matter that the Spaniards and foreigners who flocked to the mountain to win a part of the silver flowing from the cornucopia of Potosí had to break numerous laws to get there, or to suffer disease and privation once they arrived, for many a newcomer made his name and fortune there as a merchant, miner, or mill owner.

Sources exist in the archives to document this social mobility, but they are not yet easily available. The story of Nicolás de Guevara is probably typical. He came to Potosí in 1581 and was soon so wealthy that he could afford to gratify his pride by buying a municipal office for 42,000 pesos. It was "the most expensive office of its kind in all the realms of Spain," he wrote back home, as he generously dispatched money to four of his nephews there; and when he wanted to marry a Peruvian-born (criolla) first cousin, a papal dispensation was arranged. Ecclesiastics, too, had their lives affected by acquiring wealth suddenly. A Dominican friar named Tomás del Castillo discovered a gold mine beyond Potosí and found himself owner of 140 varas of a rich vein. He disposed of this unexpected wealth by donating a part of the mine to the San Esteban monastery in Salamanca, and another section to the Colegio de San Gregorio in Valladolid for the support of four students from Peru, adding that "if the Colegio will not admit the students, it is not to be given the property." The Colegio de Santo Tomás in Seville was to get a smaller amount to pay for two students with the same conditions, and the monastery of Santo Tomás of Avila was given a part of the mine with the understanding that the funds would be spent on clothing for the friars there; besides other similar gifts to the Colegio de Santo Tomás in Alcalá de Henares and the monastery of Santa Catalina in Plasencia, this loyal Dominican ordered that a part of his mine in the fastnesses of South America should be used to ornament the chapel in the sepulchre of Santo Domingo in Bologna. To understand the full impact of American treasure on Europe, it will be necessary to take into account the many scattered donations by Potosinos for their friends, relatives, and favorite churches in the old world, as well as the "donations" and "loans" by rich miners to the Crown in anticipation of future favors, and not merely the official production of the mine as recorded at the time the "royal fifth" was taken.

Almost every aspect of life, including religion, was directly influenced by the river of silver flowing from the mountain. Miners spent ostentatiously not only in life, by conspicuous donations to churches and monasteries, but also in death, by arranging for sumptuous funeral ceremonies. Sports were very popular and produced large sums for those who organized pelota games. Viceroy Toledo was hostile to this sport, believing that it attracted idle folk and wasted time better spent in mining silver. Since wealth came quickly and at times spectacularly to Potosinos, whether by trading or by mining, the idea was fixed in Spanish minds, even more firmly than before, that men achieve fortune by chance or by the sweat of other men's brows, not by their own efforts. Thus manual labor, never valued highly in sixteenth-century Spain, was even more depreciated in the new world and at the same time old taboos against noblemen were weakened. The tradition of a society whose ideal was that of the gentleman, the caballero who did no obvious work and certainly did not soil his hands, was strengthened by life at such mining camps as Potosí.

This opulent way of life was transmitted, in some parts of the Peruvian viceroyalty, to the mestizos and Negroes. In 1579 a friar indignantly reported from Quito to Philip II that most of the Spanish ladies there considered it beneath their dignity to suckle their own infants. They brought in Indian nurses, and so did the mestizo women. The mestizo servants of the Spaniards had in turn their own Indian servants, and if "a Negro goes to the market for his master, he takes along an Indian to carry home the meat." Spaniards who never ventured across the seas, observing the lordly manners and free-spending ways of their cousins returned from America, looked upon them as a wasteful lot and deplored their excesses in drink, dress, and deportment. Capoche reveals a more realistic view of the character of his countrymen, whether in Europe or America, in explaining why the mountain of silver had been unknown for so many centuries. He explains that God kept these riches hidden because He knows that Spaniards "desire mineral wealth so keenly" that only by making available to them a treasure like Potosí will Christianity be brought to such a remote and harsh land as Peru.

Capoche particularly insists on the outstanding role played by Indians in discovering and exploiting silver deposits in and near Potosí. In the early days the governors ignored royal instructions to please the Spaniards, and had not encouraged or permitted Indians to participate in or profit from the furious hunt for mines. Declining production and increasing pressure from the Crown changed all that, and Viceroy Toledo unleashed Indians for the great search. Now Indians find a new mine every day, exults Capoche; even Indian women own rich properties, and he records the owner of one mine as "Don Diego Ylla, an Indian priest," which surely must be a textual error. The existence of an Indian priest in Potosí at that time would be a sensational discovery, and it is unlikely that an Indian had reached the priesthood anywhere in South America by 1585. Wealthy Indians were known at Potosí as early as 1562, and it is clear from the "Relación" that a number of Indians joined with Spaniards to exploit mines. But no Indian is listed by Capoche as owning a mill to reduce the ore, and as time went on it is likely that the Indians lost in one way or another the mines they had discovered.

Was the social mobility of the Indians confined within certain limits? So it would appear from the "Relación"; at least it is clear that there grew up in Potosí no industrial proletariat of technicians and workers such as was developing in Europe at the time which eventually brought about a transformation of life in the old world. The mass of Indians continued to labor for the Spanish elite just as they had for the Incas, except that work in the mines was an unusually harrowing experience. But the social and economic changes that went on in Potosí during the period 1545-1585 altered to some extent the ideas of conquerors and conquered alike. Above all Potosí provided an opportunity for the spectacular flowering of the spirit of personal profit, and Capoche documents this drama in sober factual terms.

V

Did Capoche's "Relación" have any effect on the new viceroy's policy and action, as it was apparently intended to do? We know that the document was completed in Potosí on August 10, 1585, and it seems likely that the viceroy's agent Pedro de Córdoba Mesía carried it promptly to Lima for consultation with the Conde del Villar, who finally reached his post on November 25, 1585 and was accorded the traditional and ostentatious reception ceremony. He was so exhausted, however, by the long journey from Spain that considerable time passed before he could attend to the many pressing affairs of the viceroyalty. Finally, six months later, the viceroy despatched his first detailed report, informing the king that he had decided to appoint the trusted and competent Córdoba Mesía as visitador to bring order to Potosí. As a preliminary to action, the viceroy brought together some of the wisest theologians in Peru to consider the many vexing problems relating to the treatment of the Indians and also held a junta of the most experienced persons to consider in his presence the many papers and suggestions available on Potosí so that the visitador would go forth with as good advice as possible. Many of the specific recommendations drawn up by this latter group--which included the Jesuit José de Acosta--were also in the "Relación." The maintenance of the socavones was strongly supported, as advised by Capoche, as were the continuation of the right of Indians to collect ore and sell it, and the preservation of the office of protector of the Indians, the lowering of the price of mercury, and the encouragement of Indians to refine as much metal as possible with their own guaira method which required no mercury. All these and other reforms Córdoba Mesía was to put into effect. During the course of this lengthy report to Philip II, the Conde del Villar referred several times to the relaciones he had received from capable experts, though never mentioning their authors by name. In the end Córdoba Mesía did not go as visitador to Potosí, for "he excused himself," but it seems reasonable to assume that Capoche's document played a part in the decisions the viceroy took relating to Potosí.

The "Relación" continued to be known after the Conde del Villar returned to Spain in 1589 for Juan López de Cepeda, the veteran president of the Audiencia de La Plata, owned a copy of the entire document. Capoche held Judge López in high esteem, and may even have sent the copy when he learned that Córdoba Mesía had declined the appointment as visitador, so as to have a friend in the Audiencia. The Jesuit Acosta, who served in Potosí during one or two years and was present at the junta convoked by the Conde del Villar, described Potosí in his Historia natural y moral de las Indias in words so reminiscent of the "Relación" as to suggest that he knew the manuscript, though he did not refer to it specifically as he did to other material of which he availed himself.

The official historian Antonio de Herrera had access to all documents in the archive of the Council of the Indies and could requisition others, so that it is not surprising to run across phrases made familiar by Capoche in the large Historia general de los hechos de los castellanos en las islas y tierrafirme del océano (1601-1615). The able and prolific seventeenth-century Council official, Antonio de León Pinelo, collected documents on Potosí, including the "Relación," in preparation for his never-completed history of the mine and quoted Capoche as one of his authorities in his genial work, Paraíso en el Nuevo Mundo, in which he precisely located the Earthly Paradise in Andean America. He had clearly become infected by what might be called "Potosí fever"--the tendency to glorify and magnify everything connected with the mine--for he carefully calculated that the silver production up to the time he wrote "would be sufficient for a bridge or road from Potosí to Madrid 2071 leagues long, four fingers thick, and fourteen varas wide." Other writers referred to the "Relación," but it was not widely available; even the historian Juan Bautista Muñoz, whose scouring of the Spanish archives in the years 1780-1790 was an exceedingly thorough operation, seems not to have been aware of its existence. Nor does Orsúa y Vela list it among the many works he used in his voluminous and still largely unpublished work with the characteristically high-flown title Historia de la Villa Imperial de Potosí: Riquezas incomparables de su famoso cerro, grandezas de su magnánima población, sus guerras civiles, y casos memorables.

The real importance of the "Relación" lies neither in its immediate influence on viceregal actions, nor in the use made of it during the period of almost four centuries it has circulated since Capoche dedicated it to the Conde del Villar and despatched the original Ms. with "retrato" to Lima in time for it to reach the viceroy as soon as he arrived from Spain to assume the burden of governing the vast viceroyalty of Peru. Today we find the "Relación" valuable because it provides one of the most revealing documents we have on the economic and social structure of one of the greatest colonial cities of the new world, and because it illustrates in a dramatic fashion some of the basic problems involved in writing the history of Spanish America. The first point is evident from the previous description of the work, and it is likely that the full utilization of the economic, political, and sociological material in the "Relación" will eventually enliven the somewhat arid monographs on Spanish colonial municipalities in the New World.

The significance of Capoche's work to the general historiography of Spanish America requires some explanation. The "Relación," if studied in connection with the other material on Potosí, raises the basic question of the point from which new world history can best be presented: from Spain or from America? The "Relación" does, indeed, help us to understand one of the decisive periods of Philip II in Europe. These were the years during which Elizabeth's sea-dogs harried the Spanish empire. Potosí's treasure helped Philip prepare for the great trial of strength with English; the Spanish defeat of 1588 was felt in America, especially in Potosí where production was stepped up to help meet the Crown's ever-increasing needs. It is not surprising, then, to see that the king and Council of the Indies gave immediate attention to the mining correspondence and statistics on silver production among the impressive quantities of official documentation which arrived with each fleet from America. López de Cepeda, who owned a copy of the "Relación" and as president of the Charcas audiencia kept closely in touch with Potosí affairs, sent a long report to the king on December 9, 1586, emphasizing the increase in silver production and the "loans" by the Potosinos to the Crown of 323,000 ducados. But even this was not enough, and Philip II wrote posthaste to the Conde del Villar instructing him to collect all possible money to supply his "grandes y precisos" expenses. The viceroy scraped every possible barrel and proudly announced on July 13, 1589, in one of his last letters from Lima, that he had been able to remit more gold and silver than in any previous shipment from Peru to Spain. Potosí could be, and often was at least among royal officials at the court, looked upon as being primarily a producer of revenue for a hard-pressed Crown. Thus to them the history of the mine could best be viewed from the mother country.

Potosí also illustrated some of the basic problems faced by Spaniards in the lands they conquered overseas and for this problem we must shift the focus of interest from Madrid to Potosí. Both Capoche and the Viceroy Toledo, who was responsible for fastening the mita system of forced labor on the Indians for hundreds of miles round about Potosí, expressed a keen desire to help the Indians. Capoche didn't like the mingados, the Indians who were not under the mita but who came voluntarily to Potosí to work, usually in the ingenios. Perhaps Capoche as an operator of ingenios came into direct and daily contact with the mingados and may have been disadvantaged by their apparent laziness and inconstancy. Be that as it may, Capoche denounced the cruelty and oppression of Spaniards toward the mitayos who were forced to work in the dangerous mines. And Toledo waxes mightily indignant when the audacious Jesuit Luis López in 1580 charged that Indians were bought and sold with ingenios and were being decimated by their addiction to liquor. The viceroy referred to his ordinances to demonstrate that all possible measures had been undertaken on behalf of the Indians, and insisted that they had just as much opportunity as Spaniards to discover mines for their own profit. But the result was oppression and death for many Indians, despite the desire of Capoche, Toledo, and Conde del Villar, and others to protect them. As Capoche himself stated: "More blood of the Indians than ore goes into producing silver." Spain desired to Christianize and civilize the Indians, but the Crown desperately needed money and Spaniards in America could neither supply this aid nor support themselves in the style to which they wished to be accustomed unless Indians and others did the work. The "Relación" shows how impossible was the attempt to reach both objectives.

Besides presenting in dramatic colors the fundamental dilemma of Spain in governing her New World, the "Relación" also clearly indicates the special "American" quality of Potosí's history. As Roberto Prudencio, the Bolivian scholar, has pointed out, Lima and Buenos Aires were largely Spanish cities transplanted to America.

> They lacked the humus necessary to create that new atmosphere of culture which was distinctly colonial. Potosí was much different . . . Potosí was the unique and extraordinary fruit of a native plant, born from the magic injection of the Hispanic spirit. Potosí accomplished in a supreme way what we new Americans seek today and which the republic has lost: the creative genius that has resulted from the magical fusions of the two spirits, the two worlds: the Hispanic and the Indian. Thus Potosí has been able to work out its own way of life, its own style; that is to say its own culture, thanks to that amalgamation which it knew how to achieve so marvelously.

If this be true, one must look at the history of Potosí from the standpoint of this new Hispano-Indian creation in America, and not only from that of the bureaucrats in Spain concerned with the royal treasury.

The historian today, trying to comprehend the truth of a complicated subject sometimes obscured by rhetoric and various types of nationalistic propaganda, will conclude that the "Relación" clearly indicates the need for a comprehensive approach to the history of Potosí and for an investigation of documentation in both American and European archives. A fuller story and a better perspective will be achieved if the history of the mine is viewed from Spain and from America.

The philosopher of history may also see in Capoche's story an excellent example of what Oswald Spengler calls a Faustian drama, peculiar to our western culture, of man's "uncontrollable longings for freedom, solitude, immense independence." Sociologists may have a difficult time classifying Potosí, for it does not show the normal pattern of a pre-industrial city. But the rapid and radical social changes Potosí underwent produced a distinct ethos worthy of their scrutiny. Anthropologists, who have already noted the importance of cities as a center of acculturation, will find much information in the "Relación" that shows the process of cultural osmosis in Potosí altering the ideas and habits of Indians and Spaniards alike. And although it may be considered a typical example of the many historical documents composed by Spaniards to describe and explain their actions in America, in one respect it is unique. The "Relación" offers a detailed view of life, labor and technical developments by a mill operator who was both an acute observer and an active participant in the scene he recorded.

Many adventurous Spaniards rushed to Peru after the mine was discovered in 1545, but Luis Capoche of Seville is the only one known to have produced a substantial volume which provides a close-up view of the life, labor, and technical developments of one of the largest and least studied cities of colonial America, the Villa Imperial de Potosí.

CHAPTER 13.

THE PORTUGUESE IN SPANISH AMERICA WITH SPECIAL REFERENCE TO THE VILLA IMPERIAL DE POTOSI

My special concern for the development of Luso-Brazilian studies led to the organization in 1950, with the powerful and competent assistance of Francis M. Rogers, of the first International Colloquium on this subject under the auspices of the Library of Congress and Vanderbilt University. My own research focussed on Spanish America, but as I studied the history of Potosí, the famous silver mine in colonial Peru, I discovered that Portuguese had played a significant role in its development. Why was this so? As notes accumulated in my files, as colleagues in several countries aided me with advice and bibliographical citations, the reasons began to emerge. A preliminary version of my findings was presented at the Third International Colloquium on Luso-Brazilian Studies held in Lisbon in September, 1957.

Notes continued to roll in, and wherever I looked some Portuguese influence in Spanish America appeared as if by magic! Then the editor of the Revista de historia de América in Mexico City called to my attention the fact that I had published an article in its first issue back in 1938, but nothing since. He was preparing issue number 50 and diplomatically suggested that it would be "convenient" to include something from my pen in this commemorative issue. The notes proved to be too voluminous, and my other responsibilities too pressing, to make No. 50, but I did manage to complete the study, with copious footnotes, for No. 51.

Revista de Historia de América, No. 51 (Mexico City, 1958), 1-48.
Reprinted by permission.

The Portuguese in Spanish America With Special Reference to the Villa Imperial de Potosí

I

Portuguese writers have not devoted much attention to pondering the unique characteristics of their countrymen, or to searching for the soul of their nation. Nor have they been much concerned to systematize their attitudes toward Spaniards or to express in words their feelings toward these neighbors who have shared with them for so many centuries the Iberian peninsula. Yet the Portuguese do in fact consider themselves to be profoundly different from Spaniards, and woe to any foreigner who fails to recognize this fact.

Another curious fact is that relatively few studies have been made of the long-sustained and involved relations between the Portuguese and Spaniards in the New World. Although for more than three centuries Spain and Portugal ruled a large part of the American continent and during the period 1580-1640 were joined together under common sovereigns, historians of Spanish action have rarely concerned themselves with Brazil and students of Portuguese history have infrequently consulted the considerable quantity of manuscript material available in the archives of Spanish-speaking lands of their common heritage.

The ancient and acute rivalry of Spaniards and Portuguese in the exploration of Africa and in the opening up of the Atlantic has long been carefully studied and well documented. The participation of Portuguese navigators and sailors in Spanish maritime achievements is also a familiar story, for throughout the sixteenth century Portuguese were found in most Spanish ships, from the time of Columbus until Quirós. Magellan was probably the best known Portuguese in Spanish naval service but there were many others. The Portuguese did not limit their participation to expeditions by sea, as the famous narrative by "The Gentleman of Elvas" of De Soto's travels makes clear, although few references to Portuguese are to be gleaned from the official list of passengers authorized to go to the Indies.

This Portuguese contribution to the history of Spanish America has never been properly studied. No David Lopes has risen to describe the linguistic results of this movement, no detailed examination has been made of the Portuguese in a particular area comparable to Luis de Matos' monograph on the Portuguese in sixteenth-century France, and the subject is barely mentioned in the bulky 3-volume *História da espansão portuguesa no mundo* or in the 19-volume proceedings of the *Congresso do mundo portugués*. In fact, from the available publications one might reasonably conclude that neither Spaniards nor Portuguese have ever been seriously interested in the subject.

This mutual indifference, however, appears to be turning into a more active awareness, and this awareness could mark an important advance toward a more complete understanding of both Iberian cultures as they developed in America. The participation by Spaniards in the extraordinary conquests of the *bandeirantes* and the richness of documentation in Spanish and Spanish American archives on this subject, as well as the Portuguese sources on Spanish achievements, are beginning to be noted today. Historians are pointing out that Spaniards collaborated in the hunt for gold in the earlier Portuguese entradas in the backlands of Bahia, that records exist to show that one famous sertanista, Antonio da Silva, died near Potosí, and that books by Cervantes as well as The Lusiads were carried in their luggage by bandeirantes as they pushed out the colonial frontiers of Brazil on a vast front. A thorough search in Portuguese repositories and in Brazilian archives from Belém do Pará to Porto Alegre is likely to yield much information on Spanish American contacts with Brazil during the colonial period. These documents may lead to new interpretations; already one Brazilian historian has declared that so many Spaniards became bandeirantes that it is clear their vigor made a decisive contribution to the rapid and bold conquests of the Paulista and other expeditions which so effectively enlarged the frontiers of Brazil in the colonial period.

It may well be that the Spaniards who went to Brazil were fewer than the Portuguese who settled in Spanish America; if so, this fact will be useful to the historian who wishes to compare the work of the two similar but quite different Iberian peoples in the New World. This essay has a more limited objective: to bring together some notes on the Portuguese in Spanish America, with particular attention to their connection with Potosí, and especially on the seventeenth-century História de Potosí by Antonio de Acosta, a Portuguese who spent many years in that famous silver mining center.

From the early years of the sixteenth century the Portuguese warily eyed the exploits of Spaniards in the New World and waited eagerly for news of mineral discoveries there. The semi-mythical Portuguese explorer Aleijo Garcia may have been the first to alert his fellow countrymen to the possibility of great wealth from gold and silver in South America by his penetration of the Inca Empire from Brazil. He is even supposed to have passed in 1524 within a hundred miles of Potosí--the great mountain of silver in the high Andes--which was not to be discovered by Spaniards until 1545, and then by men from Peru and not by Portuguese or Spaniards from the south. The hopeful vision of a great mountain of treasure waiting to be discovered powerfully stimulated both Spaniards and Portuguese and led many expeditions and many disappointments. One adventurous Portuguese who took up the challenge was the soldier and traveler Antonio Rodrigues who became a member of the first significant Spanish expedition to the Río de la Plata region in 1535, which was led by Pedro de Mendoza. Rodrigues, along with other Portuguese, was led to join the expedition "assim por vaidade como por cobiça de ouro e prata." He was present at the founding of Buenos Aires and of Asunción, and traveled over a wide territory with Spanish soldiers for 18 years before entering the Jesuit order in 1553.

It was known to the Portuguese king as early as May 20, 1537, that Francisco Pizarro had obtained much gold in Peru because Oporto merchants had bought it in quantity from Spaniards; this helps to explain why so many Portuguese tried to penetrate the interior of South America from the Atlantic side. Spaniards pursued this hope of a "Sierra de Plata" both from Peru and from Paraguay; the disappointment of Domingo Martínez de Irala in 1547 when his great expedition crossed the dangerous Chaco wilderness to search the Andean foothills only to learn that Spaniards from the north had already discovered Potosí was bitter indeed. As the Portuguese soldier Antonio Rodrigues described their feelings: "Nos voltamos muito tristes, por não achar ouro nem prata."

The movement of individual Portuguese to participate in and profit from the Spanish territories in the New World continued. As early as 1550 we find a Portuguese named Gaspar Collazo doing business in Potosí, and in 1552 another Portuguese is recorded in Asunción. In

1565 the Portuguese Rodrigues Almeida discovered a silver mine at Huantajaya near Arica on the far Pacific coast. Because Spanish authorities throughout the New World were vigilant on behalf of family solidarity, there appears among the many royal orders on the subject one dated December 7, 1568, providing that Antonio Muñoz, Portuguese, be sent by the Audiencia of Charcas to Spain "a hacer vida con Beatriz Muñoz, su mujer."

This steady seeping of Portuguese into Spanish dominions in America was not only discouraged by Spanish authorities, it was specifically prohibited, at least at certain times. For example, the order of July 15, 1568--reaffirmed frequently later--stated that "gypsies and Portuguese" were not to be allowed to enter and when discovered were to be ejected. This instruction was evidently drawn up in part at least because of the fear that foreigners might profit unduly to the detriment of Spaniards.

But the Portuguese continued to come. In 1590 a Portuguese merchant of Macao, João de Gama, made his way to Mexico from China by the northern route to Acapulco where he was arrested by the authorities and his papers seized. Many of the Portuguese merchants apparently entered Spanish America in connection with the slave traffic, and some of them doubtless went to Potosí. Philip II had promised in Tomar in 1581 to give Portuguese the privilege of providing Negro slaves for Spanish America, but took no action for years. In 1588, the Portuguese Duarte Lopes presented a "Parecer" recommending a detailed plan which finally led to the first _asiento_, approved in 1591 on behalf of the Portuguese trader Pedro Gomes Reinel. Duarte had derived his knowledge of the slave trade from a visit he had made to Venezuela in 1586, and other Portuguese travelers made their way to Spanish America. Padre Gaspar Afonso spent some time in the Caribbean in the closing years of the sixteenth century and his account, as published in the famous _História trágico-marítima_, mentions the presence of Portuguese wherever he went. In Santo Domingo he discussed the low price of meat with a "português rico e honrado," talked with a Portuguese priest who had been shipwrecked and had survived for more than two years on fruit alone, and was warmly received by various Portuguese merchants eager to welcome him and bestow gifts upon him. In Cartagena "um português honrado de Faro, de grão crédito naquela terra" was most hospitable, and another received him in his home and displayed emeralds to the value of some 20,000 cruzados. Potosí and its wealth were also known to Padre Afonso; he learned in the city of La Vega in Santo Domingo of a new method for treating silver ore, which had resulted in greatly increased production at Potosí and had won for its inventor great wealth. The presence of a Portuguese priest in the Caribbean and his encounter with other Portuguese as he travelled about was evidently no unusual occurrence; almost anywhere in the Spanish Indies Portuguese could be found and often in comfortable circumstances.

It must be emphasized that no special legislation protected or fostered this movement of Portuguese to Spanish America. On the contrary, Juan de Solórzano Pereira held that Portuguese were particularly discriminated against among foreigners; José María Ots Capdequí makes it clear that even during the period 1580-1640, when Portugal was politically united with Spain, the Portuguese in Spanish America received no concessions whatsoever, and we know that some orders were sent to the Indies expressly forbidding the residence there of "Portuguese and other foreigners." Bundles of naturalization papers attest to the fact that a Portuguese desirous of acquiring Spanish citizenship in America had to follow the usual involved legal procedure. Despite these conditions and restrictions, the Portuguese did in fact play an important role in the development of Spanish America. Prof. Ots Capdequí describes their work as follows, basing his remarks on investigations in the Archivo de Indias and the Archivo de Protocolos in Seville:

> Unas veces otorgando contratos de arrendamiento de servicios que habían de ser prestados en Indias; otras otorgando poderes para el cobro de determinados créditos que en Indias también habían de hacerse efectivos. En ocasiones, aparecen mercaderes portugueses prestando dinero a maestro de naos. No faltan ejemplos de individuos de nacionalidad portuguesa que figuran como pilotos y marineros de las naos pertenecientes a las flotas y armadas de la carrera y guarda de las Indias. Un Duarte Rodríguez, mercader portugués, otorga poder para que reciban en su nombre, dos cajones de cochinilla que se envían de las Indias. Varios carpinteros portugueses conciertan con la Reina y con los jueces y oficiales de la Casa de Contratación para ejercer su oficio en Castilla de Oro. Hay portugueses vendedores de esclavos y otros que disputan juros sobre la renta de almojarifazgos de Indias.

Though the official regulations were not relaxed when Philip II took over Portugal in 1580, it is probable that only after that date did Portuguese begin to arrive in significant numbers in Spanish America. The story of the family of the famous Antonio León Pinelo illustrates the ease with which the Portuguese entered Spain and Spanish America during this period. His grandfather, Juan López, and other members of the family having been burned as Jews in Lisbon in 1595, his father, Diego López de Lisboa, fled shortly afterward to Valladolid with his wife and two sons, one of whom was Antonio. The father soon went on to Buenos Aires alone and by 1604 had been able to get the rest of the family across the ocean. The family moved next to Córdoba where Diego became an encomendero, and two more children were born. When Antonio's mother died, his father moved the family to Potosí where he became a wealthy merchant. When Antonio and his brother went to Chuquisaca to enter the university, their father not only accompanied them but--thanks perhaps to the wealth he had obtained in Potosí--became a student also, and apparently obtained a degree as licentiate. He later became a priest and the "mayordomo, gran privado y confesor" of Archbishop Fernando Arias and accompanied Arias to Lima when Arias was appointed archbishop there in 1630. On the death of the Archbishop in 1638 López went into seclusion, for the eye of the Inquisition was presumably still upon him, but at his death was buried in the Sagrario of the Lima Cathedral at the foot of his protector, whose will had expressly arranged this.

All the sons of Diego López de Lisboa had significant careers. Juan became a Jesuit, Diego was an active oidor of the Audiencia of Lima, and Antonio de León Pinelo served many years as one of the principal officers of the Council of the Indies and died as Cronista Mayor de las Indias. His brilliant career as administrator, bibliographer, historian, and legal scholar has not yet been fully told, but it is clear that his connection with Potosí was important in various ways and included the composition of a legal brief entitled La defensa de la Villa Imperial de Potosí.

José Toribio Medina believed that Antonio and the other members of the family systematically concealed their Portuguese origin, since it would lead to knowledge of the auto-de-fe in Lisbon in 1595. At any rate it is a remarkable fact that Antonio de León Pinelo--this grandson of the Jew burned in Lisbon--was responsible for the preparation of the Recopilación de leyes de las Indias, which Spanish historians usually cite to prove the justice and the benevolence of Spanish action in America.

Further research will doubtless add many valuable details to the story now known in broad outline of how the Portuguese went to Spanish America and what they did there. It is clear that they travelled and settled in many parts of this vast territory after 1580, particularly in Peru and the Río de la Plata area. By the middle of the seventeenth century they were by far the most numerous foreign element in the population of Buenos Aires and were solidly entrenched both economically and socially. The first teacher (1605) in Buenos Aires was a Portuguese named Diego Rodrigues from Lamego, and the earliest ecclesiastical records of Buenos Aires reveal a large number of Portuguese residents there in the period covered 1611-1617.

Portuguese artistic influence was strongly felt there, too, as the Argentine scholar Héctor Schenone has demonstrated. In architecture, silver work, and wood carving, Portuguese style was so closely followed in Buenos Aires as to give porteño development in these fields a special character. Ecclesiastical and other archives provide much material on this subject, and the names of many Portuguese artists in Buenos Aires are known. In one field, Schenone writes, Portuguese influence was supreme: "El mobiliario reproduce casi exclusivamente, durante la segunda mitad del siglo XVII, formas portuguesas combinadas a veces con las españolas, pero preponderando siempre aquéllas."

Portuguese influence continued to be felt later on, too, for the first printer in Buenos Aires was a Portuguese named José de Silva y Aguilar.

Peru was another center of Portuguese activity. José Toribio Medina records that they had made themselves the "dueños del comercio de Lima". Although the Portuguese language was spoken almost exclusively in one street of Lima, Portuguese were to be found all over the city: ". . . Herbían por calles vendiendo con petacas a la manera que los lenceros en essa corte: todos los mas corrillos de la placa eran suios; y de tal suerte se habían señoreado del trato de la mercancería, que desde el diamante al comino todo corria por sus manos. . . desde el mas vil negró de Guinea hasta la perla más preciosa."

Many of the Portuguese in Lima were well to do and this generated suspicion and dislike among the Spaniards, who also suspected them of being Jews. Thus many Portuguese were involved in the autos-de-fe of the Lima Inquisition. Medina describes the situation in strong terms:

> Habíase, en efector, desencadenado en Lima furiosa tormenta contra los mercaderes portugueses, dueños entonces del comercio del Perú, atizado y mantenido en el tormento por la Inquisición de Lima. . ."

The movement against the Portuguese for their alleged adherence to the Jewish faith spread to Cartagena and Mexico. One of the best descriptions of Lima, Cuzco, and Potosí in the early years of the seventeenth century came from the pen of an anonymous writer considered a Portuguese Jew.

Portuguese-Spanish relations in South America have usually been described in terms of their rivalry, especially in the broad Río de la Plata area and this story has been excellently documented. An important, though less well known, activity of the Portuguese was their persistent and successful attempts to gain a share in the profit from the silver pouring out from Peru. The celebrated Portuguese bishop of Tucumán, D. Francisco de Vitória, was the only one of the merchants who after 1584 sent quantities of silver to Brazil in ships which brought back African slaves, iron, clothing, food, and various kinds of manufactured articles. A valuable letter of another Portuguese merchant, Francisco Soares, given much detail of the illegal traffic current in 1597. As Luís Ferrand de Almeida shows in his résumé of this significant document:

> Navios portugueses de 30 a 40 toneladas subiam frequentemente o Rio da Prata, levando acucar, arroz, tafetás, chapéus e outros géneros, regresando ao Rio de Janeiro 'carregados de reaes de prata'. Por outro lado, os negociantes do Peru vinham a Pernambuco, Baía e Rio de Janeiro empregar os seus capitais na compra de mercadorias, chegando a trazer '15 a 20.000 ducados em reaes de prata e oiro'. O proveito que se tirava deste comercio era de tal ordem que F. Soares tinha receio de não ser acreditado. Com lucros de 100 a 500%, julgava possível atingir mesmo os 1.000%. Entendia que era de considerar a ida as minas de Potosí, as mais ricos do Peru, e acrescentava: 'Se os negociantes portuguezes e hespanhoes tivessem conhecimento deste commercio, não mandariam nem arriscariam tantas mercadorias para Carthagena, como fazem. Por isso, este Río é um grande commercio, o mais proximo e mais facil caminho para ir ao Perú'

The researches of Charles R. Boxer, Alice P. Canabrava, and others make unnecessary further attention here to the large and illegal trade between Peru and Brazil. It was, of course, not officially documented in any large way but it is likely that much additional information on the subject will be discovered in the archives of Europe and the Americas. One indication of the presence of Spaniards in Brazil may be seen from the fact that <u>peruleros</u>, or silver merchants from Peru, have been considered responsible for naming Copacabana in Rio de Janeiro after the ancient shrine of this name on an island in Lake Titicaca in Upper Peru. We may reasonably conclude that the story of the relationship between Peru and Brazil in the colonial period will be a significant segment of the history of Portuguese-Spanish interaction in America when fully known.

III

In the story of the penetration of Portuguese in South America, the silver of Potosí will be very important. As Paulo Prado has observed:

> a prata do Potosí foi assim durante séculos a grande miragem que atraía as populacões do litôral atlântico . . . Da contiguidade do Peru . . . vinha a obsessão do Potosí ou da prata, mais viva a anterior a do ouro, nas preocupacões ambiciosas dos pioneiros da colonia portuguesa.

Portuguese were to be found in Potosí as early as 1550, only five years after the Spaniards had first stumbled upon the existence of the mountain of silver there. By 1575 Portuguese were so prominent in Potosí that they participated actively in the "fiesta y solemnidades" which took place when the Iglesia Mayor was completed in October of that year. The eighteenth-century Bartolomé Arzáns de Orsúa y Vela describes it thus:

> en la calle Luizitana los famosos portugueses levantaron un gran obelisco de grandisimos maderajes, particularmente pinos y cedros, donde hizieron un rico altar con quatro rostros. En toda este lucidísimo obra estavan varias figuras de escultura, que significaban las virtudes, con sus versos y letras que lo declaraban.

The recently printed Relación de Potosí (1585) by Luis Capoche contains references to Portuguese miners who worked and suffered in the tunnels of Potosí.

The most important single contribution to the development of Potosí made by a Portuguese was undoubtedly the discovery of mercury by the poet Enrique Garces, on whom the Peruvian historian Guillermo Lohmann Villena has recently brought to light much information. Garces, born into a noble family of Oporto, went to Peru in 1547 where he became a merchant in Lima. After a period as a bookbinder in Guayaquil, he returned to Lima in 1556 and married there. Of a lively and alert intelligence, with a scientific bent, he recognized that red powder used by the Indian women to enhance their beauty and by the Indian men to inspire terror in their enemies was cinnabar. He also knew that mercury was to be found near cinnabar deposits and learned, by great skill and pertinacity in questioning Indians, that the powder came from near Huamanga where he searched for and found some mercury. In 1558 he travelled to Mexico where Bartolomé de Medina was introducing the patio method of treating silver ore, which involved the use of mercury to precipitate the silver in the ore. Garces then realized the possibilities inherent in his discovery and, associating himself with a young Mexican miner named Pedro de Contreras, returned to Peru in 1559 with Contreras and three quintals of mercury from Almadén in Spain to compare with the Peruvian product. He obtained from the Viceroy in Lima a 12 year license to exploit mercury, demonstrated the patio method to the Viceroy, and indirectly thus made possible Potosí's greatly increased silver production when Fernández de Velasco applied the use of mercury there on a large and systematic scale in 1572.

Garces also made other mining improvements and inventions in Peru, and some years later was able to retire to Madrid where he spent some of his Peruvian profits in various literary endeavors, the most notable one being the third Spanish translation of The Lusiads in 1591. Though omissions, errors, and inexactitudes have been discovered in this rendering of the Portuguese text into Spanish--as in the case of the two previous Spanish versions--Lohmann Villena believes that Garces exerted a significant literary influence in Peru and that when this is recognized "habrá que conceder a Garcés algunas páginas más de las que ahora disfruta en los manuales y tratados de historia de la literatura."

Cervantes himself praised Garces thus in La Galatea:

> De un Enrique Garcés que al Piruano
> Reino enriquece, pues con dulce rima,
> Con sutil, ingeniosa, i facil mano,
> A la mas ardua empressa en él dió cima.
> Pues en dulce Español al gran Toscano
> Nuevo lenguaje ha dado, i nueva estima,
> Quien serà tal que la mayor le quite,
> Aunque el mesmo Petrarca resucite?

Garces was not the only Portuguese poet who had an important connection with Potosí inasmuch as Duarte Fernandes, who is known to have gone there from Lima in the early years of the seventeenth century, was of Portuguese origin though born in Seville. The cultural history of Potosí, when it has been more fully studied, will quite possibly be found considerably richer than has been supposed with Portuguese writers playing their part in its unfolding just as Portuguese artists actively contributed to the embellishment of Buenos Aires.

Some of our knowledge of the presence of Portuguese in Potosí comes from census records. On February 20, 1610, for example, President Alonso Maldonado de Torres of the Audiencia of Charcas forwarded to the Council of the Indias a 12 page list of foreigners in his district. The name, age, and method of entry into Spanish America are given for each foreigner included, and occasionally it is stated how much money each person had. The Portuguese list required almost 6 pages, and information was given on the towns in Portugal from which they came.

Another kind of evidence on the position of Portuguese in Spanish America during the first quarter of the seventeenth century, particularly in Potosi, is provided by Lourenço de Mendoça in his _Suplicación . . . en defensa de los Portugueses_, a 58 folio work printed in Madrid in 1630. Mendoça was a somewhat controversial figure who had been born in Sesimbra near Lisbon and had entered the Jesuit Order in 1602 at the age of 17. Shortly afterwards he was expelled, but continued his education and was eventually named a prelate in Rio de Janeiro where he made some interesting reports on the number of Portuguese ecclesiastics who abandoned their religious work to set out for Potosí to seek their fortunes. Eventually he became commissary of the Inquisition in Potosí, despite opposition by the Spaniards in Lima, and composed a detailed and passionate plea that his fellow countrymen in Spanish America be better treated by Spain. When Portugal recovered its independence in 1640, he elected to stay on the Spanish side and refused to recognize the Duke of Braganza as King; this led to his being declared a traitor to Portugal by the ecclesiastical courts of Lisbon in 1642.

Mendoca's _Suplicación_ of 1630 becomes, therefore, in the light of his life a rather unusual document. For he declares that the Portuguese are quite as true and loyal subjects of the crown as the Spaniards themselves. Yet the Portuguese are considered Jews and even Indians look down on them with scorn, he laments. Stressing the debt Spain owes to Portugal because of the help given to Columbus by Portuguese, he points out that the Portuguese are not robbers, spies, heretics, nor have they been cruel to Indians in the way Las Casas described the Spaniards to have been. Indeed, they have been peaceful elements in Spanish America, the Inquisitor maintains, especially in turbulent Potosí which so badly needs peace. During the terrible wars between the Vicuñas and the Vascongados, the latter tried to enlist the aid of the Portuguese but without success, he reports. Everywhere in the world, except in Spanish America, Portuguese are treated with honor. But in Potosí the law prohibiting them has been applied with rigor; the jails are full of Portuguese treated as though they are spies of some foreign king or enemy. Yet they have made an important contribution in Peru, particularly in Potosí,

> en el oficio de mineros del cerro, en el de beneficiadores de metales, en los ingenios, y en el de carpinteros de aquellas

> fábricas, que de los que acuden a estos oficios y ocupaciones son en gran parte portugueses.

The arguments of the Suplicación failed, however, to soften the hearts of the royal officials in Madrid, for on May 14, 1631, an order was issued to the Audiencia de Charcas instructing it "to move against the Portuguese who have entered the Indies through Buenos Aires, of whom many are to be found in Potosí."

Was Mendoça exaggerating the handicaps suffered by Portuguese in America? Was he himself responsible, as Inquisition official, for helping to fill the prisons of Potosí with his countrymen? Certainly Duarte Gomez Solis, writing shortly before the Suplicación appeared, held an entirely different view:

> Pues claramente se sabe, que en las mas remotas partes donde habitaban, siempre está suspirado por Portugal y trata bien de los Portugueses. . . Portugueses en el mundo tienen mas credito y opinion que ninguna otra nación.

Mendoça may have been exaggerating somewhat to emphasize his argument, for the Historia de la Villa Imperial de Potosí by Bartolomé de Orsúa y Vela, mentioned above, states that Portuguese participated actively in practically all aspects of the tumultuous life of Potosí, becoming engaged not only in mining and fiestas but also in amorous adventures and in the civil wars that raged among the various "naciones" there. When Portugal recovered its independence in 1640 and the Spanish authorities hastily investigated the Portuguese at Potosí, it was found that twenty of the sixty Portuguese listed were very wealthy and that one of them, Antonio Alonso de la Rocha Meneses, had built up a fortune of two million pesos. The Spanish were naturally on the alert, and took all possible precautions to control the Portuguese at this strategic place, "el nervio principal del reino". The rich Antonio Alonso was exiled, four million pesos belonging to other Portuguese were seized, and the Audiencia maintained a vigilant attitude lest the Portuguese engage in subversive actions together with other foreigners at Potosí. How great the threat posed by the Portuguese at Potosí was believed to be, may be seen from the attitude of the Audiencia of Charcas, which in 1641 refused to permit a zealous Visitador General to open up the ancient and bitter records of the civil war between the Vicuñas and Vascongados in Potosí in search of material for possible further prosecution. For, the royal judges declared, the kingdom was:

> tan mesclado con portuguezes y por aquella parte abierto a la comunicación del Brasil por mar y por tierra con que se deja entender el cuidado, recto y prevensión que se debe tener en conservar la quietud y aunar las voluntades de los súbditos para la mejor defensa de los puestos convecinos y para evitar que con ocasión de algún ruido que puede suceder, no la tomen los enemigos para intentar alguna entrada que les sería muy fácil.

The Viceroy thereupon ordered that the Visitador's operations be stopped and that he be sent back to Lima in custody.

It seems clear that neither the Spanish kings nor their subjects in Potosí ceased to look upon the Portuguese with some reserve and even suspicion. In 1654, for example, the town fathers of Potosí refused to obey the order of the Viceroy that Captain Rodrigo Montero Cardozo be allowed to serve as a town officer, because he was Portuguese.

Throughout the seventeenth century the Portuguese remained constantly aware of the economic attractions of Potosí, and the Spaniards remained equally concerned over possible Portuguese aggression. The silver mine was now widely known and its riches widely coveted: one of the principal reasons which led Governor Raimundo of Maranhão to send out Pedro Teixeira in 1638 to explore the Amazon was to form "such an alliance with the natives that the Dutch might be deterred from making any attempt on Peru by this channel." As João Pandiá Calógeras, the Brazilian historian, observed, the illusion of other Potosís yet to be discovered in Brazil led to a series of fruitless expeditions. One of the most forceful statements of the possibilities of trade was made by Manuel Fernandes Cruz at Pernambuco in a recommendation to the king on August 20, 1650. This "antiguo morador" of Brazil pointed out that Buenos Aires and other routes to Peru were open by means of which Portuguese could "infestar as Indias--ilhas e terra firme de Nova Espanha--tanto mais que, como distava muito de Castela a notícia lá chegaria demasiadamente tarde". Perhaps the economic relationship of Potosí and Brazil is best shown by the fact that when silver production fell at the Villa Imperial, Brazilian economy was at once adversely affected, and that the clandestine Potosí trade was still remembered in Brazil on the eve of independence in 1822.

About 20 years after Enrique Garces was arranging in Madrid for the publication of his translation of The Lusiads, another Portuguese --the semi-mythical mameluco, Belchor Dias Caramuru--was in Madrid trying to interest Philip III in explorations for vast silver mines. The "sertanista de grandes viagens, fazendeiro de muitas terras" did not succeed, but he was only one of the many so dazzled by the wealth of Potosí that the search for another mountain of silver justified to them almost any sacrifice that might be involved. As late as 1694-1696 two expeditions were launched in Brazil which the illusion of Belchor Dias had set in motion.

Thus in Portugal, as elsewhere in the world, Potosí symbolized incalculable wealth. Dom Lopo Hoces, the Portuguese admiral, declared in 1639 that the pine forests of Lusitania "erão dignos de ser guardados como o proprio cerro de Potosí", and the Senate of Macao requested the King in 1640 to concede them free trade with Manila, in these words: "Pois havendo passaje tão franca de São Lucar à Nova Hespanha, não hé rezão que a fonte perenne de Potosy deixe a Castella para correr à China". Padre Antonio Vieira mentioned Potosí in one of his sermons, but for a very different reason: "Eu nunca fui ao Potosí, nem vi minas; porém nos livros que descrevem o que nelas se passa, não so causa espanto, mas horror".

Vieira's statement is significant. Where did he get his information on Potosí and the terrible working conditions there? His deep interest in economic development helps to explain his conviction that mines would be a danger rather than a strength for Portugal; he asked:

> Que utilidades se tem seguido a Espanha do seu famoso Potosi e das outras minas desta mesma América? A mesma Espanha confessa e chora que lhe ñão tem servido mais, que de a despovoar e empobrecer. Eles cavam e navegam a prata, e os estrangeiros a logram. Para os outros é a substancia dos precioses metais, e para eles a escória.
>
> Aqui vereis qual é o fruto das minas, e o que fazem rico esses rios de ouro e prata, trazidos de tão longe. Com as suas enchentes inundam a terra, oprimen os povos, arruinam as casas, destruem os reinos.

As causas naturais destos efeitos tão lamentáveis. . . O luxo, a vaidade, a ostentaçao, a delícia, os palácios, as casas de prazer, as fábricas e máquinas, esquisitas e outras cousas tão notáveis como supérfluas.

. . .E quando as mesmas frotas voltavam carregadas de ouro e prata, nada disto era para alívio ou remédio dos povos, senão para mais se encherem e incharem os que tinham mando sobre eles, e para que se excogitarem novas artes de esperdiçar e novas invencões de destruir.

Vieira's attitude did not, however, influence Portuguese governmental circles. The search for silver continued and eventually some Portuguese came to believe that their sovereign's jurisdiction reached as far westward as the mountain of silver; indeed, in 1695 and 1696 various groups of mamelucos set out to capture Santa Cruz de la Sierra, whose capitulation would have meant inevitably the fall of Potosí as well.

During all these years, however, while the Portuguese sought in vain for another Potosí, contraband silver flowed regularly and freely from Peru to the outside world through Buenos Aires and Brazil. Although the Spanish authorities learned of this movement, which was reported to amount in 1605 to 500,000 cruzados, and tried to prevent it, it continued unabated, as Charles R. Boxer shows in his substantial chapter on "The Road to Potosí".

Thus both the economy and the imagination of the Portuguese were deeply involved with that Cerro de Potosí, of which one of its loyal citizens wrote in this exhuberant fashion, which helps us to understand the powerful attraction this mountain of silver exerted:

La muy celebrada, siempre inclita, augusta, magnánima, noble y rica Villa de Potosí; orbe abreviado; honor y gloria de la América; centro del Perú; emperatriz de las villas y lugares de este Nuevo Mundo; reina de su poderosa provincia; princesa de las indianas poblaciones; señora de los tesoros y caudales; benigna y piadosa madre de ajenos hijos; columna de la caridad; espejo de liberalidad; desempeño de sus católicos monarcas; protectora de pobres; depósito de milagrosos santuarios; ejemplo de veneración al culto divino a quien los reyes y naciones apellidan ilustre, pregonan opulenta, admiran valiente, confiesan invicta, aplauden soberana, realzan cariñosa y publican leal; a quien todos desean por refugio, solicitan por provecho, anhelan por gozarla y la gozan por descanso.

El famoso, siempre máximo, riquísimo, e inacabable Cerro de Potosí; singular obra del poder de Dios; único milagro de la naturaleza; perfecta y permanente maravilla del mundo; alegría de los mortales, emperador de los montes, rey de los cerros, príncipe de todos minerales; señor de cinco mil indios (que le sacan las entrañas); clarín que resueña en todo el orbe; ejército pagado contra los enemigos de la fe; muralla que impide sus designios; castillo y formidable pieza, cuyas preciosas balas los destruye; atractivo de los hombres; imán de sus voluntades; vasa de todos los tesoros; adorno de los sagrados templos; moneda con que se compra el cielo; monstruo de riqueza; cuerpo de tierra y alma de plata; (que con más de mil y quinientas bocas que tiene llama a los humanos para darles sus tesoros, siendo otros tantos ojos para ver sus necesidades, y tanta su liberalidad que les da el corazón por esos ojos); a quien las cuatro partes del mundo conocen por la experiencia de sus efectos; sus católicos monarcas lo poseen (qué mayor grandeza!), los demás reyes lo envidian, las naciones todas lo engrandecen, aclaman poderoso, aprueban excelente, ensalzan portentoso, subliman sin igual, celebran admirable y elogian perfectísimo.

Although Spanish opinion was consistently enthusiastic about Potosí, an occasional Portuguese doubted that mineral wealth was necessary to his countrymen. In the eighteenth century one Portuguese writer set out to prove that the mines in Brazil were prejudicial to the best interests of Portugal because of their cost to the crown and because they drew labor away from agriculture. "O homen pode vivir sem ouro, e até mesmo sem vestidos, tães são os Indios do Brazil, mas nintuem pode vivir sem alimentos." This feeling was never expressed in Potosí, so far as the documents now known testify. Production and still more production was the constant cry of Spaniards, from the King and Viceroy down to the miners overseeing their sweating Indian laborers in the hot depths of the tunnels which were dug deeper and ever deeper in the mountain of Potosí so that no silver there would escape their feverish search.

IV

Not only did the Portuguese go to Spanish America and engage profitably in many enterprises there, they also wrote careful descriptions of the Spanish portion of America. The 1557 Relação of "The Gentleman of Elvas" has already been mentioned. Another important Portuguese contribution to our knowledge of Spanish America is an interesting manuscript in the Hispanic Society of America, in New York, entitled: "Derrotero del hemisferio occidental de las costas atlántican de Europa y Africa, con referencia especial a las posesiones y descubiertas portuguesas y españolas. Mapas originales dibujados y miniados en vitela por un piloto portugués residente en el Perú, hacia 1575. Con una relación de la Villa de Potosí y sus riquezas minerales, manuscrito original, con un plano y una hermosa vista miniada de principios del siglo XVII (hacia 1605), y con otras noticias geográficas, astronómicas y náuticas en manuscritos de fines del siglo XVI".

Early in the seventeenth century a Portuguese prepared a brief but valuable report on Peru, as stated above, and submitted it to the Estate's General of Holland. The author had resided fifteen years in Lima and had visited other parts of Peru including Potosí. He described the mining camp as having 4,000 Spanish households and more than 40,000 Indian workers who lived in straw huts on the edge of the town. He was struck, like most visitors, by the atmosphere of the boisterous silver center: "Pululaban en la villa los bravos, jugadores de profesión y demás gente maleante". But he also added, in that somewhat uncritical spirit which visitors to Potosí often have exhibited under the influence of their first and usually overwhelming impression of the Villa Imperial:

"Aqui estan las mejores maquinas y artificios que en el mundo nunca se han feito".

The most important Portuguese report on Peru was probably a <u>Historia de Potosí</u> composed by Antonio de Acosta, or da Costa. Orsúa y Vela, the eighteenth century <u>Potosino</u> whose massive work on Potosí will shortly be published, quotes extensively from the work which he considers one of his principal authorities for his own copious history of the vicissitudes of the Villa Imperial. He describes Acosta as a "noble lusitano que escribía en su idioma", and states that his work was published in Portuguese in Lisbon, though he does not give the date, after which the volume was translated into Spanish by the Andalusian D. Juan Pasquier who died before completing his task, which was to have included bringing Acosta's Historia up to date. The other two histories frequently referred to by Orsúa y Vela were by Captain Pedro Méndez and Bartolomé de Dueñas, both Peruvians, who likewise failed to carry their works to conclusion "on account of various circumstances". Acosta's history was thus the only one, of the four upon which Orsúa y Vela largely depended, reported finished by its author.

No copy of Acosta's work has yet been located, despite the best efforts of my bibliographical friends in Portugal, and so complete is the silence on Acosta of the standard bibliographies, that the question must be asked whether his Historia de Potosí ever existed. Acosta's name does not appear on any list of foreigners in Potosí that has come to light thus far. Arzáns de Orsúa y Vela, however, cites him so confidently and so frequently that it seems likely that Acosta actually prepared a volume which was either never printed or issued in such a limited edition that no copy has survived to the twentieth century. Lacking that single copy, in either manuscript or printed form, we have the Arzáns de Orsúa y Vela "Historia" as our only source of information on Acosta's history. Orsúa y Vela declares that Acosta's story was largely concentrated on the three "destrucciones" of Potosí: "the shedding of blood in those memorable wars of the Vicuñas, the flood when the Cari-Cari dam burst, and the depreciation of the currency effected by President Don Francisco Nestares Marín".

One cannot wholly dismiss the possibility that Arzáns de Orsúa y Vela may have perpetrated a huge hoax on his fellow historians of Potosí by creating Acosta and his Historia--and perhaps other works he so confidently quotes--out of his own imagination. The diabolical skill of such recent bibliographical forgers as Thomas J. Wise makes one hesitate to pronounce flatly on the subject. Yet we do know that Arzáns de Orsúa y Vela was a schoolmaster in Potosí who was known for many years to have had devoted himself to collecting all manner of documents on the history of the town and also gleaned from its older inhabitants their personal recollections of the past events of the Villa Imperial. An analysis of his sources and his use of them leads one to the conclusion that he was indeed what he was supposed to be: a schoolmaster determined to preserve for posterity as much information as possible on the glorious annals of his city. Until contrary evidence is produced it is reasonable to assume that the writer whose work Arzáns de Orsúa y Vela considered an important source for his own Historia did indeed live and write.

About Acosta himself, Arzáns de Orsúa y Vela says little, except that he was "Portuguez de nación". We are told that he had been in the Villa Imperial only four days when the sad news of the death of King Sebastian in Africa reached him. This had occurred on August 4, 1578, so he probably arrived at Potosí some time in 1579. As a loyal Portuguese, he inserted in his history "una lastimosa exclamación declarando las virtudes, sumo valor, y miserable ruina deste desgraciado Rey; y callando su muerte concluya con solo dezir, que de embidia el fiero Marte consiguio el no tener opossitor en el mundo; pero que a su tiempo volveria".

Acosta was a loyal Potosino, expressing that pride in the wonders of the Villa Imperial which appears in the writings of nearly all who have been drawn to relate its glamorous history. Orsúa y Vela considers him a "verdadero historiador", lauds him as one who describes events as they actually happened without adding or subtracting anything, refers to his work as a "muy acreditada y agradable Historia", and from his steady dependence upon its material clearly believes Acosta to be a discreet and trustworthy source.

Acosta, who appears to have been an eyewitness of many of the incidents and actions related in his Historia and to have resided in Potosí from 1579 until about 1657 (for his last reference is to events in this latter year), must have come to Potosí in his early youth and lived on to an advanced age. This is not so surprising as it may seem for, despite the rigors of the Andean location of Potosí at about 14,000 feet above sea level, some Potosinos lived to a ripe old age: Capoche mentions a miner who lived to be 120 years old and in his old age climbed to the top of the mountain of silver "from time to time when he felt like it".

Acosta weaves many different kinds of material into his story. He speculates on how Potosí received its name, affirms that hailstones as large as doves' eggs fell upon the town during one violent storm, remarks upon the wealth gained by tavern keepers, and gives details on the discovery of certain exceedingly precious stones. He describes the terrible hurricanes that afflicted the town; the scenes are so vivid that one almost hears the wind whistle through the narrow and crowded streets. He notes the uncovering of strange bones during the excavation for the Dominican church. He calculates--like many other writers on Potosí--how much silver has been extracted from beneath the mountain and at one point exclaims that the quantity was great enough, if piled up all together, to rise to the same height as the Cerro itself. He gives meticulous details on the numerous and costly fiestas that Potosinos organized at every possible opportunity, and seems to delight in setting down information on the follies and foibles of the Potosinos such as the time two groups fought naked from the waist up during one of the intense cold spells Potosí frequently suffered.

Acosta's piety and interest in the city's religious life is strong; he reflects faithfully the spirit of his age which has been termed "un siglo piadoso". He gives numerous accounts of miracles, demons, and catastrophes visited upon the town for the sins of its inhabitants, as well as examples of great charity and also of the lack of it. Acosta knew one Potosino so holy that after his death he was venerated as a saint; twenty years after burial in 1625 his body, Acosta assures us as an observer when the tomb was opened, "estaba entero, y tratable, despidiendo de si una fragancia admirable; efectos de la gloria que gozaba y goza su alma". And he naturally furnishes information on his fellow Portuguese: how they fought on the side of the criollos against the Vascongados; how one perished in a somewhat comical amatory adventure, how a Portuguese medical doctor lived in Potosí, and how nobly General Pereyra served as corregidor there. Acosta evidently always maintained his pride as a Portuguese; he emphasized that General Pereyra had been born in Cubillan in Portugal. We do not find anywhere in Arzáns de Orsúa y Vela's long account any depreciation of Portuguese miners or residents in Potosí. This Spanish American historian always refers to them respectfully as a very important element in the annals of the town.

Thus, Acosta's Historia de Potosí must be accepted as much more than the story of the three "destrucciones" visited upon the silver center by the civil war of 1623-1626, the breaking of the Cari-Cari dam in 1626 which inundated Potosí, and the debasing of the currency in 1650, although these topics are indeed dealt with at length.

V

Whether Antonio de Acosta's Historia de Potosí is ever found or not, all who are concerned with the history of the Iberian peoples in the Americas will do well to give increased attention to the reciprocal influence of the Portuguese and the Spaniards as they left their imperishable mark on the peoples and lands of the vast New World. To know this story more fully, we need more studies similar to Miguel Acosta Saignes' work entitled Historia de los portugueses en Venezuela. This small volume produced by a Venezuelan scholar gives a model account of the contribution made by the Portuguese in one particular American country from the conquest until today. It includes examples of their linguistic influence, tells amusing stories, including one of how a sixteenth century Portuguese failed to keep the Indian maiden he fancied, provides a useful bibliography of the scattered material on the subject, and uses census data to demonstrate how varied were the occupations of the Portuguese resident in Caracas in 1607:

> Seis encomenderos, un barbero, un médico, cuatro plateros, un espadero, un artillero, tres zapateros, un carretero, dos sastres, nueve agricultores que en el censo se indican con la palabra 'campo'; dos pulperos, un herrero, un tratante, es decir, vendedor ambulante; un albañil, un carpintero y un factor de negros, esto es, un representante de negreros, para recibir los navíos y realizar las operaciones de venta en la ciudad. Como se ha visto, cierto número de portugueses aparecen sin oficio determinado. La mayor parte de los lusitanos residentes en Caracas eran casados.

The Portuguese obtained a contract for peaceful colonization in Venezuela a few years after Bartolomé de las Casas tried in vain in 1520 to establish farmers on the coast of Tierra Firme; in fact, it is the well-known peaceful action of the Portuguese which Prof. Acosta Saignes exalts in his concluding chapter:

> Hemos visto los portugueses, pues, batallar desde los tiempos del descubrimiento: fueron navegantes, pilotos, guerreros, colonizadores, comerciantes, artífices, agricultores, artesanos, artistas, gobernadores. No hubo actividad que no desempeñasen durante la colonia. Y a pesar de haber participado en los combates, su ejercicio en Venezuela muestra que siempre tendieron más a los oficios pacíficos que a las empresas bélicas.

Here we have one more spontaneous illustration of the peaceful nature of Portuguese in their contacts with men of a variety of cultures in tropical lands.

When more fully investigated, the relationship between Portuguese and Spaniards in the New World will be seen as much more than a clash of military and political interests. Hostilities certainly existed, but toward the end of the colonial period the Spanish governors of Chiquitos and the Portuguese governors of Matto Grosso actually sent "ambassadors" to each other, and the documents on these friendly frontier contacts deep in the heart of the South American continent tell of these "ambassadors" exchanging rich presents and courtesies in an amicable spirit. This frontier relationship will also appear as a continuous and fruitful interpretation of ideas and practices between the two Iberian peoples, or the "Hispanos" as Gilberto Freyre calls them in his latest attempt to make the world aware of the contributions of Brazil to the development of an ethnic and cultural pluralism.

Two major obstacles face those who study the history of the Iberians in the New World. The first is the unmanageable amount of widely scattered material involved in making a serious investigation. The second is the combination of patriotic and political prejudices which underlie the traditional interpretations that new studies may challenge.

To the Iberians, few foreign historians render a just verdict when writing about either Spain or Portugal. To non-Iberians, both Spaniards and Portuguese seem at times unduly sensitive to any interpretation which appears to them to cast a shadow upon their respective glorious national accomplishments. The fact that both Spanish and Portuguese historians carry on research largely on their own history increases the natural tendency of each nation to exalt its own.

History also becomes inextricably enmeshed in present politics in Spain and Portugal. Many Portuguese have gone to Spanish America, but only a brave man would point out that this fact leads to a question: Why didn't they go to Portuguese-speaking lands instead? Why, if Portuguese policy has always been so successful in Africa and elsewhere--as official circles continue to affirm--did so many go to other lands, especially to Spanish America where they sometimes labored under severe handicaps? In fact, Portuguese have continued to settle in non-Portuguese speaking lands. In 1910, the 22,303 Portuguese immigrants in Hawaii were more than one-tenth of the population of the islands and equalled half the entire white population of Angola, Portugal's largest overseas territory.

The answer to such a question about Portuguese emigration cannot be easily given, but it must be pointed out that in this time of acute self-consciousness felt by all colonial powers Portugal has assumed a defensive attitude. As one minor but perhaps significant example of what is often referred to as the Portuguese inferiority complex, the foreigner entering Portugal from Spain at Tuy sees this declaration in large letters in the customs office: "Portugal is _not_ a small country." Below this statement is a map on which Portuguese overseas territories are superimposed on the countries of Europe to support this assertion. Has this Portuguese sensitivity been caused by the leyenda negra against Portugal--by the attitude widely held in Europe and elsewhere that Portugal had an unpleasant history and an uncertain future? No thoroughly documented monograph on anti-Portuguese feeling has been compiled yet comparable to the numerous studies on the leyenda negra against Spain, though abundant materials doubtless exist. Probably the anti-Portuguese feeling has as ancient roots as a Swedish scholar--the late Sverker Arnoldsson--has demonstrated is true of anti-Spanish sentiments, and probably Portuguese insistence on their maritime priority has helped to keep alive the leyenda negra against Portugal.

Portuguese-Spanish rivalry was so intense in the sixteenth century on the question of their respective geographical discoveries, and the politico-economic stakes were so high, that one censor in Spain recommended that certain maps of Mexico be not published because--even though correct--they would contradict previously held contentions of Spanish authorities _vis-a-vis_ Portuguese claims. The reasoning of the censor clearly reveals how he would utilize history for naked national purposes. The maps in question should not be permitted to appear

> para que no acontezca perjudicarnos nos mismos, confesando con nuestros papeles y escrituras en contrario de nuestras pertenen-

> cias, y dar ocasión a los adversarios [the Portuguese] de defender y corroborar sus razones, y hacer lo que nosotros vamos haciendo ahora en ir examinando las historias, libros y relaciones de ellos que en los primeros descubrimientos inconsiderablemente escribieron según la verdad, para fortificar nuestras razones y pertendencias [sic] y condenarlos con la confesión y testigo de los mismos portugueses.

The priority of the Portuguese over other Europeans in exploring many parts of the world is today an article of faith in Portugal, perhaps the tenderest subject of all. Non-Iberians have sometimes become irritated by this claim; one Italian geographer declared that when writing on their discoveries Portuguese historians were so patriotic that Baron Münchausen was by comparison an exact and sober witness. Nevertheless, no historical congress under Portuguese auspices is complete without detailed and enthusiastic treatment of this subject. The committee sponsoring the International Congress on the History of the Discoveries, held in Lisbon in September, 1960, for example, published a learned contribution by a Russian scholar on Arabic nautical knowledge which upheld the idea that the Portuguese were unique in their contacts with Islamic science and that Vasco de Gama was aided by an Arabic pilot. Both the Portuguese Congress authorities and the Russian author had their own special interests in mind, for the Portuguese prudently omitted the original preface which included a stirring anti-colonial declaration denouncing "The Portuguese, Dutch, French, and English [who] one after the other plundered the riches of the nations of Asia and Africa, oppressing and debasing the human dignity of these nations."

At this same 1960 Congress a rather bizarre communication was read which claimed the priority of the Portuguese over the Spaniards in the discovery of America by asserting that Portuguese blood flowed in the veins of certain Indians in New England before Columbus reached the New World. When one non-Portuguese participant advised caution in accepting this thesis, the Lisbon newspapers reported that only the Spaniards present applauded. One Portuguese writer has developed an ingenious theory to solve the awkward problem posed by Columbus and his voyages--the great Discoverer was really a Portuguese! This remarkable approach has not yet won many supporters, even in Portugal, but the historian who treats almost any aspect of the connection between the Spaniards and Portuguese in the New World must keep in mind the deepseated and emotionally held conviction of most Portuguese that they were the first to explore many parts of the world and that in particular their priority over the Spaniards in America is an indisputable fact.

The Portuguese also hold--and with considerable justice--that they have had and still have the most Christian and most benevolent policy toward other peoples, particularly those of a different culture or color. They consider Spaniards more cruel in general: "In Portugal we do not kill the bulls." Generalizations on comparative cruelty lead more often to heat than to light, but this desire to exalt their nation is such a fundamental part of Portuguese life that it cannot be dismissed lightly by historians if they would truly understand this remarkable nation.

Sometimes non-Portuguese writers absorb this Portuguese viewpoint so thoroughly that they lose their perspective and become apologists rather than historians. Charles R. Boxer in a review article has critically examined a work on Africa by S. R. Welch, whose interpretation he characterizes in this way:

> With few and insignificant exceptions, Portuguese and Roman Catholics can do no wrong and never have done any worth mentioning. . . He stresses ad nauseam that Portuguese expansion was totally different from that of all other colonial powers; that they hardly ever indulged in the slave-trade, and that they were always the kindest and most considerate of masters. . . He claims time and time again that 'at no period of their expansion were the Portuguese the aggressors' and that Portuguese missionary aims were never concerned with imperial expansion. Last but not least, he insists repeatedly that 'there is no racial question anywhere in the Portuguese colonies, and there never will be.'

Professor Boxer disposes of Welch with the comment: "This, of course, is utter clap-trap", and quotes chapter and verse to show how far Mr. Welch has departed from the facts of history.

Another peril, or at least problem, for historians--no matter what their nationality--who treat the history of the Iberians in America, is that so large a part of the story has been written by ecclesiastics. Has the modern history of any other nation been so exclusively compiled by clerical historians? Their solid documentary publications which Robert Streit lists in his impressive Bibliotheca Missionum afford sufficient testimony on this point. Yet ecclesiastics present, naturally, their view of history and the very weight of their contribution makes it difficult for the historian to achieve a balanced view which includes non-religious topics. Again, the various religious orders whose enthusiasm and devotion were so vital in both Spanish and Portuguese America emphasized, most naturally, their own orders and thus generated what might be called Ordenspatriotismus.

The most powerful patriotism, however, and the one more likely to dismay historians attempting objectivity, is the patriotism of the state. Portuguese at all levels of society are thoroughly saturated with a sense of history--or the vice of history, as one writer describes it--and today are emotionally as well as politically committed to the preservation of their overseas territories (not colonies) in the face of the growing conflagration in Africa.

> Portugal has always maintained, in spite of the many eye-witness accounts to the contrary, that the natives under her jurisdiction enjoyed a peculiarly free and happy life,

according to one writer, who goes on to state that allegations of cruelty and oppression were only to be accounted for by "sinister motives on the part of those who made them."

The argument today runs something like this. Portuguese policy in Africa is the best of all policies, and through the centuries the Portuguese have developed a way of handling the people and problems of Africa which has made possible her present enviable supremacy. Indeed, Portugal was right from the start: a leading official spokesman of the Portuguese government delivered a carefully-wrought address to the 1960 International Congress on the History of the Discoveries designed to prove that Portugal today is following in Africa the precepts laid down by Prince Henry the Navigator over 500 years ago. To paraphrase the dictum of the nineteenth-century historian Edward A. Freeman that "history is past politics," one sometimes feels that in Portugal today history tends to be present politics.

But fresh winds are blowing, too. Portuguese scholars and others are beginning to agree with Francis M. Rogers who, in his suggestive essay entitled "The Four Dromedaries of the Infante Dom Pedro", has persuasively called for a new approach to Portuguese studies. Professor Rogers bids all concerned with Portuguese culture to place Portugal "and its great accomplishments in a much broader framework" than heretofore, and lists a numer of topics of fifteenth century Portuguese history which merit further study in such a framework.

Other suggestions for new directions which historical studies in Portugal might profitably take come from a young Portuguese scholar, Vitorino Magalhães-Godinho, who has produced a series of studies on Portuguese economic history while living in France and Brazil. In a recent analysis of Portuguese historiography he recognizes the past achievements of Portuguese historians, and the work of such contemporary scholars as Professor Virginia Rau, but also insists that many gaps remain to be filled:

> Carecemos de roteiros de bibliotecas e arquivos, de inventários de coleçoes, de análises e edições críticas de fontes, de catálogos modernos de moedas, de um tratado de bibliografia portugûesa. Faltam-nos um tratado atualizado de numismática, una história desenvolvida de Direito. A geografia histórica está quase em branco. Não existe também una história social, humana de lingua portugûesa. Nada quanto à evolução.dos preços, demografia histórica, circulação interna, história de propiedade eclesiástica ou da propiedade nobre, regime senhorial no século XVI, classes sociais na época moderna e contemporânea. Quase nada quanto ás numerosas feitorias, á rota do Cabo, ao açucar nas ilhas, ás familias de mercaderes e emprêsas comercias. Vazio completo o do mercado da mão-de-obra.

In the light of what is now known--fragmentary as this may be--about the action of the Portuguese in Spanish America, may we not add to the exhortations by Professors Godinho and Rogers a further suggestion? Let us not limit our investigations to the minutiae of Portuguese voyages in the Atlantic before Columbus or confine the story of Portugal in the New World to the history of Brazil, challenging and important as these subjects undoubtedly are. Let us also study what the poet Enrique Garces accomplished for Spain by his discovery of mercury in Peru, what the Portuguese artists wrought in the Rio de la Plata, what Antonio de Acosta the "noble lusitano" achieved by his preservation of the history of Potosí, and what the Portuguese have contributed to each one of the Spanish American nations from the discovery period until today; in short what the Portuguese did in Spain's far-flung empire. Above all, let the fresh winds of controversy blow away the chaff. Only thus will the world hear the full story of the dynamic achievements of Portuguese speaking people in the New World.

CHAPTER 14.

A NOTE ON THE LIFE AND PUBLICATIONS OF COLONEL GEORGE EARL CHURCH

What began as a pious exercise in memory of the Rhode Island engineer, Colonel George Earl Church, who had donated a manuscript history of the Villa Imperial de Potosí by the eighteenth-century Potosino Bartolomé Arzáns de Orsúa y Vela to Brown University Library eventually became a considerable research enterprise. Colonel Church was not only a capable technician but also an attractive personality whose flair for languages and history made him a persona grata wherever he went. And he went to many places--Argentina, Mexico, Bolivia, Brazil, Ecuador, Venezuela, and finally settled down in London where he died. Material about him and his imaginative enterprises in Latin America turned up in London, Washington, D.C., Petropolis and Rio de Janeiro in Brazil, and in Sucre, Bolivia. I thoroughly enjoyed piecing together the story of his life from a variety of sources. The editing of the manuscript history on Potosí occupied Dr. Gunnar Mendoza of Bolivia and me for the better part of five years and Brown University Press published the large work, of over a million words, in three volumes, in 1965.

Books at Brown (Providence, Rhode Island, 1963), 131-145. Reprinted by permission.

A Note on the Life and Publications of Colonel George Earl Church

When the story of American enterprise in developing Latin America becomes fully known, the dreams and accomplishments of that engineer-entrepreneur George Earl Church will constitute an important chapter. He worked and traveled during a long lifetime in the vast region between Patagonia and Mexico, and by his writings helped to make known the geographical characteristics and economic potentialities of the area, particularly Bolivia and the Amazon Valley.

Colonel Church was born at New Bedford, Massachusetts, December 7, 1835, a descendant of Richard Church, who in 1632 came to Plymouth, Massachusetts, from Oxford, England, and was married to Elizabeth Warren, whose father arrived on the *Mayflower* and was an ancestor of General Warren, who fell at Bunker Hill. On his mother's side, Church was descended from Edward Winslow, who also came on the *Mayflower* and was three times elected Governor of Plymouth Colony. Through his mother Church was also directly connected with the Pease family of Yorkshire, England, well-known as having built the first steam railroad in England.

The immediate ancestors of Colonel Church removed to Rochester, Massachusetts, in 1725, and there acquired about 500 acres of land within sixteen miles of Plymouth Rock. Church's father died while he was quite young, and in his eighth year his mother settled in Providence, Rhode Island, where he attended the public schools and attained high rank in the senior class of the high school. At the age of 16 Church decided upon civil and topographical engineering as a profession, and after being employed for some time on surveys for a state map of Massachusetts obtained a position on a New Jersey railroad, but was soon after transferred to a railroad under construction in Iowa as assistant engineer. Later he was employed as Resident Engineer on the Hoosac tunnel in Massachusetts, and then served as Chief Assistant Engineer on another railroad though only 21 years of age.

The financial crisis of 1857 left Church without a job, and he then embarked on the first of many adventurous expeditions to Latin America. Contracted to work as an engineer on one of the Argentine railroads, on arrival in Buenos Aires he found the country in such a disturbed condition that work on the railroad had stopped, but he was almost immediately appointed a member of a mission of military and topographical engineers organized to explore the southwestern frontier of Argentina and to report on the best system of defense against the Indians. The mission members had an exciting experience and Church had his first taste of life on the frontier; in nine months they rode horseback more than 7,000 miles, and with a covering force of 400 cavalry fought two severe battles with the Indians. Each member was required to submit his own plan for the defense of the frontier, and, although Church was the youngest and least experienced of the party, his plan was adopted. He also began to extend his acquaintance with influential Latin Americans, which became a life long practice; for example, he met Domingo F. Sarmiento for the first time after the frontier mission was over.

In 1860 Church was again able to work as an engineer, and he surveyed and located the Great Northern Railway between Buenos Aires and San Fernando. When the first news of the outbreak of the Civil War in the United States reached Argentina he hurried home, was soon commissioned as a captain in the Seventh Rhode Island Infantry, and was sent to the front. He served successively as captain, colonel, and brigade commander of volunteers in the Army of the Potomac, distinguishing himself at the battle of Fredericksburg.

Church continued his interest in Latin America after the war was ended, and was naturally present in Providence when the Argentine Minister Domingo F. Sarmiento, famous educator and later president of his country, delivered an address on December 27, 1865, before the Rhode Island Historical Society. Sarmiento remembered meeting Church in Buenos Aires some years before and commented favorably on his discussions in Providence with Church as well as with other citizens of Rhode Island who had contributed to South America's material progress. Sarmiento was also impressed by the interest manifested in Providence in South American history and culture, and remarked:

> What was my astonishment, however, on visiting the Library of Mr. John Carter Brown, the distinguished book lover, to find in Providence a most complete and instructive collection of Spanish authors, especially of those who have written about South America from the early days of the conquest to our own time. After admiring that rich treasure, I was able to understand the praise of the talented English historian, Arthur Helps, author of an excellent history of the Spanish conquest, who declared that he had obtained documents relating to Spanish America from this library in Rhode Island, which the library of the British Museum, rich in rare books, had been unable to supply him. What I do not understand, unless we appeal to those mysterious sympathies which I referred to in the beginning, is how it happens that this treasure, which all South America would envy, is to be found in Providence. If, for example, a writer wished to treat the war that is at present ravaging Paraguay, Brazil, and the republic of Río de la Plata, he would have to come to Rhode Island. Here, he would find in this rich collection of books on the Jesuit missionaries and the frontier wars between Spaniards and Portuguese, the geographical description of every inch of the soil of those countries, as well as the causes of the present war and of the subsequent tyrannies that flower from the theocratic governments of Guarani missions. . .

At the close of the Civil War Church went back to railroad building in Rhode Island, but he could not forget Latin America and became interested in the French invasion of Mexico which was then deeply agitating the public in the United States. He studied the subject intensively, for he was at heart a researcher, and prepared such a substantial article that the New York Herald published it entire in sixteen columns of its edition of May 25, 1866. The study was soon printed in revised form as a small book with the title Mexico. Its Revolutions: are they evidences of retrogression or progress? A historical and political review. Matías Romero, the Mexican Minister, found the work so valuable that he had copies sent to the State Department and to every member of Congress. The Minister was also apparently partly responsible for having James Gordon Bennett appoint Church a special correspondent for the New York Herald in Mexico, to report on the progress of President Benito Juárez and his Liberal army.

After exciting and dangerous experiences while travelling overland to Mexico with General Lew Wallace, Church found Juárez in Chihuahua and followed the Liberal forces during the last campaigns against Emperor Maximilian in 1866-1867. Church shared the fortunes of Juárez and his army in their march southward to Durango and Zacatecas, and remained with them until the capture of Maximilian. During this period some forty-nine letters from Church were published by the Herald. San Luis Potosí struck off five medals to commemorate the recapture of that important city by the Liberal army--one in gold for President Juárez, a silver one for each of the Cabinet Ministers, and a silver one for Colonel Church, which was presented to him with considerable ceremony. His journalistic mission had now ended and, though offered by the government a large grant of land in Coahuila as recognition of his services to the Liberal cause, he returned to New York and for a while served on the editorial staff of the Herald where he enjoyed writing trenchant leading articles.

Soon Latin America called again. General Quintín Quevedo, who had been accredited by Bolivia as Minister to Mexico to congratulate the government on the downfall of Maximilian, arrived in New York with a letter of introduction from President Juárez to Church, for General Quevedo had been also commissioned to enlist the services of some competent person to open Bolivia to the world of commerce by way of the Amazon. He offered the position to Church who, after considerable study of the project, accepted the responsibility for cutting a canal or building a railroad through a tropical forest to avoid about 250 miles of falls and cataracts of the river Madeira, the main branch of the Amazon, in the heart of South America some 1600 miles from the sea. One of Church's admirers thus described the project and the man invited to undertake it:

> In view of the political and financial condition in Bolivia, the ignorance of the outside world in regard to her natural resources, the fact that the obstructions were mainly in the empire of Brazil, and the great distance of the scene of operations from civilization, the execution of any one of these projects, it was evident, involved titanic labors and demanded the services of a man possessed of a rare combination of qualities. He must be familiar with South America, its language, its history, and its people. He must be a civil engineer of great technical and executive ability. The negotiations with the two governments immediately interested in the enterprise required that he should be a gentleman of high social standing, and, in order that his representation might carry weight in the great financial centers of the world, it was essential that he be well-known as a man of high personal character and unflinching integrity. Extraordinary as were these requirements, the Bolivian Government was fortunate in being able to secure, for the work of organization, the services of a man fully prepared to meet all the exigencies of the situation. This remarkable person. . . was Colonel George Earl Church, whose name is to-day familiar to all persons of intelligence and education from Panama to Patagonia and whose life, for nearly half a century, has been largely devoted to a study on the physical geography and commercial development of South America.

For over ten years after accepting the invitation of Bolivia, Church devoted his extraordinary energy and talents to the great task. In 1868 he proceeded via England to Buenos Aires en route to La Paz, where he soon received the necessary concession from the Bolivian government for the opening of a route to the sea via the Amazon. The agreement, dated August 27, 1868, provided that Church was to organize the National Bolivian Navigation Company for the purpose of canalizing the falls of the Madeira and Mamoré and of establishing steam navigation on the rivers above the falls. He then hastened to New York by way of Peru and Panama; but getting no financial encouragement in the United States he continued on to Europe. There he discovered that the project would not be supported unless the Bolivian Government guaranteed the bonds to be issued to raise the necessary funds. So he returned to Bolivia and in November, 1869, not only won the desired authorization but also was entrusted by the Bolivian government with the responsibility for negotiating with Brazil. Church had been realistic enough to insist that one of the stipulations of his concession be that Bolivia should obtain from the Empire of Brazil the right to construct a railroad on its territory around the falls of the Madeira river.

After unsuccessful efforts for over a year, Bolivia requested Church to undertake this delicate mission, and it is noteworthy that United States Minister Markbeit attributed the failure to the "swordpoint relations existing for three centuries between the old Spaniards and Portuguese" which had "lost little of their bitterness at the date of independence of those countries and their formation into empire and republics." Church accepted the diplomatic task, crossed the Andes to the Pacific Coast, and sailed via the Straits of Magellan to Rio de Janeiro, arriving there in the midst of the great yellow fever epidemic in February, 1870. He aroused Emperor Pedro II's interest, and after 70 days of negotiation was able to sail in April for New York with the desired railway concession from Brazil plus the verbal promise that Brazil would throw open navigation on the Madeira to all nations. Brazil, possible fearing friction with Bolivia, preferred to grant the concession to Church personally, and in these terms the imperial decree of April 20, 1870 was promulgated. As the American Minister in Rio reported to Washington: "The action of Brazil in this matter has been marked by unusual promptness, an earnest desire to comply with our wishes, and a liberality which will be best understood when I state that the Government has actually granted more than Colonel Church wanted."

Minister Markbreit was even more laudatory of Church's diplomatic efforts:

> All these operations have been undertaken and pushed ahead under the most extraordinary difficulties. None of these, not even the Franco-Prussian war, the recent revolution in this republic, Peruvian and Chilean opposition to the loss of Bolivian trade by the Pacific Coast etc., have been able to impede the steady march forward of the National Bolivian Navigation Company. . . .
>
> Henceforth the commercial and friendly relations of Bolivia and Brazil must necessarily become very closely interwoven. For the first time, in fact, since the occupation of this continent by the Europeans, is a real solid effort being made to turn Portuguese American and Spanish American interests into a common channel, and make South America more homogeneous.
>
> In solving this problem between Bolivia and Brazil, Colonel Church is doing a great service to every republic at the headwaters of the Amazon, and also to civilization.

While in New York Church obtained a charter from the United States government for the organization of the National Bolivian Navigation Company, and then went on to London where he organized the Madeira and Mamoré Railway Company Limited, to which company he transferred his Brazilian concessions. He began loan negotiations and contracted with a London company on May 18, 1871, to build the Madeira-Mamoré Railway.

Church then left for Bolivia via New York, and on July 30 reached Sucre, where the Bolivian Congress confirmed his negotiations for the loan and the construction contract.

From Sucre Church rode to Cochabamba and on to Santa Cruz de la Sierra where he fitted out an expedition to descend the Mamoré with Leathom Earle Ross, an English engineer representing the Public Works Construction Company of London. On November 1, 1871, the party reached the site of the terminus of the projected railway:

> . . . In the presence of the entire party, consisting mainly of half-clad Indian boatmen, in the heart of a vast tropical wilderness, fifteen hundred miles from civilization, where the interior country was absolutely unexplored and, except by primitive savages, uninhabited, Colonel Church went through the rude ceremony of turning the first sod for a railway, that, with the faith of a Columbus, he firmly believed and fondly hoped would open to immigration and to the commerce of the world a country unsurpassed in latent wealth by any unoccupied territory of equal extent on the face of the globe.
>
> No more inspring subject for poet's pen or painter's brush could be suggested than the scene here presented by this soldier and citizen of the great Republic of the North, standing amid the wild surroundings at the head of navigation on the Madeira and pointing out to the sister Republic of the South, for centuries the victim of foreign oppression and internal strife, the pathway of future peaceful progress and commercial development.

This was the description of a friend and admirer. Now let us hear what the novelist H. M. Tomlinson had to say when he visited the same spot in 1910:

> The Madeira traverses a country notorious even on the Amazon for its fever, and quite unexplored a mile inland anywhere on its banks; the rubber hunters, too, have to reckon with wandering tribes of hostile Indians.
>
> The country is like that today. Then judge its value for a railway route in the early seventies. But Colonel Church was a New Englander, and again he was a visionary, so therefore most energetic and compelling; he soon persuaded the practical business folk, who seldom know much, and are at the mercy of every eloquent dreamer, to part with a lot of money to buy his Bolivian dream.
>
> We do really find the colonel, on 1st November, 1871, solemnly cutting the first sod of a railway in the presence of a party of Indians, with the wild about him which had persisted from the beginning of things. What the Indians thought of it is not recorded. Anyhow, they seem to have humored the infatuated man who stopped to cut a square of grass in the land of the Parentintins, the men who go stark naked, and make musical instruments out of the shinbones of their victims.

Church and his little party made their way to London by December 14, 1871 via the long stretches of the Amazon and rendered such a glowing account that an English contracting company actually undertook the job in 1872, but was forced to confess utter defeat within a year. The jungle had won. The contractors declared that "the country was a charnel-house, their men dying off like flies, that the road ran through an inhospitable wilderness of swamp and porphyry ridges alternating, and that, with the command of all the capital in the world, and half its population, it would be impossible to build the road." This failure led to involved legal and political problems, whose story has been told elsewhere and need not be repeated here.

Church was not a man to be daunted by obstacles, and he again made the long journey to Bolivia, via New York, Panama, and Peru, reaching La Paz on July 26, 1872. In his reports to and discussion with the Bolivian government he was accompanied by Samuel G. Arnold, ex-Governor of Rhode Island, as a member of the Board of Directors of the National Bolivian Navigation Company. Church proceeded to consult with the Bolivian Congress in session in Sucre, which confirmed the loan and construction contract. It was while in Sucre at this time that Church met Captain George Chaworth Musters, author of At Home With the Patagonians, who had joined a tribe of the Tehuelches Indians and who was the first white man to ride from north to south through the heart of Patagonia. Probably it was also about this time that Church met Emeterio Villamil of La Paz "who spoke thirteen languages fluently, including the Aymara Indian tongue," whose manuscript on Aymara Church possessed. It was from such contacts as these, plus his own wide reading and extensive explorations, that Church acquired his deep and detailed knowledge of South America, perhaps unrivalled at that time.

One aspect of Church's activities on behalf of his enterprises is worthy of special notice. He published almost as constantly as he traveled and negotiated. His publications were all designed to inform the public of the geography and prospects of South America and to forward his various enterprises, especially the Madeira-Mamoré railroad. In 1870, for example, he brought out in London a report on the rapids of the Madeira river, and prepared for the Fortnightly Review an enthusiastic report on "Bolivia and Brazil in the Amazon Valley." This great area, "as large as 49 countries the size of England, is more healthful than the Mississippi Valley," and is "a casket of riches." The lands through which the Madeira and Mamoré course "are rich and beautiful beyond description. Every product known to South America is now produced there, and can be increased almost indefinitely in quantity." The Indians are outstanding specimens of manhood, and are superior to all the other many natives of the New World he has known from the headwaters of the Mississippi to the Straits of Magellan. "They have immense endurance, muscle, and courage." He praises higher education in Bolivia at the University of Chuquisaca in Sucre, though "of course general education is in a lamentable condition, even as bad as it is in many parts of Europe." Church thought well of General Mariano Melgarejo, the president of Bolivia, which will surprise those who have based their opinion of this dictator on such works as Los hechos y dichos del General Melgarejo. Church described him as "the most dashing and best drilled soldier of Spanish America, has good judgment, a moderate education, converses well in Spanish, Quichua, and Aymara. . . . He is full of desire of progress, and lends his most earnest support to everything that promises to bring modern civilization into the Republic."

To Church, progress meant a commercial outlet for Bolivia's products eastward down the Amazon. The only obstacle between the markets on the other side of the Atlantic Ocean and the heart of Bolivia was the line of rapids of the Madeira, but a railroad of 168 miles would cut off the curves of the river and avoid the rapids. And Church concluded the article with a burst of promoter-prose, probably designed to induce British investors to subscribe to the loan he was at that time about to float: "Facilities for construction are very great, and abundant labour is to be found in Bolivia. Easy gradients, no rivers of moment to cross, no swampy ground, and very little excavation and embankment, render it light work to the engineering science of the present day. The estimate of its cost is £625,539 sterling."

The actual conditions encountered in the Amazon were far more difficult, as Neville B. Craig has described in great detail in his Recollections of an Ill-Fated Expedition to the Headwaters of the Madeira River in Brazil. But throughout the decade Church not only traveled widely to carry on negotiations but also persistently sustained a series of legal actions in the London courts and continued to publish. Sometimes these publications were scientific reports, such as the translation of the results of the investigations by the Kellers, the Prussian engineers who had prepared a report for the Brazilian government.

In 1875 he compiled a good-sized book which included the principal historical and geographical reports on the Madeira Valley from 1749 to 1868. His purpose was to demonstrate the riches of the country drained by this river and "to call attention to the vast system of natural canals which are destined to play a great role in the commercial and political history of South America." He also wanted to provide an accurate and impartial description of the country traversed by the Madeira river to confound those "interested in defeating the efforts of Bolivia to open a trade agreement to the Atlantic" who have sought for and accepted many doubtful sources from informants who "possessed the primary qualification of never having been within a thousand miles of the district they professed to describe." Church gave as an introduction a brief chronological statement on the exploration of the Madeira from Inca times to 1872, when he found Sr. José Augustín Palacios in La Paz, "a Bolivian engineer of much talent and painstaking observation," who had explored the Madeira rapids some years before. Then followed several reports from American, Bolivian, Czech, German, and Portuguese pens on the Madeira river regions, and Church saw to it personally that such important newspapers as the Times of London received review copies of the book.

After the failure of the London company Church shifted the scene of operations to the United States, and in 1876 a Philadelphia construction firm agreed to take on the project. The story of this ill-fated attempt is faithfully chronicled by Neville B. Craig in a minor classic not yet widely enough known to students of American and Latin American history. One ship foundered in the Atlantic en route, disease struck down many, and one group of Italian workers were so dissatisfied with conditions in the Amazon construction camp that they fled to the jungle without food or supplies and disappeared forever. The jungle again triumphed and the survivors of this fracaso struggled home in miserable condition. Church finally abandoned the entire project after almost ten years of effort, and the railroad was not to be achieved until the Brazilian government undertook the work a quarter of a century later with greater knowledge of conditions and greater resources.

During the years of the attempt by the Philadelphia contractors Church continued his publication campaign. In 1877 he prepared yet another substantial volume on the railroad project and also caused a review copy of this work to be sent to the Times. This report was a detailed history of the Madeira project, the Bolivian loan, and Church's legal struggle in London courts, together with copies of the concessions by Bolivia and Brazil, copies of various contracts and correspondence, plus excellently prepared maps and information on the trade routes projected. In the same year, 1877, Church published a carefully researched article to show why the Purus river was not a better route for communication between Bolivia and the outside world than the Madeira. For this presentation he used the available printed material, reports on his own explorations including his unpublished travel diaries, and information from a Franciscan who had recently visited the area. He also attached a detailed map, based upon data in Brazilian government archives. The Church Collection in Brown University Library shows how carefully Church prepared for his publications because it contains numerous other maps, charts, pamphlets, and official publications which formed a part of the arsenal of information he had collected.

The enterprise roused considerable controversy over the years in Bolivia, as will be seen from the "Memorandum sobre materiales relativos a George E. Church en la Biblioteca Nacional de Bolivia" by Gunnar Mendoza printed below.* The Brazilian concession also led to controversy and was in the end cancelled, as indicated in the reports by Richard Graham and José Honório Rodrigues, printed below, on some of the Brazilian sources in the Arquivo Nacional in Rio de Janeiro and in the Museu Imperial in Petropolis. Also printed below is the "Report on the Records of the Department of State in Washington, D.C. Containing Information on George Earl Church" by Julia B. Carroll which demonstrates how complicated was the Madeira-Mamoré project and how persistent Church was in pushing it. This "Report" in addition is an impressive record of the many interests and activities of Church, and all four bibliographical statements will prove useful to anyone concerned with Church and the Amazon.

Even Church's energy and persistence could not triumph and all his Amazonian efforts failed. The tangled web of political and legal complications was almost as formidable an obstacle as the heat, the disease, and the geographical problems encountered by the engineers, to which was added the unpreparedness of both the London and the Philadelphia construction companies to operate in the tropics. Church's Bolivian partner José Francisco Velarde attributed the failure to the bitter opposition by the commercial interests on the Pacific Coast and to the attempts of the Bolivian government to embarrass Church after the contract had been signed. Velarde considered the project as essential for the good of Bolivia and praised his associate in these words: "Su cooperación i su entusiasmo no han escaseado, a despecho de los obstáculos de todo jénero que se han presentado para impedir la realización de tan querida idea." A Peruvian geographer also enthusiastically supported the project and described Church as "un magnámino corazón, gran filantrópico y fanático por la libertad." Another admirer of Church was the Emperor Pedro II, who supported his idea that Brazil should undertake the construction of the railway but "political sentiment was then averse to letting any foreigners build what Brazilians regarded as the key to the heart of South America."

This "Note" is not the place to attempt a detailed analysis of the Church project for the Madeira-Mamoré, but there obviously is a great deal of material for such a study and probably even more may be found by an assiduous student. And whatever may have been the true reasons for the failure of the project, it is clear that the results were bad for Bolivia. The American Minister Markbreit reported to Washington on November 7, 1872, at the time Church was negotiating in La Paz, that "judging from the encroachments of her ambitious neighbors

*The reference "printed below" in this paragraph refers to bibliographical material omitted from the present version, but included in the original printing of the article.

the only method for the preservation of her national integrity is to push forward such commercial and military roads as have been projected by Colonel Church and others."

The road was not built; Bolivia did not achieve her commercial outlet through the Amazon to the markets of the Atlantic world, and her subsequent territorial losses are now part of history.

A few months after the second failure of the Madeira-Mamoré enterprise Secretary of State James G. Blaine accepted Church's offer to report on the political and commercial conditions of Ecuador, especially its relation with Colombia and its attitude toward and connection with disturbances between Bolivia, Chile, and Peru. Church remained in Quito three months, during which he collected information and acted on behalf of the English foreign bondholders to negotiate the readjustments of the national debt of Ecuador. He rode north as far as the boundary with Colombia to investigate the feasibility of a railroad development, and afterwards went to Lima where he wrote his report to the United States government entitled Ecuador in 1881 which was later published as a special message of President Arthur to Congress.

This report proved to be a comprehensive description of Ecuador--its geography, climate, diseases, products, exports, minerals, population, wealth, race relations, habits, government, army, financial affairs, trade, Amazon River trade routes, Panama Canal, religious conditions and the clergy, education, Galápagos Islands, military affairs, and immigration. This mass of information was "derived principally from original sources and personal observation" and revealed Church as a first-rate investigator and expositor, whose aim was to "analyze Ecuador as a problem containing many elements typical of more than one South American country."

Church did not hesitate to describe the reality of Ecuadorian life, such as the oppression of the Indian:

> He still belongs to the estate upon which he works, held there by inexorable law which forces him to work out a debt once contracted with his employer. . . . The advance he receives he riots away, and the purchase money of his freedom, which he can never redeem with his wages of 10 cents per day, binds him for life. He is thrashed and knouted like a Russian serf, and today bunches of lashes may be seen hanging at the doorways of the shops of the "Christian" Quito which sells, for various prices, according to the size demanded for girls, women, boys or men.

The other classes also came in for condemnation: "the thriftless Indian habit of spending money before it is earned has impregnated all classes, and is one of the principal national faults."

The Civil War veteran also cast a professional look at the Ecuadorian army and found it wanting in almost every respect:

> The men of the permanent army are badly drilled; they nearly all stoop: not one of them is "well set up." Although well clothed, they wear their uniforms in a slovenly, careless manner; their caps are placed all kinds of ways upon their heads; their accountrements, their rifles, their buttons are unpolished. Tall men stand in the ranks beside the short ones, and they are all unassorted. They march and carry their arms without precision and regularity, and do not show that elasticity and spring of step which is the charm of good troops. All of this might be corrected, for the material is good and might be made into excellent fighting regiments.

> The minister of war tells me that 'the army is organized upon the Prussian system'. Be that as it may, a Prussian officer would not recognize it.

Church's orderly mind, accustomed to accumulating factual data on every problem under consideration, found the lack of governmental data distressing:

> It is an unsatisfactory work to try to get any accurate data from the Ecuadorian government. Its archives, if they ever existed, have been distributed around the country by revolution and theft, until they are now reduced to a few mule loads. The finance minister confessed to me that he had no means of supplying a table of exports and imports for the past ten years, much less the previous years.

On the national debt, Church drew up a very detailed statement and, after describing the underhanded machinations of the government in this field, concluded in a rather benign mood that "a country which produces governments entertaining such ideas of honor and probity is naturally a most interesting philosophical study."

On religion and on the clergy he has no such mild approach: "Ecuador is undoubtedly the most intensely Roman Catholic country in the world. Spain in the days of Charles V and Philip II was not more narrow and illiberal. The clergy have confessed and preached the nation into such a condition of fanaticism that there is no room for morals, Christian charity, or godliness." Yet his reaction to García Moreno the famous clerical dictator has elements of justice in it which one would not expect from a New England Protestant and his eloquent description has been too little known even to historians dedicated to this important figure in Ecuadorian history:

> García Moreno, in 1861, here appears prominently upon the scene, in some respects the most remarkable man that South America has produced: daring, fearless, determined, an iron will, a tireless physique, a patriot, honest and economical, a scholar of great accomplishments, a gentleman, a tyrant by nature, a relentless executioner when he deemed it necessary, a maker and breaker of laws, and, above all, as truly moral, devout, and religious a fanatic as ever knelt to plant the holy cross upon the soil of the New World. On the 18th July, 1873, he consecrated the entire republic "to the holy heart of Jesus".

In this theocratic state heretics could not even be buried:

> At length the death of a British minister brought the problem to a solution; they could not feed his corpse to condor and raven; and so on a bleak hill north of the city they built a wall around about one hundred feet square of Ecuador, called it the "Protestant Cemetery" and semifortified its crest to prevent the corpses being unearthed by a fanaticism which the teacher of the gospel of Christ had educated to a point he could not control.

Church gives much fact as well as interpretation. We are given a list of the ecclesiastical offices in the whole country, and are told exactly how much it cost for an Indian to be married or buried by a priest.

The picture Church gave was inevitably a somber portrait, but he was convinced that "at present the elements upon which to build a thriving nation are so buried in discord that they are difficult to discover. . . The energies of the upper class are feeble. There is no spirit of enterprise, nor faith enough in each other's honesty to combine to inaugurate and carry out public works. . . Half the population oppress the other half, and these race relations alone bring curses enough on the land; but when to these are added the fanatical intolerance with which the clergy have narrowed down the Ecuadorian brain to its present dimensions, one can understand why Ecuador is so little respected by other nations."

Whatever else one may conclude concerning Church's account of Ecuador in 1881, it is clear that he must have worked hard during his three months in Quito and that this officially printed account did not attempt to give the public in the United States a pretty or a comforting view of Ecuador.

On the completion of his work in Ecuador Church traveled to Chile where he completed another frank report of 222 pages, still in manuscript, on South American affairs. Finally he returned to the United States via the Straits of Magellan, Uruguay, Argentina, Brazil, and England.

Church thereafter made his home in London, from which he carried on his numerous projects. In 1888 he published there a detailed proposal for a railway in Venezuela 223 kilometers from Caracas to Valencia. As usual he had studied the available literature, especially Humboldt, and gave a brief history of Venezuela from independence to the time of Guzmán Blanco. He believed that the proposed railroad would be of great value in maintaining internal peace for 'it is a notable fact that the revolutions of Spanish American states have ceased, once systems of railways have been built, offering easy and rapid communication between the centre of government and outlying districts."

The Venezuelan project evidently did not find approval but in 1889 Church contracted to build a railroad in Argentina at a cost of one million pounds which he successfully completed in two years despite the Baring crisis. In 1895 he spent three months in Costa Rica on behalf of the foreign bondholders of that country and while there drew up an elaborate report to the Costa Rica Railway Company on the condition of their line.

Church now had more time for his geographical and historical studies, and he built up a respectable library on the exploration and history of the Americas. He had joined the Royal Geographical Society in 1872 and was an active member. He published a number of articles in its Geographical Journal, and his letters in the archive of the Society show that he was consulted regularly on questions pertaining to the history and geography of Latin America. He was elected to the Council of the Society in 1898, "the first and only Fellow of the Society not a British subject to be so elected," and in 1902 he was further honored by election as Vice-President of the Society. He became a member of other scientific societies, including the American Society of Civil Engineers, the Hakluyt Society, and the Royal Anthropological Institute of Great Britain and Ireland. He wrote the article on the Amazon for the Encyclopedia Brittanica, and planned a volume to be entitled "South America: an outline of its physical geography and commercial history." In 1898 at the Bristol meeting of the British Association for the Advancement of Science, as President of the Geographical Section, he read a widely-acclaimed paper on "Argentine geography and the Ancient Pampean Sea."

During this period Church evidently played a lively and respected role in those golden years of London society in the decade before World War I. His first wife having died many years before, in 1907 he married Anne Marion, widow of Frederic Chapman. He never forgot his first great enterprise, the Madeira-Mamoré Railroad. In 1904, at the time international tension was mounting in South America over the rubber regions of the Amazon, he published a substantial article urging Bolivia, Brazil, and Peru to define their boundaries so that the railroad might be built to open up that "area of South America which probably has no superior in fertility and varied natural resources." In this article he also gave a backward glance at the tangled history of his efforts to build a railroad, and told of his long conversations with Emperor Pedro II which resulted in Brazil throwing open to the world the navigation of the Amazon. At his death he left a large part of a work on the Indians of South America which was posthumously published in 1912 under the editorship of his "old-friend" Clements R. Markham, who described Church as "an eminent authority on South America" as did the obituary note in The Geographical Journal of the Royal Geographical Society which termed him "one of the foremost authorities on the history and geography of South America."

During his residence in London he apparently acquired the manuscript of the Primera Parte of the Arzáns history of Potosí, for the late Henry R. Wagner saw a manuscript history of Potosí in Church's collection and unsuccessfully tried to purchase it. The manuscript formed a part of the library of books and maps which Church owned at the time of his death on January 4, 1910. Church's will provided that most of his books and the Potosí manuscript be offered to Harvard University on condition that they remain a separate collection. If this condition was not met, as proved to be the case, the collection was to be offered to Brown University, which accepted the gift. Thus it was that the Primera Parte of the manuscript history of Potosí finally came to rest in Providence, a city with a long connection with Latin America.

This note on the life of this "North American Captain of Industry in Latin America" is not designed to be a full account of the travels and activities of this remarkable man, but to give some idea of the character and accomplishments of one who tried to make Bolivia and indeed all of Latin America better known to the world. It was his energy and his concern for the history of Bolivia which finally led to the presence in Brown University Library of the Potosí manuscript and to its publication by Brown University Press as a part of the university's bicentennial commemoration.

CHAPTER 15.

THE SOURCES USED BY BARTOLOME ARZANS DE ORSUA Y VELA FOR HIS HISTORY OF POTOSI

In 1933 I first saw a large manuscript history of the Villa Imperial de Potosí in the Biblioteca de Palacio in Madrid, which had just been opened up to students by the Spanish Republic. Written by a loyal Potosino in the eighteenth century, the work had waited two centuries for a publisher. It had to wait even longer, because it was so voluminous and because support for such projects is usually hard to find. Then Emilio Ravignani agreed to include it in a documentary series he directed in Argentina, but before this could be accomplished Juan Perón came to power and Dr. Ravignani was one of the many cultural figures abruptly dismissed by the dictator.

Finally Brown University decided to sponsor the work as a part of its bicentennial publications, for its library had a copy of the manuscript and Lawrence Wroth of the John Carter Brown Library understood the importance of the history of Potosí. With the invaluable assistance of Gunnar Mendoza, Director of the Biblioteca Nacional of Bolivia, we managed to prepare the work for issuance in three large volumes. The present article was based upon a larger study which formed a part of the introduction.

Jahrbuch für Geschichte von Staat, Wirtschaft und Gesellschaft Lateinamerikas, 2 (Cologne, 1965), 119-144. Reprinted by permission.

The Sources Used by Bartolomé Arzáns de Orsúa y Vela for his History of Potosí

1. General

Many historians have attempted to explain why they write, what their views on history are, and the nature of the materials used in their work. Bartolomé Arzáns de Orsúa y Vela follows this hallowed tradition, and provides his readers with an extraordinary amount of information on the sources from which he constructed, during the years 1700-1736, his own "Historia de la Villa Imperial de Potosí", which covers the history of his mining center in colonial Peru from the time of its discovery in 1545. Over 40 authors have already written on the "varios casos, grandezas y otras particularidades de este Villa", he explains, including 14 chroniclers of Peru, and he has consulted all of them besides "varias relaciones, noticias, archivos y otros papeles manuscritos que ha diligenciado mi curiosidad." In addition, as the reader will see for himself, Arzáns quotes sections from a vast array of printed books on the Indies, which range from the early 1553 "Chronica del Peru" by Pedro Cieza de León and such standard works as those by Diego Fernández, Bartolomé de Las Casas, the Inca Garcilaso de la Vega, Antonio de Herrera, Juan de Torquemada, and Antonio de Calancha down to publications that appeared as he was writing his work in the first third of the eighteenth century. The "Bibliography" in Tomo III of the forthcoming publication will be ample illustration of the fact that he must have had available in his own home a considerable personal library or have had access to ecclesiastical or private collections in Potosí. Some of the more enlightened citizens of the Villa Imperial probably did read widely, as even the limited information now at hand demonstrates, and despite various restrictive laws, it is likely that Potosinos could if they wished have the same kind of opportunity as has been described for other parts of the Spanish empire: "los colonos de América Española leyeron y gustaron en aquellas centurias de las obras de los ingenios más celebrados de todos los tiempos, en idénticas ediciones que en la península hispana y muchas veces en el propio idioma en que los autores volcaron sus inquietudes". Though sometimes one gets the impression that Arzáns must be endeavoring to arouse his reader's wonder by the very multiplicity of references to learning old and new, sacred and profane, no one can even dip casually into the "Historia" without concluding that its author had a large reservoir of information collected from many sources.

Arzáns was able to take from these many writings "lo cierto y averiguado", but he views his task as a formidable one: "sacar a luz el compendio historial de la Villa Imperial de Potosí, sus incomparables riquezas, sus guerras civiles y casos memorables". The wealth of material he has been able to consult comforts him somewhat as he recognizes his own deficiencies and as he contemplates the immensity and complexity of the Herculean enterprise he has undertaken as a loyal son of the Villa Imperial. Even so he stands aghast: "¿Que pluma, que imaginación, que entendimiento, que sutileza podrá explicar cumplidamente la gran riqueza que se ha sacado y se saca hoy del Cerro de Potosí; la máquina de milliones de plata que ha dado de quintos a sus católicos monarcas; las grandezas de su nombrada Villa; la caridad y liberalidad de sus moradores; la fe y veneración que tienen al culto divino; y asimismo los piadosos castigos (pues siempre lo son) de la mano de Dios que ha experimentado por sus culpas, ocasionados, si más de la riqueza de sus habitadores y sobra de corporales bienes, también efectos del dominio riguroso de sus estrellas a que el libre albedrío pudieran oponerse?"

As the reader of the "Historia" will soon discover, Arzáns does not limit himself to written documents; he also weaves into his account many of his own personal experiences and many examples of oral tradition which has long been a characteristic element in the annals of Potosí.

The historian who confronts Potosí today has an even greater accumulation of documentation available than Arzáns, and the editors have provided some indications of this in their notes to the text and in the Apéndice in Tomo III on "Fuentes inéditas para la historia de Potosí". More manuscripts will surely turn up and future investigators will not only be almost overwhelmed by the sheer quantity of raw material awaiting their study, but it is also quite possible that they will be able to extract more meaning from the documents than previous historians, just as the tailings that remained after the early, crude exploitation of Potosí later yielded a rich harvest due to improved methods. New insights, too, may be developed, as knowledge of Potosí and its place in the history of the world becomes better known in somewhat the same way that new minerals are being extracted which were not known to or valued by colonial miners. Even now, however, the documentation available for the study of the history of the Villa Imperial de Potosí is as impressive in size and significance as the enormous amounts of silver that the Cerro has yielded since 1545.

2. Captain Pedro Méndez

Though Arzáns does not state exactly when Captain Méndez reached Potosí, it is clear that he was the first of the historians to reach the Villa Imperial. He was a grandson of that attractive Renaissance figure, a follower of Erasmus, Diego Méndez, and "criado de don Cristóbal Colón", and was born on the island of Española. In Arzáns' leisurely style we learn of Diego's troubles with Governor Nicolás de Ovando and that he had had a natural son named Juan by doña Ana de Quindos before leaving Spain. This son became rich and respected in Española, had two sons in marriage, and the chronicler Pedro Méndez was one of them.

Spaniards and their descendants moved rapidly and ceaselessly around the empire--at least in those early days of explosive conquest--and we next find Pedro Méndez in Mexico where he saw a document about Potosí sent from Lima which whetted his curiosity, for it included a sketch of Potosí and told of the square-shaped cloud that was supposed to hover directly above the Cerro whenever Potosí was in full production. This was perhaps in the year 1558 when the cloud had moved away from the Cerro, it was said, and silver production fell calamitously for 18 months, and the outraged Potosinos "clamaban al cielo, representábanle las necesidades que padecerían, suspiraban y hacían otros extremos pidiendo plata". Méndez was skeptical of this phenomenon and "pasó muy mozo" to Potosí, principally to see the cloud. He was disappointed: "No me pareció como lo había visto pintado, pues era más un celaje (que acaso se veía algunas tardes) que nube como se decía que ordinariamente coronaba el Cerro". Arzáns quotes Méndez on the high prices prevailing in Potosí in 1565, and he witnessed the uprising of the Potosí merchants in 1569 against the corregidor called "General Avendaño". If we estimate that Méndez was 15 years old on arrival at

Potosí about 1560, he was approximately 77 years of age in 1622 when the civil war between the Vicuñas and Vascongados began, in which Arzáns says he actively participated against the vascongados. And Arzáns states that he died in 1631, so that he had presumably reached the ripe old age of 86 years. This is not so surprising as it may seem for, despite the rigors of the Andean location of Potosí at about 14,000 feet above sea level or higher than Mont Blanc, the "king of the Alps", some Potosinos enjoyed lengthy life spans like those ancients described in the Bible. Luis Capoche mentions a miner 120 years of age who was able to climb to the top of the mountain of silver. It will be remembered that Arzáns' own wife died "at over 80 years of age", and the legal records of Potosí contain a number of references to miners who had long resisted the cold, the altitude, and the harsh living conditions to be found in the Villa Imperial.

The next most ancient historian, Antonio de Acosta, knew Méndez well, since they were contemporaries in Potosí for half a century, and describes him as of "gallarda disposición, buena estatura, de briosos movemientos, afable, generoso, bien criado, de bien engrandecidos pensamientos, en todas buenas partes extremado, de grandes facecias, admirable en discreción natural, de un ingenio cabal, vivo y levantado y gran hombre de a caballo por extremo". Méndez fought as a captain in various battles against the Indians on the Tomina frontier and later had the misfortune to incur the enmity of three persons who wrote falsehoods about him to the viceroy. Moreover, "un cierto escritor de los sucesos de Potosí" also wrote to the viceroy "echando juicios o maquinando razones de estado forjadas de su malicia propia". The historian was taken in 1627 to Lima as a prisoner, where his fate was an unhappy one. "No le fueron admitidos sus descargos ni prueba de que era mentira cuanto la imputaban, ni bastaron los ruegos de toda la Villa para que se mirase y atendiese a su inocencia, porque los cargos eran terribles, pues habían informado a su excelencia diciendo haber escrito contra su persona muchas indecencias y notas de su gobierno y lo mismo contra la real audiencia de La Plata, y que en las guerras de las vicuñas había sido contra las reales justicias capitaneando escuadrones, y que en dichas guerras se había hecho cronista, escribiendo y aprobando lo malo por bueno en sus escritos, alabando los vicios de los malos y vituperando las virtudes de los buenos".

The "Historia de Potosí" of Captain Méndez, which covered the period 1545-1626, was included among his effects at the time he was seized in Potosí. It was examined by persons "doctas y religiosas, y en toda ella no hallaron ninguna cosa impura sino solamente la verdad con que escribía los memorables sucesos de Potosí". Two copies were quickly made, and Méndez took the original with him when he was carried off a prisoner to Lima. There he seems to have been acquitted in general, but he was not allowed to return to Potosí as he requested. Though importuned to publish his work, he never did so and died in Lima four years later in 1631.

Arzáns held Méndez and his history in high esteem. He called him a "gran investigador de las grandezas de Potosí", frequently quoted the work, and lets the reader know what a conscientious truth-seeking historian he himself is by his comment on the work of Méndez: "Ella es, sobre lo muy elocuente y entretenida, muy verídica porque he comprobado muchas de sus claúsulas con archivos, libros y privilegios tan escondidos que no se le puede sospechar de cosa en contrario de lo sucedido que diga ni argüir de importuna". Méndez included in his "Historia" information on prices of daggers, hats, and clothes which Arzáns feels compelled to explain and half-apologize for: "Menudencia parece ésta para historia tan grave; pero si la historia es maestra de la vida humana, hasta estas poquedades ha de sufrir para que se vea a lo que llega la codicia de los mercaderes". Méndez has another side, too, doubtless more pleasing to the literary Arzáns, for in telling of the tumults in 1570 Arzáns says "lo celebra con la agudeza de sus dichos y otros chistes en menosprecio de aquellos capitanes y soldados del campo".

All the Villa was sorry that the "Historia de Potosí" of the brave Captain Méndez was never published, and no one more than the historian Arzáns who narrates with satisfaction the unpleasant and untimely deaths of all three of the enemies of Méndez, and who explains his unusually lengthy account of his life in this way: "Heme detenido y me detendré algo más en dar noticia de este ilustre cronista, que lo deseaba y que viniera la ocasión a las manos de declarar a los curiosos que deseaban saber quién es este capitán Méndez tan citado, quién es este autor tan repetido, para pagarle con esta memoria las muchas noticias que me ha dado".

Was Captain Méndez the first, at least chronologically, of all the figments of the imagination of our historian? As Gunnar Mendoza has stated:

> La más antigua de las crónicas potosinas en que Arzáns dice apoyarse es obviamente la del capitán Pedro Méndez que ya actuaba en Potosí en 1564. Esto querría decir que Méndez fue actor o testigo directo de cuanto relata desde ese año (por lo menos) hasta la guerra de vicuñas y vascongados en que también participó. Siendo así ¿cómo pudo incurrir en inexactitudes tan graves como las que acusa la "Historia" sobre épocas y nombres de gobernadores de Potosí que pasaron bajo su vista? En estos capítulos la "Historia" no sólo presenta en el gobierno de Potosí a personas que no lo tuvieron realmente (por lo menos en las circunstancias y tiempos que se dice), sino que no da cuenta de otros que tuvieron realmente a su cargo dicho gobierno y protagonizaron sucesos importantes.

Méndez might have fallen into these errors through sheer inability to remember all the details of a complicated history over a time span of more than half a century, for he is presented to us principally as a man of action rather than as a cloistered scholar. Or was Captain Méndez's "Historia de Potosí" the first of a long series of inventions by Arzáns, who was prepared to conjure up before the astonished gaze of his readers a galaxy of historians, and whose imagination was fertile enough to compose a series of chronicles and even provide their reputed authors with exciting biographies? If so, Arzáns performed a deed of double daring, and also cleverly protected himself against charges of inaccuracy, if later scholars such as Dr. Mendoza discovered him in a variety of large and small errors.

3. Don Antonio de Acosta

It is not surprising to learn that the author most frequently quoted by Arzáns was Don Antonio de Acosta "un noble lusitano que escribía en su idioma", because Portuguese miners, merchants, ecclesiastics, officials, and visitors were to be found in Potosí--as in many other parts of the Spanish empire--from the earliest days. They not only engaged profitably in many enterprises there, but also wrote careful descriptions of what they saw in the New World. . . .

Arzáns often refers to Acosta as a "testigo de vista", and his experience in Potosí was even longer than that of Captain Méndez, but says little more about Acosta, except that he was "portugués de nación". We are told that he had been in the Villa Imperial only four days when the sad news of the death of King Sebastian in Africa reached him. This had occurred on August 4, 1578, so he probably arrived at Potosí some time in 1579. As a loyal Portuguese, he inserted in his history "una lastimosa exclamación declarando las virtudes, sumo valor y miserable ruina deste desgraciado rey; y callando su muerte concluye con sólo decir que de envidia al fiero Marte consiguió el no tener opositor en el mundo, pero que a su tiempo volvería". The last citation to Acosta's work comes in referring to silver production for Acosta--like most authors who wrote of Potosí--could not resist the temptation to calculate how much silver the great Cerro had produced. Acosta apparently consulted the financial records kept by the royal officials and arrived at an estimate of 3,020 millions of pesos extracted during the period 1545-1657, and even this immense sum did not include the silver mined illegally and not included in the official registry. If Acosta were 20 years of age on reaching Potosí in 1579, he was a patriarch of 97 in 1657 at the time he made this estimate.

When or why the "noble portugués" began his "Historia de Potosí" Arzáns never tells us, but he does assure us that the work was printed in the Portuguese language in Lisbon, though he does not give the date, after which he says the volume was translated into Spanish by the Andalusian don Juan Pasquier who died before completing his task, which was to have included bringing Acosta's "Historia" up to date.

Arzáns describes the work in his own Prólogo as being "harto limitado", being largely concentrated on the three "destrucciones" of Potosí: "el derramamiento de sangre en aquellas memorables guerras de los vicuñas, la inundación de la laguna de Caricari y la rebaja en la moneda que hizo el presidente don Francisco de Nestares Marín". Despite this limitation, Arzáns considers the Portuguese a "verdadero historiador", qualifies his work as a "muy acreditada y agradable Historia", and from his steady dependence on its material and his respectful attitude toward Acosta clearly believes him to be a discreet and trustworthy source. Arzáns does not follow even Acosta blindly, however, for he does not accept a particular date as given by the Portuguese historian because he himself had discovered, "buscando ciertos papeles", the correct date.

We learn, too, something of Arzáns' views on history from his discussion of his sources. A poet such as Juan Sobrino may compose his story in a different way from other historians, "pues él como poeta pudo y quiso contar o cantar la cosa no como fue sino como debía ser", but Captain Méndez and Acosta wrote their history "no como debía ser sino como fue, sin añadir ni quitar a la verdad cosa alguna". And then Arzáns concludes his little homily on the nature of history with one of those classical flourishes he was so fond of making: "Y esto no es cosa nueva, que a fe que no fue tan piadoso Eneas como Virgilio lo pinta, ni tan prudente Ulises como le escribe Homero".

Acosta weaves many different kinds of material into his story. He speculates on how Potosí received its name, remarks upon the large fortunes gained by tavern keepers, gives details on the discovery of certain large precious stones, and describes the terrible hurricanes that occasionally afflicted the town in such a vivid way that one can hear the wind whistle as it sweeps through the narrow and crooked streets, and see the market goods being sold in the plaza by Indian women swirled away in the air by the violence of the wind. Acosta records the uncovering of a strange skeleton during the excavations for the Dominican church which had teeth as large as doves' eggs, and calculates that so much silver had been extracted it would rise to the same height as the Cerro if all piled up together. He gives meticulous and exuberant detail on the numerous and costly fiestas that Potosinos organized at every possible opportunity, and Arzáns often refers the reader to Acosta for more information.

Because Acosta's experience goes so far back into the early years of Potosí, his description of the first feverish days of the mining center is especially valuable. The Spaniards hurriedly threw up a town, "pues (como dice Acosta) cada cual hizo su casa con tante prisa que careciendo de la forma hubieron de quedar sin calles por donde pasar; y así en espacio de 18 meses se hicieron más de 2,500 casas para más de 14,000 personas que entre españoles e indios había". Acosta also appears to have subscribed to the same theory as Arzáns that a history should be full of spicy stories; he proudly relates how the andaluz Gaspar Martínez resisted the temptations of a lewd woman and then became one of the most pious friars in that pious Villa Imperial, how some Potosinos foolishly fought each other naked from the waist up on a bitter winter day. As Arzáns tells this incident, basing his account on Acosta, these fighters sallied forth to the fray "unos y otros desnudos de la cinta arriba con espadas y rodelas, que entonces aún era sobrante el frío para matarlos, y es prueba bastante de la locura de aquellos hombres ponerse a pelear desnudos. Pero ellos experimentaron que lo que no hizo el frío hicieron los aceros, pues habiendo peleado todos valerosamente (si hay valor donde sobra la locura) más de dos horas quedaron muertos 13 hombres de una y otra parte." As an example of the bloody gusto with which such encounters are told in Arzáns' "Historia," let this example stand for the scores of similar battles imbedded in his work. "Fue muy notable en esta batalla la fortaleza del brazo de Diego Tamayo, el cual tiró a su contrario Luis de Merlo una fiera estocada, y fue tan poderosa que atropellándole la rodela entró por las entrañas, y pasándole el cuerpo salió la punta más de una cuarta a tiempo que Pedro de Melim defendiéndose de su contrario llegó de espaldas a juntarse con las de Merlo, que no se las hizo buenas, y como estaba desnudo como todos se le metió aquella punta por los riñones, y así cayeron muertos entrambos predidos en la espada de Tamayo."

One may speculate, too, on the possibility that Arzáns was partial to Captain Méndez and the Portuguese Acosta because they both included popular sayings in their histories, such as this cantina that originated in Potosí:

> Si Potosí se os acaba,
> acudid luego a Andacava;
> si os faltare Potosí
> ahí tenéis a Tollosí;
> si Potosí se acabare
> comenzará Carecare.

Acosta's piety and interest in the city's religious life is strong; he reflects faithfully the spirit of his age which has been termed "un siglo piadoso." He gives numerous accounts of miracles, demons, and catastrophes visited upon the town for the sins of its inhabitants, and examples of great charity and also of the lack of it. Acosta personally knew one Potosino so holy that after his death he was venerated as a saint; twenty years after burial in 1625 his body,

Acosta assures us as an observer when the tomb was opened: "estaba entero y tratable, despidiendo de sí una fragrancia admirable; efectos de la gloria que gozaba y goza su alma."

Arzáns follows Acosta's practice of not disclosing the names of ecclesiastics in certain circumstances which might reflect dishonor on them, and provides a number of edifying religious stories, of which the following is a typical example:

> Tiene esta Imperial Villa otro tesoro más apreciable que el de sus minas, el cual es una milagrosa imagen de Cristo crucificado que se venera en la iglesia de San Francisco, la cual sin saber quién fue su artífice, de dónde vino ni quién la trajo, fue hallado dentro de un cajón de cedro a las puertas de dicha iglesia, cuyas maravillas, favoreciendo a los vecinos y moradores de esta Villa y en particular a los indios, escribiré en otra parte.

Acosta naturally pays considerable attention to his fellow Portuguese, and provides much information on their participation in the affairs of the Villa Imperial: how they fought with the criollos against the vascongados, how a Portuguese doctor lived there, and how splendid a corregidor was General Pereyra and how rich was Antonio Alonso de la Rocha Meneses. It is easy to see that Acosta always maintained his pride as a Portuguese and at the same time was a loyal son of Potosí who gloried in its grandeur.

But did this "noble portugués" actually live in Potosí and, if so, was he really the author of a history that was printed in Lisbon? No copy of Acosta's "Historia de Potosí" has yet been located, despite prolonged efforts and much skilled searching by my bibliographical friends in Portugal, and so complete is the silence on Acosta of the standard bibliographies that the question must be asked whether his detailed account of the Villa Imperial ever existed. His name does not appear on any list of foreigners in Potosí that has come to light thus far, and no one else has even mentioned the work. Arzáns, however, cites him so confidently and so frequently that it almost seems likely that Acosta actually prepared a volume which was either never printed or issued in such a limited edition that no copy has survived to the twentieth century. Lacking that single copy, in either manuscript or printed form, we have Arzáns' work as our only source of information on Acosta's history. One cannot wholly dismiss the possibility that Arzáns may have perpetrated a huge hoax on his fellow historians by creating Acosta and the printed work in Portuguese completely out of his own creative imagination.

If in truth Arzáns is the real author of the material he describes so carefully as coming from the pen of Acosta and numerous other historians, he must have long planned the deception. For at the time he was completing the "Anales", in 1702 at the age of 25, he lists Acosta and many of his principal sources for the "Historia" in such a way that he must have had access to all those writings or had already formed in his mind his grand scheme and exactly how he proposed to manufacture his sources for the mystification of his readers.

4. The Poet Juan Sobrino

Arzáns does not list Sobrino in the Prólogo as one of his principal sources, but it appears that the poet was one of his favorite authors. Another matter of interest is that none of the four historians mentioned in the Prólogo--Acosta, Dueñas, Méndez, and Pasquier--have yet had their names discovered in contemporary documents, whereas an "alferez Juan Sobrino" appears several times in the documents on the civil war that erupted in 1622 between the vicuñas and the vascongados. He figures as one of the minor leaders of the vicuñas, and in 1623 was charged with being one of the band that had broken into the house of the corregidor, don Felipe Manrique, killed a half dozen men and wounded a number of others, and then set fire to the house of the king's appointee before escaping unscathed.

Arzáns states that the "historiador poeta" participated actively in the wars, wrote some of the events of this terrible episode in the history of the Villa Imperial, but had completed only five libros at the time of his death in 1649.

Sobrino left unfinished his composition "en que iba escribiendo en octavas los memorables sucesos de Potosí". The composition was left "en borradores" to his son Marcos "el cual también ejercitó la poética ciencia y escribió en adelante algunos sucesos particulares, aunque anduvo omiso en sacar en limpio lo que su padre trabajó con tanta curiosidad." Arzáns cites the poem fairly frequently, always refers to it as an "obra elegante", and evidently had a soft spot in his heart for this fighter who was also a man of letters. He always takes Sobrino seriously, quotes lines from his verses--"salieron una noche, en la cual alumbrándoles la luna (como dice el poeta Juan Sobrino en una de sus octavas que comienza diciendo 'La luna llena se mostraba a Géldrez')" --and mentions that he also wrote a theatrical piece entitled "Prosperidad y ruina de los ingas del Perú" which was shown in 1641 as a part of one of the innumerable fiestas the Potosinos indulged in. After three days of bull-fighting, "hízose una rica y vistosa máscara de caballeros y otra en competencia los famosos mineros; representáronse cuatro comedias, siendo la última de ellas nueva y muy digna de representarse en los mejores teatros del mundo". This was, of course, the creation of "nuestro poeta historiador", and Arzáns gives a minute description of its contents before concluding: "Fue muy aplaudido esta comedia tanto por lo nuevo de ella cuanto por los verdaderos e inauditos sucesos que en ella se representaron. Para los indios fue de mucho sentimiento levantando grandes alaridos conforme se declaraban".

Though it is far from certain that the "alferez Juan Sobrino" was the poet who composed the elegant octavas, it need not surprise us that the poetry was written in Potosí even in the tumultuous period of bitter fighting between the vicuñas and vascongados. Diego Mexía recalls with pleasure in his "Primera parte del parnaso antártico de obras amatorias" (Sevilla, 1608) the happy though poverty-stricken years in the early part of the seventeenth century that he spent "en esta imperial villa con mi familia, como en seguro porto, esperando pasase el rigor deste airado invierno, y donde con quietud he gozado de los bienes del entendimiento, sobre quien no tiene la fortuna dominio ni imperio alguno. He desenvuelto muchos autores latinos, y he frecuentado los umbrales del templo de las sagradas musas". The poet Duarte Fernández, Portuguese in origin but born in Sevilla, went from Lima to Potosí at about the same time. But, according to Marcelino Menéndez y Pelayo,

> quien verdaderamente enriqueció aquel cerro con venas de poesía más previosas que la plata de sus entrañas, fué el sevillano Luis de Ribera, uno de tantos excelentes y olvidados ingenios de nuestro siglo de oro, el cual el 1 de marzo de 1612 firmaba en Potosí la dedicatoria de sus "Sagradas Poesías" a su hermana doña Constanza María de Ribera--'libro precioso y de lo mejor que se

ha escrito en su linea' dice con razón D. Bartolomé J. Gallardo. Ribera es castizo y elegante poeta; su dicción y estilo saben más al siglo XVI que al XVII; sus versos tienen el sabor dulce y suave de los del M. León y la lozanía de los de Herrera y demás de la escuela sevillana. El gusto del autor es muy severo y clásico; nada de oropel ni argentería: oro macizo.

Thus the poet Juan Sobrino, if in truth he lived in those turbulent years of the early decades of the seventeenth century, inherited a relatively rich literary tradition even in the Villa Imperial.

5. Bartolomé de Dueñas

Arzáns does not devote much space or attention to Dueñas, though he cites him frequently and includes him among the principal sources listed in the Prólogo, where he is called a "peruano" though in a previous writing, the "Anales", he is described as "castellano viejo". Dueñas was serving as secretary to General Velarde in 1651 when President Francisco Nestares Marín imprisoned him because he had written to the president's patron in Spain--don Diego Arce Reinoso--informing on all of the harm done by Nestares Marín in Potosí. The president was a testy and powerful official who not only imprisoned Dueñas but also embargoed all his goods including his historical writings. The reprimand Nestares Marín received from his patron did not cause him to alter his imperious way; in fact, he became even more dogmatic. "Por esto ni se acabó de perfeccionar ni se trató de darlos a la imprenta, que cierto se perdió una obra elegante según los borradores o traslado de ellos que tuve en mi poder, de donde saqué lo más conveniente para poner en esta Historia". Dueñas was finally enabled to escape to Quito with the help of his former employer General Velarde and in this way passes out of the picture and is never heard of again in the "Historia".

6. Juan Pasquier

Another shadowy figure among the gallery of Potosí historians was don Juan Pasquier who, as mentioned above, is described by Arzáns as an "andaluz" who translated Antonio de Acosta's history in Portuguese into Spanish and added other material concerning events that had occurred during his own lifetime. This is puzzling, because Acosta is quoted by Arzáns as writing at least as late as 1657, and Pasquier suddenly passes off the scene in 1658 after completing chapter 30 of book II "de su famosa historia, y aunque comenzó este autor el libro III, estorbó la muerte su prosecución, que le sobrevino de un corrimiento en el costado, conque quedó imperfecta su obra". Arzáns also tells us that Pasquier fought alongside his Peruvian-born son in 1648, and it appears that he was gently bred as he deplores the bad manners and deeds of some of the Spaniards who arrived in Potosí to make their fortunes in any way they could.

Arzáns considers that Pasquier wrote with great "elegancia", and uses his version for one of the most swashbuckling stories in the "Historia". This was the account of the two beautiful and noble doncellas, Doña Ana and Doña Eustaquia, who assumed male clothing and roamed the streets of Potosí at night bravely fighting all comers with resounding success. Arzáns apparently realizes that this tale might require some special corroboration, and before beginning the narrative he remarks that not only was Pasquier a "testigo ocular" of the dashing and in truth almost unbelievably doughty deeds of Doña Ana and Doña Eustaquia, but adds that he has also learned of their exploits from "tres venerables ancianos que hoy viven y las conocieron de vista y comunicación".

At the end they are discovered and decide to enter a convent but Doña Ana died before this, by falling from a horse during a bull fight in Lima, and Doña Eustaquia died soon after by heart-break. Arzáns learned these details by way of their Negro servant, who told don Diego Melgarejo who in turn informed our historian. Arzáns almost "doth protest too much", for he still seems anxious to assure the reader that all this really happened. So he caps his tale with the assurance that he had seen paintings of the two female paragons in the village of Chayanta, thanks to one Juan de Itulaín who knew them well and in fact had painted them.

Arzáns usually refers to Pasquier as "autor más moderno" though he certainly was not much more "moderno" than Acosta or the other principal sources, if the figures given above are correct. Arzáns states that as a small boy he knew Pasquier's younger son Pedro who was saved miraculously while swimming. After his body had been under water for half an hour he was pulled out and "(¡cosa maravillosa!) lo hallaron y sacaron vivo sin lesión ninguna". Pasquier reports on an even more remarkable example of the power of the "santa imagen de Jerusalén". The story is worth repeating in all its detail so that the reader can appreciate the style of the author in narrating the miraculous tales that are to be found in many chapters of Arzáns' work.

> En unos ranchos que estaban abajo de aquel donde era venerada esta santa imagen (que después se llamó de Jerusalén) vivía Juan Mamani, indio ladino, muy devoto de esta soberana Señora; el cual habiendo reñido con otros indios y pasando el disgusto muy adelante tuvieron modo para llevarlo al Arenal (que dista de allí un cuarto de legua) adonde aquellos crueles enemigos derribándolo en el suelo, lo degollaron dividiéndole la cabeza del cuerpo. Trajéronlo así a su rancho, y viéndolo su mujer e hijos, clamaron a la madre de Dios de Jerusalén (de quien todos eran muy devotos) diciéndoles que cómo habia permitido aquella desgracia, siendo su marido quien le festejaba con toda su pobreza. Esto sucedió a deshora de la noche, y no cesando de clamar a la Virgen su mujer e hijos fueron a su capilla y a sus puertas decían llorando mil ternezas, pidiendo por la vida del difunto.
>
> Fueron tales las veras con que lo hicieron que aun antes de acabar su oración fueron sabedores de cómo Juan Mamani estaba en el rancho vivo y sano. Fueron allá, adonde mucha gente estaba admirando el prodigio, y dando gracias a Dios y a su Santísima Madre le besaban la señal de la herida, porque el buen indio decía que la madre de Dios de la capilla le había pegado la cabeza. En esto era ya de día, y así acudieron multitud de españoles e indios a la noticia: todos lo miraban y tocaban, besándole una señal que para testimonio del milagro la había quedado en el círculo del cuello, delgada como una hebra de seda nácar. Todos lloraban de alegría viendo lo que merecía un pobre indio devoto de la madre de Dios a quien daban las debidas gracias por tal beneficio. El favorecido Juan Mamani con su mujer e hijos se mostraron muy agradecidos, pues sirvieron a esta soberana Señora con mayores veras hasta el fin de sus días.

Beyond including in his translation and amplification of Acosta numerous examples of a wonder-working providence, which Arzáns notes with awe and unction, it does not appear that Pasquier had any special contribution to make. Arzáns always refers to him favorably, and seems to be fond of him since he quotes him as late as 1734, but his citations to Pasquier's work are frequently only one of several references to the same event. Why Pasquier felt it necessary to translate Acosta's work from Portuguese into Spanish we are never told.

7. Las Guerras Civiles

Arzáns devotes more space to recounting the disastrous wars between the vicuñas and vascongados than to any other event in the "Historia", for almost all of Libro VII concerns this bitter and bloody conflict that afflicted Potosí from 1622 to 1625. The cruelties inflicted on each other by these rival bands exceeded those of Rome, France, and Granada, we are assured, for it was war to the death: "no había padres para hijos ni hijos para padres, no había parentesco ni amistad, todo fue crueldad, falta de razón, de ley, de caridad y de temor de Dios y de la justicia real". It is a story full of horrifying details, frequent examples of sadism, and some heroism. One Bolivian historian has wisely explained the universal significance of the wars in this way:

> Bien considerada esta lucha intestina tiene la significación de todo un trance crítico de la Colonia en el Alto Perú, a través del cual puédense palpar en su entraña temas fundamentales y característicos de aquella etapa decisiva en nuestra historia, y, aun más, temas que acaso superviven hoy.
>
> La localización del conflicto en un pueblo como Potosí; el esquema distributivo de los bandos según el principio regional tan propio del genio íbero y tan presente en la empresa indiana desde los inicios así como en la evolución posterior de nuestro pueblo; la participación activa de los grupos sociales coetáneos típicos: de raza--españoles, criollos, mestizos, indios, negros, extranjeros--, de trabajo--mineros, agricultores, mercaderes, artesanos, eclesiásticos, magistrados, militares, intelectuales, aventureros--,de casta--burócratas, hacendados, mitayos, esclavos, soldados--; ciertos sugestivos rasgos de insurgencia juvenil; la conmoción que suscita en toda la estructura gubernativa, del virrey para abajo; su trascendencia intelectual; su contenido patético: bastarían estos elementso para sugerir la riqueza históricamente reveladora del episodio.
>
> Potosí hace entonces las veces de un formidable centrifugador donde a impulsos del violento giro bélico queda documentalmente condensada la substancia del sistema colonial indiano.

Wars attract historians, and the guerras civiles were no exception. Arzáns states that eight printed works were available as well as five manuscript histories from which he was able to extract "lo más conveniente y menos escandaloso de estas guerras para la brevedad y decencia de esta "Historia" adonde se verá la verdad de todo." Besides these formal histories, Arzáns quotes verbatim from a number of letters and other documentary sources, especially the statements of various leaders who justified and explained their actions, and gives the reader the impression that as he writes he sits surrounded by all kinds of evidence on these most calamitous years in the history of the Villa Imperial. The events are related in tremendous detail, the exact hour of events being given frequently, and at the height of the conflict in February, 1624, a day by day record is provided. At the end of each year a statistical report on the damage is rendered, and at the end of 1624 Arzáns includes a summary for the three years 1622-1624: "son los que murieron españoles de varias naciones y peruanos 3,332, y los mestizos, indios, mulatos y negros 2,435. Asimismo los que perecieron en los caminos y pueblos del contorno de esta Villa fueron por todos 685. Los heridos en general que escaparon con vida 3,728. Los robos en esta Villa y sus contornos 2,172, y las casas que se abrasaron en rigor de las llamas en los dichos tres años pasaron de 200."

The flow of blood stopped from time to time even in these years, because Potosinos could not live without fiestas. In 1622 they interrupted their preparations for war long enough to commemorate the death of Philip III, and on June 20, 1624, they began weeks of costly celebrations to honor the canonization of San Ignacio de Loyola. No expense was spared and Arzáns recounts with delight the grandiosity of it all, quoting a "Relación" printed in Sevilla. For 14 days there were masses and sermons, with 40 quintales of white wax used, after which the streets of Potosí were gloriously decorated and on every hand one saw remarkable tableaux which Arzáns describes. At one point, for example, one saw

> Apolo con su cítara en las manos y las nueve musas sentadas en ricas sillas. Todas estas hermosas ninfas estaban con instrumentos músicos en las manos, y en unas tarjas que a sus pies estaban iban escritos sus nombres con letras de oro, y en versos se declaraban los regocijos en que cada una preside. Sus nombres eran Terpsícore, Polimnia, Euterpe, Urania, Calíope, Clío, Malpómene, Talía y Erato. Dejo de especificar la gran hermosura de sus rostros, la riqueza y variedad de sus vestidos y la multitud de preciosísimas piedras y perlas con que se veían adornadas sus cabezas, cuellos y manos.

The pious Potosinos marched up and down in procession along these richly decorated streets for a couple of weeks, rested up for a couple of days, and then went on for another 14 days of regocijos de la plaza, which included toros, comedias, saraos, sortija, máscaras, justas y torneos.

Whether all this expense of pesos and energy was possible for a community that had waged fratricidal war for two years remains to be seen after more archival investigation, and it may turn out that Arzáns introduced this period of gayety and peace as a literary device to give his readers some relief from the terrible story he had been telling.

The truce ended, a priest is killed, as well as a child, and the war is on again. But the conclusion of the bloody conflict is in sight. At last the fighting ceased in 1625 after prolonged and intricate diplomatic negotiations, peace was agreed upon by the contending parties in the Franciscan church, and was sealed--as in the case of European wars--by a wedding: "se determinó que doña Eufemia Castillo, hija única (y singular en hermosura) de don Francisco Castillo [captain of the vicuñas], se le diese por esposa (con más 600,000 pesos de dote) a Pedro de Oyanume, hijo del capitán Francisco de Oyanume [chief of the vascongados], que así se hizo con demostraciones de alegría en toda la Villa".

How well does Arzáns use the great variety of sources he so punctiliously lists? We do not know, as not a one of the histories he lists is now known to exist or even to have ever existed. Dr. Mendoza has demonstrated, in the careful notes to the text of Libro VII in the "Historia", that Arzáns has mixed up and altered names of actors in the drama in the same imaginative way as in other sections of his work. He does not favor one side over the other, thus preserving the objectivity of the true historian. Arzáns criticizes one of his sources, the Augustinian Juan de Medina, because he supported the vascongados, being one himself though he attempted to hide this fact. We are told that Medina was not welcomed by his brother friars in Potosí because of the "nota de contrario y apasionado en sus escritos" and that he had to complete his 580 fojas work in Chuquisaca.

The other historians cited are the well-known Acosta, Dueñas, and Méndez; two works in verse, by Pedro de Guilléstegui and Juan Sobrino, with copious quotations from the latter; two by friars, the Dominican Francisco Jaramillo and the Franciscan Marcos de Guadalajara y Javier; Dr. José Velázquez of the Colegio de San Cristóbal in La Plata; and a work by a priest whose name in unknown. Not one of these works upon which Arzáns states that he is basing his story is known today, a fact which helps to explain Mendoza's characterization of the bibliography on the guerras civiles as "abigarrada, paradójica, llena de peripecias y se diría que presidida por un hado fatal de frustración."

The only aspect of the civil wars which Arzáns analyzes as a historian is that problem posed by every war--who or what caused it? He rejects the accusation of some that the vascongados were responsible, and holds that "todos hicieron disparates iguales, y que así los de una parte como de la otra estuvieron muy acordados y concertados años atrás para hacer unos mismos desatinos". He believes that the sins of the Potosinos and the stars had some influence, and quotes Captain Pedro Méndez approvingly when he stated: "Era cosa de notar ver venir a Potosí hombres humildes y ángeles en su condición, y la plata los ensoberbecía y tornaba en demonios según sus atrocidades". Historians today may emphasize the economic, political, familial and provincial reasons for the conflict, but there was always present the widespread and overwhelming desire for wealth--a desire which was increased to explosive proportions by the feverish atmosphere of Potosí. The historian of Chile, the Jesuit Alonso de Ovalle, Arzáns refers to approvingly for Ovalle considers that the Cerro itself has a magic effect on the Potosinos: "los que viven en la Villa de Potosí y se crían junto a aquel prodigioso Cerro de la plata tienen unos ánimos tan intrépidos y levantados, como se ha experimentado en las inquietudes y revoluciones que allí ha habido". Of all the works on the civil wars, printed and in manuscript, cited by Arzáns, this book by Ovalle is the only one known today.

Ovalle's view on the reasons for the ills of Potosí seems sound. From the earliest days the Villa had attracted the most daring, unscrupulous, and silver-thirsty Spaniards and foreigners, which is well-documented. Though José de Acosta praised and wondered at the great security of the silver route from Potosí to the Peruvian coast, the Villa Imperial lived a rough and tumble life from its earliest years. A spectacular robbery occurred in 1561, a report of 1564 mentions the "perjudicial presencia de muchos estranjeros en la provincia, griegos, italianos, corsos, franceses, alemanes y portugueses", ecclesiastics revolted in 1578 and conspired with others to kill the Governor of Tucumán, Juan Fernández attempted a revolt in Potosí in 1580, and the war between the various bandos began in 1581. Mestizoes rose in 1585, and so many vagabonds were found in Potosí that the crown frequently ordered the royal authorities to induce them, "with discretion and skill", to go off to war or on explorations. The guerras civiles attracted men from far and wide, reports Arzáns, as each side called upon its friends and relatives in distant parts to rally around, and given the nature of the Potosinos it is not surprising that the guerras civiles occurred. As Diego Muñoz de Cuéllar, "el ministro comisionado por la Audiencia de La Plata, para averiguar y castigar los excesos en uno de los momentos más críticos, dijo una vez: 'confieso que no conozco seis hombres en Potosí de quien poder hacer segura confianza'; y otra: 'no hay en ella quien tenga sano el ánimo'."

Fortunately for students of the guerras civiles, two excellent volumes by Bolivian scholars are available to enable them to understand what happened and to check on the veracity of the account by Arzáns. Gunnar Mendoza's critical comments have already been referred to, and he bases his remarks upon his carefully organized analysis and description of the manuscripts in Sucre, a model archival report. Alberto Crespo R. has produced a well-written and substantial narrative of the wars, based on the rich documentation in Sevilla. Taken together these two volumes are not only valuable sources of information and ideas; they also demonstrate conclusively that the historian who would know the full story of what happened in colonial Spanish America must use the manuscript resources of both Spain and the New World, for these resources complement each other.

Crespo comments in some detail on the work of Arzáns, particularly as it appears in the "Anales", and he criticizes him for depending too exclusively on oral tradition. "Nadie como él ha contribuído a dar hechizo y prestigo al nombre de Potosí, pero también a desfigurar, muchas veces, su verdadera crónica". It is a fantastic, novelistic account, full of exaggeration. "Para él, los hechos no sucedían sencillamente; detrás de ellos estaba, si no el aliento divino, el impulso mágico". Yet Crespo admires his "hondo poder de evocación", admits that a considerable part of Arzáns story is about the same as one gets from the manuscripts in the Archivo de Indias, and that at times "refiere con exactitud detalles como la avaricia y la ambición del corregidor Manrique, que eran ciertas, o reproduce literalmente la copla amenazadora que apareció pegada en las esquinas de la plaza y dedicada a la intención del cuitado oidor Muñoz de Cuéllar".

Further researches will undoubtedly prove that many of the specific statements made by Arzáns on the most tumultuous period of Potosí's past are wrong, or are only partly correct; but probably they will also conclude that Arzáns has given us an essentially true picture of the social anarchy that characterized the years 1623-1625 in the Villa Imperial. Yet despite all the space and attention Arzáns devotes to his sources, many mysteries and uncertainties remain. Until copies turn up of the works Arzáns cites so frequently and apparently in good faith, the watchword must be Caveat lector!

CHAPTER 16.

WHAT NEEDS TO BE DONE ON THE HISTORY OF POTOSI?

After a historian has been investigating a subject for a long time, he begins to understand what is not known, and eventually sets down his thoughts on possible research projects. At least this was my experience with Las Casas.* When Jorge Hardoy was organizing a section on urbanization for the XXXVIII International Congress of Americanists held in 1968 in Stuttgart, he invited me to prepare something on the Villa Imperial de Potosí, whose history had absorbed much of my time during the previous decade.

Thus was born the present article. The Internacional Reunión in Potosí proposed here has not yet been held, but surely it will come to pass some time.

Verhandlungen des XXXVIII Internationalen Amerikanistenkongresses, IV (Munich, 1972), 77-85. Reprinted by permission.

*"What Needs To Be Done on Bartolomé de Las Casas", Estudios hispánicos. Homenaje a Archer M. Huntington (Wellesley, Mass., 1952), 229-232.

What Needs To Be Done on the History of Potosí?

A simple and not inaccurate response to this question would be: almost everything. Research in the history of this great silver center in colonial Peru remains in its infancy despite the valiant efforts of Bolivian scholars such as Armando Alba, Mario Chacón, José de Mesa and Teresa Gisbert, Gunnar Mendoza and Guillermo Ovando-Sanz, to whom should be added others in the New World as well as European scholars such as Marie Helmer and Inge Wolff. The reasons for this situation are not hard to find. They lie in the sheer immensity of the task: the enormous quantity of manuscript records available, the relative scarcity of historians interested in the viceroyalty of Peru when compared with those concerned with the viceroyalty of New Spain, and the difficult political and economic conditions of Bolivia in the twentieth century when so many of the modern studies of Spain's colonial history have been undertaken.

Conditions are changing, even though slowly, and the next generation will doubtless witness a decided improvement in the quality and quantity of historical writing on many aspects of the past of this silver mountain some 15,000 feet above sea level in one of the most remote parts of the Andes. Though we who study the past are not expected to predict the shape of things to come, and have not been markedly successful at doing so, it may be useful to indicate in a tentative spirit some of the problems and topics which deserve to be treated when the history of Potosí becomes of larger interest than it is today.

One caveat should be entered as a preliminary observation. We are gathered together at this session of the XXXVIII International Congress of Americanists for a discussion of urbanism, but of course the history of any city involves inevitably the history of its surrounding territory. The favelas of Rio de Janeiro, São Paulo, and other cities in Southern Brazil--is their history not also a part of the economic underdevelopment of Northeastern Brazil? Cannot the same be said of other Latin American cities, indeed of all cities? All history in a sense is urban history if regarded in this broad way. The reciprocal influence on each other of cities and countryside thus becomes a fundamental concern in our attempts to understand the way in which Potosí grew from almost nothing in 1545, when its silver was first exploited by the Spaniards, until its emergence during the next 100 years as the largest and richest urban center in all the Americas.

Let us begin with law. The study of the legal system created in the New World by Spain is looked upon by some with scorn or superciliousness, as merely an unpleasant manifestation of dry legalism and hypocrisy. For how could any people really enforce as many noble laws as Spaniards devised for their American realms? Yet no one has seriously studied the "Código Carolino", the late eighteenth-century mining code which minutely sets forth the experience of over 200 years of the Spanish effort to regulate the principal economic activity of the empire. The prolonged discussions and debates which were involved in the elaboration of this comprehensive description of mining principles and practices at Potosí await the attention of a historian trained in law and administration as well as in mining ethnology. Once this study has been made, we will have one more opportunity to learn whether developments in Peru were different from those in Mexico, and thus to understand more clearly the complexities of the Spanish empire. For the Potosinos insisted that the mining code for Mexico did not fit their conditions and needs; hence they required a new and different approach, which resulted in the "Código Carolino" which has not yet been printed, let alone analyzed. Ideally speaking, the study of Potosí mining law should be a part of the ambitious project formulated by the Chilean legal scholar Alamiro Avila Martel in his proposal for the publication of a "Cuerpo de documentos y estudios sobre el derecho de minería indiano".

Or let us take the history of agriculture, one of the least known aspects of Spanish American history. We know that Potosí could never have mushroomed into an immense urban conglomeration of a reputed 150,000 inhabitants by 1650 had it not been able to draw upon a large surrounding territory for food. No extensive investigations have been made, so far as I know, to determine where the food came from and in what quantities, what the problems of transport were, and, to what extent the mining operators were forced to concern themselves with food supply problems to ensure silver production. Here again we see the tendency of some historians to concentrate on silver production--the exportable product--without much regard to the total economic structure of society. Was the ample supply of dried potato (chuño) in truth the chief means of harnessing thousands of Indians to the production of silver at Potosí, as one writer has declared? Or did a more complex and complicated economic relationship exist between the huge area which supplied food and Indian workers and the mine itself? How far did the waves of economic influence reach from Potosí to far-off towns in Chile and northern Argentina--even Paraguay? The traffic in mules alone became an important part of this trade relationship, whose dimensions are just now beginning to emerge thanks to recent researches by Nicolás Sánchez Albornoz and others. Scattered municipal archives and archivos de protocolos as well as the better known collections in Madrid, Potosí, Sevilla, and Sucre will have to be explored if this vital and yet untold story is to be known. Silver production statistics are essential, of course, but let our quantitatively-minded historians also concern themselves with figures on chuño production and on the consumption of the popular liquor chicha and coca as well if they would give us a more complete picture of the impact of Potosí silver on Spanish colonial economy.

Another serious gap in our knowledge of Potosí may be seen in our ignorance of the detailed role of the municipality. Cabildo records are extant in large quantities, but have never been examined to locate and use the information imbedded in them of value to the economist, political scientist, and sociologist as well as to the historian. Yet we have long told our students that the cabildo affords an excellent vantage point from which to survey the whole panorama of Spanish colonial life in its grass roots manifestations. It is clear, too, that the silverhappy miners employed ecclesiastical ostentation and municipal office holding as ways to apply their sudden wealth so as to enhance their personal prestige. Another outstanding activity of the Potosí cabildo was its efforts to influence the Council of the Indies and other administrative units in Spain and in the viceregal capital Lima to take action favorable to the miners. Lobbying was an expensive but necessary method to defend the mining interests of the Potosí cabildo, whose history when told will reveal one of the most aggressive groups in the empire.

Cabildo fortunes cannot be separated from those of the royal audiencia in nearby La Plata which attempted--often unsuccessfully--to curb the pretensions of the Potosí municipality. Here we are faced with the solemn fact that there are few detailed accounts of the audiencia, which Clarence Haring declared "was the most important and interesting institution in the government of the Spanish Indies". Anyone who would seriously study the Audiencia of Charcas will find it a major task because of the bulk of records still extant and because of the volume of business it transacted; yet the municipal history of Potosí will not be fully understood until its long and at times bitter administrative contentions with the Audiencia of Charcas are better documented than they are now. The battles between these two institutions were epic, for the Potosinos were powerful and arrogant, and the audiencia was described in these terms by Gabriel René-Moreno:

> La Audiencia de Charcas! Hasta hoy la historia no ha echado sino miradas rápidas y lejanas al predominio absoluto, a la tiranía sangrienta, a la jurisdicción dilatadísma, a la soberbia incalificable de la Audiencia de Charcas. Algun día se habrán de referir la maña con que en su remoto distrito sabía ese tribunal arrogarse las facultades de soberano, el desenfado con que acertaba a burlar las órdenes del virrey, la audacia con que a las leyes sobreponía, la impunidad de casi tres siglos con que contó su despotismo en el Alto Perú.

Fortunately Padre José María Barnadas is now at work in the archives on this huge subject.

The technological history of Spanish mining in America has just begun to attract the attention of such competent specialists as Modesto Bargalló, and Potosí will prove to be a rich field for the historian of science to cultivate. A dozen years ago I brought together bibliographical information on this subject in the hope that others would open up this vein, but little has been done. Yet many manuscripts are to be found in both America and Spain on the many devices and methods both Spaniards and foreigners worked out to extract every possible ounce of silver from the mine. When the true dimensions of these technological contributions to mining are carefully examined, Professor Bargalló believes that the conviction held by many that Spaniards were unscientific will have to be revised.

The value of Potosí's historical records to anthropologists has yet to be fully understood. One basic element of Hispanic imperial policy was the repeated effort made to organize the new world natives. The bringing together of dispersed groups of Indians in native hamlets or "civil congregations" was designed to provide for their more effective indoctrination and administration. Some 250,000 Indians were resettled in New Spain alone between 1602 and 1605, but thereafter except in the Jesuit "reducciones", no large scale attempts were apparently made. Potosí was another and more exploitative kind of resettlement, for the mita system of forced labor there which operated for over two and a half centuries annually uprooted thousands of Indians from an area stretching out hundreds of miles from Potosí. The eighteenth-century Potosino historian Bartolomé Arzáns de Orsúa y Vela reserved his loudest laments for the dire effects on the Indians of the mita, which the seventeenth-century jurist and experienced colonial official Juan Solórzano Pereira called "a subject no less profound than the mines themselves". This system, by which one-seventh of the able-bodied men from all the villages in a great area around Potosí were regularly drafted to the mines, brought dreadful consequences for the Indians. To be sure, hospitals were established for them and "protectors" appointed for them, but year after year they went on dying from accidents and overwork. Potosí's name was so terrible to them that Indians chosen in the villages for the mita were sent off to the sound of funeral music, and those who escaped destruction in the bowels of the great silver mountain usually returned to their villages in miserable condition--often minus an arm or a leg, or debilitated by disease.

The cultural changes resulting from this forced moving about of thousands of Indians has yet to be studied for its anthropological importance. When the mita Indians were brought to the mining camp they met there not only an alien culture--the Spanish, organized along radically different lines from their own--but also different types of Indians from the many villages supplying miners, for the Inca empire was a mosaic of conquered tribes. Potosí thus may be looked upon as a kind of historical laboratory to study the reaction of the mita Indians to life in Potosí--the "detribalization" and "proletarianization" of the native labor force. And those who survived their mita service to return to their villages, often far distant from Potosí, must have become what anthropologists today term "cultural brokers" who probably brought new ways, new ideas, and a new technology to the Indians scattered throughout the large territory from which mita Indians were recruited.

What effect did the silver mountain have on the Spaniards and other Europeans who flocked to Potosí for rapid profit despite the hard conditions of life there? Who can doubt that the tradition of sudden riches or sudden poverty must have stimulated those freewheeling Europeans in the Andes to excesses of all kinds? Agricultural life is subject to fluctuations, too, and is dependent upon rainfall and weather; but mining has always been a most hazardous occupation and at Potosí "rags to riches" and "riches to rags" experiences were commonplace. The adventurous strain in Spanish character was doubtless intensified, and the psychological effect of Potosí on its inhabitants over the long colonial period will surely become one of the most significant, even though difficult to assess, parts of its history.

One approach to this psychological story would be to cull from the existing chronicles and other documents the stories of notable individuals who flourished in the shadow of the great silver mountain --the miners, Indian chiefs, foreigners from many lands, ecclesiastics, prostitutes, governors, desperadoes, millionaires. These biographical vignettes would be much truer to life than Ricardo Palma's Tradiciones Peruanas, and much more dramatic. Such stories would include saintliness as well as statistics, poetry, civil wars, private vengeance, and the distribution of property, to mention only a few topics.

The documentation on the economic, political and social life of the Potosinos is incredibly rich, and its surface has been barely scratched by historians. When this documentation becomes more widely known, it will be seen that what happened in that remarkable urban center in colonial Peru--the Villa Imperial de Potosí--holds significance for a large rural area as well, and that the repercussion of events in that far-off Andean region was even felt around the world. For Potosí was placed on maps drawn in Asia not many years after the mine was discovered, and a sixteenth-century colored representation of the great silver mountain has recently come to light in a Turkish manuscript. Indeed, the iconographic history of Potosí--another subject awaiting investigation--will probably prove to be one of the most impressive proofs of world-wide interest in Potosí during its time of grandeur.

Even if everyone were to agree to the foregoing catalog of needs, and I have of course omitted a number of important topics, the question naturally arises: what can be done now to induce students of history to set to work in this rich field of inquiry? Two steps, at least, may be undertaken. The first one, the publication of guides to manuscripts on Potosí, may seem a very modest proposal indeed but it is an indispensable first step. For example, the remarkable catalog and digest of documents on the famous civil wars (1622-1625), meticulously prepared by Gunnar Mendoza, should eventually arouse sociologically-inclined historians to analyze these turbulent years in Potosí. Likewise the catalog prepared over 30 years ago by José Vázquez Machicado of the manuscripts in the Archive of the Indies and recently published by Armando Alba in Potosí should encourage research in that apparently inexhaustible collection in Sevilla. A third solid guide on labor at Potosí, already compiled by Dr. Mendoza and practically ready for publication, brings together in organized form a guide to the mass of information on this vital subject whose importance steadily increases in the eyes of many historians. Once these and other guides become widely known, there should be a much more rapid development in Potosí studies than ever before.

Guides to manuscripts may be not enough to reveal to the world the historical treasures of Potosí. More needs to be done to galvanize our historical colleagues into action. It was for this reason that in 1955, after publishing the year before what I erroneously thought was my last work on Bartolomé de Las Casas, and while in Spain visiting all its universities, I sent out the following notice and invitation:

> From the plains of Castile, Lewis Hanke salutes his friends at the beginning of the New Year, and takes pleasure in sending them his first study on the History of the Villa Imperial de Potosí.
>
> With this publication, I take an affectionate farewell of my old companion Bartolomé de Las Casas and enter a new field of history--the fantastic and fascinating story of the celebrated Villa Imperial, which largely remains unwritten. To stimulate interest in Potosí and to bring together in an informal way all who work to aid in the telling of this story, there has been established an Association of Friends of the History of the Villa Imperial de Potosí. The Association is necessarily international, for the friends of the Villa Imperial are scattered in many countries of the world. It is chartered in no country, has no constitution, no dues, no President, no Vice President, no library--only a temporary Secretary. The first purpose of the Association is to discover who is interested in the subject and to draw up a list of such persons, with their complete addresses and information on what part of the history they are working. Everyone who has published or proposes to write a historical study on any aspect of La Villa Imperial is cordially invited to become a Founding Member of the Association. . . .

The establishment of the Asociación "Amigos de la Historia de la Villa Imperial de Potosí" may have served the useful purpose of alerting widely-scattered scholars to their common concern with Potosí, but no great result was noticeable. Then another idea was discussed--to organize a meeting in Bolivia of all those interested in Potosí. Over the years Armando Alba, Gunnar Mendoza, José de Mesa and Teresa Gisbert, Guillermo Ovando-Sanz, and I discussed with many persons--indeed, with anyone who would listen to us--the proposal for a "Reunión de Investigadores de la Historia de Potosí". It would be international in membership, with everyone invited who manifested a concern with any aspect of the subject. It would be ample in scope, though naturally focussed on the Villa Imperial.

The "Reunión" has, unfortunately, not yet been held. Perhaps the time has come to make another attempt. The International Congress of Americanists is an ideal body to aid the enterprise, and I therefore present the attached resolution for consideration by the present Congress.

Finally, I do earnestly hope that, whether or not a minor miracle permits the Reunión to take place, the attention it deserves will henceforth be paid to the history of the extraordinarily significant and fascinating Villa Imperial de Potosí whose uniqueness has been described in this way:

> The truly unique aspects of Potosí, however, were its size and dramatic history. Other mining centers existed in the empire and developed somewhat similar societies and sets of institutions. But Potosí came to exhibit those common characteristics of all mining societies in such a theatrical way that it became symbolic of the process that was going on everywhere. Perhaps herein lies the real justification for assigning to Potosí a long and significant chapter in the history of Spain in America. Just as the vociferous and learned Dominican Bartolomé de Las Casas, although not the only defender of the Indians, most persistently captured the imagination of his contemporaries and later generations as The Defender, so Potosí exemplified, in the gaudiest and most memorable colors, the passion for wealth that drew many Spaniards to the New World. Bernal Díaz del Castillo, the famous and articulate foot-soldier of Cortez, exhibited the remarkable combination of <u>Gott Und Gewinn</u> which characterized the Spanish conquest of America when he exclaimed: "We came here to serve God, and also to get rich". As the mountain of Potosí towers above the surrounding peaks, so will this mine, once its story is adequately told, stand as the towering symbol for the spirit of all Spaniards who came to the New World to get rich.

* * *

A Resolution on the History of the Villa Imperial de Potosí

<u>Considering</u>

That the history of the Villa Imperial de Potosí requires further study in its anthropological, artistic, cultural, economic, political, sociological, and technological aspects

<u>Recognizing</u>

That extensive archival records exist which are available for research on Potosí

<u>Believing</u>

That a meeting of scholars concerned with Potosí would be a valuable stimulation to their further efforts

Those who sign below*, having discussed in recent years the need for such a meeting, recommend that the XXXVIII Congress Internacional

---

*The signers were Armando Alba, Mario Chacón, Teresa Gisbert, Lewis Hanke, Gunnar Mendoza, José de Mesa, and Guillermo Ovando-Sanz.

de Americanistas, at its meeting in Stuttgart-Munich in August, 1968, approve in principle the organization of such a meeting and express the hope that appropriate Academies, Universities, and other cultural and scientific institutions will work toward the realization of an international conclave of scholars desirous of making better known to the world the history of the Villa Imperial de Potosí.

Addenda:

After this essay was completed there came to my attention a mimeographed study by the Argentine scholar Marcos Kaplan which underlines how necessary is the detailed study of such urban centers as Potosí for an accurate understanding of the reality of life in colonial Spanish America. His *Estado y urbanización en América Latin I. El período colonial* (Santiago, Chile, 1969) was issued by the Comité Interdisciplinario de Desarrollo Urbano, Universidad Católica, Santiago de Chile. Professor Kaplan's analysis appears to me perfectly sensible and sound in its presentation of the general lines of Iberian empire purposes and policies. What is lacking is a detailed picture--never yet presented by historians--of the reality of such economic and political centers as Potosí--in modifying or evading the legal restrictions laid down by the mercantilist, absolutist policies of Portugal and Spain. Thus Potosí presents a great challenge to historians, who now have an opportunity to present a more substantial and meaningful picture of colonial life.

PART IV

SPANISH VICEROYS IN MEXICO AND PERU

CHAPTER 17.

VICEROYS, ARCHIVISTS, AND HISTORIANS

Historians usually take the precaution of writing about their research projects after they have accomplished them and the results are printed for the world to see. But sometimes it may be useful to describe work in progress to inform colleagues of ongoing investigations and problems encountered.

At least so it seemed to me, when Drs. Burrus and Hammond were planning the Homenaje to express our gratitude to the Director of the Archive General de Indias, as he was about to retire.

Homenaje a José María de la Peña y Cámara, Ernest J. Burrus, S.J., and George P. Hammond, eds. (Madrid: Ediciones José Porrúa Turanzas, 1969), 93-103. Reprinted by permission.

Viceroys, Archivists, and Historians

Students who have once worked in the Archivo General de Indias yearn to go back there as often as possible during the rest of their lives, if I may judge from my own experience since I first met Pepe Peña there in October, 1932. We who study the history of the New World are attracted to Sevilla not only because of the great mass of manuscripts there on the accomplishments of Spain in America or because of the imperishable enchantment of the city itself, but also by the quality of the human beings who serve in the archive, from the _porteros_ who patiently deliver bundles of documents day after day for eager researchers to the _jefe_ who directs the institution. Irene A. Wright eloquently expressed the spirit of all of us held in thrall by the archive in her poem which begins:

> These are the Archives of the Indies!
> Here--in these tall cases, built from marble floor
> Toward domed, arched ceiling--
> Here are stored, in blue-wrapped bundles, pack on pack,
> The papers passed between old Spain and her far colonies.
> These are the records of their government
> From days when they were conquered, one by one,
> Until those other bitter days when, one by one,
> In revolution they wrote "Finis" at the close
> Of these colonial records.
> These are the Archives of the Indies.

Perhaps the most striking characteristic of the archive is its seemingly inexhaustible resources. Many a researcher has gone there to study one project, and has discovered half a dozen other important topics to keep him occupied for the rest of his life--and his students, too. My first objective there was documentation on the life of Bartolomé de Las Casas; but soon my investigations came to focus on an even larger and more varied subject, the struggle for justice in the Spanish conquest of the New World. Though there is still so much to do in this field that historians will doubtless be arguing disputable points relating to this struggle at least throughout the next century, eventually I was drawn to another absorbing part of Spanish American history, the almost incredible story of the Villa Imperial de Potosí. And in my attempts to understand Potosí, it was an archivist and historian--in this case Gunnar Mendoza, Director of the Archivo Nacional of Bolivia--who aided me and, moreover, who influenced me to devote a considerable part of my time during the last ten years to its history. I may someday write about the triangular relationship that developed between Dr. Mendoza, Potosí, and myself; but this is another story for a later time. Right now, I am concerned with my present struggle to publish some of the enormous documentation available on the viceroys who acted for the king in Spain's vast American empire and to show how Dr. Peña has skillfully guided and assisted my efforts.

When did I first realize the significance of the viceroys and the need to prepare their _memorias_ for publication? Who knows when a subject first insinuates itself into the mind of a student of history? The viceregal project may have first occurred to me while having a cup of coffee with France V. Scholes or some other friend in the cafe across the street from the archive, or during an informal discussion among members of the Peña de Historiadores Americanos which Dr. Ulises Rojas of Colombia organized some years ago to provide an opportunity for researchers to meet after the archive closed. At any rate, the idea entered my mind somehow; and thereafter it remained there to agitate my days and nights whether I was earning my bread at the University of Texas, Columbia University, or, as now, at the University of California, Irvine.

But projects require funds, and the search for these and for academic support requires time and persistence as well as justification. So when Doctor Ralph Gerard, Dean of the UCI Graduate Division, last year invited faculty members to submit requests for research assistance, I prepared the following statement:

Preliminary Proposal for a UCI Viceregal Project

Spain established in America one of the most extensive empires the world has ever seen, and developed a remarkable bureaucratic structure to govern it. The key official was the Viceroy, the personal representative of the King in the two great viceroyalties organized in Mexico and in Peru shortly after they were conquered in the sixteenth century. In the eighteenth century, additional viceroyalties were set up in Buenos Aires and Bogotá.

Each viceroy was supposed to draw up a formal report of his administration as a record of important events and as advice for his successor. Not all viceroys complied with this royal order; but the many reports, sometimes extensive, which were written are official documentary sources of prime value to anthropologists, economists, geographers, historians, political scientists, and indeed everyone concerned with the Spanish Empire in America or colonial administration in general. Only a small number of the reports has been published, sometimes in restricted editions or without adequate editorial apparatus. No other European power in the period 1492-1810 appears to have required such reports of their principal colonial officials, so that this corpus of material represents a unique and valuable historical source.

For some years I have been conferring with colleagues in the United States and in Spanish-speaking lands, but my work on the history of the Villa Imperial de Potosí has prevented much action. This project has now ended, and I should like to devote the next three to five years to the viceregal project if sufficient funds can be obtained.

Procedure

The Institute of Latin American Studies and the Department of History of the University of Texas sponsored a discussion on viceregal reports some years ago, with the following scholars away from Texas participating: Woodrow Borah (University of Californit, Berkeley); Ernest J. Burrus, S. J. (Institutum Historicum Societatis Jesu, Rome); Charles Gibson (State University of Iowa, now of the University of Michigan); Wigberto Jiménez Moreno (Instituto Nacional de Antropología e Historia, México); J. I. Rubio Mañé (Archivo General de la Nación, México).

The discussion revolved around a tentative project statement developed as a result of correspondence by Ricardo Donoso (Santiago de Chile), Lewis Hanke, and Guillermo Lohmann Villena

(Madrid), plus various suggestions sent in by José Rafael Arboleda, S. J. (Bogotá); E. J. Burrus, S.J. (Rome); Guillermo Céspedes (Sevilla); James F. King (Berkeley); José M. Mariluz Urquijo (Buenos Aires); Enrique Ortega Ricaurte (Bogotá); José de la Peña (Sevilla); Stanley J. Stein (Princeton); and José Torre Revello (Buenos Aires).

There was general agreement that these *memorias* should be printed, and it was recognized that this would involve considerable funds and cooperation on an international scale. In order to achieve this work in the discernible future, many correspondents and the discussion group in Austin urged that all proposals not absolutely necessary be eliminated, and agreed upon these conclusions:

1. Contents

All known viceregal reports should be included, preceded by copies of the laws under which they were prepared. Important reports drawn up by *visitadores generales* or by *audiencias* during the absence of a viceroy would also be considered. Reports by captains general should be omitted, as well as *juicios de residencia*.

2. Editorial Apparatus

The reports should be presented in a modernized Spanish text, on the basis of the best version available, and accompanied by the following materials--also in Spanish:

1. A general statement on the viceregal reports--their preparation, their value, other documents to be used, etc. No attempt would be made to give a detailed analysis of individual reports, but once the volumes were published institutions such as the Panamerican Institute of Geography and History and national academies of history would be encouraged to prepare such studies.

2. For each viceroy there would be a brief biographical statement, plus a succinct bibliography to include such available information as the *residencias*, *correspondencia*, and modern studies. Similar information would be provided on the periods when a viceroy was not in residence so that there would be a brief running account of the whole viceregal period.

3. Index. A person, place, and simple subject index should accompany each volume. The question of a consolidated index at the end of the series, to include a detailed subject index as well as person and place index, was considered. No general agreement was reached, except to defer the decision until later.

3. Publication

The prime consideration here would be an edition sufficiently inexpensive so that it could be purchased by institutions and individual scholars, and a publisher whose distribution facilities are well-developed through the Spanish-speaking world as well as elsewhere.

4. Organization and Sponsorship

It was recognized that the project would require international sponsorship by a relatively large number of institutions, though it was also felt that a small Advisory Committee would be needed for effective administration.

* * *

Plans, such as this one drawn up in Texas in 1960, are useful and necessary; but no matter how soundly prepared, they do not always produce funds. So my conversation continued with colleagues in Madrid, Washington, and other places--indeed, wherever anyone would listen to me. Then one day, by one of those fortunate circumstances made increasingly possible by the inventors of the airplane, Ricardo Donoso, Guillermo Lohmann Villena, and I met at Columbia University and decided to make a pronouncement to the world, as follows:

Declaración de Manhattan

Los que suscriben:
Guillermo Céspedes del Castillo, Catedrático de la Universidad de Sevilla;
Ricardo Donoso, Director Honorario de la Sociedad Chilena de de Historia y Geografía;
Lewis Hanke, Profesor de Historia en Columbia University;
Guillermo Lohmann Villena, historiador;
J. I. Rubio Mañé, Director del Archivo General de la Nación, México;
han discutido en los últimos años la necesidad de encarar la publicación de un cuerpo documental que incluya las Memorias de los Virreyes y Capitanes Generales que ejercieron sus funciones, en ambos hemisferios, durante la época colonial.

La importancia de esos documentos para el estudio de la historia social política, administrativa, económica e intelectual de la América Española ha sido unánimemente reconocida por historiadores, geógrafos y economistas.

La circunstancia de que fuentes tan valiosas para el estudio del pasado americano se encuentren dispersas en ediciones limitadas, hoy difíciles de obtener, y que no exhiben las apreciaciones críticas más indispensables, justifica, en opinión de los que suscriben, promover la publicación de una edición crítica, preparada por especialistas en la historia americana.

Los que suscriben esperan que esta iniciativa cuente con el apoyo, intelectual y material, no sólo de las Universidadas, Academias, Sociedades científicas y culturales, sino de las instituciones sabias que consagran su actividad a la investigación histórica.

Animados de la intención de llevar adelante esa idea, los que suscriben se dirigen a sus colegas americanistas, deseosos de recibir, no sólo el apoyo más decidido a su iniciativa, sino cuanta sugerencia conduzca a la efectiva realización de sus propósitos.

Es el própósito de los firmantes presentar esta iniciativa como una ponencia al XXXVI Congreso Internacional dé Americanistas que se reunirá en España en agosto-septiembre de 1964.

* * *

The Declaración de Manhattan was later signed by Eduardo Arcila Farías (Venezuela), Gabriel Jaramillo Giraldo (Colombia), José M. Mariluz Urquijo (Argentina), and José Manuel Pérez (Cuba), and was duly presented to the International Congress of Americanists as it met in Spain in August, 1964. But none of those "Universidades, Academias, Sociedades científicas y culturales" or even those "instituciones sabias que consagran su actividad a la investigación histórica" rushed to our aid with grants.

Thus when Dean Gerard last year resolved to allot funds to enable me to make another attempt to get this long-deferred project underway, we felt that fate had intervened to save the idea or at least to enable those interested to find a way to publish the _memorias_. And when my old friends, George P. Hammond and Ernest J. Burrus, S. J., invited me to participate in the _homenaje_ volume being prepared to honor José de la Peña, another old friend, it seemed appropriate to set down the history of the viceroy project to date. For scholarship does not consist of the finished product alone--the monograph replete with footnotes or the printed collection of documents. The final accomplishment of a work of historical scholarship is always the result of its conception, its plan--often made with the helpful counsel of fellow scholars--and the laborious confronting of problems while the work goes forward. All these elements go into making the complete record of an enterprise in research.

Such a record is essential, at least for the viceroys project. Its story is particularly meaningful for those of us who remember with gratitude the friendship and unfailing stimulation of Pepe Peña. For he not only possesses a deep and rare knowledge of the riches in the archive; but he has had that magic ability to make each investigator--whether the greenest student with "stars in his eyes" on his first visit to the archive or the oldest _veterano_ feel that he, the director, had an absorbing concern with his own individual historical research topic. So it was with my work, and so it was with the viceroy project, for Dr. Peña answered my pleas for help with the following letter which I still preserve among the growing mass of papers related to the enterprise:

> Desde luego, pueden ustedes contar con autorización para obtener microfilms de las memorias virreinales que ustedes localicen en sus trabajos. A mí me interesa expecialmente su proyecto, porque yo, personalmente, tengo hecho un trabajo sobre las instrucciones que se daban a los virreyes cuando eran nombrados para el cargo. Tengo estudiada la evolución de las instrucciones para los virreyes de Nueva España y del Perú desde los orígenes hasta comienzos del siglo XVIII y con sistematización de su contenido. Sobre ello di dos o tres conferencias en los cursos de La Rábida, hace poco más de diez años. Hasta ahora no había tenido ocasión de dar los últimos toques a ese trabajo y publicarlo, pero tengo el propósito de hacerlo en la primera ocasión.

This reply reveals another trait that has endeared Pepe Peña to all who entered the archive during his long stewardship. He not only evinced keen interest in your work but he himself had a study in progress on the same or a related subject! And, finally, this letter also reveals that he has been so devoted to the projects of others that he has not been able to complete his own. It is the earnest hope of all your many friends on the other side of "the Ocean Sea", querido Pepe, that now you will be able to give those "últimos toques" to your own writings.

CHAPTER 18.

SPANISH VICEROYS IN AMERICA: A GENERAL VIEW

My interest in the work of viceroys in Mexico and Peru developed slowly, for other subjects absorbed more of my time. The University of St. Thomas invitation to deliver the Smith History Lecture in 1972 obliged me to bring together my thoughts on some subject, and Spanish viceroys seemed the best topic for me to present.

I did not realize then that viceregal history was to occupy me so steadily for many months thereafter. At the time this volume goes to press, a ten volume documentary series entitled Los virreyes españoles en América durante la Casa de Austria is slowly being brought out in Madrid through the Biblioteca de Autores Españoles.

To accompany the documents, the Institute of Ibero-American Studies in the University of Cologne published in 1977 in its Lateinamerikanische Forschungen series, my three volume Guía de las fuentes en el Archivo General de Indias para el estudio de la administración virreinal española en México y en el Perú, 1535-1700. A final volume of the Guía is now in progress on the manuscripts available in Spanish American archives on the same subject.

Spanish Viceroys in America. The Smith History Lecture 1972. University of St. Thomas, Houston, Texas. Reprinted by permission.

Spanish Viceroys in America: A General View

I.

One of the fundamental questions everyone who studies the history of Spain in America tries to answer is: What was the true nature of her rule and its effect on the peoples of her far-flung empire, especially the Indians, and on the structure of society established there? Was Spain's rule bad or beneficent? This is the simplistic way some, especially those in English-speaking lands, have approached the complicated subject of Spanish rule. All too often historians have drawn facile comparisons between the different kinds of empires established in the New World and have reached their conclusions through clearly national or cultural biases. A cynical writer might declare: "Tell me whether your historian speaks English, French, Spanish, or Portuguese, and I will tell you which empire he considers the best."

Today, when empires everywhere have disappeared or are crumbling, we are in a better position than earlier to analyze the past and to avoid such a pointless question as "What would have happened in the sixteenth century if the New World had been discovered and colonized on a grand scale by, say, the English or some other European power?" Nor do we need to bemuse ourselves by speculating how the Indian cultures would have developed in the New World if it had never been discovered by Europeans. These questions have been raised; it is indicative of how culture-bound we are that no one asks what kind of world we would have today if China had been moved to harness its vast power and had sent conquering armies eastward across the Pacific to dominate the Americas.

Let us ignore these unanswerable questions and begin by recognizing that the Spanish Conquest cannot and should not be categorized as basically good or bad. Then it follows that we must try to understand the institutions, values, and individuals that the enormous energy of Spain implanted in the New World. Her explorers, soldiers, and ecclesiastics were men of flesh and blood who acted out their joint purpose of conquest and conversion to the Christian faith with a special Spanish zeal. The particular circumstance that Spain had been at war with the Moslems for centuries had created a militant Spanish Christianity. And that the Pope had given his blessing to the conversion of the encountered peoples endowed the Spanish thrust in the new lands across the ocean sea with a unique character. The Empire developed in the enormous region from California to Patagonia inevitably bore the imprint of Spain's institutions and individuals in that sixteenth century when Spain's power dominated the continent of Europe.

Power arouses envy. Power engenders fear. So we need not be surprised that Spain's actions in America have provoked controversy from the moment that Columbus first set foot upon a small Caribbean island.

I first became involved in this age-old controversy some forty years ago while I was studying in the great Archive of the Indies in Sevilla, Spain, and trying to interpret the Spanish conquest of America as a struggle for justice by the Dominican friar Bartolomé de Las Casas and other Spaniards who believed that the conquistadores should follow truly Christian principles as they opened up the New World. Though it soon became clear that many Spaniards, lay and ecclesiastic alike, were involved in this struggle, Las Casas had the loudest voice and exerted the greatest political influence on behalf of the Indians. For a number of years I devoted much of my time available for research to the life and writings of this dominating figure of the sixteenth century. Eventually it was borne in upon me that I should escape from the influence of this powerful defender of the Indians whose treatises, composed over four centuries ago, annoyed and angered some of the outstanding figures of his time, and which still powerfully move the hearts and minds of his readers. One of my friends had concentrated so long upon the writings of another historical figure that, he once confided, it required the services of a psychiatrist to separate them--and I wished to escape this sad fate. So I turned deliberately away from Las Casas to the fantastic and little-known history of the Villa Imperial de Potosí, that enormous mountain of silver in colonial Peru around which developed a most turbulent and luxurious mining society soon after its discovery in 1545. But I found that Las Casas and his ideas on how the Indians should be treated were an integral part of that story too. . . .

Thus Potosí was no real escape from Las Casas and the controversies his doctrines provoked! So I decided to abandon the history of the Imperial City, for a while at least. Besides historians need a change of pace from time to time, and I turned to the viceroys Spain sent to Mexico and Peru during the sixteenth and seventeenth centuries, the time of the Hapsburgs, during which Spanish institutions were firmly established from Mexico to Chile and in far-off Manila in the Philippine Islands. . . .

II.

Viceregal rule must be considered as an integral, indeed fundamental, part of what Clarence Haring described as "one of the most extended and spectacular movements in the history of civilization. . . the Expansion of Europe." Europeans discovered more territory in the seventy-five years after Columbus than in the previous thousand years, and Spain was in the forefront of this powerful movement of people and ideas which ushered in the age we call modern. To quote Haring again:

> Spain reserved to herself the greater part of the two American continents. It was almost entirely under her auspices that the Western Indies were first explored and conquered. Within three generations Spaniards discovered, subdued, and colonized the most extensive territorial empire the world had ever seen, performed prodigies of valor and endurance, and created a civilized and sophisticated society in the midst of a virgin wilderness.

One may add, too, that Spanish action was distinct from that of all other European powers which limited their efforts to establish isolated trading posts for commercial interchange with native peoples around the world: "For a long time this limited economic relationship was the only form of colonization carried on by privileged merchant companies along the coasts of Africa, India, China, and Japan." Spaniards developed a society in America, in which European customs, ideas, and technology exerted a radical change in the lives of the native peoples there which led to what has been described as "the greatest cultural change of all time."

The administrative structure that eventually took shape in Spanish America became as complicated and unwieldy as the great empire to be governed, and displayed some characteristics considered essentially

Spanish. Spaniards were great bureaucrats, very legal-minded bureaucrats at that, and no empire during the threé centuries Spain ruled America manifested a more closely or more carefully controlled panoply of administrative officers to enforce the royal will. The viceroy stood at the apex of the pyramid. A political scientist who wished to study in depth and amplitude Spanish imperial administration could do no better than to focus upon the activities and responsibilities of the viceroys sent to the New World to govern the great empire established there following the astonishing conquest.

The Council of the Indies was the supreme authority, under the crown, but it was in Spain far from the scene of the action. Though no single royal officer overseas enjoyed complete authority over anything, the viceroy's position was unique. For he represented the king, and was paramount so far as anyone was in America. In some respects, the viceroy in America enjoyed an even more prestigious position than Spanish viceroys in Naples who were more dependent on the Spanish crown. Some writers have tended to believe that the viceroys in Peru particularly accumulated "almost all the power of the monarchs themselves", and enumerated their many opportunities to determine ecclesiastical, economic, governmental, and military affairs. Others emphasize the restrictions placed on their actual exercise of authority, and point out that by the seventeenth century the viceroys represented an impoverished and weakened central government which "faced resistant, tenacious, and deep-rooted local interests." Viceroys were always charged with serving as a shield for the Indians against the ever-increasing demands of criollo (American-born Spaniards) landowners and mine owners. Eventually such viceregal interposition led to serious friction and helps to explain the disenchantment in later criollo generations which led to the revolutions of 1810.

The character and ability of any given viceroy were very important, of course, in determining his actual influence, but his power could be enormous; he was officially responsible for the enforcement of the hundreds, even thousands, of laws that flowed unceasingly from the king and Council of the Indies to America on almost every subject: whether Indians might ride on horseback, on unmarried women going to the Indies, the amount of powder to be used in salutes, the provision of oil and wine for church services. Viceroy Luis de Velasco was instructed in 1556 to see that the royal treasury officials in Mexico were in their offices for three hours each Monday and Tuesday morning. Despite the avalanche of crown orders, the viceroy lived in the New World, was influenced by conditions there of which the royal councillors in Spain were often ignorant, and daily confronted the problems great and small which the new society produced. Historians, however, have devoted little time to investigating the life and work of these key officials, especially during the period up to 1700 before Bourbon monarchs ruled in Spain. Why is this so?

While the viceregal system endured, contemporary writers recognized the significance of the viceroys, and their power for good or ill. Juan de Matienzo, one of those trained civil servants who helped to make possible the achievements of Viceroy Francisco de Toledo in sixteenth-century Peru, discoursed on the qualities viceroys needed in his Gobierno del Perú, as did the seventeenth-century fiscal officer Francisco López de Caravantes. The first general law code compiled for Spanish officials responsible for the administration of the empire in America contained a large and detailed section on the powers of viceroys. Juan de Solórzano Pereira naturally included a large section on viceroys in his Política indiana, which became the standard work on

Spanish administration in the Indies on publication in 1648. Writers in colonial Spanish America produced many chronicles and legal treatises which also usually treated viceroys and their activities at some length. In the eighteenth century viceroys in Mexico, as an indication of the size and importance of their task, organized into an impressive archive the mass of the papers that had accumulated over the years, and Ambrosio Cerdán de Landa Simón Pontero published in Lima a valuable guide to the principal events of each viceroy's rule in Peru together with a copious bibliography of books and manuscripts on the subject which is still useful.

The revolutionary wars for independence beginning in 1810 changed all this. A propaganda campaign against Spain was launched, with the aid of new editions of the Bartolomé de Las Casas denunciations of Spanish cruelty in his *Brevíssima relación*. Historians inevitably became more interested in depicting their new national heroes than in examining the records of the colonial powers whose viceroys, they felt, had oppressed them. One governor in revolutionary Yucatan felt so strongly against Spain that he ordered all colonial manuscripts burned, so that no record would remain of a system he believed wholly wrong. Once their independence was achieved, many Spanish Americans wished to forget all about their colonial past, that world they considered alien, whose values they repudiated, and in Colombia the nineteenth century saw convents and other buildings associated with Spanish rule destroyed or converted to national purposes. In Chile, Andrés Bello as rector of the newly organized university in Santiago permitted one of the younger and more fiery professors, José Vitorino Lastarria, to deliver at the formal opening in 1844 his famous anti-Spanish historical memoir, "Investigations on the Social Influence of the Conquest and of the Colonial System Established by Spaniards in Chile." Lastarria concluded: "The conquest was a cruel enterprise, animated by an inhuman desire for wealth, at the cost of a barbarous subjection of the Indians and of the establishment of an absolutist, backward, and reactionary system." If one held this view, and many did throughout the nineteenth century, why study viceroys?

Historians, therefore, largely ignored viceroys during the nineteenth century, though occasionally some biographical information was collected and some of their formal reports were printed, in rather indifferent editions. The situation did not change markedly even after 1900. Those who denigrated Spain's rule in America still flourished, such as one Venezuelan writer who wrote a biting criticism entitled "The Administrative Incapacity of Spain." Unfavorable opinions were expressed elsewhere; the French scholar Desdevises du Dezert declared that Spanish viceroys in America were "veritable satrapies in Oriental style, except that viceroys didn't remain in their posts more than a limited time." Revolutionary Mexico from 1910 on had of course no interest in colonial viceroys, and the Mexican government's non-recognition of the Franco regime after the Spanish Civil War made it difficult for Mexican scholars to work in Spanish archives during the last half century. Only the Argentine diplomat-historian Roberto Levillier recognized the importance of viceroys by publishing much of the correspondence of sixteenth-century viceroys in Peru and by writing a three-volume biography of one of the greatest--Francisco de Toledo.

The vigorous school of historians founded by Herbert E. Bolton in California began to display some interest in viceroys after the First World War, but most writers reflected the general disdain for them. As our own Texas author, Katherine Anne Porter, somewhat superciliously and certainly inaccurately declared: "The viceregal court was composed entirely of Spanish nobles who lived in perpetual luxurious exile; the Indians and Spanish were slowly forming a new intractable, unpredictable race, and all were ruled extravagantly and unscrupulously by a long succession of viceroys so similar and so unremarkable it is not worth while to recall their names." Even C. H. Haring, whose influence was felt by many in the field of Latin American history during the last generation, adopted a similar view, for he wrote that most of the viceroys left nothing much behind them except their portraits to be found in Lima and Mexico City. So why study nonentities?

III.

Historians who did occasionally venture into the viceregal field often seemed to confirm the unflattering picture given by Haring and others by investigating only minute problems of marginal interest, or by emphasizing the ostentatious ceremonies and disputes over protocol at viceregal courts. Thus the Peruvian scholar Manuel Moreyra Paz-Soldán tackled what he termed an "enigma" in the life of Viceroy Marqués de Montesclaros. The question was whether or not this viceroy was a widower when he arrived in Lima in 1607. The Peruvian historian published an immensely learned article on this subject, concluding that Montesclaros had been a widower. A few years later he found more documentation and reversed himself! Another Peruvian scholar devoted himself to the health of the Viceroy Count of Chinchón, and dug out of the archives a medical report of 1636, from which we learn that the Count had been bled "more than 50 times" by his physicians. The viceroy must have enjoyed an iron constitution to withstand such treatment, for he did not die until 1665. And, thanks to still another Peruvian scholar, who located the wills of Peruvian viceroys preserved in the notarial archives of Madrid, we learn from Count Chinchón's last will and testament that at the time of his death he owned, among other things, a painting by Titian.

The funeral ceremonies of viceroys and above all the ornate receptions organized when a new viceroy reached Mexico City or Lima have been paid much attention. The obsequies of Francisco Guerra, who died in 1612 in Mexico City and who happened to be both Archbishop and Viceroy, may be taken as a sample:

> The embalmed body, arranged in pontifical robes of purple taffeta garnished with gold and silver, rested in the chapel on a catafalque, covered with black gold-bordered velvet, and surrounded with candles. The interior of the chapel was draped in black. The head of the corpse reclined on a black velvet cushion, ornamented with gold and silver, and bore on the brow a mitre. Close to it rose the guidon of the captain-general, a rank held by the deceased in virtue of his office as viceroy. At the left shoulder rested the pastoral staff, and in the right hand the archiepiscopal cross; at the feet were two royal maces of gilt silver, and between them the prelate's hat.
>
> For three days a constant stream of visitors appeared at the chapel to give a last look at the beloved face, while friars and clergy held vigils, masses, and chants here as well as at other temples. The bells tolled solemnly all the while, and nearly every person exhibited some token of mourning, especially officials and men of means.
>
> On the 25th a vast concourse gathered at the palace to escort the body to the cathedral tomb. First marched the school children

> with white lighted tapers; then came thirty-eight brotherhoods, according to age, with standards, crosses, and other paraphernalia; the different monastic orders, closing with the Dominicans, to whom belonged the deceased, followed by over four hundred members of the clergy, the prebendaries of the Chapter being last. Then came the coffin, having at the feet the prelate's hat, and a cap with white tassel, the insignia of a master of theology. Behind were borne the cross and guidon, draped in black, between two kings-at-arms. On either side of the coffin strode the viceregal guard, while halberdiers assisted in keeping back the crowd. Following the guard came the deacons; the commercial court; the university representation, with sixty-four of its graduated doctors bearing the insignia of the faculty; the municipality, preceded by their mace-bearers; the audiencia, with three nephews of the deceased; the royal officers, bearing a black standard with royal arms in gold; three companies of infantry in lines of seven, with arms reversed, marching to the sound of four muffled drums and two fifes; the maestre de sala of the viceroy, bearing aloft on a half-pike the arms of the deceased, gilded on a black surface; the master of horse and chamberlain, leading a steed in deep mourning with a long train; another gentleman of the court, on horseback, bore the guidon of captain-general, with royal arms on crimson velvet. The procession closed with the servants of the palace, led by the major-domo.

The receptions of viceroys, usually expensive and solemn exhibitions of Castilian etiquette in its most baroque phase, have also been the subject of extensive historical investigation. In truth, there were many curious episodes in viceregal history, especially in the seventeenth century which Jorge Basadre has so aptly characterized as "un siglo autoritorio y piadoso" in his absorbing volume on the Count of Lemos. This very religious viceroy often served as altar boy and played the organ at church services; he was implacable against sin, and is supposed to have driven many hundreds of undesirable Spaniards from Lima, and established a home for "repentant females." This was of course before the days of the women's liberation movement, and if anything untoward happened it was the women who were supposed to repent! Lemos was indubitably preoccupied with reforming the morals of Spaniards in Lima, as this story, discovered by a Peruvian historian, illustrates: "The Count of Lemos, with his rectitude and example, had been able to correct the licentious habits of the Spaniards living in the viceregal capital. On the night the Viceroy died there sallied forth from the nunneries where they had been kept sequestered more than 400 prostitutes, and these worldly women began again their indecent dances."

One author alleged that Lemos was so occupied in religious services that he did not prepare the expected viceregal reports, but this assertion was quite unfounded, for the numerous and lengthy letters he sent to the king--many of which I saw in the Archive of the Indies in Spain last summer--testify that he was a devoted, energetic, and astute administrator. He sought justice, too, and became so enraged at the dreadful lives of the Indians in the great silver mine at Potosí that he abolished the _mita_ system requiring their labor. It was this viceroy who coined the unforgettable phrase: "No es plata lo que se lleva a España, sino sudor y sangre de los indios." (It is not silver that is carried away to Spain, but the sweat and the blood of the Indians.)

Viceroys in Mexico have received similar treatment. Genealogical details concerning the Spanish Grandees sent to America as viceroys are given much attention as well as curious aspects of their careers. One recent article, for example, provides genealogical data on Viceroy Marqués de Falces and his wife, Doña Leonor de Mur, together with a list of the large number of luxury goods she took with her to Mexico in 1566. Another viceroy loved music, and included several trumpeters in the crowd of relatives and servants that accompanied him. We know a good deal about the burial arrangements of certain viceroys, and it has been established by careful historical investigation that the Countess de la Coruña died after, not before, her husband's appointment as viceroy. Special attention has been given to the story of the only non-Spanish Vice Queen, the Bavarian Doña María Ana Riederer de Paar, who gave birth to three daughters in Mexico, and whose funeral rites were so sumptuous that the king reprimanded her husband the Viceroy Marqués de Guadalcázar in a royal order dated December 12, 1619. What happened to viceroys en route to their posts has been occasionally documented. Recent general works on viceroys have been undistinguished.

If one turns to biographies on individual viceroys, one must repeat the question raised by Hugh M. Hamill, Jr., at the Third Meeting of Mexican and United States Historians held in 1969 in Oaxtepec: "Where have all the scholars gone?" Hamill was referring to the astonishing lack of biographies on Mexico's historical figures in general, but the same question could be raised specifically concerning the scarcity of biographies of viceroys in Hapsburg Peru and Mexico alike. And Hamill's observation also applies: "This is curious in a society where personalist leadership has played such an important role." Donald Chipman reviews the problems and possibilities of biographical studies, including valuable data on viceregal studies recently published or in preparation. His judgment applies to Peru as well as to Mexico: "One must conclude that the status of biography in the historiography of New Spain is alive but hardly well. This is not surprising when one remembers that there are relatively few scholars working in <u>any</u> aspect of colonial history."

One almost overwhelming difficulty in preparing the biographical studies of viceroys must be emphasized: the enormous mass of manuscript material, and its dispersion in many repositories. The importance of the latter fact is clear. Though Sevilla and Madrid collections hold most of the viceregal documentation, the student may also have to go to Austin, Asunción, Berkeley, Bogotá, Buenos Aires, Cambridge (Massachusetts), Caracas, Chicago, Guatemala, Lima, London, Mexico, New Orleans, New York City, Paris, Quito, Rome, Sucre, Santiago de Chile, Washington, D.C., and perhaps elsewhere. A copy of one viceregal <u>Relación</u> is in the Royal Library in Copenhagen, and the painting of one sixteenth-century Peruvian viceroy is in Prague. Who knows whether relevant manuscripts may turn up in Leningrad and Moscow when their collections are fully open to non-Soviet scholars?

Viceregal material may also be hidden away in private European or American hands. For example, the Library of Congress in Washington, D.C. has only recently acquired a large collection of manuscripts originally assembled by George R. G. Conway and presented to the Library by H. P. Kraus. One of the manuscripts is a 522 folio order-book of Viceroy Luis de Velasco (El Viejo), 1548-1552, in which are entered his patents, land-grants, tribute ordinances, and viceregal decrees, together with a few orders by his predecessor Viceroy Antonio de Mendoza. Among the approximately 1,000 documents in this volume is much information on measures undertaken by Velasco to regulate Indian affairs, land distribution, building of highways, and patents for inventors' devices and developments of machinery, especially mills and forges for improving the extraction of gold and silver. Another newly opened collection of material in Madrid, the Archivo del Duque del Infantado, holds over thirty bound books of manuscripts relating to Juan de Mendoza y Luna, Marqués de Montesclaros, who served as Viceroy in both Mexico (1603-1607) and in Peru (1607-1615). This private collection will be very useful in supplementing the information found in the Archive of the Indies and elsewhere. The Kraus gift to the Library of Congress and the opening of the Duque del Infantado Archivo make one wonder how much other rich and hitherto unavailable viceregal material will be made known in coming years.

The great quantity of manuscripts already known, however, is undoubtedly the greatest obstacle to writing biographies of viceroys, particularly if the works are to be of the "life and times variety", as they should be. Few of the reports and very few of the copious letters of the viceroys have been published. On such a fundamental subject as Indian labor, especially on the infamous mita system, so many papers had accumulated over the years that Viceroy Duke of La Palata complained that the sheer quantity of evidence and special studies hampered his own investigation of this hotly disputed institution.

The viceregal correspondence awaiting historians in the Archive of the Indies in Sevilla has to be seen to be believed. Bundle after bundle of minutely detailed letters on all aspects of colonial administration, often accompanied by extensive reports on matters referred to in the letters--Indian tributes, silver production, lists of persons who should be considered for appointment, reports on foreign corsairs in the empire, Negro uprisings, and friction with ecclesiastics. As the viceregal governmental machinery developed, trained secretaries became a permanent part of the apparatus of administration so that whoever happened to be viceroy was able to count on these civil servants for information and advice. Many of the official reports (Relaciones) submitted by viceroys at the end of their rule were probably written in large part by these under officials.

Yet only a handful of these viceregal letters have been published, and almost none of the remarkably detailed accompanying reports which are sometimes veritable monographs. When something does appear--such as the recently published report on the Indian population of Lima prepared in 1613 for Viceroy Marqués de Montesclaros--the information is hailed at once as of fundamental importance for understanding the social and economic history of the empire. The correspondence of most of the viceroys has the great advantage of being well-organized, in four categories: Ecclesiastical affairs, civil affairs, economic affairs, military affairs. There is probably no section of the Archive which would require less work to organize for microfilming purposes.

Local documentation as well, in archives scattered throughout the empire, contains much information on how Spain governed her realms in America and on the kind of society that developed there over the centuries. But the principal and indispensable source has scarcely been touched by historians--the mass of viceregal documentation brought together by Viceroys and transmitted to the king and Council of the Indies in Spain.

IV.

In view of the remarkable quantity and variety of documentation in Europe and America known to exist, one is not surprised that historians have not known exactly how to handle the difficult and complicated problems involved in viceregal biographies. One student decided that the Duke of La Palata's work as viceroy in seventeenth-century Peru was simply too vast for a doctoral dissertation, and limited her story to his struggles with the Church, which were bitter, prolonged, and recorded in tremendous detail. Another scholar concentrated on the literary aspects of his viceroy, for a number of them had literary pretensions and encouraged poetry contests; and another was so intimidated by the size of the task that he limited himself to a general overview of his viceroy's activities rather than attempting an analysis in depth.

The Peruvian historian Jorge Basadre has applied the most imagination to the problem of how to deal with viceregal history. Faced with the enormous masses of manuscripts, he worked out an ingenious plan to present three general views of Peruvian life at approximately one-hundred year intervals, as seen through the life and time of three viceroys: Viceroy Francisco de Toledo (1569-1581), Viceroy Count of Lemos (1667-1672), and Viceroy Manuel de Amat (1761-1776). During an enforced exile in Spain while his University in Lima was in revolution, Basadre was able to carry on research on the Count of Lemos, whose story he completed brilliantly in a "slice of history" volume rather than as a biography of the viceroy.

Parenthetically it may be remarked that Basadre was most wise in not starting with Viceroy Toledo, for the material on this royal officer is simply fantastic. Roberto Levillier has published a three-volume biography, as well as many volumes of pertinent documentation, and at least as much remains unpublished. Special studies continue to appear. Even so, much remains to be done before the achievements of this energetic and competent royal representative are fully known. For example, he is called "The Solon of Peru", yet a rigorous analysis of the many ordinances he drew up has yet to be made. These ordinances remained in vigor many years, and some of them are supposed to have been based in some part on Inca law. To what extent was their dependence on Inca precedents really true? We do not know, nor do we have a satisfactory edition of the laws themselves.

Eventually San Marcos University quieted down, and Basadre returned to Peru; he completed the volume on Lemos but he did not continue with his plan to write the other viceregal works and was not even able to set down much specific information on the undoubtedly large numbers of manuscripts he consulted. Yet Lemos continued to interest historians, and two more volumes were published on this "pious and authoritarian" ruler.

This may seem unfair to other viceroys; why should Lemos have three books written about him while many others have not been treated at all? The same may be said of Viceroy Antonio de Mendoza who established royal government in New Spain in 1535. Two good biographies were produced almost simultaneously a generation ago by an American and a Spaniard, and later a third biography appeared. The result may be described as a patchwork quilt without much rhyme or reason. We appear to need badly some minimal planning in viceregal studies.

The main question today is what should and could be done, in the light of all the considerations set forth above. First of all, let us recognize that some progress has been made in recent years. The question of the influence of the origin of the institution of viceroys in Spain and their early development in America has been taken up by outstanding scholars. The many laws and regulations concerning viceroys have been recently compiled; and certain other studies have appeared and a few doctoral dissertations have been prepared. Some new approaches have been suggested, the significance of viceregal sources for economic history has at last been recognized, and some stimulating but not wholly convincing theories of bureaucracy have been applied to Spanish administration in America. We have indeed much to be thankful for as we contemplate the past and peer into the future!

V.

After my disengagement from Bartolomé de Las Casas and the history of the Potosí silver mine, I began to dream of publishing a corpus of fundamental documentation on viceroys. Eventually it became clear that the eighteenth-century Bourbon viceroys were receiving considerable attention, particularly from the historians at the University of Sevilla; I was also impressed by the fact that the viceregal correspondence increased in sheer quantity by leaps and bounds after 1700. Therefore I determined to limit my plan to those viceroys who had served during the Hapsburg period, that is up to 1700, and to include the following material on each viceroy whenever possible:

1. Biographical Sketch and Brief Statement on the Principal Events of the Viceroy's Period

2. Royal Instructions

Each viceroy went to the New World equipped with many royal orders on his behalf and copious instructions on what to do. Though eventually these instructions tended to be somewhat repetitive, they represented what the crown thought should be done and what each viceroy was to strive to achieve. Very little use has been made of these instructions, with the exception of the Swedish historian Magnus Mörner in his recent splendid volume on race relations.

3. Relación

Each viceroy was supposed to draw up a formal report on his administration to serve as a report to the king on important events of his rule and as a guide for his successor. Not all viceroys complied with this royal order, and some died in office before a report could be made; but the many relaciones that were completed constitute official documentary sources of value to anthropologists, economists, geographers, historians, political scientists, and indeed to everyone concerned with the history of the Spanish empire in America or colonial administration in general. No other European power of the time appears to have required such reports, so that this corpus of material presents a unique and valuable historical source.

Some of the relaciones have already been printed, but often in restricted editions or without adequate editorial apparatus. They are all out-of-print items today. The text of each relación will be based on the best manuscript or manuscripts available. For those viceroys who did not prepare relaciones, or whose report is not to be found, a selection of his correspondence will be given. The same will be done for those periods when an Audiencia was serving as the interim governing power, except when the Audiencia had prepared a report of its own, in emulation of viceregal procedure. Though the relaciones have different characteristics from the viceregal correspondence, they are a fundamental source which cannot be overlooked. The inclusion of both kinds of basic materials has certain evident advantages.

Some viceroys were so energetic that they prepared careful reports on how they found their viceroyalty on arrival, and all such special reports found will be included. Other viceroys, like the Conde de Lemos, disagreed with the relación his predecessor left him and compiled a kind of counter-relación. These too will be included when found.

4. Residencia Material

The "cargos" or charges against each viceroy will be included and the Sentencia whenever they are available. The *residencia* or judicial inquiry carried on at the end of each viceroy's rule to determine whether he should be punished for any mistakes while in office produced an enormous quantity of material, for the proceedings were often very detailed with much evidence given pro and con by witnesses. The stout volumes in which the *residencias* were usually bound have been scarcely touched by historians, though they are obviously of considerable value. The proceeding, for example, against Viceroy Count of Castellar in seventeenth-century Peru resulted in a monster manuscript containing some 37,000 folios. Anyone who has examined these impressive collections of paper, as I did last summer in Sevilla, cannot help but be astounded at the vast quantity of evidence against Viceroy Castellar and his associates taken down word for word by official notaries from a host of witnesses in all the far corners of Peru: Oruro, La Paz, Guayaquil, Huánuco, Cajamarca, Chimbo, Chillaos, Chachapoyas, Arequipa, Huancavelica, Cuzco, Huamanga, and other places in the vast reaches of the Viceroyalty of Peru. Viceroy Castellar died before the *residencia* trial was ended, but his widow responded to the numerous charges against the Count with a series of letters, reports, and witnesses for her side.

The wives and widows of viceroys should merit a separate work sometime, for they were valiant defenders of their husbands' reputations and their families' interests. The wife of one viceroy complained bitterly to King Philip II that he had sent her husband off to Peru for many years' service there, leaving her to cope alone with their fifteen children. Perhaps Professor Charles R. Boxer will include some of the notable vicequeens in his forthcoming Bryn Mawr lectures on "Women in the Iberian Empires."

Though the *residencia* material will be listed, only the charges against each viceroy will be printed, together with the final *Sentencia* or Sentence handed down by the king and Council of the Indies after they had reviewed the evidence. Taken together, the *Relación*, the viceroy's image of his own rule, and the *Residencia* documents provide contemporary and sometimes contrasting opinions on Spanish viceregal administration.

5. Catalogue

A list will be given of the indexes of the general letters sent back by the viceroys to Spain. Certain other important manuscripts located in various archives will be included, so that anyone who wishes to investigate any specific viceroy will be able to find here an indication of what material exists. This Catalogue will be based primarily on an examination of the many *legajos* of viceregal correspondence in the Archivo de Indias, but pertinent items from other sections of the archive will also be included.

6. Bibliography

An annotated list of articles, books, and unpublished doctoral dissertations, as well as a list of important viceregal documents previously printed, will be included.

* * *

When completed this project will provide a substantial amount of source material for the study of colonial Spanish America, all of which will be published in Spanish with the texts modernized. The documents on which this project is based are often covered with dust, and in some cases they appear not to have been consulted since they were filed away in the sixteenth and seventeenth centuries by some hard-working secretary on the staff of the Council of the Indies. Yet they often retain their freshness and pertinence to later times. What the Mexican historian Ernesto de la Torre Villar remarked about the relación of the first viceroy in Mexico, Antonio de Mendoza (1535-1550), might well be applied to others: "There is in this Relación magnificent observations on the Indians, their qualities and their defects, on the economy, religious life, colonists, laws for the regulation of society, in short, it gives a total view of the organization of the recently created viceroyalty. Some of Viceroy Mendoza's psychological and political observations in his report are fundamental and even now retain their value."

But for the student of history, mass is not enough. No matter how much viceregal correspondence and other documentation is to be found in the archives, the key question remains: What is its use? This brings us to the question of interpretation.

For over four centuries, in fact since Bartolomé de Las Casas printed his terrible indictment of Spanish rule in America, the famous or infamous "Very Brief Account of the Destruction of the Indies" in 1552 in Sevilla, opinion has been sharply divided on the nature of Spain's action in America. Was it largely bad, or largely beneficent? Or a mixture of the two? This large and unresolved problem constitutes an important part of the work of many historians of the Spanish empire, yet they are far from agreement and I myself have recently engaged in polemical writing on the subject.

Let me conclude this brief account of the large subject of viceroys by stating that no better way exists, in my opinion, to examine the true nature of Spanish rule in America in all its variety and contradictions than by using the enormous documentation on viceroys. If we analyze the documents that flowed increasingly from America to Spain for three centuries, if we avoid losing ourselves in genealogical minutiae or other relatively peripheral matters, if above all we do not look at the New World solely through the eyes of a particular viceroy, or give what might be called "a view from the viceregal palace", but instead avail ourselves of the vast source materials on the many problems the viceroy faced, then we may draw closer to the reality of Spanish America in all its richness of human drama than we have hitherto been able to do.

Though this rich viceregal documentation may provide a solid foundation, we will still need much patient labor by historians and many special studies before any adequate synthesis or interpretation of Spanish American history can be attempted comparable to the work of Richard Hofstader, projected shortly before his death in 1970. For he had at hand an "extraordinary proliferation of first-rate historical monographs" which scholars have produced during the last twenty years. No such harvest is available for the historian of Spanish America. Thus the finished construction must wait, but the bricks are available in great abundance.

In conclusion, though I am suspicious of most generalizations, let me hazard one of my own. Even when the monographs have been prepared, I cannot imagine that all questions will be answered, or that controversy over the true nature of Spanish rule in America will be stilled. I am sure, however, that the viceregal documentation and the specialized investigations derived from it will disclose that the Spanish empire was made up of a remarkable variety of men and women who transferred an old society to a new world and developed there a mixed society such as the world had never seen before. The story of their lives will be well worth hunting for among the thousands upon thousands of pages of manuscripts, as well as for the fundamental forces of society that will also be found there. Together, the history of these individuals as well as the customs, the institutions, the laws, the values that they brought from Spain to America will be found useful in deepening our understanding of both the past and the present, and perhaps even of the future.

CHAPTER 19.

EL VISITADOR LIC. ALONSO FERNANDEZ DE BONILLA Y EL VIRREY DEL PERU, EL CONDE DEL VILLAR (1590-1593)

One of the pleasures of research in the Archivo General de Indias in Sevilla is the regularity with which interesting manuscripts turn up on topics one is not studying. During the years of combing through the many legajos there on viceregal administration I had paid no special attention to the residencias, those judicial enquiries at the end of each important official's term of office to determine whether he had broken the law.

Then arrived an invitation from the Academia Nacional de la Historia in Caracas to participate in a conference on audiencias and residencias. I remembered running across some items on Visitador Alonso Fernández de Bonilla who inspected both the Audiencia de Lima and Viceroy Conde del Villar. As I looked further, there turned up a rich and curious collection of documents which served as the basis for the following article.

Memoria del Segundo Congreso Venezolano de Historia, II (Caracas, 1975), 13-29. Reprinted by permission. Translation by Celso Rodríguez.

El Visitador Lic. Alonso Fernández de Bonilla y El Virrey del Peru, El Conde del Villar (1590-1593)

I. Introducción

La historia de las visitas generales en la América española ha sido oscurecida por el problema de definir sus funciones-- era esencialmente la misma institución que la residencia?--pero al margen de su conformación jurídica, una pregunta más fundamental es si esta institución cumplió una finalidad provechosa. Ernesto Schäfer, estudioso alemán, un tanto dogmático, que ha hecho una gran contribución a nuestro conocimiento de América durante el reinado de la Casa de Austria, ha dado una opinión muy pesimista sobre la utilidad de las visitas generales:

> Efectivamente ha quedado conservado sólo una parte muy pequeña de todas las actas de Visitas. La pérdida al fondo no es demasiado lamentable, porque por lo menos 7/10 de cada acta de Visita no contenían más que las contestaciones de los testigos a los interminables interrogatorios, y estas contestaciones por su uniformidad y pesadez protocolaria son tan largas como fútiles. En cambio, la pérdida de casi todas las sentencias definitivas pronunciadas por el Consejo de Indias es muy sensible, porque éstas, a juzgar por las pocas aún conservadas, rendirían un cuadro detallado de la verdadera conducta de los visitados y serían muy valiosas para la historia de la cultura.

En verdadero estilo teutón, Schäfer continuó dando una lista del material existente en al Archivo General de Indias, pero nadie, por lo que yo he podido verificar, ha analizado todavía esas miles de páginas manuscritos con intención de evaluar el verdadero significado de las visitas generales. Mi estudio actual de las inspecciones del Lic. Alonso Fernández de Bonilla al gobierno del virrey Conde del Villar en Perú, desde 1585 hasta 1590, no tiene como propósito ofrecer un detalle completo de esta visita, sino proveer una reseña general de este caso, indicar qué documentación existe y también sugerir el valor que tales investigaciones judiciales pueden tener para el historiador que hoy día desea comprender la empresa de España en América.

II. El Virrey

Don Fernando Torres y Portugal fue nombrado virrey del Perú el 31 de marzo de 1584, pero no llegó a Lima hasta el 25 de noviembre de 1585. Gobernó mediocremente por poco más de cuatro años, al cabo de los cuales entregó el cargo virreinal el 8 de enero de 1590 a don García Hurtado de Mendoza, marqués de Cañete. El historiador peruano Rubén Vargas Ugarte, S. J., ofrece una interpretación condescendiente y en general favorable de su actuación en el Perú: "Hombre fiel, discreto y bueno, Villar no sobresalió por sus dotes pero, en conjunto, nos le hacen apreciable. Ni las circunstancias ni el tiempo le permitieron realizar alguna obra señalada, pero podía alejarse del Perú satisfecho, porque había puesto lo mejor de su voluntad y de su inteligencia al servicio de su Rey y de sus subordinados. Este es su mejor elogio."

Una investigación minuciosa de la acción del conde del Villar como virrey lo revela como persona arbitraria, pues suprimió el sistema de alcaldes electivos en Lima y designó un corregidor, pero esta innovación solamente se aplicó durante tres años. Sentía aversión por la Inquisición y ni siquiera acompañó a los funcionarios del Santo Oficio en los autos de fe, lo que dio lugar a una real cédula ordenándole específicamente que así lo hiciera. El virrey debió sentirse muy satisfecho cuando el 5 de octubre de 1586 se enteró por el fiscal de la Inquisición, Juan Alcedo, quien se hallaba en su lecho de muerte, que doña Catalina Morejón era la amante del inquisidor Antonio Gutiérrez de Ulloa mientras su esposo estaba ausente de Lima. Para evitar un escándalo mayor el conde del Villar la desterró. Con posterioridad el Consejo Supremo de la Inquisición ordenó a Juan Ruiz de Prado que investigara a Ulloa pues había otros cargos contra el inquisidor.

A menos de un año del incidente de doña Catalina, la Inquisición llamó a Juan Bello, secretario privado del virrey, para que respondiera a las acusaciones que se le habían hecho. El conde del Villar estaba cargado de años y achaques y dependía muchísimo del joven secretario de gobernación, en quien confiaba plenamente el manejo de los asuntos del Estado. Era un cargo de extraordinario poder y responsabilidad: "era Juan Bello quien escribía la cartas a Su Majestad, estaba al corriente de los más secretos asuntos del gobierno, y por cuyas manos pasaba, además, la casi totalidad de los negocios tocantes a la jurisdicción real en el Perú". Al principio el virrey expresó su solidaridad con el secretario y envió a su capellán y confesor para asegurar a los inquisidores que tenía absoluta confianza en Juan Bello y que debía ser reintegrado a sus ocupaciones lo antes posible, a menos que los cargos contra él fueran probados. Luego el virrey se vio impelido a modificar completamente su posición, pues se enteró por su joven y disoluto hijo y por su sobrino, de moralidad y comportamiento igualmente dudosos, que Bello había hecho una deposición secreta ante la Inquisición sobre los asuntos virreinales. En realidad, así lo había hecho en un testimonio de lo más sórdido, que revelaba la escandalosa conducta de los parientes del virrey a los que Bello se había opuesto. De este modo, Jerónimo de Torres, hijo del virrey, y su sobrino Diego de Portugal se aprovecharon del viejo y enfermo conde del Villar, y Juan Bello fue sumariamente arrestado por el virrey haciendo más vehemente la acérrima enemistad que ya existía entre la Inquisición y el virrey.

La situación y los problemas económicos demandaron la mayoría del tiempo del conde del Villar cuando no estaba ocupado en contrarrestar lo que él consideraba los artibrarios intentos de la Inquisición de socavar la autoridad real. Sobre las condiciones en Potosí se ha publicado la detallada _Relación_ del minero Luis Capoche, que ofrece una excelente descripción de este centro minero, y entonces sumamente importante. Para una reseña de los problemas administrativos, ver la correspondencia del virrey que ha sido publicada. Uno de los primeros censos del Perú fue preparado en este período, el que indica que allí había paroximadamente 3.000.000 de habitantes en 1586.

Son numerosos los manuscritos existentes para llevar a cabo un estudio del gobierno del conde de Villar, y se hallan en distintos lugares; muchos de esos documentos se refieren al desarrollo económico de las minas de plata de Potosí. Se hicieron importantes informes sobre los indios, cuestiones geográficas y asuntos económicos, y unos pocos documentos originales están en la Lilly Library en Indiana University (Bloomington, Indiana).

El virrey partió para España antes de que llegara el visitador general, y por eso nunca se encontraron. En vista de las turbulentas relaciones del conde del Villar con la Inquisición, conviene destacar que la persona encargada de hacer la visita general era un inquisidor de México, el Lic. Alonso Fernández de Bonilla.

III. El Visitador General

Con frecuencia el rey y el Consejo de Indias confiaban la delicada e importante misión de visitador general a funcionarios de la Inquisición; en realidad, el colega superior de Bonilla, el inquisidor Pedro Moya de Contreras, había sido designado para realizar la visita general en México en 1573, al mismo tiempo que ejercía el cargo de inquisidor. El había establecido la Inquisición en México en 1571 y no apreció el celo de Bonilla cuando más tarde pasó a formar parte de los miembros de la Inquisición. El 24 de marzo de 1574 Moya de Contreras presentó al Inquisidor General un informe desfavorable sobre lo que él consideraba que eran dudosas acciones de su colega inferior. Ambos inquisidores se dedicaron activamente a sus obligaciones, que incluían una considerable concentración en asuntos financieros y juntos rastrearon al judaísmo y la herejía en México. Se conoce poco sobre la historia de las primeras comunidades judías en México, pero después de 1571 "nombres, sucesos, títulos y en verdad los testimonios de todo el panorama de la vida judía han sido conservados".

El 19 de julio de 1589, el Lic. Bonilla recibió en México despachos desde España sobre la visita general que debía realizar en Perú. El transporte era difícil pero confiaba en poder embarcarse en enero o febrero a lo sumo. Su promesa de fidelidad y cuidado reflejó bien el espíritu de un burócrata de la Casa de Austria en América:

> Y a la partida y de todos los puertos que tomaré daré a V. M. cuenta de mi viaje. Y llegado al Perú entenderé en mis comisiones con fidelidad y cuidado a que me obliga la confianza que V. M. hace de mi. Y aunque procuraré corresponder con todas mis fuerzas a tan grande favor, lo que más ofrezco es una voluntad al servicio de Dios y de V. M. libre de otros respectos que me obliguen más que al de la causa pública.

De ahí en adelante la correspondencia del Lic. Bonilla constituye un expresivo ejemplo del valor histórico de tales cartas, como tan bien lo ha expresado el Dr. Ismael Sánchez Bella:

> La correspondencia de los visitadores generales enviados a un virreinato. Su calidad humana--son cuidadosamente seleccionados por los consejeros de Indias, muchas veces entre inquisidores, y poseen sólida formación jurídica, integridad e independencia--, el rango de que están revestidos muy frecuentemente, de consejero de Indias, a título honorífico a veces--pero con frecuencia de derecho y de hecho--; otras, titulares de obispados y aún arzobispados en Indias, y los amplios poderes que reciben como visitadores generales, a veces unidos a la facultad de residenciar a virreyes, les permiten actuar con gran libertad y obtener pública y secretamente, una información riquísima, que se recoge en el voluminoso expediente de la visita, pero del que se adelantan juicios e informes en la copiosa correspondencia de carácter confidencial que van enviando al Consejo de Indias y al rey en los largos años que suele durar la visita.

Por la correspondencia de Bonilla sabemos de su largo y difícil viaje desde Acapulco, de donde salió el 18 de marzo de 1590 hasta que finalmente llegó al Callao el 2 de agosto, donde poco después su escribano real Juan de la Fuente murió a causa de las penurias sufridas. El Lic. Bonilla no se sintió lo suficientemente bien hasta el 26 de setiembre, para anunciar públicamente la visita. Después de esto sus cartas informaron con regularidad y en detalle acerca del progreso de la visita y las anotaciones y comentario que contienen estas cartas indican que recibieron una atención rápida y cuidadosa.

Para el 10 de octubre de 1590 Bonilla había redactado las 126 preguntas que contenía el interrogatorio sobre el virrey y los funcionarios fueron despachados a distintos lugares del virreinato para obtener pruebas. Después de dos años y medio Bonilla redactó 108 cargos individuales contra el conde del Villar, y el 26 de marzo de 1593 fueron anunciados oficialmente a don Diego de Portugal y al Dr. Alberto de Acuña en su carácter de procuradores del virrey.

Para entonces el conde del Villar ya había muerto en España, pero Bonilla informó al rey el 15 de marzo de 1593 que remitía los documentos de la visita porque "aunque se ha muerto, importará verla para la inteligencia de aquel gobierno y dejado aparte lo que de ella resulta y lo que la gente de su casa infamó el gobierno del conde. Dice que no podría juzgar de su persona cosa que desliga de las obligaciones de caballero, buen cristiano, limpio, y de buena intención y verdadero trato".

Eventualmente los legajos de la visita llegaron al Archivo General de Indias, donde ahora permanecen a la espera del investigador que tenga el tiempo y la paciencia para leer los cientos de páginas manuscritas coleccionadas por el Lic. Alonso Fernández de Bonilla durante su examen del gobierno del conde del Villar. La defensa de los procuradores del virrey y la sentencia del rey y del Consejo de Indias no han sido encontradas, pero existe suficiente información para inquirir acerca de la visita general y tratar de responder a la pesimista opinión de Ernesto Schäfer.

IV. Preguntas

Aún no ha llegado el momento de tratar de analizar y describir esta visita en detalle, pero el historiador que examine las numerosas fuentes manuscritas disponibles puede al menos formular estas preguntas:

1. Por qué Felipe II y el Consejo de Indias ordenaron la visita?

Esta es una pregunta fácil para contestar! Además de las normas españolas de realizar investigaciones periódicas a sus funcionarios administrativos, habían llegado quejas desde el Perú a la corte real. Esto no es extraño, porque el Perú había demostrado ser mucho más difícil de gobernar que México, donde dos competentes virreyes, Antonio de Mendoza y Luis de Velasco (el Viejo) habían establecido firmemente el poder español en los primeros treinta años (1535-1564). En Perú había estallado la guerra civil en los primeros tiempos, el primer virrey había sido muerto por los rebeldes y Perú no experimentó un gobierno estable hasta el de Francisco de Toledo (1569-1581). Pero este virreinato era de gran extensión y complicada naturaleza. No sabemos la verdadera dimensión de la corrupción y mala administración que hubo hasta que llegó el Lic. Bonilla, pues la documentación de las residencias a los virreyes anteriores aparentemente se han perdido, pero los papeles del primer visitador Diego Bribiesca de Muñatones son copiosos y significativos. También es significativo que este visitador haya sido arrestado por actuar ilegalmente, y sólo fue perdonado años después de su muerte. Por lo tanto, podemos dar por descontado que había mucho para inspeccionar y corregir en el gobierno del Perú.

2. Cuál fue la actuación del Lic. Bonilla como visitador del virrey?

En este punto la respuesta no puede ser categórica. El visitador redactó 108 cargos contra el virrey en dos años y medio aproximadamente, que no fue un lapso inusual para tal tipo de investigaciones. Pero las inspecciones a la Audiencia de Lima, a otras instituciones y a otros funcionarios, que estaban incluidas entre los deberes del visitador, en un asunto distinto y será referido luego.

Se justificaron los cargos contra el conde del Villar y fueron redactados con responsabilidad? El interrogatorio o lista de 126 preguntas que se hizo a los diferentes testigos cubren una multitud de asuntos, pero representan imparcial y totalmente los aspectos del gobierno virreinal que debían ser investigados? Ciertamente, la acumulación de cargos no ofrece un panorama correcto de lo realizado positivamente por el conde del Villar, ni siquiera de las condiciones en que ejerció su autoridad en el Perú, porque el principal objetivo de todo visitador, incluyendo Bonilla, era encontrar lo que estaba equivocado y recomendar soluciones. Y quién puede decir si los testigos que trataron de responder a las 126 preguntas no fueron especialmente seleccionados para que dieran la respuesta que deseaba el visitador?

En el caso del conde del Villar, ni siquiera tenemos sus descargos o defensa tal como le presentaron sus agentes, pues estos papeles faltan en la documentación existente sobre la visita. Vargas Ugarte considera que muchos de los cargos eran en realidad "defectos del sistema y en todos los gobernantes recaían por igual, como el descuidar la paga de los indios chasquis, el abuso de llevar a Huancavelica indios de provincias lejanas. . . y el que no se repartieran los mitayos en la debida proporción y con la debida equidad, así en Huancavelica como en Potosí". Vargas Ugarte acepta que ciertos cargos fueron correctos: "Mayor fundamento tienen los cargos en que se le acusa de haber consentido muchos desmanes de su hijo don Jerónimo, cuya vida estaba lejos de ajustarse a lo que exigían la moral y las leyes y el cual, prevalido del parentesco que le unía al virrey, admitía gajes y obsequios, con fines torcidos y se dejaba cohechar por cualquiera".

Nunca sabremos con seguridad cómo juzgar esos 108 cargos. Aunque contáramos con la defensa del virrey, ésta había sido preparada por su sobrino don Diego de Portugal, que había estado igualmente envuelto con don Jerónimo en las escandalosas actividades que empañaron el gobierno del conde del Villar. Más importante aún, no sabemos lo que decidieron Felipe II y el Consejo de Indias, después de haber examinado los cargos, los descargos y la demás copiosa evidencia que tenían a su alcance. La sentencia, como ocurre con tantas otras visitas, no se encuentra entre los papeles de la de Bonilla, aunque puede estar oculta en algún lugar del Archivo General de Indias, y algún investigador afortunado tal vez tropiece con ella.

Si lo juzgamos por su correspondencia, ciertamente, durante los tres primeros años de su actuación en el Perú, parece que Bonilla se mantuvo bastante activo. Disfrutaba de la confianza del rey pues cuando en 1592 se produjo en Quito el conflicto sobre la alcabala, Bonilla fue designado para investigarlo y en el mismo año el rey lo nombró Arzobispo de México. Además, Juan de Cepeda, Presidente de la Audiencia de Charcas y hombre difícil de conformar, opinó favorablemente del visitador. Cepeda había recomendado que los factorajes de los azogues fueran tomados en Charcas o en Potosí y no en Lima, como el virrey creía que era mejor. Bonilla apoyó a Cepeda y vencieron la objeción del virrey, lo que naturalmente le agradó al presidente. Como Cepeda le informó al rey el 12-III-1593, esto fue "lo más acertado, tomando a mi cargo mandar desenmarañar y sacar a luz cuentas tan confusas y engañosas que así se deslizan entre las manos como el azogue".

Una vez que los cargos contra el conde del Villar fueron redactados y enviados a España, la labor de Bonilla se hizo claramente más lenta y al final su visita fue una de las más largas de las efectuadas en las Indias, y una de las menos satisfactorias.

3. Cuál es el significado de la visita del Lic. Bonilla al conde del Villar?

Aunque basándonos en la documentación de la visita del Lic. Bonilla no puede arribarse a una firme conclusión acerca de cómo el conde del Villar ejerció sus funciones, esa documentación puede ser de considerable utilidad para los historiadores que traten de reconstruir la realidad del gobierno español en Perú durante esos años. La información sobre la enconada disputa entre el virrey y la Inquisición nos ayuda a comprender la constante tensión entre la Iglesia y el Estado que caracterizó a la administración española en América. Los testimonios de los numerosos testigos que respondieron a las 126 preguntas del interrogatorio, ofrecen datos repetidos y a veces contradictorios, pero en general revelan los aspectos más negativos de la vida en Perú, como también lo hace el memorial de Juan Bello a la Inquisición.

La correspondencia del visitador, la de los oficiales reales, y la minuciosa información sobre cuestiones financieras que proveyó Bonilla, constituyen en su totalidad valiosas fuentes sobre aspectos vitales de la dominación española, con implicaciones de relevancia para el historiador. Como lo ha señalado Vicenta Cortés Alonso para un período anterior en el Caribe, "los asientos de las cuentas del tesorero Alonso de la Puente, contador Diego Márquez y veedor Gonzalo Fernández de Oviedo, de 1514 a 1526, dan una panorámica de la conquista y asentimiento de Panamá, de los caciques, entradas, orfebrería indígena, etc., casi día por día". Este tipo de minucia ha de ser utilizada eventualmente por aquellos historiadores que acepten el desafío proclamado por Waldemar Espinoza Soriano, que acertadamente puntualiza que ningún estudio serio o completo ha sido realizado todavía en ninguna de las seis instituciones básicas en las españolizadas sociedades aymará y quechua--"mitas, yanaconaje, reducciones y municipios, tasa y tributación, cacicazgos, comunidades de tierras y encomiendas".

Debe destacarse una contribución especial de la documentación de la visita de Bonilla. Vargas Ugarte descubrió y fue el primero en señalar que incluye varios documentos fundamentales sobre los repartimientos, como uno del virrey Francisco de Toledo, que puede ser de provecho para los estudiosos de la historia económica de este período. En realidad, la visita contiene gran información para el historiador económico, pues trae datos sobre el movimiento de navíos, cuentas de almojarifazgo, registros de tributos y listas como la "Relación de las partidas de mercaderías y esclavos que resultan por los registros de los navíos que vinieron al puerto de Callao de esta ciudad de los Reyes el año pasado de 1587, que están por evaluar y cobrar los derechos reales que a S. M. pertenecen, y los navíos en que han venido y por qué cuenta y de qué parte es como sigue". Asuntos relativos a la defensa, información biográfica, y en verdad muchos otros aspectos del gobierno virreinal son tratados en los cientos y miles de páginas de documentos de la visita de Bonilla.

A veces tanta minuciosidad abruma. Sabemos lo que se les debía pagar a los chasquis, cuántas gallinas y huevos daban los indios para la casa virreinal toda esta información debidamente declarada en testimonios jurados firmados por los caciques. En conjunto esta documentación, casi tan fresca e inutilizada como cuando Bonilla mandó aquellos papeles a España, debidamente sellados, según la cédula real ordenada, ofrece una visión amplísima y a la vez básica de la vida peruana económica, social y política. Esta visita, por lo tanto, será una fuente notable para todos los historiadores que deseen evitar lo que el escritor peruano Felipe Barreda Laos decribió como peligros cuando declaro:

> La historia virreinal de América vive amenazada por dos conjuraciones: la de los eruditos sin imaginación que renuncian a todo esfuerzo de evocación, y convierten la historia en recopilación, más o menos ordenada, de documentos, intercalando narraciones que son verdaderos desiertos de aridez y arenales sin vida; la de los "hispanófilos" e "hispanófobos", los cuales deforman la realidad histórica, considerando la Historia de América no como realidad básica, intrínsicamente verdadera y respetable, sino como simple valor subalterno de la historia de la Metrópoli; como recurso de propaganda política y cultural.

Los manuscritos coleccionados por el Lic. Bonilla, no nos dirán todo. Una fuente de igual importancia, y a veces todavía más valiosa, ha de ser la correspondencia virreinal tan acertadamente elogiada por Manuel Moreyra Paz-Soldán. Pero la visita de Bonilla nos indica que una parte esencial de los pormenores de la historia de España en el Nuevo Mundo ha de constar en la documentación reunida por los visitadores, que revelará parte de la información requerida por Luis E. Valcárcel, en lo que llama "ese mundo disimulado por el historiador colonial", y correctamente afirmó que "los archivos guardan muchas revelaciones sobre la vida de millones de hombres olvidados". Porque las visitas, naturalmente, incluyeron mucha información sobre los conquistados, así como sobre los conquistadores. Uno de los pocos historiadores que ha utilizado los documentos de las visitas expresó que: "Todas las visitas trataron, en gran medida, acerca de los indios. Colectivamente, ofrecen un conocimiento perspicaz de sus hábitos y costumbres y la aculturación que resultó de su contacto con los españoles . . . La visita, ya fuera religiosa o civil, suministra importantes datos al historiador, al antropólogo y al etnólogo que se dedique a investigar la Florida española". Aunque el autor se refiere a una frontera provincial, lo mismo puede decirse en cierta medida de las visitas en cualquier lugar del imperio español. Y observa además que las visitas religiosos también están incluidas, así como la visita civil de Bonilla que estamos considerando ahora. Se conoce menos todavía de las visitas religiosas, pero con seguridad futuros investigadores les han de prestar, mayor atención porque complementan en cierto grado a las visitas civiles.

Podemos concluir estos comentarios generales sobre el significado histórico de las visitas agregando que probablemente nunca se podrá determinar con exactitud si los cargos contra el conde del Villar fueron justos y correctos, pero algunos de los documentos necesarios para preparar una historia cabal del Perú se encuentran en la visita de Bonilla. Y contamos con esa documentación porque el rey y el Consejo de Indias, a pesar del costo y la frustración que causaban las visitas, ordenaron que se realizaran estas investigaciones mientras España gobernara el Perú, y los documentos fueron preservados para los historiadores por dedicados archivistas y administradores españoles.

V. Epílogo

El conde del Villar ya había partido cuando el Lic. Bonilla llego a Lima en 1590, y por ello el proceso contra el virrey no encontró mucha oposición, especialmente porque uno de sus procuradores o agentes era el escandaloso don Diego de Portugal, que en años anteriores había sido responsable por muchos actos licenciosos gracias a la protección y ceguera del virrey. La inspección a los demás funcionarios fue un asunto distinto, pues sufrieron de inmediato las acciones del visitador. Como lo ha señalado Ismael Sánchez Bella: "Los oficiales reales de Lima, al exigirles en 1592 el pago de los alcances que les hace el visitador Bonilla, tienen que vender sus esclavos para poder pagar". Cuando los oficiales reales vieron que los resultados de la investigación de Bonilla les resultarían dañinos, intentaron "la apelación ante el Consejo de Indias, huyendo del carácter ejecutivo y riguroso que tenía la Visita". Al principio el fiscal Núñez de Avendaño favoreció la visita y había notificado al rey en una carta fechada el 29-XII-1590: "Cada día veo por experiencia que es más necesario el Inquisidor Bonilla que por mandado de V. M. vino a visitar esta real audiencia". Pero él también cambió de opinión a medida que Bonilla comenzó a descubrir lo que consideró que eran anormalidades financieras.

La principal crítica al visitador fue su lentitud. Llegó a completar los cargos contra el virrey en 1593, pero la investigación a la audiencia y a otros funcionarios se hizo interminable. El virrey García de Mendoza, en su carta a Felipe II del 18-V-1593, sólo se quejó de las excesivas deliberaciones de Bonilla: "El dicho visitador procede en su visita muy cuerdamente, aunque va tan despacio que en tres años que ha que la comenzó no ha dado cargos a ninguno de los de la Audiencia". El virrey le aconsejó al rey que lo apurara, "porque al paso que lleva entiendo que no se acabará en muchos años y tanta dilación es de mucho inconveniente así por la gran cantidad de dinero que se gasta como porque los oidores respecto de estar en visita tienen con los relatores, abogados y negociantes más contemplaciones de las que serían menester".

Sin lugar a dudas Bonilla <u>no fue</u> un hombre de acción. Cuando en 1592 Felipe II lo nombró arzobispo de México, esperó un año y medio antes de ser consagrado en Lima por el arzobispo Mogrovejo. Felipe II también lo designó visitador en Quito, después del desagradable disturbio que tuvo lugar allí el año anterior a causa de las alcabalas, pero no le pareció necesario ir. Bonilla mantuvo correspondencia con la Audiencia de Quito y firmaba sus cartas al rey "El Arzobispo de México", pero no aceleró el ritmo de su visita y cuando el virrey García de Mendoza terminó en 1596 su período de seis años, el visitador todavía estaba en el Perú ocupado con la visita.

El rey y el Consejo de Indias tal vez se impresionaron favorablemente con la aparente dedicación de Bonilla por los asuntos financieros y su comprensión de cual era el interés del monarca, pues en diciembre de 1595 escribió a Felipe II: "Las dos cosas más preciosas que V. M. tiene en este reino son el cerro de Potosí, que es de plata, y el de Huancavelica de azogue".

Llegó a Lima el nuevo virrey, Luis de Velasco, tan competente como su padre, y la visita continuó año tras año. Aparentemente nunca se había estipulado una duración precisa a visita alguna, y Felipe II fue probablemente el monarca español que apreciaba la necesidad de proceder con cuidado, cautela y prudencia en las funciones de visitador, y hasta toleraba inspecciones tan largas como la de Bonilla. El virrey Velasco se empezó a quejar, y el 14-IX-1597 el rey le ordenó al visitador que completara su trabajo dentro de los tres meses. Ni siquiera esto hizo apurar a Bonilla, pues recién en marzo de 1599 le informó al secretario del virrey que había completado la visita. Pero esta no fue más que una acción dilatoria, porque un mes más tarde Velasco le comunicó al rey que Bonilla no había entregado todavía los cargos a la Audiencia, por consiguiente, el virrey recomendó que el rey instruyera al visitador que "agora diese los cargos sin hazer aucto perjudicial de suspensión ni condenación en manera alguna y que todo se remita así a ese real consejo".

Pero esto tampoco produjo una reacción en Bonilla, y el arzobispo de México murió en Lima en 1600, sin haber ocupado ese alto cargo y sin haber completado realmente su visita. Francisco García Durán debió ser encargado para finalizarla y el 28-IV-1603 le informó al rey que hasta esa fecha se habían utilizado en la visita 43.601 hojas de papel.

No fue sino hasta el 28-IV-1603 que la Audiencia informó al rey en esta lacónica nota: "La visita desta Real Audiencia ha trece años que dura, y va conclusa en esta flota. Suplicamos a V. M. la mande y despachar".

Sumariando esta larga visita, probablemente la de más duración en el imperio español, uno solo puede maravillar de la persistencia de un visitador tan consciente y tan lento como el Lic. Alonso Fernández de Bonilla. Cómo se arregló para pasar un mes detrás de otro compilando evidencias de corrupción y fechorías? Tal vez su experiencia anterior como Inquisidor en México lo había acostumbrado a contemplar y estudiar las peores facetas de la vida. De cualquier modo, su presencia en Lima durante una década debió haber actuado como un freno en las acciones de los funcionarios a quienes les hacía la visita y en realidad debe haber disminuido las actividades administrativas en general, pues quién podría dejar de pisar firme sabiendo que el visitador Bonilla estaba allí observando!

PART V

TEACHING AND TEACHERS

CHAPTER 20.

HOW A HISTORIAN WORKS: A REPLY TO A STUDENT QUERY

When the graduate students in history at Columbia University in 1963 or 1964 invited their professors to explain how they worked, my initial response was to doubt my ability to say anything useful on the subject. And even if I did, would the graduate students listen? Besides, I was busy on the history of Potosí, struggling to complete a publication that had been on my mind for thirty years, and didn't want to stop for interruptions.

So I didn't reply at first. My wife finally convinced me that I should try; more, she participated so fully in the thinking and the writing of this brief statement that it really is a joint effort. This collaboration convinced me that the wife of a historian is the person to answer all such queries.

Homenaje a Jaime Vicens Vives, I (Barcelona, 1965), 81-84. Reprinted by permission.

How a Historian Works: A Reply to a Student Query

The choice of a historical subject to study is almost as personal as the choice of a wife or husband and may have almost as long-term consequences for a young scholar's future. Certainly he must make both of these choices himself, although his professor may have some influence on the selection of the research topic. "The right to be consulted and to warn"--to borrow Walter Bagehot's observations on the role of the British monarch--seems to me the professor's role.

Today's young scholar is caught between two compulsions: one, to find and attack a problem ample enough to deserve the effort he will put into studying it and, second, to limit his study to manageable proportions so that he can fulfill as soon as possible the requirements leading to the degree he seeks in order to be ready for professional employment. How he, or she, resolves this problem must be an individual's responsibility.

Time available, personal interest, circumstances--and luck--play at least as large a role as advice in a scholar's development, as may be seen from the following account of my own experience.

My latest study and favorite work is Aristotle and the American Indians (London and Chicago, 1959) because it sums up much of my earlier work and offers, I believe, historical perspective on a problem which continues, as it has done throughout history, to plague the world: the basis for relations between unlike races of mankind.

Since I began graduate work in Latin American history in 1930 my major effort has been to understand from the vantage point of the 20th century the clash--not of arms--but of ideas on the nature of man which arose during the 16th century Spanish conquest of America. Here came a great European power, conquering and colonizing, and it encountered in the New World many strikingly different cultures, all strange to the Spaniards who believed their mission was to explore, to conquer, and to Christianize.

Within the framework of their own time and system of ideas, which were little affected by the Reformation except as it alarmed the Spanish Church and added urgency to the effort to spread the faith in the New World, the Spanish nation both at home and in America was agitated by questions which had important implications for the treatment of the natives they met. Were these plumed and painted peoples men, or sub-men incapable of receiving the Christian faith and western civilization? How, and in what order, should the dual mission to conquest and Christianize be accomplished?

What first directed my attention to the excitement of ideas that marked the era of conquest was my discovery, as I searched in the library for a suitable dissertation topic, that one man, Bartolomé de Las Casas, a Dominican, had taken his stand, after some years as a complacent participant in the exploitation of the Indians, as their defender and spokesman against the treatment his own countrymen accorded them. Moreover, he had fought for fifty years, basing his arguments on Christian doctrine, to change the hearts of Spaniards and to fashion the laws of the Indies to favor peaceful and orderly relations between the Spaniards and the natives. A year and a half in Spanish archives, first on a grant from Amherst College and then on a Harvard fellowship, opened up to me the fascinating story of the struggle for justice which I discovered so many Spaniards had waged during precisely those years when, according to the clichés about the Spanish conquest, the Spanish presence in America had consisted almost entirely of mass murders and heartless exploitation. Various articles, volumes of documents, and monographs resulted from this time. One was The Spanish Struggle for Justice in the Conquest of America (University of Pennsylvania Press, 1949), a thorough revision and amplification of my doctoral thesis. The struggle to write The Struggle, during years when my principal duties were in the Hispanic Foundation in the Library of Congress, should be mentioned because it gives my answer to the question "What conditions are necessary to produce good writing?" The possibility of travel, time--even if snatched in weekend blocks, evenings, and "vacations"--and still more the understanding of one's wife and children that this preoccupation is a necessary effort to be respected and when possible aided, and patient writing and re-writing, always aiming for greater clarity of thought and simplicity of style: these are the conditions, often difficult, under which good writing may be done. About ideal conditions I cannot speak; one does the best he can under the conditions in which he lives.

In addition to the historical research made possible by travel and study, I was fortunate enough to receive a post-doctoral grant from the Social Science Research Council which enabled me to spend some months observing an American anthropologist at work in a Guatemalan village. I have always believed that this experience deepened my concern with the native peoples and enlarged my understanding of the problems which the Spaniards met in their far-flung explorations. Because in the written records of this now distant time Spanish voices spoke so much more loudly than those of the Indians, the historian in the Latin American field must never fail to keep aware of the Indian realities that were so meagerly documented and sometimes only reflected in Spanish documents. This fellowship also enabled me to travel the length and breadth of Brazil, an exhilarating experience during which I came to appreciate anew the intimate relationship of geography and history which is particularly powerful in Latin America.

At present I am editing a large manuscript on the colorful history of the Imperial City of Potosí, the site of the great silver mine discovered and exploited by the colonial Viceroyalty of Peru, now modern Bolivia. I happened upon this manuscript in Madrid in the Royal Library in 1934. But only now, with the indispensable aid of a Bolivian scholar, Dr. Gunnar Mendoza, and the very generous sponsorship of Brown University, which owns one of the manuscripts and will issue the work during the University's Bicentennial anniversary in 1964, is this remarkable account to be made available to scholars. The history of South America's once largest city (about 150,000 souls in 1650) will offer future scholars, I believe, as rich a lode of information in many fields as it ever did the Spaniards in silver production during its heyday, when vale un Potosí connoted immeasurable riches.

Luck has played a part in this project, and the publication of the history of Potosí, like the history itself of this silver mine located some 14,000 feet up in the Andes, has had its fantastic and unexpected ups and downs. Some twenty years ago, for example, the publication of this work was all arranged for through the good offices of an Argentine friend who was the Director of the Instituto de Investigaciones Históricas of the University of Buenos Aires. Then Juan Perón came to power, removed my friend, and the project collapsed. Now due to the fact that Brown University happens to be celebrating the completion of its first two centuries and wishes to provide a contribution to history by making available to the public the manuscript donated to it fifty years ago by an American engineer, Colonel George E. Church, who was interested in Bolivia and its history, the almost incredible story of the Potosí silver mine is finally about to be published.

The story of Potosí is the other side of the coin of the Conquest: it deals with the struggle for riches, but fascinatingly mixed with mining technology, religious contention, the composition of society (since it drew men of many nations), dramatic events hitherto unknown, and, that perennial delight of historians, informed gossip. My attempt to define the historical problems the history of Potosí poses has appeared in Spanish as a publication of the University of San Francisco Xavier in Sucre, Bolivia and in English by Martinus Nijhoff of The Hague. The Brown University publication will greatly enrich our understanding of certain aspects of the history of Latin America and will, I hope, stimulate further research in this neglected field.

Our concern today with Latin America, its problems, its relationships to ourselves, needs historical perspective. This I tried to give in two paperback volumes: _Modern Latin America: Continent in Ferment_ (2 vols., 1959) which attempts to provide historical background for better understanding of present and impending changes there. My plan is to continue to study and to interpret the realities of this important group of nations, both Spanish and Portuguese speaking, whose world roles are growing and whose futures are so bound up with our own.

To return to the problems the young student of history faces, let me stress that whatever subject matter he chooses he must feel genuine concern for and strong attraction to it, and must learn both to read and to speak in the languages he needs for the study and travel involved. As he works into it, let him learn the value of consultation with others in his field in whatever country they may be. There are few ivory towers today and none should be inhabited by historians. And only if he gives himself with tenacity, enthusiasm, and good heart to his enterprise can he produce writing that will satisfy him and attract readers. A writer who is not read fails in his true function: to communicate what he has learned and thus to add to the sum of usable knowledge gained in his own time.

CHAPTER 21.

STUDYING LATIN AMERICA: THE VIEWS OF AN "OLD CHRISTIAN"

The study of Latin American history in the United States has greatly improved since I first started to read on the subject as an undergraduate at Northwestern University under I. J. Cox in 1922. The angle of our vision has broadened, we have been aided by new approaches and methods from the social sciences, and both students and professors have become more deeply aware of Latin American culture by living there. Indeed, there has been a kind of revolution in my own lifetime, and I tried to describe and interpret the changes I have seen in the following article delivered in 1966 as the Charles Wilson Hackett Memorial Lecture at the University of Texas.

But the revolution is by no means complete. We must henceforth devote much more attention to the teaching of Latin American history, and the conclusion of this lecture explains why I am now in my "pedagogical phase."

"Studying Latin America: The Views of an 'Old Christian'," is reprinted from Journal of Inter-American Studies, Vol. IX, No. 1 (January, 1967), 43-64 by permission of the Publisher, Sage Publications, Inc.

Studying Latin America: The Views of an "Old Christian"

I

Latin Americanists must be prepared for sudden shifts in the winds of circumstance. Less than ten years ago a gathering of scholars at the Newberry Library in Chicago lamented the lack of support for their disciplines, and drew up an impressive list of tools and monographs needed to advance the field. Presumably the specialists returned to their campuses refreshed by this heady and cathartic experience of thinking adventurously, but they found no change there in the attitudes of their university administrators or the majority of their colleagues, who still believed that Latin America was an area of peripheral value; the professors were not discharged, of course, for they had tenure, but the promise of the early flurry of Latin American area developments that had occurred in the 1940's was not fulfilled.

Even foundations, usually eager to tread new paths and reach for some stars, adopted a cautious attitude, immediately following World War II, toward spending money on Latin American studies. I still remember a dinner meeting at the University of Texas some ten or twelve years ago at which a senior officer of the Rockefeller Foundation counselled moderation in the development of a Latin American program there. The University could not adequately treat all of Latin America, he explained; propinquity and past developments indicated that the Institute of Latin American Studies at Texas should largely limit itself to the study of Mexico. That may have been at the time sound advice--though the University authorities did not so consider it and the President and the Institute decided not to apply for a Latin American grant if the University would have to agree to restrict its sphere of activity to Mexico alone, important as that segment of Latin America undoubtedly was. And thus it was that I enjoyed a stimulating and valuable experience for some seven years of attempting to administer an Institute of Latin American Studies at a major center almost without outside funds.

Even foundation officials are not omniscient, however; the year after the Newberry Library meeting in 1958 Dr. Fidel Castro came to power in Cuba, Washington and the public "discovered" Latin America again, and within a year or two the Ford Foundation--whose resources exceed those of any other foundation--decided that Latin American studies in the United States and institutions in Latin America required assistance. This combination of government and private support has been responsible for the most dramatic development of academic interest in Latin America that has yet taken place in the long history of "boom" and "bust" that has characterized this field in the United States. Never before have so many libraries been able to strengthen their collections on both Brazil and Spanish America, an activity in which the Latin American Collection of the University of Texas, under the vigorous and competent direction of Dr. Nettie Lee Benson, continues to show the way. Never before has the Conference on Latin American History of the American Historical Association been able to sponsor so many and such valuable projects; never before has the academic marketplace been so attractive to graduate students; never before have so many professors and students been able to visit and study in Latin America for such prolonged periods; never before have our research facilities and salaries been able to pull to our faculties so many scholars from Latin America as to create a kind of "brain drain" from those countries. An impressive Latin American Research Review has been launched by some 30 institutions, and its generous budget for its first two years of existence approximates the budget of the Hispanic American Historical Review for its first 48 years. Indeed the best single index to the booming state of Latin American studies and Latin American affairs generally is this quarterly record of research in progress and of information useful to investigators. Even publishers--those fairly accurate barometers of public and private attitudes--are now willing and at times eager to launch books on Latin America, though there is still a tendency to stress the "Two Minutes to Midnight" or "Rampant Communism in Brazil" type of book intended to make our flesh creep and thereby to reap an easy profit.

All these are remarkable events to a veterano like myself who completed a Master's essay on the Liberator Simón Bolívar during the days of Calvin Coolidge; who waited out in Spain two of the depression years living with my wife and two boys on a modest fellowship, designed to keep barely alive one thin graduate student, supplemented by borrowing from relatives; who emerged from the long period of study for the doctorate only to find that post-depression developments had killed university expansion; who was a participant in the inter-American projects of World War II as a Library of Congress staff member, when money flowed rather freely under the aegis of Nelson Rockefeller; who survived the long years of drought that set in about 1945 and lasted until about 1960; who, finally, has witnessed the enormous proliferation of courses and research activities during the last five years-- a proliferation so great that the Center at the University of California at Los Angeles announces that it "provides the framework within which approximately 150 faculty members representing 38 departments and eight schools and colleges may become more effectively involved in teaching, research, and services related to Latin America." The research projects at this Center range from "Aztec Linguistics" through the "Biology and Control of Structural Pests in Latin America," to "The Impact of Peace Corps Volunteers in Slum Communities in Peru," and the "Avifauna of Nicaragua."

Not only do we find a multiplicity of activities under way at some universities; there has also been a jungle growth of area studies at institutions large and small throughout the land. The Newberry conference concluded that up to 1958 area research on Latin America lagged, though paradoxically enough Latin Americanists had pioneered the concept of area studies in the pre-World War II years. Following the "re-discovery" which Castro set off, all this changed rapidly. Institutions and individual scholars forgot or decided not to heed the advice of Professor Robert Wauchope of Tulane University, whose reflections on the problems of multi-discipline area research are among the soundest we have. "Area study is a complex and difficult activity," stated Professor Wauchope, "and one which, like marriage, should not be entered into inadvisedly." Though here and there a scholar today sounds a discordant note by referring to the foundation "commissars" who have "been fashioning a tortuous rhetoric to justify the millions which must be poured, willy-nilly, into 'area programs'," one hears of no universities or scholars refusing largesse from foundations or Washington: we now have "major centers," "secondary centers," and probably eventually will have "tertiary centers," and perhaps even other classifications will appear.

Viewing all these changes and developments with the perspective of 40 years--it was in June, 1926, that I gave my first course on Latin American History, a feeble effort that I was allowed to make at the

1926 Summer Session of the University of Chicago--what may one say about our present affluence with funds flowing from Washington and private benefactors alike?

First of all one cannot repress a strong feeling of satisfaction --so many capable graduate students, easier publication possibilities for serious works, so much useful activity. The program made possible by the Rockefeller Foundation of translating Latin American books through university presses, in which Frank Wardlaw and the University of Texas Press have played an important role, is in itself a far-reaching and substantial stimulus to a deeper knowledge of Latin America. But will the present lush phase of development merely underline the validity of the charge by one of our Latin Americanists that "despite sometimes useful or even handsome accomplishments, Latin American studies [in the United States] since the 1920's have been a fairly ridiculous tail to a politico-commercial kite"? Though one may take this extreme statement with several grains of salt--Latin Americans and Latin Americanists like to make sweeping generalizations which may or may not have a close relation to facts--one cannot examine Latin American studies today without feeling some reservations and some doubts, or without desiring to stand like the goose on the ramparts of Ancient Rome, to warn of possible disaster. Latin American studies are booming, but steady and responsible growth of our Latin American programs must be our principal objective today, in the university world at least, for a boom-bust approach can lead to frustration, disappointment, and mediocrity.

Specifically, our efforts must reach down into the grass roots of our educational system. Hubert Humphrey stated in 1964, before his election as Vice-President:

> It is this attitude of understanding and respect that must permeate not only our leadership, but our entire society. This will not be easy to accomplish--as most adults in this country were educated in schools where the overwhelming majority of textbooks and reference books either ignored Latin America or reflected a condescending attitude toward Latin Americans. Written chiefly by authors sympathetic to a northern European cultural inheritance, which historically has been fundamentally unsympathetic to Latin culture, these books have been all too important an influence in shaping the attitude of generations of Americans. Change in popular attitude comes slowly. A full appreciation of the importance of Latin America will come only when our education system begins to reflect the priority stated by President Kennedy when he described Latin America as the most critical area in the world.

My purpose in the rest of this paper is to present both the positive advances and the doubts in the light of the experiences and predilections of an "old Christian," somewhat like those other more authentic old Christians of fifteenth and sixteenth century Spain who grew up in an older tradition and looked upon the newcomers, the "new Christians" with some reserve. But in my case, it is with hope and respect, too, that I view the entrance into Latin American studies of so many new participants, coming from so many directions and disciplines.

II

Expansion is king today in Latin American studies. The sheer size and distribution of the research under way is staggering. Besides the academic developments in the United States already mentioned, Congress has continued to produce quantities of documentation on Communist penetration into Latin America, and to publish many reports of its numerous committees and individual members who visited the area to review government operations there as well as such detailed studies as the large volume on United States-Latin American Relations prepared several years ago by universities and research organizations at the request of Senator Wayne Morse's Subcommittee on American Republics Affairs.

Elsewhere in the Government a vast amount of research is being carried out; some 500 studies relating to Latin America were sponsored by Federal agencies during the period 1957-1964, and an estimated 30 million dollars were spent on them. The present budget of the government for similar activities is a closely guarded secret, but it undoubtedly is large. Our embassies in Latin America are now extensive establishments, staffed with many kinds of experts from anthropologists and agricultural experts to political and cultural officers in considerable profusion. On my first trip to Latin America in 1935, I didn't think of going to the U. S. Embassy for anything except my mail; today, our embassies can be very helpful to the visiting scholar. The ambassadors and their staffs are no longer surprised to have professors studying in their countries, as they were when Carl C. Taylor started, in the early 1940's, the research program of the Department of Agriculture on rural sociology in several Latin American countries. The embassies were then rather unprepared for such projects, and somewhat surprised at the prospect of having sociologists in their midst. One ambassador asked the scholar in his country to attend all embassy meetings and functions insofar as possible as a member of his official staff. Another ambassador told the sociologist preparing one of those volumes, that have been so useful to all of us, that members of the embassy staff could probably answer all the questions that he would want to ask, "and requested, if not dictated, that in all his contacts with the host-country the sociologist should be accompanied by an embassy officer." Such days are definitely over, and the academic presence of the United States in most Latin American countries today is an important and ever pervasive force.

International agencies also pour forth a steady stream of valuable publications, sometimes resulting from extensive and expensive investigations. The United Nations, the Organization of American States, and such specialized agencies as the Inter-American Development Bank have published a multitude of factual and challenging reports. Indeed, the Bank's annual Social Progress Trust Fund report has become since its first appearance in 1960 one of the basic sources of data for developments in its field of action.

Latin American studies are beginning to become popular outside the United States too. Canada's interest in Latin America, for example, has steadily increased during recent years. In the not-too-distant future regular courses will probably be offered on Latin America in a number of Canadian universities whether or not Canada decides to join the Organization of American States.

European developments are notable as well. Five centers are planned for Britain; France and Germany are busily engaged in strengthening their university resources and economic relations in the field; and in European academic circles generally more interest in Latin America exists than ever before. The Ford Foundation supported a conference in Italy in 1964 looking to some kind of concerted action or at least exchange of information on Latin American programs in Europe. Increased European interest will mean an even larger and richer literature on

Latin America, and it is also likely that the Latin American nations will be somewhat less solely dependent on the United States for financial support. The official visit of President Eduardo Frei Montalva to England, France, and Italy in July, 1965, was designed to increase Europe's assistance to Chile and to emphasize Latin America's growing desire to move out from under the shadow of the United States.

Soviet Russia has become increasingly concerned with Latin America since 1945. Her Latin Americanists now participate in international conferences, keep up-to-date on publications relating to Latin America that appear outside Russia, particularly in the United States, and Soviet interest in underdeveloped countries of the world, including those in Latin America, has evolved during the past decade into a major undertaking. As one study states:

> This is evident by the growth of periodical literature and monographic studies, academic meetings, the organization during the summer of 1960 of the Soviet Association of Friendship and Cultural Cooperation with Latin American Countries, and the founding early in 1962 of a special Institute of Latin American Affairs at the Academy of Sciences of the U.S.S.R. The aim of the Institute is to publish works on Latin American history, politics, economics, and culture, to coordinate Latin American studies and research within the U.S.S.R. as well as in the countries of the Soviet bloc, to establish and to maintain contacts with Latin American countries, and to train Soviet personnel qualified in Latin American affairs. The Institute plans to publish a two-volume abstract on Latin America, a volume of articles on the recent national liberation and working-class movements, a symposium on contemporary problems of Brazil, and a volume dealing with 'the success of socialist construction' in Cuba.

The Japanese interest in Latin America that began before World War II has now strongly revived. Universities there are adding scholars trained in Latin American studies to their faculties, publications are being brought out, and organizations have been established to foster economic and cultural relations. The People's Republic of China has apparently begun to concern itself with Latin America only in the political and propagandist sense, if one may judge from the list of publications available in English.

Perhaps the most significant change has occurred in Latin America itself. More and more, her scholars and institutions of higher education are increasing their research and are devoting their energies to an examination of their own problems. In economics notable results have been achieved; in anthropology and sociology substantial progress has been made, while the realistic study of governmental administrative and political processes is under way. The coming generation of Latin Americanists in the United States and elsewhere will profit as never before from the insights and the contributions of Latin American scholars as they turn their attention to studying their own society with the tools of modern social sciences.

A second kind of expansion--an expansion of ideas and approaches to the study of Latin American phenomena--is another noticeable part of the scene today. A U. S. Government contract makes it possible, for example, for a university anthropologist to participate in a symposium at the 132nd annual meeting, last December, of the American Association for the Advancement of Science: the topic was "Drinking Patterns in Latin America," of Indians of course as the drinking patterns of other sectors of the population don't seem to interest our scholars.* The analysis of doctoral dissertations accepted since Castro and now in preparation would illustrate how far our attention has been directed toward "scientific" studies of the decision-making process, voting behavior, economic interest groups, and the like in Latin America. Graduate students in the social sciences are more likely to arrive in Latin America armed with questionnaires, a collection of theoretical concepts derived from European or American models, or some methodological procedures derived from an analysis of political processes in, say, New Haven, Connecticut, than they are to reach their research areas steeped in the political philosophies and value systems of Luso-Hispanic peoples. Some hilarious and also depressing encounters must have taken place in Latin America when such students began to test in the field their models and research designs developed in the United States, handicapped as they sometimes were by an imperfect command of Portuguese or Spanish, or unaware of the basic cultural values of the people they were studying. No wonder that some observers reached these conclusions: "In some disciplines there is an opportunistic attitude toward Latin American studies, coupled with a belief that a mere transfer of techniques from other areas is sufficient, and an underestimation of the importance of psychological insight resulting from intimate contact with actual conditions and from mastery of tool languages." Please note that the quotation does not come from Kalman Silvert's report on the Camelot Project of a couple of years ago, where precisely these points were made, but from an analysis by Irving A. Leonard in 1943. A leading Latin American sociologist, writing in 1964, was even more blunt in his description of the activities of American social scientists in Latin America:

> (a) they produce an accumulation of data, irrelevant for the knowledge of the social structure of the region or its different national societies;
> (b) they do not contribute all that would be necessary and possible to the development of autonomous thought and the formation of higher personnel for social research;
> (c) they do not increase or facilitate the creation of a "universe of communication" among Latin American institutions and sociologists; on the contrary, they distort it.

Another characteristic of Latin American studies today in the United States is the increasingly directed nature of research. The government spends much more money on research relating to Latin America than all the other institutions combined, and spends this money inside and outside of universities. Often the investigations are directed toward a specific objective, and sometimes make possible valuable experience for individual scholars, or result in the excellent country manuals, prepared with army funds, such as those on Bolivia, Brazil, Colombia, Panama, and Venezuela. Occasionally, government funds support basic research, as in the case of certain air force projects in Latin America. But directed research holds dangers, too: one of our universities offers excellent three-year fellowships--thanks to a Ford grant rather than a government subsidy, I believe--but as set forth in the announcement "the fellows will be required to write a dissertation

---

*Dr. Henry F. Dobyns brought to my attention after this article was first published that anthropologists have started to study drinking patterns of non-Indian sectors of the population of Latin America.

relating to social revolution in Latin America." Surely universities, of all institutions, should provide a home for individual research. As France V. Scholes so eloquently argued in 1958, at the Congress of Mexican and U. S. historians in Austin, in his paper on "Freedom for the Historian":

> I hope that this Congress recognizes and will assert the right of the individual historian to pursue his labors in his own way and according to his own lights; the right freely to choose his own subject for investigation; the right not to be placed under pressure, direct or indirect, by any agency, private or governmental (including universities). . . I can only deplore the policies of some agencies which sometimes seem to profess more wisdom than the individual scholar in regard to what should be studied or what merits long-range investigation; and in particular I wish to register protest against the current emphasis upon and preference for projects which deal with contemporary problems or the contemporary scene. . .
>
> A revered friend once told me that I spend my time dusting off the documentary cadavers of the past. Perhaps! But I do believe and know that these "documentary cadavers" often have more life and vitality in them than some of the arid conceptualizations that are sometimes palmed off as history.

It is too soon to estimate the significance of the impact of these two different kinds of expansion upon the principles and practices of those who study Latin America. The growth of scholarly interest outside the United States will certainly bring new facts and fresh viewpoints. The application of new tools to such fields as history can be a valuable exercise, though I do not expect tremendous results immediately in the field of history as we historians are notably resistant to change. We are assimilationists, but we absorb new ideas slowly and hesitantly.

Historians in the past have had to cope as best they could with theologians, metaphysicians, and biologists. As one wise historian has said: "The work of the great majority of practicing historians still remains untouched--or unredeemed, if you will--by the influence of social science. They go about their business unaware of content analysis or computer programming. Sooner or later, however, most of them will be touched in one way or another. They will be using new concepts and vocabulary without necessarily being aware of the origins of either." And we may enjoy with this same historian the conviction that the newcomers whom I call "new Christians" to our field have something to their credit: "At least they are not preoccupied with God, apes, or infinity. They do share with historians a common concern with man--a man who 'behaves' instead of 'acts,' but is still a man."

One may be sure, too, that the newcomers, who usually concentrate on contemporary Latin America, will find it difficult to find adequate sources for their studies. Archives in Latin America are rarely open for students to use. As Bryce Wood remarked at the conclusion of his detailed examination of the armed conflicts in Latin America during the period 1932-1942: "'History is too important to be left to historians,' appears to be the motto of diplomats and officials of foreign offices who jealously guard the fundamental records." Not only are the government, ecclesiastical, and private archives rarely open to researchers but, even when open, their lack of organization makes it difficult and time-consuming to consult their material, indispensable as it is to the understanding of the contemporary scene.

There is also a general reluctance among Latin American historians to concern themselves with contemporary history. Some exceptions may be found, but the only major investigation in modern history there has been undertaken by that remarkable scholar, Daniel Cosío Villegas, and even his "Historia moderna de México" project was sparked by a Rockefeller Foundation grant. His project, too, is working backwards toward the middle of the 19th century and not toward the present. The more widely accepted attitude has been expressed by the Venezuelan historian Guillermo Morón, speaking of recent events in his own country:

> For the period up to the present day, it seems wise to leave a blank, since we lack the perspective for an impartial view. . . There is real difficulty in attempting to evaluate the present administration. There are certain extraordinary things, as for example the fact the very day after the new Constitution had been approved all constitutional guarantees were suspended, and the country was ruled for two years with no such guarantees in force. . . . Contemporary times are complicated and stability is brittle and crumbling.

One may, of course, produce his own sources by the questionnaire method, an activity which some Latin Americans look upon with amusement, skepticism, and fear. The questionnaire-researchers will probably be faced with another obstacle: lack of faith among Latin Americans in the scholarly nature of the projects so eagerly pursued by American scholars in Latin America. Project Camelot in Chile, Operación Simpática in Colombia, and the recent charges that Michigan State University was a cover for C.I.A. activities in Southeast Asia are bound to make it more difficult than ever for our researchers to study contemporary Latin America, above all such topics as "social revolution," the ideology of the military, and the influence of the Communists. The method of collecting information by interviews also encounters formidable obstacles in some countries. A doctoral candidate in history at Columbia University discovered last year in Argentina that informants were not helpful on the political maneuverings of the period before 1946. As he reported, they had "either forgotten what happened, tried to forget what happened, or acquired new and largely irrelevant perspectives on given historical situations." He concluded: "Unfortunately, it looks as though the interview, as a method of research on pre-Peronist Argentina, is of little or no practical value to the modern historian." One may add that "oral history," as developed in the United States, has not yet been cultivated in Latin America to any important extent, and its growth may be hampered by the same obstacles that the informant method has to face.

If our researchers stay in Latin America long enough, they are likely to learn that research models constructed in the United States may have to be applied cautiously, if at all, in actual Latin American situations. They may come to see, as the Mexican economist Edmundo Flores stated: "In studying underdeveloped countries we have to be aware of tremendous cultural biases and poorly supported evaluations . . . the understanding of works in the social sciences particularly requires explicit and overt recognition of the values of the writer and of all the values of the society that is being analyzed."

What these values are will require careful attention. I doubt that the philosophies and ideas of St. Thomas Aquinas, Dante or Francisco Suárez dominate the thinking of the increasingly powerful forces in Latin America insistent on the need for change, although one of our Latin Americanists calls for much more attention to their writings as basic to our true understanding of Latin America. But what values do these various groups hold? Anthropologists point out the existence of some dozen types of groups and subgroups in Latin America, from primitive Indians to sophisticated urbanites. Whose values must we study? And how far does the older value system in Latin America--even the system erected in the colonial era--affect thought and action in Latin America today? In a recent discussion among historians on "Colonial Institutions and Contemporary Latin America" at the American Historical Association annual meeting, one participant concluded that the colonial value system "had been more impervious to change than the structure of institutions" and suggested that those concerned with promoting the rapid modernization of Latin America "should become increasingly aware that the process involves much more than directing capital flows or altering the terms of trade."

Two final observations on research development. Almost no support has been provided for Latin American social scientists to study our own underdevelopment, our own racial situation. Is this not a serious lack in any overall assessment of the present situation? And not one of our many institutes or centers is primarily a research center. They give courses, arrange lectures, receive ambassadors and other dignitaries, conduct relations with foundations and the governments, lobby with their colleagues to employ Latin Americanists in the departments where there are none, constantly strive to have their university authorities devote enough time to their problems, and otherwise disperse their limited energies in many ways. All of these are perhaps necessary and potentially valuable services, but nowhere is there the concentration of research as at, for example, the East Asian Research Center at Harvard. One result is that the quality of research accomplished by professors hard-pressed on many fronts varies greatly. The sheer quantity of time and energy absorbed in the administration of centers and projects is impressive but also distressing.

But research problems do not pose the most difficult challenge in studying Latin America. The real question before us, in my opinion, is how to put Vice President Humphrey's exhortation into practice. How can we ensure that Latin America will become an integral part of instruction in our educational system?

III

Though it may seem to some that doubts concerning the health of our Latin American studies today are treason or worse, I am convinced that teaching will largely determine whether a sound and steady growth will be achieved in the long run for the United States. Of course research cannot be entirely separated from teaching, but the future depends to a considerable extent, in my opinion, on how we teach and where we teach about Latin America. Though this applies to some extent to all Latin American subjects, I shall confine my remarks to history teaching, as it is the one most familiar to me and is probably the field in which most of our students take courses.

Our future also depends on our conception of the place of Latin American history in the educational structure of the United States. Let me warn you that I have been thinking what Senator J. W. Fulbright calls "unthinkable thoughts." They may be summarized as follows:

(1) The study and teaching of Latin American history should not aim at inculcating "Panamericanism" or to promote the "Good Neighbor" concept, or to defend any particular political action or economic policy of the United States in Latin America, not even to fight Communism

there! Nor to define, as one historian has described his interests, the "cultural and institutional imperatives of the past which shape contemporary process."

(2) Latin American history will have an important place in our educational system only if it is recognized as a subject worth studying as a significant segment of world history, which will throw light on another culture than our own.

(3) To achieve this object, Latin American history must be taught as the development of a civilization similar to ours but also different in some respects, and it must be taught at the high school as well as the college level. The primary purpose must be to produce better educated citizens, and not specialists.

Each of these "unthinkable thoughts" requires some explanation.

The influence of cultural nationalism has never been stated more clearly than by Herodotus, the Father of History. Herodotus, after visiting the Egyptians, concluded that they were a puzzling people. Women went to market in Egypt while the men remained at home to weave. Just the opposite occurred in Greece. And, most strange, the Egyptians wrote from right to left. He noted, however, the surprise of the Egyptians at his observations concerning their writing habits. It was not they who were strange, the Egyptians maintained, who wrote from right to left, but the Greeks, who wrote from left to right. This kind of ethnocentrism thus has existed for a long time and one should not be surprised to find it a powerful force today from Maine to Patagonia. All students, therefore, need to have "windows on the world" opened up for them to allow them to learn about other people, other cultures, and other points of view. Howard Mumford Jones in a recent provocative report on "Uses of the Past in General Education" describes this situation as a need for what he calls "de-education" and "re-education". As he explains it: "By de-education I mean the ability to get outside one's own cultural pattern, and by re-education I mean cultivating the capacity to accept some simpler culture at its face value, not to look down at it."

Of course it doesn't have to be necessarily a simpler culture; one might very well study a sophisticated culture. The possibilities are numerous--Russian culture, Chinese culture, African culture, Arabic culture, etc. There are many "windows on the world" for our students to look through. Our 20th-century American--thanks to the growth of area studies since World War II--has a wealth of material to draw upon. Moreover, the spirit of our age seems to be more favorable than any time since the sixteenth century toward the study of other cultures. For the interest of a people, of a nation, in the culture of other peoples is a relatively recent phenomenon and far from universal even today. So far as I know it was the Spanish missionaries who went to America in the wake of Columbus who first displayed a lively interest in another culture than their own. Medieval travellers did report on the strange customs they encountered, but with the Spanish missionaries there was an organized effort for specific objectives. A priest who accompanied Columbus on his second voyage first studied the Indian languages he found on the island of Hispaniola, and soon there developed a remarkable drive among the early friars to learn to speak the many languages of America, in order to convert the Indians. But some Spaniards studied Indian cultures partly because their curiosity was aroused, such as the Franciscan Bernardino de Sahagún, the first anthropologist in America.

In the years since the Spaniards first studied Indian cultures, however, studies of other cultures were sporadic everywhere until recently. In the United States, the American Council of Learned Societies in the 1930's began its important pioneer work. Then World War II boomed all language study and some cultural studies for strategic purposes. Area studies development since the end of World War II has been notable. In years to come it is likely that historians will consider our present age as a remarkable one, not only for its achievements in outer space but also because the United States has devoted so much attention to the study of many languages and many cultures, some of them quite remote from our own culture. The United States has indeed made astonishing progress during the last 20 years in African, Arabic, Chinese, Japanese, Russian and other studies and this development will surely mean a greater and greater enrichment of the educational offerings of our high schools and colleges, and thus of the understanding by our students of other cultures.

But Latin American history has certain obvious advantages which make it an unusually valuable, and available, "window on the world." Spanish and Portuguese are relatively easy languages--at least in comparison with the languages just mentioned--and Spanish is more widely taught in our colleges today than any other. To study a culture, a knowledge of the language is certainly highly desirable; thus Latin American history enjoys the advantage of offering no great linguistic barrier to students. Again, many Latin Americans live in the United States and their presence--increasingly felt in cities far beyond New York--also helps to make possible learning about their culture. Moreover, Latin America as a travel area is open--except for Cuba--and 1.5 million American tourists visit Mexico every year, which helps powerfully to explain her economic stability. Thus students who read about Latin American history in class may also know a Latin American, or visit some part of that large and varied area which includes primitive tribes, sophisticated urbanites, ancient archaeological sites, exciting modern architecture, painting, music, and literature. Therefore if we are agreed that American high school and college students would benefit from an exposure to another culture as a part of their fundamental education, the study of Latin American history offers many advantages for both the students and the professors, who will have to learn how to teach Latin American history. Nor does one visit suffice. Many of us have favorite aunts or uncles who made the grand tour of Europe back around the time of Theodore Roosevelt and who ever afterwards considered themselves experts on the state of Europe generally. But the world does not stand still, and the changes which are occurring in Latin America and elsewhere require periodic visits of our professors if they are to be adequately prepared for the classroom. The Scarborough Report in Britain some 20 years ago stated that a specialist should re-visit his area at least every three years and few would deny the reasonableness of this recommendation.

This brings me to my next point. How can the history of more than 200 million people to the south of the Rio Grande be presented most effectively to our students?

My answer is a simple one. Latin American history should be looked upon not as a "crisis" subject, but as the unfolding story of a culture, a civilization both interesting and worthy of study. It is natural that the coming of Castro, the Bay of Pigs fiasco, the missile crisis, and U.S. intervention in the Dominican Republic should stir our students to an increased awareness of Latin American affairs, but a "current events" approach in which attention focuses on transitory dictators, military juntas, economic crises will not, I am convinced, provide the kind of course required by the nature of the world in which we live and by the place of the United States in the present and foreseeable world.

What should be included in a course--perhaps to be called "a History of Latin American Civilization"? Much more on the art, literature, and philosophy of the people of Latin America from pre-Columbian times to the present; much less on the rather dull political events that clutter up many of our presentations. For, contrary to the newspaper presentation of Latin America, this vast area is much more than a festering mass of economic discontent and political turmoil. One need not be a pollyanna to see that much more is to be found there. This may shock some who feel that the only true history is "contemporary" history and that anything that happened before 1900 should be studied today only if it can be shown that today's problems had their roots in that far-off age. As Howard Mumford Jones wrote:

> The past is not the present. On the contrary, the past is significantly different from the present--that is why it can be useful to us, and that is why it has meaning and imaginative charm. General education is impoverished when we neglect this central truth in an anxiety to prepare everybody for today's world. . . difference enriches: likeness palls.

The presentation of a course on Latin American civilization is much more possible of achievement now because many of our younger scholars have been able to live and work in Latin America, thanks to fellowship grants from the government and foundations. Even though there is altogether too much emphasis on recent events--as though the last few weeks or months or years were always the most significant--and on studying revolutions, still the fellowship holders learn a lot about Latin American life that is not usually included in their doctoral dissertations. On their return, these well-prepared younger scholars are bound to try to incorporate in their teaching and in their research what they have absorbed in Latin America. They are finding out how relatively backward we are in teaching about Latin America at any level, when compared with the teaching of U. S. history or European history; one need only look at the materials available for instruction. Maps, paperbacks, textbooks, collections of readings, "problems" books--none of the instruments for teaching Latin American history seem to me to be comparable in quality or in variety to what students take for granted in U. S. or European history. Part of this cultural lag is undoubtedly due to the fact that more students take these other courses, so that a much larger market exists for teaching materials on Latin America. But it is also true that we simply have not devoted enough energy or imagination to the task.

One obvious way to present a course on Latin American Civilization in such a way as to challenge and interest our students would be to use the comparative approach. I do not mean comparison with Africa, Asia, or any other underdeveloped area outside the hemisphere, though such an approach might be useful under some circumstances. But the American hemisphere has been and still is a great laboratory in which experiments have been tried out in many fields, and we should be willing to use this experience for educational purposes. For Frenchmen, Englishmen, Spaniards, Portuguese, and many other people have participated in the exploration and colonization in the Americas but we have not yet adequately incorporated this historical experience into our teaching of history at any level. Our students learn about Columbus and his brave companions in the first chapter of all the textbooks on U. S.

history, and then the textbook usually turns to discuss the Pilgrims and the first Thanksgiving. If there is any additional information given, it is likely to be a reference to the destruction of the noble Indians by the cruel Spaniards. Why could not our courses on Latin American Civilization incorporate some material comparing what went on in the Spanish and Portuguese empires with what occurred under British and French rule? I am not proposing a history of the Americas--though separate courses with this orientation might be developed for advanced students in colleges--but rather the recognition of the fact that different types of colonial cultures developed in the Americas, and that most students would already have some knowledge about the British and French experience in the New World to serve them as background. In unrolling the history of Latin American Civilization, we should make use of this knowledge by drawing comparisons--when possible and when appropriate--with Spanish and Portuguese experience in such fields as Economics, Education, Land, Religion, Science, and Slavery. . . .

The incorporation of these and other similar topics into a carefully organized course on the history of Latin American civilization, the preparation of interesting teaching materials on these topics, and the training of teachers to plan and direct such courses would require careful consideration. But one immense advantage of our present study of Latin America--at least as seen from the perspective of an "old Christian," or perhaps I should call myself an Old Believer in the significance and attraction of Latin America--is the energy, imagination and financial support devoted to the area today. In conclusion, therefore, I salute the Old Believers who have labored in the vineyards over the years--I am mindful of the fact that the first university in the United States to pool its resources on Latin America and to present its varied courses as an area program, back in 1915, was the University of Texas--and I also salute the "New Christians" who have brought to the movement their vigor and vision. The ecumenical spirit is needed in universities as well as in churches, so that both "Old Christians" and the newer variety may discover sources of mutual strength for deeper, richer studies and teaching on Latin America. Whether the present state of affluence lasts or not, if we use our tremendous resources wisely enough Latin American studies will be more varied, more interesting, and more significant in our national education than ever before.

CHAPTER 22.

TOWARDS AN INFORMED CRITICAL JUDGMENT ON HISTORICAL FILMS

How to use films effectively in classroom teaching has been discussed by historians for a long time. In 1923, at the first annual meeting of the American Historical Association that I attended, there was presented a silent film on "French and Indian Wars in North America" based on a book in the Chronicles of America series and impressively narrated in person by Dixon Ryan Fox. This production seemed to me a feeble effort, but the subject roused in me some interest in the subject.

Almost fifty years later the American Historical Association announced a program to cut down Hollywood films for use in classrooms and invited suggestions. With foundation funds the AHA produced four such films, one of which was Juárez. For each film a booklet of documents was prepared to give some historical depth and provide additional material to stimulate discussion. The program was developed on the assumption that a film never was sufficient by itself, and that students needed selected documents to enable them to understand the true contribution of the film.

The annual meetings of the AHA now regularly include several programs on films and history and there is a much greater range of films and more sophistication in their use. But the fundamental problem remains: how may they best be used for sound instruction in history?

Benito Juárez and the French Intervention in Mexico, Lewis Hanke, ed. (Armon Books, Cambridge, Massachusetts, 1971), v-x. Reprinted by permission.

Towards An Informed Critical Judgment on Historical Films

The principal questions one must ask about a historical film are: Is it so absorbing as drama that it recreates the epoch for the viewers, and is it essentially true to the facts of history as we know them? Juárez answers affirmatively both questions on the whole satisfactorily, though certain episodes introduced solely for dramatic effect cannot be justified. But does this movie adequately portray the complexities and uncertainties of the period of Mexican history when the full-blooded Zapotec Indian Benito Juárez led the reform movement in Mexico and successfully opposed Emperor Maximilian who was supported by French arms? Here the answer must obviously be no.

Life is always infinitely more complicated than any attempted dramatization of it. One can appreciate the strength of the movie Juárez, particularly the impressive art of Paul Muni and Brian Ahearne as they portray Juárez and Maximilian respectively. One can gain a vivid impression of the reaction of the French occupation forces and the Mexican people toward each other. One can learn something of the beauty and variety of the landscape and the towns of Mexico. Above all, one can feel the immediacy of Juárez's strongly held conviction that he must prevail over Maximilian for the sake of Mexico's integrity as a nation whose future must be determined by Mexicans themselves.

What the film cannot provide is an explanation of the historic past of Mexico that helps explain the bitter civil war between the Liberals and the Conservatives there, which had opened the way for foreign intervention. Nor can it adequately show the powerful play of international political influences at work throughout the period. For this we must turn to history, and to a brief account of the half-century of turmoil that preceded the landing of Emperor Maximilian in Vera Cruz in 1864.

During the years when Juárez struggled to maintain his government and to expel Maximilian, Mexico suffered from all the political and social problems that it had experienced since it had declared its independence from Spain in 1813. These years were a prolongation of the colonial period, with the Church and the Army continuing to enjoy much power and privilege, and a small number of aristocrats controlling the wealth of Mexico with little thought for the welfare of the masses. During these years of neo-colonial rule, no stable government or unified political parties developed. A short-lived empire under Agustín Iturbide (1822-1823) was succeeded by years of tumult during which an irresponsible army officer, Antonio López de Santa Anna, dashed in and out of power, to the detriment of all. So disunited did Mexico become by 1846 that an expansionist, aggressive United States was able to invade her soil easily and take away more than half of her territory as spoils of war.

The Mexican-United States War marked the beginning, however, of a move toward national regeneration, in which the Liberals began slowly to coalesce their authority and to sharpen their political objectives. In those years of confusion and uncertainty we can now see a steady Liberal determination to cut down ecclesiastical and military prerogatives, as well as an unyielding Conservative determination to oppose changes which would diminish those ancient privileges. When General Santa Anna was finally forced out of power in 1855, after influencing

Mexican events in an erratic and personal way for over 30 years, the Liberal attack on the neo-colonial social and economic structure of the country began in earnest.

Reform laws followed thick and fast: The Juárez Law (1855) limited the jurisdiction of ecclesiastical and military courts; the Society of Jesus was banished (1856); the Lerdo Law (1856) required the Church to sell its enormous holdings of land, estimated to be from one-third to one-half of all valuable land in the country; and the Constitution of 1857 provided for freedom of speech and of the press, abolished hereditary titles and forbade monopolies, declared the State supreme over Church, and granted religious freedom to all. Juárez became President in accordance with this Constitution in December 1857, and until his death in 1872 he was the dominating figure in Mexico.

The immediate result of the 1857 Constitution was the "War of Reform" (1858-1861). The United States recognized the Liberal regime (April 6, 1859), which enabled it to negotiate foreign loans and to buy armaments. Soon thereafter Juárez issued the famous "Laws of Reform" disestablishing the Church, suppressing all religious orders, and confiscating all ecclesiastical property not sold according to the Lerdo Law. Civil registration of births, marriages, and deaths became compulsory. One pro-Liberal American summarized the confrontation between Church and State in 1861 as follows:

<u>Liberal Creed of Reform and Civilization</u>

Constitutional government in place of dictatorship.
Freedom of religion.
Freedom of the press.
Nationalization of church property.
Army subordinate to civil power.
Free and full opening for colonization.

<u>Reactionist or Church Creed</u>

Inviolability of church property, and re-establishment of former exactions.
The military and clergy responsible to their own tribunals.
Roman Catholic the sole religion.
Censorship of the press.
No immigrants except from Catholic countries.
A central dictator, subject only to the church, or, if possible, the restoration of a monarchy or a European protectorate.

There is no need to tell here the complicated story of Conservative-Liberal struggles in the succeeding decade or the intricate diplomatic maneuvering in Europe which led to the English, French, and Spanish expedition of 1862, which ostensibly was formed to collect the financial claims of their nationals but which soon became an effort by Napoleon III alone to establish a great Latin Catholic empire in Mexico to block the southward expansion of the United States and provide France with raw materials for her industries. These were the days, as Lord Bryce observed, "when Louis Napoleon was trying to establish for France a hegemony over the Romance-speaking peoples of Europe, the days when his <u>Life of Julius Caesar</u> was published . . . It was the fashion for his literary court to represent the French people as the heirs of ancient Rome, and modern perpetuation of her spirit and her greatness."

The scene for the tragedy depicted in the movie <u>Juárez</u> was set when the Archduke Ferdinand Maximilian Joseph, a brother of Franz Joseph, Emperor of Austria, and a Hapsburg descendent of the Emperor Charles V under whose banner Cortez conquered Mexico in the sixteenth century, landed in Vera Cruz with his ambitious and politically minded wife, Carlota. He had devoted entire days on shipboard "to the annotation of a manual of Court etiquette, with meticulous instructions for the benefit of the Mexican Chamberlain," which was poor preparation for confronting the grave problems of Mexico.

The film Juárez faithfully presents the naiveté and ignorance of Maximilian as he gradually learned some part of the reality of the country he hoped to govern in a just and liberal way and as he came to realize the determination of the Liberals under Juárez's leadership to expel his foreign administration. But the story of domestic Mexican politics which swirled around Juárez and the efforts of Maximilian to control the Church cannot be depicted in sufficient detail in a movie, where the director always must keep in mind the need for drama and opportunities for his stars to display their art.

Juárez was produced in the years immediately preceding World War II, when nations were girding themselves ideologically and militarily for that great conflict. Warner Brothers spent $2 million, gathered a cast of over a thousand persons, and selected a group of outstanding actors for the principal roles--Paul Muni, Bette Davis, Brian Ahearne, Donald Crisp, Claude Rains, and John Garfield. As Time reported, "It is not only the most ambitious in Warner history, but by all odds the most spectacular picture of the year." The beetle-browed labor leader John L. Lewis himself made one of his rare appearances in non-labor circles by turning up, in full evening regalia complete with starched shirt, at the Manhattan premier of "the most political and patriotic canto in the whole Warner cycle of epic biography." One reviewer declared, "Neither Paul Muni nor Bette Davis is the star of the film, although they are given co-star billing. Democracy really plays the leading role." It was perhaps for this reason that even a Dutch Socialistic review devoted considerable space to a Hollywood movie.

Juárez was exhibited widely and received a welcome in many countries, including Mexico, although there the initial hostility was so intense that an order from President Lázaro Cárdenas was needed before the picture could be shown publicly. Its Mexican premiere, however, proved to be a resounding success; indeed, as a New York Times reporter wrote, it conquered Mexico.

Today, the Zapotec Indian Benito Juárez and his reform program continue to enjoy official governmental support, as is evidenced by the 10-volume edition of his writings recently sponsored by the government. As President Adolfo López Mateos stated in his introduction to this collection, "The sectarian passion which even now attacks Juárez a hundred years after his death is, in fact, a demonstration of his greatness . . . the more that is known about Juárez the statesman, the reformer, the patriot, and the man, the more we respect him." Other voices in Mexico have been raised to urge that Juárez be studied as a historical figure of fundamental importance to an understanding of Mexico and not merely used as a symbolic figure to revive old but still lively Conservative-Liberal dogmatisms. We on the other side of the Rio Grande can do no less: to recognize Juárez for his key role in the long and still-troubled history of his country, and to attempt to understand him through the film for its dramatic representation and through documents for their additions and modifications to the limited vision of the movie media. Together, the film and the readings offer students an excellent opportunity to exercise critical judgment on what they read and what they see. This, after all, is one of the principal reasons we study history.

CHAPTER 23.

THE CARE AND FEEDING OF LATIN AMERICANISTS: SOME REMARKS ON THE MOST IMPORTANT INSTRUMENT IN TEACHING—THE TEACHER

When E. Bradford Burns, President of the Pacific Coast Council on Latin American Studies, was preparing the program for the twentieth annual meeting of this active regional association in 1974, he decided to emphasize teaching. Knowing my interest in this subject, he invited me to deliver a luncheon address which explains the presence of this article.

Proceedings of the Pacific Coast Council on Latin American Studies, 4 (1975), 1-10. Reprinted by permission.

The Care and Feeding of Latin Americanists: Some Remarks on the Most Important Instrument in Teaching--The Teacher

In some modern and innovative educational circles teachers seem to be almost passé. They are surrounded by the latest machines produced by educational technology--cassette programs, learner feedback systems, and the like--and unless they have ready access to a computer terminal they may consider themselves deprived of an essential tool of their trade. Films of course are such standard equipment today that one institution of higher learning is rumored to have constructed a special movie house, with popcorn machines in the lobby, to make the students feel perfectly at home and among familiar surroundings. They can munch buttered popcorn while accumulating credits for graduation. For some the conclusion is clear: if one has enough machines, teaching will not only be easy but also full of contemporary significance.

If we follow another line of educational philosophy, we may come to believe that teachers are not really needed at all in the learning process. According to Ohmer Milton, Professor of Psychology and Director of the Learning Research Center at the University of Tennessee, the whole structure of higher education must be radically changed. For him two points are of outstanding importance: "First, we must stop thinking of ourselves as custodians of students and their learning. Second, students must assume full responsibility for their learning." Though Professor Milton's book entitled _Alternatives to the Traditional: How Professors Teach and How Students Learn_ was published only last year, his remarks on the custody of students already sound a bit dated. Certainly anyone who has had much connection with college and university students in the last five years can testify to the fact that the custodial aspect of higher education has ceased to be a major concern of faculty and students alike in many parts of the country. If we take Professor Milton's second point seriously, one might conclude that if students do in fact assume full responsibility for their learning teachers would probably have a diminished and perhaps inconsequential role in the educational process. On still another front we find Monseñor Ivan Illich, that whirlwind sage of Cuernavaca, who is accustoming us to the idea that classrooms themselves are wrong. We must "de-school" society, we are told, if we are to be saved. I understand that students who go to Cuernavaca to learn Spanish at the Illich Center find themselves in classrooms rather constantly--but this appears to be an exception to his philosophy.

Thus whether we look upon the teachers as principally experts on educational hardware, or whether we agree that students have full responsibility for their own education, or whether we perceive the classroom as the enemy and look upon a society without schools as the ideal --our future as students and teachers will indeed be far different from the system under which many of us grew up. But need we accept all these propositions? At the risk of being classified as a hidebound traditionalist, let me state my fundamental position: the teacher, at least in Latin American studies and particularly in history, the fields I know best, is more important than ever before. We are, or should be, trying to help our students to learn about a way of life--in some respects much different from our own--and this task requires all the knowledge and experience and teaching instruments we can manage to acquire in preparing ourselves for the difficult assignment.

Let us begin with the Graduate School. Should we not encourage all graduate students in history to select one of their fields for the general examination far from their principal interest? If so, graduate students in Latin American history will have some knowledge of another area of the world, and students from other areas will bring their perspectives to our field. How valuable, for example, has been Carl Degler's Neither Black Nor White? For one of the charges made against Latin Americanists in years past was that they were well-meaning enthusiasts who had little knowledge of other areas, and even today such an experienced practitioner in the field as the Swedish historian Magnus Mörner feels that we know all too little about European history, even the Iberian background.

Another weakness is the training of graduate students, according to another diagnosis. Certainly in my undergraduate days--now some time ago as I received a bachelor's degree just half a century ago--our professors didn't pay much attention to the art of the teaching process. One became a teacher by the mysterious process of osmosis.

Do we not need to work harder than ever before to assure some teaching experience for all graduate students, not just for the favored few who enjoy teaching assistant jobs? Princeton, the University of Massachusetts in Amherst, and doubtless many other universities are now attempting to devise arrangements which will encourage an interchange with community colleges in their region. Courses on teaching in community colleges could be offered in the universities, directed by a community college teacher, while graduate students might serve as interns in community colleges. Other similar arrangements with other institutions including some in Latin America might be worked out to make certain that our graduate students would all have some experience in teaching before facing classes alone. Too many of my generation suffered culture-shock when they met their first classes--a traumatic experience, good neither for the students nor the teacher!

Another problem with my generation, though not so acute today, was the lack of experience of our graduate students in Latin America. During the 1960's money flowed so freely that many if not most of our graduate students had an opportunity to learn about Latin American life outside archives and libraries. Now that travel funds are harder to get, we must hope that graduate students will somehow or other be able to manage a period of travel and residence in Latin America, as such experience is an essential part of their preparation as teachers. And they need to return, as regularly as possible, to maintain familiarity with the ever-changing scene in Latin America.

Graduate study can provide negative lessons, too, as some of you may already know. My own reaction to the three seminars I took was that I learned how not to organize this kind of course. All three professors were outstanding scholars of their time, but there was little discussion of teaching problems or, indeed of research training. One of my professors had his three graduate students at his home for tea once a week and it was a delightful experience though bibliographically and structurally far from perfect, as I soon discovered on first trying to work in Spanish archives. Samuel Eliot Morison assigned each student in his seminar a topic so specialized that no general discussion was possible. Indeed, I can't remember even the topic I worked on in his seminar on U. S. colonial history. I do remember working on Mary Rowlandson of Indian captivity fame, for the Dictionary of American Biography was a chore he assigned. The only deposit in my mind of this seminar was the joke one student propounded as we had a field day visiting old houses in Massachusetts. What was the dullest, most moribund town in all New England?

This was just the sort of enquiry to appeal to cynical graduate students! The correct answer we were told was: Topsfield. Why? Because this Massachusetts town was so dead that on a quiet, summer evening one could hear the arteries harden around town as the old folks sat on their front porches. James Westfall Thompson at the University of Chicago was still another and more dramatic type. He seemed to delight in developing an adversary relationship with the students, which put me off, though he never tried to browbeat me. I learned something from each of these professors, but it was largely in how not to direct a seminar.

We must stress the importance of graduate training and experience because teachers of Latin American history today, and in the foreseeable future, confront a special and challenging situation. There are more students and more institutions than ever before, but the traditional requirement of United States history or Western Civilization has disappeared or is being eroded away. This is a relatively new phenomenon, the product of the late 1960's and early 1970's. As late as 1969, when I was negotiating with the University of Massachusetts and requested an opportunity to offer a general course of the "Columbus to Castro" type, there was some question raised in the History Department there as to the desirability of such a course. Should not all students, at least history majors, be required to take Western Civilization? Otherwise these students would leave the university without any knowledge of such important events as "the investiture struggle", to quote one senior faculty member. Today, throughout the country, there are few history courses--or indeed courses in any specific subject--with a "tariff" on them, as my colleagues in American history at the University of Texas used to term the legislative-imposed requirement that no one could graduate from the University without a year's course in American history.

The conclusion is clear. Henceforth students in many four-year institutions will be offered a number of general orientation--or survey --courses. African History, Asian History, Middle Eastern History, Russian History, World History, and perhaps others will compete with Latin American History for students, along with the usual courses in United States History and Western Civilization which will probably continue to be popular, especially if they are not required, and students will be able to take these courses in relatively small classes. The days of a Herbert Eugene Bolton holding forth to a mass of 1,000 students in the history of the Americas are gone forever. Even United States history and Western Civilization, despite the large sums of money poured into textbooks and readers by publishers, and despite their attraction for students who prefer not to stray far from traditional paths, will probably survive only if they are taught to much smaller classes.

Therefore we in the field of Latin American history must compete henceforth for students. Eight years ago I tried to bring this fact of life to the attention of my colleagues in the Charles Wilson Hackett Lecture at the University of Texas, Austin, in a piece called "Studying Latin America: The Views of an 'Old Christian'." In 1966, expansion was king in Latin American studies, and the sheer size and distribution of research under way was staggering. The amount of research under way is still staggering: witness the research inventory appearing regularly in the Latin American Research Review, but there is still too little attention paid, in my opinion, to the problems of presenting Latin American history in a meaningful way to our students--especially to those students who are not going to become Latin Americanists, but who should become intelligent citizens.

The performance of our teachers in the classroom is no longer a peripheral concern to administrators or to students. In 1966 there were plenty of jobs. Graduate students interviewed chairmen of departments, asking what fringe benefits were offered, how small a teaching load was involved, what were the publication opportunities, how soon would a summer growth grant be available? Those days are gone, and gone forever I believe.

The question today is: how can we best prepare our graduate students to become effective teachers of Latin American history--so effective that they will be able to compete with the other general courses in history being offered to students in many institutions? No one has the complete answer, so far as I know, but the following suggestions occur to me:

I. We should look upon ourselves as generalists, as well as specialists.

By this I mean that we must give particular attention to the broad, orientation, survey-type course. Something better than the "Columbus to Castro" course may eventually develop, but always we should attempt to make this course as sound and as interesting as possible. In practical terms, this means the achievement of a proper balance between Portuguese America and Spanish America, as well as between the colonial and the modern period.

When I received a bachelor's degree in Latin American history in 1924, I had read almost nothing about Brazil. Then fifteen or twenty years later Gilberto Freyre's The Masters and the Slaves burst upon us, followed by Samuel Putnam's splendid translation of Euclydes da Cunha's Rebellion in the Backlands. For all too long our students learned about Brazil in these two important volumes, but of course they were not enough to provide a balanced and detailed view of the subject. During the past ten years there has been a remarkable production in English on Brazilian history, so that at long last our teachers have access to a wealth of valuable studies, many by younger scholars who employ the latest ideas and tools in their presentation. We probably need, however, several summer institutes or semester-long programs in Brazil to give our teachers with largely Spanish American backgrounds an opportunity for some first-hand contact with the great continent that is Brazil. It may not be a continent in the strictly geographical sense of the term, but anyone who has travelled in the Amazon area will know what I mean.

On the other problem of balance--colonial versus modern--I should say little, lest someone think that I am beating my own drum. But if anyone doubts that there is an intimate relation between the past and the present in Latin America, let the doubter read the sophisticated discussion of this subject by Woodrow Borah, Charles Gibson, and Robert Potash. They were responsible for a brilliant session at an annual meeting of the American Historical Association when they focussed their attention on "Colonial Institutions and Contemporary Latin America."

Another advantage to giving due weight to the history of the colonial period is that a school of younger scholars such as James Lockhart is helping to dissipate the old notion that before 1810 there was no change or movement or regional variation. A good example of this refreshing influence is the article by William B. Taylor in the August issue of the Hispanic American Historical Review entitled "Landed Society in New Spain: A View from the South." Here he rejects the old clichés about haciendas, and adds more evidence to show that "regions dominated by stable, monolithic, financially secure Spanish estates were the exception rather than the rule." Professor Taylor's research underlines what other historians have been emphasizing more and more:

there was change, there was development, there were regional variations in the period before 1810. In my view only historians who have done some specialized work will be able to present a generalized view of Latin American history which is both convincing and cautious. But if they insist on offering courses which are too specialized in content or approach they will fail in their larger objectives. They will also fail to attract the general student.

II. We should not look upon Latin America as only a "crisis" subject.

In a sense, of course, a crisis is always upon us whether we recognize this fact or not. But is it not dangerous to use current interest in Chile, or Cuba, to attract students or justify courses? My views on this have not changed since 1966:

> Latin American history should be looked upon not as a "crisis" subject, but as the unfolding of a culture, a civilization both interesting and worthy of study. It is natural that the coming of Castro, the Bay of Pigs fiasco, the missile crisis, and U.S. intervention in the Dominican Republic should stir our students to an increased awareness of Latin American affairs, but a "current events" approach in which attention focusses on transitory dictators, military juntas, economic crises, will not, I am convinced, provide the kind of course required by the nature of the world in which we live and by the place of the United States in the present and future world.

Unless there is chronological depth, political balance, and some attention to the values in some respects different from our own, which are to be found in Latin America, we will not be providing our students with a substantial picture of Latin America sufficient to interest them as undergraduates and to help them maintain this interest after their formal education is over.

The specific content and tone of every class should reflect, to some extent, the life experience and training of the teacher. Likewise, of course, the teacher must study the members of the class to determine how best to introduce the subject to them. I hope, too, that our teachers will never be wholly dependent upon other persons for their films, slides, and other such devices. Most teachers take their own snapshots as they travel about in Latin America, and these can be revealing personal documents of absorbing interest to students even though the photographs may lack technical finish. The resulting course, or courses, will thus reflect to some extent the personal experience of the teachers as they struggle to convey to their students some of the flavor and variety of Latin America. Teachers of art courses have long used their own slides, which are more flexible than TV, films, or video tapes for one can linger over a particular slide if need be.

But we might well be more systematic in our evaluation of teaching approaches and teaching instruments, old and new, which brings me to my third, and last, suggestion.

III. We should have an annual publication for teachers of Latin American history.

The *Hispanic American Historical Review* has an important role to play, and it discharges this faithfully. But its task does not include any special emphasis on teaching. *The History Teacher*, valuable and promising as it is, has to cover the waterfront, so that we cannot expect it to pay special attention to Latin America. Summer workshops such as that being planned by G. Micheal Riley of the University of Wisconsin, Milwaukee, for teachers will be helpful. But there should be some focal point for all those concerned with teaching methods, teaching instruments, and publications on Latin American history teaching. Now we have no way to keep up to date Jane Loy's pioneer guide to films on Latin America. Film and History may eventually help, but this pioneer publication is still barely established and the field of films is enormous, and growing.

Professor D. Anthony White of Sonoma State College worked out last spring a new type of course on "Revolt in Mexico, 1810-1821", which was a cooperative project with his students in researching and writing historical fiction on the struggle for independence in Mexico. This fall he is initiating a similar course on the Mexican Revolution of 1910. Just a few days ago there came to my attention a report on "Topics in Latin American History: Urbanization and Violence" by James A. Sandos and Richard P. Hyland of the Department of History in the University of California, Berkeley, which grapples with the concepts and practical problems in using books and media material in courses on Latin American history. There must be many other such reports floating about in academe searching for sympathy and informed scrutiny. Where can we get a thorough professional evaluation of these courses and ideas? Nowhere at present, so far as I know.

To fill this need, I have recommended to the Conference on Latin American History of the AHA that it sponsor and publish each spring a near-print publication to be devoted wholly to ideas, publications, and problems in teaching Latin American history. I am convinced that many interesting experiments are being tried in many different kinds of institutions throughout the country. We should encourage them all to report succinctly on their experiences so that their ideas may be tried out elsewhere and evaluated by colleagues in other parts of the country.

This proposed annual volume would also include reviews of textbooks, readers, films, cassettes, and might also publish from time to time critiques by Latin American historians. One of the most valuable articles of this kind was prepared years ago by Jorge Basadre, but there must be other Latin American, and European, scholars who have had enough experience in our institutions to warrant additional evaluations. Once established under a vigorous and imaginative editor, aided by a broadly based Editorial Board, this volume should prove to be a stimulating and indeed essential tool if the teaching of Latin American history is to survive and prosper in the years to come.

May I add that we could do worse than refer back to Jorge Basadre's observations on the teaching of Latin American history in the United States, which he expressed a quarter of a century ago in his Introduction to the Pan American Union report on Latin American Courses in the United States. It is all worth reading today, and it is unfortunate that we have no up-to-date report on the same subject, with information on the readings and films used in the various courses. Basadre devoted his closing remarks to "A Few Words About Professors." To prove that history sometimes repeats itself, his opening words were: "There was a time when these courses were in great demand and teaching personnel was limited; but now that the years have produced a considerable number of graduates in Latin American Studies, greater selection is possible." Then Basadre went on to discuss the need to learn languages, visit Latin America regularly "to avoid the stratification of judgments and opinions, and in order to keep currently informed of the changes which sometimes occur so rapidly in the Latin American scene." Basadre also called for a "feeling of cordial fellowship, accompanied by a vast patience" if our teachers are to "accept and appreciate the differences in the ways of living in the two Americas." He also warned that the U.S. teacher "must have a moderate supply of skepticism or caution and be capable of his own table of values, in order to distinguish that which is fundamental from that which is of only fleeting notoriety in Latin American life, so that he will not be carried away by the influence of personal friendships or superficial impressions. He should also acquire a selective standard of preferences or tastes and he must especially avoid any 'missionary complex' to participate in the internal struggles and quarrels of Latin American countries." Are not these observations still valid today?

One of the great and unsolved problems facing higher education today is how to recognize and stimulate effective teaching. Most institutions give lip service to the principle that advancement in the teaching profession is increasingly based on performance in teaching as well as on other criteria, and there is a tremendous amount of attention given now to evaluating teachers, as well as an awareness of the need to do so. What is lacking thus far, it seems to me, is some public method, some review outside the teacher's institution, similar to the scrutiny which publications receive through professional journals. I realize that book reviews can be unsatisfactory measures of the worth of a book; as editor of the Hispanic American Historical Review for six years I learned how difficult it is to judge fairly and competently the articles submitted to it. Reviews of books sometimes leave something to be desired, from the standpoint of the author. But over the years historians and indeed all scholars have been convinced that it is one of the few recognized ways we have to take the measure of historians.

Let me hasten to express my admiration for the work of the Pacific Coast Council on Latin American Studies for the sessions on teaching, both at the meeting last year and at this twentieth meeting. Would that all regional councils on Latin American studies were as active!

A special annual publication on teaching ideas and teaching instruments on Latin America will not solve all problems. There still remains the impact of the individual teacher, the ingenuity and imagination he or she musters to present the complexities and varieties of Latin America. Students vary in their receptivity too. I don't have time to elaborate on this, but every teacher knows that there are good years and not so good years, depending to some extent on the kind of student in the class. We must take for granted henceforth, I believe, that our classes will include a wide and interesting variety of human beings.

One final word. Latin Americanists must ever be grateful for the fact that we have a remarkable part of the world to study. We were not the first "area study", for the medievalists and those who studied the ancient world of Greece and Rome preceded us, though they don't talk so much as we do about it. But one of the encouraging aspects of Latin American life is that writers look upon publication as a means of expressing themselves--the way they deposit their grain of sand. They continue to write and to publish under circumstances that would discourage most of us. There has come to be in this country an emphasis on publication for promotion alone; publish or perish is the sacred phrase. Some publish and perish, because their output is so parochial, so forced, so mechanical. It has always seemed to me that one of the lasting rewards of studying Latin America and of knowing Latin American scholars is that they usually publish for the right reasons. They believe they have something to say, and they want to say it.

When we add to this the stimulating fact that there are so many good topics awaiting investigation, I find it difficult to resist concluding that we are favored by the fates. If this spirit has indeed come to influence Latin Americanists, as I am convinced it has, our teachers will continue to express their individuality in teaching as well as research, and they will be all the better for a sustained and searching evaluation of their teaching and their publications.

PART VI

OTHER TOPICS IN LATIN AMERICAN HISTORY

CHAPTER 24.

GILBERTO FREYRE: SOCIAL HISTORIAN

While visiting Brazil in 1938, thanks to a Social Science Research Council post-doctoral fellowship, I had an opportunity to see much of that tremendous country and to study its geography. In those days Brazil was considered an exotic country whose history was rather peripheral to the main current of Latin American affairs. Today Brazil and its more than 100 million people are the focus of much research, and our students are flocking into courses on its history.

During my prolonged experience in Brazil almost forty years ago, I began to read its history and fell under the spell of Gilberto Freyre, whose Casa grande e senzala had been published a few years before. I had an opportunity to know him in his home in Apipucos, Pernambuco, and we had some memorable times together inspecting old fazendas and discussing his views on how Brazilian history should be written.

His was a fresh and imaginative approach, and I determined to learn about Brazilian history through his writings. I felt that Spanish America as well as readers in the United States should know about his interpretations. As I read his books on the ship returning to New York--those were the days when one still ordinarily travelled by ship--and a motley crew we were for American chorus girls who had been hoofing it in Buenos Aires and a Yankee prize-fighter were also tourist class passengers, I became convinced that Freyre was successfully working a revolution in the writing of Brazilian history. More, he was creating a new image for Brazilians of themselves--a past marked by a relatively peaceful mixing of African, European, and Indian elements to form a new and unique nation.

During the last decade a large and important literature has appeared, largely in Brazil, to challenge and revise some of Freyre's basic assumptions, as Emília Viotti da Costa points out in "O mito de democracia no Brasil."* My pioneer essay on Freyre must be considered therefore as a part of the cultural climate of its time; it was the reaction of a North American who visited Brazil when race relations were first being studied in Brazil. Both Freyre and the revisionists today reflect some of the intellectual and political interests of their different times.

*Da monarquia à república: momentos decisivos (São Paulo, 1976), 227-242.

Quarterly Journal of Inter-American Relations, I, No. 3 (Cambridge, Mass., 1939), 29-44. Reprinted by permission.

Gilberto Freyre: Social Historian

Works of history are not written in a vacuum, and historians, no matter how sternly objective they attempt to be, are not bloodless creatures removed from the hurly burly of life. The histories written during any given epoch are, therefore, valuable bits of evidence to the future historian for they often reflect the dominant intellectual and political interests of that epoch. Particularly is this true for Latin America where historians are not so closely confined to the academic heath as in the United States and may be generals, statesmen, or politicians as well as writers of history. They may even make history, and then sit down to compose large works on the subject, as did Lucas Alamán of Mexico and Bartolomé Mitre of Argentina. It will be no shock to future historians, then, if they come to find that the works of the Brazilian historian Gilberto Freyre are a revealing guide to the most significant problems of present-day Brazil. His principal volume thus far, Casa grande e senzala, has stirred the Brazilian intelligentsia to its variegated core and has roused enthusiastic debate on the past, present, and future of Brazil.

Not all opinion on the book is favorable. Freyre has been accused of showing himself not only an opponent of the Jesuits but an enemy of the Church itself, and one critic who is sympathetic to the Jesuits has gone so far as to suggest the desirability of a modern "auto-de-fe" to burn the author and his book. Other writers--some of them ecclesiastics--have rushed to support him and it may almost be said that there exists today in Brazil a Freyre cult and that he runs, perhaps, as much danger from hordes of uncritical admirers as from any other single quarter. At any rate, from President Getulio Vargas down to the intellectuals pacing up and down the Avenida Rio Branco in Rio de Janeiro, and including many lonely thinkers scattered over the vast spaces of Brazil, the works of Freyre have inspired a lively interest in Brazil's past and a serious concern for her future which seems, to one foreigner at least, wholly admirable and wholesome. The following description of the man and the evaluation of his works is presented not as a definitive and critical estimate of Freyre's historical labors--for the writer is not qualified to perform such a feat--but as an introduction to the thought and writings of one of the most influential and interesting intellectual figures in Brazil today.

* * *

Gilberto Freyre was born in March, 1900 in the city of Recife, capital of the State of Pernambuco, and is descended from some of the most ancient families in this great sugar region, one of his forbears being the Dutch gentleman Gaspar van der Lei, who came to Brazil in the seventeenth century in the company of Prince Maurice of Nassau. After joining the Catholic church, this Dutchman married the daughter of a great plantation owner named Mello, whose forefathers were among the first Portuguese colonists to settle in Pernambuco during the sixteenth century. Throughout the following centuries the Wanderley family seems to have remained largely aloof from mixture with Indians and Negroes and married--for economic and social reasons--within the family circle. During the nineteenth century there was some admixture with Spanish blood, Freyre itself being a Spanish name.

At the age of seven Gilberto Freyre entered the American Baptist School in Recife where he remained ten years. Here he experienced a severe religious crisis under the pressure of the evangelical atmosphere. Afterwards he lost his interest in Protestantism and came to feel that it was contrary to his deepest intellectual and spiritual tendencies. It is a tribute to the sincerity and tolerance of both Freyre and his former teachers at this Protestant school that they have remained friends through the years.

During this formative period, Freyre began his literary career at the age of thirteen by editing the journal O Labaro, sponsored by the school's Sociedade Litteraria Joaquim Nabuco. About this time, in order to pay part of the costs of his education, he began to teach Latin in the school, the students being older than himself. This responsibility produced a somewhat precocious independence and an essentially serious attitude.

After graduation from the Baptist School in 1917, Freyre continued his education in the United States and secured his B.A. degree from Baylor University in 1920. Here, too, he continued to help support himself--by translating and writing. The most significant impulse in his development came when he entered the Graduate School of Columbia University and fell under the spell of Franz Boas, the grand old man of American anthropology, and other Columbia teachers in the social sciences who were stimulating the study of cultural history. At a time when many theses presented for the master's degree revealed all the unlovely traits of a mediocre academic exercise, Freyre's "Social Life in Brazil in the Middle of the Nineteenth Century" was a well written study on an absorbing topic based upon a wide variety of primary sources. It was promptly published in the Hispanic American Historical Review. Freyre also found time during his days at Columbia--he continued graduate work there after his M.A.--to direct a review with a Chilean student friend.

From the United States Freyre went to Europe on a grand tour, visiting museums, libraries, and lecture halls in England, France, Germany, Belgium, Spain, and Portugal. In 1925 he returned to Brazil and at once demonstrated his organizing talent by editing a volume commemorating the first centenary of the Diario de Pernambuco. In this year he also was responsible for the First Congress of Regionalism in Brazil at which he insisted upon the necessity of integrating Brazilian life according to a regional concept rather than by the artificial, state system set up by the first republican constitution.

After a visit to the United States to work in the Library of Congress and the rich Oliveira Lima Collection of the Catholic University of America, Freyre was appointed Professor of Sociology at the Normal School of Pernambuco. From the first he inspired his students to begin their investigations in their own home districts. This belief in the significance of regionalism also found concrete expression in the journal A Provincia, which he directed during 1928-30, and in his propaganda for a museum in Recife which would contain carefully chosen objects representative of the regional aristocratic traditions--such as furniture, textiles, and decorations from the old plantation days as well as pieces of popular Brazilian art and folklore. In furtherance of this movement to inspire the Pernambucanos with a deeper sense of their own culture, he also encouraged the planting of trees and flowers typical of the region along the streets and in the gardens of Recife.

Freyre's advanced studies, then, did not separate him from contact with public life--he has never led a purely academic existence--and in 1931 he was so involved in politics that he accompanied the Governor of Pernambuco, Snr. Estacio de Albuquerque Coimbra, to European exile.

This journey permitted him to make investigations in the Portuguese archives and to meet the Portuguese historian J. Lucio de Azevedo. Then he was called to Stanford University to deliver a series of lectures and to direct a seminar on Brazil.

Once more in Recife in 1932, Freyre started to write his Casa grande e senzala which, as the anthropologist Roquette Pinto observed, "was born a classic"("nascia obra classica"), and will be considered at length later in this essay. In 1934, the year of its publication, Freyre organized in Recife the First Afro-Brazilian Congress in which the attention of scholars in Brazil and abroad was called to past and present Afro-Brazilian problems. Two volumes of papers made up of material hitherto widely dispersed were subsequently published.

Other works followed, and with the appearance of Sobrados e Mucambos, Nordeste, and Conferencias na Europa he definitely made for himself an important place in the contemporary Brazilian intellectual world. He also directs the series, now being issued by José Olympio, entitled Coleção de Documentos Brasileiros, and has in preparation an edition of a diary kept by the French engineer and socialist Vauthier during his visit to Brazil in the 1840's, a volume entitled Ordem e Progresso on Brazil under the republic, and a study of English influence in Brazil.

During these years of active literary production, Freyre has not lost his interest in teaching or in communicating to his students his own intense absorption in Brazilian problems. In 1935 he was called to the faculty of the newly founded University of the Federal District in Rio de Janeiro and there established a Department of Sociology and Anthropology. This department was later abolished by conservative administrators although Freyre continued on the faculty as professor of social research until his resignation at the end of 1937.

Anthropologists have often been looked upon (in Brazil and Europe alike) with some suspicion as dangerous fellows with advanced ideas who might possibly prove harmful to Church or State. The French government in 1846 prevented the organization of an anthropological society and when Broca finally started one in 1859 he was sworn to keep the discussions within orthodox limits, and a police agent was assigned to attend meetings for two years to see that this agreement was fulfilled. About the same time the Society of Anthropologists in Madrid was suppressed after a short and checkered career. It is not to be wondered at, therefore, that Anthropology has not yet won a secure place for itself in Brazilian universities. Freyre has continued to teach from time to time, but it is with the influence of his pen that this article is chiefly concerned. Though not yet forty, Freyre has helped to liberate the writing of Brazilian history from the grip of genealogists, chroniclers, and official historians who had previously dominated the scene under the aegis of the various historical societies--or "cemeteries," as they are called by some of the younger and brasher historians.

* * *

Before entering upon a description and evaluation of Freyre's works, it is necessary to state the idée maîtresse which animates all his work. The central fact of the history of Portuguese colonization, as he sees it, is the rapid and general mixture of races, Indian, Negro, and Portuguese, which has taken place in Brazil under unusual--practically unique--conditions, for the process has been largely a friendly one. This mestiçagem has softened the slavery system and has bestowed upon Brazil, Freyre feels, the blessing of a psychological unity and the possibility of a social democracy based upon _mestiçagem_ in which men of deverse origins may seek equal social and cultural opportunities, and may find their own level independent of color and economic or social position. The ills usually attributed to _mestiçagem_ in Brazil--such as corruption, immorality, a relaxing luxury--came not from _mestiçagem_ but from conditions created by a patriarchal slave society based upon a one-crop plantation system. This _mestiçagem_ was brought about not simply by force of the circumstance that Portuguese colonists did not bring their women but was a policy favored on the whole by the government and expressive of the deep-seated tolerance of the Portuguese. This resulted in a vigorous hybrid race and Brazil may look forward to a dynamic culture "formada pela confraternizacão de raças, de povos, de valores morais e materiais diversos, sob o predominio de Portugal e do cristianismo." So runs the argument and almost lyrical affirmation of Gilberto Freyre on the past and future of _mestiçagem_ in Brazil.

It should be said at once that Freyre was not the first to arrive at this conclusion. Carl Frederick Ph. De Martius in that shrewd and wise paper entitled "Como se deve escrever a historia do Brasil" stated that mixture of races in Brazil might produce a sublime result--"uma nação nova e maravilhosamente organizada"--that this mixture must have been fore-ordained in heaven and that one of the principal tasks of those who would write the history of Brazil would be to set forth the singularity of the conditions under which three races had met and intermingled there in a way unknown to previous history. The study of this mixture of races and cultures Freyre has chosen as his life work.

He has given us in the introduction to _Casa grande e senzala_ a glimpse of his first formulation of this concept. During his student days at Columbia University, he felt that a great responsibility rested upon him and his generation to solve the problems of Brazil. The one which disquieted him most was _mesticagem_. One day--after three years of absence from Brazil--he saw a group of Brazilian sailors--mulattoes or _cafusos_--crossing Brooklyn Bridge. They seemed to him to be caricatures of men and he remembered with bitterness the contemptuous phrase of an Anglo-Saxon tourist who referred to "the fearfully mongrel aspect of the Brazilian population." If mixed races were really inferior, as many people seemed to believe--particularly if Negro blood were a considerable part of the mixture--what hope was there for Brazil? It must have been a poignant moment in the life of the young and earnest student.

Shortly afterward Boas, the anthropologist, revealed to him "the true value of the negro and the mulatto." Freyre learned, as he says, "the difference between race and culture and came to discriminate between the effects of purely biological relations and those of social influence--between cultural heritage and environment." The mixed races were not doomed, therefore. It was this comforting anthropological concept which gave Freyre hope, provided him with a fruitful approach to his country's past, and became the cornerstone underlying all his historical works. Throughout his volumes, wherein is amassed a great wealth of fact from a variety of sources, and presented with rare literary ability in a compelling emotional style, this single idea gives coherence to the mass and furnishes the key to his thought.

* * *

Freyre's picture of largely peaceful race mixture in Brazil becomes even more striking when compared with the practices of other colonizing nations toward the colored races. Indeed, one cannot fully appreciate the profound implications of his historical works unless such a comparison is made. The survey of conflicting racial theories which follows is, therefore, an attempt to provide a suitable background against which Freyre's point of view may be properly understood.

Cotton Mather records that the early English settlers of New England considered it "a religious act to kill Indians" and, as John Lawson remarked of the English colonists in the Carolinas, "We look upon them with Scorn and Disdain and think them little better than Beasts in Human Shape." A similar sentiment prevailed more recently amongst the Dutch Boers in South Africa where the watchword of the Voortrekkers in matters regarding natives was "No equality in Church or State."

It was in the United States, though, that these theories seem to have had their most luxuriant growth. Before the Civil War, Anthropology--or what passed for this discipline--was primarily engaged in showing that the Negro was no real human being but a domestic animal that might be treated as his owner saw fit. Gliddon, one of the prominent students of the period, stated that "the blacks do not belong to the same creation as the whites. Their organization dooms them to slavery, and precludes them from improvement." According to W. S. Jenkins, whose Pro-Slavery Thought in the Old South (Chapel Hill, 1935) is a valuable compilation of interesting information on the subject: "The whole defense of slavery turned on the theory of types of man. If Negroes were of the same species, they were capable of the same enlightenment; consequently, they should not be held in bondage which was opposed to this improvement." Nott, with Gliddon one of the most forthright upholders of slavery, affirmed that he was ready to support emancipation on the day when sufficient proof had been accumulated to show that the Negroes were capable of development, and he, naturally enough, did not live to see that day.

In the light of the prolonged controversy in Europe and the United States it is highly significant that no similar one seems ever to have broken out in Brazil. True, some writers have declared that the white immigrants of Brazil have contributed more than all other strains, and the exact part played by the Negro in Brazilian culture remains to be ascertained--(one critic of Freyre's works states that the Negroes furnished only blood and strength like cows and oxen)--but no outspoken theory has grown up to assert the intrinsic inferiority of Negroes to whites. And Freyre is only one of a number of important Brazilian students who have seriously studied Negro culture.

Our knowledge of the way Spaniards in the new world handled the problem of mixed races is still far too scanty to warrant making dogmatic declarations. It seems, however, to be true that Spain did not encourage her aboriginal population and mixed races to develop as much as did the Portuguese in Brazil. In the Spanish colonies the diverse races and mixtures tended to remain, on the whole, separate, and preserved their own speech, dress, occupations, food, and way of life.

Before leaving this topic, it may be proper to pose, even though it will not be possible to answer, the following question: Why have the Portuguese been more tolerant of color differences than the other European peoples--even their Iberian brothers, the Spaniards? Arnold Toynbee seems to think that the repugnance some people feel for others sprang from Protestantism, and that "the modern western race theory has been distilled out of the theology of Protestantism by the genius of a de Gobineau." But the prevalence of such theories among the American subjects of the Catholic kings of Spain would appear to demolish this explanation. How then can the lack of prejudice among the Portuguese be accounted for? Should we accept the suggestion of J. H. Oldham that the more intimate our contact with another people, the more ready we are to endorse the Psalmist's verdict, "He fashioneth their hearts alike?"

* * *

But enough of theories! It is time to examine Freyre's historical works. Casa grande e senzala is a stout volume of over five hundred pages, now in its third edition, which portrays the Brazilian family in the colonial period as seen in the relationship between the casa grande (plantation manor house) and the senzala (slave quarters). Five chapters, each of about one hundred pages, consider respectively "The General Characteristics of Portuguese Colonization in Brazil: The Formation of an Agrarian, Hybrid, Slave Society," "The Indian in the Formation of the Brazilian Family," "The Portuguese Colonist," and then two chapters on "The Negro Slave and the Sexual Life and Family Life of the Brazilian."

This intimate picture of Brazilian life under the patriarchal, one-crop (sugar) slave society is based upon a wide variety of relatively unused sources. Unpublished family letters, parliamentary documents, reports of public health committees, ecclesiastical records, theses of medical students, and the works of foreign travelers have all yielded their quota of facts. In the breadth of his intellectual interests, Freyre reminds one of Henry Buckle, who began the bibliography of his History of Civilization in England with Abd-Allatif's Relation de l'Egypte and ended with Wrangel's Narrative of an Expedition to the Polar Sea. Like Buckle, too, Freyre believes a historian must be a man of many talents. He must be anthropologist, sociologist, folklorist, psychologist, and it is well if he can be also a student of human geography and genetics. For formal documents are not enough in a country where primitive and semi-primitive peoples are to be found.

As illustrative of Freyre's method, the first chapter on the general aspects of Portuguese colonization contains more information on nutrition than on administration, and more space is devoted to syphilis than to religious activity. "Brazil was syphilized before it was civilized" is one of Freyre's telling phrases. Negro influence in nutrition is emphasized and it is pointed out that not miscegenation but bad diet and syphilis--scourges that still afflict Brazil--were responsible for many of the unlovely aspects of Brazilian colonial life. Most important of all, Portuguese tolerance of colored peoples and hospitality to strangers--aided by the lack of formidable geographical obstacles--helped to create a united society in which disharmonies were quietly resolved.

The chapter on the Indians describes the breaking down of their culture by the paternalistic civilizing policy of the Jesuits and by the plantation which bound some of these nomadic people to the soil. Freyre does not give us, however, a clear picture of the various Indian tribes in Brazil at the time of the conquest, probably because Brazilian ethnology is comparatively undeveloped.

More revealing is the following chapter on "The Portuguese Colonist" who, says Freyre, lacked the warlike and religious preoccupations of the Spanish conquistador as well as the rigidity of the stern English Puritan. He was dominated by no fixed idea. Although an aristocrat, he was a temporizer, who had no inflexible convictions to prevent him from mingling his blood and culture with Indian natives and Negro slaves. Thus no black legend grew up depicting the Portuguese conquests in

America as a series of atrocious crimes. We may ask, however, whether Spain's leyenda negra developed because the conquistadores were more bloodthirsty than the Portuguese or because Spanish misdeeds were more skillfully broadcast by the Spanish Bishop Bartolomé de Las Casas, whose passionate indictment of his countrymen in the Brevísima relación de la destrucción de las Indias rang round the world. Be that as it may, the Portuguese colonists had greater cosmopolitanism and social plasticity than any other Europeans in the Americas. Ethnologically and socially they were a most heterogeneous lot. This whole chapter abounds in information on and suggestive interpretation of the psychology of Portuguese people who, though they mixed freely with all classes and all colors, created a civilization which has remained until today, in Freyre's opinion, profoundly and predominantly Portuguese.

The two final chapters of Casa grande e senzala deal with the place of the Negro in aristocratic plantation life in colonial Brazil and with his contribution to Brazilian culture. These two hundred-odd pages are richly informing on all aspects of Negro life--its African origins, its mythology, its diseases, and its linguistic, dietary, and other cultural contributions. It is in these chapters that Freyre's attention to sexual matters is so pronounced that the narrative becomes almost sexual history rather than social history.

Standing out crystal-clear in the mass of occasionally repetitive material is the main idea, namely, that the eroticism, luxury, laziness, and sexual depravity often considered as the Negro contribution to Brazilian life, are not inherent defects of Negro character, but characteristics of a slave society. He buttresses this argument with examples drawn from life in the southern part of the United States before the Civil War. Having disposed of these unpleasant aspects--and be it said that he never glosses over the most unlovely facts, Freyre would have the true and positive contributions of the Negroes in language, mythology, and material culture acknowledged and considered a component part of Brazilian culture.

This description of Casa grande e senzala may close with a mention of Freyre's treatment of a minute linguistic problem which gives point to his chief contention. Portuguese philologists permit only one way of placing personal pronouns; thus, diga-me, façame, espere-me. On Brazilian plantations this inflexible rule disappeared and various usages developed. The Negro slaves, in speaking to their masters would say, not diga-me but me-diga, which has come to be employed as a more intimate expression between children and friends than the formal Portuguese phrase. Freyre maintains that to suppress either the Portuguese or the Brazilian form would be unfortunate.

Casa grande e senzala portrayed the leisurely, almost vegetable, existence of the patriarchal, plantation, colonial society; Sobrados e Mucambos describes its decadence. Following an excellent introductory chapter on Brazilian society about 1800, Freyre begins his dramatic account of the decline of the rural aristocracy, which set in about the time João VI fled to Brazil to escape Napoleon, and Brazil's social and economic center was shifting to the cities. There existed no longer an integrated, static social group ruled over by senhores de engenhos but the beginnings of a new society with different values, whose leaders were young, educated, and deaf to the call of plantation life.

The impact of the nineteenth century and the re-Europeanization of Brazil, as Freyre terms it in a brilliant chapter, not only created a gulf between men and women, but a milieu favorable to the rise in Brazilian society and public life of the mulattoes and the bachareis (young men with a degree in medicine or law). The last chapter of

Sobrados e Mucambos, an essay on this development, is one of the best Freyre has written. A great transference of power took place, then, from the rural patriarchs to a bourgeois aristocracy--in which the bacharel or doctor, at times a mulatto, held an important place.

The mulattoes did not always achieve their desires--Tobias Barreto, for example, despite his intellectual attainments never won the woman he loved because her family considered him too negroid--and some of them never shook off a feeling of inferiority. But Freyre also states that it is precisely that region--Bahia--where mestiçagem was most intense which produced the largest number of Brazilian leaders in the nineteenth century.

* * *

The evaluation of Freyre's historical writings at this time and by this writer must be considered a tentative effort by one who is far from expert in the field. However, certain universal problems are always involved in evaluating any history, and it is proposed to examine here Freyre's sources, method, viewpoint, and style.

The extraordinary variety and richness of the sources he utilizes have already been mentioned. In the discovery and use of historical material he has always displayed energy and resourcefulness. As he explained in his first published study he had been obliged "to fight his way through the accounts of prejudiced, uncritical, and superficial minds--through periodicals, lithogravures, manuscripts, books of travel, and diaries."

The material foundations, therefore, upon which Freyre has raised his historical structure are sound, and so copious is his information on some matters that he has difficulty at times in handling it.

Some omissions may be noted. Comparatively little use is made of the vast mass of badly organized material piled up in the publications of the various Brazilian historical societies--particularly of the Instituto Historico e Geographico Brasileiro. In a work devoted to a plantation society (Casa grande e senzala) slight attention is paid to agriculture, and in a volume dealing with the re-Europeanization of Brazil in the nineteenth century (Sobrados e Mucambos), no clear account of the intellectual progress of the country is given. Whether Portugal continued to exert an intellectual and social influence in Brazil is not stated. Probably the manuscript materials for such studies are scarce, and certainly adequate guides to whatever manuscripts exist are still to be made.

Most historians display some particular point of view in their work and Freyre is no exception. He would emphasize the contribution of the Negro and would exalt the value of mestiçagem.

Freyre's defense and advocacy of mestiçagem present special problems for, as Bryce observed, "the subject is one of extreme interest [but] comparatively few data for positive conclusions exist." Emotions have been aroused and academic opinions have been voiced, as described above. In Brazil, Lacerda, on the basis of his general knowledge and observation, has paid tribute to the intellectual and imaginative powers of mestizos but adds that as a rule they squander what they have, are irresistibly fond of ostentation, are unpractical in their affairs, versatile and intemperate in their enterprises. The upper layers of Brazilian society, moveover, still find a certain difficulty in accepting miscegenation wholeheartedly--perhaps as a result of their contact with Europe and the United States. And at least one Portuguese anthropologist considers mestiçagem "um risco para todas as sociedades humanas, desde a Familia até ao Estado; um risco tomado sobre as gerações futuras. Como ninguém pode prever a sua impetração, deve desaconselhar-se."

When Freyre champions race mixture he is, then, entering a field where controversy still rages. The need for serious study of this problem is great for, as Bryce stated, the subject "deserves to be fully investigated by men of science. The difficulties are obvious, because the concomitant and perturbing conditions are so numerous." And it is to be earnestly hoped that Freyre, with his intense interest in the problem and his scholarly background, will go on to provide the facts to support his belief.

Brazilian critics have raised questions concerning Freyre's sources, method, and point of view. Fewer objections have been raised to his style. Even those who dispute his ideas acknowledge that his prose is vivid and interesting. His grammar is not orthodox, however, and some complain that he has no regard whatsoever for its rules. The reason for this probably lies in the fact that Freyre deliberately writes Portuguese as that language is spoken in Brazil by the common people. Freyre is here in good company, for the poet Jorge de Lima and the novelist José Lins do Rego also follow this policy. Freyre himself recognizes that his style is not pure or perfect, but there is no doubt that he has charmed many a would-be opponent by the vigor and beauty of his prose. Even one with a superficial knowledge of the Portuguese language can appreciate the power and expressiveness which Freyre commands.

* * *

In closing this study, the relation of Freyre's work and thought to the political and intellectual currents of his time may be suggested. One of Brazil's most vital necessities is to achieve a cultural unity which will assure political stability for this vast country with its heterogeneous population. Some Brazilians believe that the only possible way to avoid cultural chaos is a return to that one certain and definite tradition, the Portuguese, and that only by a complete immersion in this culture stream may a fundamental unity be attained. Others insist that, given the variety of Brazil's population, such a return would be impossible. In the light of this lack of social unity--or this anarchy as some describe it--the contemporary importance of Freyre's viewpoint becomes clear. The cultural consolidation of Brazil requires, he believes, that the contributions of all elements of the population be recognized and, even though the resulting cultural fusion will be deeply influenced by their Portuguese heritage, a new and stronger race will emerge which will have a distinctive character born of that fusion on a new continent. Such a belief may not be susceptible of proof and it may turn out to be just another one of those sweeping generalizations on racial problems born of hope, but the fact remains that Freyre's doctrine contains political dynamite and has a definite connection with urgent political problems of Brazil at this moment. The danger of Fascist and Nazi ideologies winning a dominant place in the hearts of Brazilians has recently been widely asserted in the press of the United States--and, of course, in view of the traditional hospitality accorded foreign intellectual movements in Brazil, this danger becomes more than a theoretical possibility. Those who fear the influence of totalitarian dogma in Brazil would do well, however, to ponder these words of Freyre:

> It is this past marked by almost fraternal collaboration of African culture--and indigenous culture as well--with the Euro-

pean, which gives Brazil one of its strongest traces of individuality. It is this which sets us apart today from those European groups for which there can be no compromise, no temporizing, between one culture and another, between one race and another, and for which there exists only the exclusive domination of one race, of one culture, which considers itself superior. In our immigration policy, we Brazilians cannot act in contradiction with this past, which constitutes a powerful national tradition and which does not permit us to welcome, on our soil and in our life, peoples radically opposed to that which has been and continues to be fundamental in Brazilian evolution--a free intercommunication of cultures and a thoroughgoing mixture of races within an essentially Brazilian framework.

In conclusion, one prophecy will be ventured. The historian living one hundred years hence will probably not only be able to discover this definite relationship of Freyre to the fundamental political and social problems of his time but will also go far before he finds, in his search among the records of our intensely nationalistic age, a nobler basis upon which to erect a nation than that which is provided in the pages of *Casa grande e senzala* and *Sobrados e Mucambos*.

CHAPTER 25.

FREE SPEECH IN SIXTEENTH-CENTURY SPANISH AMERICA

Some of my friends thought "free speech" was too strong a phrase to use in connection with Spaniards in sixteenth-century America. So it is if you have in your mind the old ideas of Spain as a nation of cruel conquistadores, dominated by fanatical inquisitors. My researches in the Archive of the Indies in the years 1932-1934 had brought to light a great mass of letters and reports by Spaniards speaking freely of what and whom they did not like in America and what they wanted the king and Council of the Indies to do. So I decided to analyze these complaints and recommendations, and in the following article I tried to explain the situation which so puzzled some of my friends.

The Hispanic American Historical Review, XXVI (1946), 135-150. Reprinted by permission.

Free Speech in Sixteenth-Century Spanish America

The fortunate student who has labored in the Archivo General de Indias quickly learns that Spaniards in sixteenth-century America not only wrote voluminously and composed extensive reports but also that they expressed their opinions with an astonishing freedom. Start digging almost anywhere in the tons of historical records in that great repository in Seville and on every aspect of Spanish rule in America you will find hundreds of letters and reports giving advice, admonishing, exhorting, lamenting, and threatening--letters written to the mightiest monarchs of Europe by their loyal subjects across the seas. Ferdinand and Isabella, Charles V, and Philip II were all powerful rulers who usually brooked little opposition. From the very beginning of the conquest, however, and throughout the sixteenth century, friars, conquistadores, colonists, Indians, judges, and a multitude of royal administrative officials sat down in all the far corners of Spain's New World empire to compose personal messages to their king, explaining what and who was wrong, and describing the measures needed to remedy the situation. The Spanish monarchs even tolerated public discussion of such dangerous questions as whether the wars against the Indians were just and whether Spain held a just title to the Indies.

So outspoken were these informers, particularly the ecclesiastics, that Spain's enemies seized upon their accusations to create the "Black Legend" of Spanish cruelty and obscurantism. Spaniards have naturally resented this and have tended to consider those who spoke freely of conditions in the Indies almost as traitors. Only recently has it been brought out that the widespread criticism allowed, and even stimulated, in America by the Spanish government really constituted one of the glories of Spanish civilization. One of the principal leaders in advocating this view has been the Cuban scholar José María Chacón y Calvo, whose _Criticismo y colonización_ represents a new and important development in the study of the history of Spain in America. It is also worthy of note that the twenty-sixth Congress of Americanists which met in Seville in 1935 approved unanimously the proposition, put forward by various Spanish-American delegates, that the men who criticized Spain's colonial practices--Antonio de Montesinos and Bartolomé de las Casas, Domingo de Soto and Francisco de Vitoria--should be considered as "authentic representatives in the New World of the Spanish conscience." To an outsider who has participated only vicariously in the great tradition of Spain's empire overseas, this clasping of the thistle to the bosom and proclaiming the freely expressed criticism in sixteenth-century America as a glorious heritage and not treason, seems both sensible and noble. It is the purpose of this essay to set forth this hitherto unemphasized aspect of Spanish rule in the Indies, to show what this freedom was, why it was exercised, and what were the consequences.

Liberty and freedom of speech have an ancient and honorable tradition in Spain. An examination of the records of the Cortes, or Spanish parliament, in the sixteenth century shows that the kings allowed it great liberty in expressing opinion and giving advice, although the advice was seldom followed. Even during the rule of the strict Philip II, the Cortes never hesitated to tell the king just what they thought of his own life and work, or to point out to him how he might improve both.

The freedom of speech customary in the Indies during the sixteenth century, which was so deplored by such administrators as Viceroy Francisco de Toledo and considered so surprising by historians, was therefore a natural development. The great distances lying between the various parts of the colonies and the court, the royal policy of playing off one group against another, and the fact that the king by virtue of the patronato real was also largely responsible for the spiritual welfare of the Spaniards and the Indians, help to explain the vast flow of correspondence and special representations from towns, friars, colonists, and viceroys to the king and Council of the Indies in Spain.

The king's loyal subjects did not sugar-coat the pill of their criticism. At a time when princes were usually approached in a genuflecting and laudatory spirit--witness the fulsome praise bestowed in 1504 upon Philip the Handsome by Erasmus in welcoming him back to Rotterdam--the tone of the remarks made by Las Casas before Charles V at Barcelona in 1519 provides a startling contrast. After reciting the iniquities practiced by Spaniards in the Indies, Las Casas declared:

> I am certain that I am rendering Your Majesty one of the greatest services that a vassal may make to his prince, and I do this not because I desire any kind of reward or prize, because I am not doing this to serve Your Majesty, since it is certain (speaking with all respect and reverence due such a great king and lord) that I would not move from this spot to another spot to serve Your Majesty, except for the fidelity I owe as a subject, unless I thought and believed that I was thereby making a great sacrifice to God.

And some ten years later he told the king and Council of the Indies that he much feared that they would be denied salvation because of the misery they permitted in the New World. Archbishop Juan de Zumárraga adopted a somewhat similar attitude in calling to the king's attention the enslavement of Indians in Pánuco province and elsewhere, writing "if it is true that Your Majesty has granted permission for this you should, out of reverence to God, do humble penitence for it."

Other Spaniards expressed similar sentiments, though more tactfully. Judge Tomás López once wrote to the king, preliminary to describing a number of distressing situations that needed remedy, that it was the duty of loyal vassals to tell him the truth rather than agreeable pleasantries. Probably the most elegant statement came in the letter written to Charles V in 1543 by some Dominicans in New Spain, in which they said: "O invincible Caesar, the wise Plato considered that prince to be fortunate to whom God had given a republic whose subjects should freely dare to state and make known the truth; and that republic was fortunate if its prince listened to such loyal exhortations in a royal and thankful spirit."

Thousands of friars acted upon the assumption that the king would want to know what was going wrong and would remedy the situation once this was known. Their spirit was not servile but independent and their words were charged with an honest indignation. Less learned folk wrote to their far-off king too; and Cunninghame Graham has well characterized their attitude while describing the manner used by Pedro de Valdivia toward Charles the Fifth:

> that independent, democratic style that Spaniards may have received from their long contact with the Moors. Like them, while understanding thoroughly the difference that exists between a Sultan

and a camel driver, the camel driver never forgets he is a man, and in his manhood equal to any other of the sons of Adam. Thus, though Valdivia kisses in all his letters 'Your Catholic Majesty's feet and hand,' that does not in the least prevent him from standing for what he considers are his rights.

The nature and treatment of the Indians provided the subject matter for most of the speeches in the Indies and for most of the letters to Spain. Allied to these questions were the justice of Spanish rule in America, royal administration in all its multiple aspects, attacks by individuals on the character and policy of other individuals, and there was at least one record of public opposition to the Inquisition and to usury. Sometimes these letters were brief heart-rending appeals, sometimes they were prolix, detailed, and confused accounts, and in one instance a whole syllabus on royal errors in the New World was drawn up by a relatively unimportant functionary. In one case an official sent in a document of 109 chapters solely devoted to Indian problems, which still exists in the Archivo General de Indias, with frequent marginal notes, to show that the Council of the Indies received and carefully considered it. These communications were usually directed to the king and Council of the Indies, but many friars sent their information and accusations to Las Casas, for him to present to the royal authorities. The files of letters from all parts of America to Las Casas bulged so that they almost filled his cell in the convent of San Gregorio in Valladolid where he lived after renouncing the bishopric of Chiapa. In his will he requested that these letters be organized chronologically, according to the province from which they were sent, so that "if God decided some day to destroy Spain because of the destruction caused in the Indies, the reasons for His Justice would be clear."

Ideas and complaints did not remain hidden in correspondence. They achieved the permanence of print. At least the writings of Las Casas were never prohibited, whereas those who wrote books to defend the Spaniards and Spanish policy found it more difficult, and sometimes impossible, to obtain royal permission to publish. Certain of the writings of the principal opponents of Las Casas, such as Juan Ginés de Sepúlveda and Gonzalo Fernández de Oviedo, never were printed until the nineteenth century, whereas Las Casas was able to distribute--all too freely, in the opinion of some of his contemporaries--his published and unpublished tracts throughout Spain and the New World. As one contemporary writer, Pedro Gutiérrez de Santa Clara, declared in his _Historia de las guerras civiles del Perú_, Las Casas defended the Indians "in the presence of the King our Lord and before the members of the Royal Council at court, before the Viceroy Antonio de Mendoza, before the governors, captains and bishops of all the cities, towns, and other places in the Indies through which he passed. And this he did without fear or trepidation of any kind because he declared that he did this to serve God and our King."

Moreover, no one from the king downward was exempt from criticism. Friars usually denounced conquistadores, although a few of the fiercest critics Las Casas ever had were other friars, town councils fulminated against friars, and even such saintly figures as Bishop Vasco de Quiroga were accused of maltreating Indians. Not all the fierce denunciations of cruelty to the Indians came from the lips or pens of ecclesiastics. One of the bitterest charges was made by Licenciate Fernando de Santillán, judge of the royal audiencia in Lima, who on June 4, 1559, reported that in Chile the Spaniards had killed many Indians, setting dogs on some, burning others, mutilating still others by cutting off their noses, arms, and breasts, and in other ways cruelly destroying them.

Of course there is a natural diversity among men, which leads them to different conclusions, as Viceroy Antonio de Mendoza pointed out in the instruction he left to his successor in the difficult post of governing New Spain. What makes the freedom of speech enjoyed in sixteenth-century America so notable is that the Spanish rulers not only permitted but did almost everything they could to encourage it, as the following consideration of the laws and regulations of the time shows.

As early as August 14, 1509, King Ferdinand ordered that "no official should prevent anyone from sending to the king or any one else letters and other information which concern the welfare of the Indies." The king's letter to Admiral Diego Columbus of November 14, 1509, provides interesting background information, for it explains that the previous governor, Nicolás de Ovando, prevented the citizens of Hispaniola from sending letters, "which was a great disservice to the king," and then refers to the order stopping this. Columbus is instructed to obey this order and "not to impede or allow anyone else to prevent any person from writing to us as he wishes. Everyone is to have entire freedom to write, for no matter what they write I will see that what they say will harm no one unless he merits it." On June 15, 1510, the king ordered Diego Columbus and the royal officials "henceforth not to restrict anyone who wishes to send or bring books or accounts or letters or other writings, but on the contrary everyone may write as he pleases."

Not everyone could, however, speak as he pleased in the New World. The first ecclesiastic to preach against the enslavement of the Indians, the Dominican Antonio de Montesinos, roused such a storm of protest in 1511 that King Ferdinand brought the complaints of the colonists to the attention of his council, which voted unanimously to punish Montesinos as well as the rest of the Dominicans who supported him. In a very strong letter dated March 20, 1512, King Ferdinand ordered Diego Columbus to ship the friars home to their superior "to have them explain what moved them to do such a thing--to take such a novel and groundless attitude." But, added Ferdinand, perhaps the friars failed to understand the legal and theological basis for the enslavement of the Indians, which had been formally considered and approved years before. Therefore the Admiral was instructed to show the Dominicans the papal donation and other letters and "to speak to them in the best manner possible." If they agreed not to raise similar questions in private or in public in the future, they might stay in Hispaniola. If not, they were to be sent home at once for punishment "because every hour that they remain on the island holding this dangerous opinion will do much harm to all the affairs of that land."

The friars did not stop preaching in favor of the Indians, however, nor were they punished. Montesinos went to Spain but only to carry on the fight there in convent and council chamber, with the result that the first code of ordinances to protect the Indians and regulate their treatment--the laws of Burgos--was promulgated in December, 1512. Friars hurried back to Spain, with or without the necessary authorizations, to defend the Indians. When pressed to show by what right they traveled, they would reply--as Las Casas is supposed to have done on one occasion--"with the license of charity."

The prohibition of 1512 against the free-speaking friars was reaffirmed on July 22, 1517. This order brought out the fact that the Dominicans had been announcing in sermons that the Indians could not be commended justly to Spaniards and that Spaniards must release them --although, the king asserted, "it is notorious that the Indians have no capacity to live by themselves and to understand the faith, and that to commend them to Spaniards is the best way to effect these desired ends." Preaching against the encomienda system caused disturbances, the king added, and must be stopped.

The history of "scandalous preaching" in the Indies would require a whole volume. Sometimes the friars attacked the royal judges as instruments of the devil because of the tributes required of the Indians, at other times the friars were accused of subversive preaching, and one soldier wrote to the king, "I can assure Your Majesty that these friars, or at least most of them, as soon as they leave their monasteries, lose all chance of going to heaven." Once, at least, indignant colonists tossed a free-speaking Augustinian out of the pulpit in Mexico, and most royal officials at one time or another complained to the king that the constant talk by friars on behalf of the Indians greatly wearied them.

The king tried from time to time to keep the peace by ordering ecclesiastics, as he did on January 25, 1531, "not to preach or speak against persons in authority so as to produce a scandal but to reprove them privately and send word to the king." Later on the pendulum swung the other way, and on September 7, 1543, a royal order was sent stating that _encomenderos_ had been impeding the faith, and that friars who preached against them should not be interfered with so long as they had the necessary authority from their ecclesiastical superiors. It is clear that the friars were never wholly silenced in the sixteenth century, and any investigator who has worked in the archives will be able to cite additional illustrations to those referred to in this paper.

In some other countries and in some other centuries of Spanish history the ecclesiastics were usually stout supporters of the prevailing ideas and tendencies of the age. English bishops declared to their king in 1624, for example, "Defend us with the sword and we shall defend you with the pen." And in the First World War, the religious groups in the United States almost unanimously supported their country's position. Not so with the ecclesiastics in sixteenth-century Spain. They presented a real and stubborn opposition to the acts and theories of their fellow Spaniards. As the conquest spread from the islands to the mainland, all royal officials were warned to allow citizens there complete liberty to write or to go to Spain to present their views. The Audiencia of New Spain was similarly instructed, on July 31, 1529, "on pain of perpetual banishment from our kingdoms and from the Indies." For the king had heard that this audiencia had ordered all letters and other writings received in New Spain by all persons brought to the audiencia in Mexico City for examination before delivery. This must be stopped, King Charles declared, and the audiencia was not to impede letters going to or from New Spain, "nor is the audiencia to interest itself in finding out what is in the letters or who carries them." Another very strong order was issued on February 25, 1530, reaffirming one promulgated December 15, 1521, when the king had learned that the captains and pilots of ships were being menaced by certain persons who wanted others to be forbidden passage to Spain to prevent them from informing the king. Transgressors were to lose their property and any office or privilege they enjoyed.

This order, repeated later for other parts of the empire, sets forth very clearly the royal view. It reads:

> We order and emphatically maintain that now and henceforth at

all times when each and every royal official and all other persons who are citizens and residents and inhabitants of the Indies, islands, and Tierra Firme of the Ocean Sea wish to write and give an account of everything that appears to them to be convenient to our service or if they wish to send messengers or come themselves, they shall be allowed to do these things and no one (including captains, pilots, and sailors) is to be permitted to place any restriction or hindrance or obstacle, whether directly or indirectly, under penalty of losing all favors, privileges, and positions granted by us and loss of all property and under pain of our displeasure.

And in order that everyone may know of this order and that no one may pretend ignorance of it, we order that this letter be proclaimed publicly by the town crier before a notary public in the town squares, markets, and other customary places.

That such laws were necessary may be seen from the difficulty Bishop Zumárraga was having in Mexico at that time to get his letters to the king. The audiencia kept a sharp lookout and confiscated the bishop's reports against it. Finally he arranged with a Basque seaman to smuggle a letter to Spain, which was successfully concealed in a barrel of oil on shipboard. Throughout the sixteenth century the crown constantly struggled to keep the channels of communication from the Indies open, as the series of orders and the reissue of orders to this effect clearly testify. It is true that in 1558 the viceroys and audiencias were ordered to consider all complaints and suggestions first, but the way of appealing to the king if no redress followed was clearly marked out.

Nor did the Spanish authorities passively await information. They asked for it, in the most specific terms. The ecclesiastics who accompanied Diego de Almagro were requested on May 31, 1531, to send back by the first ship "trustworthy information on the quality and the ability of the Indians and an account of what should be ordered for them so that we may consider this in our Council of the Indies and approve what may be just, and in the service of God and for the welfare of the Indians and without prejudice to or charge upon our conscience."

The king was desirous also of hearing from the diverse groups in his empire. On August 8, 1551, for example, he encouraged Indian representatives of towns to come to Spain to inform him but was realistic enough to add that they must not be allowed to come on private business or because of the "industry of some Spaniards." One of the most revealing incidents in the whole history of free speech in America may be seen in the royal order of May 27, 1582, in which Philip II bitterly complains to the bishop of La Imperial because "he had not reported the inhuman treatment of the Indians of Chile by the Spaniards." Perhaps the only modern counterpart of this practice was the invitation President Lázaro Cárdenas of Mexico gave for any citizen of Mexico to telegraph collect any complaint he wished to make.

The dangers inherent in this policy of no censorship were obvious, and were pointed out by responsible ecclesiastics and officials from the time it was ordered. An anonymous memorial of 1516 warned that informers on Indian affairs should not be believed implicitly, for each one had his own particular interest, a warning that was repeated more than once. Martín Cortés, second Marquis of the Valley, represented the attitude of many persons in America when he wrote to the king on October 12, 1563: "Your Majesty and your Royal Council of the Indies should understand clearly that there is no story so improbable concerning events here that witnesses may not be found to swear to its truth, for exaggeration flowers in this land."

Towards the end of the century, the king attempted to have the flood of communications to him organized and summarized before being brought to his attention. Philip II also wanted his correspondents to write clearly, for on October 17, 1575, he informed his officials in the Indies, from the viceroys down, that their letters should be "brief, clear, substantial, and decent, without generalities, using words which will most appropriately convey the meaning of the writer." Of course Philip, methodical monarch that he was, did not content himself with passively receiving whatever information happened to be sent to him. He seems to have invented that twentieth-century scourge, the questionnaire. No contemporary bureaucrat or sociologist has ever contrived more detailed or longer lists of questions than Philip sent to the Indies in his ceaseless quest for information.

Never during the sixteenth century did the crown attempt to stop the free flow of news--good and bad--from the New World to Spain. The historian today who digs away in the Archivo General de Indias in Seville becomes painfully aware of the results of this policy, for literally tons of reports and letters of the most controversial and divergent nature have been piled up on every topic of colonial administration--mute but incontrovertible evidence that the policy was effective.

Did free speech influence the government of the Indies? A complete and definitive answer to this question would require volumes of documents and many qualifying answers. But we know that every set of ordinances promulgated by the crown--the instructions for Governor Ovando (1501), the Laws of Burgos (1512), the New Laws (1542), the Ordinance of Discoveries of 1573--were all drawn up because of complaints from America. No subject was too small or petitioner too humble for the highest authorities in Spain to consider the matter. When the Indian Don Pedro de Henao wrote to the king from Quito in 1588 urging that Spaniards collect their own tributes rather than make the Indians do so, the Council of the Indies approved and so ordered it; and when the Indian Don Bernardo of Mexico found it difficult to get about because of old age, a royal order dated at Toledo on January 24, 1539, granted him permission to ride a horse, notwithstanding the law against Indians doing this. Nor was any part of Spain's empire too far away to command the attention of the king. When the Bishop of Manila, the vigorous Dominican Domingo de Salazar, insisted on making the Chinese converts to Christianity in the Philippines cut off their pigtails as a visible symbol of their emancipation from heathenish customs, the opponents of this extreme measure carried their protest to Philip II and won. Nor was any problem too important to raise, for the king allowed and even encouraged the discussion of such a tender issue as the justice of his own right to rule the New World.

This condition barely outlasted the sixteenth century, for we find Juan de Mariana lamenting in 1601 that "no one dared to tell kings the truth." This Jesuit historian may have exaggerated somewhat, but it is certain that there was much less free speaking after 1600. And later on in the seventeenth century criticisms of the colonial system were found inconvenient, and the unfavorable report of Pedro Mexía de Ovando was confiscated and destroyed. Any study of sixteenth-century Spanish America, therefore, must keep in mind the policy of the crown to permit and even to encourage free discussion of affairs of the New World. This policy was so faithfully followed that enemies of Spain were able to quote Spaniards on Spanish cruelty and oppression, thus laying the basis for the "Black Legend."

Today this freedom of speech in the sixteenth century is coming to be understood for what it really was--an imaginative and courageous attempt by Spain to shoulder the heavy burdens placed upon her by her political and ecclesiastical dominion in the Indies, and one more illustration of the intense individualism of Spaniards whether at home or abroad. This period of free speaking coincided with the greatest age Spain has ever known, and the best-known official chronicler of the deeds of the Spaniards in the New World, Antonio de Herrera, well understood that this was no accidental relationship. If freedom of speech were not permitted, Herrera stated, during the course of an investigation of charges that he had written ill of some famous conquistadores, "the reputation of Spain would fall rapidly, for foreign and enemy nations would say that small credence could be placed in the words of her rulers, since their subjects were not allowed to speak freely." Though speech became less free in the Indies after 1600, Spaniards continued to describe frankly and fearlessly their own shortcomings. . . .

CHAPTER 26.

MEXICAN MICROFILM DEVELOPMENTS

The Library of Congress has always had a broad approach to the kind of collections and services necessary to support the activities of the Senate and the House of Representatives. During the leadership of Archibald Macleish and Luther H. Evans, the Library paid particular attention to Latin America. One sign of this was the opening on October 12, 1939, of the Hispanic Room and there followed many other indications of a continuing interest in the culture of the nations south of the Rio Grande. As Director of the Hispanic Foundation during the years 1939-1951 I had a grandstand seat for all these developments, and in 1949 the Library sent me to Mexico to initiate the microfilm program described in this article.

The Library of Congress Quarterly Journal of Acquisitions, Vol. 6, no. 4 (Washington, 1949), 9-13; Vol. 8, no. 2 (1951), 12-14.

Mexican Microfilm Developments

The Library of Congress assumed responsibility for the Microfilm Laboratory of the Benjamin Franklin Library in Mexico City in November 1948, and thereby entered a new phase in its acquisition of Hispanic source materials. The step was an important but not an unexpected one, for the Library's interest in Mexicana goes back to almost the beginnings of the institution. Thomas Jefferson's concern to purchase for his private library everything published on the Americas is well known, and as early as 1809 he wrote to Dr. Banjamin Barton: "Mexico is one of the most interesting countries of our hemisphere, and merits every attention".

The Mexican Minister to Washington in 1830, Sr. José María Tornel, helped to establish the present healthy and extensive exchange and gift relationship between Mexican institutions and the Library by presenting a copy of the "instructions of the Count Revillagijedo, viceroy of Mexico, to his successor in 1794". It is worth emphasizing that this first important acquisition from Mexico was a copy of a manuscript and was a gift. The war with Mexico brought a practical and urgent need for acquiring information on our neighbor, and on August 4, 1848, the Joint Committee of Congress on the Library resolved: "That the Librarian be authorized to purchase all the constitutions and laws of Mexico, and also to subscribe for a newspaper published in Vera Cruz and for one published in the City of Mexico". Here we see the emphasis on law and legal literature which has become of ever increasing importance in the tradition of the Library and which is reflected faithfully in the Library's microfilm program now being undertaken in Mexico.

The half-century after the Mexican War was a long period of slow gestation for the Library as a whole, including the Mexican collection. Yet even then the material available was used, for it is recorded that during the dark days of the Civil War, Mr. William H. Seward, Secretary of State, visited the Library and "posted himself on the history of Mexico and the life of Napoleon". The inauguration of the new building in 1897 led to a re-examination of the purposes of the Library. The Librarian, John Russell Young, stated that "The interblending of Spanish-American history with that of the United States makes it advisable that we should continue to strengthen ourselves in that department . . . it would be wise in the development of the manuscript department to note particularly what pertains not only to the United States, but to America in general. Canada, Newfoundland, Nova Scotia, the West Indies, but more especially the countries to the south--Mexico, Central and South America--should have especial attention".

The Handbook of Manuscripts in the Library of Congress (1918) demonstrates how well this policy was put into effect, for there is much Mexican material listed. Moreover, it was used, for the Manuscripts Division reported in 1919, "The papers called for show an increasing interest in Central and South American history, and in the history of Spanish control in America". Since the Handbook appeared, the flow of Mexican material has continued, most of it by gift. Mr. George R. G. Conway, an enlightened and devoted collector-historian of Mexico City, presented 46 volumes of typewritten manuscripts from the Archivo General de la Nación in Mexico City and elsewhere, relating for the most part to Englishmen and the Inquisition in Mexico, 1559-77. The Bancroft Library of the University of California, through its Librarian, Herbert Ingram Priestley, presented to the Law Library a microfilm copy of the first legal code printed in America, the ordinances issued by Viceroy Antonio de Mendoza in 1543 and printed by the famous Juan Pablos. In 1929 came the Connor collection of several thousand pages of transcripts and photostats of manuscripts in Spanish archives relating to the colonial history of Florida, accumulated by Jeannette Thurber Connor.

Another type of gift was made by Dr. Silvio Zavala of the Museo Nacional de Historia of Mexico who, while carrying on research in the Library of Congress in 1939 as a Guggenheim Fellow, lent to the Library his collection of microfilms of manuscripts on Indian labor in Mexico during the colonial period so that enlargements could be made. These manuscripts form a part of the Archivo General del Hospital de Jesús, formerly the papers of the Hernán Cortés family. During the last ten years, Professor France V. Scholes, of the University of New Mexico, has transferred, on behalf of the Division of Historical Research of the Carnegie Institution of Washington, some 30,000 pages of reproductions of manuscripts in Mexican and Spanish archives relating mainly to Yucatan in the sixteenth century. In 1941, for example, 13,027 prints, 22,779 photofilms, and 267 pages of typewritten transcripts were received from this source.

The most important acquisition, however, was the collection of original manuscripts on Mexico and Peru donated by Mr. Edward S. Harkness in 1929. The Mexican documents consist of 2,600 folios and are mostly the product of sixteenth-century law suits in which the conquistador Hernán Cortés and his son Martín Cortés, the Marqués del Valle, were involved. The greater number have to do with the proceedings in criminal suits against the alleged participants in the conspiracy to overthrow the Government of New Spain and crown the Marqués del Valle. As an indication of the continuation of the pleasant policy inaugurated by Minister Tornel in 1830, the Library presented in 1944 a complete set of microfilm enlargements of the Mexican portion of the Harkness Collection to the Museo Nacional de Historia, of which Dr. Zavala is Director.

Music as well as manuscripts was acquired. A gift is recorded, for example, of a "collection of Mexican bugle calls, containing the Degüello, a composition of very early origin". The late John Lomax, however, was responsible for the most creative work in this field, for he collected the Hispanic folk music still cherished by the Spanish-speaking population of Texas. In 1936 he spent some weeks there recording the music of "Los Pastores," a miracle play brought from Spain over 300 years ago by the Franciscans. Handed down orally for all these years, the text and the music have undergone many changes which Lomax recorded for the Archive of American Folksong of the Library, with the help of Father Tranchesi, Pastor of Our Lady of Guadalupe Church in San Antonio. He also recorded "Las Posadas," the singers coming from the Guild of San Antonio Midwives.

Another type of Mexican material assiduously collected by the Library is that on Indian languages. The Schuller collection in 1913 laid down an excellent foundation, which was steadily strengthened by reproductions of manuscripts and books largely purchased from the Maya scholar William Gates. The manuscripts, written mainly in the sixteenth and seventeenth centuries in various Indian languages and dialects of Central America and Mexico, comprise dictionaries, vocabularies, grammars, calendars, compendiums, discourses, sermons, and treatises on doctrine which afford a wealth of source material for a knowledge of native American languages.

The Library's acquisitions have also reflected the turbulent years of the Mexican Revolution. In 1921 extensive files of Mexican newspapers covering the years 1911-20 were received. There are 149 separate titles in the collection, and papers of practically all parties and the personal organs of the various revolutionary leaders are represented. Besides the better-known papers--such as El Demócrata, El Heraldo de México, El Universal, and Excelsior--there are papers of which only a few numbers were ever issued, either because money or paper was lacking, or because they were suppressed and their editors banished. The heat and the struggle of the Revolution are shown by the titles of these papers--El Gladiador, La Guillotina, El Hombre libre, Regeneración, El Renovador.

All this rich harvest of acquisitions was largely unplanned and came to the Library by gift and exchange, or occasionally by purchase. The microfilm development currently under way in Mexico is a planned project, but it is not the first of the Library's attempts to bring to Washington and to make available documents from Mexico or bearing on Mexican history. For in 1913 the Library of Congress entered into a cooperative arrangement with the University of Texas to obtain transcripts from Mexican archives. Other similar material relating to the history of the Southwest under Spanish rule was acquired in 1915 through Prof. Herbert E. Bolton of the University of California and through Prof. Eugene C. Barker of the University of Texas. Later, beginning in 1926, further acquisitions from the Mexican archives were made through Prof. Charles W. Hackett of the University of Texas.

Work in Spanish archives was begun in 1914, under the direction of Dr. William E. Dunn of the University of Texas and was continued at varying rates of speed until the Library undertook in 1927 its first large-scale operation for copying manuscripts in foreign archives relating to the history of America, with funds provided by Mr. John D. Rockefeller, Jr. Some 2,500,000 pages of material were reproduced during the seven-year period the project was carried on, and a considerable portion of it came from Spanish and Mexican archives.

The Mexican portion of the Rockefeller project was started in September 1929, by Prof. France V. Scholes. For three years representatives of the Library searched in Mexican archives for documents on the history of the Southwest and on Mexican-United States political and economic relations. The principal archives used were the Archivo General de la Nación, probably the largest and most important single collection of colonial manuscript material in the Western Hamisphere, and the Archivo General de la Secretaría de Relaciones Exteriores. Other archives in which work was carried on to a lesser extent were the Secretaría de Fomento, Colonización e Industria, Secretaría de Gobernación, Secretaría de Guerra y Marina, and the Biblioteca Nacional. Thus only archives in Mexico City were utilized, although Dr. J. Franklin Jameson, Chief of the Manuscripts Division, manifested an interest as well in provincial archives in Saltillo, Monterrey, San Luis Potosí, and Querétaro. It should also be pointed out that the European phase of the project brought in information on Mexico. Besides the material from Spanish archives, the papers of Father Pichardo were copied in Paris, and from Berlin came reproductions of the political correspondence with the Prussian Legation in Mexico up to 1867, and Prussian reports and documents on the arbitration between Mexico and the United States, 1838-41. From the Haus-Hof-und Staatsarchiv in Vienna came almost 15,000 photostats of papers Emperor Maximilian sent from Mexico in 1866, as well as the series of Austrian diplomatic correspondence with her representatives in London, Paris, Rome, Madrid, Brussels, and

Washington relating to this ill-starred affair. An interesting printed item on the same episode, acquired in 1939, is a complete file of the daily newspaper published in Mexico City in French during the first half of Maximilian's rule, L'Ere nouvelle: Journal des idées et des intérêts franco-mexicains.

The effect of all this copying of material was notable in the development of American historical writing. As Dr. Waldo G. Leland stated: "Practically the entire body of primary sources of American history located abroad, especially in the archives of the principal colonizing countries, is being made available in Washington, under conditions as to use far more satisfactory and conducive to good work than those under which the originals themselves must be studied".

As a consequence of these activities, the Library of Congress has been able to compile a number of bibliographies and guides. Among those emanating from the Government Printing Office in the past decade are the following:

Colonial Printing in Mexico; Catalog of an Exhibition Held at the Library of Congress in 1939 Commemorating the Four Hundredth Anniversary of Printing in the New World. 1939. 60 p.

A Guide to the Law and Legal Literature of the Mexican States. By Helen L. Clagett. 1947. 180 p. (Latin American Series No. 13).

A Guide to the Law and Legal Literature of Mexico. By John T. Vance and Helen L. Clagett. 1945. 269 p. (Latin American Series No. 6).

Mexican Government Publications: A Guide to the More Important Publications of the National Government of Mexico, 1821-1936. By Annita Melville Ker. 1940. 333 p.

The steady and healthy development of scholarly and popular studies on Mexico and the Southwest must be attributed in part to the availability of primary source materials brought to Washington under the Rockefeller project. Since the conclusion of the program in 1932, the Library has continued in a smaller way, with the James Benjamin Wilbur bequest and funds appropriated by Congress, to obtain reproductions of materials related to the Harkness manuscripts, such as the Residencia of Hernán Cortés from the Archivo General de Indias in Seville, Spain.

The presence of Luther H. Evans, Librarian of Congress, in Mexico City in December 1947, as a member of the United States delegation to the UNESCO Conference, made possible the first move toward a new program of microfilming Mexican materials. At that time Dr. Evans offered to the Mexican Government, on behalf of the National Archives and the Library of Congress, a microfilm copy of the diplomatic correspondence existing in the National Archives between the Department of State and the American Embassy in Mexico prior to 1906. The offer was made in the belief that "the study of these documents by the historians of both countries will contribute in an effective manner to a greater understanding of our history and relations", and Dr. Evans also expressed the hope that the Library of Congress would be able to continue its program of copying similar materials in Mexican archives as further steps toward the same end. The microfilms were subsequently presented to the Mexican Government by Ambassador Walter Thurston in a ceremony held April 7, 1948, in the Ministry of Foreign Relations in Mexico City.

The technical means of carrying on a microfilm program were made possible when the Library assumed responsibility for the Microfilm Laboratory of the Benjamin Franklin Library in November 1948 as a result of conversations between the Department of State and the Library. The Benjamin Franklin Library, which is generally recognized as one of the most effective of the cultural and informational undertakings abroad of the United States Government, had established the laboratory in 1944, with the assistance of a Rockefeller Foundation grant. Since then, under the direction of Mr. George T. Smisor, it has played an important role in familiarizing Mexican scholars and institutions with the possibilities of the microfilm technique. With this well-equipped laboratory a part of the Photoduplication Service of the Library of Congress, the facilities were available for a microfilm program which was speedily developed by the various divisions of the Library concerned.

Following the pattern of planned cooperation established at the time the first copying work was undertaken in Mexico in 1913, the Librarian called a meeting on December 27, 1948, at which representatives of the University of Texas, the University of California, the Newberry Library, and others spoke on their own interests in the field and discussed arrangements by which duplication could be avoided and by which the most useful results could be achieved for the Nation. . . .

. . .This program began in November 1948 when the Library's Photoduplication Service assumed responsibility for the Microfilm Laboratory of the Benjamin Franklin Library in Mexico City and appointed George T. Smisor to direct its operations. By the time this program comes to an end on June 30, 1951, a total of almost a million exposures will have been made for the Library of Congress and for other institutions in the United States, particularly for the University of California at Berkeley, and for individual scholars. Work has been carried on in the libraries and archives of the States as well as in the major repositories of material in Mexico City.

The largest body of material copied consists of the official gazettes of all the Mexican States and Territories up to 1924. The Law Library began to collect such periodicals seriously about twenty-five years ago when the late Law Librarian, Dr. John T. Vance, spent several months in Mexico. He discovered that copies of the gazettes prior to 1924 were difficult to obtain and in some cases no complete collections were to be found anywhere.

The official gazettes, especially for the nineteenth century, constitute an important body of information on the legal and legislative developments of the time. During this period relatively few books were produced and the gazettes are one of the few regular sources available on the various Mexican States. Here are to be found court decisions and judicial notices, State budgets, reports of legal commissions, records of State Senates and Chambers of Deputies, articles on constitutional reforms, texts of treaties signed by Mexico with foreign nations, mining laws, voting returns of the municipalities, amparo proceedings, and a considerable quantity of miscellaneous data bearing on the whole round of governmental and legal activities during the first century of Mexico's life as a nation.

In addition, the gazettes include agricultural, economic, educational, and political news of value to the historian. In Coahuila, for example, the ranchers sometimes announced their cattle brands, with designs, in the gazette; and in other States municipal territorial boundaries, population statistics, the official calendar, and much miscellaneous information were printed. Some of the gazettes had correspondents in the United States, who seem to have reported principally on mayhem and sudden death. Even the advertisements in these periodicals reveal much of interest to the social historian, for they show the commercial expansion of the United States and other countries--the forward march of the billiard table and the sewing machine. A detailed list of all gazettes microfilmed will be available from the Photoduplication Service after June 30, 1951, and positive copies of any part or all of this material may be purchased after that date.

Another large project has been the microfilming of the diplomatic correspondence between the Ministry of Foreign Relations in Mexico City and the Mexican Legation in Washington for the period 1853-98. Twenty-two volumes of indexes and over 200 volumes of correspondence are being copied. This correspondence deals with all aspects of Mexican-United States relations for the period. The correspondence also includes much information on Mexican relations with Europe because during the rule of President Benito Juárez the Mexican Foreign Office kept in touch with its diplomatic representatives in Europe through the Mexican Legation in Washington. A positive copy of these diplomatic records will be presented to the Ministry of Foreign Relations in accordance with the agreement made in 1948 between Dr. Jaime Torres Bodet, then Foreign Minister, and Dr. Luther H. Evans.

The microfilming of all the available unpublished indexes to the manuscripts in the Archivo General de la Nación in Mexico City is another important part of the Mexican project. This great archive contains the largest body of colonial manuscript material in the Western Hemisphere. It is rich in information on Mexico and on the Spanish Empire generally, and its tons of manuscripts are indispensable for the historian of that part of the United States once under Spanish control. Of the approximately 22,500 bound volumes in this archive over half have been indexed. Some of the principal sections such as "Tierras," "Reales Cédulas," "Hospital de Jesús," "Historia," "Inquisición," "Universidad," "Correspondencia de Virreyes," and "Minería" have been completely indexed and will be a valuable guide to a large amount of original material which must always be of interest to historians in the United States. An index of special interest is the one listing manuscripts on Yucatan, which was prepared with the assistance of the Carnegie Institution of Washington.

Another project to copy Mexican material is now being carried on in Paris as a joint undertaking with the Colegio de México. The manuscripts included all relate to the period of the Maximilian intervention in Mexico and were discovered by a representative of the Colegio de México, which will issue a guide to the documents.

The completion of the projects described above will make available to students a great mass of historical, legal, and other material which, when considered in conjunction with the documents already in the Library of Congress and in the National Archives, will make Washington one of the principal centers in which Mexican studies can be seriously pursued.

The branch microfilm laboratory in Mexico has also been of substantial assistance in developing the use of microfilm there. Mr. Smisor has advised a number of Mexican institutions on microfilm techniques, and the use of microfilm for library and historical purposes in now well established in Mexico.

To continue work in Mexico, the Library of Congress has recently entered into an agreement with the Instituto Nacional de Antropología e Historia for a cooperative microfilm program. The Instituto, through its Museo Nacional de Historia and under the direction of Dr. Silvio A. Zavala, will provide technical supervision, the cost of microfilming, and a guide to the material copied, while the Library will supply the film and make a positive copy for the Museo. Dr. Zavala plans to equip one of the splendid rooms of the Museo, which is in the Castle of Chapultepec, as a microfilm reading room and reference center for historical students. The Castle occupies a commanding position overlooking the metropolis of Mexico City and is surrounded by well-kept gardens. These gardens offer good opportunities for peripatetic discussion, which seems to be as necessary for historians as microfilm. At this center will be brought together copies of the printed and unprinted guides to Mexican manuscripts and other basic bibliographical tools which will create a workshop for investigators such as has never been available before.

Microfilm copies of much scattered manuscript material in Indian languages and on colonial history which were made by the Benjamin Franklin Library, in cooperation with various Mexican institutions and scholars, have been transferred to the Museo and it is hoped that other similar transfers will be made in the future. Emphasis henceforth must be placed on making the mass of Mexican material that has been microfilmed better known, and to do this effectively guides need to be prepared and reading facilities must be available. The concentration of the microfilm in the new center in Mexico City and in the Library of Congress in Washington is an important step in this direction.

CHAPTER 27.

THE OTHER TREASURE FROM THE INDIES

Commemorative events fall so thick and fast in the Hispanic world that one might spend much of his time at Congresos delivering papers and visiting with colleagues. One of the most fruitful conferences of this kind that I have attended was the reunion organized by Richard Konetzke, Director of the Iberoamerican Institute at the University of Cologne in 1958 in honor of the Emperor Charles V. Often there are amusing and informative informal conversations which add spice to the formal events. The meeting in Cologne was made memorable for me by my first meeting with the venerable Spanish scholar Ramón Menéndez Pidal, who saluted me as a Lascasista tolerable.

In my paper at Cologne I tried to explain why historians must always be grateful for the extraordinary interest of Spaniards in preserving the record of their actions in the New World.

Karl V, Der Kaiser und seine Seit, Peter Rassow and Fritz Schalk, eds. (Cologne: Böhlau-Verlag, 1960), 94-103. Reprinted by permission.

The Other Treasure from the Indies

Historians have long speculated concerning the effect of gold and silver from the New World on the fortunes of Spain in Europe. We in the Americas have sometimes been inclined to feel that this treasure exerted a profound and possibly determining influence. We know that only the timely arrival in late 1519 of Mexican gold from Hernán Cortés saved Charles from bankruptcy at about the time his election as Holy Roman Emperor was announced in Barcelona. "It was the first real indication of the wealth of the Indies", stated Roger B. Merriman, "a foretaste of the way in which the preponderance of the Habsburgs in the Old World was to be supported by the resources which they could draw from the New". We also know that other loot from Montezuma's Empire reached Brussels shortly afterward to astonish Albrecht Dürer with the artistic ability of the Mexican Indians. It seems clear that aid from America's treasure continued, though somewhat erratically, throughout the reign of Charles V; that the discovery in 1545 of the fabulous silver deposits at Potosí in the high and arid Andes of far-distant Peru came just in time to relieve the royal treasure; and that the real flood of treasure from America started about 1550 when Pedro de la Gasca returned to Spain with most of the treasure available in Peru. This treasure must have loomed large in the eyes of the court for we find that even in retirement at Yuste the Emperor could be moved to great wrath when corrupt officials in Seville dissipated the expected and badly needed quintos levied on silver and gold production overseas.

Yet the real impress of this outpouring of treasure has been long debated. Prices did rise sharply, as Earl J. Hamilton demonstrated in his classic studies, and it seems reasonable to suppose that wealth from the New World may have encouraged the expansive-minded monarch to be even more expansive. The returns from the Low Countries, however, and especially the steady, large ecclesiastical revenues Charles received in Spain--as James A. Llorens has recently set forth in an unpublished doctoral dissertation--may have been even more significant than American gold and silver. It must be recognized, though, that we do not have as exact information as would be desirable on American treasure, and we probably never will have despite the interest and importance of the subject. Charles R. Boxer, Fernand Braudel, Alice P. Canabrava, and others have presented studies which indicate a flourishing contraband trade between Peru and Brazil in which silver from Potosí played a key role. Detailed statistics on illegal mining activities and contraband trade are not ordinarily preserved, and thus we will probably never learn with any exactitude how much treasure from America actually reached the Spain of Charles V. We must, of course, encourage the efforts of scholars to probe into these secrets and we must also applaud the work of such lonely officials as Armando Alba of the Casa de Moneda at Potosí and Gunnar Mendoza at Sucre to collect and preserve the financial records--but it is unlikely that the full story of the amount of New World gold and treasure that reached Europe will ever be ascertained.

Another treasure awaits historians, however, and I take my text from Ramón Carande who has done much to explain the economic affairs of Spain. Professor Carande has written, in one of those sentences pregnant with meaning that make his Carlos V y sus banqueros a contribution of such enduring value:

> El español de las Indias demostró poseer, junto a otras, excepcionales dotes de observador. Registra en los viajes de descubrimientos y en las campañas de colonización, cuando descansa con la pluma en la mano, tal cúmulo de datos que sus escritos llegan a difundir enseñanzas comparables por su riqueza a las más valiosas de las recogidas allí.

It is this other kind of treasure from the Indies--the extraordinary wealth of documentation which both excites historians by its richness and depresses them by its quantity--which awaits those who concern themselves with the New World aspects of the epoch of the Emperor Charles V.

* * *

Historians must ever be grateful for the keen sense of history and the almost unconscious and certainly widespread recognition by the early Spaniards that their actions in the New World would one day be carefully scrutinized by posterity. Columbus started the practice of writing about America, and many followed his example. . . . Eventually this concern that the record of their deeds be known and the nature of the overseas lands be described led the Council of the Indies to establish, not long after Charles died, the office of a Cosmographer and Cronista Mayor whose obligation it was to devote himself to writing the history of the Indies on a year-round basis. As stated later in the Recopilación de leyes de Indias, (Libro II, Título 12, ley i), the position was established for this reason:

> Porque la memoria de los hechos memorables y señalados, que ha habido y hubiere en nuestras Indias se conserve, el Coronista mayor de ellas, que ha de asistir en nuestra Corte, vaya siempre escribiendo la historia general de todas sus Provincias, ó la particular de las principales de ellas, con la mayor precision y verdad que ser pueda, averiguando las costumbres, ritos, antigüedades, hechos y acontecimientos, con sus causas, motivos y circunstancias, que en ellos hubiere, para que de lo pasado se pueda tomar exemplo en lo futuro, sacando la verdad de las Relaciones y papeles mas auténticos y verdaderos, que se nos enviaren en nuestro Consejo.

In the days of Charles V the writing of history in and about America was not so much an officially approved activity as it was a manifestation of the Spaniard's conviction of his high destiny in the New World and of his Renaissance zest for life. The ever-present ecclesiastics shared this feeling, too, for scarcely a decade after the Franciscans reached New Spain they appointed one of their number to compose a history of their accomplishments to date. . . .

It is true that the Crown stimulated its representatives to report carefully and in a detailed way on the new dominion; the conquistadores were even "charged with prying out the secrets of those new lands to see if there were mosques and Moslem priests". At times, too, such a chronicler as Gonzalo Fernández Oviedo y Valdés seemed to be indulging in exaggerated accounts of the New World for the benefit of the folks at home. He wrote, for example, that he had heard of a Peruvian monkey that "was no less extraordinary than the griffins," for it had a long tail, with the upper half of its body covered with many-hued feathers and the lower half with smooth, reddish fur. It could sing, "when it felt like it," in the same dulcet tones as a nightingale or a lark. Oviedo also noticed that roosters crowed less frequently and less raucously than in Spain, and even the tom-cats of the Caribbean made so little noise at night that his studies were not interrupted as they often had been when he was at the University of Salamanca. . . .

Most of these chronicles are well-known, of course, though it is instructive to learn that Marcel Bataillon of the Collège de France can discover new and interesting facets of the work of such a familiar historian as Francisco López de Gómara; that only now the director of the Archivo General de Indias, José de la Peña y de la Cámara, is opening up hitherto unknown biographical material on Oviedo; and that Manuel Giménez Fernández of the Universidad de Sevilla is bringing together, through patient exploration of the archives, a quantity of information on the life and Historia de las Indias of Bartolomé de las Casas, whose doctrines and actions have been the subject of controversy for over 400 years. Dibble and Anderson have not yet completed their monumental edition of the Florentine codex of Bernardino de Sahagún's anthropological work, which is being translated for the first time into English and provided with copious notes.

The broad interests of these early chroniclers, which today would be dignified by some such resounding phrase as "interdisciplinary coordination," must be recognized too. They viewed the conquest in the round, and discoursed on disease and death, art and cooking, linguistic matters, child-raising, and a galaxy of other topics which interested them in the New World. Even Las Casas, best known for his staggering statistics of Indians killed during the conquest and for his polemical writings, also revealed a concern for education, a competence in psychology, and an interest in nature that even now are not fully appreciated.

All these and other similar chronicles have long been known and used; indeed, one may say that they have been exploited by historians in the same way that the early miners at Potosí drew off the richest deposits of silver lying easily accessible at hand. In both cases, however, much valuable material was left untouched for future generations to use. Even such a standard and obvious source as the official reports drawn up for their successors by the hundred or more viceroys in Peru and Mexico have not been adequately or fully published, though active consideration is being given now to remedying this deficiency. And the "encomienda"--that basic economic, social, and religious institution--has yet to find a historian who has made full use of the pertinent though scattered and somewhat refractory manuscripts.

The laborious process of locating and editing this additional historical material still goes on. Robert S. Chamberlain, who was a member of the Carnegie Institution of Washington group working on Yucatán, in the course of carving out a solid monograph on The Conquest and Colonization of Yucatán, 1517-1550, came upon many fresh manuscripts concerning this difficult and little-known episode in the Spanish conquest. Yucatán was a poor land, populated with war-like Indians and powerful native priests; hence after almost ten years of strenuous effort the Adelantado Francisco de Montejo sent this bitter and pessimistic despatch to his King:

> In these provinces [of Yucatán] there is not a single river, although there are lakes, and the hills are of live rock, dry and waterless. The entire land is covered by thick bush and is so stony that there is not a single square foot of soil. No gold has been discovered, nor is there anything [else] from which advantage can be gained. The inhabitants are the most abandoned and treacherous in all the lands discovered to this time, being a people who never yet killed a Christian except by foul means and who have never made war except by artifice. Not once have I questioned them on any matter that they have not answered, 'Yes,' with the purpose of causing me to leave them and go somewhere else. In them I have failed to find truth touching anything.

The letters of friars also reveal a pungent and noteworthy quality of observation. Vast quantities of manuscripts exist in European and American archives on the Indians, but the following letter by the Dominican Domingo de Betanzos sums up succinctly one fundamental aspect of this spiny and persistent problem:

> Esta de verdad es materia en la qual un abismo llama otro abismo. . . todas las cosas de aquestos indios son un abismo de confusion lleno de mil cataractas, del cual salen mil confusiones e inconvenientes. De tal manera que aunque lo que se ordena sea en si bueno y con sancta intención provehido, quando se viene a aplicar a la subjeta materia sale dañoso y desordenado y redunda en daño y disminución de aquellos a quien bien queremos hazer.
>
> Si quieren veer el misterio muy a la clara miren con diligencia las opiniones de todos los que en esta materia an de hablar. . . tan diversas y contrarias, las unas de otras por via ninguna se podran concordar, e lo que más es de considerar cada uno esta tan fixo e araigado en su opinion que le parece que dezir lo contrario es blasphemia e desatyno.

The voluminous private correspondence of Spaniards in America, who exercised a most unusual freedom of speech at least during the epoch of Charles V; the truly impressive number of "legajos" of judicial and notarial records in which are embedded valuable historical data; and the biographical statements drawn up by conquistadores seeking a pension or preferment from the Crown all will undoubtedly produce some day a rich yield if systematically worked over. The "residencia" manuscript records alone constitute a largely unexploited collection of considerable value for reaching a more realistic picture of life in America than the rosy views which official documents sometimes produce. The most weighty proof of the almost inexhaustible detail on certain aspects of the achievement of Spain in America is to be found in the many-volumed opus of Huguette and Pierre Chaunu, Séville et l'Atlantique, 1504-1650, which surely marks a significant advance in this field. When these official data are joined with the economic information of a "local" character--such as the early account books of the "haciendas" of that same Diego de Ordaz who was so eager to peer down into the smoking volcanoes--we are confronting an almost frightening quantity of economic data.

The number of stimulating historical problems to be found in this copious documentation is as impressive as its sheer bulk. Even in such a relatively well-worked field as that of legislation on the Indies, Richard Konetzke has demonstrated that the mass of laws that Spain produced in such bewildering variety has not yet been fully exploited by historians. The analysis of the origins of the Spaniards who went to the New World has just begun to receive the attention it deserves. And what more curious commentary on Spaniards and on the shock of a conquest that brought together peoples of such different development can be found than item 24 in the 1512 Laws of Burgos, the first code drawn up to regulate Indians, which provides: "That no one may beat or whip or call an Indian dog [perro] or any other name unless it be his given name."

Perhaps we need not agree with the dictum that "History to be interesting and valuable should be recorded by persons of talent and prejudice or by chambermaids who listen at keyholes," but has the time not come for a much greater emphasis on the social and economic history of Spain in America? Once this truth has been recognized, the historical data recorded concerning the America of Charles V will prove to be a treasure trove which will give historians cause for delight as well as for professional profit.

Besides this impressive documentation made up of the observations, chronicles, correspondence, and judicial records, one other aspect of this other treasure from the Indies should be mentioned. Europeans did not generally follow the lead of Dürer in exclaiming over the artistic ability of the Indians--in fact, America seems to have made relatively little artistic impact on Europe in any way--but the New World did pique European curiosity and led to far-reaching speculation on the nature of man. As Francisco Romero, the Argentine philosopher, has expressed it, "There was developed during these years a new philosophy, a new vision of the cosmos, and a new science of nature".

Francisco de Vitoria made one of the most lasting contributions in the realm of international law in his famous treatise De Indias where he remarked, with a refreshing and amusing candor, that "The Indians are stupid only because they are uneducated, and that if they live like beasts, so, for the same reason, do many Spanish peasants". And he also asserted that discovery alone gave the Spaniard no more rights in America than a canoe-load of Indians would have acquired had they "discovered" Spain.

This preoccupation with the New World was not limited to Spain, for the German Franciscan Nicolas Herborn--who, incidentally, requires greater study than he appears to have received to date--looked at the New World through both light and dark spectacles, and the world has since continued to do so! On the positive side Herborn, writing in 1532, rejoiced at the prospect of a wholly Christianized America in the not too distant future. He foresaw a bright and shining spiritual conquest--in which the Indians would be like so much soft wax in the hands of the devoted friars. But on the other hand he feared that the destruction of the Empire in Europe was at hand. Believing that God had turned on the Jews for repudiating Christ, Herborn predicted that the Empire would be taken from Germany because it had fallen away from the Catholic Church, and then would be given over to the Indians who were destined, he thought, to represent the staunch and solid phalanx of Christ in a vigorous and developing New World free from the religious dissensions which were splitting Europe asunder.

Of all the ideas churned up during the early tumultuous years of American history, none had a more dramatic application than the attempts made to apply to the natives there the Aristotelian doctrine of natural slavery: that one part of mankind is set aside by nature to be slaves in the service of masters born for a life of virtue free of manual labor. Learned authorities such as the Spanish humanist Juan Ginés de Sepúlveda not only sustained this view with great tenacity and erudition but also concluded that the Indians were in fact such rude and brutal beings that war against them to make possible their forcible Christianization was not only expedient but lawful. Many ecclesiastics, including the Indian apostle and the Dominican friar Bartolomé de las Casas, opposed this idea scornfully, with appeals to divine and natural law as well as to their own experience in America. . . . Inasmuch as I have recently published a little volume dedicated to this controversy, entitled *Aristotle and the American Indians*, I will say no more here on this absorbing topic.

As a conclusion, one generalization may be hazarded concerning both treasures from America. In one respect at least the prospecting for mineral wealth and its primitive extraction in the Emperor's New World domains was markedly similar to the task historians face today in the location and utilization of that "other treasure". In both cases there can be seen plenty of work for all available hands. The Crown insisted that Indians as well as Spaniards--indeed, everyone--be encouraged to participate in the feverish hunt for silver and gold so urgently needed in Europe. And despite the opposition of Spaniards, the natives did discover mines. Thus began an economic and social movement in America, marked by considerable social mobility--a movement that is still going on.

So today, the sheer size of the mass of documentation yet to be located and studied is so enormous that historians will doubtless work over these sources for many years, just as Spaniards extracted mineral wealth from the New World for almost three centuries. Moreover, a variety of specialists must be drawn into the labor--anthropologists, economists, geographers, and sociologists, to suggest but the most obvious of the disciplines whose members will find rich data for their studies. In fact, none of the representatives of the social sciences and few of the humanities will go away empty-handed. Let us therefore invite all interested scholars to the common task--and I appeal especially to my colleagues in Germany and other European countries.

If this attack is carried on along a broad front, can anyone doubt that this "other treasure from the Indies" will help us to achieve the objective set up by the late Carl Becker of Cornell University: "The attempt to reconstruct, and by imaginative insight and aesthetic understanding, make live again that pattern of events occurring in distant places and times past", which we call history? Even if we do not wholly achieve this objective, will not the rich and copious historical documentation produced in and about the New World during the epoch of the Emperor Charles V be a powerful aid in deepening and perhaps transforming our knowledge of America, and of Europe, in those decisive decades of the sixteenth century?

CHAPTER 28.

EL FUTURO DE LAS INVESTIGACIONES SOBRE MESTIZAJE EN LAS AMERICAS

One of the most unstudied and important subjects in Latin American history until recent years has been mestizaje--the mixing of races. Over thirty years ago while being considered for appointment to the faculty of the School of Advanced Studies in Princeton, I proposed this as a topic for prolonged research. The School made no appointment in Latin American history then, or indeed later, and I became principally concerned with other investigations.

When the Academia Nacional de la Historia in Peru invited me to participate in its conference on mestizaje, the subject still interested me and the following paper resulted. Just recently a French scholar at the University of Nice, Claude Mazet, sent me a copy of his substantial 1975 monograph, Recherches Historiques sur le Pérou: La Population de Lima au XVI-XVII Siècles: Parroquia de San Sebastián (1562-1689). It was, he wrote, an attempt to produce a mini-study of the kind recommended in this article.

Today we know much more on the difficult subject of mestizaje, thanks to the researches of Magnus Mörner and others. But there is still much to be learned.

Revista histórica, XXVIII (Lima, 1965), 371-375. Reprinted by permission.

El Futuro de las Investigaciones sobre Mestizaje en las Américas

Al clausurar toda reunión académica, como este "Seminario sobre Mestizaje" que la Academia Nacional de la Historia ha tenido la iniciativa de patrocinar, es necesario hacerse esta pregunta: ¿Cuál debe ser el próximo paso que deberíamos dar? ¿Cómo reducir a la práctica las ideas discutidas y las resoluciones tomadas?

Es costumbre entre los profesores universitarios, al menos en mi país, emplear días y días discutiendo posibles proyectos de investigación, que se desearían comenzar, si sólo se dispusiese del tiempo y el dinero necesario. Muchas de estas discusiones, tenidas en los Estados Unidos, fueron organizadas por el Doctor Waldo Leland, Director del American Council of Learned Societies, el cual empleó su vida escuchando a infinidad de profesores que le proponían proyectos de posibles investigaciones y publicaciones. Después de tales conferencias, tenidas en los fines de semana, el Doctor Leland solía proponer a los presentes una pregunta final: "Y bien, caballeros, ¿qué piensan ustedes hacer el próximo lunes por la mañana para llevar a cabo estos proyectos?"

Aunque desgraciadamente no he tenido la oportunidad de estar con ustedes durante todas las reuniones de este Seminario, yo quisiera hacer la misma pregunta a todos los presentes, y a todos aquellos interesados en el complicado y fundamental problema del mestizaje en América. Si queremos hacer avances serios en este campo, ¿cuáles son los criterios que hemos de mantener claros en nuestra mente? ¿Cuál es el futuro de estos estudios sobre la fusión de razas y culturas en América? Fusión de razas y culturas que ha sido descrita por Pedro Henriquez Ureña con estas palabras: "La conquista y población del Nuevo Mundo por las dos naciones hispánicas dio origen a una sociedad nueva, probablemente distinta de cualquiera de las ya conocidas y, con seguridad, nunca igualada en cuanto a la magnitud del territorio en que se extendía".

En primer lugar, debemos reconocer que estamos siendo testigos de una enorme expansión en el interés mundial por América Latina. Hace poco tuve necesidad de revisar todos los estudios americanistas que han aparecido en los últimos seis años. Pude constatar, con sorpresa y admiración, el sinnúmero de publicaciones que han visto la luz no solo en los diversos países de las Américas, sino incluso en países alejados de nuestros círculos intelectuales como Japón, Rusia Soviética, las dos Alemanias y Checoslovaquia. Existe, en progreso, un desarrollo notable de los estudios americanos en las Islas Británicas, con nuevos centros en vísperas de establecerse en Londres, Oxford, Cambridge, Liverpool, y Glasgow. En Francia hay un notable avance en el número de profesores y cursos universitarios dedicados a América Latina. Hace poco me encontré, por ejemplo, con el Doctor José Durand de Lima como catedrático en la Universidad de Tolosa, quien me explicó el avance en Francia. En Alemania existen varios centros Universitarios, y el año pasado se publicó en Colonia el primer Anuario sobre el tema. En España continúan los varios institutos publicando libros y estudios sobre los diversos aspectos de la acción de España en el Nuevo Mundo.

Por todas estas manifestaciones de interés, podemos deducir que ahora más que nunca la investigación de lo latino-americano ha dejado de ser una cosa de familia, y se ha convertido en algo universal. Todo el mundo se interesa por esta gran área, y no es una coincidencia fortuita que uno de los líderes, precisamente en este campo del mestizaje, sea un sueco, el Doctor Magnus Mörner. Tengo entendido que el Doctor Mörner ha enviado una ponencia a este Seminario. El hecho de que él no se encuentre aquí personalmente es mi propia culpa! En estos momentos el Dr. Mörner está actuando en substitución mía como Profesor Visitante de Columbia University, y gracias a su presencia en Nueva York, yo me encuentro aquí en Lima con ustedes. Junto con el antropólogo Marvin Harris, el Doctor Mörner va a ofrecer un Seminario sobre Mestizaje en América Latina, que será uno de los primeros organizados en mi país. También sobre el mismo tema está organizando un Coloquio, que tendrá lugar en Nueva York hacia el mes de diciembre, y será patrocinado por Columbia University y Cornell University.

Esta gran explosión de publicaciones y cursos sobre América Latina nos traerá consigo grandes ventajas. Me refiero a la interpretación o mejor dicho interpretaciones de la historia de este continente. Es verdad que todavía hay libros y discusiones alrededor de ciertas figuras como la de Fray Bartolomé de Las Casas, pero ni un Don Ramón Menéndez Pidal ha podido convencer al mundo que Fray Bartolomé era un "paranóico". Hoy, la mayoría de los historiadores del mundo ven en Las Casas una de las glorias de España y de América. Como ha dicho muy bien la poetisa chilena Gabriela Mistral, Las Casas y los españoles que lucharon por la justicia en América son un honor para la humanidad.

Además de este gran incremento en los estudios americanistas, nuestra generación se ha liberado, al menos parcialmente, de las sombras de las revoluciones independentistas. Hace una semana, un historiador colombiano habló en un Seminario en Bogotá contra lo que él llamó la historia "heroica". Los defectos de esta historia heroica son según él:

a) exagera el papel jugado por el héroe: y tiende a convertir la historia en una sucesión de biografías.
b) sobrecarga el relato con detalles íntimos de la vida del héroe, detalles que no guardan relación directa con su rol histórico.
c) se preocupa de la historia de una minoría--los héroes-- y descuida la de la mayoría--que es un pueblo en su totalidad-- que también tiene su historia digna de ser estudiada.

Hoy día hay más y más interés en el cultivo de la historia del pueblo, y uno de los aspectos fundamentales es el proceso de mestizaje. ¿Pero en qué forma debemos confrontar este proceso? Tenemos que reconocer que estamos todavía en los comienzos de nuestra tarea, aunque investigadores como Angel Rosenblat, Richard Konetzke, George Kubler, Magnus Mörner y otros ya han dado magníficas aportaciones al campo. Sin embargo existen varias actitudes de parte de los historiadores que han creado dificultades al trabajo, y han oscurecido la verdad. Esas actitudes son:

I. <u>Romanticismo</u>: Para los que siguen esta pauta, la fusión de razas en América es un hecho laudable, una gloria de España o una gloria de América, según la línea política del historiador. Perfume y flores llenan sus páginas, y citan documentso solamente para ilustrar su verdad. Naturalmente, esta actitud no es más que una evasión de la realidad, y una evasión de la función de un investigador verdadero.

II. <u>Pesimismo</u>: Según el pesimista, el mestizo era un malcontento entre dos mundos, un hombre "marginal" para emplear la palabra de los antropólogos. No es difícil encontrar en la documentación ejemplos que "prueban", para el bando de los pesimistas, la mala conducta de los mestizos.

Por supuesto que tenemos que admitir que el proceso del mestizaje es uno de los problemas históricos más difíciles de estudiar. Podemos comparar la falta de documentación en este campo con el silencio de los documentos sobre la plata extraída clandestinamente de las minas de Potosí sin pagar el quinto real. Muchos mestizos no quisieron registrar su ascendencia como tales en sus papeles familiares, y por eso el historiador del mestizaje tiene que ser necesariamente una combinación de psicólogo, detective, paleógrafo, etc.

Dadas todas estas circunstancias, quisiera sugerir los siguientes procedimientos para adelantar en el futuro los estudios sobre este tema:

I. Un moratorium de diez años en el pronunciamiento de generalizaciones sobre el mestizaje. Estamos en la infancia de estos estudios. Es prudente recordar esta verdad, y es necesario rechazar la tentación de lanzar a los cuatro vientos aseveraciones y conclusiones, que aun no han sido fundamentadas en la roca viva de la investigación.

II. Fomentar lo que yo llamaría mini-estudios. Hablamos de latifundio y minifundio. Tal vez podemos emplear la palabra mini-estudio para indicar la investigación en pequeña escala. Permítanme un ejemplo. En todos los países de América existe una documentación más o menos completa, en los archivos eclesiásticos, con datos sobre bautismos, casamientos, y entierros. Muchas veces estos documentos contienen una información excelente sobre la cualidad mestiza de los individuos. Sería interesantísimo saber si hubo variaciones de pueblo a pueblo, de región a región, de siglo a siglo. Si pudiéramos llevar a cabo este trabajo, verdaderamente benedictino, en diversos países y en diferentes regiones, tendríamos con el tiempo una documentación más segura, más amplia que la que hoy está a nuestra disposición.

Otro ejemplo de mini-estudio sería el análisis de la actitud de los cronistas ante el problema del mestizaje. Angel Rosenblat ha comenzado esta tarea, pero hay mucho más por hacer. Basten dos ejemplos. Antonio Vázquez de Espinosa en el siglo XVII no se fijó mucho en el asunto; tampoco el historiador de Potosí Bartolomé Arzáns de Orsúa y Vela en el siglo XVIII. Por qué? Solamente después de un minucioso estudio de lo que los cronistas han escrito podremos entender cómo los historiadores de la colonia han enfocado el proceso del mestizaje.

Otro tipo de fuente para un mini-estudio serían las relaciones de los virreyes. Hubo una gran variedad de virreyes en América, y en general confrontaban sus problemas de administración en una variedad de modos y con un cuño personal. ¿Cómo confrontaron los diversos virreyes, en casos concretos, este mundo nuevo del mestizo? Aquí tenemos otra posibilidad de mini-estudio.

Todos ustedes pueden sin duda pensar en otros ejemplos de investigación en pequeña escala, que nos darían en el futuro una base más firme para el conocimiento del proceso del mestizaje en América. Ojalá que este Seminario, debido a la sabia iniciativa de la Academia de la Historia, sea sólo el comienzo de esta interesante, necesaria e importante investigación.

Quisiera concluir con otra estimulante frase de Pedro Henríquez Ureña que, al hablar del "florecimiento del mundo colonial", escribió así:

> Ya hemos visto cómo las nuevas experiencias convirtieron en hombres nuevos a los españoles y portugueses que se establecieron en el Nuevo Mundo. A fines del siglo XVI, sus descendientes, algunos de ellos de pura sangre europea, pero en su mayoría con alguna mezcla de sangre india, eran hombres de un tipo nuevo, "el nuevo indígena", que vivían dentro de un medio único, crisol de dos culturas. También los indios, por lo menos aquellos que aprendieron a hablar el lenguaje de los conquistadores, eran

distintos de como habrían sido: la vida había cambiado para ellos lo mismo que para los recién llegados.

El Mundo Nuevo era, por tanto, un mundo de cambios, pero tal vez el cambio más perdurable y más significativo para el futuro de América fue ese proceso de fusión que llamamos mestizaje.

CHAPTER 29.

A MODEST PROPOSAL FOR A MORATORIUM ON GRAND GENERALIZATIONS: SOME THOUGHTS ON THE BLACK LEGEND

No serious student of the work of Spain in America can avoid grappling at some point in his career with the problem presented by the Black Legend interpretation. This unfavorable view of Spain was made popular in many lands by the writings of Las Casas and others, and still flourishes. Here are my observations on a subject which will doubtless always be an important topic in Spanish American history. For opposing views, see Professor Benjamin Keen's articles in The Hispanic American Historical Review, XLIX (1969), 703-731, LI (1971), 336-355.

The Hispanic American Historical Review, 51 (1971), 112-127. Reprinted by permission.

A Modest Proposal for a Moratorium on Grand Generalizations: Some Thoughts on the Black Legend

Benjamin Keen's stimulating contribution on the Black Legend illustrates how almost inexhaustibly the colonial period provides challenging controversies that lead us to re-examine basic views on the history of Spain in America. Though this is not the place to discuss all the questions he raised, the time may have arrived for writers on the Spanish Conquest to declare a moratorium on the striking off of generalizations and judgments and to enter the archives for further research. The purpose of this note is to indicate why a moratorium is needed. Let us begin with one of the more obvious simplicities.

Keen analyzes the development of Charles Gibson's thought on the Black Legend and refers, among other points, to his "sombre picture of an Indian population. . . so demoralized that it found relief from its misery in drinking on a scale rarely seen in history." What Gibson actually wrote, in that dramatic last sentence of his solid work on _Aztecs under Spanish Rule_, was: "If our sources may be believed, few peoples in the whole of history were more prone to drunkenness than the Indians of the Spanish colony." Now even such an energetic and competent scholar as Gibson would find it an impossible task to go through all the sources available on drunkenness "in the whole of history" so thoroughly as to write that last sentence with complete justification.

Undeniably there was much drunkenness among Indians under Spanish rule in America. The reasons for this, however, may not be as simple as Keen and Gibson suggest. The eighteenth-century Mexican Jesuit Francisco Javier Clavigero explained Indian addiction to liquor in this way: "Actualmente y siempre han sido sobrios en el comer: pero es vehementísima su afición a los licores fuertes. En otros tiempos la severidad de las leyes impedía abandonarse a esta propensión: hoy la abundancia de licores y la impunidad de la embriaguez trastornan el sentido a la mitad de la nación." The latest study on the condition of Indians before and after the conquest in Peru by Nathan Wachtel makes additional points relevant to this question. Under Inca rule neither wine nor coca was permitted to the ordinary Indian; a consumer society developed after Spaniards came. The activity of merchants and work in the mines created conditions which promoted greater Indian consumption of food, even meat, than before. Coca became a highly valued and widely sold product, and wine drinking reached such proportions that Fray Benito de Peñalosa declared in 1629: "Todos los males de la América española procedían de haber plantado viñas en el Perú." While this seventeenth-century generalization may not be wholly true, the taverns of such mining centers as the Villa Imperial de Potosí did in fact become famous on account of the amount of liquor consumed in them as well as for large fortunes made by their owners.

An argument may be made, therefore, that greater access to hitherto denied goods was at least in part responsible for the Indians' addiction to drink under Spanish rule. But alcoholism remains one of the important relatively unstudied topics in Spanish colonial history. The causes of this phenomenon are complex matters which cannot be adequately explained by sweeping pronouncements.

Keen's own attempt to clarify and resolve the issues relating to the Black Legend introduces a number of doubtful generalizations of the "Let the laws be obeyed, but not enforced" interpretation which I thought had been decently interred long ago. He condemns the White Legend for substituting "the texts of laws and pious expressions of goodwill, generally unimplemented, for the reality of Indian-Spanish relations." How does anyone know that the laws were "generally unimplemented"? Or to cite other expressions Keen employs, the laws were "on paper"; the general ordinances of 1573 were given merely "lip service." Keen also holds that "the essence of Philip's Indian policy was profoundly anti-Lascasian. During his reign Indian tribute and labor burdens increased and Indian living standards declined." Was it royal policy to aim at despoiling the Indians, even if Philip's practice did in fact cause some of these results?

Let us analyze this simplistic view of Philip II's Indian policy, in the light of what actually happened in northern Mexico, an example Keen gives to support his interpretation. He states that "the period after 1573, the year of the promulgation by the Council of Indies of the general ordinance which, according to Hanke, put the ideas of Las Casas on the law books, saw no cessation of 'war by fire and sword' and slavehunting against the Indians." Evidence for this, we are told, may be found in Philip W. Powell's monograph. But the facts brought out in this volume on Indian-Spanish relations in northern New Spain emphatically do not support Keen's view; rather they reveal a long battle over whether war should be used, a battle the "hawks" eventually lost.

When Viceroy Martín Enríquez de Almanza arrived in 1568 he, according to Powell, "was virtually forced by prior circumstances to pursue a policy of 'war by the sword'"; but, even so, debate continued on the justice of the policy. On May 20, 1578, Philip II ordered Viceroy Enríquez to study the minutes of the 1546 meetings of the Council of the Indies and of the Bishops of New Spain to discover how to encourage the formation of congregations of Indians by rewarding those who entered such congregations voluntarily with remission of their labor services. Philip also instructed the viceroy to prevent violence and to work with such patience, though with all deliberate speed, as to attract the Indians to the royal plan of resettlement. But not until 1585 did the efforts of those who insisted on peaceful persuasion rather than the sword triumph. As Stafford Poole demonstrates, in his detailed and substantial study of the dispute, the ecclesiastics at the Third Mexican Provincial Council in 1585 strongly condemned war, even against the wild Indians in northern Mexico: "We do not find nor do we feel any justification for making war by fire and blood."

During the period 1585-1600, as Powell relates, Viceroy Manrique de Zúñiga and others finally worked out a basic pattern of pacification. Powell calls it a "peace by purchase" (supplies of food, clothing, and all the paraphernalia of sedentary living) and "peace by persuasion" (diplomacy and missionary effort). Henceforth the crown increased its efforts to bring together Indians and to organize a mission system. And these peaceful efforts did not remain a pious program, talk without action. The pacification policy took effect; most of the hitherto warlike Chichimecas settled down. To make certain that the official policy had been carried out, Viceroy Conde de Monterrey named two capable officers--the royal accountant Diego Infante del Aguilar and Captain Juan de Vergara Osorio--to conduct a careful and systematic inspection of results accomplished. The 3,300 page manuscript record of their visita in 1601-1602 still exists in the Archivo General de Indias. Powell has studied this report in detail, in a substantial article published after his monograph.

To summarize on this point, Philip II supported peaceful persuasion, not force, after 1585, even on the warlike Chichimecas in northern

Mexico, as Powell's monograph conclusively proves. Philip II also supported programs to civilize the Indians by urbanizing them, both in Peru and Mexico. The crown policy does not seem unreasonable, difficult as it was to enforce in America. After all, Spaniards wanted both to Christianize and to profit from the Indians, and they could no neither if the Indians were dead, which would have been the case if "war by fire and sword" had been generally used. The epidemics of the early 1570s, which inaugurated the "century of depression," made a peaceful policy particularly attractive to Spaniards dependent on Indian labor.

Moreover, laws are worthy of study whether always enforced or not, for they reveal the psychology of a people. Sixteenth-century Spaniards were a legalistic and moralistic people whose laws and polemics tell us what they thought life ideally should be. One of the best ways to find out what evils the Spanish crown was attempting to abolish is by studying the laws themselves. Some of the most telling descriptions of Spanish cruelty to Indians, for example, appear in the texts of royal orders--so much so that the seventeenth-century jurist Juan Solórzano y Pereira was ordered to remove from the manuscript of his Política indiana some of the ordinances designed to prevent mistreatment of Indians so that notice of these incidents would not reach foreigners. Historians will have much less material to work with if they ignore the traditions and attitudes imbedded in sixteenth-century Spanish law. They also will be ignoring one of the fundamental aspects of the intellectual history of Spain. The result will be a homogenized product, not history, for the "in-dwelling spirit" of Spanish society, to borrow one of Américo Castro's eloquent phrases, cannot be understood if the Spanish sense of law is disregarded.

Questions of fact are also involved in any serious consideration of the general role of Indian law. If Spaniards in America were so ready to disregard the law, why did so many of them dread it? Those who rebelled against the New Laws of 1542 designed to protect the Indians did so because they feared their enforcement, and they did not rest until they managed to get some of the more stringent ones watered down. Those who opposed Bartolomé de Las Casas and even threatened him with physical violence while he was bishop in Chiapa feared the laws he proposed. Those who tried to suppress the Third Mexican Council opposed its conclusions on laws respecting Indians. Obviously some Spaniards in America considered the laws a genuine threat to their interests. There would have been no need to fight "generally unimplemented" laws which were "pious expressions of good will."

The answer to the question of the enforcement of Indian law must be sought in the archives. Here we are all indebted to the pioneering investigation of Woodrow Borah. His contribution on "Social Welfare and Social Obligation in New Spain: A Tentative Assessment" leads the way to a field of research all too often underrated in the past. His remarks on the positive acts of the Spanish regime in setting up hospitals and in establishing the Cajas de Comunidad must be taken into account in any judgment on Spanish action in America. His observations on the General Indian Court, which handled Indian law suits in New Spain, are particularly pertinent:

> For the period the court was an innovation that looks bold even today. Although there were special provisions for hearing Indian cases in other parts of the Indies, nowhere else did they reach such full development or come to a system of tax-supported legal aid. In Mexico the General Indian Court operated as a genuinely country-wide institution that once called to jurisdiction of a

> case could not be disregarded. The voluminous records surviving in Mexico City indicate that its services were used extensively. It was active to the end of the Spanish regime.

Whether Borah's forthcoming history of the General Indian Court will show that the laws designed to protect the Indians were generally ignored remains to be seen. But whatever conclusions he reaches, they will be based on archival research rather than upon undocumented generalizations.

My principal question, however, concerning Keen's position has to do with his assumption that the seriousness of the effort Spain actually made on behalf of her Indian subjects should be measured "not by the volume of legislation or of debate on the subject, but by such pragmatic criteria as Indian population trends and living standards." These "pragmatic" standards may seem appropriate to us today, with medicare and other social security measures being extended to larger and larger segments of our society, but should historians always put on twentieth-century spectacles to look at the sixteenth century? And if we are going to include population trends, should we not recognize that behind those seemingly "hard" facts on population trends expressed in stark mathematical terms there often has lurked many a prejudice? In a review of the considerable literature that has developed on the subject since the sixteenth century, Rolando Mellafe recently wrote: "Sobre pocos temas de historia colonial hispano-americana se ha opinado con más libertad e irresponsabilidad que sobre los de población, y no es corriente que un problema histórico se cargue de tanto sentido polémico e intencionalidad ideológica." Even today, when methods have improved, does not the recent Woodrow Borah-Angel Rosenblat exchange on this controversial subject suggest caution rather than confidence when it comes to calculating how many Indians were in America in 1492 or 1519?

The reasons advanced for the decline of Indian populations are also contradictory and controversial. Generalizations flourish here with tropical luxuriance. Juan Friede recently provided historical documentation to prove that epidemics caused great loss of life among the Indians in two mining communities in New Granada in 1629, but then seems to contradict himself by delivering this generalization: "There are numberless documents which definitely attribute the decrease of the Indian population to excessive work, malnutrition, flight, segregation of the sexes, ill-treatment, cruelty, conscription for expeditions, enslavement, the <u>mita</u>, etc. Hundreds of archival documents refer to these factors rather than the plague as the cause of the decline." Friede makes no attempt to document this opinion, which can only be held by those who are willing to ignore the known information on epidemics and disease. Mellafe warns that this problem, too, is a complicated one, with various kinds of questionable interpretations at large: "Al respecto hay ficciones y malos entendidos, se repiten conceptos sin valor científico alguno." He emphasizes that one must distinguish between periods and that conditions differed from area to area. Even the size of an Indian family varied substantially, and the growth of mestizos helps to explain the decline of Indian population, for Spanish males preempted Indian women who therefore bore fewer Indian children. The "pragmatic criteria" of population statistics, by which Keen wishes to measure Spain's effort, must be studied with a full knowledge of the variations, subtleties, and undetermined quantities involved.

"Living standards" are tricky as population trends. Would such standards be the same for Spaniards as Indians? If different, in what way? Indians may have held different opinions on what constituted a desirable living standard. The royal chronicler Antonio de Herrera solemnly reported what one "indio discreto" is said to have responded when a sixteenth-century Spaniard asked what were the greatest benefits brought the Indians. The answer must have surprised the Spaniards, for the Indian praised these Spanish contributions: the egg, because it could be eaten cooked or raw and by the young as well as the old; the horse, because it increased their mobility and relieved them of burden bearing; and the candle, because it prolonged day into night. Thus living standards depend to some extent on what one values in life. Does Keen mean housing conditions, medical assistance, calories per person per day, or something else? Whatever criteria are adopted, how did living standards under Spanish rule compare with those of the Indians before the conquest? Did these living conditions improve by the end of Spanish rule as some historians claim?

If possession of land becomes a basic factor in assessing "living standards"--an element which as Gibson remarks Las Casas largely left unmentioned in his catalog of Spanish abuses of Indians--present generalizations may be misleading. Keen depends upon Gibson's documentation from the Valley of Mexico to show that Indians did lose much land. But they lost little in Oaxaca, as has recently been demonstrated by the patient work in local archives there of William B. Taylor, one of Gibson's students: "The Valley's pueblos and caciques generally retained sizeable holdings, certainly more than sufficient to meet basic needs and escape dependence upon an alien landholder." Taylor also finds that Indian lands were not reduced to isolated or mountainous regions, as Frank Tannenbaum once suggested; and that land holdings of Spaniards in Oaxaca were generally small and highly fragmented. We need more studies of this kind before we can appreciate the variety of landholding arrangements in effect throughout the empire. The idea that conditions, practices, and laws varied throughout the empire is a concept at least as old as Rafael Altamira's _Autonomía y decentralización legislativa en el régimen colonial español, siglo XVI a XVIII_ (Coimbra, 1945), which is a restatement of his earlier studies on the subject, to which Silvio Zavala has also made important contributions. All these questions, and perhaps others too, must be confronted if the "population trends and living standards" argument is brought forward, and much research will be required if they are to be adequately answered.

For sixteenth-century Spaniards, certainly for Philip II and his advisors, the standards would have been different, to some extent at least, from those applied by Keen, as we can see by the section in the 1573 law in which they justified the conquest by ticking off the various benefits, including material ones, the Indians would enjoy under Spanish rule:

> The Indians should be brought to an understanding of the position and authority which God has given us and of our zeal in serving Him by bringing to His Holy Catholic Faith all the Western Indies. They should also learn of the fleets and armies that we have sent and still send for this purpose, as well as of the many provinces and nations that have rendered us obedience and of the many benefits which they have received and are receiving as a result, especially that we have sent ecclesiastics who have taught them the Christian doctrine and faith by which they could be saved. Moreover, we have established justice in such a way that no one may aggravate another. We have maintained the peace so that there are no killings, or sacrifices, as was the custom in some parts. We have made it possible for the Indians to go

> safely by all roads and to peacefully carry on their civil pursuits. We have taught them good habits and the custom of wearing clothes and shoes. We have freed them from burdens and servitude; we have made known to them the use of bread, wine, oil, and many other foods, woollen cloth, silk, linen, horses, cows, tools, arms, and many other things from Spain; we have instructed them in crafts by which they live excellently. All these advantages will those Indians enjoy who embrace our Holy Faith and render obedience to us.

Those who today judge the conquest solely from the material viewpoint--population trends and standards of living--and who dismiss as rhetoric the other Spanish justifications set forth in the 1573 law, may find themselves in the position of the _indigenistas_ so mordantly described by the Mexican painter José Clemente Orozco:

> In their opinion the conquest was not as it ought to have been. Instead of sending cruel, ambitious captains, Spain should have sent a numerous delegation of ethnologists, anthropologists, civil engineers, dental surgeons, veterinarians, doctors, rural school teachers, agronomists, Red Cross nurses, philosophers, philologists, biologists, art critics, muralists, and learned historians. . . .
>
> Upon arriving in Veracruz Spaniards in allegorical carts decorated with flowers would debark from the caravels, and in one of them Cortés and his captains, each carrying a little basket of Easter lilies, a great quantity of flowers, confetti and streamers for use along the road to Tlaxcala and the great Tenochtitlán; the conquistadores would then pay homage to the powerful Moctezuma, establish bacteriological, urological, X-ray and ultraviolet ray laboratories, a Department of Public Assistance, universities, kindergartens, libraries, and savings and loan associations. The Spaniards, instead of accepting the frequent gifts of Aztec and Toltec maidens, should have brought handsome girls from Andalucia and Galicia to be offered to Moctezuma and Cuauhtémoc. Alvarado, Ordaz, Sandoval and the other heroes of the conquest should have been assigned the task of guarding the cities in ruins so that nothing would be lost of the tremendous pre-Columbian art. The Spaniards should have learned the seven hundred eighty-two different languages then in use here; respected the indigenous religion and left Huitzilopochtli in his place; given free handouts of seeds, agricultural machinery and livestock; constructed houses and given them to the peasants; organized the _ejidos_ and cooperatives; built highways and bridges; taught new industries and sports, all in a nice way, gently and with affection.

Orozco omitted only one point. He did not include the idea, advanced by some writers, that the Indians would have been better off if Spain had never established her empire in America. Even Las Casas once declared that, if force had to be used to convert the Indians, it would have been better to leave them unChristianized.

These quotations illustrate some of the unsolved problems involved in attempts to understand the Black Legend. As students of history, do we not need to view the Spanish conquest in a somewhat different perspective from that of either Philip II or the present-day "pragmatic" writers? As France V. Scholes has written, in one of the soundest and most concise interpretations on the subject: "The attempt to combine the economic and the ecclesiastico-humanitarian motives of empire created problems of tremendous historical significance." Whether the attempt to convert the Indians to Christianity was "good" for the Indians or not, these efforts influenced Spanish action in America to a remarkable degree.

This attempt led to the struggle for justice which was, it seems to me, unique to Spain in the early modern period. (Here is an example of how hard it is to abandon one's own generalizations!) These struggles were vigorously fought, in Spain and in America, and by no means always resulted in benefits for the Indians. But the real effects of those struggles on New World society in many cases remain to be studied. For those who believe that the struggle for justice ended by the time Philip II began his rule, it may come as a surprise that one of the most bitter and prolonged battles to protect the Indians was fought in Potosí at the end of the eighteenth century, between the criollo Pedro Vicente Cañete who defended the mita vigorously and learnedly, and the peninsular Victorián de Villava who with passion and erudition attacked it mercilessly. This event has been studied, but many other subjects await historians. For example, the audiencia, which Clarence H. Haring judged to be "the most important and interesting institution in the government of the Spanish Indies," has received little attention. The few monographs published thus far do not fully utilize the copious archival material available, though detailed study of its labors in various parts of the empire and over a considerable span of time would perhaps be the best single method to determine whether or not royal laws were given merely "lip service." Ernst Schäfer, whose fundamental researches on the workings of the Council of the Indies required years of labor in the Archivo General de Indias, believed that the high quality of the audiencia judges was responsible for the effective administration of justice: "De los muchos centenares de letrados españoles en las Indias, al final, muy pocos fueron los que se mostraron indignos de su clase." Las Casas recognized the key role the audiencia played in protecting the Indians. In 1566, in the last year of his long life, he successfully argued against the abolition of the audiencia in Guatemala.

Some of the laws undoubtedly were not enforced or only partially enforced, for the King's justice was applied with varying success according to the period and the particular region concerned. One of the best ways to learn about such matters would be to examine the residencias of the audiencia judges. As the Peruvian historian Raúl Porras Barrenechea remarked, unless one studies these documents "no se puede escribir fundadamente la historia colonial." Such an investigation would above all make clear to what extent royal policy laid down in Spain was actually implemented in America, at times in the face of the powerful opposed interests of the Spanish colonists and church officials.

Even after archival investigations a variety of interpretations is bound to appear, depending upon which aspect the historian chooses to emphasize. Two significant recent contributions--the volumes by Pál Kelemen, and by Stanley and Barbara Stein--almost seem to treat different parts of the world and different ages, though both focus on the Latin American colonial period.

Latin America has become in recent years the patient on the psychiatrist's couch; we may expect, therefore, to see more interpretations appear as historians with one eye on the present or on the future contemplate the past. As Luiz Aguiar Costa Pinto observed: "What is under debate is the whole heritage of the archaic society--the economic, political, and intellectual heritage--its structures, its values, its prospects." As this debate proceeds, we shall be fortunate if we escape a grossly anachronistic "presentism" with everything in the past irrelevant and unforgivable if it does not measure up to our noblest ideals today or if it can in any way be connected with Western civilization, the only fomenter of war, imperialism, disease, cruelty, superstition, and hypocrisy. We may be entering a period similar to that following the early nineteenth-century revolutions when the Spanish colonial period was considered by many historians in the newly emancipated nations to have been wholly bad: "Consumada la Emancipación, padecimos por explicable enojo y con eco que resonó por decadas, un afán de borrar, casi diría de aniquilar, el ciclo histórico que a esas luchas había antecedido."

In the end, an overall interpretation of Spain's work in America usually leads to large, general questions. We may agree, at least I certainly do, with Juan Friede when he makes clear that the "reality in America," rather than the mere enunciation of laws and theories, is the stuff of history. But ultimately we return to the essential nature of colonial rule in America, and to a judgment on how Spain handled those problems created when she attempted to combine the "economic and ecclesiastico-humanitarian motives of empire."

These judgments lead to generalizations, and so long as they are not expressed in simplistic "Black Legend" or "White Legend" terms they can be helpful in understanding the complex history of the Spanish conquest. For example, it would be difficult to find a juster balance than that of Edward G. Bourne, whom Keen and others rightly praise:

> What, in fact, did Spain attempt in the New World and what did she accomplish? She undertook the magnificent if impossible task of lifting a whole race numbering millions into the sphere of European thought, life, and religion. . . . Even if the attempt was in some degree a failure, it was a failure after the fashion of failure of Alexander the Great to establish a permanent Asiatic Empire, a failure that has left an ineffaceable impress on succeeding ages. . . .
>
> Yet the conception was grand, and the effort to realize it called forth the best that was in the men who labored either consciously or unconsciously for its accomplishment. Like all great events in human history it has its dark sides, and unfortunately these dark sides, through the influence of national jealousy and religious prejudice, have commonly been thrust into the foreground by non-Spanish writers.
>
> The great permanent fact remains, however, after all qualifications, that during the colonial period the language, the religion, the culture, and the political institutions of Castile were transplanted over an area twenty times as great as that of the parent state. . . .
>
> The work of Spain in the New World, defective as it was and adulterated with selfish aims, offered an extraordinary field for the display of national and individual character. . . . The colonial legislation of Philip II's reign, whatever its defects, reveals a profound and humane interest in the civilization of his over-sea dominions. . . . The long arm of the king was stretched out to protect the weak and the helpless from oppression and error. It did not always do it, but the honor of the effort should not be withheld.

Many historians today will accept Bourne's conclusions as essentially sound, and some will also agree that our field needs more theoretical approaches--more imaginative speculations on Spanish American history. But would it not be well for us now to concentrate for a while on particular historical problems, such as the activities of the audiencias in their attempts to enforce the multitude of royal laws in the various regions of the Indies or the landholding arrangements in various parts of the empire? Has the moment not arrived for a temporary moratorium on questionable generalizations presented as historical fact?

CHAPTER 30.

THE CONGRESSES OF MEXICAN AND AMERICAN HISTORIANS IN RETROSPECT

The discussions which historians from Mexico and the United States have been conducting regularly since 1949 constitute an unusual and perhaps unique development. When the organizers of the Third Reunion held in 1969 in Oaxtepec discovered that I could not attend, they asked me for a statement to be included in the program. My reply was in the form of a historical recollection of the previous meetings and a suggestion for the future:

> When Dr. Silvio Zavala first began to discuss with me the desirability of bringing together historians from Mexico and the United States to consider matters of mutual interest, we had no fixed plan nor were there any previous binational meetings of this kind in the Americas to guide us. The project really developed as one part of Dr. Zavala's imaginative program for the establishment of the Commission on History of the Pan American Institute of Geography and History, through which he aimed to stimulate historical endeavours in many ways. In the years immediately following World War II there was growing in Mexico and the United States alike a concern with cultures and events far beyond their national boundaries. As we conferred with historians in both countries, we tended toward an ecumenical approach, with some emphasis on comparative treatment of common historical experiences. The specific topics agreed upon after extensive consultations reflected this approach, for the program of the First Congress of Historians from Mexico and the United States, which convened in Monterrey, Nuevo León, September 4-9, 1949, included sessions on "The Teaching of History," "The Preservation and Organization of Historical Sources Materials," "Economic Relations of Mexico and the United States," "The Frontier Provinces," "Literary History," "Comparative Historical Development of Land Systems in Mexico and the United States," and "Intellectual History."
>
> The participants, we felt, should also reflect a broad spectrum of historians. Thus we made a point of inviting historians from the United States who cultivated other fields than Latin American

---

Contemporary Mexico. Papers of the IV International Congress of Mexican History, J. W. Wilkie, M. C. Meyer, and E. Monzón de Wilkie, eds. (Berkeley: University of California Press, 1976), 13-22.

History, such as Merle Curti, Paul Gates, and Edward Kirkland. From both countries came many well-known specialists in Latin American history as well as younger historians who later made their mark. The French historian François Chevalier and such Latin American scholars as Jorge Basadre and Mariano Picón Salas together with the Spaniards Javier Malagón and José Miranda gave an international flavor to our deliberations.

One of the high points of the Monterrey Congress for me was the remarks of that universal man, Alfonso Reyes, who began his banquet talk on "Mi Idea de la Historia" by referring to himself as "un convidado inoportuno" and then went on to present a moving description of history as an ingenious combination of scientific research, acute interpretation, and artistic expression. Another address of unusual general significance was the statesman-like appeal of Luther H. Evans, Librarian of Congress, for international cooperation in the preservation, organization, and microfilming of historical documentation in the Americas and elsewhere.

The Second Congress which took place in Austin at the University of Texas in 1958 was even more universal in scope and participants. The program focussed on the frontier, partly because of the presence of that individualist Texan Walter Prescott Webb, but there was also an ecumenical spirit present, perhaps because the Secretary General of this Congress was the medievalist Archibald R. Lewis. Thus besides such veteranos who had been at Monterrey as Arturo Arnáiz y Freg, Carlos Bosch García, Edmundo O'Gorman, Carlos Pérez Maldonado, Antonio Pompa y Pompa, France V. Scholes, and Arthur P. Whitaker there appeared several medievalists--Charles Julian Bishko, Robert S. López, Claudio Sánchez Albornoz, and Philippe Wolff--who tackled "The Medieval Iberian Frontier." The session on "The Frontier and Ranching in the United States and Mexico" provided an opportunity for comparative treatment, and was held appropriately enough on Professor Webb's ranch "Friday Mountain" near Austin.

The session devoted to "The Great Frontier Concept" revolved around Webb's thesis and provoked wide-ranging evaluations by Geoffrey Barraclough (England), Sir Keith Hancock (Australia), Arthur R. M. Lower (Canada), and José Honório Rodrigues (Brazil). The last session of the Second Congress brought together a number of unusual papers on a permanent theme: "The Historian's Task from Mexican and United States Viewpoints."

Now we are on the eve of the Third Congress, whose principal spirit is Lic. Daniel Cosío Villegas, one of the Mexican authorities upon whom Dr. Zavala and I leaned while the First Congress was in the process of becoming. I well remember a discussion in my temporary home in San Angel in early 1949 when Don Daniel, with his characteristic candor, expressed a certain skepticism concerning international conclaves. At the closing session of the Monterrey Congress he freely admitted he had been wrong, and surprised us all by speaking in an optimistic vein. The Congress had yielded beneficial fruits, he stated; he had been impressed in general by the quality of the participants and their papers. His faith had been renewed "en la increíble vitalidad de México." He had been particularly pleased to find at Monterrey North American historians whose speciality was not Latin American history. But he did have some recommendations for future congresses, and proceeded to give some useful suggestions.

Now in the same spirit of warm appreciation for all those who have worked so hard to bring together historians of Mexico and the United States during the last twenty years, may I venture to present another recommendation. Our Congress has almost come of age. Has not the time come for a modest continuing organization to carry on the necessary consultations between congresses? Thus far the life of the congresses has been uncertain, somewhat precarious, as we have no more visible evidence of support than the fakir in India who throws a rope up in the sky and then proceeds to climb up. We should always try to preserve sufficient spontaneity and flexibility to make certain that the successive meetings reflect the developing concerns of the historians, but would it not be a step forward to have the Third Congress appoint a small committee to be responsible for deciding when and where the Fourth Congress should meet, and to make such other decisions as may be necessary between meetings?

Many aspects of our world have radically changed since those pioneer congresistas first met in Monterrey, but at least one constant remains--the need felt by historians on both sides of the Río Bravo to discuss subjects of mutual concern. Therefore the Third Congress of Historians of Mexico and the United States at Oaxtepec will surely perform a useful and an imaginative function, and this veterano warmly salutes its organizers and participants. Hail!

When the Fourth Meeting was being organized, the program committee invited me to give in Santa Monica a luncheon talk which explains the following retrospective view which also contains some suggestions for the future.

The Congresses of Mexican and American Historians in Retrospect

Slightly over half a century ago, during my initiation ceremony as a university freshman into a social fraternity, there occurred this phrase which has stuck in my head ever since: Watchman, tell us of the night! Perhaps these words remained fresh in my memory, when many of the events and impressions of those far-off years have faded away, because I must have sung them many times as a boy in the church which my parents took me to in the small towns in which I grew up. For just recently I found in The Methodist Hymnal the song from which this magic phrase comes:

> Watchman, tell us of the night
> What its signs of promise are.
> Traveller, o'er yon mountain height
> See that glory--beaming star.
> Watchman, doth its beauteous ray
> Aught of joy or hope foretell?

Exactly what meaning my fraternity brothers intended by the use of this phrase in the initiation ritual I was not sure then, or now, but its sonorous not to say portentous words seemed to provide an opportunity to examine one's past with an eye to future developments. Let us at any rate take it in this sense, and have a look at this unique and exhilarating institution which has brought together now for the fourth time historians and others concerned with Mexico. Has anything like it ever been seen on land or sea or in the air?

So far as I know, the scholars of no other two nations in the Americas have organized such gatherings. Brazil in 1922 and Argentina in 1936 sponsored large all-American meetings made possible because they were commemorative occasions; but these were handsomely supported by their respective governments as official, one-time affairs and thus may be considered as comets which flashed across the skies once and then disappeared forever. Certainly they represented no continuity of effort to understand the history of America or of any part of the New World continent. Nor has the Pan American Institute of History and Geography, which approves and recommends the organization of bi-national meetings, had much influence toward this desirable end. It would, in fact, be extremely difficult to get nations together on this basis because of historical or boundary problems. For example, historians in Ecuador and Peru, Peru and Chile, Argentina and Brazil, to name only a few, would encounter much resistance to the idea. Let us hope that this resistance will be overcome in the future, for I maintain the conviction that historians in countries which have had friction and misunderstandings particularly need to have such meetings. My experience with Mexican and U. S. historical sessions encouraged me to contemplate a reunion of Cuban and U. S. historians. On my last visit to Havana, in 1958, I found Cuban historians of widely differing political views eager for a meeting. Alas, events overtook us before the necessary arrangements could be made.

The American Historical Association has convened twice in Toronto, and a generation ago the Carnegie Endowment for International Peace funded a number of conferences and investigations by Canadian and U. S. scholars. Although the Carnegie Endowment published a small shelf of useful monographs produced by this collaboration, no ongoing discussions were stimulated or made possible. Neither sessions of the American Historical Association in Canada nor the Carnegie project deposited any sediment in which the tender plant of international discussion could grow.

Has any effort similar to the meetings of Mexican and North American historians been carried on outside the Americas? Probably the Scandinavian nations have done something, and an informal conference of Anglo-American historians has been held in London for some years, but one wonders whether any two nations with the kind of historical relations experienced by Mexico and the U. S. have developed such fairly regular meetings, at least during the uneasy and tumultuous years since the end of World War II. Decisions on the place and nature of each session have been made on a joint basis, the proceedings of each meeting have been published and thus made available to those not fortunate enough to have attended the sessions, and a healthy combination of young and old, men and women, from both Mexico and the U. S. have attended in increasing numbers as have our colleagues from other countries. All this has come to pass without the existence of a Constitution, By-Laws, officers, dues, or any other apparatus of organized professional groups with which we are familiar. Nor do we pass resolutions deploring this or that, or hasten to set up committees to investigate the horrors which are thought to exist here and there, and thus far what James Lockhart has described as the "moral outrage of the developmentalists" has not gripped us.

Without our being united by an emotional commitment to immediate action or by a deep desire for change, these four meetings have been possible simply because the participants have been interested in the programs devised for discussion. To quote Lockhart again, they have been motivated by the same force which moved the social historians he was talking about: "a positive fascination with their subject." Indeed, we seem to be witnessing a kind of folk "happening", which we ordinarily associate with the gatherings of rock music enthusiasts at such famous places as Woodstock and Watkins Glen. Mexicanists wherever they may live increasingly are attracted to our meetings and like lemmings swarm over land and through water to be present when our reunions are held. So noteworthy have these movements been that it is likely that future historians of mass migrations will consider these meetings as among the most interesting and colorful in the story of international conferences of our times.

What has been the basis for this success? For a resounding success the reunions have been; let us not forget this fundamental fact. Each one of the sessions since the pioneer one in Monterrey in 1949 has been a mini-miracle. Some of the success has been undoubtedly due to the places selected for the sessions. How could a conference fail in Monterrey, Austin, Oaxtepec, or Santa Monica?

Even more important has been the special competence displayed by the principal organizer of each of the four sessions. As one who was close to Silvio Zavala in the establishment of the first conference I can testify to the impressive administrative talents of this scholar who also contributed notably to the institutional and legal history of Spain in America. For the Austin meeting in 1958 we all benefited from the wide-ranging intellectual interests of a medievalist, Archibald R. Lewis, whose spirit was ecumenical enough to permit a deep concern with Latin America.

Those of you who were privileged to be at Oaxtepec in 1969 need no words of mine to emphasize the influence there of Daniel Cosío

Villegas. One cannot attempt to confine the manifold and remarkable activities of Don Daniel by referring to him simply as a "historian", though I am tempted to do so for the distinction it may give to the rest of us who cultivate this field. Our present session of course could not have been brought off without the unusual gifts of that quantitatively-oriented historian James W. Wilkie, who has been fortunate enough to double his own strength by the help of his wife Edna Monzón de Wilkie. Many other competent and devoted scholars have powerfully helped to make these four mini-miracles.

Attractive location and inspired direction by the unusually gifted academic entrepreneurs who organized the four conferences were thus of basic importance in assuring the continuity of the dialogue on the history of Mexico. But there were other perhaps not so obvious but certainly as significant forces: the variety of the topics discussed, and the independent spirit with which they were treated. Each conference has had a somewhat different focus and the result has been a fresh and healthy variety of approaches to the main topic--Mexico--whose varied culture of course has been responsible for making possible such an orientation to our meetings.

One may wonder why more attention has not been given to the study of women's role in Mexico, the history of medicine and public health, or the history of films, but of course no meeting or even series of meetings can cover all possible topics. A special effort needs to be made, though, to diminish the usual emphasis on the political approach. And certainly an exclusively social sciences orientation is not satisfactory.

One favorable circumstance of all our sessions thus far has been the fact that there has been no desire to soften or avoid debate on critical issues. As Rafael García Granados stated in Monterrey, we must not teach a spineless history in a misguided attempt to preserve thereby international harmony. And he illustrated this remark in this way: "En un Congreso Internacional del que no quisiera acordarme, diplomáticos disfrazados de historiadores comenzaron sus peroraciones sosteniendo la conveniencia de la dulcificación de la Historia, para terminar disputando sobre los agravios mutuos recibidos por sus países." There has usually prevailed in our discussions a certain civilized discourse, which I believe was set for all of us by the presence and words of that great Mexican humanist Alfonso Reyes at the first meeting in Monterrey. For Don Alfonso honest and informal discussion was the objective, and such disagreements as have occurred in our sessions usually result from our different perspectives on matters of substance. I well remember the lively meetings in Austin when Walter Prescott Webb, the grand old man of Texas history and of frontier theory, discovered that some of the other distinguished participants there simply did not support his thesis. For Webb such discussions with his peers who "marched to a different drum" merely enhanced the pleasure that this salty and independent Texan derived from the reunion.

Nor has this spirit of independence been limited to conferences. Readers of Historia Mexicana and The Hispanic American Historical Review will be able to testify that historians of Mexico and the U. S. feel free to speak frankly to each other in between sessions of our conferences. And there are some who may suspect that individuals such as Edmundo O'Gorman and myself have made a special effort to exhibit this spirit of independent historical interpretation over the years in our different approaches to the life and thought of Bartolomé de Las Casas, whose 500th birthday will be commemorated in 1974.

But enough of the past! It is time to attempt to answer the question posed by that phrase: Watchman, tell us of the night, What its signs of promise are?

I have been stimulated in this direction by noticing that the last session on our program at Santa Monica will be focussed on "Present and Future Projects" and on "Analysis of and Lacunae in the Congress." With a warm appreciation of the extraordinary efforts of many institutions, of scholars from Mexico, the U. S., and other countries in making possible the four sessions of our unique conferences, let me set down my tentative thoughts on possible subjects for future consideration. These proposals I have formulated myself. No committee has been at work to guide my hand, and the suggestions are set forth in the knowledge that they will be examined by others in an independent spirit. I have been led to examine this question with a special interest because as Vice-President of the American Historical Association I have come to see that the international affairs of our members, now more than 14,000 strong, need much more attention than they have received. It is true that the Council of the AHA unanimously voted in December, 1948, to serve as one of the sponsors of the Monterrey Congress, which was the first time I believe, and perhaps the last, that the AHA took a direct interest in an international meeting of this kind. The first Soviet-American historians' colloquium took place in Moscow in October, 1972, under the sponsorship of the AHA, but this was a small and modest effort in which only a handful of scholars participated. There is much more that should and could be done by the American Historical Association in this international field. If elected President in December, one of my principal preoccupations in 1974 will be to improve the international relations of the AHA. The experiences that Mexican and North American historians have had during the last quarter of a century is a unique experience, which will be a valuable record to keep in mind as the AHA attempts to improve its relations with historians in other countries. The International Congress of Historical Sciences will bring together several thousand historians in San Francisco August 22-29, 1975, for the first such meeting in the Western Hemisphere, but there are other ways, too, to bring about greater understanding among historians and we must explore all possible avenues.

Now let us turn to a few specific points on the future of our own conferences, based on the meetings held since 1949 in Monterrey. First of all I am beginning to believe that we may soon experience collectively what the psychologists call "an identity crisis." We started out as meetings of "Historians from Mexico and the United States" and after three sessions under this banner we are now an "International Congress on Mexican Studies." This new, large, canopy is a perfectly logical one to construct, and may be the best one under which to operate. It has sometimes seemed to me that the only sure way to bring scholars together in a really useful professional spirit will be to organize meetings on various kinds of studies on an international basis. If this pattern prevails, there might then be an International Congress on Mexican Studies in Europe, from time to time, organized perhaps in cooperation with the vigorous and growing group of Mexicanists in Europe.

But if you transform the meetings from sessions of "Historians from Mexico and the United States" to an "International Congress of Mexicanists", note that you have thus eliminated in any formal way at least participation by specialists on North America, to say nothing of historians of the United States. Now I am not unmindful of the faults of historians; in fact at Monterrey in 1949 I was allowed to give a luncheon talk on "The Professional Diseases of Historians", which fortunately for the development of friendly relations with my colleagues was not printed in the Proceedings. But the strongest support for Mexican studies in the United States will probably always be provided by the Conference on Latin American History of the American Historical Association, and it is to this body of some 1,000 members which we must look for continued interest. May I observe, in what I hope will be looked upon as an objective statement by non-historians, that historians in both Mexico and the U. S. interpret history in a flexible way so that representatives of other disciplines are usually present at conferences organized by historians. Moreover, Woodrow Borah, Charles Gibson, and the late José Miranda, for example, have been as likely to be found at anthropological meetings as at conferences of historians.

Note, too, that we have shifted from reunions of historians to meetings on "The New World Looks at its History", the subject at Austin in 1958, on "Investigaciones Contemporáneas Sobre Historia de México" at Oaxtepec in 1969, and now to "Contemporary Mexico." There has been a steady narrowing of focus, so far as the subject is concerned, though there has been a notable and welcome development in participation by non-Mexicans and non-North Americans. Except for participation from Latin America outside of Mexico, for this is almost non-existent. It is exceedingly rare to find a Brazilian, an Argentine, or a Chilean, for example, making a serious investigation of any Mexican phenomenon--even of the Mexican Revolution.

Now let me pose the most sticky question of all. Must our deliberations always be focussed on Mexico, whether Mexican History or Mexican Studies? Why not a session on United States History, or Comparative History, or at least some theme which is not exclusively Mexican? Would not this kind of topic increase even further international participation, and might even attract scholars from other Latin American countries? One topic which would surely arouse much interest among historians everywhere is "Comparative Revolutions in the Americas." The U. S. is getting ready to commemorate the events of 1776; why could our next meeting not be devoted to this great topic with special emphasis on Cuba, Mexico, and the U. S? The American Historical Association has at work under the direction of Professor Richard Morris of Columbia University a Committee on the Commemoration of the American Revolution Centennial, and some joint enterprise could possibly be arranged if enough scholars are interested. Revolution would provide an excellent theme for historians in the Americas, as would Indians. As one who has spent a lot of time over the years with indigenistas, I have long wondered whether the time has not arrived to give more attention to Indians. They constitute much too significant a subject to be left entirely to the indigenistas! Any topic of course would be useful if it brought together scholars from Mexico, the U. S., and other countries to discuss matters of common concern.

Such an orientation would be very valuable for our historians at least, who all too often are concerned only with U. S. history, and also for our Mexicanists, who sometimes find their departmental colleagues so immersed especially in European or U. S. history that they have never met a Mexican historian and thus exhibit a certain provincialism. This ignorance on the part of too many members of the American Historical Association naturally impedes the development of Latin American and Mexican History in our universities. Now that Mexico City has such excellent conference facilities as to attract such groups as the American Association for the Advancement of Science, why should not the AHA meet sometime there? But would Mexican historians and Mexican historical groups be interested in discussing anything except Mexican history?

Needless to say, if we could ever move the American Historical Association to hold a meeting in Mexico there would inevitably be significant sessions included on Mexican history, but these alone would not provide for sufficient meetings between Mexican historians and U. S. historians not specifically concerned with Mexican history.

One of the obstacles to a fruitful meeting of the American Historical Association in Mexico is the scarcity of Mexican scholars who have studied U. S. history, or indeed any other field of history than their own, in a professional way. Perhaps the proposed AHA session in Mexico City would serve a double purpose in enlarging the vision of all those historians who think only in terms of the history of their own country. I am convinced that the practice and interpretation of U. S. history would be measurably improved if scholars outside the U. S. concerned themselves with our history and thus brought new views and possibly hitherto unused documentation.

And I note that it has also been observed in Japan that Latin Americans are very absorbed in their own history. One Latin Americanist at Sophia University in Tokyo has pointedly inquired, in the last issue of the Latin American Research Review, after describing Latin American Studies in Japan:

> This report has analyzed the state of studies on Latin America in the country which is one of the greatest economic powers of the world and which, according to the prediction of Herman Kahn, will be the country of the twenty-first century. And now let me ask, what does Latin America know about Japan? How many research centers and university departments are there which teach that Japan is no longer the land of cherry blossoms, because the fouled air of the great cities kills them, nor the land of Mount Fuji, because the smoke of the blast furnaces wipes its stylized figure from the landscape, nor the home of the geishas, because they prefer the easier road of the nightclubs? Where are the translations into Spanish of Nobel prizewinner Kawabata? If Latin Americans want the Japanese to understand the reality of Latin America, Latin Americans must also try to understand the reality of Japan.

I have put forward this revolutionary idea of an AHA annual meeting in Mexico City with the full realization that it may find favor neither in Mexico or the U. S. I know it will be difficult to convince the Council of the AHA, which decides such matters so far as our historians are concerned, that a Mexico City meeting would be practicable and would be approved by our membership. But such a meeting, if properly prepared, could be a milestone in the history of relations between Mexican historians and North American historians, whose first important event was the 1949 session in Monterrey.

No matter how the problem of this "identity crisis" is revolved, there is one topic to which all future meetings might well give more attention: I refer to Teaching. How little attention has been paid to this subject in our conferences! I have been told that there was a flurry of excitement created in Oaxtepec during the discussion of Mexican textbooks, but this seems to have been caused by some special circumstances. It is now clear to everyone, I trust, that significant research has been produced on Mexico during the years since World War II by scholars in a number of countries, particularly on Mexican history broadly conceived. But I doubt that sufficient effort has been devoted to incorporating in the courses on Mexico--whether given in Mexico or elsewhere--the new data and new insights discovered by the researchers. One may also ask whether enough attention has been given to the teaching process itself. Have the textbooks and other teaching aids proved to be adequate for providing an honest and interesting account of Mexican history in the U. S. and of North American history in Mexico? A few years ago the American Historical Association sponsored a project for an examination of history textbooks in Great Britain and the United States with respect to each other's history. In August, 1973, there was held at the California Institute of Technology a ten-day conference of teachers from Great Britain and the United States, organized at the initiative of British officials. Plans call for a second conference in York, England, next year, and the hope is that similar means of communication can be maintained therefore. The British Historical Association publishes an excellent journal called Teaching History, and as many of you know there is now located in Long Beach another excellent journal The History Teacher which pays appropriate attention to problems of teaching Latin American history in the U. S. And I cannot forebear from mentioning that the Pacific Coast Council of Latin American Studies plans, under the leadership of its active President E. Bradford Burns, to devote much attention to teaching.

How much more are such activities as those now engaged in by British and North American teachers needed between history teachers in Mexico and the United States! And why not examine the history teachers, too? How much do they know of the language and culture of the foreign nation whose history they are teaching? Have we used films, music, and slides enough despite the existence of a few excellent films such as "Memorias de un Mexicano"? I have been encouraged to suggest more attention to teaching because of the efforts of the Latin Americanists in the U. S. in recent years and because of the activities of such Mexican scholars as Josefina Zoraida Vázquez.

What "identity" this conference decides to seek, and whether "Teaching" or some other compelling topic is added to our agenda, there will still remain the tricky question: Has all the expenditure of time, energy, and money required by our folk happenings, our four conferences, been worth the effort? John Franklin Jameson, long-time editor of the American Historical Review and one of the key figures in the development of the American Historical Association during the first third of this century, was convinced that the international relations of historians were important, even essential, for the future peace of the world. Even while the First World War raged, he was thinking of post-war historical relations, but he raised some pertinent questions in a letter to Alexander S. Lappo-Danilevski on August 3, 1917:

> Interesting as these international congresses of historians have been, and valuable as it has been to bring such men into mutual acquaintance, it may well be felt that these congresses might have done more to promote the progress of historical science than merely to provide an opportunity for the reading of various papers and for social intercourse. Might they not, one may ask, have brought about some concrete steps of progress, some definite achievements of an international character? . . . It is even possible that the sense of having a common work to do, international enterprises under way, might do something more to bring the historians of warring countries once more into friendly relations, than if there were prospects of nothing else than the reading of isolated papers.

Unfortunately the International Congress of Historical Sciences did not develop any of the various specific tasks proposed by Jameson, except for a bibliography which has had only a limited usefulness. But he had put his finger on an important point, which needs some consideration during the session next Sunday morning on "Reflections on Contemporary Mexico."

Even if perfect agreement were reached on the proposition that the conferences should engage in some common tasks, what should these projects be? What can be done most effectively on an international basis? Many specific proposals can doubtless be found, and everyone will have his favorites. Two that appeal to me are:

I. The Organization of Historical Source Materials and Questions of Access to Them.

A number of projects have been completed on microfilming and others are under way. Is anything else needed now? Do scholars in Mexico or the U. S. have adequate access to the sources they need for the study of contemporary Mexico, or for any other period?

II. The Collection and Organization of Photographs, Slides, and Films for Teaching and Research on Mexico.

My impression is that these materials are widely scattered in Mexico, the U. S., and elsewhere. What can and should be done to make them better known and more available for teaching and research? It may well be that our conferences should not attempt to launch large projects involving substantial sums of money which would undoubtedly be hard to find. But could not the conference organize informal working parties on a shoe-string basis to explore in the years between our sessions on what needs to be done and then try to encourage some institution to do the job? My own feeling is that we might well act as a catalyst, but probably would encounter problems in doing much more. Discussion of other possibilities by other participants in this conference will surely reveal some unsuspected aspects of the subject.

One final suggestion. Although I recognize that the social sciences approach and especially the quantitative methods now very popular have made significant contributions, I hope that we do not forget that Mexico has produced and long been noted for her art, literature, music, and philosophy. Have these humanistic contributions been given sufficient emphasis in any of our four sessions? I know that strenuous attempts have been made to do so, but could not even more be accomplished? Why could the next reunion not follow the lead of the International Congress of Anthropological and Ethnological Sciences, which commissioned an opera by Gian Carlo Menotti for its 1974 meeting in Chicago? The resulting work, Tamu-Tamu, was given its world premiere. performance in Chicago September 5. Why shouldn't the organizing committee for our next meeting show some similar pizzazz, or perhaps I mean panache, by commissioning a symphony, ballet, film, opera, or some other artistic creation on perhaps some theme such as mestizaje in the Americas?

To return to my beginning remark: Watchman, tell us of the night. I hope that all of you will agree with me that a bright future for our conferences does indubitably exist, provided we maintain the variety and spirit of independence that have characterized the first four meetings, and provided the leadership that made possible those four mini-miracles continues to be available. Let me close these remarks, which some may view as too optimistic or too revolutionary, on a sober note.

Can we continue to survive unless there is somewhat more continuity in our meetings? Nine years elapsed between Monterrey and Austin, and eleven years between Austin and Oaxtepec, but only four years between Oaxtepec and Santa Monica. Would it not be better to aim at meeting every five or six years so that the Happenings will be held at a fairly regular rate? This is but a detail, however, and this watchman does, to quote the religious hymn, definitely perceive both hope and joy in contemplating the future of the beaming star which has thus far guided our sessions.

CHAPTER 31.

THE *PROBANZAS DE SERVICIOS* AS HISTORICAL SOURCES: JOHN FRANKLIN JAMESON'S VIEWS ON THE HISTORY OF SPAIN IN AMERICA

Some forty-five years ago, while searching in the Archivo General de Indias in Sevilla for manuscripts on Bartolomé de Las Casas, I came upon a sketch of an elaborate coat of arms presented to Philip II by an Indian in Quito. It was included in a document drawn up by Cacique Sancho de Velasco to describe his services to the crown, services which he considered so important that they should be rewarded by various honors including a coat of arms. This "Probanza de Méritos y Servicios" was the first one I had ever seen, and the sketch was an attractive illustration of how Indians had become a part of the Spanish machinery of empire. So, like many another student in the archive, I made a note on the document for possible future use. The idea of writing something about these probanzas began to take shape slowly in my mind, but other topics absorbed most of my attention.

Then Stuart B. Schwartz produced a stimulating essay on "State and Society in Colonial Spanish America: An Opportunity for Prosopography"* which renewed my interest in probanzas. Shortly thereafter an invitation arrived to participate in a volume being planned to honor an old and valued friend, Irving A. Leonard, and at long last I produced the following article.

*In New Approaches to Latin American History, edited by Richard Graham and Peter H. Smith (Austin, 1974), 3-35.

In Chang-Rodríguez, Raquel and Donald A. Yates (eds.). Homage to Irving A. Leonard: Essays on Hispanic Art, History and Literature. Published under the auspices of the Latin American Studies Center of Michigan State University. New York: Editorial Mensaje, 1977. Reprinted by permission.

The Probanzas de Servicios as Historical Sources: John Franklin Jameson's Views on the History of Spain in America

Jameson is usually remembered in historical circles today as the editor who first achieved and then maintained for many years the ecumenical distinction of the American Historical Review. Probably few Latin Americanists consider him a pioneer in their field. His letters, however, make it very clear that his view of American history was broad indeed. He included a volume on the Spanish documents of the Southwest in the series he edited on Original Narratives of Early American History, and was responsible for commissioning Herbert Eugene Bolton to prepare the Guide to Materials for the History of the United States in the Principal Archives of Mexico (1913) which retains its usefulness even today.

Jameson was also instrumental in launching The Hispanic American Historical Review. When its first issue appeared in February 1918, there was included a welcoming letter from President Woodrow Wilson who expressed the hope that the review should lead "to very important results both for scholarship and for the increase of cordial feelings throughout the Americas", for Jameson had used his influence to see that a busy president took time out to compose this message to a fledgeling historical review. It was this letter which may have led the Soviet writer I. R. Lavretskii to charge in 1959 that "Wilson called on the journal to influence American public opinion in a direction useful to ruling circles of the U.S."

Jameson also had ideas about history as is demonstrated by his slim but pathbreaking volume on The American Revolution Considered as a Social Movement (1926) and by his AHA presidential address on the place of religion in the history of the United States. His insights into the history of Spanish American history are less well known, but they seem very fresh today when more and more attention is being paid to the history of people. In 1925, long before C. H. Haring's classic volume on The Spanish Empire in America appeared, in a letter to the veteran researcher in Spanish archives, Irene A. Wright, Jameson declared: "We have now a pretty fair supply of studies of the Spanish system, of the institutions of Spain's colonial empire, and we have many studies of individual episodes and of the history of administration or events in particular countries or provinces. All these, and what has been printed about the financial history of the empire, help to explain the want of ultimate success to which you allude".

It was characteristic of the historical zeitgeist of the 1920's in the United States for our historians in the days of Calvin Coolidge to take for granted that Spain had failed as an imperial power. The only question was to explain why. This appears to be a permanent strain in the attitude of some of our countrymen, whether righteous Republicans at the time of the Spanish-American War or the "progressive" left-leaning historians of today.

Jameson also raised other questions. He remembered the complacency of the earlier New England historians when they studied the character of the people who established the English colonies. As William Stoughton remarked in his 1668 election sermon: "God sifted a whole Nation that He might send Choice Grain over into this wilderness". Jameson pointed out that as late as 1925 we knew a great deal less about the "character of the mass of human beings" that came to Spanish

America than we knew their English counterparts. Why had so little attention been given to this movement? Jameson also held a firm opinion on this:

> I doubt if the Spanish American mind is sufficiently self-critical to grapple with it, and Native Sons of the Golden West and other North American students do not stay long enough in Spain to permit of the examination of such a theme, for it cannot be found in any small number of legajos nor interpreted by one who does not know well the different parts of Spain. As I see it, one would have to salt down the little bits of information as one came upon them, during a considerable period of time, before he would be able to answer such questions as, How large a part of those Spaniards who settled in Colombia, in Venezuela, in the regions of La Plata came from Asturias or from Galicia or from Andalusia, how large a part of them were gentlemen, and what did that mean? What was the actual character and mental furnishings of this or that element in the great migration?

No one attempted to answer these fundamental questions in Jameson's day; indeed, we have just begun to study them in recent years. There was one lonely scholar, Alice B. Gould of Massachusetts who, at the time Jameson was writing to Miss Wright, was "salting down little bits of information" as she searched for data in Spanish archives on the sailors who went with Columbus. The actual production of this remarkable blue-stocking was not large, and the mass of other material she accumulated like a pack-rat over the years and left unpublished at her death will probably never see the light of day.

Who can doubt that Jameson was on solid ground when he stated over half a century ago:

> Quite apart from the question whether anything can be discovered in this way as to the reasons for Spanish colonial success or the opposite, one of the greatest, and on the whole the most peculiar, of the fundamental facts of American history is that it springs from and represents the most extensive human migration in the world's history, and it would be well that we should know more of the nature of that migration. I wish, in short, that I knew as much about the conquistadores and those who came with them as I do about the Pilgrim Fathers, or the other choice grain, and some not so choice, that came to New England in the seventeenth century.

The records available for studying the "peculiar" history of those who emigrated to Spanish America from Europe in the colonial centuries are copious, scattered, and largely unused. They may be divided into these general categories:

1. Licenses to emigrate.

A few years before Jameson made his pronouncement on the need to learn more about the emigrants, Luis Rubio y Moreno published a Catálogo metodológico of passengers who received licenses to go to America in the sixteenth century, and ever since historians have been mining the rich collection of manuscripts on this subject in the Contratación section of the Archivo General de Indias in Sevilla. A generation after Jameson's statement, Cristóbal Bermúdez Plata began to publish some of the license documents, a task that Peter Boyd-Bowman has carried forward in recent years. A substantial beginning has been made, but much remains to be done. Even when all these records are known and organized, their usefulness is distinctly limited, as Juan Friede has pointed out.

2. Notarial records.

Wherever the emigrants went to in Spanish America they began to buy and sell, marry, engage in litigation on all manner of subjects, and in other ways to leave a rich deposit of information about their artistic, economic, and social activities in the manuscript volumes of notaries in the New World. These voluminous and widely scattered documents have only recently begun to be studied, notably in the publications of James Lockhart. The wills left by emigrants have scarcely been noticed by historians, except in isolated instances. Certainly they have been but rarely analyzed to determine some of the principal problems in the history of the emigrants: "Their regional origin, their characteristics, the social classes to which they belonged, the customs and traditions they possessed, and the dialects, beliefs, and superstitions they introduced into America".

If the licenses for emigrants tell us something about the people who went to Spanish America, the notarial records reveal more of the social fabric and commercial life they created in the New World, for these documents contain an incredible amount of particularized data in title deeds, powers of attorney, rental agreements, mortgages, quitclaims, legacies, wills, dowry settlements, contracts for personal and professional services, business agreements, apprenticeships, guardianships, the collection or settlement of debts, mining claims, and the sale of real estate, cattle, horses, and slaves. And the lists of property of those who died reveal what they had acquired overseas.

3. Church records.

When ecclesiastical archives in Spanish America are fully open to historians, and when they are organized for use, they will surely provide a great quantity of information. Meanwhile the many thousand rolls of microfilm taken by the Mormon Church in Mexico of parish records, Inquisition documents, and notarial manuscripts offer excellent opportunities for significant investigation. The Inquisition records alone will yield much juicy detail, particularly of the kind that today would be included in The National Enquirer, on the seamy side of colonial life. The anthropologist Noemi Quezada Ramírez has even mined these documents to produce a monograph on Amor y Magia Amorosa entre los Aztecas (1975).

4. Private Correspondence and Memoirs.

Our poverty in this category of sources is astonishing and depressing. Letters written by the people of Spanish America are just beginning to be used by historians, and one must search long to find any diaries, memoirs, or family papers that have done so much to enlighten us on the actions, feelings, and thoughts of colonists in English America. Most Spaniards in America from the viceroy downward engaged in business but how few are the letters and reports of these merchants. Even when such basic source materials were produced, they have rarely been published. One exception is the memoirs of the knowledgeable Cádiz merchant Raimundo de Lantery, but only one part of them has survived and it remains a rare item privately printed in Spain. Hence it is virtually unknown; I do not recall seeing a citation to it by our scholars today. Much documentation of this kind must be lurking in many places. Literature may help out here, for such a volume as

Tales of Potosi (1975) can tell the percipient reader much about the everyday life and values in this Peruvian mining community. But we do not yet have a volume on Spanish America comparable to the work by Agustín G. de Amezúa y Mayo on La vida privada española en el protocolo notarial. Selección de documentos de los siglos XVI, XVII y XVIII del Archivo Notarial de Madrid (1950).

5. "Merits and Services".

Most students who work in Spanish or Spanish American archives run across many documents usually entitled "Probanzas de méritos y servicios" which were drawn up by thousands of Spaniards in America throughout the colonial period. They were intended to justify requests for some kind of preferment, pension, or assistance from the crown. Some individual probanzas have been cited in monographs, but few have been published in the original Spanish, and only a handful have been translated into English. Certain legajos, especially in the Indiferente and Patronato sections of the Archivo General de Indias, are filled with these documents and they are also to be found in almost every archive and manuscript collection with a serious interest in Spanish American history. One of the best ways to bring this material to the general attention of students would be to publish a carefully selected volume of probanzas, comparable to the volume of private letters that has just appeared.

All of the potential sources mentioned above deserve fuller treatment than can be given in this brief paper. Attention will be limited, therefore, to the "Merits and Service" documents because of their special significance. Let us recognize, too, that the elite such as the conquistadores, the encomenderos, the great churchmen, and royal officials require less attention because they were more likely to make their voices heard. Viceroys, judges, corregidores, and rich Potosí miners, for example, often presented probanzas which were formidable documents, at times printed in elegant fashion, testifying to their splendid accomplishments for the crown. Widows of important officials filed probanzas, hoping for support.

The statements prepared by the lesser figures drawn to America will best satisfy Jameson's desire for more information on "the character of the mass of human beings". Their probanzas will provide much raw data for the historian who patiently reads the thousands of pages available. He will learn much about the history of the times as well as the claims of the individuals. The conquistadores naturally devoted much attention to their military exploits, including references to their previous services in the King's armies in Flanders, Italy, and Spain. The hazards of war in America are shown in stark and revealing detail. Juan Velázquez de Núñez, kinsman of the ill-fated first viceroy of Peru, was captured by the rebel Gonzalo Pizarro and condemned to death. Through the influence of the Bishop of Lima his punishment was softened; they cut off one of his hands, and imprisoned him in a convent. It may well be that the general information imbedded in the probanzas will prove to be their principal historical value.

These probanzas not only concern the derring-do of soldiers. Relations with the Indians are treated, such as the famous pacification of the Cacique Enriquillo by Bartolomé de Las Casas on Hispaniola in the early days of the conquest. One Spaniard who applied for assistance referred in his extensive probanza to his special contribution as a salad chef for Francisco Pizarro, for the famous conquistador loved salads and kept an expert in preparing them always at his side. General Lope de Mendoza boasted of his contributions in building bridges over perilous rivers in Peru, which saved many lives. He also enforced the laws, as corregidor in Quito improved the streets, built fountains to embellish the city, cared for the hospitals, and organized an expedition of 200 soldiers to go to Chile when trouble erupted there. Ecclesiastics less often drew up probanzas but there are some examples, such as those relating to Friars Alonso de la Veracruz, Pedro de Angulo, and Diego de Porres and many more will surely be found.

Jameson did not include Indians, Negroes, or mestizos in his history of the people who made up Spanish America as he was thinking of the "emigrants" in a restricted sense. Historians today will naturally wish to explore the sources for information on these other groups as well. The church records will provide much data, and some of the Indian caciques got into the probanza act as well. The Tlaxcala archive contains many statements on the services rendered by the Tlaxcaltecas in the Spanish conquest of Mexico. Cacique Principal Francisco Aymoro of Charcas not only presented his biography but also described his father's services. Ralph Roys and France V. Scholes discovered notable documents on the Xiu family in Yucatán, which concentrated on their claim to nobility status. Cacique Sancho de Velasco in Quito in 1569 even manifested such a high opinion of his worth that he demanded a coat of arms whose exact description he set forth in some detail. This cacique was wealthy and powerful enough to be able to have a representative at the court to press his claim. His petition, and an impressive sketch of the coat-of-arms he devised are to be found today in Sevilla. In most cases these caciques mentioned their services in governing their own people. If enough of these probanzas are found, we will be able to determine how much credence we should give to Immanuel Wallerstein's recent undocumented generalization: "Spain did not have the administrative energy to create a large bureaucracy in the Americas. Therefore they used the old expedient of empires, the cooptation of local chieftains into the political system as intermediary agents of the Crown and the Spanish settlers".

For obvious reasons Negroes presented fewer probanzas, but there is at least one. Francisco Vioho, "Moreno libre, nacido en Guinea, y naturalizado en la Ciudad de los Reyes del Perú" described his brave fighting in Chile and requested that he be appointed Captain in one of the three Negro regiments in Los Reyes. From these few and somewhat spotty indications, it is clear that many sources exist to answer Jameson's questions, especially if we broaden the enquiry to include all the people who made up the population.

For the historian interested in biography in this field today, the best way to begin will be to read Stuart B. Schwartz's excellent article. One of the first preliminary steps to be taken thereafter is the location and cataloging of the thousands of existing probanzas. As no bibliographical hero of the quality of José Toribio Medina, supported by a large foundation, is on the horizon, there will be the need for a group, or several groups, of dedicated researchers who will need plenty of what Schwartz terms _sitzfleish_. One limiting factor is the relatively weak development of local and regional historical and genealogical societies in Spanish America, of the kind that have made such valuable contributions in New England to the history of the people of English America.

The town histories and genealogical works which Jameson probably knew about since his boyhood in Amherst, Massachusetts, were the product of local scholars often animated by a powerful genealogical fervor which they inherited from their English ancestors. Such enthusiasm appears to be unevenly distributed in the world; there seems to be no tradition in Spanish America comparable, for example, to the "Korean genealogical tradition in recent centuries that perhaps finds no peer anywhere on earth for zeal and accuracy".

Is it not clear from the sketch given here that, except for the Mormon microfilming, relatively little has been done to make known or to use the extraordinary documentary resources awaiting historians who wish to carry out the studies called for by Jameson? Even when genealogists have worked in these sources, their contributions are not always widely enough known to historians, as apparently is the case in United States history as well. Another sobering thought is that no volume on Spanish background has yet been written comparable to Wallace Notestein's _The English People on the Eve of Colonization_ (1954).

Once the sources are known, we will still have to be on guard to ensure that this monstrous documentation yields truth rather than merely loaded representation by interested parties. Spanish authorities in the sixteenth century were aware well of the potential for self-glorification by those who prepared probanzas. However, the assessment of the true value of documents is one of the standard tasks of any historian. Methodological problems will also be encountered, and here too Schwartz shows the way.

In conclusion, let me hazard the opinion that we need more studies of both the elites and the masses. Today we hear much about writing history from the bottom up, surely a laudable but not wholly new enterprise. But when dealing with a society as hierarchical as Spanish America was in the colonial period, with privileges and even dress controlled by rank, historians will not be able to give a true picture of that society by neglecting the great and the powerful. If we are fully to understand the history of the Villa Imperial de Potosí, for example, we must include not only the story of the Indians sweating and dying in the bowels of the mine, but also the account of the formal investiture of José Sáez de Elorduy as a member of the Alcántara Order, which took place in all its ritual glory in the San Agustín church there. There is still much to be done in this area. How many flesh and blood biographies do we have of viceroys, archbishops, conquistadores, or encomenderos? Even though the analysis of the non-elites will surely yield unexpected and important results, the whole society functioning according to its own values is what we must seek to understand.

As we attempt to comprehend the reality of the life of the people of Spanish America centuries ago, we must never forget that we are dealing with an ancient culture in which the individual has always played a powerful and pervasive role. Thus we must have individual biographies, whether of the elite, or of the men of Cajamarca, but based upon the wealth of material available. I still remember the impact Irving A. Leonard's biography of Carlos Sigüenza y Góngora had on me many years ago, as well as his later chapter on the life and poetry of Sor Juana Inés de la Cruz.

To conclude this introductory essay on a large subject: sources, no matter how rich or how numerous, are of little use until they are discovered, organized, and analyzed. But for the kind of biographical recreations which have distinguished Leonard's contributions through the years, one must have, along with documents, literary skill, and imagination.

PART VII
GENERAL HISTORY

CHAPTER 32.

MATERIALS FOR RESEARCH ON TEXAS HISTORY IN EUROPEAN ARCHIVES AND LIBRARIES

One of the most active state organizations to foster the study of history has long been The Texas State Historical Association. Its membership was a healthy combination of academics and citizens concerned with the past of Texas, which enabled it to support a solid historical journal and to organize annual meetings.

In the years following my appointment to the University of Texas faculty in 1951 I became aware of how much had been done to make available the documentary sources for the history of the state, and I was also convinced that even more could and should be done. Thus when the Association invited me to participate in one of its annual sessions, I had a topic that only needed to be written up.

The Southwestern Historical Quarterly, LIX (1956), 335-343. Reprinted by permission.

Materials for Research on Texas History in European Archives and Libraries

How can students of the history of Texas be certain that the important materials for their research, now located in European archives and libraries, are made available for use in connection with the rich treasure of sources already gathered in Texas and in other parts of the United States? One possible solution may be simply stated. The University of Texas, through the Eugene C. Barker Texas History Center, in cooperation with the Texas State Historical Association and all other interested persons and institutions in Texas and elsewhere, might lead the way by establishing a Historical Manuscripts Commission to give continuous attention to the problem. Before suggesting the possible objectives and activities of such a commission, a brief survey of achievements to date in making research materials from Europe available in Texas may be helpful.

The story of the extensive and prolonged search by United States historians and institutions for manuscript material bearing on American history has been told by Roscoe R. Hill with a wealth of detail in his report entitled American Missions in European Archives. The first American scholar to exploit the resources of European archives was Jared Sparks (1789-1860), professor of history at Harvard University. George Bancroft, William H. Prescott, Francis Parkman, Buckingham Smith, Henry Charles Lea, John Gilmary Shea, and others used quantities of material from the archives of France, Great Britain, Italy, and Spain during the nineteenth century.

The task was so large that institutions began to work as well as individual scholars. States and state historical societies especially became interested in European manuscript materials which resulted in the acquisition of much information about the records in European archives as well as large collections of transcripts. As Dr. Hill points out:

> New York was the first state which actively undertook the securing of handwritten transcripts from European archives. Provision for the undertaking was made by an act of the State Legislature passed on May 2, 1839. By this act, the copies of documents "relating to or affecting the colonial or other history of New York" could be secured. On January 15, 1841, John Romyn Brodhead was appointed to carry out the mission. He was a graduate of Rutgers College and had served in the American Legation in Holland. His instructions, given by Governor William H. Seward, gave him much discretion in carrying on the work in Holland, England, and France. He spent three years in the task and received a yearly salary of $2,000 and expenses of travel. As a result of his investigations, he selected and copied thousands of documents in the principal archives of Holland, England, and France. These copies formed eighty volumes which were deposited in the New York State Library. Later they were published by the state.

Massachusetts, New Jersey, North Carolina, and Virginia successively carried on similar enterprises.

With the coming of the twentieth century more planning and more funds were devoted to projects for obtaining material on American history from European archives, particularly by the newly established Carnegie Institution of Washington. Dr. J. F. Jameson, who for the period of 1905-1928 ably directed its Department of Historical Research, described what he considered the proper functions of his department to be in these words:

> The normal processes of historical work would commonly be said to be four: The finding of the original materials, printed or unprinted; the putting of them into accessible and well-edited print, if they have not already that form; next the production of monographs; and, finally, the composition of general histories. Unless under circumstances quite exceptional, the last two processes are better left to the free action of individual scholars. Given the materials, they will produce monographs and histories in the future, as they have in the past, and of a better flavor than those which might be turned out by an organized institution. In the main, it must be the proper function of an organized and permanent institution, disposing of ampler resources than most individual historians can command, to carry on the primary, fundamental, and costly tasks of finding the materials or guiding men to them, and of printing such of them as are unprinted and most deserve print, selecting those which are likely to give the greatest possible aid and incitement to the production of good monographs in important fields.

In order to avoid duplication, the Carnegie Institution first investigated the nature and extent of manuscript material already available in the United States and led to the preparation by C. H. Van Tyne and Waldo G. Leland of their _Guide to the Archives of the Government of the United States in Washington_. An examination of previous research projects in European archives was also made, and in addition James A. Robertson compiled a list of the copies of material from Spanish archives then in United States repositories, together with a list of 1075 such documents that had been published. A third project resulted in David M. Matteson's _List of Manuscripts Concerning American History Preserved in European Libraries and Noted in Their Published Catalogues and Similar Printed Lists_.

All of this work was preliminary to and supplementary to the main labor of the Carnegie Institution's Department of Historical Research, which was the preparation of guides. Substantial volumes were published, as the result of prolonged residence abroad by some of the country's best scholars, on manuscripts in Great Britain, Spain, France, Italy, Germany, Austria, Switzerland, and Russia. Representatives of the Carnegie Institution also worked in Scotland, Ireland, the Netherlands, Denmark, Norway, and Sweden. Reports on these last mentioned countries were not published but most of the notes from these missions are now deposited in the Library of Congress. In some respects these guides have never been superseded. For example, the basic work on Mexican archives still is Herbert E. Bolton's _Guide to the Materials for United States History in the Archives of Mexico_, which had been started while Bolton was teaching at the University of Texas.

Some documentary publications were issued by the Carnegie Institution, among them the three-volume collection edited by Charles W. Hackett entitled _Historical Documents Relating to New Mexico, Nueva Vizcaya and Approaches Thereto, to 1773_.

This carefully planned and long-range Carnegie program probably constitutes the most important single effort in the United States, or perhaps any other country, to locate and describe materials on its history in foreign archives, and provided a splendid collection of printed guides which in turn were indispensable instruments for the successful completion of large scale copying projects, of which the most significant was that of the Library of Congress. Started in 1927, supported by a half million dollar grant from John D. Rockefeller, Jr., this so-called Library of Congress Project A brought copies of over two million pages of manuscripts to Washington and had a notable effect on the development of American historiography. As Dr. Leland has stated:

> Practically the entire body of primary sources of American history located abroad, especially in the archives of the principal colonizing countries, is being made available in Washington, under conditions as to use far more satisfactory and conducive to good work than those under which the originals themselves must be studied.

While this Carnegie program was developing, Texas historians and the University of Texas of course were not idle as the interesting papers presented in connection with the dedication of the Eugene C. Barker Texas History Center testify. As Miss Winnie Allen stated at that time:

> Miss Lilia M. Casís, as a graduate student working under Herbert E. Bolton, made the first transcription of a Spanish document relating to Texas history. This transcript was made in longhand, in Mexico, under the patronage of the president of the University of Texas, David F. Houston; it became a part of the Library in April, 1903, and is still in the files. The process of transcription was appreciably speeded up by the use of the typewriter and carbon paper, and, after 1906, by a joint agreement entered upon by the Department of History of the University of Texas with the University of California, the Newberry Library, and the Library of Congress, which enabled each of these institutions to acquire a greater number of transcripts at a lower cost than if each had been working independently. This project was in operation until the middle twenties under the supervision of Miss Elizabeth West, Herbert E. Bolton, Eugene C. Barker, William Manning, Charles W. Hackett, William E. Dunn, and Charles Cunningham. The University of Texas now had a total of approximately 124,797 pages of transcriptions from the Archives of Mexico, Spain, and Cuba, touching upon every phase of colonization in New Spain.
>
> Dr. Carlos E. Castañeda has selected, copied, and calendared a total of 30,516 pages of photostats from the Matamoros and Saltillo Archives, the Archivo San Francisco el Grande, and several other local archives in Mexico. These volumes, together with the transcripts from the archives in Mexico and Spain, the Nacogdoches Archives, and the Bexar Archives, constitute the principal source material which Dr. Castañeda has used for writing the six volumes of his monumental history of Texas which he has completed, and which, under the title of _Our Catholic Heritage in Texas, 1519-1936_, has been published under the auspices of the Knights of Columbus of Texas.
>
> In the field of the German colonization of Texas, our most extensive holdings are the 17,277 pages which were transcribed

> under the supervision of Dr. R. L. Biesele from the photostats of the Solms-Braunfels Archives loaned to us by the Library of Congress.

In addition to these transcripts, there should be mentioned the valuable and extensive original manuscript material which is available in Texas, particularly the Bexar Archives, the Austin Papers, and the wealth of material to be found in various private and public collections in the state. For the Spanish side of Texas history there is available the valuable Guide to the Latin American Manuscripts in the University of Texas Library by Carlos E. Castañeda and Jack Autrey Dabbs, supplemented by their splendid Calendar of the Manuel E. Gondra Manuscript Collection. Recently their calendar to the Juan E. Hernández y Dávalos Manuscript Collection was completed, and it may safely be said that no university in the United States has been more faithful in providing information for the public on its manuscript collections than the University of Texas through the contributions of Castañeda and Dabbs. Would that other universities--such as California--did likewise.

You may well ask what remains to be done, if so much has been accomplished already. To answer this question let us look at California, another great state whose history also requires that European archives and libraries be utilized. There the University of California has taken the lead, with financial assistance from a patriotic association named The Native Sons of the Golden West and later the state legislature, in locating and copying manuscript material in Europe. Beginning in 1911 there was established a Native Sons of the Golden West Fellowship which permitted ordinarily one or two graduate students to go to Europe for research each year. Dr. Hill gives a good account of this fellowship which was held by thirty persons during the period 1911 until 1933. Eighteen of these worked in Spain alone, ten others used French, English, and Portuguese archives as well, and of the remaining fellows, one did his research in England and the other in Germany. As Hill points out each Native Sons fellow

> was engaged in the investigation of a special topic, but many carried their studies much beyond the original assignment. Ordinarily, the basic study was used in fulfilling the requirements for the doctor's degree, but often the published works of the fellow extended much beyond the thesis as will be noted below. In connection with the publications by the fellows, a vast amount of information on the various archives is presented. List of documents and general descriptions of the fonds investigated are given in the bibliographies. Naturally, these are descriptions of those records relating to a specific subject, but they serve to reveal the richness of the resources available in each case. In some instances, more formal guides to materials relating to California, the approaches thereto and the West, were produced. In addition, large quantities of transcripts were often secured and numerous fellows have deposited their collections with the Bancroft Library of the University of California, thereby adding much valuable material to that important collection of records relating to the Pacific Coast Region.

One of the by-products from the fellowship was Charles E. Chapman's Catalogue of Materials in the Archivo General de Indias for the History of the Pacific Coast and the American Southwest, which was a substantial volume of 775 pages. Another such guide is Abraham P. Nasatir's 559 page French Activities in California: An Archival-Calendar Guide. Eugene Albert Taliatberro, a fellow in 1924-1925, produced a dissertation on "The Development of Texas, 1715-1724." Besides the publications and doctoral dissertations prepared by the Native Sons fellows who based their investigations on materials in European archives, sixteen other graduate students at California used the data obtained in Europe by the fellows for their doctoral dissertations.

The Native Sons fellows not only amassed historical notes in archives; they also had an opportunity to live in Europe, become acquainted with life there, and improve their linguistic skills. Their experience abroad, therefore, not only provided excellent research materials for themselves and other students but also helped to enlarge their understanding of the ways of other people and of cultures different from their own, which has been considered a useful part of a historian's training since the days of Herodotus.

It will be remembered that the Carnegie guides paved the way for a large scale copying program undertaken by the Library of Congress. The Native Sons fellowships preceded similarly a copying enterprise by the Bancroft Library of the University of California with funds from the state legislature to the amount of almost $100,000. In 1950 some 110,000 exposures of largely nineteenth century business records of British companies that had operated in California and Mexico were made and work was started on the photography of some 550 volumes of reports from British diplomatic and consular representatives in Mexico during the period 1822-1905. Equally significant copying was done in Mexico, some 218,000 exposures having been made, mostly from the rich sections in the Archivo General de la Nación, Californias, Provincias Internas, and Correspondencia de los Virreyes. The Bancroft Library program also includes extensive microfilming in Portugal and Spain, and some work in France and the Netherlands.

To return to Texas, it is well to emphasize the large amount of material already collected in Austin and the steady effort that has been put into making it available through guides and calendars. Of importance also is the material on Texas in European archives which has been obtained, such as the French material by Bishop Lawrence J. FitzSimon of Amarillo and the microfilm copies of material in Belgium archives on Victor Pirson which Professor Joseph Schmitz of St. Mary's University in San Antonio has been using for his research. It is precisely because so much has been done that one ventures to suggest that the time has perhaps come for a long-range effort to plan and develop a program which would eventually bring to Texas the material in European archives to be used in conjunction with the rich collections now here.

The archives of the foreign offices in Paris and London must hold a quantity of diplomatic correspondence on Texas. The records of British companies that played an important role in the development of the economic world during the last hundred years are extensive. The Companies Registration Act of 1844 has resulted in the building up of an archive in London which has the corporate records of all English and Welsh limited companies, both public and private, including articles of incorporation, prospectuses, annual reports of finances, shareholders and in some cases operations, and changes in corporate structure and management. Among the 500,000 companies, representing interests in all parts of the world, included in this archive there must be a rich harvest of data for the economic historian of Texas.

The archives of Spain, Italy, and other countries are certain to yield material on Texas. Dr. Harry Ransom of the University of Texas has found that Swedish archives have reports on Texas by Sir Swante Palm. Most probably other repositories of Texana in Europe can be found.

To locate this material and to arrange for its selection, reproduction, and calendaring will require persistent and patient work over a period of time, and funds. Has not the moment come to meet this challenge?

Some organization will be needed, but whatever machinery is set up should be so flexible as to use the skill and devotion of individual historians. If the University of Texas Board of Regents should appoint, for example, a Historical Manuscripts Commission it would naturally endeavor to enlist the support and assistance of a number of institutions and individuals. The Commission could serve as a planning and fomenting group. Some support might be obtained in the form of Fulbright grants to enable individual scholars to work in European archives. Could we not achieve some day a Eugene C. Barker Fellowship to enable a succession of Texas graduate students to carry on research in European archives?

This proposed Commission might also give attention to the copying of Texas material in Mexican archives such as those in Saltillo. Dr. Nettie Lee Benson has reported that a considerable quantity of manuscripts are to be found there which some time should be microfilmed, at least in part. The Commission also might concern itself with the prompt publication of reports on material thus acquired in foreign archives and it would appear that the *Southwestern Historical Quarterly* would be an appropriate instrument for this purpose. Unless the material is made known to students, it will not be used, and if it is not to be used, there is no point to obtaining it.

The Historical Manuscripts Commission would have a hard job to do, but over a period of years it might well perform a valuable service for the history, and hence for the people, of Texas.

CHAPTER 33.

EARLY AMERICAN HISTORY AS A PART OF THE HISTORY OF WESTERN CIVILIZATION

One of the problems for Latin Americanists, in the United States at least, is how to avoid provincialism. The student or professor interested in Latin American history, for example, should not be so narrowly concentrated on his field as to forget about the larger questions of history or the position of Latin American history in the long sweep of the history of Europe. Sometimes professors, at other times libraries, help students to see the larger view.

The Rhode Island nineteenth-century merchant, John Carter Brown, and the library on the Americas up to about 1800 that he had established in Providence, have been a source of inspiration to me since my graduate school days. I travelled rather frequently from Cambridge, Massachusetts, just for the pleasure and profit of talking with Lawrence C. Wroth who so ably directed the library in those years. When the new Librarian, Thomas R. Adams, organized a meeting in 1960 on the Early History of the Americas, I was pleased to have an opportunity to present my views on how all interested in this great subject may learn from the books and other research materials brought together at the John Carter Brown Library, now an ever increasingly used part of Brown University.

The John Carter Brown Library Conference: A Report of the Meeting Held in the Library at Brown University on the Early History of the Americas (Providence, Rhode Island, 1961), 29-43. Reprinted by permission.

Early American History as a Part of the History of Western Civilization

When Mr. Adams invited me to speak on this topic my understanding was he wanted no long discourse, and certainly such a distinguished and knowledgeable audience as this needs none. I conceive my role here to be somewhat like that of a bull in the ring: to charge about and perhaps make some extreme movements but in the end to be disposed of. My hope, too, is that our discussions this afternoon will not be comparable to a Spanish bullfight--where blood is expected to flow freely and the bull always dies--but to a Portuguese bullfight in which the bull is not killed. Everybody wins in a Portuguese bullfight: the bullfighters, who perform incredibly dexterous and graceful deeds while mounted on superb Arabian horses; the bull, who is persuaded to leave the field, by a half-dozen docile bullocks, when the afternoon's ritual has been completed; and the spectators, who have enjoyed this combination of skill and pageantry. Once, years ago in Lisbon, I attended a bullfight in which everything went so well that the bullfighter was rewarded with a huge bouquet of roses, and he thereupon was escorted around the ring to the plaudits of the crowd while his colleagues vied for the opportunity to embrace him. Just to indicate how differently such affairs are handled in Spain, let me report on a bullfight that is reported to have occurred just last summer in Alicante. The bull was despatched so promptly and so expertly by the matador that the crowd enthusiastically awarded him both ears and the tail of the defeated animal. These were cut off, and the matador went around the ring holding in his hands the symbols of his great triumph. Then, to everybody's surprise, the bull got up again--having been stunned, not killed--and charged the matador, who finally took so long in killing the animal that the crowd turned on him and insisted that he give back the ears and tail as a sign of his disgrace.

* * *

In approaching any such large topic as "Early American History as a Part of the History of Western Civilization," one must naturally have in mind certain basic propositions. Some of the thoughts that have occurred to me are:

1. <u>John Carter Brown Library Lies in a Very Rich Bibliographical Belt</u>.

The 500-odd miles that stretch down the East Coast from Cambridge and Worcester to Washington contain a very large proportion of all the printed books on the history of all the Americas up to 1801. Some outstanding items or collections on particular areas may be elsewhere in the United States or in Europe, but they must be few indeed.

2. <u>John Carter Brown Library Is the Only Research Collection Built Up Exclusively on a Broad All-American Basis</u>.

Other collections in this rich bibliographical belt and elsewhere in the United States have developed outstanding collections on one or more aspects of British, French, Portuguese, or Spanish America, but only John Carter Brown Library has carved out as its field the vast area stretching from Greenland and the Arctic to Patagonia, "the entire Western Hemisphere," to use Lawrence Wroth's phrase in his volume on *The First Century of the John Carter Brown Library*.

3. <u>The State of the Book Market</u>.

A third fact of life which every library must keep in mind is the state of the market. Like most students who use rare books but do not buy them, my knowledge of the book market is quite limited. But it is clear that since Mr. Brown bought, in 1846, for ten guineas the first Latin edition of the 1493 letter in which Columbus announced the discovery of America, the price of this book and all other such Americana has gone up astronomically. Another fact which must daunt at times the most enthusiastic librarian, even though he has vast sums at his disposal, is that the number of copies of the foundation books upon which the history of the Western Hemisphere rests is <u>not</u> increasing. Of course there may be some spiritual descendent of the famous forger Thomas J. Wise now happily and skillfully plying his trade, to the end that in due course some choice items will appear on the market. But this is not likely; even if another forging genius appears, who wants specimens of this doubtful art?

If we take for granted these three circumstances--the rich bibliographical belt in which Providence is situated, the fact that the Library is the only collection devoted exclusively to the Western Hemisphere as a whole and the present state of the book market--what should we conclude?

In order to give that balance prescribed in early treatises on oratory and declamation, I propose to suggest three ways in which the Library--in the light of the three circumstances just outlined--can continue and even extend its contribution to the development of the study of the history of the Western Hemisphere as a part of the history of Western civilization. To begin with the obvious:

1. <u>The John Carter Brown Library Should Continue to Serve the Individual Scholar</u>.

I still cherish a long letter Lawrence Wroth wrote to me back in 1932 describing the holdings of the Library on Bartolomé de las Casas. Though I was then one of the graduate students pullulating at Harvard, Dr. Wroth wrote me the kind of detailed, friendly, and persuasive letter that I thought librarians of rare collections usually reserved for wealthy friends from whom they hope to extract several thousand dollars to purchase a much needed item. I am happy to see that in the "Program" that Mr. Adams has prepared there is a place for this kind of assistance to go on and that he contemplates even increased and improved physical arrangements for the individual reader who comes here to take advantage of the resources of the Library. The proposed Bibliographical Center will, of course, be of tremendous aid to the individual worker, and we will all agree, I am sure, on Mr. Adams' proposals. The sordid matter of financing them we will leave to President Keeney and his colleagues.

My next point may be more controversial.

2. <u>The Development of Photographic Reproductions on a Planned and Systematic Basis</u>.

Mr. Adams states that "a secondary part of the program is to continue to add to either the main Brown University Library or John Carter Brown Library these 'substitutes' wherever we cannot get the original." Of course a book is a copy--a <u>printed</u> copy--of some "original" item.

Now I know that "microfilm" is a nasty word in some circles and that even the words "photostat" and "microcard" cause some delicate stomachs to turn over. However, Brown University already has a splendid collection of some 2,300 items on microfilm as recorded in its <u>List of Latin American Imprints Before 1800, Selected from Bibliographies of José Toribio Medina, Microfilmed by Brown University</u>. The project was carried out in Chile, with Rockefeller Foundation funds, and might well be extended on a planned and systematic basis. A large number of desirable items are in collections outside Chile, and Medina did not cover the water front. He did supremely well, of course, by publishing over three hundred volumes and articles--mostly bibliographical--in his lifetime, but during the last quarter century a host of bibliographers has grown up who have made their reputations by printing bibliographies with the phrase "Not in Medina" in their titles.

Let me give two illustrations of what I mean by extending the John Carter Brown Library on "a planned and systematic basis."

Dr. Wroth has pointed out that one of the Library's richest fields is the work of historians in the second half of the sixteenth century who wrote on the discovery, exploration, or colonization of America. And he states that the Historia of Francisco López de Gómara who coined that unforgettable phrase--"Except for the coming of Christ, the most important event since the world began was the discovery of the New World"--is to be found in thirty-seven of the forty-four known editions. Why not obtain a negative microfilm now of the seven editions not here, and even if copies of them come on the market sometime in the future at reasonable prices, the microfilm copies will have served a good purpose. López de Gómara is a useful example for my purpose here because I happen to know that Professor Marcel Bataillon of the Collège de France has started, with his usual skill and persistence, to work on the Historia of López de Gómara, and it is quite likely that the next generation will show increased interest in this significant book.

One more illustration and I shall move on to my third and last point. The Library has sixty-eight per cent of all the printed books on the native languages of America issued before 1800 as recorded in Viñaza's Bibliografía española de lenguas indígenas de América, and in addition fifty manuscripts and a number of printed books not included in Viñaza. Native Indian languages is a field in which much important work remains to be accomplished, and it is a rich field. . . .

Other regions of America are rich too; I remember finding many years ago in the Archive of the Indies in Sevilla a long and mournful letter from a sixteenth-century friar near Bogotá who despaired of ever communicating with Indians. He complained that even though he had learned one native language, the Indians on the next hilltop spoke an entirely different language.

Today signs multiply of a growing interest in the subject. The Instituto Tecnológico of Monterrey, Mexico, has recently acquired the splendid collection of sixteenth-century imprints brought together by the banker Salvador Ugarte, and the American Philosophical Society has a committee at work to prepare a guide to the rich materials in the Society's collections. A half-dozen universities and the Smithsonian Bureau of American Indian Ethnology are at work, and the American Indian Ethnohistoric Conference will hold its eighth annual meeting next week at Indiana University. Finally, a remarkable group of missionary linguists called the Wyclif Translators are manifesting a zeal worthy of the great figures of the past who labored to bring Christianity to the New World.

Why not work out a co-operative venture to assure the existence in Providence of every book on Indian languages of the Americas up to 1800, to the end that any library or individual anyhwere could obtain at a reasonable price a photographic copy of one or all of the basic texts? Of course any project such as this one would have to be related to the undertaking now under way to microprint all available items in the Evans bibliography.

This service, indeed the whole program proposed to extend the Library's present photographic holdings on a planned and systematic basis, would be a great boon for all concerned with Indian languages--particularly for those outside the rich bibliographical belt of the East Coast.

Unless my former boss in the Library of Congress, Mr. Verner Clapp, and his colleagues of the Council on Library Resources can devise a photographic copy of a book that feels and looks and smells like the original article and gives the user the same emotional feeling and scholarly data, I suspect that we are entering a long period in which rare printed copies (books) and photographic copies in various forms are going to have to learn to coexist. If this be true, let us adjust our hair shirts as comfortably as may be possible and proceed to my last point.

3. The Stimulation of Comparative Studies on the History of the Hemisphere to 1800, Including Its Impact on Europe and on the Far East.

One obvious enterprise for the Library to undertake would be the utilization of this great collection for comparative studies in the history of European exploration and colonization in the Americas up to 1800, not forgetting the impact of America on Europe and Asia. So many persons present have participated so actively in many similar developments that I feel somewhat timid about even referring to them, but it may be useful to set down as examples some of the operations now going on. The Folger Library, under the dynamic direction of our Chairman, serves as a stimulating center for researches on British culture in Shakespeare's day, and the Institute of Early American History and Culture at Williamsburg performs a valuable service in its field. The International Colloquium on Luso-Brazilian Studies, which held its first meeting in the Library of Congress under the presidency of Professor Francis Rogers, considers the expansion of Portugal in the New World, and the Instituto de Cultura Hispánica in Madrid gives attention--albeit in a somewhat propagandistic spirit--to Spanish action in America. The Pan American Institute of Geography and History has been at work on a "History of the Americas," in which Dr. Waldo G. Leland has had an active role, and has had a tonic effect in exercising the general muscles of particularistic historians, but the project has also revealed how much monographic investigation needs to be accomplished before works of synthesis can be written. The Institute of Caribbean Studies at the University of Puerto Rico has as one of its objectives comparative studies in that area, including investigations of the contemporary scene. The new journal Comparative Studies in Society and History, under the guidance of Professor Sylvia Thrupp and others, has provided an outlet for comparative studies on a broad, indeed, a world front.

Scholars concerned with the comparison of British, French, Portuguese, Spanish and other colonizing activities in the Americas up to 1800 are widely scattered, and need to have opportunities to discuss with each other problems of mutual interest.

What kind of topics would be discussed if meetings were sponsored by the Library? Economics, including international trade, Education, Indians, Land, Religion, Science, and Slavery are some of the topics which come to mind at once. Others, which would be fun to tackle, would be:

1. Americanism.

Soon after the first Europeans stepped ashore in the New World, they began to notice differences between their new home and the old. Oviedo, one of the earliest Spanish historians, went into these differences in considerable detail, pointing out that people, plants, and animals experienced changes as they crossed the ocean. Language was affected too; Oviedo worked up as an appendix to his history a list of the new words needed in Spanish America. He even asserted that roosters crowed less raucously in America, and did not disturb his sleep as they often had done during his student days at the University of Salamanca.

This theme is a vast and tricky one. How far was this feeling of Americanism merely a reaction to attitudes of high-hatted Europeans who looked down on their American cousins? The work of the Italian scholar Antonello Gerbi, who has just published in Mexico in Spanish a notable contribution on this subject, will be highly useful. The essential European part of early American history is well illustrated by this theme, too, and the variety of responses to roughly similar conditions might be instructive.

2. The Enlightenment.

How did the ideas of eighteenth-century Europe spread to the Americas and what happened to them there? Why did they have different effects in the various areas? Philosophers, historians, and others will find this a challenging question.

3. Linguistics.

Were different methods developed to learn the native languages by missionaries and others in the several areas and, if so, why? And what were the policies on teaching the natives the language of the colonizing powers?

Given the richness of the Library in Indian languages and the almost alarming growth of linguisticians on our university campuses today, the discussions of such topics might be lively.

Or perhaps something more general should be attempted. How valuable to all students of the early history of America would be a volume similar in competence and imagination to the American Indian and White Relations to 1830 by William N. Fenton, Lyman H. Butterfield, and Wilcomb E. Washburn, but conceived of course on a comparative basis.

4. Medicine.

United States historians have been showing the way recently in this field, and their influence might well have a beneficial effect if a comparative study were made. The Spanish experience was important, too, and its story has been barely scratched by researchers. How many in this room have heard of the extraordinary smallpox vaccination globe circling expedition that started out in 1803 from Spain led by Francisco Javier Balmis to carry the newly discovered vaccine to her far-flung dominions? Professor S. F. Cook has described it thus:

> Seldom, perhaps never, in the history of medicine has there embarked an expedition so grandly conceived, so well executed, so uniformly successful as that of Balmis. Certainly, no new therapeutic procedure of similar magnitude has ever been made available by a single agency to such a wide segment of the world's population. By it the discovery of Jenner was made available to the populations of the West Indies, Mexico, Central America, much of South America, the Philippine Islands, the East Indies, and China. Through this one act on the part of the corrupt and decadent government of Spain more lives probably were saved than were lost in all the battles of Napoleon. Yet this magnificent experiment in social welfare and public health has gone substantially unnoticed and unrecorded by both medical and political historians.

Twenty-two orphan boys were taken along, as the vaccine was transported in these human containers. At the beginning of the voyage a small nonimmune boy was vaccinated with a potent preparation of cowpox virus, and when the reaction was at its peak another boy was vaccinated, and so on across the Atlantic.

The organization of discussions on these and other topics--for my list is designed to be suggestive rather than definitive--would of course require careful consideration. They should be called, perhaps, conclaves rather than conferences, colloquia, or congresses. A "conclave," in my dictionary, means an intimate meeting of a few persons. The topics and participants would be prudently selected, preliminary homework would be expected, and a volume of proceedings would be published to spread the results far and wide.

What would be the results of such conclaves? They might help all of us to discover what comparative studies are. Professor Thrupp, who has had more experience in this vineyard than most of us, recently wrote me: "There is a lot of hard work to be done before very many historians will have any clear notion of how and why comparative studies are to be attempted."

Though it would be difficult for me to explain what comparative studies are, I can tell you what I think they should not be in the comparative study of European colonization in America. They should not be based on the supposition that the Americas have a common history and that the history of our vast continent and of the many different kinds of people in it from the Eskimos in the north to the Fuegian Indians in the south culminates in the establishment of the Pan American Union in Washington. To put it more simply, I do not subscribe to Herbert E. Bolton's theory that the Americas have a common history in the sense that he meant it. Years ago a Mexican historian, Professor Edmundo O'Gorman, who had served as a visiting professor at Brown University, wrote a brilliant essay on this question and disposed rather effectively of this theory which rests insecurely upon what may be called continental chauvinism. A volume has been written on *The Western Hemisphere Idea: Its Rise and Decline*, and a Master's thesis has been prepared on Bolton's rather weak philosophical underpinnings. Let us draw a veil over this concept and move on to the assumption that the record of what went on in the Americas up to 1800 is an important part of the history both of the Western Hemisphere and of Europe. Some common elements certainly existed, but this is a far cry from the position advocated by Bolton and others.

Perhaps the most significant fruit to be expected would be the widening of the horizons of all of us. Here I tread on delicate ground. Let me begin by confessing that we in Latin American history all too often limit ourselves to the study of Spanish America and omit or pass rapidly over Portuguese America. Now that Brazil with its sixty-five million people is becoming a world power, the situation will have to change, but up to now we have been woefully neglectful of Brazil.

I do not know what the situation is in Canada, but my impression is that their universities and scholars pay relatively little attention to the other parts of the hemisphere. The same may be said of Latin Americans although on certain formal occasions many profess a continental vision. With respect to the host of United States historians who teach United States history in our universities, I am told that they also show relatively little interest in the other cultures of the hemisphere, that they rarely have to carry on researches abroad, and that they rarely have a good knowledge of foreign languages. I know that it is difficult for the Fulbright Committee to find competent scholars in United States history to lecture abroad in French or Spanish. I will not include Portuguese as a language of interest to United States historians lest you begin to wonder whether life on the plains of Texas has not softened my brain!

In conclusion I should like to pay tribute to the vision of John Carter Brown in establishing the geographical scope of his collection as "the entire Western Hemisphere." In that handsome and meaty volume entitled Essays Honoring Lawrence C. Wroth, George Kubler suggests that this decision may have been based on a sort of manifest destiny feeling, and Mr. Brown began to buy Spanish Americana in 1846, at the time of the Mexican War, according to the late Henry R. Wagner. Neither the Wagner nor the Kubler essay is completely convincing on this point. I suspect that the decisive steps were taken in the early years through the influence of John Russell Bartlett, the friend upon whom Mr. Brown leaned for advice. Educated in French Canada, with broad intellectual interests, he had a valuable exposure to life below the Rio Grande during the period 1850-1853 when he served as the United States Commissioner for determining the boundary with Mexico after the war. In his Personal Narrative he tells of these border experiences: how he relished the social affairs at which the Mexican ladies displayed their grace in dresses which would be admired in New York; how he was surprised to find a Mexican general who spoke English, and indeed several languages, with great correctness, and was familiar with the works of Addison, Milton, and Shakespeare; how he inspected the archives in San Antonio and observed: "The Northern States have spent immense sums in sending agents to England, France, and Holland to procure similar papers from the State archives to illustrate their colonial history. Texas possesses in her own record offices voluminous documents of equal value, in which the scholar and historian of every State feels an interest second only to that of her own people." Bartlett also displayed that ambivalent attitude of many English-speaking persons toward the work of Spain in America; he manifested a real respect for the amazing feats of Spanish explorers, but he also exhibited a patriotic Yankee feeling that a better job was done north of the Rio Grande.

Libraries, however, do not prosper merely because of a sound beginning. A continuing concern is also required. The contributions of George P. Winship and Lawrence Wroth were also decisive, and they, too, by their purchases and personal publications demonstrated that they had an all-American view.

I like to think, too, of John Carter Brown's original decision as another illustration of that unprovincial spirit of the United States in the second third of the nineteenth century when Motley was delving into the records of the Dutch Republic, when Emerson was learning about the philosophies of the East, when Parkman was writing his imperishable histories of the French and British in Canada, when Prescott was publishing best sellers on the conquests of Mexico and Peru, when John L. Stephens was bringing to popular notice the ancient Mayan civilization of Yucatan, and when Ticknor was laboring in his study on a history of Spanish literature which was to remain a standard work for generations. And all of these works are still readable despite the passage of more than one hundred years.

Whatever may be the true explanation of how that merchant and manufacturer of Providence, John Carter Brown, came to embark upon his career as a collector in his fiftieth year, no one today can fail to see that the library which bears his name has become a great institution not only devoted to collecting Americana, but in the true American tradition it has grown from a "gentleman's library" into a living part of an academic community and is now a national institution with certain international projections as well. Whatever may be the specific recommendations that come out of this conference, we can all rejoice that the Library's Committee of Management adopted an ambitious program last year, and that Brown University decided to hold this special kind of bibliothecal "town meeting" to discuss, in President Keeney's discreet and felicitous phrase "the Library's proper place within the framework of scholarship."

EPILOGUE

After finishing this peroration, I happened to look through the slim and elegant volume recording the ceremonies that took place when the newly completed John Carter Brown Library building was dedicated on May 17, 1904. The present Mr. John Nicholas Brown was there, as he is today, but on that occasion he had attained the ripe age of four years and it was his heavy responsibility to hand over, at the symbolic moment, the keys to the Library, to President Faunce of Brown University. There were speeches then, too, and the content of the address by Frederick Jackson Turner of the University of Wisconsin reminds one of the old saw that not only does history tend to repeat itself but historians sometimes repeat each other. For Professor Turner closed his remarks in this way, and in the same spirit I end my paper:

> Rightly to appreciate the John Carter Brown Library demands that this community rightly appreciate and provide for the support of investigation and for the highest type of scholarship. Its scope, indeed, suggests exploration and discovery. . . .
>
> Because it is so clear that with the rich historical resources of the libraries of this city and with the scholars already at work here, Brown University can become the mother of a long line of historical scholars, I wish to urge upon this audience the greatness of the opportunity and the need of such provision for research, fellowships and professorships, as shall recognize the importance of historical studies in this University and the value of the John Carter Brown Library.

CHAPTER 34.

DO THE AMERICAS HAVE A COMMON HISTORY?

Due to the imagination and support of Alfred A. Knopf, there came into being a Borzoi Books on Latin America series which made possible the launching of thirty volumes in the decade beginning in 1964. Our aim in the series was to set forth a challenging idea or controversial topic, with many source materials from historians in Latin America and elsewhere. Our hope was to arouse interest among students by exposing them to a variety of approaches to historical issues, so that they would not have to depend exclusively upon textbooks.

Don Alfredo has retired from his long and fruitful publishing career, and the series now languishes. But I am happy to learn that the Center for Latin American Studies at Arizona State University plans to republish a number of the Borzoi Books in up-dated editions.

As general editor, I felt it necessary to do more than work with the manuscripts of my colleagues and decided to produce a volume on Bolton's theory which had long interested me. Here is the introduction for my volume in the series.

Do the Americas Have a Common History? A Critique of the Bolton Theory (Knopf, 1964), 3-50. Reprinted by permission.

Do the Americas Have a Common History?

1. Background

The idea that the Americas--North and South--have shared a common historical experience developed slowly in the nineteenth century, and was not fully elaborated until Herbert Eugene Bolton devoted his presidential address before the American Historical Association in 1932 to the theme of "The Epic of Greater America", in which he declared:

> There is need for a broader treatment of American history, to supplement the purely nationalistic presentation to which we are accustomed. European history cannot be learned from books dealing alone with England, or France, or Germany, or Italy, or Russia; nor can American history be adequately presented if confined to Brazil, or Chile, or Mexico, or Canada, or the United States. In my own country the study of thirteen English colonies and the United States in isolation has obscured many of the larger factors in their development, and helped to raise up a nation of chauvinists. Similar distortion has resulted from the teaching and writing of national history in other American countries.
>
> Our national historians, especially in the United States, are prone to write of these broad phases of American history as though they were applicable to one country alone. It is my purpose, by a few bold strokes, to suggest that they are but phases common to most portions of the entire Western Hemisphere; that each local story will have clearer meaning when studied in the light of the others; and that much of what has been written of each national history is but a thread out of a larger strand.

The idea of a Western Hemisphere with separate interests from those of Europe goes back at least as far as Thomas Jefferson's letter of 1808 in response to overtures from Cuban and Mexican leaders of incipient independence movements, and the revolutionary wars that began in Latin America in 1810 roused considerable political interest in the area and its problems. There had been increased commercial and cultural relations since about 1800, but little consciousness in any of the American nations that they shared a common history. Vera Lee Brown Holmes wrote in her history of America:

> While the newer American republics admired the eldest member of the family and paid her the compliment of imitation in many respects, there were few interests in common and fewer occasions for inter-American cooperation. The bases of unity, though fundamental, were as yet inchoate, unexpressed, and largely unrecognized. The American colonies had freed themselves from Europe but had not yet built a common house.

The subject of a common history was not even much discussed in the United States and when it was, the idea was seldom looked upon with favor. The influential North American Review, edited by the historian

Jared Sparks, included in 1821 this blunt statement in an unsigned review of a work on Paraguayan history:

> We have no concern with South America: we have no sympathy, we can have no well founded political sympathy with them. We are sprung from different stocks, we speak different languages, we have been brought up in different social and moral schools, we have been governed by different codes of law, we profess radically different forms of religion. . . . How can our mild and merciful peoples, who went through their revolution without shedding a drop of civil blood, sympathize with a people, that are hanging and shooting each other in their streets, with every fluctuation of their ill organized and exasperated factions? It does not yet appear that there exist in any of those provinces the materials and elements of a good national character; of a character to justify our putting our own interests at hazard, by interfering in their present contest. . . . We hold it to be a maxim clearly established in the history of the world, that none but the temperate climates, and the climates which produce and retain the European complexion of skin in its various shades, admit of the highest degrees of national character.

Such political leaders as James Madison also held an unfavorable view of the societies to the south. In 1823, the year that the Monroe Doctrine was enunciated, he attributed the slower increase of population there to the "vicious institutions of Spanish America, where Nature was not less bountiful" than in the United States. The _leyenda negra_ which decried all things Spanish was indeed widespread. Alexander Hill Everett, diplomat and later editor of the _North American Review_, emphatically believed the Iberian colonies of America inferior to the English colonies, and his declaration in 1827 indicated why he felt that there was such a gulf between the United States and Ibero America:

> The United States ever since the formation of its first settlements furnishes a splendid commentary on the advantages of our position, even under the colonial system. These advantages, however, did not lie. . . in the facility afforded us by the great extent of the territory, taken in connexion with the original scantiness of the population, for obtaining by labour an abundant supply of the means of subsistence. . . . There is not difficulty in finding countries where labour will produce abundant fruits. The difficulty is to find a place where men are permitted to enjoy the fruits of their labour, and this was the signal distinction of the United States, even as colonies. This blessing of Providence (for it is one and nothing else) will turn a sandbank or an iceberg into a paradise of plenty, as it has been seen to do in Holland and Switzerland; and will make the wilderness blossom like a rose, as it has done with us.

Alexander H. Everett's older and more famous brother, Edward, was just as firm in his convictions and, contemplating the history of Spain and Portugal in America, could find no good: "From the extreme southern point of Patagonia to the northernmost limit of New Mexico, I am not aware that any thing hopeful was done for human improvement by either of the European crowns which added these vast domains to their territories."

John Quincy Adams probably reflected the views of many in the United States; he "was impartially prejudiced against Spaniards and Spanish Americans alike, for he had swallowed whole the 'Black Legend' of the inveterate cruelty, faithlessness, and fanaticism of the Spanish people, and he still regarded the Spanish Americans as Spaniards even after they began their struggle for independence against Spain." Those who held such views were not likely to feel that they had a common historical experience worthy of mention.

Historians and publicists on both sides of the Atlantic continued to compare the work of the various European powers in America in the light of their own predilections, but the thought of a common history shared by the nations of the new world--or by some of them at least--did not die. Buckingham Smith, for example, struggled in the 1850's to make North Americans conscious of the valuable Spanish content of their own history by proposing the publication of a large "Documentary History of that part of the United States once under Spanish domination," but the project languished and then disappeared. . . .

Meanwhile historians in various parts of the Americas were beginning to give some attention to a history of the Americas. Hubert Howe Bancroft in California, Diego Barros Arana in Chile, and Justin Winsor in Boston all published historical works continental in scope during the second half of the nineteenth century. Imposing as these histories were in the vast quantity of facts presented and bibliographical references compiled, they appear to have had little or no intellectual underpinning of theory. The temper of the times was nationalistic; Carlton J. H. Hayes has characterized the years following 1875 as the period of "Babylonian Captivity" of American historiography, which saw the trend away from European history toward purely American themes. The first president of the American Historical Association, Andrew D. White, saw little hope, in 1884, for the American scholar who wanted to specialize in the history of a country other than the United States or Britain.

Daniel de Leon had initiated courses on inter-American relations at Columbia University in 1884, but it was Bernard Moses, who had first offered a course on "Spanish American History and Institutions" in the spring of 1895 at the University of California, who began the campaign to broaden the teaching of American history in the United States and thus laid the basis for Bolton's approach to the history of the Americas. In a paper delivered at the time of the Spanish American War on the subject of "The Neglected Half of American History", Moses declared: "American history, in its proper sense, embraces all attempts to found and develop civilized society on this continent, whether these attempts were made by the English, the French, the Portuguese, or the Spanish."

Another scholar who would broaden the base of American history was William R. Shepherd, whose introductory remarks at a 1909 session of the American Historical Association dedicated to the topic "The Contribution of the Romance Nations to the History of the Americas" clearly anticipated many of the essential ideas of "The Epic of Greater America." He declared, "Balance is an element too often lacking in the history of America as it is written and taught today."

2. Development of Bolton's Theory

These exhortations seem to have produced no great change in the teaching of American history but the pioneer work of Moses in Berkeley paved the way for Herbert Eugene Bolton, who established a vigorous school of historians with inter-American interests in the period beginning in 1911. He had grown up as a boy in Wisconsin in the provincial and narrowly nationalistic atmosphere which Moses had so boldly attacked. Bolton once described that environment in the picturesque and dramatic way that made him such an effective lecturer:

> My early environment and outlook were typically Yankee "American," that is to say, provincial, nationalistic. My unquestioned historical beliefs included the following: Democrats were born to be damned; Catholics, Mormons and Jews were to be looked upon askance. The Americans licked England; they licked the Indians; all good Indians were dead; the English came to America to build homes, the Spaniards merely explored and hunted gold; Spain failed in the New World; the English always succeeded; their successors, the Americans, were God's elect; American history all happened between the 49th parallel and the Rio Grande; the Americans virtuously drove the Mexicans out of New Mexico, Colorado, Texas, Arizona, and the rest, and thereby built a great empire. Every one of these concepts is false in whole or in part, but it took me half a lifetime to discover it.

The radically different interpretation of the history of the Americas, which Bolton expressed in his 1932 address on "The Epic of Greater America," was a long time growing in his mind. During his first university teaching experience, at the University of Texas in 1901, he came into direct contact with the Spanish heritage, learned that the manuscript sources for the true history of the Southwest were largely unused, quickly applied himself to studying Spanish so that he could read the documents, and formulated views on the significance of the rule of Spain in American history. Professor George P. Garrison, Chairman of the History Department at Texas, had visited archives in Mexico City and Saltillo in 1900, had begun with Lilia M. Casis to make transcripts of Mexican documents bearing on Southwestern history, and had been instrumental with L. G. Bugbee in calling the rich Texan archive in San Antonio to the attention of historians. In 1903, Garrison published a volume _Texas: A Contest of Civilizations_ which is marked by a pro-Anglo bias and which explains the rise and fall of Spanish power in the Southwest as a manifestation of evolutionary principles and "the survival of the fittest." The Garrison interpretation was representative of the views then prevailing among United States historians. If Bolton had read in his student days such a monograph as Frank W. Blackmar's _Spanish Institutions of the Southwest_, he would have seen Spanish institutions disparaged in comparison with the Anglo-Saxon, for those were the days when Herbert Baxter Adams' "Teutonic School" at Johns Hopkins University dominated American historical thinking. Darwin himself had believed that United States history represented "natural selection" at its best and the Anglo-Saxon emigration of the West the climactic event of all history. "For American historians Darwin seemed to have provided a scientific basis for their confidence in the superiority of Anglo-Saxon political institutions." In such an atmosphere, the history of other cultures in the Americas received little attention.

In 1904, E. G. Bourne's _Spain in America_ began to turn the tide; here for the first time there was available a well-written, accurate, and fair-minded volume in English, which received the accolade of a paperback edition almost sixty years later. Bourne's volume did not lead, however, to regular courses on Latin American history at his university, Yale; it was not until 1963 that this institution had a faculty member on tenure who devoted all his time to this subject.

Bolton was chosen, while at Texas, to compile the Guide to the Materials for the History of the United States in the Principal Archives of Mexico, projected and directed by John Franklin Jameson for the Carnegie Institution of Washington. This work in Bolton's hands was no narrow list of U.S.-Mexican diplomatic documents but a wide-ranging guide which remains, after half a century, the best volume available on Mexican archives as a whole, with special attention to the Spanish borderlands. The preparation of this Guide and later publications required several extended visits to Mexico, during which Bolton came to have an intimate acquaintance with the manuscript treasures there, and laid the basis for his many later documentary publications. Bolton allowed nothing to interrupt his laborious cataloguing of manuscripts in dusty archives. The story is told that when Pancho Villa raided the town of Juárez, everyone fled in haste except Bolton and two peons. The guerrilla leaders were so much interested in his activities that they appointed him head of the archives and he was allowed to continued cataloguing in peace.

In the fall of 1909 Bolton left Texas to join the Stanford faculty, after which he moved to the University of California at Berkeley where he remained until his death in 1953. During the long productive period he steadily developed and strengthened his approach to American history. In 1911 he was encouraged to learn that the widely-respected historian and editor of the American Historical Review, John Franklin Jameson, was also convinced that the Spanish contribution to United States history had not been adequately realized by United States historians. In December of the same year, at the Ithaca meeting of the American Historical Association, Bolton made known his own convictions on this point.

Ever since Hubert Howe Bancroft had published in San Francisco his massive collection of volumes on the history of Western America from Panama to the Pacific Northwest, California had been a good place to feel fresh winds blow. It was natural, therefore, to find California historians continuing to extend their horizons. The Panama-Pacific International Exposition at San Francisco in 1915 had planned a special meeting of the American Historical Association, but instead a historical congress was held which drew scholars from many countries. The papers presented were edited by Bolton and H. Morse Stephens as The Pacific Ocean in History. Among the scholars present were Rafael Altamira from Spain, E. Larrabure y Unánue from Peru, and León María Guerrero from Manila. This gathering of historians in San Francisco may have been responsible for arousing interest in Peru in continental history, since a Chair of History of the Americas was established in the Universidad de San Marcos in Lima, Peru, about that time.

Bolton's passion for documentation was recognized by his appointment in 1916 as director of the Bancroft Library, which became under his dynamic guidance a principal center for research in Western American and Latin American history. He became Chairman of the History Department in 1919, a position he retained until his retirement in 1940. During these years he built "a good small department into one of the nation's leaders." These years also mark the beginning of his intensive research when he not only produced a long shelf of books but also supervised 300 master's theses and some 100 doctoral dissertations. In the summers he traveled many hundreds of miles by horse or mule to trace the routes of such far-ranging explorers as Coronado, Kino, Portolá, and Anza.

In 1920 Bolton published a textbook, with significant assistance from his former student Thomas M. Marshall, called The Colonization of

North America, 1492-1783, in which principal emphasis was placed on non-English colonies and on those English colonies that were not among the original thirteen. In so doing he publicly challenged for the first time the traditional values held by the United States historians of the generation influenced by the Johns Hopkins school who had generally felt that their chief responsibility was to follow the spread of Anglo-Saxon civilization westward across the continent. The Bolton-Marshall volume had an entirely different objective:

> This book represents an attempt to bring into one account the story of European expansion in North America down to 1783. Text books written in this country as a rule treat the colonization of the New World as the history, almost solely, of the thirteen English colonies which formed the nucleus of the United States. The authors have essayed to write a book from a different point of view. It has been prepared in response to a clear demand for a text written from the standpoint of North America as a whole, and giving a more adequate treatment of the colonies of nations other than England and of the English colonies other than the thirteen which revolted. This demand is the inevitable result of the growing importance of our American neighbors and of our rapidly growing interest in the affairs of the whole continent, past as well as present.

Two years later, in 1922, at the American Historical Association meeting in New Haven he advocated that college courses be offered on Greater America. He had already established such a course at California in 1920. In a jocular address a few years before his death he said:

> I did not expect any students in such an unheard-of course and made no preparation for it. The first day 772 registered, to my dismay, and the second semester 1,248. There were no textbooks, no maps, no apparatus. That year I worked harder than ever. I spent day and night reading, made a day-by-day syllabus of one mimeographed page, drew maps on manila paper. . . . For a quarter century I lectured to more than a thousand students twice a week.

The course caught on so promptly with the undergraduate body "as to shift the whole structure of the department." In the years that followed, Bolton improved the teaching apparatus and in the early years of W.P.A. projects, he arranged for the preparation and drawing of a large collection of meticulously compiled maps which the Department of History at Berkeley still preserves.

In the syllabus Bolton carefully worked out for the course and later published, he deplored the distortion which resulted from "the teaching of national history alone" in the Americas: "The day of isolation is past. The increasing importance of inter-American relations makes imperative a better understanding by each of the history and culture of all."

Bolton also set forth what he considered another great advantage of the course on the history of the Americas:

> One shortcoming of the usual first-year course in United States history given in this country is that it covers essentially the same ground as the courses taught in the grammar grades and again in the high school. It lacks freshness. This element of freshness is admirably provided by a synthetic course in the history

of the Western Hemisphere in which the United States is put in a new setting.

The popularity of the course made possible the appointment of graduate students as "section hands," and thus attracted many to Berkeley for their advanced study. So many were drawn by Bolton's prestige and the possibility of a job that Bolton was honored with two collections of Festschrift essays, probably a unique distinction in the annals of history in the United States.

Historians recognized Bolton's achievements by electing him president of the American Historical Association; he was the first historian west of the Mississippi River to be so honored. Though he confessed to one correspondent that he was racking his brain "for something to say" in the presidential address, it is clear that "The Epic of Greater America" constituted his mature thought on "some of the aspects of Western Hemisphere history." In a letter to Guy Stanton Ford, who had been a fellow-member for two years of Frederick Jackson Turner's seminar at Wisconsin along with Carl Becker, Bolton explained that his interpretation of the role of the Spanish Borderlands was but a part of a larger concept. In an earlier paper at a Colorado conference he had "presented sharply the differences between the Spanish Borderlands and the heart of the Spanish empire, and then proceeded to interpret very broadly the significance of the borderlands in the contrasts and interrelations of Spanish and Anglo-American peoples in North America."

Now Bolton was moving on to a larger view. "The most expansive idea which interests me," continued Bolton in the letter to Ford written during the period when he was preparing his presidential address, "is the presentation of American History as Western Hemisphere History, instead of Brazilian History, Canadian History, or United States History. It is inconceivable that we should not have histories of Europe as well as histories of Germany, France, England, etc. It is just as absurd to assume that the Western Hemisphere has developed in isolated chunks and yet we in the United States have proceeded on that assumption."

Nor did even this "Epic of Greater America" concept absorb all of Bolton's thoughts in the spring of 1931. He also requested funds of the administration of the University of California for assistance in connection with his research on "a synthesis and interpretation of the history of Spanish North America. It will embrace the old administrative unit called New Spain, including the Isthmus, Central America, and the Northern Borderlands, from the discovery to the end of Spanish rule about 1822. I hope to do for New Spain what Parkman did for New France."

Bolton delivered his presidential address before the American Historical Association at Toronto in December, 1932, during the depth of the Depression, and followed Carl Becker whose 1931 presidential address on "Everyman His Own Historian" presented the practical idea that the past must be used for the purposes of the present. Charles A. Beard, who succeeded Bolton as president in 1933, also insisted in his address, "Written History as an Art of Faith," that history should be useful to society. The historian who studied the length of wigs in Restoration days or cotton prices in the Alabama of the fifties "would be a strange creature if he never asked himself why he regarded these matters as worthy of his life and labor." It is not surprising, therefore, to find that Bolton included political as well as academic considerations in his address. Speaking at a time when the Good Neighbor Policy was being developed, he again called boldly for a change in the method and teaching of history in the Americas. In his picture of new world events and personalities he almost succeeded in cramming into one long address the essential material in the year-long course he had been giving so successfully since 1920. To be sure, he included some doubtful history, too, for toward the end of the paper he sounded a Pan American political note: "The essential unity of the Western Hemisphere was revealed by the Great War. . . . It is a significant thing that all America, from the north pole to the south pole, was either on the same side of the great struggle or remained neutral. There was emphatic Western Hemisphere solidarity."

He also expressed the hope that his new synthesis would set in motion a host of researchers in the same way that Frederick Jackson Turner's thesis of the great role of the West had unleashed historians to work on frontier topics. The study of fresh and challenging aspects of Greater America would, moreover, rescue United States historians from their doldrums:

> A report by a recent committee of historians complains that many doctoral thesis subjects in United States history have been cultivated past the point of diminishing returns. A larger synthesis of American history, I am sure, would do much to relieve this rather pathetic situation. Who has written the history of the introduction of European plants and animals into the Western Hemisphere as a whole, or of the spread of cattle and horse raising from Patagonia to Labrador? Who has written on a Western Hemisphere scale the history of shipbuilding and commerce, constitutional development, arbitration, the effects of the Indian on European cultures, the rise of the common man, art, architecture, literature, or science? Who has tried to state the significance of the frontier in terms of the Americas?

Bolton also emphatically called for action: "It is time for a change. The increasing importance of inter-American relations makes imperative a better understanding by each of the history and culture of all. A synthetic view is important not alone for its present day political and commercial implications; it is quite as desirable from the standpoint of correct historiography."

An eye-witness account assures us that President Bolton made the rafters ring, without aid of amplifying devices, in the large Toronto hall where the members of the American Historical Association had gathered on foreign soil for the first and only time in its history. But he evidently did not convince many of his colleagues, either then or later, for they continued to teach American history in the traditional way. Though the lavishly illustrated textbooks they used usually began with the discovery by Columbus, the next event depicted in any detail was the landing of the Pilgrims from the *Mayflower*. Does this reflect what the theologians term "invincible ignorance" on the part of United States historians? As one professor of Latin American history has noted:

> Years ago I grew tired of being lectured to and being told that the Bolton thesis is pernicious by U.S. history colleagues who couldn't be sure of spelling Ecuador correctly or be quite sound on the question of whether Chihuahua is north or south of Tierra del Fuego. My crotchety character takes other forms too. After hearing a sweeping generalization about "American History" I'm apt to reply, "If you're referring to the history of the United States, as I presume you are, etc." It achieves nothing: I might as well try to alter the stars in their courses.

Or does the indifference derive from a deep-seated feeling in the United States that the *leyenda negra* was essentially correct, and that Edward Everett was right over a century ago when he looked south across the Rio Grande and could see nothing hopeful done for human improvement there? Perhaps the Alliance for Progress, in publicizing the economic difficulties of Latin America and in ignoring the advances made there, contributes today to this view.

Or are most of our undergraduate students essentially apathetic toward the study of international relations, as one investigator charges, and might this attitude have been engendered by the parochial, "patriotic," and nationalistic American history taught in our schools? Or did the reluctance of our universities and colleges to act on Bolton's advice to establish broad courses on the history of the Americas result from the essential conservatism of most of our academic communities where "the reform of a college curriculum has been compared in difficulty to the task of moving a graveyard"?

A historian must ask, finally, are there some sound reasons for refusing to lump together all the nations of the new world? The reception and discussion of Bolton's "Epic of Greater America," to which we now turn, will reveal that all these considerations--and others, too--are involved in the question: Do the Americas have a common history?

3. Discussions of the Bolton Theory

The first reaction to "The Epic of Greater America" was apathy and silence. Turner's frontier hypothesis had been accepted immediately "almost without critical test," and during the succeeding years had "inspired and been exploited in a multitude of tomes and monographs" by numerous scholars in American history who "with extraordinary industry and enthusiasm, and in great detail, have applied and tested it." If the Bolton Papers in the Bancroft Library are a true indication, little interest was manifested by Bolton's colleagues in his approach. Several historians wrote him to praise the address, but no more. If the peoples of the Americas do have a common history, their divergent intellectual development had apparently made them largely unaware of it so far as their historians were concerned.

Though undoubtedly skepticism was felt by some members of Bolton's audience at Toronto, the first public attack was mounted in January, 1939, by the philosophically minded Mexican historian Edmundo O'Gorman who deplored what he considered to be Bolton's emphasis on material progress and failure to reckon with "spiritual manifestations." Moreover the "larger historical unities and interrelations of the Americas" indicated by Bolton seemed to O'Gorman to be "unities which may be found in any group of men, simply because they have all been born and raised, they all eat and work. Larger unities, no doubt, but unities of Nature and not of human nature, which is the essence of history."

Bolton apparently chose to ignore the controversy which O'Gorman's attack set off, or he may have felt that he and the Mexican writer were talking about different things. All his life he "accentuated the positive," wrote reviews of contributions of other scholars with the greatest reluctance, and was, in the words of a long-time colleague at Berkeley, "straightforward, simple, and steadfast" in both his personal life and his historical labors. Once this colleague had shown to Bolton a document proving that one of the captains he proposed to write about had been a conniving scoundrel. Bolton "was a good deal shaken; the man had betrayed his trust; the planned volume was dropped. It was not in Bolton's nature to expose the rascal, but he would have no more to do with him."

O'Gorman's charge that Bolton did not appreciate the cultural elements in his history of the Americas must have wounded him to the quick, for he had always considered himself a true friend of Latin America who had tried to recognize its achievements. It may be that Bolton intended his article entitled "Some Cultural Assets of Latin America"--written in a highly laudatory vein and intended to impress an official State Department conference on cultural relations--to answer the criticism that he had no appreciation of the cultural development of Latin America. Bolton's original views became more accessible about the time of the conference, through the publication by his friend Professor William E. Lingelbach, one of the few colleagues who had sent letters of congratulations after his presidential address, of a collection of essays by Bolton called Wider Horizons of American History.

In 1939, the same year that O'Gorman's attack first appeared, support for the idea that the Americas shared a common historical experience came from an unexpected quarter--from the poet Archibald MacLeish, whom President Franklin D. Roosevelt persuaded to accept the direction of the Library of Congress. MacLeish had perhaps never heard of Bolton or read "The Epic of Greater America" but he had a feeling for the unity of America at a time when Europe was rushing toward war, and his participation in the discussion is a good illustration of the fact that the theme of the history of the Americas has attracted some non-historians. On October 12, 1939, MacLeish dedicated the Hispanic Room of the Library of Congress in words that might have been spoken by Bolton:

> We dedicate here a room and a division of the Library of Congress which has been set apart for the preservation and the study and the honor of the literature and scholarship of those other republics which share with ours the word Americas; and which share with ours also the memories of human hope and human courage which that word evokes--evokes now as never before in the history of our hemisphere. . . .
>
> America has shaped and qualified and redirected the lives of men living on her continents for four hundred years. But we who are born in America and live our lives here, have not very well understood our relations to these continents, nor our debt to them, nor in what way they have altered us and changed our bodies and our minds.
>
> From the beginning of the sixteenth century there has been accumulating on these continents a body of recorded American experience of the very greatest importance to anyone concerned to understand the American earth and the relations of that earth to the men who live upon it. Because this experience has been recorded in several languages and because it has been deposited in scattered places--places as far apart as Santiago de Chile and Bogotá and Buenos Aires and Mexico City and New Orleans and St. Louis and Quebec--because, furthermore, it has been overlaid with the continuing importation of European literature and European thought--for all these reasons the recorded American experience has not influenced the common life of the Americas as it should have influenced it. It has not been useful to an understanding of the Americas as it should have been useful.

As the war deepened in Europe, the discussion of hemispheric history continued to be related to contemporary events. At a conference on Inter-American Solidarity at the University of Chicago in August, 1941, the Cuban historian Herminio Portell-Vilá invoked the Cuban patriot José Martí to support his view that the Americas have much in common and that "it would be a great mistake for the two Americas to ignore any longer their common destiny." In December, 1941, shortly after Pearl Harbor, much attention was given to the theme at the annual meeting of the American Historical Association in Chicago. Jorge Basadre, the Peruvian historian, delivered a luncheon address on "The United States and the Disunited States" in which he declared that differences do not make for real disunity between North and South America. Many common forces are evident in the evolution of the American peoples, he felt, such as similar colonial divergences from Old World patterns, common immigrant traditions, formation of national consciousness, similar social ferments and political experimentations; and finally, "the same dangers, the same enemies, the same challenge, the same destiny."

The theme "Do the Americas Have a Common History?" was further investigated at this meeting by a panel of historians from Canada, Colombia, Mexico, and the United States. All agreed that, in certain respects at least, the Americas did have common experiences susceptible of synthetic treatment, excepting only Edmundo O'Gorman of Mexico who returned to the attack. Starting off with a quotation from the Mexican philosopher Antonio Caso that "History which generalizes is history which falsifies," O'Gorman himself went on to generalize as follows:

> Spanish colonization is animated by a medieval spirit; whatever it contains that is modern is a blemish in it. Anglo-American colonization is of pure modern inspiration; whatever it contains that is medieval is, in it and for it, an unjustified limitation. The Puritan, the man whose defect in his time was that of being too modern, saw in America, literally and vitally, a golden land of promise, of liberation; for the Spaniards, America is, without hyperbole, an unredeemed and black land, the vast empire of the Devil. . . .
>
> In my judgment, the profoundly important aspect of the problem which must be solved lies in the sphere of spiritual and moral forces. I believe that until now the relations between the two Americas have had as a basis a deep lack of comprehension, not in the purely intellectual sense, but a spiritual incomprehension which has originated from a mutual and reiterated ethical disesteem. Recall the extraordinary book of José Enrique Rodó, which, unjust or not, is a beautiful and facile expression of an authentic sentiment of the Hispanic-American creole soul. "Although I do not love them I admire them," says Rodó, directing himself to the Latin youth of the New World and referring to the North Americans. Do not let us forget either the brilliant José Martí, who notes as the greatest peril of "our America [the Latin] the disdain for the formidable neighbour who is unacquainted with it." And what should be said of the feeling Bolívar expressed in these words of his--"The United States, which seem destined by Providence to infest America with wretchedness in the name of Liberty?". . .
>
> There is no sense, then, in speaking of a "common history" of the two Americas, because either it is common history in the broad sense of being human history, and then nothing concrete is being said, or it is common history in the sense of some "great unities" based on some supposed resemblances and then it is fallacy.

The repercussion of this debate was not felt to any great extent in the Americas outside the United States. Historians in both French and English-speaking Canada seem to have preserved a complete silence, even though all four papers presented at Chicago were published in the Canadian Historical Review. One lone Argentine historian, Enrique de Gandía, who considered the dispute in 1941, saw weaknesses in the arguments of both Bolton and O'Gorman. A Peruvian Aprista leader, Luis Alberto Sánchez, does not even mention Bolton in his own "New Interpretation of the History of America" which appeared in 1943. Mexican intellectuals were similarly apathetic, and O'Gorman himself seems to have lost interest in the subject, since in his writings on historical ideas since his 1941 paper at Chicago he rarely refers to the dispute.

Even Bolton's students did not carry high the torch. When the second Festschrift volume, Greater America was published in 1945, one of its announced major purposes was to present "concrete evidence of Bolton's influence in creating a school of Western Hemisphere historians," and the 123-page bibliography of the writings of Bolton's students was described as "impressive evidence of his influence on his students, whose positions, productivity and wide geographic distribution insure the spread and perpetuity of the concept of Western Hemisphere history." But not one of the many contributors undertook to expound, analyze, or evaluate his concept.

The idea did not die, however, though it manifested itself in devious ways. Following the close of World War II there followed in Latin America one more "examen de conciencia" in which the theme of comparative colonization was as passionately debated as current political problems. As the Venezuelan historian Eduardo Arcila Farías showed in 1950, during the course of a lengthy and penetrating analysis, authors who engage in colonial comparisons usually have allowed their historical judgments to be influenced by the contemporary scene:

> It is currently asked why the United States has attained the immense development which today astonishes the world, while the majority of the republics of Spanish origin carry on a languid, anemic, lazy existence and appear to march wearily on urged by the whip of modern demands. The answer to so serious a question is always sought in one's own origins, frequently to fall, with a simplistic criterion, into the dangerous pit of racial prejudice. Or else the problem is reduced to solely a question of method.
>
> Had Spain copied the supposed Saxon "method," which never existed, the Central and Southern American republics would be as outstanding today as the powerful Northern State. And it occurs to very few to seek the causes in the original conditions of the old colonies and in their subsequent development as independent nations. . . . The immense and at times harsh differences that the observer finds between the peoples situated on either side of the Rio Grande have interposed themselves like a turbid mirror darkening the past.

Arcila Farías concludes by urging historians to recognize that many different types of colonial activity resulted from the diverse geographical and other conditions met by the colonizing powers and to avoid generalizations based on clichés deriving from political or religious biases. But he is not sanguine concerning the possibility of achieving this objective approach:

> For at stake are spiritual interests so diverse and sometimes so opposed that it is impossible to unite them. A Catholic will

always assert that Spanish colonization excelled over the Saxon insofar as the former brought Christianity to large human masses throughout the continent; the Puritans will maintain the same point of view, but in behalf of their religion. A third will say to these two that it is solely by accident that North America is Protestant and not Catholic. It will be a difficult task to convince Catholics to admit the superiority of Protestantism or vice-versa.

Contradictory opinions also circulated. José M. Gallardo had welcomed the Bolton approach, but emphasized the need to use literature as an important source, and the literary critic Samuel Putnam reported that he had successfully tested Bolton's idea in 1946 while teaching a comparative course at the University of Brazil on the literature of Brazil and of the United States. One recent literary historian, the late Stanley T. Williams, has greatly eulogized Bolton's productiveness and his idea, "which like some other theories of history can never be fulfilled." And William Z. Foster faithfully applied the Communist party line doctrine by declaring that Bolton's work "suffers from characteristic bourgeois shortcomings, distortion, and superficialities," although he concluded: "A general history of the western hemisphere as a whole has become very much needed now because of the growing attempt of United States' imperialism to reduce the entire hemisphere to the status of an armed, dominated, and thoroughly controlled Yankee hinterland."

As examples of the state of discussion in the United States twenty years after Bolton spoke in Toronto, three selections are given. Philip C. Brooks, who studied under Bolton, presents an analysis of the strengths and weaknesses of the ideas in the "Epic of Greater America," the economist Sanford Mosk enters the lists, and Arthur P. Whitaker holds in his exposition of "The Atlantic Triangle" that "the mystic notion of New World unity is less a help than a hindrance to the historian who seeks to record and explain the reality of American life." These views were drawn up just at the time when the History of America Program of the Pan American Institute of Geography and History began to get under way, and with this project the discussion enters a new and expanded phase.

4. The History of America Program

The Bolton theory was responsible, in part at least, for the History of America Program sponsored by the Pan American Institute of Geography and History. There was need for greater systematic knowledge in each American nation of the history of the other nations of the continent. Ignorance of each other's history had long been widespread in the Americas, as well as an intense nationalism, and misunderstanding existed even among the Latin American nations themselves. Some tended to look down on the people of other countries and sometimes referred to them as "tropical types." The Argentine jurist Carlos Calvo wrote to Bartolomé Mitre in 1864 that their country would surely settle accounts in due course with "that colossus with feet of paper, the Empire of Brazil." Similar unfavorable comments could be found in most countries about one or more of their neighbors. Such a climate of opinion was not conducive to even cordial relations much less understanding or appreciation of hemispheric history.

Part of the difficulty lay in ignorance of each other's history. Albert W. Bork emphasizes this when he declared: "Since 1804 when a

Compendio de la historia de los Estados Unidos (puesta en castellano por un Indio de la Ciudad de la Paz) appeared from the press of E. Pochard in Paris, there has been no very outstanding history translated and published in Spanish except Kirkland's [A History of American Economic Life]." Other reasons for the indifference to United States history in Latin America are pointed out by Ramón Ruiz who explains that resentment of United States treatment of such topics as the war with Mexico, and the conviction of Latin Americans that United States historians "are unable to penetrate the soul" of Latin America are also potent influences. Other explanations are given, too, but the result is that Latin American universities almost universally "ignore the history of their powerful and successful neighbor." One may add that Canada has shown only a faint interest in the history of Latin America, and that Spanish America devoted little attention to Brazilian history. Few historians in the Americas are familiar with the other cultural areas in the continent. It has recently been stated that "the Anglo-American historian is in many ways like the amateur genealogist, interested in his own racial past, but not interested in any part in which he cannot biologically share," and this generalization applies as well to many historians in other parts of the Americas.

Brazil is a special case, for her historians seem to take it for granted that Brazil is a country apart which has reached a greater maturity than Spanish America. Brazil avoided the long wars of independence and the subsequent civil commotions which so afflicted Spanish America, has not been a victim of oppressive dictatorships, recognizes no Indian problems, has a peaceful racial history, and is dedicated to seeking peaceful solutions for all problems. Moreover until almost the end of the 19th century Brazil was an empire and the republics in the continent tended to distrust her because of her different form of government. The result has been a kind of gulf between Brazil and other nations in the Americas.

Brazilians have often felt, therefore, that their historical development has been unique. As one prominent scholar wrote: "What is this 'North America' and 'South America' but purely geographical concepts? It is a pity that these terms as well as 'Latin America' are used to include Brazil which is quite distinct." The note that Brazilian experience in the New World has been something quite different from merely the history of Portuguese in America was early sounded in interpretations of Brazilian history. Carl F. Ph. de Martius, the German scientist who spent much time in Brazil in the 1830's, composed a classic paper on "How the History of Brazil Should Be Written" in which he set forth the concept so popularized today by Gilberto Freyre that the mixture of races in a new world was the unique contribution of Brazil to the world. This mixture must have been foreordained by God, Martius wrote in 1841, and he stated that one of the principal tasks of those who would write the history of Brazil would be to set forth the singularity of the conditions under which Indians, Negroes, and whites had met and intermingled there is a way unknown in previous history. This racial mixture might very well produce a sublime result--"uma nação nova e maravilhosamente organizada."

Brazilian historiography has also emphasized the links between Brazil and Portugal and their mutual opposition to Spanish America rather than hemispheric ties. In recent years Freyre has been proclaiming the existence of a somewhat mystical union between Portuguese and other tropical peoples--luso-tropicalismo--which further turns attention away from the American continent. And the present day movement in Brazil to establish an independent foreign policy with a special influence in such non-hemispheric matters as African development and opposition to nuclear weapons will be another influence to de-emphasize Brazil's role as simply a large nation in the new world. Brazil now is, or wants to be, a world power.

Even Brazil, though, has some part in the history of the idea that the Americas have a common history. The French-born Benedictine Frei Camilo de Monserrate proposed in 1856, while director of the National Library in Rio de Janeiro, that the history of all the American nations should be taught in Brazil, and stated that "the teaching of the national history cannot be complete except as parallel to the history of other American nations. Many problems in Brazilian history cannot be treated and resolved in a more or less definitive way without using data provided by the history of other countries of the New World."

The proposal did not prosper. Benjamin Franklin de Ramiz Galvão bitterly complained that the 1886 program for the teaching of Modern History included everything that agitated Europe from 1453 to 1859 but the American items were limited to the Independence of the United States and the War with Mexico. "Our Brazilian youngsters," he lamented, "are taught from a manual prepared in France, for French students, and according to French views. May these lines call from their lethargy our professors and instill in them the courage to edit a history adequate for the needs of an American people!" This passionate appeal also went unheeded.

Another indication of the way some Brazilians felt toward their Spanish-speaking neighbors and the United States can be seen from the sharp attack on the idea of fraternity in the Americas by Eduardo Prado in 1893. Writing during the early and agitated years of the Republic, Prado declared that the American fraternity was an illusion and that the fact that Brazil and the United States are found on the same continent is a geographic accident "to which it would be puerile to attribute an exaggerated importance. . . for we find ourselves separated not solely by great distance, but by race, by religion, by character, by language, and by the traditions of our people." As for the Iberian nations of America:

> there are more hatreds, more enmities among them than there are among the nations of Europe. . . . The disordered and horrible history of all these nations is a river of blood, a constant massacre. . . . The characteristic mark of all of them beyond the tragi-comedy of dictatorship, constituent assemblies, and insurrections which fill their existence is the ruinous state of their public treasuries. . . . The ministers of Finance of the Spanish-speaking republics, by means of loans which are never repaid, have extracted more money from European pockets than Europe ever obtained from the gold and silver mines of America.

The early years of the twentieth century saw some change, for Joaquim Nabuco was appointed the first Brazilian Ambassador in Washington and the Baron Rio Branco said some kind things about the Monroe Doctrine in 1908, but it would be a mistake to exaggerate the Pan American spirit in Brazil even then. There was still reserve in Brazil toward Spanish America, and Manoel Oliveira Lima's pioneer work on _The Evolution of Latin America Compared with That of English America_ (1914) did not lead to any consideration of hemispheric history as a whole. Only in 1931 was some limited attention given to the history of America in the secondary schools as a part of the educational reforms of Minister Francisco Campos. Finally, in 1939 by the establishment of Chairs of the History of America in the various Faculties of Philosophy, the subject was introduced to Brazilian universities.

Bolton's presidential address evidently did not reach Brazil, for there is almost no discussion of it by Brazilian historians today though many seem to be sympathetic to the concept without knowing it by name. Hélio Vianna of the University of Brazil published a statement in 1935 on "Bases sociológicas de formação americana," in which he insists that English, Portuguese, and Spanish-speaking peoples of America are fundamentally different from each other despite certain political and social similarities that can be found in their historical evolution. Later, however, in 1948, in commenting on the Argentine historian Enrique de Gandía's discussion of the Bolton thesis, Vianna believes it important to achieve "a continental sense" to protect Americans from disruptive forces arriving from Asia and Europe. Such a transformation can only come, he feels, from an exact understanding of America as a whole. Such an understanding will come more from an examination of original differences than from a search for similarities. He favors a realistic study to achieve a solid continentalism, and not one fostered by "americanistas de emergencia."

Though later research will doubtless present a more complete and accurate picture of the state of historical thinking and nationalistic feeling in the years before World War II, it seems clear that the historians of the Americas have had little opportunity to study each other's history, or to know each other. This situation was radically changed in the period after 1946, largely due to the work of the Pan American Institute of Geography and History through its History of America program, which proved to be a unique aspect of the development of the idea of hemispheric history. The concept underlying the Program was formulated at the first meeting of the Commission on History of the Pan American Institute of Geography and History at Mexico City in 1947 at the suggestion of Arthur P. Whitaker and Silvio Zavala.

The Institute, an inter-American governmental institution but working according to professional standards, had translated into Spanish Bolton's presidential address, had established in 1938 the Revista de historia de América to serve as a historical journal for all the Americas with articles in all four languages of the continent, and published a stimulating volume of Ensayos sobre la historia del Nuevo Mundo (1951).

Under the energetic direction of Silvio Zavala, President of the Institute's Commission on History, and with the strong support of Dr. Whitaker, a Program rapidly developed under Pan American Institute auspices which enlisted the support of several governments and the Rockefeller Foundation. As the "Introduction to the Project for a History of America" states, the collaborators were "to provide a pattern for a general history of America" but there was to be no attempt to impose one, or to write such a history. The historians drawn into this enterprise became aware that the objective of the project and possible means of reaching it underwent constant unplanned alteration, since the difficulties of cooperative work are well known and especially since the directors of the project made no attempt to arrive at agreement on basic assumptions. Each collaborator was given the utmost liberty, a circumstance which, as Ralph E. Turner points out in his "Comments", sharply contrasts with the kind of planned "scientific and cultural history of mankind" upon which UNESCO was then engaged.

The extensive correspondence and discussion that accompanied the development of the History of America Program constitutes one of the most valuable parts of the project. Historians in the past had found it difficult to find the funds for inter-American Congresses, and even those few that had been held, such as the ones at Rio de Janeiro in 1922 and at Buenos Aires in 1936, were relatively large gatherings whose objectives were partly ceremonial. Now scholars came together as small groups of professionals to discuss a carefully prepared program, and anthropologists were present as well as geographers and historians. Such meetings were held in several countries including Cuba, where dictator Fulgencio Batista provided all the necessary funds, with no strings attached, as a part of the José Marti centennial. Never before had United States historians been so exposed to the idea of hemisphere history, for the progress and problems of the Program were considered at length at no less than three annual sessions of the American Historical Association. Samples from the records of the 1952 and the 1956 meetings are given to provide a sort of laboratory view of how the experiment was conducted. Anyone who reads these documents carefully will find many of the topics included in the previous discussion of the Bolton thesis, although Dr. Zavala apparently never wished the Program to tackle this question directly.

5. What Resulted from the History of America Program?

What has been the result of this international exercise in historiography? Dr. Zavala lists the many publications issued, and has presented a concise review of the Program in "International Collaboration in the History of America."

One direct result has been to turn increased attention to studies susceptible of comparative treatment such as frontiers and religious developments. Another more indirect influence has been the increased interest shown by philosophers in the discussion of inter-American problems. At congresses of philosophers in Buenos Aires, New York, and elsewhere, the question of the unity of the philosophies of the Americas has been posed. Risieri Frondizi of Argentina believes that Latin America and the United States have a different historical past: "we speak a different language; we feel and think a different way; we have different ideals and aspirations; and so have a diversity of philosophical interests. Philosophers in the United States are concerned with questions of epistemology, methodology, semantics, and logic while in Latin America the central problem is man and his creation." Even in the face of such diversity as is to be found among Peruvian Indians, Brazilian Negroes, and Argentines of Italian descent, Frondizi believes that Latin Americans have a unity and differ from Americans of the United States, though the philosophic ideas of both originate in Europe. He feels philosophers in the United States to be abstract, technical, theoretical thinkers sealed away in ivory towers from their real world, while the Latin American thinker has "his feet firmly grounded in the cultural, social, and human reality in which he lives."

The Mexican scholar Leopoldo Zea, who has played an important role in the historical activities of the Pan American Institute of Geography and History, has emphasized the importance of the history of ideas for an understanding of the history of America. He stimulated a series of volumes on ideas in individual countries, established a *Revista de historia de las ideas* and has written extensively himself on the subject. He has never discussed Bolton's theory explicitly but he has given attention to those images Latin America and the United States have of one another which influence their thoughts and their actions. Latin America has been conscious of the presence of the United States in the continent, throughout its history; Zea shows how the United States "sometimes has been thought of as the expression of the spirit of all the liberties, at other times as the expression of the most crude materialism." The United States, however, has generally

> not been able to feel for Latin America any interest beyond the purely material one--the interest of a manufacturer in markets which furnish an easy outlet for certain products, or the interest of an industrialist in the raw materials which enable him to manufacture such products, or that of a financier who wants to broaden his field of speculation. . . . Little or nothing did each know of the spirit of the other. Ibero-America, feeling herself impotent in the field of the material, sublimated her impotence by considering herself the maximum expression of spirit in America, while assigning to North America a purely material role. For her part, North America saw in Ibero-America nothing but a group of half-savage tumultuous peoples, worthy only of despotic government.

This last remark demonstrates that, despite the passage of years since Edward Everett enunciated a similar view in Boston in the 1820's, the essential views of some historians have not greatly changes. When a Venezuelan composes an article on "La idea de la unidad de América," he is thinking only of Spanish America; when a Brazilian prepares a study on "Atuais tendências da historiografia brasileira," there is no mention of anything but strictly national themes; and when a United States historian presents a paper for the International Congress of Historical Sciences at Rome in 1955 on "The Central Themes of American History" he is referring only to United States history and chooses to limit himself to national topics. When historians gathered at the University of Texas in 1958 for the Second International Congress of Historians of the United States and Mexico scholars came from many countries, but none of them mentioned Bolton. The volume of the proceedings of the Congress is entitled *The New World Looks at Its History* (1963), but not one of the participants supported, refuted, or modified the ideas of Bolton on the history of America. The Spaniard Jaime Delgado goes even farther and, writing from a "Hispanist, Roman Catholic, anti-liberal point of view," maintains in his *Introducción a la historia de América* that the history of the United States has no place in American history, since its colonial period is a part of English history and its later times a part of universal history. For Delgado, the history of America is largely the history of Spain in America, though Brazil has a slight part because of its recent tremendous growth.

Silvio Zavala, director of the History of America Program, has concluded that inter-American unity is a complex phenomenon but believes that

> The American focus allows us to see an over-all picture of parallel colonial experiences. Although not always connected, they are the result of the expansion of various European nations during approximately the same moments in time, in geographic areas where some real connections were possible, and through forms of society and culture whose comparison, in their similarities and diversities, permits us to obtain a more complete knowledge of each particular colonization and region and ehlps to define the general outlines of the history of the hemisphere in this era, as well as its relations with the rest of the world.

Richard Morse has worked out a different focus, for he has set forth an analysis of the settlement of Latin America which

> hinges neither upon the national culture and traditions of the settlers nor upon a localized and culture-bound definition of a given New World "frontier." What is stressed is the process of change and innovation that affects any migration of people, whatever their cultural heritage and motivations, who venture forth from a mature society into an empty continent. Such a stress, it is felt, is the one most likely to yield fruitful hypotheses for a comparative history of the Americas.

Arthur Whitaker, one of the principal architects of the Project for a History of America of the Pan American Institute, believes that "In retrospect, Bolton's essay seems to mark the end of one period of historical writing rather than the beginning of another, and to express the political mood of romantic Pan Americanism associated with Franklin Roosevelt's Good Neighbor Policy." And he concludes:

> Despite several centuries of the common experience of development in a New World environment, the history of the Americas has so far successfully resisted the efforts of American historians to integrate it in accordance with the Western Hemisphere idea. Save in the political realm, the record of that experience is largely one which is held together either by the common ties of the Americas with Europe or else by the covers of a book.

A State Department geographer has even pointed out that there is no such thing as "the Western Hemisphere," except in a conventional sense.

Though it may be too soon to judge the full effect the Bolton idea has had on historians in the United States, the comprehensive guides on historiography by Michael Kraus and Harvey Wish indicate relatively little impact to date. Kraus gives a good general description, emphasizing Bolton's Spanish borderlands approach as a regional historian, Wish includes a brief paragraph on Bolton but does not refer to "The Epic of Greater America," while the British historian H. Hale Bellot writes: "The Southwestern and Californian school, of which the leader is Professor H. E. Bolton, working in an area in which the social foundations are Spanish, finds itself driven to make American history more than the history of the United States." We see, too, that the very detailed _Harvard Guide to American History_ does not refer in its copious bibliography to "The Epic of Greater America" or Bolton's _Wider Horizons in American History_. In the realm of teaching aids, three university textbooks have appeared but their sales are probably modest and they are largely used on the West Coast or the Southwest, as if to illustrate Bolton's remark in 1929:

> It is we in the borderlands who have the strongest historical bonds with our Latin neighbors. We of all North Americans best know and appreciate their brilliant minds, their generous hearts, and their delicate culture. We of all North Americans most prize the unmistakable Spanish touch which our fore-runners gave our once Spanish lands. It would be only fitting if we of the borderlands should be foremost in a fair-minded appraisal of our common historical heritage, foremost in the study of our common problems and foremost in making closer and stronger the bonds of true international understanding.

One of the few, perhaps the only, United States historian who has concerned himself recently with the theoretical problems involved in Bolton's concept is Edwin C. Rozwenc, who has stated:

> If America, as Henry Adams once observed, is primarily a vision, the time has come for American historians to investigate the web of values and beliefs that are related to the master myth which asserts the newness of America, the novel possibilities of American historical development. The influence of traditional ideas and institutions was very great in the minds and hearts of the Europeans who went to the New World, but the necessity of building a social fabric where no European society existed at all encouraged rearrangement of European ideas and practices. America is an extension of Europe, but its sense of the past and its vision of the future have been inescapably altered from the beginning.
>
> Moreover, if we are seeking to answer the question--What is America?--we must expand the area of our inquiry to include all of the cultures and countries which are embraced by the word America. Hence the symbolic meanings attached to the Virgin of Guadalupe are as important to our investigations as the symbolic meanings attached to "virgin land." In particular, historians in the United States must free themselves from excessive emphasis upon the agrarian primitivism of Turner.

6. Final Questions

In looking back on the discussion of "The Epic of Greater America" since Bolton first delivered it in Toronto, one wonders whether his central idea has been fully understood. William Binkley wrote in 1941 that critics of the idea fail "to understand that a synthesis does not necessarily tie the nations themselves together into a unified system, but that it is concerned, instead, with presenting a comprehensive view of the similarities, contrasts, and interrelations of their past experiences as a means of providing a basis for a clearer understanding of the local or national history of each of them."

Another question is whether Bolton was deliberately aiming to shock his distinguished audience of historians into thinking more broadly, which every teacher tries to do in one way or another; Bolton had been essentially a teacher from the day he met his first class in 1900 as Professor of Economics and Civics at the State Normal School in Milwaukee. And was he also trying to awaken historians to the importance of the rich and varied materials awaiting those willing to venture beyond the relatively narrow and well-worked field cultivated by scholars who limited themselves to United States history? All his life he poured over archival records, made long journeys over the rough terrain whose history he was describing, and encouraged students to do the same. The meager correspondence he preserved--he seems to have thrown away the bulk of it, and some of his most valuable letters were destroyed in the Berkeley fire of 1923--testifies to the fact that his graduate students who discovered an important document in a foreign manuscript collection reported it promptly because this was the kind of letter Bolton appreciated.

If Bolton were alive today, he might be surprised to see so much attention paid to his concept of Western Hemisphere history, for his emphasis had always been upon research and publication rather than ideas. For example, at the inauguration of the Institute of Jesuit History of Loyola University Bolton denounced "so-called histories of

America" in a ritual sort of way, but his speech devoted considerably more attention to advising the Jesuits to obtain money to organize their archives to make possible the preparation of solid historical monographs. He envisaged these studies as a "multitude of topics, biographical, regional, institutional, cultural, scientific, or whatever subject may commend itself. Books can be written on the Jesuits as explorers, geographers, cartographers, ethnologists, botanists, astronomers, linguists, _Américanistes_, historians, agriculturists, importers of European crops and domestic animals, founders of schools, colleges and universities, as architects, as musicians, as medical men, or as business managers."

Perhaps Bolton should be looked up to as essentially a stimulator of other scholars, despite his own massive contributions. And he preserved a puckish humor until the last, for one graduate student remembers him, aged about 80, giving advice like this: "Don't ever write a definitive work, young fellow; it kills off the subject. Leave a few mistakes and your students will have great fun catching up the old man."

One may also ask whether historians refused to accept Bolton's views because they fail to understand that he acknowledged differences in the Americas even though he did not judge it wise to emphasize them. In conversations with students and in the syllabus for his popular course on the "History of the Americas," he recognized these differences. In comparing Hispanic American revolutions with those of the English colonies he wrote: "In the two cases there were various similarities and many contrasts." But he chose to underline the similarities, doubtless because of so much previous emphasis on the gulf between the United States and the nations to the south. In the face of an almost solid phalanx of United States historians who had never visited Latin America, knew little Spanish or Portuguese, and still subscribed to many of the clichés of the "black legend" of innate Spanish cruelty, obscurantism, and failure, he chose to dwell on Spanish achievements; his fundamental attitude toward life was positive.

Bolton may not have stressed sufficiently that his approach appears to be most meaningful for the colonial period, and he waxed so enthusiastic about the Americas that he has been grouped with Charles Beard and other continental isolationists who flourished in the early 1930's. However this may be, there is no doubt that Bolton produced history that was read, and that he was a bold and imaginative force.

His ability to convey the hardships and the glory of the history of Latin America influenced another leader, Samuel Eliot Morison, to urge the example of Bolton as an inspiration for young historians in his own presidential address in 1950:

> The historical profession will have little use for timid pedants, whose ambition goes no farther than to get a firm footing on one of the lower steps of the academic escalator, proceeding painlessly from one professorial grade to another until overtaken by death and oblivion. It wants men and women of courage as well as of honesty and balance. A historical career can be a great adventure, and not in ideas alone; witness the lives of Bolton and Trevelyan, men who write history that sings to the heart while it informs the understanding. . . . We want more bold and positive characters to enter the profession.

If Bolton himself may have been partly responsible for the indifference of so many United States historians toward his views, can we not also ascribe part of their apathy to the kind of graduate training they received? Many historians believe their own training could have been sounder, and the American Historical Association itself has been sufficiently concerned to undertake an investigation of the problem. Typical of some of the criticism heard at present is the observation by Oscar Handlin, in the article referred to above, which is reminiscent of Bolton's strictures against the narrow outlook of United States historians:

> There is something pathetic about the Ph.D. dissertation, laboriously compiled, meticulous in its apparatus, factually accurate but intellectually arid, and generally marking the end rather than the beginning of a writing career. The qualities evoked by training toward these ends are not, however, such as in themselves to produce original scholarship. The ability to raise meaningful and unexpected questions, to exercise critical judgment in arriving at broad conclusions, and to discover relationships between the experiences of the present and the data of the past are not discouraged by the graduate schools and the profession in general; they are simply, and in the nature of the case almost inevitably, overlooked.

Or are the historians themselves the victims of a nationalism which in many colleges and universities manifests itself by courses on "American" history which are required of all students, so that most of our history departments are necessarily staffed to a considerable degree with those competent in United States history alone? It may be, too, that the present indifference to the Bolton theory is one more illustration of Roland Van Zandt's charge that "the American historical mind, traditionally empirical and anti-philosophical, has remained immune, in all substantial effects, to the great polemic of our time."

A final question might well be a political one, or one with the kind of political overtones that have been so often heard in discussions of the Bolton idea. Now that European discussions and maneuvers concerning the Common Market have revealed a disunited Europe, with many economic and political divergences deriving partly from history, will the thought of a common history of the Americas seem so far-fetched after all? Or, to raise a political issue on this side of the Atlantic Ocean, should we consider the opposition to the history of the Americas a Pan Latin American nationalism? The current wave of continental nationalism in Latin America merits careful consideration, and if it succeeds, "Nuestra America," so often celebrated in oratory, will speak --not English--but French, Portuguese, and Spanish.

Certainly we may hope that Bolton's proposition will be scrutinized more seriously in the future. Charles Beard's economic interpretation of the Constitution achieved greater notoriety than "The Epic of Greater America" on its first appearance, but it was 50 years before detailed studies were carried out along the lines suggested by Beard. Bolton's ideas may eventually be given a similar scrutiny, perhaps by someone who chances to read this book!

The purpose of this Introduction is to raise questions rather than to answer them, and to show that discussion of the complex issues involved in hemispheric history still continues. The glitter of Germán Arciniegas' brilliant prose sparkles over many of the problems, and the remarks by Charles Griffin in the concluding selection demonstrate that historians sometimes change or modify their opinions.

Historians are usually slow to change, however, Though some national professional associations meet in many different parts of the country, the American Historical Association--partly for the practical reason of size--usually holds its annual meetings in Chicago, New York, or Washington, D.C. A session is now scheduled, however, for San Francisco in 1965, thus fulfilling a dream cherished by the West Coast members since 1900. The Association has come together on foreign soil only once--in Toronto in 1932 when Bolton delivered his presidential address --and another session in Toronto is planned for 1967. If the Association ever goes to Mexico City we can be sure that the ideas expressed in "The Epic of Greater America" have at last begun to take root among historians in the United States.

CHAPTER 35.

IBERIAN CIVILIZATION IN THE OLD AND NEW WORLD

Norman F. Cantor had the imagination to invite historians to discuss with him their convictions and experiences. So it came about that we spent a day together in his home during which he asked me various questions, and I tried to answer them. He is a skilful editor, and *provocateur*, as the following record of our conversation demonstrates.

He prefaced our discussions with these words:

The Historiographical Context

The role of the Spanish and Portuguese peoples in overseas exploration, settlement, and empire building during the sixteenth century is one of the great achievements of European history, and one that has not been given its due in traditional historiography, particularly in the English-speaking world. Liberal Protestant historiography was more concerned to denigrate the Iberian achievement, when it did not ignore it, than to appreciate the magnitude of the task that the Spanish-speaking Catholics undertook and to examine dispassionately the qualities of the first important overseas European societies. Recent historiography, while not blind to moral failings of the Spanish-American empire, particularly its treatment of the native peoples and cultures, has taken a very different perspective on Iberian civilization in the Old and New World. We now recognize the political skill and military power of Spain and Portugal under Habsburg rule, and we are coming to appreciate both the governmental and cultural attainments of the Iberians in the New World. Furthermore, the disappearance of the European overseas empire in our own day has allowed historians to examine in a less partisan spirit the institutions and social structures of the Spanish- and Portuguese-American empires. In addition, twentieth-century experience with multi-racial societies and with the problems of the government and modernization of pre-industrial societies allows us to consider the history of Latin America from a fresh and highly relevant standpoint.

Norman F. Cantor, ed., *Perspectives on the European Past, Conversations with Historians* (New York: Macmillan, 1971), Part I, 322-343. Reprinted by permission.

Iberian Civilization in the Old and New World

Norman F. Cantor

What do you consider to be the most fruitful approach to the relationship between Iberian history and the history of Latin America?

Lewis Hanke

The best approach for an American is to stand in the New World and look at the history of the Iberian nations in Latin America. In the past, most historians have stood in Europe and studied the ideas, institutions, practices, and influences given by Europe to the New World. However, the manuscripts and publications upon which the story rests are to be found in the great centers of the New World as well as the European archives. The Archivo General de la Nación in Mexico City, the great archive in Buenos Aires, the national archive in Rio de Janeiro, and even archives in little-known towns are overflowing with material. In the sleepy little town of Sucre, in Bolivia, there is a remarkable collection of manuscript material and rare printed items on practically every aspect of the history of Spain in America. The material has been collected and organized by a Bolivian scholar with little material support from outside; he is one of the archival heroes encountered occasionally in that part of the world.

To understand Latin American history , one must go beyond the archives to appreciate what might be called the mestizo--the mixed race --complexion of New World history. I don't mean here the physical mixing of races, but rather that mixture of institutions and ideas which characterizes Latin American history. For example, in order to avoid manual labor in the silver mines, the Spaniards adopted an old Inca institution by which one seventh of the men in any village had to serve in the mines for a stated period of years. Thus they adapted for their own purposes an ancient local method of exploitation. The Spaniards also patterned much of their legal code in the New World after the code of the Incas. Francisco de Toledo, the greatest viceroy Spain ever sent to Peru, based his ordinances and much of his whole style of government on ancient Inca law. The mixture of men, of blood, of ideas and institutions, gives Latin American history its special flavor and meaning.

Does the history of Latin America exist as an entity--as a distinct subject?

It does in the United States and in certain other parts of the world. In Latin America they are inclined to consider all the countries together during the colonial centuries, but they see a rupture in this unity after about 1810, with the emergence of strong nationalistic feelings. After 1810 and the wars for independence, Argentine historians study Argentine history, Brazilian historians study Brazilian history, and so forth. However, a number of Latin American thinkers have recently been giving increasing attention to the problems of common background and common interest among their nations.

A certain unity is imposed upon Latin American history by the European heritage. The unifying effects of the European tongues--Portuguese in Brazil, Spanish throughout most of the rest of Latin America --can hardly be overestimated. Although the accents of the New World differ from those of the Old, the literature and history of the two worlds are parts of a total civilization which seems cohesive to me. Another important factor is the common religion. Although the number of Protestants in Latin America is increasing, and Jews have played an important part there since the sixteenth century, still the cast of civilization--the structure of society, the way people think and feel --is strongly colored by the Catholic faith. Then there is a vaguer set of circumstances concerning ways of life, how people look at things, what political theories appeal to them, and how they organize their families; all these things, I believe, were very much influenced by the European background.

The theme of revolt lends continuity to Latin American history: through the centuries, the Indians, the Negroes, and the _mestizos_ have risen up against oppression. The revolutionary movements of the nineteenth century were not isolated instances; revolution seems to be endemic in Latin American history. Today there is a new kind of revolution throughout the area--a revolt against tradition. There is enormous popular sentiment against the traditional, hierarchical Spanish-Portuguese way of life. Latin Americans blame this tradition--in which the many were exploited by the few--for their difficulties in entering the modern world.

Geographically, of course, there is unity in the great area of Latin America, which stretches from the Rio Grande to the southernmost tip of South America--an area so vast that all of Europe between Madrid and Moscow could lie in Spanish America and be lost. But what gives Latin American history its special charm is the variety of responses of its separate parts to the European heritage, and this variety may derive partly from geographical considerations. Geography, of course, is not just facts about rainfall and the length of rivers. We must seek to understand what the French call human geography--the study of the total influence of environment upon man. I think it was Schopenhauer or Nietzsche who said that Latin America would never be able to struggle to its feet because nature was so overpowering there. Latin American history offers historians an excellent opportunity to compare what two similar (but slightly different) nations achieved in an enormous area under similar (but slightly different) geographical conditions.

What special problems are involved in research in Latin American history?

To begin with archives: the amount of material left in Latin America by the Spaniards (who were bureaucrats _par excellence_) is staggering. Despite the popular image of the lazy Spanish-American, I don't believe that any other empire in history was as carefully constructed as the Spanish empire. When I look through the documentary records of this great work I am both exhilarated and depressed. I am exhilarated because I can go to the archives and find out the kind of instruments--the kind of shovel, the kind of seeds--taken by a colonizing expedition to America in 1519. I can find out when the ship sailed, how many mariners were on board, what was the captain's name. But I am a little depressed by the bulk and diffusion of the material.

The Spaniards were among the most historically minded people in the world. Columbus began the tradition of writing about the New World, and everybody followed him. The Spanish Crown stimulated the writing of history. I think until the Scottish Royal Historiographer was established in the eighteenth century there was no other European nation with official chroniclers; a system of historians for Spanish America was established by Philip II in 1572. Not only that, but the Spaniards seem to have invented the questionnaire about 1569 to expedite the administration of their empire. Questionnaires were filled out by every governor in the New World and returned to the Crown. The questionnaire of 1569 included about fifty questions: the kinds of

Indians in the town, their language, the prevailing winds, crops, local history, and so on. By 1601, this questionnaire had become a printed volume of three hundred pages. The royal government also commissioned ecclesiastical histories of the New World.

One can think of the historical documentation of the empire as in two parts: the records of the central government, and the local records, which are scattered all over America in local archives. Even Paraguay (today one of the poorest and most backward nations in Latin America) has a magnificent archive. In its capital city of Asunción, founded in about 1540, there is a splendid archive with manuscripts concerning territory now in Uruguay, Brazil, Argentina, Chile, Peru, and Bolivia. One of the tendencies of historians (and I'm glad to say we are now getting away from it) has been to emphasize the work of the central government--what the Council of the Indies disposed, or what the viceroy decided. If we are going to understand the social and economic history of Latin America, we must consult local archives, including municipal records and parish registers. In the colonial period, the parish registers recorded the ethnic origins of man and wife, which is helpful in tracing the slow emergence of the _mestizo_ race. When you combine the large and imposing central governmental records in Spain with the local records in America, you have a highly impressive body of historical documentation.

In dealing with all this material one must reckon with a set of prejudices. The Spanish and Portuguese tended to overemphasize and even distort what they accomplished in the New World; later on, when the Spanish-Americans and Brazilians became independent, they tended to underplay the achievements of the mother countries. Written history has been affected by these fundamental prejudices, which we describe as the _peninsular_ and the _creole_ attitude: the attitude of the Spaniard or Portuguese with wealth and an important office versus that of the colonial--born in the New World--for whom opportunity and riches were not so readily accessible.

In the nineteenth century, and more particularly in the twentieth, there has been an attempt to bring the Indian into Latin American history. History is usually written by conquerors--one does not find much documentation by the conquered. It is difficult to find out just what the Indian people thought of their conquerors, although anthropologists and others have made significant contributions to this question in recent years. Social scientists have made it clear that the mass of people in Latin America have not shared in Iberian civilization; indeed, one sociologist has said that at least half of the people in Latin America today make their living from the land, and that the majority of them are using instruments and methods which are no more advanced than those used by the Egyptians at the dawn of history. This may be one of those grandiloquent phrases enunciated by sociologists, but it certainly is true that life is crude in the rural provinces of Latin America. Historians have learned from social scientists to question the traditional elitist approach to Latin American history, which emphasized the dominance of Spanish institutions in the New World.

One of the major problems of historians of Latin America is economic, of course, and Latin American historians have had to struggle against their environment. In both Brazil and Spanish America the collection, decipherment, and publication of any material requires an heroic effort. There has been little government help for historians in most parts of Latin America, and historians from outside Latin America simply do not have the instruments--bibliographies, for instance--which historians of Europe or the United States take for granted. Thus we have documentary problems, problems of diverse interpretation, and a very unequal development of the apparatus of scholarship. If you are looking for problems, we have them.

<u>What is the condition of the archives in Spain itself today?</u>

In terms of protection and organization, they are in excellent condition. There is a great deal of material, and there are archival guides to important collections. I am thinking not only of the great archives of Seville but also of the colonial archives in Lisbon and the great national library of Madrid as well as the great collection that was formerly the king's private library. France V. Scholes and I were apparently among the first historians to go through this library fairly systematically--that was under the Republic, in 1933, when any historian could use the library. We discovered then that it held a tremendous wealth of material.

In Spain the archives are generally accessible, but in Portugal the ancient, exclusivist attitude still exists. Even back in the fifteenth century, when the Portuguese were making their great explorations and discoveries, they did not publish their materials but kept everything to themselves--and to some extent they still do. It is possible to get into the public archives if you are an historian, but to get into the private collections is very difficult.

Another aspect of the European archives is that just as Peruvian silver traveled all over the world, so the manuscripts concerning Latin America have strayed far afield. For instance, the first volume or so of the municipal records of La Paz, Bolivia, are in the British Museum! These manuscripts traveled because certain ambassadors had acquisitive instincts, or visitors saw manuscripts neglected and brought them home to be preserved, or archival material was captured by conquering armies. Nobody really knows all the reasons why manuscripts move, but they do, and Spanish manuscripts have moved a great deal.

<u>Who are the most important historians of Spain, Portugal, and Latin America--those who have shaped our understanding of the development of Latin American civilization--and of the main historical trends and interpretations?</u>

If I confine myself to the twentieth century, I would begin with Rafael Altamira--the man who first acquainted Spain with the need to study the history of Spanish America. After the Spanish-American War of 1898-1900, a famous generation of philosophers and thinkers speculated about what had gone wrong: Why had Spain lost the war? One explanation was the Spanish indifference to their true historical experience. Altamira established the first chair of Spanish-American history in Spain in about 1906 or 1907--rather late, considering how long Spain had been in the New World and the magnitude of the Spanish achievement there. Altamira worked hard and got his students interested, and they produced imaginative and broad-ranging studies and research projects, elevating the level of the doctoral dissertation in Spain and assuring the continuation of Altamira's work through successive generations of historians.

Altamira understood law as an integral part of the structure of Spanish life--not as a rigid external structure, but as the core of social life. He emphasized the administrative decentralization of Spain in the New World. To study the laws of the Indies and the ordinances devised by Spain to govern American political affairs, ecclesiastical affairs, mining regulations, and maritime activity was not enough: Altamira believed that one must find out how the Spanish laws were applied in the different provinces of the New World, how the different ways of life in the various provinces influenced the Spanish laws. The <u>enco-</u>

mienda, for example--the system through which the Spanish government (from shortly after Columbus until the early eighteenth century) rewarded conquistadores by allowing them to exact services and tribute (not land) from a certain group of Indians--was not a uniform system throughout Spanish America. The encomienda in Chile was quite different from the encomienda in Venezuela. Only recently, during the last ten or fifteen years, have scholars in the various countries been studying local records to apply this basic concept of administrative decentralization.

Another man I admire greatly is Jaime Vicens Vives in Barcelona, who died in 1960. He was not primarily concerned with Latin America (his field was the place of his native Catalonia in the general history of Spain), but his high standard of bibliography influenced Spanish historiography. His Index of Spanish History was established in 1955 and has continued since his death to be the best available annotated bibliography of Spanish-American history.

It is difficult to mention any one Portuguese scholar as the leader in the study of Brazilian history. Portuguese scholars tend to look upon Brazil as only one part of their larger empire--Cabral, after all, was going to India when he happened to discover Brazil. Perhaps the name of Karl von Martius--a scientist and a foreigner--should be mentioned here. Von Martius was in Rio in 1838 when the first historical society was established in South America, and he won a prize in 1839 for his essay on how the history of Brazil should be written. Von Martius was a German--not a Portuguese or a Brazilian--but his essay seems to me the starting point of Brazilian historiography. Von Martius believed that the distinguishing characteristic of Brazilian history is the way in which the Portuguese, the Indians, and the Negroes have mixed and developed. He also emphasized the geographical dimensions and variety of Brazil, from the Amazon in the north--that river which is really a moving lake on which oceangoing vessels can travel for two thousand miles--to the southern plains, which resemble the plains near the Rio Grande.

The work of the Brazilian historian Gilberto Freyre was brought to the attention of English-speaking readers by Alfred A. Knopf in New York long before there was any boom in Latin American studies. Freyre's The Masters and the Slaves is perhaps the most widely read book on Brazilian history in the United States and in Europe. Freyre, I believe, gave substance to Von Martius' idea of the history of the Portuguese in Brazil as the history of the mixing of races, especially as this mixing took place on the fazendas--the great plantations.

We might emphasize here the importance of the fazendas in Brazil, especially in the northeast where sugar was raised. Like the English gentry, the Portuguese lived on the land. They controlled the people on their land in a feudal, despotic way, according to Freyre. Even the Church was subject to the master, since the priest usually was a younger son or a nephew. In this, Brazil was quite unlike Spanish America, in which the old Spanish urban tradition thrived. Spaniards were town people who established towns all over their new world, but the Brazilian gentry lived on their land.

Freyre's work gave a special character to our thinking and writing about Brazilian history. His was a broad-brush treatment (only recently has the archival and monographic history to which we are accustomed been established in Brazil) which emphasized the way in which the owners of these great fazendas raised large numbers of children--some legitimate and some not--and established a racial basis for Brazilian society. It should be said that Freyre developed some of his ideas on racial aspects of history while he was a graduate student at Columbia University in the early 1920's, where he studied with Giddings, the sociologist, Franz Boas, the anthropologist, and the historian James Harvey Robinson.

A third historian I should mention is Ricardo Levene of Argentina, who was both an historian and an entrepreneur of history. He taught for many years, published documents and popular histories, and it is said that even Juan Perón was one of his students. He was devoted to the care and support of the documentary archives and was able to find funds for their support, with the result that Argentina has a remarkable collection of guides to municipal and provincial archives. Another Argentinian--a contemporary of Levene's--was Emilio Ravignani, who directed the best historical review in Latin America. He also sent representatives to Spain to copy documents on every aspect of Argentine history. There is no one in Argentina today--or indeed in South America--who can compare with these men; we are still suffering from the effect of Perón and later dictatorships on the university tradition.

Mexico is another great center for history, and here I would mention particularly Silvio Zavala and Edmundo O'Gorman of the University of Mexico. These men are at opposite poles in historical interpretation, but each one has made an important contribution toward focusing ideas and publishing documents on Mexican history.

The Chilean José Toribio Medina, who almost never left Santiago, published between two and three hundred volumes of documents and bibliography. His outstanding work was bibliographical: for instance, he published eight volumes listing all the books published in Mexico in the colonial period. This was more than a mere catalogue: he made a study of each author (often based on Spanish manuscripts) and an analysis of the contents of each book. He noted where copies of each book could be found and added other useful information. Medina set up and printed his own books, with the help of his wife, and they worked day and night. I don't know of any historian or bibliographer who comes near him in accomplishment.

Today, as never before, professional historians are at work in Latin America, and they are more open to the currents of the world, more conscious of the standards of scholarship, and more determined to achieve standards which will be recognized in other parts of the world. There is even a rather interesting group of Marxist historians in Latin America. Some are mere party liners, but others are something more. I should mention Germán Carrera Damas of Caracas, the author of the monograph The Cult of Bolívar. This is worthy of special notice because the Spanish-Americans rejected Spain and everything to do with Spain after they won political independence, and they sought what historians call a usable past. In the nineteenth century there grew up a special emphasis on the revolutionary period and the revolutionary heroes--Simón Bolívar, José San Martín of Argentina, Morelos and Hidalgo of Mexico. This "usable past" got out of hand, to the point where supporters of San Martín as a hero didn't like Bolívar, and vice versa. When then Spaniard Salvador de Madariaga, now of Oxford, wrote about Bolívar in a patronizing, peninsular fashion, the Venezuelans rose up in wrath and even passed formal resolutions in the Academy of History in Caracas against de Madariaga and his nefarious interpretation of Bolívar. The shadow of Bolívar still hangs over every historian in Bolivarian countries--in Venezuela, you have to write first about Bolívar or you are not an historian. Carrera Damas has published some chapters from his monograph in reviews and has received angry, insulting letters, but he is going to publish his volume of Bolívar anyway, and that takes courage. Perhaps we will see the shadow of Bolívar lifted from Latin American history.

<u>Have there been English and American historians who have made significant contributions to Iberian or Latin American history?</u>

We must certainly mention William H. Prescott, who decided back in Boston in the early 1840's that he was going to devote his life to the story of the conquest of Mexico and the conquest of Peru. It was fortunate for the United States that there were two great historians of that era: Francis Parkman, who turned the attention of his readers to the north--to the Jesuits, to the French in Canada--and Prescott, who described the glorious exploits of the <u>conquistadores</u>. Americans were very chauvinistic in the 1850's; they were not really interested in anything except the expansion of their own continent. These men helped to mitigate the parochialism of Americans, and they were great popular writers--best sellers.

After Prescott I think of Hubert Howe Bancroft, a California businessman who produced thirty-nine volumes on the Pacific basin and collected a great library which is still the nucleus of the Bancroft Library at the University of California at Berkeley. Bancroft invented oral history back in the 1880's (long before Allan Nevins developed it), and he had people go out to interview elderly citizens who remembered the old Spanish Empire in Mexico. His work is still a valuable, connected story of the great West Coast from Alaska to Panama.

In 1895 Bernard Moses gave the first course on Spanish-American history at Berkeley, and if you believe as I do that the history of Latin American civilization should be taught--not because of the Good Neighbor Policy or because of Latin American Communism but because it is an important part of the history of mankind--then you must go back to the man who established the first course. Just before the Spanish-American War in 1898 Moses told a meeting of teachers that we must cultivate the neglected half of American history--by which he meant the part which had to do with Spain and Portugal. He pointed out that we could learn something from our enemy (this was on the eve of war), that a knowledge of Spanish culture would help us to discover that there are other civilizations than our own. In this attitude, Moses was a pioneer in this country.

Among more recent historians of Latin America I should mention Henry C. Lea of Philadelphia, who devoted much of his life to a monumental history of the Inquisition--a landmark in ecclesiastical history. Roger Merriman of Harvard wrote a four-volume work. <u>The Rise of the Spanish Empire in the Old World and the New</u>, which is still a standard work. Its first two volumes (particularly Volume I on the medieval period) are not up to the standard of the last two, particularly Volume IV, which presents a masterful synthesis of the intricacies of European diplomacy in the time of Philip II. John Elliott, the young man who has recently gone from Cambridge to the chairmanship of the history department of King's College in London, is more than just a promising member of the new generation of historians. His is the most solid work we have on the revolt of 1640 in Catalonia. We should also mention John Parry of Harvard, and Pierre Chaunu, the young French scholar who with his wife Huguette has published a nine- or ten-volume work on the economic history of Spain and Spanish America in the sixteenth and seventeenth centuries. John Lynch of the University of London has contributed to our knowledge of both Spain and Spanish America.

<u>Can we view the history of the Iberian Peninsula and of Latin</u>

America as part of the general history of Spanish and Portuguese civilization?

I think we must. The medieval Iberian background is a vital and indispensable element of the history of Latin America. As Charles J. Bishko has emphasized in his work on the history of Spain and Portugal, the influence of these countries is a continuing influence in the modern world; for example, the greatest intellectual migration to Latin America came about as a result of the Spanish Civil War, at which time a number of important scholars, historians, and artists left Spain for the New World. I have mentioned Rafael Altamira: he was one of this group. Through the years, with or without political connections, Spaniards read the poetry and prose produced in Spanish America, Brazilians were in touch with what Portuguese were doing, and vice versa. Spain and Spanish America, Portugal and Brazil, form a cultural whole, and many Spanish-Americans and Brazilians studied in Europe and published their works in Europe.

There are changes in influence, of course. In Brazil today you will not find much sympathy for Portugal. As a matter of fact, the school headed by the historian José Honório Rodrigues believes that Brazil must develop a wholly independent foreign policy, independent of the United States and of Portugal. Increasingly, the younger scholars in Brazil are unwilling to support Portuguese policy in Africa. Thus far--or until recently--Brazil has not opposed outright any Portuguese policy, but there is a growing number of scholars who want to cut the umbilical cord. In spite of them, however, Portuguese and Spanish connections have been maintained with Brazilians and Spanish-Americans since the sixteenth century, and they are still important.

Did medieval Iberian history play a role in the history of Latin America, and what was its legacy?

Roger Bigelow Merriman made the striking statement that the history of Spain in America began in a cave in Covadonga. He meant, of course, that it began at that moment in 716 when the Spaniards first began to push back the Muslims. The famous *Reconquista* began in the cave of Covadonga in northern Spain and culminated at Granada in 1492 with the final expulsion of the Muslims. During this period Spain developed a head of missionary steam--a warlike attitude, a depreciation of Muslim culture, and an insistence on a unified, integrated culture of its own--which accounts for its warlike attitudes after 1492 and for the insistence that Moors and Jews and converts should not go to the New World. I've often wondered whether the Muslim theory of a just war with missionary connotations was absorbed by the Spaniards during the medieval period.

Medieval Iberian institutions had an important influence on the development of Latin America. We think particularly of the *encomienda*, the institution by which Indians were required to give service and tribute to certain Spaniards. The *encomienda* was developed in medieval Spain to reward those who supported the war back of the battle lines. Knights and others were given grants of land, sometimes grants of people, and (what they never got in the New World) jurisdictional power over groups of people as the battle line advanced. In America the institution was modified by American conditions and attitudes. The *encomenderos* never got jurisdictional rights because the Crown was always fearful that they would rebel so far away from royal authority and then there would be a new group of nobles to put down, just as Ferdinand and Isabella had to put down the Spanish nobles. Another medieval institution was the *residencia*, that system by which Spaniards always had a final judgment on royal officials. The viceroy had to stay at his post, and anybody who wanted to complain about him or his activities could do so. These residencia records became an important part of the documentation of the Spanish work in America.

In Portugal, things were not so closely organized as in Spain. The Portuguese never developed any council for Brazil comparable to the Spanish Council of the Indies. Portugal never had official historians for Brazil; they kept their activities quiet. But we are told by Gilberto Freyre that during the medieval period Portugal developed a certain kind of toleration which gave a special note to Brazilian history. There was a favorable attitude toward mixing with people of different color because for a while Muslims of different color had been the lords in Portugal, and during the medieval period dark-colored women came to be preferred over others. Freyre says that the racial democracy of Brazil had its origins in the mixing of peoples in Portugal under special conditions in the Middle Ages. Today anthropologists and others insist that the "racial democracy" of Brazil must be closely examined, and some of our anthropologists do not share Freyre's rhapsodic view of the situation in Brazil. However, it is obvious to anyone who has visited Brazil that there is a special kind of relationship between the races there, and Freyre and others say that this goes back to the medieval period.

What was the structure of government and society in the Iberian peninsula at the end of the fifteenth century?

Ferdinand and Isabella were firmly in control at the end of the fifteenth century, and Spain was ready for empire. The king and queen had put down the rebellious nobles; Spain had developed legal institutions under lawyer-type officers loyal to the Crown; it had a unified, hierarchical social structure. In August 1492, Columbus set forth from Palos in southwestern Spain, and in April of that year Granada fell to Spain, liberating the military and ecclesiastical forces for use in the New World. A third important event of 1492 was the publication of Antonio de Nebrija's Grammática Española, the first organized grammar of any European language. When it was presented to Queen Isabella, she said, "What's this book good for?" and one of her courtiers is supposed to have replied: "Sire, language is the instrument of empire." At the very moment, then, when Spain had a unified monarchy, its nobles in order, and its Church under the domination of the Crown, the Spanish language was developed as an instrument of colonization. The Spanish empire exists still wherever Spanish is spoken--wherever people are influenced by the art and philosophy which come to them through the Spanish language.

Sixteenth-century Spaniards also made an unprecedented attempt to study other languages and other cultures. When Nebrija's pupils got to the New World they threw themselves into studying its languages because they realized they could not convert Indians unless they could reach them in their own tongues. The vocabularies and grammars of the Indian languages prepared by Spanish priests--mostly in the sixteenth century --comprise a great corpus of philological material. Bear in mind the great variety of Indians in the New World: a modern anthropologist has said that even today, more separate languages are spoken by the Indians in an area of fifty square miles around the Isthmus of Tehuantepec in Mexico than in all of Africa south of the Sahara.

Not as much is known about Portugal in 1500; the heroic figure of Prince Henry the Navigator has overshadowed the study of the late medieval period. However, the situation is similar to that of Spain in that Portugal was an expanding nation, ready to take on new activities. In Portugal as well as Spain there had been a reform movement in the Church and the monasteries in the latter part of the fifteenth century, and the young friars who went out to the New World were influenced by reforming zeal as well as Nebrija's linguistic rules.

I would like to ask one question here: Why was there such a desperate effort to Christianize the Indians and not the Negroes? Missionary work went on among the Indians during the 1520's and 1530's, and the forties and fifties, when Luther had split Europe asunder. Contemporary writers pointed out that Cortez and Luther were supposed to have been born in the same year--one, they said, to split Christendom apart, and the other to make possible the development of a New Jerusalem with no troublesome Protestants. All this would come about if they could speak to the Indians and make them Christians. There was a passionate and very well organized ecclesiastical movement to win over the Indians so that the seamless web of Christendom could be woven again in the New World.

The missionaries did not only learn languages in the New World; they also studied Indian cultures. The first modern anthropologists were Spanish friars. The greatest of them was Bernardino de Sahagún, whose impressive work was written in the Aztec language in the sixteenth century and is just now being made known to the English-speaking public. Sahagún decided that in order to Christianize the Indians he needed to know everything about them--their feasts, their educational methods, their gods, everything--and he spent two years in one Indian village and then went on to another, questioning everything. This was the greatest concerted, organized effort up to that time to learn about the culture of another people.

What are the differences between Spanish and Portuguese colonies with respect to the pattern of settlement and government?

We must remember, first of all, that Brazil was never the center of the Portuguese empire as Spanish America was the center of Spain's; it was always, to some extent, a marginal land--even after sugar was developed in the seventeenth century and gold was discovered in the late seventeenth and eighteenth. Second, Portugal was never as administrative-minded as Spain. Portugal did not establish a Council to the Indies until the period between 1580 (when Philip II took over Portugal and its dominions) and 1640 (when the Portuguese were "liberated" from Spain). For those sixty years Portugal and Brazil were dominated by Spain, and there was an attempt by the bureaucratic Spaniards to organize Portuguese imperial institutions. They got them to organize a Council to India (which included Brazil) but there was never the same kind of corpus of laws and ordinances for Brazil that there was for Spanish America.

Patterns of settlement were dissimilar, too. In the early years the Portuguese gave great quantities of land to important Portuguese, but this was done only very rarely by the Spaniards. True to their administrative genius, Spain had from the very earliest days a carefully devised set of ordinances for every town. Shortly after Cortez conquered Mexico City, while the ruins of the ancient Indian capital were still smoking, a geometer walked in the ruins and laid out the avenues of Mexico City. The great law of 1573 provided a very careful plan for the settlement of towns in the New World. The land had to be high enough to avoid disease; the streets to be laid out in such a way that the winds would blow through properly; the plaza to be big enough to hold a bullfight or a procession. The church was to be on a certain side of the plaza, the town council on another. Everything was regulated in Spanish America; in Brazil, not at all. The streets go every which way, like those of medieval towns. The Portuguese stayed out on their fazendas with their slaves and their large, loosely organized families; they visited the towns only occasionally and took little pride or interest in them.

Moreover, no books were printed in Brazil during the whole of the colonial period. Think of the hundreds, the thousands, of Spanish publications which José Toribio Medina located and recorded in his great bibliographies. There was nothing like that in Brazil, nor was any university founded there, although the University of Mexico and the University of San Marcos in Lima were established by royal order in 1551. The Portuguese were not even much interested in keeping their new land free of heresy. They did not extend the Inquisition to Brazil, and many Jews and others went to the New World. When you compare the Spanish work in Spanish America to the Portuguese work in Brazil, you see that despite the common heritage--in religion, in institutions, and in medieval background--there were enormous differences in the organization of the empires.

What was the impact of America on the Iberian states and societies in the sixteenth and seventeenth centuries?

Ever since the publication of Earl J. Hamilton's classic work of thirty years ago on the rise of prices, we have known that inflation was an important effect of the influx of silver and gold into Spain and other parts of Europe. Although Hamilton's work has been criticized in recent years, I tend to believe that no one as yet has shaken Hamilton's basic thesis. The new wealth also gave to the kings of Spain a remarkable degree of independence from their parliament. In this period parliaments in certain countries were becoming more restrictive of the Crown, but not in Spain or Portugal. The money from the New World may not have been as important in percentage as people once believed, but still it was free money. The Crown got one fifth (the royal quinto) of all the silver and gold from America, and the king could dispose of this as he saw fit. The outstanding economic historian of Spain, Ramón Carande, whose fundamental work on Charles V and his bankers is one of the notable economic works of this century, has said that the king actually got more money from parliament and from the Church than from the New World. Even so, he did not have to ask for the new money, and he could spend it as he liked--against the Protestants, the Turks, the French--which gave the Spanish Crown a special dimension of independence or irresponsibility.

The influence of America on Europe is a difficult subject; it has not been sufficiently studied to draw any far-reaching conclusions. The newly rich Americans who came home and built imposing houses or churches in small villages (these are still visible today) must have had an effect on Iberian mores, but we have no documentation. New World themes were not much used in art, surprisingly; one would expect that the dramatic nature of the conquest and the new wealth would have been expressed in artistic motifs. On the whole, this is a subject on which we need more investigation.

Looking at the sixteenth and seventeenth centuries as a whole, how did the Iberian peoples deal with the problems arising from multiracial societies?

Very few women accompanied the conquistadores in the first years of the sixteenth century; the conditions of life were too hard. Thus there was mixing from the beginning between Spaniards and Indian women --we have good records on this. We know also that there was a Spanish policy in the early years of marriage to the daughters of Indian caciques (chieftains) so that the Spaniards would win property and position through marriage. In Peru we find the same thing--some of the Spaniards married Inca princesses. Some of them lived with Indian women and did not marry them; back in the early part of the sixteenth century we find am ambivalent attitude toward marriage. As the years went by, many children were born of mixed marriages and many more were born illegitimate, and there grew up a group of mestizos who were looked down upon for their illegitimacy. Often their fathers left and the Indian mother had to bring up the child alone. Some attempts were made to help them --the Crown established a special school for mestizo orphans--but there was growing prejudice, too, to the point where mestizos were not able to get important government positions and generally were not allowed to enter the religious orders. Salvador de Madariaga believes that part of the turbulence of the New World is derived from the resentment of the mestizos toward their white fathers. Mixing went on through the whole colonial period, and the mestizo society grew porportionately larger as many Indians died of disease and overwork. In the eighteenth century, despite some liberal regulations and a few changes, it was increasingly difficult for an Indian or a Negro to get a position or to go to a university.

The Spanish-American Indians had notable defenders, beginning with Bartolomé de Las Casas, the Dominican friar who attempted to protect their lives and property from the Spaniards. In Portuguese Brazil there was no great struggle on behalf of the Indians except when António Vieira, a Jesuit and one of the great figures of the seventeenth century, worked on their behalf. He was a great preacher and a diplomat of considerable power in Europe, and he had ideas on developing the Portuguese economy by incorporating conversos (new Christians) into Portuguese life. He opposed the Inquisition and defended the Indians, but not the Negroes.

One of the great mysteries of history is why the conscience of the Spaniards and Portuguese twinged more easily on behalf of the Indians than that of the Negroes. One explanation is that the Iberians had been accustomed to Negro slaves in Europe, and their consciences had thus been blunted. Also there was the tremendous desire of the priests to win the Indians for Christianity in order to build a new Jerusalem without Protestants.

In the seventeenth century there were two or three interesting Jesuit defenders of the Negroes, but there were not battlers like Las Casas. One was Alonso de Sandoval, who pointed out that some of the Negro slaves were Muslims who could read and write Arabic and were intellectually superior to their masters. He pointed out that they came from different cultures, different tribes, different parts of Africa, and he advocated the establishment of a school to study African culture. Sandoval was the first Africanist, but neither he nor any other Jesuit defender of the Negroes intended that they should be freed. They believed that the Spaniards should treat the slaves justly and kindly, that they should be Christianized, but that was all. This was not at all the idea expressed by Las Casas in 1550 when he said at Valladolid that all the people of the world are men, and opposed the Aristotelian doctrine of natural slavery. Valladolid was one of the great moments of Western history, but a new atmosphere took over in the seventeenth century. The sixteenth century was a great period of expansion, when all kinds of ideas were expressed and all kinds of hope appeared. The seventeenth century settled down to what some historians call the colonial siesta, but all through these centuries the quiet revolution of blood relationship continued, making Latin America the social and economically turbulent part of the world it is today.

<u>What is the general significance of the year 1550 for the history of Iberian civilization?</u>

The disputation in 1550 and 1551 between the Spanish Dominican Bartolomé de Las Casas and the Spanish Renaissance scholar Juan Ginés de Sepúlveda was one of the great moments in the history of mankind. It illustrates the influence of events in America upon the course of affairs in Europe and in the world. The disputation was held because the king and his council had received various letters charging that the Spaniards were cruel and unjust in their conquest, and the council decreed in 1549 that conquest must cease until the king and his advisors could determine whether or not this was true. Some of the greatest theologians and legal experts of the time sat on the commission. Unfortunately we do not have the exact voting record of the members, but we do have the basic documentation: the statements by Las Casas and Sepúlveda--both very long-winded. Sepúlveda, trained in Renaissance studies, had studied at Bologna with the great Aristotelian scholar Pomponazzi. He maintained that the Indians were natural slaves--that they should be treated well but that they could not escape from their status--and he used all the authority of Aristotle to support his views. Las Casas, who had at that time about half a century of experience in the New World, said there was no reason why a Christian nation should adopt such a doctrine. He argued that just conquest could be carried on only by Christian principles. No formal vote was taken--apparently it was a close and very touchy decision--but after a while the conquests were resumed. However, the famous law of 1573--the ordinance which governed Spanish conquest for the rest of the colonial period--expressed Las Casas' principles: namely, that peaceful means should be employed and force used only as a last resort. Embedded in the ordinance is a kind of apology or justification: the Spanish were ordered to explain to the Indians all the benefits of Spanish rule and to tell them what Spain had accomplished in bringing seeds, animals, plants, and--above all--Christianity and civilization to the Indians. These ideas have been ringing down through history ever since.

In one marvelous passage Las Casas said that all the people of the world are men, that no one is born enlightened, that all of us must learn from those who have gone before. Everyone could become a civilized, Christian being, and he emphasized education and religion as methods of bringing all the people of the world into civilized life. Here I think there is a similarity between the mid-sixteenth century and the mid-twentieth, when the revolution in transportation and communication produced another era when large numbers of people were suddenly confronted with others of very different religion, background, color, and <u>mores</u>. In our own day this brought about another dispute about the essential nature of man, and Las Casas' arguments cropped up again in the discussion over the United Nations' Declaration of the Rights of Man. The debate of 1550 appears to have a special relevance for us today.

<u>What was the role of the Church in sixteenth- and seventeenth-century Spanish culture and society; particularly, what was the place of the friars and of the Inquisition?</u>

The Church was one of the fundamental institutions of Spain and Spanish-America, Portugal and Brazil. I would like to distinguish between two periods: the early, expansive period up to about 1570, when the orders were given carte blanche to go to the New World and bring the Indians into the fold. At the same time the Crown acquired through various royal patronage bulls enormous power over the Church--

over appointments, the collection of revenues, and so on. The peculiar relationship between the church and the state in Spain and Portugal is illustrated by the famous bull Sublimis Deus, issued by Paul III in 1537 because there had been complaints from friars in America of cruelty to Indians. Paul said in this bull Indians were rational beings with souls, that their property and lives must be respected, and they must be Christianized. The bull, of course, embodies standard Christian doctrine, but it was not sent immediately to the New World. Every bull that went to America from Rome had to go through Spain and to be approved by Charles V, and in order to show his authority he held up the bull--even though he subscribed to its essential doctrine--because he had not himself initiated or approved of it.

There was a great change in about 1570. The Crown turned the screws of royal control a little tighter; the Spanish government insisted that the Indians were largely Christianized (although in fact they were not); and the great period of ecclesiastical expansion was over. The king put the friars under the authority of the bishops, curtailing their independence and submitting them thus to royal authority also. Before 1570, the friars were the ecclesiastical conquistadores who went into the New World and accomplished marvels--we're told that two Franciscans baptized 14,000 Indians in one day in 1530. After 1570, the bishops were in charge and the friars were curbed.

The Church still had an important role in nonecclesiastical activities and institutions--hospitals, for example, and universities. Many of the outstanding professors were priests. The Jesuits were famous, too, for their pharmaceutical work; they prepared drugs for the missionaries and introduced European drugs to America and American drugs to Europe. Here again there was profitable interaction between the two worlds. Ferdinand and Isabella found that churchmen were among their most loyal administrative officers, and they occupied many important positions even up to that of viceroy.

As the years went on, the ecclesiastical, missionary zeal of the churchmen diminished and they became important landowners and slaveholders--they became the capitalists of the new society, the people who had money to lend. The Church became a powerful economic institution, but it remained still a powerful ecclesiastical institution which performed many services for society. The churchmen were the historians of the New World; they had no family responsibilities and could devote long periods of time to research and writing. They carried on the literary traditions of Spain and Portugal, producing poems, novels, and histories as well as useful chronicles of colonial life. The Church was a multifaceted institution, and although it is possible to criticize it very severely for its conservatism and economic position, one must recognize that churchmen were also the preservers and carriers of civilization, just as they had been in Europe in the Middle Ages.

As for the Inquisition, that had an interesting and separate history in the New World. As I've mentioned, the Portuguese did not extend the Inquisition to Brazil, so there was a more open situation there than in Spanish America, where from the beginning there was one big problem: were Indians subject to the Inquisition? One of the early inquisitors hauled an Indian to the Inquisition about 1531 and --I believe--burned him. This was attacked by the authorities, and finally it was decided that Indians, being new Christians, should not be subject to the Inquisition. This was a great victory for toleration, in a way, and after 1570 no Indians were brought before the Inquisition.

The victims of the Inquisition, for the most part (and here we depend on the documentation provided by Medina), were the usual kind of heretics--poor Christians--or they were foreigners, or the so-called Portuguese Jews who arrived in the New World during the period of Spanish rule over Portugal between 1580 and 1640. Throughout the whole colonial period, the Inquisition in the New World was not at all the powerful institution that it was in Spain. In the eighteenth century it became more than ever a political instrument to keep out the works of the philosophers (Rousseau and others) who were deemed to be dangerous or critical of monarchy--but as in the case of many other laws in the New World, these rules were not always enforced. The Inquisition was another European institution with a special development in America because of the special conditions and circumstances there.

Would you attempt a general assessment of the favorable and unfavorable characteristics of Spanish rule in America? It has been portrayed as one of the greatest achievements of human government, and also as one of the darkest periods of history.

This is a subject on which volumes have been written. It can be summarized briefly as the white legend versus the black legend, and the conflict between those who defend Spain and Portugal in America and those who denounce them is a permanent part of our historiography. It is difficult to make any meaningful remarks in such a brief compass, but we must distinguish among the centuries and between Spain and Portugal. There was no monolithic "Spanish (or Portuguese) rule" in America; there was administrative decentralization, and no common denominator can be applied to all parts of the vast territory of empire.

Moreover, although the Spanish laws may have been very strict and very detailed, they were not always enforced. One of the phrases quoted by people who denounce Spain is *obedézcase pero no se cumpla*--"let this law be obeyed but not enforced." The true meaning of this concept has been distorted, and it has medieval precedents which are not always recognized. In the Middle Ages it was used to prevent a law devised for one situation from being applied automatically to another. Spanish-American viceroys used it not to challenge the royal authority but to delay in enforcing an unacceptable law until they had an opportunity to appeal to the authority and present their argument. Every modern judicial system acknowledges the right of appeal through certain processes.

The conflicting interpretations of the famous New Laws of 1542 exemplify this concept as well as the controversy between those who support Spanish rule and those who decry it. In 1542, as a result of a powerful propaganda effort by Las Casas and other friars, Charles V and the Council of the Indies were prevailed upon to pass a series of laws known as the New Laws. Their essential elements were (1) that no new *encomiendas* were to be granted; and when the Spaniards who held the Indians died, those Indians were to be put under the protection of the Crown; (2) that Indians were to be taken away from those who mistreated them; (3) that royal officials could not legally own Indians. A tremendous controversy resulted, and in 1545, after another propaganda campaign by those who wanted to keep the *encomienda*, some of these basic laws were abolished--an important reversal. The viceroy of Mexico or New Spain believed that these were unwise laws--certainly those Spaniards to whom they applied found them unacceptable. Fearing that the laws would lead to revolution, the viceroy suspended them; he obeyed them, yes, but he did not enforce them until he had a chance to report back to Spain and point out their disadvantages. The viceroy of Peru, on the other hand, enforced the law and took Indians away from their owners. Peru was much less civilized than Mexico; it was a turbulent land with a civil war raging, and the viceroy was captured and executed. One of the famous old rebel captains, Francisco Carbajal, put the viceroy's head on a string and carried it up and down the Andes as a symbol of disdain for royal authority. Faced with threatened revolution in Mexico and actual war in Peru, the Crown and the Council of the Indies took another look at the New Laws and abolished some of the least popular.

The actions of Spain have been the subject of a tremendous propaganda campaign since the early sixteenth century. Las Casas himself, toward the end of his life, wrote several treatises designed to persuade the king and the Council of his point of view. These were seized at once by political enemies of Spain and translated into Flemish, English, Italian, Latin, German, and Dutch. The editions illustrated by Theodore De Bry are worth far more than a thousand words: they show Indian women killing their children because they did not want to have a Spanish child; they show Spaniards killing Indians, setting dogs upon them; they show Indians committing suicide in preference to living in a Spanish civilization. These pictures carried all over Europe the idea that the cruel Spaniards were killing, indiscriminately and in the most unchristian way, the mild savages of the New World. They were the single most powerful element in the creation of the widespread idea that Spaniards are essentially a cruel people, and we still find this idea embedded in the emotional consciousness of English-speaking peoples.

No one who studies the actions of Spain and Portugal in America will defend all of them; there is no need for such a defense. We try to understand them in order to describe them honestly, and we must think first what Spain and Portugal were like themselves during the colonial period. The European nations have been criticized for failing to introduce the Enlightenment to Latin America or to develop science there, but they could not introduce what they did not have. I regard this struggle for justice in Spanish America, even though it frequently failed, as the first confrontation between European people and a large mass of people of a different color and different religion. If Spain produced a Sepúlveda--a scholar who used his learning to apply the Aristotelian doctrine of natural slavery to the Indians--it also produced a Las Casas, who was bold enough to say, "This is unchristian. This is not what Spaniards should do. You should not use force." Spain produced both these men, and if you examine the history of Spain in America you must look at both sides of the coin: the cruel *conquistador* and the Christian priest. Both represent authentic reflections of the Spanish spirit and character. This question cannot be conclusively answered, but I believe that if you study the history of Spain and Portugal in America you will find that their problems were much like those we are facing today. In questions of racial tension and social justice, it is hard to say that we have done very much better in this century.

May we consider the supposed decline of Spain in the seventeenth century? Was this just a political and military decline, or did it involve fundamental economic, social, and cultural matters? Did the burden of ruling an empire contribute to the decline of Spanish power, and how was America affected by it?

The decline of Spain is one of the great historical problems, and we must distinguish first of all between real and apparent decline. Modern historians see a decline in the seventeenth century, but contemporaries did not perceive it at all--for them, Spain remained a powerful (and widely hated) nation. One basic element of the decline was made clear to us in Earl J. Hamilton's detailed, statistical studies of the price revolution following the great influx of New World silver. Another element was the slow decline of Spain's administrative capacity. The outstanding rulers of sixteenth-century Spain--Charles V and Philip II--were great administrators by any standard, and they rode the waves of European history as none of their successors were able to do. Perhaps another element was the lack of a challenge after the sixteenth century, that great period when Spain was at the center of the European world for the first time in history. It was the home of the greatest empire of its time, developing new institutions and adapting medieval institutions to the needs of the New World. This may have been related to the cultural coming-of-age of Spain; printing was introduced in the late fifteenth century, and the debates of the sixteenth century were conducted in print.

In the seventeenth century Spain was suffering from the long, corrosive effect of the rise in prices and the resulting social and economic disequilibrium, and the rulers of Spain could no longer meet the problems of Spain. Too, the rising monarchies of Europe gave increasing competition just when Spain had fewer resources with which to meet its challengers. In the eighteenth century the Bourbon monarchs brought some of the French administrative ability to Spain, and much was done to tighten the imperial administration. French institutions such as the intendant system were adapted to the needs of the New World. They strengthened the defenses of the northern frontier of Mexico against the English, improved the colonial administration, and arranged for scientific experts or technical advisers to visit American mines. However, this period was not comparable to the sixteenth century because the Crown itself was weak (except for Charles III), and the empire lacked a central core of strong administrative authority.

In this period, problems became so complicated and the administrative apparatus so involved that continual confusion and red tape produced a kind of paralysis, a slowdown in all the operations of the empire. For example, production at the great silver mining center at Potosí in Peru went down steadily in the eighteenth century, partly because no one in authority had sufficient energy to confront the problem. Thus the great influx of silver which influenced princes in the sixteenth century diminished, the foreign experts were unable to halt the decline, and the imperial bureaucracy was too vast and complicated to work decisively or effectively.

I tend to agree with Hamilton that the emphasis on the role of the Inquisition and of censorship has been exaggerated. Hamilton said that there were certain economic attitudes, institutions, and prejudices which helped to undermine Spain over the long pull of the seventeenth and eighteenth centuries, and that these might help to explain her decline. As we look back now we can see that no empire can exist through a long period of time without undergoing tremendous changes, and of course great changes did take place in the eighteenth century, including the opening up of the intellectual life, the quickening of trade, and the appearance of the United States to the north. Remember that at the very end of the Spanish empire--after 1800--Yankee merchants and Yankee skippers were in Buenos Aires, off Chile, in Peru, and in Mexico. A combination of European and North American n influences combined with the basic situation in Spain to bring about the Spanish decline.

What was the impact of the Enlightenment on Spain and Latin America?

Here's another interesting example of the way in which a European movement affected the New World. Intellectual currents did travel across the Atlantic: some of the writings of Rousseau and other French philosophers and English philosophers came into Latin America, so far as we can tell from lists of books from libraries and from the records of the Inquisition. However, the improvement of agriculture was an important part of the Enlightenment in Spain, but this was not carried across the ocean. The cultivation of tobacco and sugar and wheat went along just as it had for generations.

In mining, some of the new chemical and physical methods of developing silver and gold were applied in the New World. In New Spain and Mexico there was established a school praised by Alexander von Humboldt (perhaps the most alert and knowledgeable European traveler ever to come to the New World) who declared it the equal of anything in Europe. He also praised the school of fine arts, but not the state of agriculture. Again, a European movement had a different development when it reached the New World.

To what extent is 1810 a dividing line in the history of Latin America? What is the relationship between the colonial period and the modern period?

Despite the arbitrariness of choosing any one date as a dividing line, I think 1810 is still significant in the political history of Latin America. It was a watershed: the time at which Spanish-Americans became conscious of themselves as different from the Old World. Because of the Napoleonic invasion of Spain and Portugal, the mother countries were in such a tumultuous situation that it was possible then for the New World to hope for real change.

How much actual change took place in the period of revolution and independence between 1810 and 1830? We must recognize that no tremendous series of social and economic changes took place as was the case in the English colonies. On the other hand, slavery was abolished in many countries--Indian slavery at least, and sometimes Negro slavery. There was a desire to throw off the racial distinctions and laws relating to racial matters which had become increasingly important in the eighteenth century.

Economically, there was great destruction, first of all. In Venezuela, we're told, about half of the male population between eighteen and fifty years of age was lost between 1810 and 1830, and in other parts of Latin America there was considerable loss of lives and property. All the ports were opened to foreign influences. British merchants and American sailors came; American ships and American goods came; there was foreign investment. The British, in particular, had naïve ideas about the money they were going to make from these newly opened nations, and there was a fever of speculation. British capital was available for almost every kind of enterprise. Some of their projects were conceived without knowledge of the realities of Latin America, and many British investors lost their shirts.

The opening of Latin America to economic influence produced an intellectual opening. Groups of scientists and artists visited Brazil, Mexico, Chile--some of our best representations of Latin America in the 1830's and 1840's came from European scholars. I mentioned before that the German Karl von Martius developed the basic interpretation of Brazilian history.

At this point perhaps I should say that we are now very conscious of the special place of Brazilian history in the whole range of Latin America studies. In times past, most of us learned Spanish rather than Portuguese and studied Spanish America rather than Brazil, but today

Brazilian history is considered an integral part of Latin American history and its subtle and interesting differences are recognized. For example, the Brazilians are proud that they are not men of force and action; they consider themselves to be men of peace, who have achieved social and political ends by persuasion. The Brazilian revolution was a primarily peaceful transfer of power from one group to another, in contrast to the bloody wars of Spanish America.

The period 1810-30 was one of great change in some respects--economically, politically, culturally--but historians now realize that many of the institutions, ideas, and practices of the colonial period endured. Even with the abrogation of the oppressive Spanish laws, the Indians were no better off under the new regimes. In some respects they were worse off without the protective laws of Spain. The wealthy, powerful Creoles who supplanted the wealthy, powerful peninsular Spaniards oppressed the Indians even more than the Spanish colonials.

Even with new ideas from Europe, there were no great intellectual changes. During the revolutionary period there was a feeling that the Church had been an oppressive part of the old colonial regime, that it was too powerful economically and should be reformed. In Peru there were some forward-looking priests--their lives and activities are just now being studied--who proposed a modern Church: a poor Church, with married clergy and a concern for the poor. Their proposals were struck down by Rome and were not raised again until Vatican II. The new ideas were forgotten, and the Latin American Church kept the position it had held in the colonial period. It was a political-economic power, a wealthy institution allied to the interests of those in power, with no concern for the people. One of the first things the Mexican revolutionaries of 1910 did was to strike at the Church.

Thus although there were changes after 1810 there were also continuities, such as the exploitation of the Indians and the power of the Church as a bulwark of conservatism. The period between 1810 and 1830 is being re-evaluated by historians.

<u>What is the importance of the study of Latin American history today in the light of the contemporary world and contemporary problems?</u>

I think we are beginning to see Latin America as a kind of microcosm of the problems of development everywhere. Today, when problems of development and underdevelopment are so much in our minds with respect to the new nations of Asia and Africa and the Near East, we look on Latin American history after 1810 as a long story of the struggle for development. Various nations which never before manifested any special interest in Latin America are now studying Latin American history and affairs; these are no longer regarded as marginal matters cultivated by a few dedicated individuals.

We see now that the problems which Latin America has faced since the sixteenth century are the fundamental problems: how do you educate a great mass of illiterate people; how do you develop the agricultural potentialities of an area where there has been no real progress for centuries? The problems faced by Spain and Portugal as expanding nations of the sixteenth century are world problems, best expressed in the 1550 disputation between Las Casas and Sepúlveda. Their arguments are now fundamental parts of such works as the contemporary civilization course at Columbia University, where the great problems of the world are presented to our students.

Latin America is no longer on the periphery of the world. It is a large, varied kind of laboratory, in which over a great expanse of territory and throughout four centuries of history men have faced many of the problems and circumstances now being faced by other nations in their struggles to enter the modern world. The study of Latin American affairs has challenged the interest of scholars in many lands, and it seems to me that this wide interest cannot help but enrich our studies.

CHAPTER 36.

AMERICAN HISTORIANS AND THE WORLD TODAY: RESPONSIBILITIES AND OPPORTUNITIES

One of the tasks of the president of the American Historical Association is to deliver an address. Though attempts have been made to abolish it, thus far the members seem to believe that every president should be permitted to deliver himself of the message he considers necessary for the times. A wide and wildly miscellaneous variety of addresses has resulted. In my case I tried to combine a message with some discreet references to my own field, because I was the first Latin Americanist to be elected to this position, for Herbert Eugene Bolton was primarily a Borderlands scholar with a deep interest in comparative history.

The American Historical Review, 80 (1975), 1-20. Reprinted by permission.

American Historians and the World Today: Responsibilities and Opportunities

Nations have long had relations with each other and have acknowledged some responsibilities to each other in the world, but have historians? Members of the American Historical Association will increasingly ponder this question as the time approaches for the first meeting in the United States of the International Congress of Historical Sciences. Some American historians have attended the other international meetings held in Europe since 1900, but the congress is expected to bring together in San Francisco in August 1975 several thousand historians, most of them Americans. The participants will read or listen to learned papers on the "grand themes of history" as well as on a large number of smaller topics, will attend receptions, and will enjoy the still powerful attractions of northern California. One may well ask to what useful end all this movement, all this expense of time and money will be directed.

My answer is a simple one. International congresses of historians do not fully meet the needs of the times and cannot be expected to do so unless the organization that sponsors them is substantially changed and unless national organizations accept far greater international responsibilities. For the AHA this means that we need to strengthen the teaching and writing in the United States of the history of all regions of the world, to recognize the increasingly significant study abroad of our history, and to foster in all possible ways the professional relations of historians on an international scale. For the ICHS to meet its challenge, this largely Western organization must review its traditional operations in various specific ways, which will be suggested later.

This may seem a Utopian proposal to those aware of the political problems encountered by the congresses and to historians everywhere who are often concerned principally with their own history. Conor Cruise O'Brien wrote:

> Most history is <u>tribal</u> history: written. . . in terms generated by and acceptable to, a given tribe or nation. . . . Historians, like other people, tend to identify with a community--not necessarily the one in which they were born--and in the case of modern historians this identification is likely to affect, and interact with, the character of their work, their career, their geographical location, and their public. Normally they write within a convention which suggests these conditioning factors do not exist, or can be ignored. Marxist historians, indeed, emphasize such factors but only as limitations on bourgeois historians.

If this be true, or partially true, why should Americans concern themselves with the history of other tribes and with other tribal historians?

* * *

Members of that large and diverse tribe which inhabits what is called the Western World can best begin to examine these questions by considering the consequences of the discovery of America on the writing of history. Herbert Butterfield has emphasized that one of the unique characteristics of the West is its "historical mindedness" and that history only in modern times has become the kind of subject it is today. Yet he and many others ignore Iberian influences, a considerable omission because in the development of history since 1492 Spain was in the forefront, at least chronologically, of all European nations, and Portugal also made significant contributions.

Historians should be grateful for the Spaniards' keen sense of the past and for their almost unconscious though certainly widespread realization that Spanish actions overseas would one day be scrutinized by posterity. Columbus started the practice of writing about America, and many followed his example, for the conquest so stimulated their imagination that they came to look upon it as the greatest event since the coming of Christ. Even as the conquistadores roamed over vast areas of land and sea and missionaries attempted to Christianize millions of Indians, they collected historical materials and composed chronicles on a monumental scale. This copious documentation constitutes another kind of treasure from the Indies, distinct from the gold and silver found there, a documentation that still excites historians by its richness and depresses them by its quantity, for every fleet from Spanish America carried homeward thirty or forty boxes of documents, often carefully indexed for convenient study by the council of the Indies.

Beginning with Viceroy Antonio de Mendoza, who arrived in Mexico in 1535, the principal Spanish officials manifested a keen interest in history. Mendoza wanted to know about the "chronicles, hieroglyphs, and pictures from Montezuma's palace which told of the migrations of the ancient Mexicans." Many other viceroys, moreover, commissioned the writings of histories or received histories voluntarily written by Spaniards on American subjects. Sometimes there was a polemic purpose, as when Viceroy Francisco de Toledo organized in the 1570s a study of Inca history to prove Spain's contention that her conquest not only had followed just principles but in fact had liberated the Indians from a tyrannical and unjust Inca rule. But even this stern official was much impressed by what he saw in Peru, and he proposed that a museum be created in Spain where "Indian art and the products of nature" in America could be studied.

Ecclesiastics were eager to have their missionary triumphs recorded. In 1536 the Franciscan chapter in Mexico City recommended that one of their number write an account of Indian life in pre-Spanish days as well as a history of the labors of the first group of Franciscans, known as "The Twelve Apostles," from the time of their arrival in 1524. The dedicated missionaries Spain sent to America were convinced that the discovery and conquest not only afforded a unique opportunity to bring the Gospel to the Indians but also, according to some, foreshadowed the rapid approach of the end of the world and the coming of the millennial kingdom. Though the traditional Church was being destroyed in Europe, or at least severely challenged by Luther, the friars were determined that a new and more powerful Church be built in America. But there was no time to be lost. Faced with an enormous diversity of native languages, which were in turn divided into hundreds of dialects, all phonetically and morphologically alien to European languages, the early friars first tried to learn Nahuatl by playing with Indian children to acquire useful phrases. Frustrated in their attempt to identify even a few words but unwilling to allow one Indian soul to suffer damnation because of their own ignorance, some of the early friars preached to the Indians in Latin or Spanish in the hope that Christian fervor would make up for linguistic deficiencies.

As the conquest proceeded and Philip II increasingly came to dominate the administrative machinery governing the far-flung Spanish empire, a demand arose for an adequate history of Spanish accomplishments as a whole. A decisive epoch for historiography began about 1570 when the council of the Indies decided that good administration required an archive containing organized information on previous laws and past events, machinery for obtaining current reports, and an official historian. A detailed questionnaire was drawn up, which every governor in America was ordered to answer with specific data on the history, people, climate, and geography of the territory he administered. Begun as a brief inquiry in 1569, this questionnaire soon grew to fifty items and--since bureaucrats never seem to have enough information--eventually became a printed volume of three hundred and fifty questions, which must have been a heavy cross for hard-pressed governors in the far reaches of the empire to bear.

The first historian was appointed in 1573, and beginning in 1578 instructions were regularly sent out requiring the principal royal representatives in America to search their archives for historical manuscripts and to dispatch the originals or authentic copies to the council of the Indies so that a true, general history of the Indies could be written. The council had a realistic view of the habits of historians, for it decreed that the appointee would not receive the last quarter of his salary until he had turned in some completed text. For almost two hundred and fifty years, until the eve of independence, Spain sent out a constant stream of orders for information and history.

Controversy inevitably developed over what constituted "true" history. To set straight the record as he saw it, one foot soldier of Ferdinand Cortez, Bernal Díaz del Castillo, composed a True History of the Conquest of New Spain, now a classic on the discovery period. Bitter and prolonged battles on the justice of Spanish dominion and the place of Indians in Spanish society produced an enormous amount of historical documentation, which continues to attract historians. We are particularly aware of these disputes today because 1974 witnessed the commemoration of the five-hundredth anniversary of the birth of Bartolomé de Las Casas, the best-known defender of the Indians and a persistent doubter of the justice of Spanish rule. Inasmuch as my volume on his doctrine has recently appeared, I will restrain myself, with some difficulty, from analyzing his role in the development of historical writing in America and his insistence that the American Indians should not be considered natural slaves according to the Aristotelian doctrine but instead should be persuaded by peaceful methods to accept the Christian faith. To prove that the Indians were not semi-animals whose property and services could be commandeered at will by the Spaniards, Las Casas prepared a large work entitled Apologetic History, in which he advanced the idea that the Indians compared very favorably with both the Spaniards and the peoples of ancient times, were eminently rational beings, and in fact fulfilled every one of Aristotle's requirements for the good life.

The main argument of Las Casas against those who considered the Indians less than human beings, an argument that entitles him to be included as a principal member in that great tribe that might be called "all mankind," may best be summarized in his own words:

> Thus mankind is one, and all men are alike in that which concerns their creation and all natural things, and no one is born enlightened. From this it follows that all of us must be guided and aided at first by those who were born before us. And the

> savage peoples of the earth may be compared to uncultivated soil that readily brings forth weeds and useless thorns but has within itself such natural virtue that by labor and cultivation it may be made to yield sound and beneficial fruit.

We see here the beginning of the great dispute today, in which William Shockley and Arthur Jensen contend that blacks are born with genetic deficiencies that limit their intellectual growth and hinder their attempts to compete with whites.

The history of the relations between Europeans and natives in the conquest period is rich in detail. Indian men loved to wear their hair long, which offended Spaniards, whose custom was to have their hair cut short. Besides, the Spaniards said long hair was filthy and that Indian women usually slept with the men whose hair they braided, which was an offense to Christian morals. In Manila one zealous sixteenth-century bishop was so opposed to allowing Chinese converts there to keep their queues that it required an order from the council of the Indies to stop him from cutting them off. Instead, the bishop and his missionaries were ordered to treat the Chinese "with prudence and intelligence, and with the kindness and mildness required to nurture such new and tender plants." In the following century Jesuits in the Philippines denounced the drinking of chocolate; in Mexico they said it was a danger to chastity for it aroused the passions. By the end of the century, however, the nutritious drink had become a standard breakfast food on Jesuit tables in Spain and the Indies.

But one custom of the Indians was not accepted--human sacrifice by the Aztecs. None of the many contemporaries of Las Casas who prepared histories of the dramatic meeting of the West with Indian culture supported his view that the practice of human sacrifice, which revolted lay and ecclesiastics alike, should be understood in the light of the Indians' own history and doctrines. Las Casas discerned, underneath the horrible and bloody aspects of these rites, a commendable spirit of religious devotion that might be directed to higher ends and enlisted in the service of the only true God.

As the conquest proceeded and as the archives of the council of the Indies in Spain began to fill, Spaniards gave more and more attention to Indians and their culture. What taxes had they paid to their rulers before the Spaniards came? What religious concepts did they have that must be rooted out to prepare them for the true faith? Did their previous habits indicate that they were capable of becoming civilized and Christian? Though ecclesiastical writers concentrated on religious aspects of the conquest, they also viewed it in the round; they wrote on art and cooking, child training, disease and death, and the many other subjects that interested them.

The greatest single figure in the study of Indian cultural history was the Franciscan, Bernardino de Sahagún. One of the earliest missionaries in Mexico, he was not satisfied with the approach involving playing with children and almost at once began to study Nahuatl and collect materials bearing on the Indian past. In 1547 his superior ordered him to work on a history, and for a decade he continued his investigations. Then in 1558 he embarked in Tepepulco near Mexico City upon a large-scale, systematic study of Aztec culture, with the aid of several of his own Spanish-speaking Indian disciples who also knew Latin. Sahagún had written down many extensive lists of items--culture elements they would be called today--on which he desired information, and he brought together about a dozen old men reputed to be wise in their own lore. Sahagún and his research assistants interrogated these informants during

1558-59; it was the first oral-history project in America. The old men illustrated their replies by preparing a series of drawings and paintings, which were explained in writing by the Indian assistants. These visual materials became an essential part of the historical documentation.

After two years of discussions with the old men and his young Indian assistants at Tepepulco, Sahagún moved to another center at Santiago Tlatelolco to test his preliminary findings, for he exhibited the fundamental skepticism of the historian who is rarely satisfied that he has complete or accurate sources. For two more years, 1560-61, he reviewed and revised all his material with the help of a new set of informants. It took him three more years to re-edit the whole manuscript, which was still in Nahuatl, and to rework it into twelve books, each one broken down into chapters and each chapter into paragraphs.

The result was a carefully organized mass of text and 1,850 illustrations on the spiritual and material aspects of the life of the ancient Mexicans as the Indians remembered them. It was decidedly not, like so much of the transatlantic literature of the period, a European view masquerading as a description of far-off peoples, but a remarkable collection of oral literature that expressed the soul and life of the Aztec people at the time of their greatness, one of the finest sources known for ethnohistory. While some other Spaniards were fanatically destroying Indian culture, Sahagún methodically brought together documentation of the functions, ceremonies, legends, and traditions of the many gods of the Aztecs, on astronomy, astrology, the calendar, and the calculation of the recording of time, which was of great importance to them. Sahagún also included their superstitions, rhetoric, philosophy, ideas of mortality, songs to the gods, and hymns to the sun, the moon, the stars, and the wind. The ancient rulers received much attention, as did their merchants and judges. The education of the children in the home and school was treated, as well as information on botany, zoology, and the animal and plant life of Mexico, mineralogy, agriculture, the preparation and preservation of edible plants, sculpture, painting, melting of metals, the jeweler's trade, house building, the raising and care of domestic animals, road building, and temple construction. The final book described the conquest of Mexico as seen by the conquered.

Sahagún's purpose was clear: to learn all about the Indian language and culture in order to help him and the other missionaries in their conversion labor. Thus he included descriptions of the ways in which Indians got intoxicated for ceremonial reasons, for Sahagún maintained that missionaries must know all about the sins of the Indians in order to correct them, just as doctors must study disease.

As Sahagún struggled through the years against obstacles and apathy he became so immersed in the study of Indian culture that he grew interested in it for its own sake and was concerned that contact with Europeans would cause the native culture to disappear or become hybridized. Thus there was dedication and urgency in his work. At last, as the result of a royal order in 1577 instructing Viceroy Enríquez Martínez to collect all of Sahagún's manuscripts for the council of the Indies, the Nahuatl text was translated into Spanish and sent to the council.

Sahagún died in 1590 without seeing a single chapter of his monumental work published. Only in recent years have complete editions of both the Nahuatl and the Spanish texts become available, based upon the various manuscripts dispersed in libraries in Florence, Madrid, and Mexico City. The first translation into any language of the entire Nahuatl manuscript has just been completed, after thirty-five-years' labor, by Charles E. Dibble and Arthur J. O. Anderson, whose English version, General History of the Things of New Spain, imparts the spirit as well as the substance of the original. This outstanding work of American scholarship, richly footnoted and based upon extensive researches by European and Mexican scholars as well as those of the editors, will enable the English-speaking world to appreciate one of the foundation works in the history of how scholars in one culture have studied another.

Sahagún must be recognized as one of the most complex Spaniards in sixteenth-century America. He was a member of a powerful nation, whose people believed themselves to have been singled out by God for His purposes just as certainly as the Puritans of Massachusetts Bay Colony were convinced that they were "God's Chosen People." He was a member of one of the most militant missionary nations that the world has ever seen, yet in an age when few persons displayed a respectful interest in any culture except their own he devoted many years of effort to understanding, from their viewpoint, practically all aspects of the life of the ancient Mexicans. For a sixteenth-century European, his was a remarkable achievement particularly when we realize that no other colonizing nation produced such a figure.

The work of Sahagún and other Spaniards who studied the history of Indian culture and the accomplishments of Spain in America have not yet sufficiently been analyzed or understood. Perhaps in 1992 when the five-hundredth anniversary of the voyage of Christopher Columbus across the Ocean Sea will be commemorated--and Spain has already appointed a commission to plan for this event--we will have an adequate examination of these works that helped to lay the basis for the modern study of history. Among the many figures who should appear in such a work, Sahagún will be seen not only as a "past glory" but as one whose work has significance for us today. As Miguel León-Portilla of the University of Mexico emphasizes, Sahagún's supreme achievement is that he found a way to discover in a different culture those elements which are common to all mankind. León-Portilla concludes that the world today, with its many distinct cultures and physically closer together than ever before because of technological advances, needs the lesson of Sahagún, for it should help us to achieve relations with other cultures through dialogue and comprehension.

* * *

Why do some historians in the twentieth century, which bears some striking resemblances to the time when Sahagún was at work, study other cultures? Why do many more historians, though occasionally attempting to develop professional relations on an international basis, continue to work only on the history of their own tribes?

Only fragmentary accounts have been published concerning the efforts of historians to create some kind of international community, which illustrates the truth of the remark by Charles Homer Haskins, "Many historians find it easy to be historically minded respecting everything save only history." Our best single source for an understanding of the development of the international congresses from the American viewpoint is the correspondence of J. Franklin Jameson, that giant among the founders of the AHA, for it provides a running account of the activities of historians in the international meetings held since the first one in Paris in 1900. When Jameson attended the congress in London in 1913, the ignorance and the indifference of the European historians toward American history pained him. He reported that no one in Great Britain "was at all interested in American history." Nor did other European historians at the congress manifest the slightest curiosity in what had happened in the United States. By 1915 Jameson was fearful that World War I would create a state of mind "which for a long time will make it difficult for the students of history in various nations to come together in a spirit of harmony," and he was sufficiently realistic to see "only a restricted scope for international endeavor in history," due to "the fact that for the last four hundred years mankind has been chiefly organized in great states." He did not expect European historians to cooperate much.

Although Jameson spent most of his life outside universities, he considered them the basis for sound historical activities. In 1919 he supported plans to establish a professorship of American history at the University of London. He also applauded the proposal that the 1923 congress should include one session devoted to our history; in fact, he wrote in a burst of chauvinism, "American history, between you and me, should be the chief pursuit of mankind henceforth." The congress meeting in Brussels in 1923 was not prepared for such a radical step as a session on United States history alone but experimented with a separate session on "the history of the American continents," which may have reflected a reluctance to schedule a session on any subject that Europeans considered as parochial as United States history and on which they were not prepared to speak. The miscellaneous and scattered papers delivered at this session must have convinced the few Americans who attended that European scholars had little knowledge of or interest in our history.

Americans were sensitive in other ways too. Haskins devoted his presidential address in 1922 to recounting American contributions to European historiography, as if to make certain that everyone understood how much had been accomplished over here. He urged Americans not to be content with receiving European history secondhand, in packages prepared by European scholars, and insisted that American historians "participate fully and directly in all phases of the historical activity of our time." This question, he declared, concerned "the future of American scholarship, its dignity, its independence, its creative power."

Eager as Jameson was to see our history properly recognized at international congresses, he was principally determined to have the congresses produce some lasting benefit for historians and history and also bring historians together in friendly relations by working for a common purpose. The establishment of the International Committee of Historical Sciences in 1926, with a permanent bureau to provide continuity and leadership, was intended to develop projects with international support. But only an International Bibliography of Historical Sciences received general support, and it has had a precarious existence. The statement made by Jameson still has some validity: "These congresses might have done more to promote the progress of historical science than merely to provide an opportunity for the reading of various papers and for social intercourse."

But what can historians do, scattered around the world as they are, following different approaches to history, living under different kinds of governments, with only a few able to attend the meetings held every five years? My own view is that we should encourage the ICHS to expand its activities between sessions on the basis of a few fundamental policies, such as the following.

First, access to archives should be liberalized. The VIth International Council on Archives in 1968 passed far-reaching resolutions on this subject. It urged that archival administrations of all countries review national regulations controlling access to documents and propose to appropriate authorities the removal of all unjustified restrictions. It recommended further that "the principle of equality of treatment between national and foreign scholars be recognized and applied everywhere." Historians surely want to have as full access to sources as possible, and international pressure might be one of the best ways to achieve it. Should not historians, therefore, join with the archivists to work toward these desirable objectives? The ICHS would be expected to devise some procedure to handle complaints, perhaps in cooperation with the archivists. The experience of the AHA with the charges against the Franklin D. Roosevelt Library proves that this might be a heavy responsibility, but no announcement of principles governing access will be worth much unless there is some machinery for inquiry and redress of grievances.

Second, historians should be encouraged to study and teach in foreign lands. Jameson had ideas on this too. He proposed that British professors of history be invited to attend and participate in the annual meetings of the AHA, an invitation that might also involve their teaching in our universities. He once succeeded in getting support from the Carnegie Endowment for International Peace, and distinguished historians from a number of British universities attended the annual meeting in December 1924. Afterward a number of these visitors went to universities to meet with their colleagues and deliver lectures. Why should some similar arrangement not be developed for every session of the ICHS? How valuable it would be, for example, to our students and our faculties if fifty or more foreign historians who will attend the meeting in San Francisco could also teach for a quarter or semester before or after the meeting. The experiences of these historians on our campuses would also enlarge their understanding of life in the United States and the variety of historians to be found here. The matching of historians with appropriate institutions might require considerable managerial expertise, but it could be done.

Third, the teaching of history should receive sustained attention. Some sporadic attention has been given since World War I to the analysis of textbooks in order to eliminate gross prejudices and nationalistic bias, but the ICHS does not seem to have considered the improvement of history teaching as an essential part of its task. This is a curious fact. The modifying of national and other prejudices in the writing of textbooks should be one of the obvious and natural objectives of historians in their international organization. But attention to history teaching should not be limited to the ever-present problem of honesty and balance in textbooks. Is it not equally important for us to exchange ideas and experiences with our colleagues in other countries in order to improve the teaching of both our own national histories and the history of other cultures? This fundamental labor can probably best be undertaken at the primary- and secondary-school level, which means that we should ask the ICHS to develop some definite program for teachers in these grades to live and teach outside their own countries. Here indeed is a large and complicated enterprise in which the AHA is not yet fully equipped to participate, but our divisional committee for teaching should be very helpful in the future.

Besides these continuing activities for the improvement of accessibility to sources, travel for historians, and the teaching of history, the ICHS should re-examine the program and organization of its congresses. There must be better ways to foster understanding among historians than to mount expensive extravaganzas every five years.

The beginnings of the movement for the closer association of historians on an international basis were made by a small band of European and American historians in the early decades of this century, and in our present desire for improvement we must not forget or undervalue the pioneer efforts that made possible the present system of meetings every five years. Nor must we forget that most international movements develop very slowly and often involve disappointments and frustrations. But a larger and more solid structure for the international relations of historians is long overdue, and let us hope that at least the scaffolding for a new structure will have been constructed by the time the AHA completes its first century in 1984. When this comes to pass, all historians, no matter which tribe they belong to, will benefit.

* * *

If Jameson could visit us today he would doubtless be gratified to see how American studies, including history, are being increasingly cultivated in universities, institutes, and special associations in Britain, continental Europe, and elsewhere. The inadequacies that lasted into the late 1950s resulted from lack of funds, faculty resistance attributed to political opposition or doubt as to the academic validity of courses on the United States, and "the absence of young scholars with sufficient academic qualifications to merit appointment to university teaching posts in American studies." Thanks in part to the Fulbright program and foundation grants to the American Council of Learned Societies to encourage these studies overseas, the situation has changed radically in recent years.

Now the shoe is on the other foot. Japanese schoolteachers who studied at the University of Massachusetts, Amherst, last summer were shocked to find so little attention to Japanese history in our textbooks, just as scholars in Japan concerned with developing Latin American studies there deplore the ignorance in Latin America of Japanese culture. Foreign historians, in the spirit of Jameson, may now be sensitive to what they view as our indifference to their increasingly important work on United States history. C. Vann Woodward deplored the parochialism of some American historians in these words: "The fault of Americans lies largely in their habit of looking within for the significance of historical experience and assessing it narrowly according to preconceptions and legends of democracy, equality, and frontier-flavored determinants of exceptionalism." This myopia also explains why Americans have been so slow "to understand the significance of the influence they have exerted beyond their borders." David M. Potter gives substance to this charge, in examining the Civil War, for he concludes, "The significance of the Civil War for world history, and particularly for the history of nationalism, has been generally neglected by historians."

The quantity and quality of foreign contributions to United States historiography since the end of World War II will probably surprise many of us, and the AHA might well sponsor the preparation of an annotated and organized bibliography on the subject. This bibliography would make clear that the increase of attention to our history abroad has not only been beneficial to the persons overseas whom Jameson worried about but would be equally useful to our own historians, for they would learn something about their own fields from foreign historians. A Dutch writer has stressed the difference between American and European scholarship: "European ideas that do not fit well into the American conception of self, that collide with the dominant official ethos of America, have long been soft-pedalled in American scholarly thought, while they prevail in European thinking." There are differences, too, between American and European conceptions of social history, for different value systems result in different views. In the light of development abroad, must we not conclude that American history is too important to be left to American historians alone?

With the ever increasing attention the AHA is giving to teaching, why could we not sponsor, in various parts of the country and on a variety of topics, a continuing series of summer seminars and colloquia that would bring together historians from other parts of the world to discuss matters of mutual interest in the teaching and interpretation of American history? The foreign participants might spend an additional month or so visiting other colleagues or working in archival or library collections. Eventually American and foreign historians might work together on some aspect of our past. Would it not be refreshing to have a Brazilian scholar join with one of our historians to study the history of race relations in the United States?

Since Sahagún's fundamental work on Mexican Indians, studies of foreign cultures by scholars outside the cultures were sporadic until recently. Our institutions of higher education were parochial, for they recognized mainly the United States and Europe as proper subjects for scholarly inquiry and usually regarded other parts of the world as outposts on the periphery of civilization. The result, as Richard D. Lambert stated in his review of language and area programs, was that "generations of Americans educated before World War II were ill-equipped to live in the postwar world of newly independent nations asserting their rights to political sovereignty and to respect for their cultural identities." Today the situation has radically changed, due to the energetic and far-sighted support for foreign area programs of the American Council of Learned Societies and the Social Science Research Council from the 1930s onward, with financial aid from foundations. World War II prompted foreign language and cultural studies for strategic purposes. Since the end of the war development has been notable, for only thirty years ago "the American scholarly experts on many of the world's areas could have been assembled in a small room, and today all the world areas are represented by flourishing scholarly associations with memberships running in some cases into the thousands." Throughout our colleges and universities one now finds a wide variety of well-trained area specialists, ready to enrich the educational offerings for their students with their hard-won knowledge of other cultures.

Many of these area specialists are historians, and now that few students are required to take courses in United States history or Western civilization, should not all history departments use their influence to encourage undergraduates to become acquainted, through a broad "civilization" course, with the history of another culture distinctly different from their own? World history will also have a place, particularly if presented with the imagination and expertise of a William H. McNeill, but the study of a single civilization has a special value all its own. Equally important would be the encouragement of graduate students in history to select one field from non-Western history for their general examinations. Enough good material now exists in English to make this a respectable and interesting possibility for all graduate students, and such a broadening of their training would also enlarge their possibilities as teachers. This training would, in addition, increase their ability to treat topics of comparative history. The stimulating contribution of Carl N. Degler on race relations in Brazil and the United States indicates what we may expect when practitioners in one field enter another.

Fifty years ago Haskins felt that one of the important obstacles to American research on European history was the deficiencies of our libraries. Today it is possible to pursue meaningful research on most areas of the world without leaving the United States, and in many fields our library resources are unsurpassed. A large volume would be required to do justice to this subject. Let these illustrations indicate the depth and range of the documentation available on foreign areas: in the period 1962-67, the Library of Congress offices abroad obtained 7.5 million publications from Ceylon, India, Indonesia, Nepal, the United Arab Republic, and Yugoslavia. Through this program forty other research libraries received sets of foreign-language publications, and 310 libraries received English-language sets. The April 1965 issue of the Library of Congress's _Monthly Index of Russian Accessions_ contained 487 pages of triple-column pages in small type.

Another way in which American historians might improve their world view would be to hold an annual meeting in Mexico City. We have met twice in Toronto: why not follow the example of the American Association for the Advancement of Science and other American professional associations by trying out the excellent facilities in Mexico City? It would be worth the trip alone to visit the Anthropological Museum there, a remarkable testimony to the Indian cultures whose study Sahagún initiated.

One possible danger must be mentioned. As our students and professors become more acquanted with the history and conditions of other tribes, will we become more sensitive to injustices committed abroad, especially to historians, and in consequence will we attempt to influence foreign nations in ways we consider desirable? Spaniards studied Indians largely as an aid to Christianizing them. Will the AHA look upon governments and historians that do not follow our ways as laggards in civilization who must be exhorted by formal resolution and even condemnation to follow our leadership on such explosive matters as civil rights and free speech?

These are gut issues on which honest historians differ. Thus far the Soviet Union's treatment of its dissident intellectuals has received most attention, but if relations between the People's Republic of China and the United States continue to increase, there will be other problems to confront. Although ethnocentrism can be found in many places--and there may be even today some Americans who would agree with Jameson that what the world needs is a large dose of American history to save it--China has one of the most completely closed civilizations ever developed in the world. Until the 1840s Chinese governmental and educational elites saw little need to study foreign languages or cultures, for all non-Chinese were considered barbarians. Those few who did study these subjects were dubbed "barbarian tamers" and tolerated because they performed an "odious and distasteful job, like sewer-inspectors," an attitude that lasted in some quarters well into the nineteenth century. Today there is a different orthodoxy in China, according to which Maoist values are enshrined as the ultimate repository of truth. Apparently we will see in China a conscious and continuous ideological orientation of historical scholarship, as has been the case for some time in other countries, which will make dissidence dangerous and unlikely.

Americans living in a pluralistic society where there is legal emphasis on individual rights and free speech look upon such cultures as subject to thought control, whether in China, Saudi Arabia, the Soviet Union, or elsewhere. Can historians from widely varying cultures find common ground to stand on? If one may judge from our experience in discussing Latin American history with Soviet scholars, the possibilities of a fruitful exchange of views must not be exaggerated. Thus far these exchanges have been limited because of financial, linguistic, and political reasons, but it is likely that the coming generation will see a more wide-ranging and intense debate than ever before as historians discuss Latin America from the standpoint of their own tribes.

A final problem must be mentioned: the function of "tribal history." Do all nations--including the United States--need parochialism, naiveté, and myths to bind together their people? Does everyone need to cultivate self-sustaining, self-satisfying, and supportive notions about the virtues and unique qualities of the tribe he belongs to? Perhaps so, and if tribal history can be kept within decent bounds by the perspectives of historians inside and outside the tribe, it may serve a useful purpose. It must be recognized, too, that not all members of a tribe accept the dominant interpretation of its history and that divergent opinions within a tribe affect the views of historians outside. A century ago Japanese educational leaders embraced the American dogma of hard work and individualism--"Boys, be ambitious" was the watchword transmitted to Japanese youth by William Clark of Amherst. Japanese Americanologists such as Yasaki Takagi, who introduced a course on the United States at Tokyo University in 1918, were convinced that America was basically "a good country of good people." The generation after 1945 was not so sure, and it aimed at viewing America objectively and dispassionately. A new school, now gathering influence, "contends that earlier American studies in Japan, following the example of American scholars themselves, have ignored the problems of America's minorities--the blacks, Indians, and immigrant groups--and is in need of fundamental reform." Today Japanese textbooks no longer reflect the simplistic image that summed up for previous generations the message of America: "Boys, be ambitious."

If myths are useful when held by members of a tribe concerning its own history, they are less innocent and less justifiable when they are invoked to explain another culture. For example, during the Vietnam War the United States stressed its opposition to Communist North Vietnam as a totalitarian dictatorship similar to those found elsewhere. The difficulty with this argument Frances FitzGerald has made clear: "The non-Communist Vietnamese leaders believed in intellectual freedom no more than the Communists. . . . Intellectual freedom, of course, implies intellectual diversity." Is not one of the important reasons for paying attention to the history of other peoples to make sure that our understanding of their culture is not based on untenable myths?

However we may answer these questions, I believe that historians in this country now face a watershed, just as did that small group of teachers and writers who founded the AHA in 1884, who aimed to raise the teaching of history to a higher level because they were convinced that the local and state spirit should give way to a larger, national view. Our problem today is to find ways of strengthening all international aspects of history teaching and writing in the United States. I am convinced--and this may be an expression of my own ethnocentrism--that no nation today has a better opportunity than our own to attempt to study other cultures without necessarily losing the necessary life-giving and life-sustaining connection with our own national roots. A minority group like the Scots or the Catalans may have some justification for giving almost exclusive attention to their own history, lest they disappear as a distinct culture. But surely the situation is different in the United States, with its many different strains of cultures, with its economic and political power, and with the need to overcome or at least diminish and channel in other directions the force of what might be called its missionary zeal.

My hope is that in the great enterprise, whose dimensions I have barely sketched, organized American historians will have an important and even indispensable part. Today the AHA has more projects, more problems, and a larger budget than ever before. Among our 17,000 members is to be found an astonishing diversity of historical interpretations, life-syles, linguistic skills, and, yes, pizzazz. Surely this remarkable aggregation of human beings will be able to influence the study and teaching of history in international as well as national ways and to strengthen the already solid beginnings made here to study seriously the history of other nations and other peoples, while continuing to help Americans understand their present and future by providing an honest and informed picture of the past. When this day arrives we shall be achieving what Jameson hoped for: recognition of the fact that the history of the modern world cannot be fully understood unless foreign historians pay more attention to our history and recognition that United States history cannot be fully comprehended if isolated from world history.

Americans will then be ready for an even more difficult step, the initiation of fundamental revisions in their own views of the world, man, and the future, which began in the century of the great discoveries and for which Bernardino de Sahagún showed the way by his studies of Aztec culture. If American historians are fully aware of their opportunities and responsibilities in the world today, they can exert a powerful influence by their teaching and research to the end that we are able to appreciate the history of other peoples without losing allegiance to our own. By studying the history of their own tribes and other tribes as well, historians should be in the forefront of all those who would seek to understand the common elements in all cultures.

Musicians and entertainers (bk. 1, no. 19)

Bathing the baby (bk. 6, no. 29)

The ruler's war array (bk. 8, no. 77)

Cleaning the teeth (bk. 10, no. 161)

Treatment of spider bites (bk. 11, no. 287)

Copperworking (bk. 11, no. 796)

The illustrations are from Bernardino de Sahagún, Historia de las Cosas de Nueva España, 5 (Madrid, 1905). Photographs reproduced from the collection of the Library of Congress.

PART VIII

CONTEMPORARY AFFAIRS

CHAPTER 37.

PLAIN SPEAKING ABOUT LATIN AMERICA

Historians may concentrate their research interests on far-off days in Latin America, but they find it difficult if not impossible to refrain from also commenting on contemporary affairs. My first venture into these turbulent waters was during my life as Director of the Hispanic Foundation in the Library of Congress. Washington was a lively place in the early 1940's, and the Library of Congress under the vigorous leadership of Archibald MacLeish was no bookish sanctuary. There streamed through the Hispanic Foundation a steady flow of Latin American scholars and statesmen who talked freely of their problems and the prospects of the world in those uncertain months before Pearl Harbor.

When George Leighton of *Harper's Magazine* invited me to try my hand at explaining Latin America to a larger public than my historical colleagues, I decided to make the attempt. In the first article I tried to dissipate some of the naive ideas held in the United States about the Nazi "threat" in Latin America, and to show that our complicated relations with the nations to the south required more careful and sophisticated attention than they had previously received. In the second article I set forth two general ideas which still seem to me to be valid: in the great area we call Latin America so many forces are at work that few generalizations about it may be made with confidence, and our national purpose should be to foster the eventual increase of democratic realities there.

Harper's Magazine, No. 1086 (November, 1940), 588-596. Only the first article is reprinted.

Plain Speaking About Latin America

I

To one recently returned from visiting most of the republics of Latin America, the almost single-hearted concentration of our press on the Nazi activities there comes as a disquieting fact. In Bogotá, Santiago, Buenos Aires, São Paulo, or Rio de Janeiro one may find in the leading papers columns of news on the United States and its multifold, sometimes bizarre activities, but in our papers information on Latin America usually takes the form of scare articles on the Nazi threat and it is not too much to say that the American public is now being subjected to a news blitzkrieg concerning Latin America. It is a hemisphere ripe for the taking, we are told, and every possible "insinuendo" is used to make us see Nazi troopers every time we peer across the Rio Grande.

The Nazi offensive there, and the many-sided fifth-column activity which supports it is, judging from our newspapers, apparently the only newsworthy topic on Latin America. Perhaps the Dies Committee has so conditioned the public palate that only raw red meat is acceptable. Our newspapers rush correspondents around the twenty republics by air, who in each capital pause long enough to sharpen their pencils and pose the now familiar question: "And how much fifth-column activity have you here?" Sometimes a correspondent spends as much as a full week in one country gathering data for his cable dispatch. And practice makes perfect, because a Congressman who recently spent one day in Puerto Rico was able to ferret out widespread Nazi activity there and to predict a serious and imminent uprising.

In the face of this menace our people are not idle. Groups of clubwomen tour the southern republics, two symphony orchestras play in the more sophisticated capitals, and a caravan of business men proposes to motor around Central and South America this fall. These and many other moves are designed, one learns, to improve our relations with Latin America and somehow or other help defeat the Nazis there.

This concentration of public attention upon the Hitler menace is perhaps natural, but may lose rather than win friends for us in Latin America; and unfortunately it comes at a time when the United States has the best opportunity presented for a hundred years to place our relations with the other American republics on an honest and lasting basis. This opportunity we are in danger of muffing because of sheer ignorance and lack of information. It is no comfort to remember that "'twas always so" and that we have always oscillated violently in our attitude toward Latin America between simplification and mystification. There was a time when all their actions were mysterious and everything was explained by a reference to those inexplicable Latins; charming of course, but quite beyond the ken of rational people like ourselves. We are just now in a simplification phase, just as we were before the First World War. In the newspaper cartoons the Latin American was always a handsome, guitar-strumming fellow with provocative mustachios who strutted in the moonlight before his beauteous señorita's ancestral home. The beauteous señorita, moved by her lover's passionate song, allowed him to squeeze her hand through the iron grating of the window of her ancestral home, and climactically tossed him a rose. It was a pretty picture and many people saw it in their mind's eye (and nothing else, except perhaps Pancho Villa leading his ragged band across the horizon) when they thought of Latin America in those faroff days before 1914. Now the one image clear to all who can read the newspapers is this: a Nazi agent lurking behind every door in Latin America. Nearly everything else to the south is seemingly irrelevant. At a time when Leland Stowe's sensational articles on Nazi activity in Norway before and during the German occupation are being sharply challenged, and when our relations to our American neighbors are of prime importance, does it not behoove us to avoid unduly simplifying our Latin American friends and their problems?

The Nazi danger exists of course, and it would be naïve to underestimate the possible havoc Hitler's agents could create in Latin America. It does not forward the cause of inter-American understanding, however, to label indiscriminately all Germans and persons of German ancestry in the southern republics as "Nazi," for they may be missionaries, escaped Jews, or solid citizens married into important and respectable Brazilian, Chilean, or Argentine families. These Germans would bitterly resent being considered Hitler's stooges and their thoughts can only be imagined on reading the statement of a well-known professor in this country who recently proclaimed, in a women's magazine with an enormous circulation, that the Latin American republics "have large German and Italian minorities (*numbered literally in the millions) which already have been organized for sinister purposes* originating in Berlin and Rome." (The italics are mine.)

If we are to combat the Nazi menace, we ought to know what it is, and the American public would be better informed on its true extent if our newspapers took Latin America seriously enough to station a few of their crack reporters in the key places--say Mexico City, Havana, Bogotá, Santiago, Buenos Aires, São Paulo, and Rio de Janeiro. For it is an ominous fact that there is not a single first-line American newspaper correspondent stationed permanently in Latin America. A great volume of news is already collected there by the Associated Press and the United Press, but our newspapers use only a small fraction. Special trips to Latin America have been made by competent reporters, and it is announced that John Gunther is getting ready to worm his way inside South America, but this is not enough. We need in our editorial offices executives who will send outstanding reporters to live in Latin America, and will see to it that the news collected there is used. We should no longer then be faced with this dangerous situation: at a time when our relations with our southern neighbors are more important than ever before, the run of the mill news, which would provide a factual background for a truer picture of Latin America, is not made available to our public in any considerable quantity and none of our outstanding reporters lives in any of those countries to paint the perspective with a skilled and authoritative pen. (As this article goes to press, word has arrived that *Time*, Inc., has again scooped the newspapers by opening up a permanent office in Buenos Aires.)

There looms an even greater danger from this blotting out by the "Nazi menace" of all other news of Latin America. The widespread movement to improve our cultural relations has been overshadowed by the persistent publicity given to fifth-column activities. Now if the United States government wishes to take a step toward improving inter-American cultural relations such a move may easily be suspect, seeming to arise more from a desire to thwart Hitler's agents or to aid us to secure the naval and air bases necessary to protect the Panama Canal, than from a genuine interest in their culture. Once the crisis is over, this political interest in their culture, if it is shallowly rooted, will topple over. Such a crash would raise an echo to be heard throughout the Americas very unpleasantly for many years to come.

II

The brief history of our attempts to embark on a cultural program under government auspices merits detailed attention, but it may be useful to consider first the case of the Germans in southern Brazil, where the Nazi menace is supposed to be greatest because of the concentration of Germans there. So far as I know, none of the newspaper writers who harp on this chord has ever lived or even visited in Blumenau, Florianopolis, Curitiba, or Porto Alegre. If the Chicago Daily News had sent one of the Mowrers to Brazil five years ago with orders to visit the length and breadth of that vast country, from the Amazon to Rio Grande do Súl, from Rio de Janeiro to Minas Geraes and Matto Grosso, here is the sort of information the American newspaper-reading public might be getting today.

Brazil is the greatest melting pot in the world. Its basic Portuguese culture has enabled it to fuse and absorb the Indian and Negro cultures into one of the most interesting mixtures known today. It is a peaceful land, with no tradition of bloody revolution or civil war. There is probably no country in the world where Hitler's racial doctrines would find scantier soil in which to root than in Brazil. Gilberto Freyre, a brilliant Brazilian sociologist, historian, and publicist, has devoted his life to proclaiming through his writings the past and present of his country in which the Portuguese, Negro, Indian, and other peoples have fused and are being fused into a Brazilian culture. Those who fear the influence of totalitarian dogma in Brazil, therefore, would do well to ponder these words of Freyre:

> It is this past marked by almost fraternal collaboration of African culture--and indigenous culture as well--with the European, which gives Brazil one of its strongest traces of individuality. It is this which sets us apart today from those European groups for which there can be no compromise, no temporizing, between one culture and another, between one race and another, and for which there exists only the exclusive domination of one race, of one culture, which considers itself superior. In our immigration policy, we Brazilians cannot act in contradiction with this past, which constitutes a powerful national tradition and which does not permit us to welcome, on our soil and in our life, peoples radically opposed to that which has been and continues to be fundamental in Brazilian evolution--a free intercommunication of cultures and a thoroughgoing mixture of races within an essentially Brazilian framework.

Now consider the Germans in southern Brazil against this background, many of them poor, peasant folk who over a hundred years ago began to come to a foreign land because their own country offered them so little. Devout Catholics and Protestants they are, and thus not likely to look with favor upon the policies of pagan Nazi Germany. During the nineteenth century and now they cling to some of their customs but there can be little doubt that the "Brazilianization" policy of the government and the whole social trend in Brazil will eventually make them true Brazilian citizens. The very generosity of Portuguese culture in its relation with other cultures will doubtless work toward the comparatively painless process of "Brazilianization." Our battleships and our air fleets will not be able to defend this Brazilian culture from the Nazi menace. Brazil has a stronger weapon than mere force, namely assimilation, and I suspect will triumph in the end, refusing to accept either Nazi leadership or our own. Incidentally, it would seem that the Brazilian attitude toward races and peoples provides a sounder basis for future development than either the Nazi doctrine or our general practice toward our own Negroes and Indians.

Such general considerations as these suggest that there is not ready at hand a simple answer to that inevitable question posed by the roving reporter who interrupts his air flight for a matter of hours to jot down all the answers on Nazi activity in southern Brazil. But a series of such articles by a discerning writer who took time to live in the country, learn its language and customs, mingle with its politicians, business men, and intellectuals might approach in authenticity and value the Russian articles of Walter Duranty or W. H. Chamberlin. And is Russia more important to us than Latin America?

III

But to return to the attempts made in this country to improve our cultural relations with Latin America. The government took the lead two years ago by setting up a Division of Cultural Relations in the State Department. Before it was born, voices outside and inside the Department were heard, insisting that the Division must not become a propaganda agency nor adopt the tactics of the Nazis and Fascists in Latin America. There resulted a situation similar to that of the well-known lass who was urged to hang her clothes on the hickory tree but not go near the water. For the Division was set up in a political department of the government and was designed to serve a political purpose. Yet the Division found itself hedged in at almost every turn by prohibitions; there were so many activities it could _not_ engage in. And it languished for lack of funds. At a time when good-will bomber flights were made to Latin America at the drop of a hat--well, at least every time a president was inaugurated there--the Division was forced to talk big and do little because money was lacking.

There was never any dearth of good ideas. Four conferences were held in Washington in the fall of 1939 on inter-American relations in the fields of art, music, education, and publications, to which important people flocked from all over the country and at which useful ideas fairly burgeoned. But all these ideas involved money for their achievement and little was forthcoming. The Division has never received sufficient funds although cash seems to be available for other purposes. I have often wondered how much those good-will bomber flights cost--the one made to Brazil last year to help celebrate the fiftieth anniversary of that republic included several expensive planes and a complement of thirty-three men. Whatever the sum, it is certain that the Division of Cultural Relations of the State Department has been forced to drag along on a very thin diet and, unless the situation changes radically, will be obliged to fall into a state of respectable desuetude.

Nor have other government attempts brought forth more fruit. A weak committee with an imposing title, the Interdepartmental Committee on Co-operation with the American Republics, was set up some two years ago under the aegis of the State Department to enable the various government agencies (Smithsonian Institution, Department of the Interior, Tariff Commission, Maritime Commission, Federal Works Agency, Civil Aeronautics Authority, Department of Justice, Public Health Service, Department of Labor, Department of Commerce, and Library of Congress) to work out a general program for improving relations with Latin America. A million-dollar plan was drawn up, but at the last minute it was decided to make each agency present separately its own part of the proposed program in its own deficiency bill. Thus, instead of forming a solid front, the agencies were divided and naturally lost. The Smithsonian Institution, for example, had to press its request for funds to prepare a <u>Handbook of the South American Indians</u> along with its deficiency request for some electrical wiring in its basement. The resulting confusion may well be imagined, and only a minute sum was granted by Congress. In June of this year, after some feverish meetings, the Interdepartmental Committee presented, at the suggestion of the budget bureau and State Department officials, a modest proposal involving a grand total of some $250,000, just about the cost of one gun sighter on a battleship. Congress voted some billions for defense but slashed the Interdepartmental Committee budget in two. The money granted will be well spent, but the sum seems unimpressive when compared with the half billion dollars proposed to Congress to facilitate loans to Latin America through the Import-Export Bank.

It seems clear, therefore, that only a modest assistance can be expected from Congress in the general cultural program, either through the Division of Cultural Relations or the Interdepartmental Committee for Co-operation with the American Republics. One must not be dogmatic, however, and this may be too gloomy a prognostication, for as this article is being written, word comes that Nelson Rockefeller has accepted President Roosevelt's invitation to serve on the Council of National Defense as Coordinator of Commercial and Cultural Relations between the American Republics. His task will be, the newspapers inform us, to

> . . . handle details of the much-amended cartel plan if it is placed in operation. Remedies for the South American surplus situation would probably receive first attention at his hands.
>
> Further, there were credible reports that Rockefeller might be asked to create and manage a counter-propaganda campaign in Latin America designed to overcome and neutralize German propaganda.
>
> The State Department's division of cultural relations, in existence about two years, has been handling mostly the exchange of students, periodicals and other literature. It has steadfastly kept away from what might be called a pro-American propaganda campaign in the Latin American nations.

Whatever his functions prove to be, it is more than likely that President Roosevelt has realized that money is needed to make the mare go, and that due provision will be made. One wonders, however, whether Mr. Rockefeller, instructed to mend both commercial and cultural fences, will be able to find much time for the second type when the first present so many difficulties. And even if he does, is it not possible that some Latin Americans may look upon this combination of business and culture as a not too subtle and streamlined version of dollar diplomacy? Anyone who realizes the hitherto inadequate efforts of the government in this vital field can only wish Mr. Rockefeller godspeed and hope that he will be able against great odds to put new life into a movement which is groping for direction and starving for lack of Congressional support.

If the government has thus far failed to make any large commitments, why did the private foundations not step in? That is the question many people are asking and there appears to be no satisfactory answer. For our foundations are clearly non-political, have worked out a wise policy of distributing funds, and have funds to distribute. True, some foundations are prohibited from engaging in activities outside the United States; others, such as the Guggenheim Memorial Foundation, are doing excellent work so far as their limited funds will permit. But what about the other great foundations, one of which proclaims in its charter as its aim "to promote the well-being of mankind throughout the world"? If the foundation officials were engaged in a careful survey of the potentialities of the Latin-American field, we might hope for the future, but so far as I know no presidents or vice-presidents have yet gone to spy out the South American land, at least in the non-medical fields. Much valuable public health work has been performed, particularly by the Rockefeller Foundation, and it would thus seem logical for some foundation to push on into the fields of the social sciences and the humanities, where problems even more difficult of solution are waiting.

Perhaps the foundations wish to emphasize their non-political nature by not climbing on the bandwagon, now that the American public realizes the political stakes involved in our inter-American relations. Perhaps the scarcity of soundly established universities and other cultural institutions in Latin America makes the foundations pause, because their policy is to assist institutions which have a reasonable hope of securing permanent support within the country. Yet some strong institutions do exist, such as the Municipal Library in São Paulo, Brazil; the Faculty of Fine Arts in Santiago, Chile; the University of Colombia in Bogotá; and the Faculty of Arts and Letters in Buenos Aires.

Perhaps the foundations have discovered that our own universities have failed to develop adequate personnel for Latin-American work and hence we lack men and women fitted for carrying out good plans, many of which already exist on paper. Although this country may boast a distinguished past and respectable present in some field of Latin-American scholarship (The Hispanic-American Historical Review has been published for over twenty years, and hundreds of courses are offered by our universities), it probably is still true that capable, well-trained workers in the vineyard are too few. Is this very situation not a challenge to the foundations?

Let us grant that the foundations ought not to enter Latin America for political reasons, that the strongly established institutions in Latin America are few, and that our own universities have not developed an adequate personnel. It is still true that Latin America remains one of the great relatively virgin areas awaiting scholarly investigation. Latin-American archives have been barely touched, the Spanish and Portuguese languages spoken in the new world offer just as valuable and interesting problems as the English spoken here, and many of the countries are virtually sociological laboratories where social processes may be watched in operation.

But emphasis need not be laid wholly on new contributions to knowledge to be made in this rich field. Latin America also offers a spacious realm for the diffusion of knowledge. Her illiterate millions must be taught to read and the world's accumulated knowledge brought to them. But how? There is no easy answer to this question, but the foundations might well help to provide one by devoting more substantial appropriations in the Latin-American field.

Our great private foundations must face many pressures of course, but if one of their functions is to seek out pressing problems and help to alleviate them, it would seem that the foundations have thus far missed this particular bus, and that only stern and purposeful running will enable them to catch it. True, some funds have been granted, mostly to institutions in this country for their Latin-American activities. Yet how much more could be accomplished if the foundations would make some decisive and courageous move, particularly in the fields of the humanities and the social sciences!

IV

At this point I hear voices exclaiming, "If the government and the foundations have shown timidity, what constructive suggestions can be made in the present impasse which you paint so darkly?" Before attempting to suggest an answer to this pertinent question, I should like to set down certain general considerations.

First, let us remember that our interest in Latin America has had a long history. Since the first struggles of the Latin-American peoples for independence, some United States citizens have taken a sympathetic and lively interest--a fact not to be forgotten during all the huffing and puffing of present day cultural ambassadors. Young men with romantic fire in their eyes fought for the rebels against Spain over a hundred years ago; statesmen realized the political stakes involved, and commercially-minded Yankees scented possible profits. David de Forest of New Haven, for example, lived and thrived in Buenos Aires during almost the whole revolutionary period. On his return to the United States he left a valuable ranch to the Argentine nation and ever afterward celebrated Argentine Independence Day by holding a gay open house for all lovers of Argentine liberty in the spacious New Haven house he built with profits won in Buenos Aires.

Even during the dullest decades of the nineteenth century this relationship never ceased. Herndon and Gibbon, those young naval lieutenants who traveled down the Amazon in the 1850's on an official expedition for the United States government, encountered an American circus playing to eager audiences in the most remote river towns. And they found that even the cloistered ladies of Andean Bolivia were quite conversant with the novels of James Fenimore Cooper. Massachusetts textiles too were on sale in Peruvian villages. It must be always remembered, therefore, that this relationship which we are trying to focus and to direct has had a considerable history.

Second, we should remember that these relations have been of the most diverse sorts. We have acted toward our southern neighbors in the spirit of the Good Samaritan and also in the spirit of Simon Legree. We have given flour to the starving Venezuelans when an earthquake ruined Caracas in 1812, and we have also furnished such colorful personalities as William Walker and such economic conquistadores as William Wheelwright, Henry Meiggs, the Harmon Brothers, and others, who swashbuckled up and down Latin America. Indeed, Americans have enthusiastically joined with Europeans to divide up this new world melon. Bond salesmen, Texas oil drillers, and large-souled New England schoolmarms (brought to Argentina by Sarmiento) have all brought their influences to bear on Latin America.

The variegated nature of present-day contacts was borne in upon me forcibly five years ago while returning by boat from South America. Besides the usual run of tourists and business men, there were aboard the following representatives of our culture: one cauliflower-eared pugilist from Brooklyn, who had been well battered by Argentine boxers; ten Broadway chorus girls who had helped to enliven the hot spots of Rio and Buenos Aires; one Armenian minister from Fall River, Massachusetts, who had just finished his second preaching tour in Argentina; one hat-maker who had been plying her trade in Uruguay (her "advanced ideas" caused the minister to worry over her soul during most of the voyage); one missionary's wife, with brood of children, from the wilderness regions of Matto Grosso in Brazil; one teacher, who had been consulting some sixteenth-century manuscripts in a Bolivian monastery. As we proceeded northward to New York, I had plenty of time to wonder what impact these representatives of American culture had made on South America.

The United States government and its responsible officials have also manifested a medley of approaches in this field. To name only an outstanding example, Woodrow Wilson in his Mobile speech in 1913 set forth a noble proposal for our relations with Latin America, but only two years later ordered the Marines into Vera Cruz. And Walter Hines Page, one of Wilson's most intimate cronies, thought it might be necessary to "shoot" the Mexicans into self-government.

This strange situation--shall we term it a basic dichotomy?--still exists. We have a "Good Neighbor" policy, but this policy is being carried out in curious ways. On the one hand, we have an official Division of Cultural Relations set up in the State Department without adequate funds and, on the other, a series of expensive goodwill bomber flights to Bogotá, Rio, and Buenos Aires, when new presidents are inaugurated there. The government says brave words concerning democracy in the New World, but the military bigwigs of Latin-American dictators are whisked around the country in army planes and Pennsylvania Avenue is clogged with tanks for their benefit.

Finally, if one nation is to foster cultural relations with other peoples, it should know what their culture is. It is essential to know, for example, that to a considerable extent Latin America and Anglo-America have had different experiences. It is true that men in all parts of the New World faced unknown dangers and developed a civilization under pioneer conditions--and of course this experience binds them together to some extent. But there is some truth in the belief held by some that Latin America has always been, and now is, closer to European thought and culture than to our own. As an example of the eagerness of Spaniards in the New World to know European thought, it has recently been discovered that among the effects of Pizarro's Dominican chaplain, Fray Vicente de Valverde, who was killed by the Indians in 1541, was found a book by Erasmus, recently issued from the press. And it is now believed by some scholars that the whole of the first edition of Don Quixote was shipped to America by astute book dealers who knew of the avidity with which books from the old country were bought in the new world. As a final example of the way in which some Latin-American intellectuals view the relationship of United States culture and their own, consider these facts:

In 1936 there was held in Buenos Aires, under the auspices of the League of Nations Committee on Intellectual Cooperation, a discussion on this topic--What is the real difference between American culture and European culture? Two aspects of this meeting--at which such intellectuals as Georges Duhamel, Stefan Zweig, Jules Romains, Afrânio Peixoto and Alfonso Reyes were present--are pertinent to this discussion:

1. No representatives of the United States sat in the meeting, although the P.E.N. conference had brought a number of our writers to Buenos Aires at this time, and

2. No one seemed to be able to give a satisfactory reply to Jules Romains when he asked what the essential difference was between American culture and European culture. Various Latin Americans made the at-

tempt, but no statement was able to prevail against the searching analysis of Romains who maintained that European and Latin-American culture were one.

With these general considerations in mind, let us see how the United States might move if money is secured for embarking upon a real campaign to improve our cultural relations with Latin America. First of all cultural and commercial matters could be better handled apart than together. We ought to provide the exchange of ideas, publications, students, and teachers, and because we believe this exchange in itself to be good, not because we thereby hope to sell more goods, or help to smooth the way for the acquisition of air bases. If this axiom is accepted, it follows that the money should be spent by recognized cultural agencies such as the American Council of Learned Societies, the Institute of International Education, the American Library Association, the Smithsonian Institution, the Library of Congress, and other similar institutions.

Second, there should be no thought of linking this cultural program with a campaign to attack the Nazis in the press and by radio on their own ground, if for no other reason than because in a campaign of vituperation we should be opposed by masters of the technic who would not be slow to expose our most vulnerable flanks. If, for instance, we supply pictures to Brazilian newspapers showing Nazi atrocities (a plan put forward by one organization), the Nazis would very likely release photographs showing North American Negroes swaying from a limb after some lynching party. It could even be a current photograph, and if the effectiveness of our blasts could be thus reduced, the relative justice of the charges would matter very little. Or the Nazis could quote from the Nation of August 10, in which the Jehovah's Witnesses were stated to have been treated as follows:

> At Odessa, Texas, about seventy innocent men, women, and children were hauled into the courtroom by the sheriff and county attorney, held until midnight without food or water, and then the thirty-five men were packed into a small upper room for the rest of the night. During five hours from midnight they were brought downstairs, one by one, and grilled by the American Legion. Purposely deprived of food and drink until ten o'clock Sunday morning, they were then loaded on a truck and carried to the county line, delivered to a mob of a thousand, guided by and including the American Legion, who stoned and drove them on foot along the railroad right of way for over five miles. They were prevented from leaving the right of way to get water; a number fainted and had to be carried. . . .

No, accusations and indignations against the Nazi war machine will hardly make friends for us in Latin America. We ought rather to strike a positive note, by letting Latin America know what we are saying, thinking, feeling, and writing. One way to do this would be to provide a carefully selected collection of our best books translated into Spanish and Portuguese. And conversely, we ought to launch a similar collection of their contemporary writing in English translation for widespread circulation in this country.

V

The suggestions put forward above do not by any means exhaust the possibilties, which include the increased intelligent use of radio.

Indeed, it must be insisted upon that this paper does not attempt to describe all the present-day activities or even outline all the potentialities of the future. But the principles enunciated might be carefully considered in planning any long-range program to bring about that greatly to be desired end, mutual understanding in the Americas. For, in my opinion, our wisest course in the grave days that lie ahead, is to bend every effort, through channels of government, foundations, and cultural institutions and through the efforts of private individuals, toward achieving a real appreciation among the peoples of the two Americas of one another's cultures. The political and commercial necessities that draw us together, so much insisted upon today, are real and must continue to be diligently pursued. But only if we of the North and the South increasingly like and understand each other, can we both face the future with confidence.

CHAPTER 38.

THE INCORPORATION OF INDIANS AND NEGROES INTO LATIN AMERICAN LIFE

Howard University sponsored a conference on "Racial Minorities and the Present International Crisis" held during that tense period before Pearl Harbor when it was becoming increasingly clear that the United States would eventually enter the World War II. This conference provided an opportunity to attack the simplistic views some Americans held on the struggle between democracy and totalitarianism in Latin America, and the relation of this struggle to the larger struggle in the outside world.

It was at this conference that I first met Ralph Bunch, then a Professor of Political Science at Howard University. He told me that he had been refused a fellowship by an American foundation, because he had proposed to study in Brazil. He felt that the foundation officials were afraid that he would absorb some "wrong" ideas about race relations there.

"The Incorporation of Indians and Negroes into Latin American Life", <u>The Journal of Negro Education</u>, X (1941), 504-509. Reprinted by permission.

The Incorporation of Indians and Negroes into Latin American Life

Latin America: Soil for Democracy?

Although the pundits in this country who discourse on Latin American affairs disagree on many points, probably most of them would agree that the problem of the clash of ideologies in Latin America is one of the most important and least understood aspects of Inter-American relations. We have tended to regard Latin America as the scene of a simple struggle between the forces of democracy and those of totalitarianism. In observing this struggle from afar, we have placed great emphasis on the utterances of the Latin American leaders. When Colonel Batista of Cuba, or President Ubico of Guatemala, or President Aguirre of Chile has declared for hemisphere defense and democracy, we have eagerly taken note. And we have been correspondingly concerned when President Vargas of Brazil seemed to move toward fascism in 1937, even though he hastened to explain that his regime was a special brand of democracy he had designed to meet particular Brazilian conditions. So urgent and so continental did the issue appear to the Foreign Ministers assembled at Havana in 1939 that they agreed to recommend to their governments "that necessary measures be taken to eradicate from the Americas the spread of doctrines that tend to place in jeopardy the common Inter-American democratic ideal."

Declarations for democracy are heartening of course, but up to now we have pretty thoroughly neglected to ask the fundamentally important question: What is the character of the soil in Latin America in which foreign ideologies--of whatever sort--must take root if they are to have force and meaning? For the struggle between the two great conflicting ideas of our time is conditioned, in Latin America as everywhere else, by the existing social structure and predispositions of men's minds.

All generalizations concerning Latin America must of course be taken with Mark Twain's barrel of salt. The fact is that the diversity among the twenty Latin American republics is such that almost any sweeping statement about the continent as a whole, particularly about its "spirit," is bound to be untrue because it ignores the profound differences among the twenty republics. Yet it is arguable that certain large social and economic classes exist generally throughout the continent. These may be roughly designated as the conservative landowning society, the cultural fusionists, and the urban industrial society. The proportionate importance of these three groups varies from country to country, but all are found in each country. And one begins to find in an examination of the interests and outlooks of these several groups an answer to the important question: What soil does Latin America offer for the growth of democracy--what for totalitarianism?

Cultural Fusionists of Latin America

The space available will permit the description of only the second group--the cultural fusionists--which has a spiritual rather than an economic basis. It is made up of poets and philosophers, drawn from various economic levels--the novelists, journalists, professors, anthropologists, and some government officials--who believe that their America must develop an individual, autochthonous culture based upon the proposition that all the races in each country must be fused into an integrated national body politic. The problem revolves around their attitude toward the Indians and mixed races and, as in the case of the great landed estates, has its roots in the conquest.

The Spaniards who overran America in the sixteenth century solemnly disputed whether the natives were rational beings, barbarians, or a sort of soulless intermediate species between men and beasts. Each of these views found adherents and the literary strife amongst them produced numerous writings of interest to the historian. Bartolomé de Las Casas, the "Apostle of the Indians" composed a magisterial treatise to prove that the Indians were eminently rational beings, and in fact fulfilled every one of Aristotle's requisites for the good life. Gonzalo Hernández de Oviedo, official historian and sworn foe of Las Casas, was one of the most prominent among the rival school. He considers the Indians "naturally lazy and vicious, melancholic, cowardly, and in general a lying shiftless people." Their marriages are not a sacrament but a sacrilege. They are idolatrous, libidinous, and commit sodomy. Their chief desire is to eat, drink, worship heathen idols and commit bestial obscenities. What could one expect from a people whose skulls were so think and hard that the Spaniards had to take care in fighting not to strike on the head lest their swords be blunted? Thus was the American Indian described in Hernández de Oviedo's *Historia general y natural de las Indias*, written at the command of the king. The din of this controversy even reached the ears of Pope Paul III who promulgated in 1537 the famous bull *Sublimis Deus* which proclaimed that the natives were indeed human beings whose souls must be won for the church and whose property and lives could not rightfully be commandeered by the Spaniards. So hotly did the dispute continue that Charles V finally ordered a social and political experiment to be performed to discover whether Indians could live like Christians. A control village was actually set up for this purpose in Cuba about 1539. This first social experiment in the new world failed, much to the delight of the "dirty dog" school of thought, which was ever afterwards steadfastly opposed by the "noble savage" group. Throughout the three centuries of colonial life, the Indian, though generally conceded a soul, was still largely confined to hewing wood and carrying water for his Spanish masters who in general used him without much reference to that soul. It is suggestive of the approach of that time that the prize winner in an essay contest, held about 1800, to determine means of humanizing Indians in Guatemala, offered the sublimely simple proposal that they be made to wear Spanish pants and boots.

The Indians entered the political arena again in the Spanish American revolutions of the early nineteenth century, serving mostly as cannon fodder but winning their freedom on paper. Francisco de Miranda, one of the early revolutionary leaders, in his eloquent appeal to the inhabitants of Venezuela, referred to the Indians and *mestizos* as "Citizens" and one of the first decrees of General San Martín stated: "Henceforward the indigenous inhabitants of Peru shall not be called Indians, but Peruvians." During the remainder of the century little change resulted in the lives of the Indians, but since 1900 a more fundamental program based upon this earlier philosophy has been embarked upon.

The poets and philosophers who hold the cultural fusionist view insist that the reevaluation of the Indian is an indispensable condition for the existence of a real nation. They feel that their democratic constitutions will be a legal fiction while the Indians and other races are not incorporated into the life of the nation. A recent illustration of this truth occurred during the Chaco War when the Bolivian Indians, who had been herded to the front by the dominant whites, sometimes threw away their rifles while the thoroughly assimilated Paraguayans fought bravely to the last. As Moisés Sáenz, present Mexican Ambassador to Peru has written:

> There must be cultural integration. A mestizo body must have a mestizo soul. Trying to apply the Nordic standard of the white men is both unjust and futile. Let our civilization bravely accept the basic fact of our Indo-Iberic mixture, let our Indians have a voice and we may create a new world.

What do these racial theories have to do with totalitarianism versus democracy in Latin America? A good deal. One essential part of the Nazi doctrine, known all over the world, is its scorn for mixed races, for Negroes, Indians, and all who are considered not pure-blooded Nordics. Some Germans appear to realize this obstacle to winning adherents in Latin America, for Indian Commissioner John Collier believes that it was to attract Indians in the Americas to totalitarianism that a German court in a test case recently pronounced a Sioux Indian an Aryan, therefore eligible to German citizenship. Even this violence to anthropological fact does not wholly solve the problem for some prominent personalities are only part Indian and thus, according to the Nazi party line, a part of that inferior scum, the mixed races. Although Nazi agents may attempt to play down this phase of Nazi thought, Latin Americans are well aware of it, and the presence in every Latin American country of refugees from Hitler's regime is a constant reminder of this idea so alien to the cultural fusionists. The leaders of this group recognize the menace of the Nazi doctrine and have called upon their followers to stand firm against it. The Apristas, a revolutionary party in Peru, who in the past have resisted every sort of foreign imperialism, including our own, are now strongly in favor of President Roosevelt's foreign policy. Their leader, Raúl Haya de la Torre, still under surveillance in Peru, has recently declared that the totalitarian racial ideas are much more dangerous than our economic imperialism. Whereas there is reason to hope, he writes, that the economic differences between the United States and Latin America may be eventually resolved, the Nazi regime with its disdain for mixed races is a graver and more permanent menace. Haya de la Torre has published articles on this subject in Mexican and Chilean newspapers as well, taking occasion to point out that feudal aristocracies in Latin America have always scorned the Negro, the Indian, and mixed races. Even though the Aprista movement may be numerically small, when their leaders enthusiastically approve of any part of the policy of the "Colossus of the North"--that is news!

Other Peruvians, such as the more conservative Professor Víctor Andrés Belaúnde, support the Apristas in their emphasis upon the fact that the future of their country is bound up with their mixed races. The Argentine writer Ricardo Rojas exults in the sense of brotherhood among all races that have found asylum in his beloved Argentina.

Brazil, where there exists a large Negro population as well as some Indians and many European immigrants, has throughout its history prided itself upon its lack of racial prejudice and upon the fact that all kinds and conditions of men have been accepted there. Brazilian intellectuals are alive to the importance of this unifying concept to their national life and such a tract as Archibald MacLeish's "The Irresponsibles" which charged our intellectuals with indifference toward the basic issue of our day, the choice between the freedom or enslavement of the human mind, could never be levelled at them. In 1933 shortly after Hitler rose to power a manifesto was printed in Rio made up of contributions of some thirty-four Brazilian intellectuals, among them such distinguished figures as Afrânio Peixoto of Rio and Plinio Barreto of São Paulo, entitled Por que Ser Anti-Semita? The burning of Jewish books in Germany, the expulsion and virtual enslavement of the Jews were not only explicitly condemned but the opportunity was taken to reaffirm the writers' belief in the soundness of Brazilian racial doctrine and practice. It was, they said, "the clamor of a group of enlightened Brazilian consciences against the action of backward barbarians" and the following statement is typical:

> Always have we been in the past, we are today, and we believe that we will always be resistant to those ignoble fools who attempt to divide mankind into pure families and impure families, into superior castes and degraded castes, into semi-divine groups and semi-animal groups. In practice all of us in Brazil follow this sound and kindly philosophy which makes all peoples brothers --disunited brothers, imperfect brothers, some tall brothers and some short brothers, some white brothers and some black brothers --but, at last, all brothers. Some peoples may be more intelligent than ours--or more ferocious than we are--none, however, in any age, under any sky has ever understood better the old and well founded and beautiful truth of human equality on the face of the earth.

These principles have been put into practice and are not mere "literary talk." Under the Brazilian monarchical regime of the nineteenth century any Brazilian--no matter what his origin, race, or color --could become Prime Minister and lead the country. Mulattoes and Negroes such as Rebouças and Saldanha Marinho, though of humble birth, were prominent in political life. It was perfectly natural for Brazilians to see Nilo Peçanha, a Mulatto of very humble origin, follow, as minister of Foreign Affairs, Lauro Muller, the blue-eyed and purely Aryan son of a poor German colonist of Santa Catarina in Southern Brazil.

And even under the pressure of events of the last eight years, the Brazilian intellectuals have held fast to this conviction, exemplified particularly well by Gilberto Freyre, Brazilian sociologist and historian. Freyre delivered a lecture in Pernambuco last June on the occasion of the celebration of the 800th anniversary of the independence of Portugal. His thesis was that the Portuguese-Brazilian unique contribution to the world was a social framework which permitted and encouraged a free intercommunication of cultures and a thoroughgoing mixture of races. Against any outside influence which would threaten this structure Freyre would fight; and his lecture was a passionate affirmation of this culture. He considers it a duty to oppose all racial imperialism which might prevent Brazil and Portugal from carrying on their vast experiment in ethnical and social democratization. Freyre no more approves Nazi Aryanism than he does the "greaser" baiting and Jim Crowism that goes on in the United States.

It is incidentally instructive to note that even the Brazilian Integralista party which was believed to have had German and Italian ideological connections did not lift its voice against those who favor the incorporation of all race elements into the Brazilian state, a fact which suggests the strength of that idea. Totalitarian doctrines, particularly Nazi racial ideas, can expect only opposition from the Latin American cultural fusionists and what is important, this group is more nobly nationalistic than any other in Latin America.

If we are inclined to dismiss their possible political influence with a shrug, it must be remembered that their writers are highly esteemed, more so than in the United States, and attain high political posts. Bartolomé Mitre, an outstanding nineteenth century Argentine historian, also served his country as a general and finally became president. How few of our historians have also been generals! And poets are especially honored in Latin America. When Amado Nervo of Mexico died in Montevideo, Argentina and Uruguay each sent a battleship to escort his body home and a Cuban warship later joined the procession into Vera Cruz. When the Nicaraguan poet, Rubén Darío, travelled through the Spanish American countries his journey was like a royal progress. Guillermo Valencia, one of Colombia's greatest poets and intellectuals today, twice ran for the presidency and it was not considered strange that a writer of verse sought the highest political position in his country. These writers, then, constitute an important and articulate group which wields a great and at times decisive influence in public affairs.

The present political significance of the cultural fusionists thus becomes clear. An essential part of their credo is that a new culture based upon a mixture of races and peoples is coming into being in the New World, which must not be halted by any influence from abroad. As the Liberator Simón Bolívar declared about 1820, Spanish Americans are neither Europeans nor Indians, though descended from them. José Martí, the Cuban patriot; Domingo F. Sarmiento, the Argentine educator; and Andrés Bello, the Venezuelan scholar--indeed all the clearest and most influential voices of the poets and philosophers of Latin America --have exalted the <u>American</u> qualities of their cultures and have felt themselves a part of a new world and not merely overseas Spaniards or Portuguese. Jorge Basadre, important Peruvian historian and present librarian of the ancient University of San Marcos in Lima, has summed up movingly the case for Peru which a cultural fusionist of any other nation of Latin America would surely subscribe to for his own country:

> We must always welcome all persons who come in good faith to collaborate with us in our national development; we must always steadfastly oppose anyone, whoever it may be, who attempts to divide us, to exploit us, or to dominate us.
>
> A great battle is in progress in Latin America. Rival European, Northamerican [sic], and Asiatic interests struggle fiercely for our markets, our raw materials, and our spiritual direction. In face of this chaos, what attitude shall we Peruvians adopt?
>
> What must guide us is love for Peru, concern for the needs of Peru, and defense of the interests of Peru.

Conclusion

The struggle to incorporate the Indian and the Negro into Latin American society is a mighty struggle and it will not be completed in this generation or the next. It is in some places a desperate struggle, and in all countries its mark may be observed. It is an epic struggle whose importance to humanity can scarcely be overestimated. At a time when Hitler's armies have rolled over most of Europe bringing with them their master's racial dogmas, we see developing in the Latin portions of the New World a mixed race society which is far from perfect but whose future is rich in its promise for humanity.

CHAPTER 39.

AMERICANIZING THE AMERICAS

As the nations of the world girded for war, many writers in the United States looked upon Latin America as ripe for dominance by some European ism, such as Communism or Fascism. This seemed too simplistic a view to me, as conversations with Latin Americans and the study of their history led me to feel that the truth was quite otherwise. So I developed a much different interpretation in the following article.

The Inter-American Monthly, I (Washington, D.C., 1942), 8, 51-54.

Americanizing the Americas

Dakar may be only 1700 miles from Brazil and the bomber may be daily diminishing the distance between the Old World and the New, but culturally the Atlantic Ocean is becoming a wider and wider abyss. The gulf is discerned most clearly in Latin America, which has definitely ceased to be a cultural colony of Europe and is just as definitely determined to preserve her own way of life despite the ever increasing influence of world events. This is an all important fact sometimes obscured today by those who view Latin America simply as a battleground where our culture competes with European influences. Such an interpretation of the forces at work ignores the one great hope and resolve voiced by Latin Americans--to work out for themselves a new culture in the New World which will not only permit them to express their own creative power but will also constitute their special contribution to the world's civilization.

Until the relatively recent past, their constitutions, women's fashions, philosophy, music, law, art, all were imported from abroad or were modeled on a foreign pattern. The upper classes yearned toward Europe and cherished the hope of accumulating enough money to live and die there, preferably in Paris. Some of the wealthier and, automatically therefore, more traveled families prided themselves upon their foreign accent and the difficulty generally with which they used their native tongue after prolonged absences in Europe. Such persons eagerly concurred in the prevalent idea, which had been philosophically explained by Hegel and Buckle, that America did not offer suitable soil for a real culture.

Today the situation is almost exactly the opposite. Today there is a widespread distrust in Latin America of European civilization and a much greater emphasis upon the need and possibility of America's creating her own culture. It may be poorer, but it must be her own. For example, Heitor Villa-Lobos, perhaps Brazil's greatest contemporary composer, did not leave Brazil until he was forty-one years old and already a national figure. His attitude toward Europe is made clear in his oft-quoted remark on reaching France. He said, "I did not come to Paris to learn; I came to show you what I have done, and to play for you the music I have composed in Brazil." And his slogan is, "Better something bad which I have developed myself, than something good derived from others." Though critics differed in their estimates of Villa-Lobos' music, none adopted the condescending attitude usually taken by Europeans on listening to American music. This latter is well expressed by the words of a Parisian who once remarked, concerning the music of a certain Chilean composer, "Yes, he is quite good, a sort of Debussy on a minor scale."

No longer will it be possible to use a purely European standard in judging the cultural achievements of the New World. But is it possible for these heterogeneous nations, geographically vast and ethnically complex, to create independent cultures and if so, what forms are they likely to take? This question has a history, a present significance, and possible future importance worthy of consideration.

Although historians have long disputed whether Columbus was seeking Asia or a New World, the Spaniards who accompanied him soon came to realize that it was in truth a New World they had reached, and the Spaniards and Portuguese who settled these exotic lands became to a certain extent new men through their experiences. Gonzalo Fernández de Oviedo, first official chronicler of the New World, gave some illustrations of the differences between the old Spain and the new Spain across the seas in his General and Natural History of the Indies, written some four centuries ago. Oviedo was obliged to use in this work no less than 485 Indian words or Americanisms. He explained to his readers that when they found these "strange and barbarous phrases" in his work, these must not be attributed to lack of knowledge or breeding on his past--for he, as he was careful to point out, had been brought up in the royal household and had consorted with nobility--but simply to the need to employ such expressions to explain adequately those things which had no counterparts at home. Oviedo described in many chapters the luxuriant flora and fauna of the New World, observing that even when Old World animals were to be found in the new lands, their characters had changed after crossing the ocean. Roosters, for example, crowed less raucously than in Spain and tom cats made less noise as they prowled amorously about at night.

Hardly had the conquistadores subdued the New World and started to organize it, hardly were the first Spaniards born in the New World, than they declared themselves different from the Spaniards. Resentment, moreover, was aroused in the American born of both Spanish and Portuguese colonies by the policy of reserving many important official posts in America for "peninsulars." This contributed powerfully to the growth of an American spirit. Indeed, rivalry between Spaniards and Portuguese who flocked across the ocean and the men born on this side became an open quarrel before the end of the sixteenth century and persisted until the wars of independence.

The revolution of 1810-1826 was a profound change, for the Latin Americans believed that they had won not only their political but also their spiritual and cultural independence. Some thinkers believed it important to translate the revolution into educational terms at once. Don Simón Rodríguez, one time tutor of the Liberator Simón Bolívar, scandalized the good families of Chile not only by exposing his own body in his anatomy class--and he was as thin and as stringy as Don Quijote--but also by declaring that American children should study America, and that Inca history was more important for them than all the battles of the Medes and the Persians.

After the Revolution

Their independence won, the American republics were free to absorb cultural influences from the world at large, and did so, particularly from France. They showed an uncompromising spirit of hostility toward Spain and rarely did a decade pass without the occurrence of a battle between the conservative, clerical pro-Spanish group and those who considered that Spanish influence during the colonial period had been so oppressive and benighted that it must now at all costs be eliminated, even in the cultural field. Sarmiento, the great Argentine educator, felt strongly on this point. His letters written during a visit to Spain in the third quarter of the nineteenth century are eloquent testimony to the anti-Spanish feeling prevalent in Spanish America. Lastarria in Chile led a campaign against the old Spanish culture there which was in favor of a new and democratic American culture.

Argentines particularly showed themselves independent with respect to Spain. Juan María Gutiérrez, for example, scornfully returned to the Royal Academy of the Spanish Language in Madrid its diploma as Corresponding Member. When the distinguished Spanish scholar, Ramón

Menéndez Pidal, made an official visit to Spanish America in 1914 with the purpose of founding Academies of the Spanish language to be associated with the Royal Academy in the mother country, he encountered in Argentina hostility, tempered with indifference. To be sure an Academy was set up, but the institution had no life, and fell apart after its first year. On its ruins was built an Argentine Academy, which proudly and pointedly made no connection whatsoever with the mother academy in Madrid. Many other illustrations might be cited, but enough has been said to indicate that there have existed active anti-Spanish cultural elements in the Spanish American countries ever since they won political independence from Spain.

Having cut themselves off to a considerable extent from their past, these new nations were helpless before the mature European culture that now poured in. A period of cultural servitude--to employ a phrase used by some present-day Spanish American writers--now followed. Dictators such as Guzmán Blanco of Venezuela fashioned all their public buildings according to the architectural standards of France of the Second Empire. Other dictators sought inspiration in other and more distant springs. There was the Central American ruler, for example, who so loved Ancient Greece that he ordered all the school houses in his land built on the model of the Parthenon. This classical influence crops up in strange places even today. When the two thousandth anniversary of Virgil was celebrated in Mexico, there was much lamenting of the decline of classical studies there, and the labor leader, Vicente Lombardo Toledano, mourned as loudly as any professor.

We can understand the spell of Greece, for our own architects have been dominated by her example. In fact, only recently the mammoth National Gallery of Art in Washington was erected in the ancient style, despite the wails of some of our modern spirits who wanted something more American.

Over a period of many years, Latin American artists and writers did not consider that they had really arrived until they had been recognized in Europe. Even writers now living belonged to a generation which preferred to publish its first books abroad. Later works might be issued at home, but prestige required at least one early volume bearing the imprint of some great center of European culture. One is reminded of our own North American singers who found it enormously helpful, even imperative, to have sung a season with La Scala and even to have Italianized their names before attempting to catch the ears of their countrymen. Some Americans, both North and South, who stayed too long abroad, lost their cultural equilibrium and never recovered it.

Toward a New Culture

In the last fifty years the tide of opinion has turned. Latin American writers and artists no longer bow in automatic obeisance before European culture, nor are they merely in revolt against their past. But great inquietud, or uneasiness, affects the hearts and minds of all Latin Americans conscious of the gravity of this moment in the world's history. No one can read their books, reviews, or daily newspapers without confronting at every turn a discussion of this problem: How can Latin America create a culture which will be her own? The question is being asked by Argentines, Mexicans, Brazilians, Venezuelans; by novelists, historians, philosophers, poets; by conservatives, radicals, middle-of-the-roaders. One and all, they are in agreement on the main point--that American countries must produce an American culture, neither imitating nor attempting to follow Europe, the United States, or Asia.

These men and women want to Mexicanize Mexico, make Argentina more Argentine, and Colombianize Colombia. Some of them, until recently, still made trips to Europe but returned saddened by the European scene and with renewed faith in America. As one Argentine professor declared last year, he returned "convinced that America is the new hope of the world. Of a New World with a new soul."

How and why did this revolution occur? What are the characteristics of this new American culture now being created?

The impact of two world wars separated by a single generation led to the widespread dissatisfaction which Latin Americans feel today toward European culture. It is a disenchantment which reaches down into every root of their intellectual and artistic life, and produces unmistakable tension everywhere.

Bulwark Against Fascism

One may say flatly at this point that the realization of a need for independence--and the determination to achieve it--are powerful arguments against the capture of the spirit of the Latin American by Nazi doctrine or Fascist theory. They make unlikely the bugaboo of Falangista Spain leading Spanish America by the nose into the totalitarian camp. Even such a well known Catholic conservative as Alejandro Ruiz Guiñazú, son of the present Argentine Foreign Minister, shows this strongly in the book he published in 1940 entitled Argentina Confronting Itself. The author had just returned from a long residence in Europe, principally Italy. Although he refers to Mussolini as "that statesman of genius" and believes him to be the most important political figure in twentieth-century Europe, Ruiz Guiñazú emphatically rejects Fascism and Nazism (as well as North American democracy), and asserts that Argentina must seek her solutions through deep knowledge of her own conditions and needs. He even urges Argentines to know their country, especially the provinces--which is quite a concession for any Porteño, or resident of Buenos Aires, to make.

The Spanish Civil War sharply divided what pro-Spanish sentiments still persisted in Spanish America. Under the best of conditions Spanish influences had been fighting a losing battle ever since the colonies won their independence. The battered Spain which is struggling to her knees today inspires pity rather than affection or respect. Certainly the Falangistas will find it difficult to carry on Nazi propaganda under the guise of cementing cultural relations with Spain's daughter republics across the seas.

Since World War I

The spiritual crisis which occurred after the first World War did nothing to restore Latin America's faith in Europe. The translated version of such works as Oswald Spengler's The Decline of the West confirmed many Latin Americans in the feeling, right or wrong, that Europe was an exhausted continent from which they had relatively little to learn. From now on, certainly, there was no uncritical admiration for her culture.

Perhaps it was the very failure of the attempt to adapt European culture to their own needs--sometimes by blind imitation--which convinced the Latin Americans that they must look for and cultivate their own distinctive values. So, at least believes Samuel Ramos, one of Mexico's most suggestive thinkers, whose Profile of Man and Culture in Mexico is one of the basic books for those who would attempt to understand the intellectual cross currents swirling in that republic.

Nor was this a Mexican phenomenon alone. Jorge Basadre, whose Peru: Problem and Possibility summed up, in 1931, the attitude of an intelligent, sensitive Peruvian toward the position of his country in America and in the world, remarked upon the widespread desire of many Peruvians of the generation after the first World War to write essays "in search of our expression." The famous work of José Carlos Mariátegui, Seven Interpretive Essays on Peruvian Reality--a volume which became the Bible for liberal thinkers in and out of Peru--was a good example of this tendency.

Not all Latin Americans have believed themselves capable of producing a distinct culture based on American conditions. The reality of America is too sad and unpromising, complained Laureano Gómez, leader of the Conservative party in Colombia. Gómez examined Colombian culture and found it pitiful. Her Spanish heritage? Consider the black and dismal picture of cruel conquistadores, and idiot kings, and obscurantist intellectual policy. The African and Indian elements in Colombia's population? These he frankly considered liabilities, until they might be thoroughly assimilated, and this he felt sure would be a long wearisome process.

When these national problems were considered alongside the tremendous geographical obstacles to Colombian unity--mountains, jungles, impassible rivers--Gómez saw little hope of any immediate Renaissance in Colombia. Where was her intellectual strength? he asked, and replied that in philosophy, in the natural and physical sciences, Colombia was a desert. True, she had many poets--dozens flourished in every village --but not one was worthy of inclusion in the standard anthology of Spanish poetry. "Colombian culture," he concluded, "is and always will be an artificial product, a fragile, hothouse plant which requires constant care and attention lest it succumb to adverse conditions." This pessimistic attitude was promptly attacked by other Colombians of more sanguine temperament, such as the present Foreign Minister, Luis López de Mesa. Yet Gómez had well expressed the negative answer to the question--Can an independent culture really be created in Latin America?

The affirmative answer is represented by many thinkers, particularly many in Argentina. Some Argentines even believe that they are developing a new language, based of course on Spanish, but reflecting New World life in the same way that the English spoken in the United States is a new and characteristically American tongue. Naturally Spaniards are slow to acknowledge this, just as some English philologists refuse to recognize the importance of changes that have occurred in the English language in the United States.

Recently Professor Américo Castro, one of the most distinguished authorities on the Spanish language, published a brilliant and irritating study entitled, The Linguistic Peculiarity of the Río de la Plata Region and Its Historical Background. The volume was irritating, at least to the Argentines, for Castro severely criticized certain Argentine expressions as corruptions of the Spanish language developed under the pretext of working out an Argentine language, which was in reality tending to become anarchical. Castro's interpretations of the "barbaric" linguistic peculiarities of the Argentines as due to their ill-advised desire to appear original, although it was really only rebellion, have led to hot discussions in Buenos Aires. It will be a long time before the sounds of battle die down. Meanwhile Spanish as spoken in the New World continues to diverge from that of the mother country, and the recent publication of a bibliography of over one thousand titles bearing on American Spanish--Mexicanisms, Peruvianisms, Ecuadorianisms, and other Americanisms--points out some lush green fields where philologists will long wander contentedly.

Buenos Aires Conference

Perhaps the most thorough debate on the existence of Latin American culture as such took place in Buenos Aires in 1936 under the auspices of the Committee on Intellectual Cooperation of the League of Nations. . . . When the New World writers insisted that an independent development was inevitable and desirable, the Europeans, particularly Jules Romains, asked to be told wherein lay the special characteristics of this new culture. What, exactly, were its concrete manifestations? Thereupon was launched a long and inconclusive debate. . . .

Well, what _is_ the answer to Jules Romains' query about the exact content of the new American culture of which he had heard so much talk?

Simón Bolívar, the Liberator, stated the problem neatly over a hundred years ago when he attempted to explain the cultural and spiritual position of the peoples he had recently emancipated: "We are neither Europeans nor Indians, but an intermediate species between the aborigines and the Spaniards. Americans by birth, we are Europeans by law--thus our situation is most extraordinary and most complicated." But Bolívar was positive, as he stated in his discourse to the Congress of Angostura in 1819, that laws devised for his countrymen ought to be based upon their own needs, customs, and traditions, not on laws made in Washington.

Such a reply would not satisfy Jules Romains, but it may serve as a point from which to look at two approaches whereby the Latin Americans have tried to express their sense of uniqueness.

The first approach, in point of time, was insistence that since this was physically a new world--with different birds, beasts, trees, flowers, crops, and people--it was automatically a distinct culture. Books written about either the physical background, or about men and women against that background, were therefore examples of that culture. True descriptions of nature offered great scope to writers, and some of Latin America's most outstanding novels were inspired by man's battle to dominate nature--such as José Eustacio Rivera's _La Vorágine_ in Colombia, or the _Doña Bárbara_ of Rómulo Gallegos in Venezuela. It was gradually realized, however, that voices _describing_ the New World were not necessarily synonomous with the voice _of_ that world.

Indianist Movement

Then arose a second and more radical approach, the Indianist movement. This has existed in one form or another since the early days of the conquest when Bishop Bartolomé de Las Casas proclaimed the virtues of the natives and lauded their culture. In every successive generation, certain Latin Americans have proposed to orient Latin American culture toward the Indians. Of the many attempts, the revolution in Mexico has produced the most concrete and far-reaching results, but the Aprista movement, started by Haya de la Torre in Peru, has also developed extensive plans for the building of an Indo-America. Aprismo and the Mexican Revolution are among the most authentically American political and cultural movements to arise in the New World.

One of the great examples of Indian influence is to be found in art and architecture for not only are there substantial monuments from pre-Conquest days but there is a vast number of churches--it is said there are 9,000 in Mexico alone--and other structures which the Indians helped build and to which they sometimes made substantial artistic contributions. Some architects like Angel Guido in Argentina have proclaimed the "imperious necessity" of seeking emancipation from Europe in the indigenous influences.

It is no accident that the prize-winning Latin American novel recently selected for translation into English, after a continent-wide contest, was _Broad and Alien Is the World_, written by Ciro Alegría, a Peruvian Aprista, depicting the struggle waged by the Indians of a Peruvian village against a rapacious ranch owner.

Native Influence

There are dangers inherent in the too widespread application of the Indianist idea. In Argentina, for instance, indigenous cultures exist only in museums. As for the Andean countries of South America, Bolivia, Ecuador, and Peru, where the Indians numerically predominate, the artists of other Latin American countries sometimes feel that the native influence has been a limiting one rather than an enriching experience--that painters, for example, have become so immersed in Indian themes that as painters they are technically and spiritually small. Even in Mexico, where the Indian has provided a truer basis for cultural development, the artist who deliberately limits himself to the seven lineal elements of Aztec design--as did Adolfo Best Maugard--must recognize that he _is_ limiting his sphere of action by putting an arbitrary limit to his artistic development.

Perhaps the most satisfactory conclusion that one may reach today is embodied in the words of Pedro Henríquez Ureña, of the University of Buenos Aires, whose wise writings have illuminated so much of the literary history of Latin America. Henríquez Ureña refuses to be drawn into the support of any one school. He claims that the problem is really a very simple one.

He advises his fellow writers to recognize fully and frankly the divergent influences at work in Latin America, and to labor as intensively as possible to perfect their own creations. His only advice is that they link themselves always to the New World in their themes, in poetry, the novel, drama, criticism, history, and all the other arts and crafts that make up that complex we call culture. Some years ago many of our own North American critics and writers were ever on the alert to discover or to create the Great American Novel, and the result was merely much self-conscious writing. Perhaps Latin American artists and writers must forget their theorizings about creating an American culture if they are to achieve one.

Brazil is a special case all by itself. No one who has visited that great sprawling country can fail to be impressed by its variety, its beauty, and the general optimism of its people. Travelers exclaim over the glories of Rio de Janeiro, and political prognosticators spend much time wondering about the real sympathies of President Vargas. Yet one of the most important facts about Brazil is that her writers believe that they have already achieved a distinct Brazilian culture, based on a thorough-going mixture of races and cultures. If this main direction can be maintained--a direction which is diametrically opposed to that of Hitler's Aryan dogma--Brazil will indeed provide a new and notable civilization of which the Americas may well be proud.

Nearer Home

Having said all this, it seems pertinent to shift to ground nearer home and to inquire what connection, if any, all these attempt to Americanize the Americas have with the present policy of the United States toward the other nations of the New World. The connection, it seems to me, is this: We are now engaged in the greatest campaign ever waged in this country to understand the peoples of the other Americas. We are impelled to this by various considerations, of which to some North Americans, the military and commercial outweigh the cultural. But it is clear to me, at least, that mutual cultural understanding and sympathy are the keystone of the arch of hemispheric solidarity. I believe that the Good Neighbor policy will ultimately stand or fall depending upon our attitude toward the desire of Latin American statesmen, intellectuals, artists, and common men for an independent existence as creative human beings.

Our Attitude

What should our attitude be toward the Latin American countries in search of themselves? First of all, we can sympathize with them, for we ourselves are still struggling to free ourselves from the European domination of our own culture. The next task will be harder; that is, to respect our neighbors enough not to be wounded if it appears that the Latin Americans do not turn with one accord toward us as to a new sun now that the light from Europe is failing. We must realize that their independence is but a sign of their growing maturity. We have been a menacing political behemoth on their horizon for so long, and are physically so overpowering in relation to them, that we are still, not surprisingly, a natural object of suspicion in spite of the Good Neighbor policy. We will tend to be even more so, if, at a time when national consciousness is running high, we seem to be urging ourselves as mentors.

If the many and diversified plans now under way to improve our relations with Latin American countries do nothing but acquaint them with our own struggle to achieve a national culture, and with the fruits of that struggle, the money and time will have been well spent. Only we must emphatically not expect or even hope for any mass conversion to our way of life and thought. Only solutions which arise out of the Latin American cultures will have any validity for Latin Americans. There is already an ever-increasing movement of men, and ideas, up and down and around the Americas. The American family of nations will be all the stronger and all the more firmly united, if the various peoples of the New World can be encouraged to work out their own cultural destinies.

CHAPTER 40.

CULTURAL RELATIONS BETWEEN THE OLD WORLD AND THE NEW: A TEXAN VIEWPOINT

Europeans have long worried about events in the New World. In the eighteenth century the French intellectual Raynal and others felt that mankind was deteriorating in America, and the German philosopher Hegel had pessimistic thoughts on the future of the New World in the nineteenth. Some of these historical precedents were in my mind when Humberto Campagnolo, Secretary General of the Société Européenne de Culture in Venice wrote to suggest that I participate in a discussion on cultural relations between Europe and America. Thus I took the precaution of obtaining from Dr. Campagnolo a promise of entire freedom to present my views. When my text reached him he didn't like certain parts of it, though he didn't specify which sections. Even at the page-proof stage he assured me that he would be willing to allow any changes I might care to make. But the article represented my opinions on the subject, so I let them stand, warts and all.

Comprendre, Nos. 10-11 (Venice, 1954), 142-148. Reprinted by permission.

Cultural Relations Between the Old World and the New: A Texan Viewpoint

The question to be discussed, Professor Campagnolo writes in his suggestions to contributors, revolved around the preponderance of America today in the world. The greatly increased power of America has created a disequilibrium of political and economic forces which represents, we are told, a danger to the free development of the creative spirit. This danger must be recognized so that "those forces may be brought into being which will both prevent political and economic ambitions from getting out of bounds and lead to such reforms as will restore to Europe the authority required by its cultural position." The politico-cultural role of the Société Européenne de Culture will be devoted, it is explained, to stimulating such a variety of opinions as will be useful in preparing the way for the discussions to be held during 1954 in São Paulo and Geneva, under the auspices of Unesco, on cultural relations between the Old World and the New.

A noble proposal, certainly, especially when each contributor is invited to respond in his own way--a welcome and even indispensable condition for a University professor in Texas! So let me begin by amplifying and re-phrasing the question somewhat. Should it not read: What possible dangers and what possible advantages to culture may be derived from the power of America?

Do many persons except in Moscow, Warsaw, Peiping, or at those "peace congresses", really believe that the United States represents only a danger to culture? And for the sake of accuracy, is it not clear that America to the Société means not Canada, not Paraguay, not Brazil, not Haiti, nor any other nation on the American continent except the United States? Of course this interpretation greatly restricts the discussion and may not be welcomed by all the participants in São Paulo, but it is difficult to believe that any American power except the United States is considered "a danger" by the Société.

It would perhaps not be appropriate to elaborate the obvious point that Russia might also be considered "a danger" to the creative spirit and to the cultural relations between the Old World and the New, but it may be remarked in passing that this danger seems a real one to some of us in the United States partly because fear of Russia rouses and consolidates many reactionary forces here which would be nuisances--not powerful blocs--in less troublesome times.

One more observation perhaps should be made before we get our teeth into the main question. Does the Société actually believe that any reform or combination of reforms will restore Europe's previous cultural dominance? Isn't this a yearning for the past which cannot be recalled? Would it not be more prudent, and also more imaginative, to look forward instead of backward? This second question would then become: How can Europe best play the cultural role in which her age and wisdom can most fruitfully be employed? If this approach is adopted, we can avoid spending a great deal of time and nervous energy on a tender subject, for one topic wisely and deliberately dropped by Professor Campagnolo relates to the present attitudes of European and American nations toward each other--their understanding, or lack of understanding, of each other's culture.

We in the United States know full well the anxiety felt in Europe about us because of our supposed distrust of intelligence, the widespread conception that we possess no religious or spiritual qualities, have no interest in pure science, are concerned solely with the present and are scornful of the past. According to this view, the United States is a soulless country, given over to materialism and addicted to a purely mechanical and quantitative type of civilization. It is reactionary, opposed to all who question capitalism, and is powerful today but its power is negative. To use the words of those who organized the present discussion: the United States today is a "danger" to the free development of the creative spirit.

Many Europeans doubt that an important or distinctive culture has been created anywhere in the New World. This unfavorable judgment applies to the Americas as a whole, for ever since the Spanish conquest some Europeans have tended to deny that a real culture could develop in the New World and the theory was once advanced that even Europeans degenerated after living in America. In the eighteenth century an award was offered in France for the best essay on the topic: "Has the discovery of America been beneficial or unfortunate?" This question seems to be current in some European circles even today for the January issue of Holiday, an American travel magazine, warns Americans going to Europe in 1954 that they must expect to be met with the following attitudes:

> Americans are too generous, Americans are too stingy; Americans give their money to the wrong people (if you are Italian, the wrong people are the French, the English, the Germans, the Belgians--if you are French, you deduct French from the list and add Italian. If you are German you deduct German and add French, etc.); Americans are too insular, Americans travel too much; Americans do not try to learn foreign languages, Americans speak foreign languages with an accent; Americans are too warlike, Americans come into wars too late; Americans drink Coca-Cola, Americans drink gin, Americans drink whisky; Americans are not religious enough, Americans are fanatically puritanical; Americans are too hard-boiled, Americans are naively idealistic; Americans don't know how to make love, Americans make love too much; Americans are too fond of money, Americans throw their money around too easily; Americans. . ."

It is important to realize, too, that even intellectuals share some of these popular and shallow attitudes and accept still other clichés which bear upon the general theme to be discussed in São Paulo and Geneva. As recently as 1936 there took place in Buenos Aires a discussion by representatives of P.E.N. clubs under the auspices of the Committee on Intellectual Cooperation of the League of Nations. Such European notables as Jules Romains, Count Keyserling, Fidelino de Figueiredo, Stefan Zweig, Emil Ludwig, and such distinguished Latin Americans as Afrânio Peixoto, Alfonso Reyes, and Pedro Henríquez Ureña were present. The Europeans were saddened to find that their own culture was no longer held in such high esteem as formerly in Latin America, and, after the polite preliminaries were over, permitted themselves to show skepticism concerning the possibility of Latin America's achieving a distinct culture of her own. No United States representatives were present and the question of its culture did not arise.

When the New World writers insisted that already a general conviction was held in many parts of America that independent development was inevitable and desirable in America, the Europeans, particularly Jules Romains, persistently asked to be told precisely wherein lay the special characteristics of this new culture. What, exactly, were its concrete manifestations? Thereupon was launched a long, fruitless, and inconclusive debate. One gets the impression from reading the record of this elegant and erudite conversation that Romains departed from Buenos Aires feeling that his question had never been adequately an- swered, and that the Latin Americans went home somewhat frustrated by the reception accorded their attempts to explain their souls to their European colleagues.

Another set of clichés has been forming on this side of the At- lantic with respect to Europe, especially since the end of the First World War. These may be summarized roughly: Europe is spent, her scholars and literature, as well as her economies and her governments, have suffered crippling blows, but, most serious of all, she has lost that imagination and vigor which made her such a leader for centuries. She is now in her old age, a splendid ruin, perhaps, but not a conti- nent whose culture will serve as a model for the United States or the world. Europe is finished, but she doesn't recognize the fact. Her desire to re-establish her cultural dominance now is a pathetic, even though understandable, attempt at self-deception. Time does not stand still, and Europe cannot be assured its former preferential position for all time in cultural matters. What Europe really needs is some kind of collective psychiatric treatment to the end that--just as par- ents must learn that children grow up and sometimes in ways not under- stood or approved by the older generation--she will learn how to be happy though not dominant.

An illustration of the projection of these two extremes in the political realm has recently appeared in <u>The Road to Safety</u> by Sir Arthur Willert. This record of 30 years' service in Anglo-American diplomacy reveals that as late as August, 1917, four months after the United States entered the war, Northcliffe and others in England were having the greatest trouble trying to persuade their Government in London that the United States "must be treated as our most important ally." Today some Americans have to be persuaded that Britain "must be treated as our most important ally."

But today should we not label these black and white extremes for what they really are--obstacles to an honest understanding among vari- ous members of the same family--and devote ourselves to the study of our cultural relations with the persistence and tact of men of good will? In this process everyone will have to stretch his moral and in- tellectual muscles if the high objectives sought by <u>Comprendre</u> are to be fully realized.

Now let us return to the first question: What possible dangers <u>and what possible advantages</u> to culture may be derived from the present power of the United States? A calm and amazingly unemotional dialogue was held in New York last month between certain intellectual voices of Europe and of the United States on the reasons for current anti-Ameri- canism in Europe. The main problem at this meeting, sponsored by the American Committee for Cultural Freedom, was stated in this way:

"How can we unify our spiritual and cultural resources without creating destructive conformity, without crushing essential diversities during an epochal moment in history when a shift in world power has en- dowed a reluctant nation, the United States, with vast, even if not ultimate power over the free world's destiny and perhaps survival?"

The Americans deplored but did not wring their hands over the evident misunderstandings in Europe about the United States, and the Europeans assured their colleagues that the price of power was unpopu- larity and envy. All agreed that anti-Americanism imperilled the free world in its struggle with Communist totalitarianism, and urged that more dialogues be held. There were no name callings at this New York conference, no facile suggestions for improvement, no resolutions. Professor Henri Peyre of Yale University, himself a Frenchman, applied the Toynbee idea that progress has come from challenge by concluding that "anti-Americanism is a constructive challenge to America which should impel America to revise its conceptions of American life."

Another lesson the United States has been learning during the last thirty years is her need to understand the other cultures of the world. The American Council of Learned Societies, which has been the leader in this pioneering enterprise, announces in one of its recent bulletins these publications which have resulted from projects sponsored by the Council:

Religious Trends in Modern China, *A List of Published Translations from Chinese into English, French, and German*, *Kuo Jo-hsu's Experiences in Painting*, *A Guide to Iranian Area Study*, *Social Justice in Islam*, *Books and Periodicals in Western Languages Dealing with the Near and Middle East*, *Russian Discoveries in the Pacific and North America*, *History of Russia in the XIX Century*, *Russia in Manchuria (1892-1906)*, *The Burmese Writing System*, *Among Arabic Manuscripts*, and *Russian Thinkers and Europe* by V. V. Zenkovskii. This last work covers the period from about 1800 to 1925 and the author defines his theme to be "the unfavorable criticisms of European culture made by Russian thinkers."

Other cultural enterprises undertaken by various institutions in the United States demonstrate the same wide ranging efforts to learn from other cultures, but in an international setting. The Library of Congress in Washington sponsored in 1950, jointly with Vanderbilt University, the first Colloquium on Luso-Brazilian Studies. Princeton University held a Colloquium on Islamic Culture last year, while the Social Science Research Council brought together a group of scholars who focussed their attention on "The Present and Future of African Studies." In my own field, Latin American history, the United States has contributed much in documentation, bibliography, and interpretation since William Hickling Prescott wrote his classic histories of the conquest of Mexico and of Peru over a century ago.

But, it may be objected, all this benefits the United States, but where is the advantage for others? A tentative and partial reply might be that the United States is being forced--for economic, political, and cultural reasons--to confront the world, and its problems are not limited to those connected with maintaining a just and fruitful relationship with Europe alone. The United States, with its material resources--recall that the Library of Congress recently microfilmed half a million exposures of Mexican provincial gazettes, many pages of Biblical manuscripts in Mount Sinai Monastery, and a large portion of the diplomatic documents of the Japanese Foreign Office--may be able to provide the world's scholars with better cultural resources than before and may be able to bring a fresh approach to the study of cultures on a world scale. One may look at *Anthropology Today* if one wants to see how broadly conceived and supported an American scholarly undertaking can be. Edited by Professor A. L. Kroeber of the University of California, published by the University of Chicago Press, this stout volume records the proceedings of an international symposium held in New York thanks to the financial aid of the Wenner-Gren Foundation, which is located in New York, but supported by a Swedish philanthropist. Many eminent foreign scholars participated but the contributions of American anthropologists were outstanding.

Many other examples could be cited, but they all would tend to show that the United States, as a result of its world position and its need to learn about other cultures, welcomes the possibility of working with other nations and with other scholars to help bring about a more just and more general appreciation of all the cultures of the world. That this desire to free ourselves from an exclusively European cultural world has a practical and urgent meaning today may be seen from the serious charges levelled by Prime Minister Jawaharlal Nehru against UNESCO on January 9, 1954, in New Delhi. He complained that UNESCO overemphasized Europe and that Western powers still treated the newly independent Asian countries as inferiors. And Maulana Abul Kalam Azad, India's Minister of Education and President of the Indian Commission for UNESCO, declared: "Today no organization can be regarded as truly international unless it functions in both East and West."

Let us not ignore the difficulties of the present world wide responsibilities of the United States, and let us discuss these difficulties as frankly and as realistically and as often as possible in print, and by face-to-face dialogues. But let us not forget that the ultimate purpose must be to seek freedom based on a common cultural heritage.

What is that common cultural heritage? Dr. Waldo G. Leland, who has done much through the American Council of Learned Societies to advance scholarship in the United States and to foster international understanding, has declared that "there are certain vital matters on which we cannot disagree. Chief among these is the absolute necessity of intellectual freedom, of freedom to seek the truth, by all the methods of science and scholarship that we possess, and to interpret this truth in complete honesty according to the best of our knowledge and according to the dictates of our consciences. Without this freedom, no progress in science and learning is possible, nor can there by any true education." Columbia University has provided another answer to this vital question, an answer which will find much support in the United States, in Europe, and indeed in all parts of the world where men cherish freedom. The Bicentennial celebration beginning in January 1954 to celebrate the establishment of Columbia University in 1754 has been focussed on "Man's Right to Knowledge and the Free Use Thereof" inasmuch as "freedom of inquiry and expression was the most appropriate subject which a free university in a free country could choose." Sixty panels of illustrations and quotations were selected by a faculty committee to illustrate what were considered the five vital aspects of the principle:

The Inclusiveness of Man
The Values of Knowledge
Man's Right to Knowledge
Man's Right to the Free Use of Knowledge
The Responsibilities of Knowledge

The little booklet reproducing these panels is a fascinating panorama of the history and implications of these five vital aspects of "Man's Right to Knowledge and the Free Use Thereof." One of the most significant panels for our discussion concerns "The Scholar and Research." Here are reproduced the words of Professor William T. Laprade of Duke University, who declared in a 1951 article entitled "Scholarship, Hysteria, and Freedom": "A scholar needs to be free to formulate and test any plausible hypothesis that may occur to him regardless of whether or not it runs counter to views currently accepted."

The same basic philosophy was formally adopted by the American Association of University Professors when in 1949 it reaffirmed "unequivocally its adherence to the general principle that no scientific theory or proposition should be elevated to the status of a dogma to which members of the academic profession must subscribe."

If these views prevail in the discussions to be held in São Paulo and in Geneva, consideration of the possible dangers and possible advantages to the culture of the world from the present power of the United States will be both stimulating and productive.

If European domination of Western civilization is a thing of the past, exactly what will be her special contribution in the future? Here allow me to confess quite openly that I never think of "Europe" or the "European scholar"; these terms are too generalized to have much meaning. Portugal and Scotland are not markedly similar, nor do Italy and the Netherlands have many cultural characteristics in common. The same might be said of the United States; Southerners and Texans who have not yet wholly forgotten the Civil War derive a special pleasure out of the "Yanks: Go Home" signs plastered on some walls in Europe. The scholars living in Europe who are making notable contributions to the fields of history in which I am interested I think of as friends and as individuals, not as "Europeans". Charles Boxer and Robin Humphreys of London, Marcel Bataillon and Robert Ricard of Paris, Virgínia Rau of Lisbon, and Manuel Giménez Fernández of Sevilla, all these and other European colleagues are producing articles and books whose quality I respect. Of course, I also respect the contributions of a number of colleagues in the United States, as well as in Lima, Peru; Rio de Janeiro and São Paulo, Brazil; Sucre, Bolivia; Buenos Aires, Argentina; Mexico City, and elsewhere in Latin America. Conversely English scholars know that their own literature and history are being cultivated deeply in the United States and recognize these contributions.

A preliminary conclusion on the nature of Europe's future cultural position vis-a-vis the United States might be phrased in this way: One does not need to fret about being a cultural leader. A leader exercises leadership. Europe will continue to influence the world by her excellence, but not by her seniority.

One answer, neither new nor startling, to the question of Europe's future cultural influences is that scholars, writers, and artists in Europe and the United States must make a more determined effort to know each other. In this task a real command of foreign languages is indispensable and it is encouraging to see how many American scholars have devoted themselves during the last twenty years to learning the languages required for their studies on European cultures. Despite our shortcomings, probably no nation's students have applied themselves as earnestly or as systematically to foreign languages as have Americans during the last generation.

We in the United States have a heavy responsibility in this work of mutual understanding because our material assistance is needed to make possible exchanges of individuals and the distribution abroad of our more serious books and learned journals. As Professor Peyre has emphasized:

> The truth is that among the disciplines more prominently and most brilliantly studied in this country are economic and social sciences, psychology, ethics; also art history, anthropology, prehistory and medieval history, archaeology, linguistics, oriental studies, history of science, literatures, literary criticism, and several others. Some of the journals published by the

practitioners of those disciplines are today the most solid and the most alive to appear anywhere, and their merits are not due to lavish financial means, but to the diligence and devotion of their editors, authors, and readers. Indeed, parallel foreign reviews, assisted by their governments, often do not have to go through the financial agonies of American magazines, niggardly supported, if ever, by foundations. It is regrettable that articles, often disparaging foreign nations and hardly fair to the latent virtues of American culture, which appear in some weeklies in New York, should be immediately reproduced, magnified, and misunderstood in European magazines, while at the same time, European scholars, educators, engineers, writers, clamor in vain for scientific and literary periodicals from our institutions of learning.

Publications are indispensable, but exchange of persons is no less so. Historians, psychologists, artists, economists, and scientists will learn to know and respect each other in their professional meetings and not in the rarefied and somewhat artificial atmosphere of an international society devoted to culture in general. A significant and encouraging fact to us in the United States is the strong support given by Congress to the government program for the exchange of specialists and scholars. We are not good "propagandizers" and the official efforts in this field have been met generally with strong criticism from many quarters, inside and outside the halls of Congress. But the exchange of students and professors has never been challenged or doubted by any significant segment of the American people or their representatives in Washington. And so powerful a force can this exchange be for cultural understanding that some of us feel that a willingness by Russia and her friends to allow such exchanges would be as important news as an understanding on atom power. Until Russia does permit students and professors more freely to enter and leave her country, the basis for a true understanding of her culture remains weak.

It may be pertinent to point out that university professors in the United States, writers for magazines and the radio, and intellectuals in general are those who are mainly responsible for keeping American "problems" such as our own unwise immigration regulations in the limelight.

Yet, despite the present unreasonable restrictions of the McCarran Act, thousands of students, professors, and experts come to the United States every year to learn and to teach. Even here in Austin, deep in the heart of Texas, our State University has some 500 foreign students from over fifty countries. We have 150 Arabic speaking students alone. The flow is both to and from the United States; thousands of Americans are studying abroad this year. Nevertheless, too few of our Texas faculty and advanced students have the opportunity to study abroad, despite valuable help from private foundations and the government Fulbright program. These opportunities must be increased if a truly broad basis of understanding is to be achieved. It must be understood, withal, that the international role of American scholarship has not been small, as Dr. Waldo G. Leland stated back in 1940. He emphasized the fact that American scholars collaborated with their colleagues of other countries in organizing a great number of international congresses devoted to various disciplines, and joined with them in a rapidly increasing number of enterprises of research and publication. These enterprises include the preparation of major tools of research, such as scientific abstracts, "bibliographies, dictionaries, and corpora of inscriptions and documents; the study of the history of prices and of business cycles; the recording and analysis of folklore and folk music; the study of dialects; statistical compilations of all sorts; comparative studies in literature and art; research in geology, terrestrial magnetism, oceanography, and biology; investigations into the causes, incidence, and possible control of numerous diseases; archaeological excavations; the preparation of geographical maps and atlases; sociological enquiries; and the editing and publication of learned and scientific journals."

This brings me to another point, or rather question. Will it not be more fruitful to work as much as possible through existing international institutions both private and official? Government sponsored organizations labor under some significant disadvantages and the role of a private, non-official association can be especially important--a point which Americans with their emphasis on states' rights and their fear of a centralized government can readily appreciate--but funds and facilities are more often available on a permanent basis to governmentally supported institutions. Every effort should be made to use existing associations, private and official, to provide a way for fostering international relations on a professional level, rather than attempting to set up new organizations unless this becomes absolutely necessary. Political and personal circumstances usually combine for a few years, at least, to permit a newly established institute or commission to be launched with enthusiasm and temporary financial support. If the organization is active and worth its salt, it will require more, not less, money as the years roll along.

Burdensome as the financial problem is or will become in time with every one of these organizations, old or new, the competition for brain-power will be just as severe and, in the long run, the crucial point. For no one nation has enough qualified scholars in any one field and often there is an astonishingly small reservoir of individuals capable and desirous of participating effectively in these various international organizations.

A regular and ever-increasing exchange of ideas and of men is what we must aim at. The Société and its review Comprendre have a role to play at a high generalized level of discussion, and meetings for a few days--such as are planned at São Paulo and Geneva--may be useful, if well prepared for in advance, and if the results of the deliberations are spread widely by the publication of proceedings. But there is a broader and more permanent movement of men and ideas on the professional level which can best--and perhaps only--be fostered through well-established international associations devoted to their special interests. Universities and learned journals sometimes tend to perform the same service of bringing men together around a subject or a concept of common interest. The freer the flow of persons and of publications, the more permanent and regular the relations between Europeans and my countrymen, the sounder basis will there be for European wisdom and European experience to exert their proper influence.

Some Americans would pose here a question. Would greatly increased contact with Europe not constitute a "danger" to the full development of our own creative spirit? To these Americans Europe itself--or at least an important part--appears determined to destroy the very cultural traditions that have taken root here in so many ways. What will be the ultimate effect upon American culture of the nationalistic and totalitarian philosophies, or the anti-intellectual movements in the arts and religion, that have been so characteristic of Europe in the last quarter-century? This "danger", if it exists, we must run. And we believe that cultural chauvinism and isolationism are now on the defensive in the United States. Can the same be said of Europe?

Wisdom flows at all levels of society, not just among intellectuals, and no restrictive relationship will be satisfactory to Americans. Indeed, one of the real difficulties in carrying on such a discussion as is being sponsored by Comprendre is that Europeans and Americans often differ markedly in their understanding of the meaning of "culture". At any rate, exchanges of persons are essential on many levels. As Clement R. Attlee warned in his hard-hitting article entitled "Britain and America" in the January, 1954, Foreign Affairs (New York), "It is only by visits to each others' homes that real understanding can be reached by the underprivileged classes. I am certain that this understanding is vitally important for the preservation of our democratic and free way of life."

Such visits and such exchanges would permit Europeans and others to assess more accurately the varied and at times apparently discordant voices of America by which Europeans tend to judge us. As Henry Wriston, President of Brown University, remarks in the same issue of Foreign Affairs: "As time goes on, world opinion will come to judge us more by what we do than by what we say in the course of doing it, and in turn, as we gain experience in world affairs, we will learn better how to talk with our own countrymen without needlessly disturbing friendly nations."

Europeans prize individualism and respect and practice frankness, as do Texans. So they will understand a mild word of caution to those Europeans who go to São Paulo. Do not, I pray, underestimate the sophistication and learning to be found in the Americas from Chile to Canada. Since the Italian Columbus sailed westward looking for India, Europeans who have remained at home sometimes have maintained curious ideas on America. It was El Dorado, full of gold; it was a degenerate continent; it was populated with noble savages; it was the population safety valve of Europe; it was a crude frontier society. Europe was the measure of all things. Pre-Colombian art, for example, was not properly understood and appreciated by Europeans--as the Hungarian born art historian Pál Kelemen has pointed out--because it did not correspond to the moods and the modes to which they were accustomed in Europe. And for a long time men and women of the New World automatically genuflected when a European approached.

The ladies of Rio de Janeiro in 1808 offered a typical example of this spirit of accepting everything European as the perfect model. They had gone down to welcome the Portuguese court fleeing from Napoleon and observed with surprise that all the ladies of the court had cut short their hair! Not knowing that the Portuguese ladies had been forced to do this for sanitary reasons during the long voyage across the Atlantic, the Brazilians rushed home and cut off their hair so that they would follow the latest and most correct fashion. It is safe to predict that none of the elegant Brazilians who meet the European delegates at the gigantic São Paulo airport--which has more traffic than that of London--will be prepared, even symbolically, to cut off her hair! No, the time is past when Europe can live on age and authority alone. The United States is today developing a highly significant leadership in linguistics, and this significance is coming to be recognized at least by Asiatic scholars. The need is urgent for the growth in Europe of a more realistic and objective assessment of the Americas based on knowledge rather than emotion or political propaganda. If this honest evaluation is not sought for and achieved, Europe's own intellectual values will be imperilled and she might fall into a cultural antiquarianism that has no bright future for anyone.

Yet, there does exist in the United States a real reservoir of understanding of Europe and her many problems respect for her achievement, and belief in her future contributions. Professor Allan Nevins of Columbia University expresses well this feeling--in the same January issue of Holiday referred to above--when he writes:

> Europe may be impoverished by wars, down at the heels, racked by anxieties for the future, hardly able in some countries to maintain democratic governments; still the glories of its letters and arts shine as resplendent as ever. We no longer think that the older nations conspire to undervalue us, nor do we complain, as Lowell did, of a certain condescension in foreigners. The shoe is on the other foot. They accuse us of condescension. But the American still acknowledges their transcendent achievement in literature, painting, sculpture, music, and architecture. Where we have produced great talent, Europe has produced great genius.

Much patience will be required on all sides if the São Paulo discussions are to be useful and much persistence will be necessary if the difficult and sometimes painful process of mutual understanding is to go on after the meeting is over. A sense of history will be essential, too, for most of the problems relating to cultural relations between the Old World and the New have had a long past.

Let us always remember, too, that the willingness to cooperate is essential. An Associated Press despatch from London dated January 12, 1954, states that the U.S.S.R. has organized 200 of its historians to prepare a ten volume "History of Mankind" which will probably appear long before the UNESCO-sponsored "Cultural and Scientific History of Mankind". UNESCO has called in historians from many countries East and West, and a Journal of World History has been recently established for the sole purpose of exchanging views and discussing differences among these historians. The UNESCO project has been the subject of lively and probing debates in Europe and in the Americas, and certainly is open to criticism on some points, but can anyone doubt which system will produce the more honest, more objective history?

Above all a fresh spirit of good will must move participants in São Paulo with a determination to reject both American continental chauvinism and European cultural imperialism. When this has been achieved and mutual confidence created on both sides of Christopher Columbus' "Ocean Sea", we will be able to work in cooperation, not in rivalry, recognizing that European and American cultures (plural!) are inextricably woven together in the great and glowing fabric of Western civilization.

CHAPTER 41.

REFLECTIONS ON THE VIOLENCE IN PANAMA

When shocking events occur in Latin America, newspapers, the radio and television rush to render judgment or predict the future. When the Canadian Broadcasting office in New York offered me in 1963 an opportunity to spend about five minutes commenting on the flare-up in Panama before its television audience, I could not resist the challenge to include in my highly compressed presentation at least some historical and interpretive material.

Historians probably should not be poised to deliver immediate opinions on all the topics of the day, but now and then such excursions into tangled contemporary problems can be useful educational experiences, at least for the historian himself. Whether the following remarks had any impact in Canada or elsewhere remains a mystery. My sister in Montreal was surprised to have me appear on her television screen, and one Panamanian living in New York congratulated me on giving an interpretation which included Panama's viewpoint. Otherwise silence reigned.

A television statement for the Canadian Broadcasting Company, 1963. Printed by permission.

Reflections on the Violence in Panama

The death of 27 persons, the wounding of over 300 others, and the widespread destruction of property last week in Panama point again to fundamental and long-unsolved problems in the relations between the smallest republic in the Americas and the United States. The Republic of Panama was born in 1903 amidst charges of imperialism against Theodore Roosevelt, and the recent clash is the most serious and potentially most dangerous conflict that has flared up in tropical Panama since the Canal was opened to world shipping in 1914. The Panamanian Foreign Minister has publicly charged that "defenseless Panamanians have been the object of vile military action by the most powerful nation of the world." The teen-age American students at Balboa High School felt that they were showing true patriotism by refusing to obey the order of the U.S. Governor of the Canal Zone, and defiantly flew the American flag alone at their school, because they and their parents disagreed with the recent decision of the U.S. government always to fly American and Panamanian flags together in the Zone in recognition of Panama's "titular sovereignty."

What conclusions may be drawn from this terrible clash? Clearly the U.S. government cannot allow American high school students to defy it. Washington's announcement today to all Americans in the Zone that they must obey the agreement to fly both flags together or leave the Zone is belated but welcome. With Castro in Moscow conferring with Khrushchev and the Alliance for Progress in trouble throughout the hemisphere, the world is watching every U.S. move in Panama. The stakes for us and for the world are too high for anything but the most careful and calculated steps by our most seasoned officials, and we must henceforth avoid chauvinistic demonstrations by naive high school students.

While Castroist elements "measurably increased" the violence of the riots, as the Secretary of the Army has said, a serious culture clash lay behind the battle over the flags--a fact rarely emphasized in the news pouring from Panama. The Americans who built the Canal had little but contempt for the "natives" who lived in dirt and disease, did not speak their language, were not of their race, had a different moral code, were alien in many ways. After the Canal was finished, many Americans stayed on and kept themselves the technical elite, taking great pride in their accomplishment. They built up in their Canal and their Zone a comfortable, complacent, and self-sufficient community depending on Panama for little except menial labor. After decades there, many of them did not even know how to ask for a bottle of beer in adequate Spanish. It is doubtful that their high schools taught Central American history or gave the American students any idea of how Panamanians felt about the Canal Zone.

The Panamanians who were looked down upon as "spigs" by the Americans, in turn developed their own clichés about the Americans, the "gringos". Most Panamanians saw Americans only as thirsty and roistering soldiers and sailors who often figured in lurid episodes in Panamanian dives, wealthy tourists, or business men who kept to their own crowd. Panamanians considered the gringo an immature, cocky, swaggering, money-mad blonde without culture who considered himself superior to all Panamanians, especially to those of Negro blood. His women were loose. His nation, the Colossus of the North, was run by imperialist bankers in Wall Street.

Given this basic misunderstanding is it any wonder that trouble has come repeatedly and with increasing violence?

What can be done now? What can be negotiated by the two governments?

We must take more seriously than ever before the conviction of many cultivated, respectable Panamanians, and not just Castroite sympathizers, that the treaty governing relations between the two countries is--to quote Panamanian Foreign Minister Solís at the United Nations in 1962: "humiliating, injurious, unjust, and inequitable." Probably Panama will demand, and receive as in past treaty negotiations, a higher rent for the Zone, better working conditions and higher status for Panamanians working in the Zone. But these concessions and the promise to enforce the decision made earlier this month--whose violation by U.S. high school students precipitated the present conflict--that the Panama flag always be flown with the Stars and Stripes in the Zone will not suffice. The thorny question of sovereignty will be raised more insistently than ever before, and apparently the U.S. has begun to realize this by its decision announced today "to discuss all differences with Panama."

If these discussions are to be better than a pause between conflicts, the U.S. must use more imagination and have available more facts on Panama than before. Shall the U.S. continue to give lip service to what it calls Panama's "titular sovereignty" in the Canal Zone by flying both flags together, yet stand pat on the assertion made by Secretary of State Dulles just 10 years ago that the U.S. has sovereignty over the Canal "to the entire exclusion of the exercise by the Republic of Panama of any such sovereign rights, power, or authority"?

What if the Canal were to be "inter-Americanized" or "internationalized"? We need more public information and more public discussion of the many and complicated economic, legal, military and political problems involved. Both countries are in the midst of tense election campaigns, so the question of sovereignty cannot be resolved immediately, but should not this period be used as a preparation for vital decisions?

The U.S. met the challenge of cutting the Canal through hills and jungles with courage, skill, and intelligence. Cannot the American public now face the true nature and dimensions of our dispute with Panama and summon up equal courage, skill, and intelligence to meet the social and political challenge produced by the head-on collision of Panamanian and American culture? In facing this challenge, we might well recall the words of Secretary of State Elihu Root before the National Assembly in Panama in September, 1906, before the canal was built:

> . . . The two peoples, the Anglo-American and the Spanish-American, are widely different in traditions, laws, customs, and methods of thinking and speaking and doing business. It often happens that we misunderstand each other, . . . that we fail to appreciate your good qualities and . . . you fail to appreciate ours; and that with perfectly good intentions, with the best of purposes . . . we clash, we fail to understand each other, . . . and misconception and discord . . . arise. Let us remember this in all our intercourse; let us be patient with each other; let us believe in the sincerity of our mutual good purposes. . . and be . . . forbearing each with the other, so that we may go on together in the accomplishment of this great enterprise.

Now that the Canal has been accomplished and has served well the people of the world for almost 50 years, can we not follow President

Johnson's oft-made exhortation: "Come, let us reason together."

Yes, let us reason with our Panamanian friends in the spirit of Elihu Root, but let us prepare to discuss more seriously than ever before the question of sovereignty.

CHAPTER 42.

THE BONES OF CUAUHTEMOC

History is past politics, declared Edward Augustus Freeman, but in Latin America today one also sees that past history is present politics. This is the lesson to be drawn, I believe, from the battle in Mexico over the bones of Cuauhtémoc, the last Aztec emperor. It is a tangled story which needs some detailed description to be fully understood. But this article attempts to show that to understand the contemporary affairs of Latin America, a knowledge of the colonial period comes in handy.

Encounter, XXV, No. 3 (London, 1965), 79-85. Reprinted by permission.

The Bones of Cuauhtémoc

Bones have played a remarkable role in Spanish American history ever since the remains of Columbus were transferred in 1509 from Valladolid to the Carthusian monastery of Las Cuevas near Seville. The controversy over whether this set of bones was ever moved (and if so, where?) is still carried on with enthusiasm and erudition. To Mark Twain's witticism about the two skulls of Columbus, one when he was a child, and the other when he was a grown man, it has been suggested that perhaps a third should be added--the skull he died with.

The most significant battle over historical bones, however, has been waged in Mexico since the dramatic announcement in September 1949 that the tomb of Cuauhtémoc had been found in the village of Ichcateopan. This last Aztec emperor, tortured and eventually strangled by Cortez, had long symbolised in the popular mind the heroic Indian resistance to the Spanish conquest. Since the fall of the Aztec capital Tenochtitlán in 1519, many Mexicans have considered Cortez a foreign oppressor who destroyed thousands of Indians, and made possible the unpleasant introduction of an alien culture. So persistent and strong has been this attitude that public opinion has always successfully opposed the erection in Mexico of a monument in his honour. Though Cortez died in Spain, he considered himself so much a part of the New World that he stipulated in his will that he and all his family should be buried in Mexico. But it was evidently judged prudent to hide his bones, for they only came to light in 1946, three years before the Ichcateopan revelation. Some cynical observers in Mexico suggested that there was a direct connection between these two discoveries; the *indigenistas*--who resented any attempt to exalt the contributions of Spain to America by publicising Cortez--had purposefully prepared Cuauhtémoc's bones as a counterfoil. That this rumour even got started indicates the bitterness of spirit between the two factions that have wrangled since the 16th century over the true nature of the Spanish conquest and the three centuries of colonial rule.

Scientific experts were marshalled for and against the historicity of the bones at Ichcateopan, and a full account of the public trial that ensued would fill a whole issue of *Encounter* since practically every approach was used except the carbon 14 method. The government immediately appointed an official commission of distinguished Mexicans, who decided (in October 1949, with one abstention) that the bones were those of several individuals and that proof was lacking to establish when they had been interred. A popular outcry greeted this decision. Violent attacks appeared in the press which insisted that the Commission was both biased and misinformed. One counter-report pointed out that the Commission had contained no physicist, no mathematician, and only one chemist. The government experts were denounced as wanting in patriotism, and their attackers were charged with Communism in the newspapers, which gave "The Bones" front-page treatment.

The Ministry of Public Instruction now felt compelled to appoint an even more formidable group to sit in judgment. This time it included not only historians and archaeologists but also representatives of outstanding Mexican cultural and scientific institutions. Geologists, chemists, metallurgists, epigraphers, mathematicians, and various other specialists were called to give testimony. Numerous meetings were held to examine the mass of evidence and artifacts that rapidly accumulated.

The Commission's first act, however, was to do conspicuous honour to Cuauhtémoc by being photographed standing guard solemnly in front of his statue in the Paseo de la Reforma. Patriotism--and prudence--required no less. The Commission then deliberated a full year, holding thirty-eight separate sessions, and receiving ten formal reports on special aspects of the problem. Despite ferocious and unremitting attacks in various newspapers and periodicals, it held essentially to its predecessor's conclusion that the bones were not Cuauhtémoc's. But the public excitement did not abate much, and this may be the reason for a lapse of over ten years before the voluminous proceedings of the Commission were published (and then only in a private, rather limited edition).

Why did the Mexicans feel so strongly on the question of these bones? The Cortez-Cuauhtémoc confrontation could occur only in Mexico --for what other country could or would mount such a testimony to its indigenous culture as the splendid National Museum of Anthropology opened in Chapultepec Park last September? But it is also true that the nature of the conquest has been continuously and rancorously discussed in Spanish America generally during the last 450 years by historians and laymen alike.

Even Peru, whose aristocratic, wealthy upper class is perhaps more faithful to Spain than any other élite group in Spanish America, has not escaped divisive discussions on the nature of the conquest. A striking monument to Francisco Pizarro stands proudly in the Plaza de Armas in Lima in front of the cathedral--for which this one-time pig herder who conquered Peru laid the cornerstone and carried the first beam on January 18th, 1535. Tourists are shown there to-day his mummified remains in a glass coffin, which reposes in a chapel. No battles have been waged over these bones. But the cruelties of the conquest of Peru are kept alive by indigenistas (Luis Valcárcel) and contemporary historical works (e.g. Juan José Vega's Manco Inca el gran rebelde). Indeed, in all of Spanish America--a vast territory in which, as R. A. Humphreys has stated, "all Western Europe from Madrid to Moscow might lie and be lost"--the disagreements over the conquest have broadened out until they have become inextricably bound up with judgments on the Spanish colonial régime as a whole.

One of the key questions on the conquest is how Spanish action in America affected the Indians. The most frequently cited author is Bartolomé de Las Casas, the best-known defender of the Indians. As the Spanish-speaking world prepared to commemorate in 1966 the 400th anniversary of the death of this controversial Spanish Dominican, his ideas and influence have rightly attracted an ever-widening interest. He believed that Indians were rational human beings, who could be converted to the faith by peaceful means alone. Conversion should involve a real understanding of Christian doctrine and should not be a superficial baptism of the uninstructed. He was convinced that the cultures of the strange beings brought to the notice of the world by the discovery of America deserved not only study but respect, and suggested that the Indians compared very favourably with the peoples of ancient times. He even maintained that the Maya temples of Yucatán were not less worthy of admiration than the pyramids in Egypt (thus anticipating the conclusion of 20th-century archaeologists). In some respects, he asserted, Indians were superior to Spaniards, and cited their family life and the industry of Indian women as examples.

The only justification for Spanish rule in the New World, Las Casas insisted, was the fulfilment of her religious mission. If "violence and intolerance" are among the characteristics of the Spanish people (as one of their greatest historians, Rafael Altamira, argued), the struggle waged by Las Casas and others to permit the triumph of mildness and Christian persuasion, even though the victory was never won, becomes all the more remarkable. Las Casas opposed the enslavement and degradation of the Indians on doctrinal, not sentimental, grounds. "All the peoples of the world are men," he proclaimed in 1550, opposing the application by a Renaissance Spanish scholar of Aristotle's doctrine of "natural slavery" to the Indians. . . .

It was Las Casas' effort to do something about the bodies and souls of the American Indians that led the Mexicans to raise a monument to him in the 19th century beside their greatest cathedral. He has become one of the most popular folk-heroes of the New World. (The splendid equestrian of Charles IV, El Caballito, is tolerated along the Paseo de la Reforma, it is said, because the Mexicans, who love horses, are enchanted by the noble charger upon which the Spanish monarch is so confidently mounted.)

Las Casas has become known to the world largely because of his allegation on the numbers of Indians killed--which helps to explain why Spain has never seen fit to honour him with a statue in Madrid. His experiences after he first went to the West Indies (in 1502) and the documents sent to him from many parts of the Indies until his death in Spain in 1566 convinced him that the conquest of America was one of the darkest pages in the annals of mankind. These convictions he set forth in the most widely read of all his many treatises, the Very Brief Account of the Destruction of the Indies (1552). This was a province-by-province description of the bloody deeds of his countrymen during the conquest, in which he claimed that millions of Indians had perished.

The words of this Spanish bishop were quickly seized upon by Spain's political enemies. They were translated into the major European languages for the greater defamation of Spain--and the modern age of propaganda began. The first English edition appeared in London in 1583, and in the next year Hakluyt, in his Discourse on Western Planting, selected some of the more gruesome passages from Las Casas to arouse Queen Elizabeth "to proper horror of Spain." The last English translation, which appeared in New York in 1898, entitled, An Historical and True Account of the Cruel Slaughter of 20,000,000 People in the West Indies by the Spaniards, was designed to incite Americans against the Spaniards in Cuba, and succeeded in doing so. Is it any wonder that so many English-speaking people have a deep-rooted feeling that Spaniards are a uniquely cruel people?

The disputes started during Las Casas' lifetime, continued throughout colonial rule, and reached a new height of passion during the tumultuous period of the wars for Spanish American independence, 1810-1825. A veritable rash of reprints of Las Casas' Very Brief Account appeared, in London as well as in Philadelphia and in Spanish America. London at that time was a centre for Spaniards, and a lively discussion took place there on the justice of Spanish rule, with a view to supporting or opposing the revolutionary movements in the New World. William Walton specifically cited Las Casas in his Exposé on the Dissentions of Spanish America (1814) and charged that Spain had deliberately suppressed the truth of the conquest and had permitted "only epic poems and romances in praise of the first conquerors. . . in which the ignorance and vices of the defenceless natives were alleged as a plea for unheard-of butcheries." In Spain, Ferdinand VII's mentor, Juan de Escoiquiz, published a three-volume "heroic" poem, México conquistado, which was a panegyric of Cortez (and prefaced by indignant notes against Las Casas), for by this time a kind of popular cult had grown up in pro-Spanish circles about the figure of the conqueror of Montezuma.

The victorious insurgents in the early 19th century were in no mood to soften their condemnation of the motherland. Their feelings have been well characterised by Stanley Stein: "Spain, to them, came with the sword and departed with the sword." The ferocity of the wars for independence created no climate for reconciliation, and Mexico even expelled large numbers of Spaniards from her soil during the years 1827-29. During the depressing post-independence period, some Spanish American thinkers attributed their nations' troubles to the kind of society they had inherited from Spain.

Interpretations of the conquest by historians have tended to become polarised. Scholars formed in the atmosphere of the _leyenda negra_ --the "black legend" of Spanish cruelty and oppression--are ever on the alert to condemn what they believe to be softness towards Spanish action in America and the creation of a "white legend." An outstanding recent monograph on _The Aztecs under Spanish Rule_ is described by one reviewer as a "footnoted edition of Las Casas." Professor Gibson's enormously detailed text and rich bibliographical apparatus point to the inescapable conclusion that "the deterioration of a native empire and civilisation" resulted and that the Indians responded to their defeat and depressed social status by addiction to drink. The sombre summation, indeed the last remark in this impressive volume, helps to explain the Cuauhtémoc complex in Mexico today: "If our sources may be believed, few peoples in the whole of history were more prone to drunkenness than the Indians of the Spanish colony."

Another example from recent historical studies may be seen in the population estimates of Borah and Cook. They calculate that some 25 million Indians lived in Central Mexico when Cortez first landed, and that by 1548 this dense population had melted away to about 6 million. These figures are bound to re-open the question of whether the statistics of Las Casas were so "exaggerated" after all--for he had stated in 1542 that four million had died in Mexico since the conquest began. The lethal forces responsible for this estimated loss of 19 million human beings may have been malaria or intestinal viruses, rather than Spanish cruelty; but the opponents of Las Casas who condemn him on the ground that the New World had a much smaller population than he claimed will now have to re-examine this argument.

The most eloquent illustration of the continuing struggle represented by the battle over the bones of Cuauhtémoc may be seen in the recent publication of a large book attacking Las Casas, written by the Spaniard Don Ramón Menéndez Pidal at the age of ninety-three. The most highly respected scholar in the Hispanic literary world to-day, Don Ramón here sets forth his passionate conviction that Las Casas was unworthy of the honour accorded to him by many, and was in fact a megalomaniac, indeed a paranoic. Looking back on the Spanish conquest through his own tinted spectacles, Don Ramón sees few dead Indians; rather, a scene of contentment and cultural advance made possible by Spaniards. When Don Ramón made known his convictions on Las Casas at Oxford in 1962 to an international group of Hispanists, he was astonished to learn in conversation with a Mexican writer that some Mexicans _still_ cherished strong resentment against Cortez and were not yet ready to forget the cruelties of the Conquest. Why did they not remember instead the benefits brought by Spain to the New World? The cultural contributions of the Indians are not mentioned by Don Ramón; he does not share at all the feeling of Albrecht Dürer on seeing in Brussels in 1520 the gifts presented by Montezuma to Cortez:

> I saw the things that were brought to the King from the New Golden Land: a sun entirely of gold, a whole fathom broad; likewise a moon, entirely of silver, just as big . . . and all sorts of strange articles for human use, all of which is fairer to see than marvels. . . . I have never seen in all my days that so rejoiced my heart as these things. For I saw among them amazing artistic objects, and I marvelled over the subtle ingenuity of the men in these distant lands.

Why do arguments about the _conquistadores_' treatment of Indians in the far-off 16th century still agitate scholars and men in the street in Spanish-speaking lands? Is this merely another instance of that powerful spirit of nationalism to be found on all continents? This is much too simple a solution.

Great advances have been achieved within the last generation in the study of sources which throw light on the realities of the Spanish American past. All periods are being studied, the amount and quality of writings both in and outside of Spanish America are impressive, and historians are adding to their traditional techniques some of the methods of the allied social sciences. Comparative analyses are being more often attempted, and lively scholars from various countries are being brought together for research and teaching in the University of Chile, the _Colegio de México_, the University of São Paulo, and other institutions south of the Rio Grande. New and exciting topics such as _mestizaje_, the history of mixed races, are being taken up by historians with the help of anthropologists and others. Yet the conquest remains a richly debatable part of the field. Why?

The Swedish historian Sverker Arnoldsson's explanation is that controversy continues because "the economic, social, and racial problems which were created by the conquest of the New World still exist." The increasing number of persons concerned with these problems are coming to realise that, as one widely experienced agricultural specialist has written in describing the desperate plight of the workers on the land:

> In Brazil, Haiti, and the eighteen Spanish American countries as a whole, at least one half of the agriculturists are dependent upon methods of extracting a living from the soil that are more primitive, less efficient, and more wasteful of human energy than those the Egyptians were using at the dawn of history.

In their distress in the face of the great task of modernising their societies, many have found relief in blaming the United States, but the complex subject of anti-Yankee feeling is a story in itself. The Brazilian sociologist, Luiz Aguiar Costa Pinto, has pointed out another basic fact:

> In these societies everything is on the table for debate, and all debate is a political debate. Development in Latin America is not only a transition from plantation system to factory system. In fact what is under debate is the whole heritage of the archaic society--the economic, political, and intellectual heritage--as well as the archaic society itself--its structure, its values, its prospects.

Though Brazil, an increasingly great power in the Americas, is different in many ways from Spanish America, Brazilians also have been scrutinising their Portuguese past in a critical spirit and are no less determined than their neighbours to modernise the society they have inherited.

In the debates to-day Spanish Americans generally tend to sympathise with Las Casas, for they consider him a turbulent but Christian and altruistic spirit who was "the first great anti-colonialist" in America. He is honoured because he emphatically and consistently opposed the unjust actions of his own people, and dared in the 16th century to criticise the society which many hold responsible for the ills of to-day. Dictatorship, the Indian "problem," corruption, the great landed estates, an oligarchical system, have all been seen as unfortunate results of the Conquest. Many Spanish Americans would agree emphatically with the geographer, James Parsons: "Everywhere in Latin America the hand of the past lies heavily on the land." Thus the histories and interpretations of the Conquest are, in effect, contemporary history.

The Conquest, then, is the "living past" of both Spain and Spanish America. How long ago the great confrontation of Spaniards and those they called Indians happened. And yet how persistently the historical consequences remain as part of our world, our time, our problems!

We may begin by debating the authenticity of the discoveries at Ichcateopan, but from the argument over the bones of Cuauhtémoc we are led inevitably to consider the obstacles--or at least some of them--that confront the "Alliance for Progress" to-day.

CHAPTER 43.

EDWARD LAROQUE TINKER

Usually I have tried to avoid formal occasions, but I could not resist the request to speak at the dedication of the Tinker Library at the Spanish Institute in New York City, April 28, 1970. These "Remarks" have never been printed so far as I know, and are included here as a personal tribute to an old friend.

Edward Laroque Tinker

My first awareness of Edward Laroque Tinker was as the author of a remarkably interesting book entitled Lafcadio Hearn's American Days, which I had stumbled upon as an undergraduate at Northwestern University beginning to study Latin American history under the guidance of one of the veteranos in this field, I. J. Cox. It was many years later, while serving as Director of the Hispanic Foundation in the Library of Congress, that Don Eduardo loomed on my horizon as someone deeply concerned with libraries and with Hispanic culture. Later, at the University of Texas, I became accustomed to seeing harnesses and other gear connected with horses accumulate in the university library along with books as successive donations arrived from the Tinker collection in New York for the Hall of the Horsemen of the Americas he established there. It was during these years, too, in 1955, when a State Department operation, which included a visit to every Spanish university, allowed me to be present in Madrid when Tinker, at the mature age of 74, received a Doctorate from the University of Madrid. Later, when I had moved to Columbia University, we spent a number of pleasant sessions together as new members of the Board of Trustees of the Hispanic Society of America--along with other freshmen trustees Ernesto da Cal and George Moore --all under the benevolent and witty guidance of Hyatt Mayor as he initiated us into the mysteries of the activities and problems of the Hispanic Society. But it is not of my personal impressions of Don Eduardo that I propose to address myself very briefly to on this occasion, when we are dedicating the library of the Spanish Institute to his memory. My purpose will be to present a few reflections on the phenomenon of Edward Laroque Tinker as a Hispanist in the United States, and some modest recommendations for the future activities of the Tinker Library.

When my old friend and colleague in many a Hispanic and Luso-Brazilian undertaking, Carleton Sprague Smith, invited me "to say a few words" I accepted with alacrity because of my many associations with and affection for Don Eduardo, and then repented at leisure when it became clear how difficult this task would be. For he was much more then a Hispanist, and had been active in many fields. More than 20 years before receiving his Spanish doctorate he had achieved the distinction of becoming a Docteur de L'Université de Paris, and had written many different kinds of books including one with the challenging and somewhat baffling title of "The Palengenesis of Craps"!

But whatever may have been his achievements in other fields, what concerns us today is his development as an amateur Hispanist. No matter how many doctorates he received or how many learned assemblies he spoke before, there was no academic dust on Don Eduardo. I think of him as one of that small and select band of his English-speaking contemporaries who were attracted by Hispanic culture as a living, unique experience of man upon this earth, and who aimed to recapture this spirit in their writings. William Henry Hudson was one of these, whose Far Away and Long Ago is a wonderful tale of the Argentine and gaucho life on the pampa, to which Tinker also made significant contributions beginning with his work on The Cult of the Gaucho and the Birth of a Literature (1948). Robert Bontine Cunninghame-Graham, the Scottish mystic, horse-lover, and copious historian on Spanish American themes was another of this group of English-speaking writers who fell under the spell of Hispanic culture. Whether Tinker ever met this Scottish individualist I do not know, but they surely would have become boon companions if they had.

Walter Owens was another, though he never was particularly devoted to horses, so far as I know. He evidently spent his days in an office in Buenos Aires, but also hearkened unto the call of Hispanic culture, for he produced unusual translations of the first Spanish epic poem in America, the sixteenth-century La Araucana by Alonso de Ercilla, as well as José Hernández's classic on the life of the gaucho Martín Fierro.

Archer Milton Huntington was another such "amateur" Hispanist, and we employ the word "amateur" in its true meaning, not as a dabbler or superficial devotee but, to use a dictionary definition, as "one who engages in a sport, study, or other activity for pleasure rather than for financial benefit or professional reasons." Huntington's poems, embodying the wisdom and grace he had absorbed during his prolonged study of Hispanic literature, his determination to bring to the United States an understanding and appreciation of Hispanic culture through the establishment of the Hispanic Society of America, all served to mark him as another of the rare breed to which Edward Laroque Tinker belonged. These amateurs have all gone, but what a rich and varied legacy have these English-speaking writers left the world as a result of their somehow having been touched by the inner qualities of the Hispanic world. And how fortunate has been Spain that she was able to inspire the affection and respect of such a gifted constellation as William Henry Hudson, Robert Bontine Cunninghame-Graham, Walter Owens, Archer Milton Huntington--and Edward Laroque Tinker.

There remains the question of the future of the Tinker Library. Today with so many collections of books, especially in the New York metropolitan area, one must ask this question of every new library: to what end? Is this new activity necessary? I realize that all this sounds suspiciously like the questions fired at witnesses in Washington by an economy-minded Chairman of the Appropriations Committee! But I speak as a long-time admirer of libraries, and of librarians. It is no mistake that the art historian Pál Kelemen has dedicated his volume on Art of the Americas: Ancient and Hispanic thus: "To the countless unnoticed librarians of our country, who are carrying on their cultural work with intelligence and patience."

It is easier to raise the question of the future of the Tinker Library than to answer it. Some negative conclusions, however, seem clear. It should not, indeed it cannot, compete with other libraries in the metropolitan area which for years have been collecting books on Spain. Nor does it seem to me desirable to limit it to works on one period such as "The Golden Age" or "Twentieth Century Spain". What is plainly needed, in my opinion, is a center where teachers giving courses in the Spanish language or in some particular field such as history and literature can turn for up-to-date and reliable information on teaching materials of value. The Pan American Union provides such a service to some extent for students and teachers interested in Latin America, but so far as I know none exists for Spain. If the study of the Spanish language and Spanish culture are to occupy their proper place in our educational institutions, the quality of instruction must be improved. Much has been achieved in recent years by devoted teachers, but much remains to be done. My hope, then, is that the Tinker Library will think primarily about its possible use to teachers who may never read a book in this room but whose work might be enriched by information collected and made available by the Tinker Library.

One final thought. Despite Don Eduardo's privileged position, he never wrote about the elite, but about the gauchos, the common men, the underprivileged in the great empire Spain established in America. One of his last publications was on popular cultural manifestations: his *Corridos and Calaveros*. Does not this indicate that the Tinker Library should include a goodly selection of works on the Spanish people, the men and women who through the centuries have helped to endow Spanish culture with such a character and with such dimensions that talented foreign amateurs have spent a goodly portion of their lives working to make their countrymen, too, aware of the special contribution of the Spanish spirit to the cultural life of the world.

CHAPTER 44.

FOUR GENUINE GENERALIZATIONS ON ACADEMIC POLLUTION CREATED BY U.S. LATIN AMERICANISTS

One of the notable developments since World War II has been the establishment of regional Councils on Latin American Studies. Their annual meetings provide an opportunity for everyone interested in Latin America to meet other scholars in the region and to broaden perspectives with programs in which representatives of various disciplines participate.

Over the years I have attended such meetings in many parts of the United States, and have found them to be professionally stimulating as well as pleasant social affairs. They also make possible forums to consider some of the general problems of Latin Americanists, such as this piece delivered in Knoxville in 1973 at the annual meeting (twentieth, I believe) of the Southeastern Conference on Latin American Studies.

SECOLAS Annals, Vol. V (March, 1974), 5-15. Reprinted by permission.

Four Genuine Generalizations on Academic Pollution Created by U.S. Latin Americanists

We tend to think of pollution in terms of dead fish floating down chemical-filled rivers, or as that yellow fog which blankets the Los Angeles area all too often, but there are other kinds of dangers menacing modern man--especially those of us who study Latin America in universities. For want of a better description I call this phenomenon "academic pollution in the Good Neighborhood."

In setting forth these dangers I shall speak plainly, in the same spirit as those ancient Aztecs so professionally studied by the Franciscan Bernardino de Sahagún in sixteenth-century Mexico. You may remember that this notable anthropologist described how Aztecs got ceremonially intoxicated in a number of different ways, but emphasized that in general Aztec society severely regulated the drinking of liquor, though it allowed those who reached the age of seventy to imbibe all they wanted. Let us substitute generalizations for liquor, and ration them very carefully among our younger Latin Americanists until they reach the magic age of seventy. You will readily understand, then, why a veterano like myself, who will be 70 in the not too distant future, feels free to describe academic pollution with all the abandon of those old Aztecs who reached confidently for the wine bottle, or whatever they called the jar that held the precious liquid.

I.

My first generalization has to do with the books and manuscripts upon which so much of our research and teaching--at least in the humanities--depends. Even though the Bolivian archivist Gunnar Mendoza has not yet completed the enormous task of preparing a guide to the Latin American manuscripts in the United States, we know that the total is great and growing. The National Union Catalog demonstrates that our collections of rare books are so impressive that Latin American scholars not infrequently find it far easier to work in Washington, New York, Berkeley, Austin, or some other center in the United States than in their own country.

How did these books and manuscripts get here? Often, perhaps usually, by perfectly legitimate means but not always. Our institutions acquiring Latin American books and manuscripts do not of course rival in skulduggery and duplicity the skilled activities of those who wheel and deal in museum circles, for there archaeological artifacts from Latin America have become such big business in recent years that The New Yorker a couple of weeks ago ran a long story on the subject, bringing out the chilling fact that there are so many middle-income art collectors today that there is a pre-Columbian department at Bloomingdales. But there is plenty of dissatisfaction south of the Rio Grande which prompted my article on this subject last year in the Newsletter of the Latin American Studies Association. This topic is too large for treatment here, but it remains a constant threat to honest and enduring relations with our Latin American colleagues.

What can be done about it? Various international organizations such as the Pan American Union, UNESCO, and the Seminar on the Acquisition of Latin American Library Materials (SALALM) are aware of the problems created by the steady movement--both legally and illegally--of books and manuscripts from Latin America to our collections, and are doing what they can. My own view is that the solid base on which we must establish our efforts in this field was set forth by Luther H. Evans in 1949 at the First Congress of Mexican and United States Historians held in Monterrey, Mexico.

Dr. Evans, as Librarian of Congress at that time, stated these principles:

> In considering our responsibilities and those of other cultural institutions of the Americas it seems to us that there are three basic principles that should be our guide:
>
> I. The cultural institutions of the several American nations should unite in refusing to countenance any improper removal from a country of its unique cultural materials and in working toward the universal recognition of every nation's prior right to unique documents constituting a part of its cultural patrimony.
>
> It is the policy of the Library of Congress that it will not buy, nor will it accept as a gift except under terms that permit its restitution, any document that appears to have been removed from another country in violation of its laws intended for the protection of cultural resources or to have been improperly removed from the collections of any library, public or ecclesiastical archives, or similar cultural institution. . . .
>
> II. The cultural institutions of the several American nations should aid each other in programs for the preservation and cataloging of their collections of historical sources, and in developing the best technical methods to this end. . . .
>
> III. The principal cultural institutions of the American nations should cooperate to preserve and disseminate by means of photoreproduction the basic rare or unpublished documents of their history and culture, including those located in Europe. We must go a step beyond aiding each other in the preservation of historical sources and disseminating information about them. We must endeavor to make it realistically possible for a scholar in any of the American Republics to make use of the most important sources relating to the history of the Americas without prohibitive travel costs.

It will be difficult if not impossible for any diplomatic action by treaty or even international convention to assure that these principles are actually put into effect. A more effective method, so far as the United States is concerned, might be to apply to rare books and manuscripts the law proposed by William D. Rogers, the President of the American Society of International Law, who "suggested that no antiquity given to a museum should qualify for a tax benefit if the donated object was without a convincing pedigree." Even though such a regulation might take some of the speculative money out of an inflated market, problems would probably remain--at least so far as rare books and manuscripts are concerned.

Do we not need, in addition, to raise the consciousness of every librarian, every researcher, every teacher concerned with Latin American studies in this country, to the end that they will do everything possible in their own institutions to make the principles enunciated by Dr. Evans a quarter of a century ago at Monterrey a reality?

II.

Let me try out another generalization on you. The coming years will probably see increased tension among Latin Americanists everywhere as the study of Latin America becomes more and more widely carried on. Has any area of the world ever been the focus of research and writing as Latin America is today? Not only do we find a notable development in the United States since World War II, which may easily be noted by reading the Latin American Research Review, but there has also been a significant increase in Western Europe, Japan, Eastern Europe, and the Soviet Union. In Latin America, too, there has been much more attention devoted to her own culture and problems than ever before.

If this be true, why worry? Let me illustrate by an example from my own field--history. As the Irish writer Conor Cruise O'Brien has so well expressed it: "Most history is *tribal* history: written, that is to say, in terms generated by, and acceptable to, a given tribe or nation, or a group within such a tribe or nation. . . ."

Let us apply O'Brien's observations to Latin America. We find that some historians in Latin America do not know what is being written by historians outside their own country because they do not have the necessary publications or languages. And now that some of the historians outside Latin America are stressing quantitative methods and behavioristic approaches, is this gap not bound to grow? We can already see a backlash, now that many foreign social scientists of the behavioral persuasion are at work on Latin American problems, especially when they apply North American methods and concepts to Latin American society.

The Director of the Social Science Center of the University of Puerto Rico had this to say in 1970:

> . . . the vast social science research on Puerto Rico conducted by North American investigators has contributed very little to a real understanding of our society. It reflects, in general, a tendency to subordinate data to preconceptions; to design and construct categories in terms of ideal modes of conduct and behavior alien to the society under scrutiny, these categories usually lending themselves to the simplistic analysis which limits the point of reference to 'mine' and seldom uses that of 'other.' As a result, some of the basic and fundamental aspects of the society have been neglected. Among these may be included child growth and development, racial prejudice, religious practices and beliefs, the attributes of social class and status differentiation, the elements of differential class behavior, the persistence of traditional and agricultural values despite the high rate of physical change, the socio-psychological effect of sterilization on approximately thirty percent of women in their reproductive stage, the effects of mass media on people's attitudes and opinion, the religious and political conservatism of the society at large, the persistence of poverty conditions among one fourth of the families of the Island, the high rate of unemployment, the inequality of educational opportunity, the increasing social differentiation between classes despite an increasing per-capita income, the limited civil rights afforded to individuals from political minority groups, the legislative and judicial processes and the effects of living in a colonial setting. These areas are no doubt high points in the Puerto Rican culture and society and yet up to very recently were never on the agenda of behavioral science research in Puerto Rico.

We sometimes think of the Iberian world as being particularly susceptible to misunderstanding by practical Anglo-Saxons anyway, but the situation may be more universal, if we are to believe Conor Cruise

O'Brien who comments on the complicated situation which exists when one culture is studied by foreign experts:

> Similarly Africans are pleased by the interests of Africanists, and people in the Aran Islands were pleased by the interests of German philologists and American anthropologists. In all these situations there seems to be a curious delight in the feeling that the stranger knows far more than oneself and yet--being a stranger--understands nothing.

Whoever has had a student from Latin America in his class on Latin American history will appreciate this remark!

What is to be done? One step might be to make it possible for Latin American scholars to study our problems, should they wish to do so. Why do American foundations always give their funds to Latin American institutions and individuals to work on their own problems? Would Latin Americans not acquire, as some of our students do, a useful perspective on their own history by studying a foreign culture? Yet how infrequently do we find an Argentine historian at work on the history of any other country, or even neighboring Brazil or Chile or the history of England or France whose culture they have greatly admired! Even Latin American graduate students in our universities often resist studying Latin American history for they wish to study Colombian history, Cuban history, etc., depending on which country they come from. Once I managed to persuade a Mexican graduate student at Columbia University to write his M.A. thesis on Brazil, but this took a lot of doing! For his doctoral dissertation, of course, he worked on Mexico.

In a selfish way we in the United States would benefit from the insights and interpretations by foreign scholars studying our culture. Or are we so self-centered and conscious of our own strength and rectitude that we are impervious to outside influence? The anthropologist Robert Redfield wrote a brilliant essay on this topic which he entitled "Does America Need a Hearing Aid?"

In conclusion on this generalization, we have an area of the world being increasingly studied by students from different countries, from different cultures, from different value systems. I have been interested in the work of Soviet historians on Latin America since 1960 when I. R. Lavretski published in a Moscow historical review a long and rather unfavorable description and analysis of the Hispanic American Historical Review in the period under my editorship. We translated the article, and it proved to be one of the most popular issues ever of the HAHR. Then in 1965 someone whom I had never heard of before or since wrote from Moscow inviting me to join him and other Soviet historians in denouncing American intervention in the Dominican Republic. When I responded explaining that many of our professors were opposed to the United States intervention and proposed that we jointly oppose all intervention in Latin America by outside forces, he replied that none had occurred except by the U.S. and that he could not publish any such statement in the Soviet Union as it would "only evoke protests on the part of our public."

But I came to exchange publications with some Soviet scholars, and was pleased to see that they brought out in 1966 a volume of essays on Bartolomé de Las Casas commemorating the 400th anniversary of his death. Then in January, 1971, I went to Moscow, Leningrad, Prague, and Leipzig with assistance from the International Research and Exchange Board (IREX) established by the American Council to foster professional exchanges with the Soviet Union and certain other countries. The article in the Latin American Research Review in 1970 by M.S. Al'perovich had encouraged me to believe that Soviet historians were ready for professional discussion. Some of them undoubtedly are, but much remains to be done before a fairly free professional exchange of opinion can take place. We must learn a new vocabulary perhaps. Dr. Lavretski in his article in the HAHR came close to labelling Professor Arthur P. Whitaker and myself as satellites of the State Departmenc because we had lectured in Latin America under the auspices of the government cultural relations program. And Dr. Al'perovich, in calling for dialogue, referred to Soviet historians as "progressive", which rather implies that others are "unprogressive" or even "retrograde." Indeed, Dr. Al'perovich included me among the "apologists of Spanish colonialism" and those whom he labels as "representatives of reactionary bourgeois historiography." As Professor Russell H. Bartley, who translated the article for LARR, comments:

> Dr. Al'perovich, a leading Soviet historian of Latin America, appeals both to his Marxist colleagues and to their non-Marxist critics abroad for a serious exchange of views of salient problems of Latin American history. Scholarly polemic, he suggests, may contribute significantly to the elucidation of historical realities, and, consequently, is an object worthy of the historian's attention. Such debate proves useful, however, only when purged of bias and preconception. Serious criticism does not admit of gratuitous epithets, and, Al'perovich adds, should be restricted solely to questions of scholarship.
>
> The coin, of course, has two faces, and U.S. scholars are not alone guilty of representing ideological verbiage as scholarly criticism. One must not seek to refute an argument, writes Al'perovich, be labeling its author a 'Marxist' or 'anti-Marxist.' The same, we might add, holds for such unscientific qualifiers as 'reactionary,' 'progressive,' and 'bourgeois.'

We hope for more exchanges in a professional spirit and the Conference on Latin American History of the American Historical Association named last year a Committee on Professional Relations with Socialist Countries, including Cuba, to see what can be done. One of the members of this Committee, Professor Russell H. Bartley of the University of Wisconsin, Milwaukee, and one of the few Latin Americanists we have who speaks Russian fluently, is now at work preparing an English translation of representative historical articles on Latin America by Soviet scholars which we hope will be published by the University of Texas Press under the sponsorship of CLAH. . . .

We should continue to search for ways to carry on a fruitful dialogue with our colleagues in Soviet Russia. But the obstacles are real, as the report on the First Soviet-American Historical Colloquium demonstrates. The discussions in Moscow last October arranged by the Soviet Academy of Sciences and the American Historical Association were judged useful on the whole, but the future worth of such sessions will depend on the themes selected for discussion and the participants: "Most important in the immediate future is to have such topics that would lead the Soviets to feel the need for sending people who are in fact their best scholars." My own experience has not been encouraging. Five Soviet historians of Latin America were invited during the last year or so by the Conference on Latin American History, with financial support from IREX, to attend the annual sessions of the American Historical

Association and then visit some of our Latin American centers. Not one accepted.

III.

Another generalization occurs to me on an entirely different subject, and may be expressed in this way: When will Latin Americanists in the United States realize that they must pay more attention to teaching methods, teaching materials, and teaching objectives if they are to survive during the next generation? I do not wish to underestimate what has been done and is now being accomplished, so I will confine my remarks to my own field, history.

Our principal professional review, The Hispanic American Historical Review, has never covered teaching in any systematic way, and I now regret that I was not aware of the need during my own editorship 1954-1960. It was only in 1966 that the subject seemed so crucial to me that I devoted my Hackett Memorial Lecture at the University of Texas to teaching and spoke there on "Studying Latin America. The Views of an 'Old Christian'."

Subsequently from time to time some of our historians have expressed interest and sympathy, and in 1971-1972 my colleague Professor Jane Loy and I obtained a modest grant from the Office of Education for an examination of audio-visual materials for teaching the Columbus to Castro course. I am happy to be able to announce that Professor Loy's volume on this subject is now in press and will be published shortly by the Consortium on Latin American Studies Programs (CLASP) and may be purchased by writing to this organization at Box 13362 University Station, Gainesville, Florida 32601. The title is Sights and Sounds. A Guide to Motion Pictures and Music for College Courses.

Much more will have to be done, I fear, before our teachers of Latin American history in community colleges and four-year institutions are fully aware of the vital need to improve teaching. I am convinced that there are a lot of good ideas and materials being experimented with here and there, but I am equally convinced that we must have some regular forum for the discussion of teaching of Latin American history. My present plan is to try to induce the Conference on Latin American History to issue a special report every year as a regular number of its Newsletter circulated to the thousand members of CLAH. It would also be very helpful if every one of our regional associations would devote time and effort to making our teaching as effective as possible.

For we stand at an important point in the history of Latin American studies in this country. A number of outstanding centers and widely scattered individual scholars have demonstrated their capacity in research. Improvement is possible, as is the case in every field, but we are no longer a minority group with an inferiority complex in terms of scholarly accomplishment. Why cannot we recognize, therefore, that we must make a special effort to improve our teaching? Is it not clear for everyone to see that students no longer have to take any particular course--that the required course is vanishing? The lesson is obvious. Unless our courses attract students by a presentation that is both imaginative and substantial, there will be no courses in Latin American history, or they will remain as highly specialized courses taught by a vanishing elite to a few students.

Is it not now equally clear from all the discussions and reports on academic administration now being debated on every campus that teaching ability is becoming an ever-more important part of appointment and tenure decisions? I am not pessimistic about our ability to compete with history teachers in other fields--after all Latin America is an extraordinarily interesting and challenging part of the history of the world--provided our historians treat teaching as seriously as they do research.

IV.

My final generalization is likely to be the most disputed and dangerous of all! Why is it that Northamericans of many differing political and economic persuasions are so confident that they know how Latin Americans should conduct their governments? Are we still under the spell of an America that has wrought a miracle in the wilderness all by our own efforts and wisdom, and thus we tend to look upon all foreigners as laggards in the march toward a better life? When we add to this complacent conviction the idea that a beneficent and generous United States is always ready to lift up an erring brother, we have a powerful concoction which has often influenced the attitudes of our citizens as they turn their gaze southward to observe the frailties and frivolities of those so unfortunate as to be born in an Iberian, Catholic world.

This curious combination of mixed motives is well exemplified by the attitude of an American businessman who declared at the turn of the century that the U.S. is honor bound to maintain law and order in Latin America. Our motives, naturally, are manifestly pure: "Our people believe in justice, and in the liberty which carries the torch of civilization over the earth." We have done everything possible to aid those unfortunate laggard Americans to the southward: "No father ever watched over his wayward offspring with more care, sorrow, and anxiety than has the beneficent government of the U.S. observed these countries, studying by what means it could bring order out of chaos, decency out of crime."

Later on Washington felt that the way to assure stability in Latin America was to assure free elections as our policy makers and some of our professors considered this the hallmark of a truly democratic society. Today a different set of perceptions seems to guide our government, though no one knows for sure what these perceptions are. For on the one hand we have the head of the Central Intelligence Agency transmitting to the White House an offer of $1 million from ITT to oppose the election of Salvador Allende in Chile. At the same time we have some of our professors determined to have the Latin American Studies Association denounce the actions of certain Latin American governments and send investigating missions to Latin America to collect documentation on the repressive acts of governments there.

Perhaps those of us who are influenced by Latin American culture are particularly susceptible to the power of the word--the ringing resolution with assumption of absolute truth by those who pass them. Certainly the Pan American Union has passed over the years such a multitude of grandiose declarations so far removed from the reality of things that one can only apply the words of Bartolomé de Las Casas to the Requerimiento, that curious manifesto embodying Spanish convictions on religious and political theory devised by a royal lawyer in 1513 to be read, in Spanish of course, to the New World Indians before carrying on war against them. Las Casas confessed that in considering the way this legal document was used he could not decide whether to laugh or to weep. Since 1889 the Pan American Union, whose imminent demise has been predicted so often that it sometimes surprises one to find it still functioning in Washington, has boldly adopted resolutions to govern continental relations on almost every problem under the sun: library exchanges, economic cooperation, the Liberator Simón Bolívar, establishment of a "family income", uniform laws throughout the continent, tourist travel; it has also in solemn convention recommended "special attention to the problem of indigenous women", technical assistance, information courses for workers rewarding their rights and duties, asylum, aggression, plant and sanitary control, obligatory leave of absence for prospective mothers, and a multitude of other matters. In 1938 the hope was expressed "that when recourse is had to war in any other part of the world respect be given to those human rights not necessarily involved in the conflict, to humanitarian sentiments, and to the spiritual and material inheritance of civilization." Back in 1930, there was even a tribute to the Department of State.

Do specialists devoted to the history of other areas of the world feel it incumbent upon them to denounce what they consider wrong-doing in those areas? Would we really welcome it were Japanese or Soviet historians concerned with the study of our history to regularly denounce the treatment of minorities, Angela Davis, corruption in government, intervention in Latin America, the Vietnam war, etc.? Has opposition abroad on such matters ever had much influence on the United States? There can be a reaction, yes, as when President Nixon refuses to receive a Swedish Ambassador in Washington or send one to Stockholm because he does not like the speeches of the Swedish Prime Minister on Vietnam. But President Nixon does not change his policy.

And why don't the Russian specialists in this country feel impelled to send off telegrams every time a Soviet scholar is sent to a mental hospital for his courage to dissent? Or those studying Africa denounce what they believe to be crimes in that great continent? Or our Middle East experts condemn either Israel or the Arab world, depending on which side they are convinced is right?

Perhaps the American continent is different, in the old Boltonian sense, or in the way that orators on Pan American Day declaim on the subject of a new people in a new world creating a new and hitherto undreamed of perfect civilization. Or are Latin Americanists more sensitive to injustices abroad and more courageous in speaking out against them?

It has also been felt by some of our historians that when a historian is put in jail unjustly by some repressive Latin American government historians in the United States should condemn this wrong by passing a resolution. If a sociologist or even an economist is similarly treated we don't seem to care so much.

Let us recognize that this is a gut issue--that no one has the complete truth on these tangled problems often sunk deep in history. Let us also make plain that every individual in this country has a right to make his opinion known, and that among any group, especially among Latin Americanists, there will be found a variety of opinions. But should we not attempt to preserve our professional associations, like the Conference on Latin American History and the Latin American Studies Association, from engaging in yearly extravaganzas at their business sessions on political resolutions? For the foreseeable future some governments in Latin America will be engaging in activities which some of us will condemn. Should we attempt to utilize our professional associations to express our opposition to torture, repression, and other unpleasant facts of life in Latin America, which are found in many parts of the world? Some of my colleagues, including some of my former students, do believe that such political resolutions should be passed. Perhaps the famous generation gap is involved here. At any rate, I continue to believe that such political resolutions are generally contraproductive, that they imply a superior moral position which we have no right to assume, and that they may even be at times a kind of patronizing intervention which a number of our colleagues in Latin America will not welcome. At the very least, we should have as full a debate as possible on these resolutions with the decision of the professional association made on the basis of a mail vote in which all members have an opportunity to participate.

Such then are my "genuine generalizations." I am sure that many persons present have other declarations on these and similar subjects, and I hope that during these and other meetings of Latin Americanists there will be opportunities to discuss them. To return to the Aztecs, even though they believed that on reaching the age of seventy everyone should be free to drink as they pleased, I do not remember that they also held to that later maxim expressed in the phrase *in vino veritas*.

CHAPTER 45.

WHO SHOULD OWN PRESIDENTIAL PAPERS?

During 1974 I prepared a brief note for each issue of the American Historical Association Newsletter, designed to bring matters of current interest to the attention of historians and to diminish the distance between the thousands of members of the Association and their president. My last contribution appeared in the December, 1974, Newsletter and focussed on a problem of hot and continuing interest, presidential papers and tapes.

AHA Newsletter, XII, No. 9 (December, 1974), 3-4. Reprinted by permission of the American Historical Association.

The President's Corner: Who Should Own Presidential Papers?

Farewell Note

This is my last piece for the Corner, and like all the others it states my personal opinion on issues before the association. Eventually the Council, increasingly a yeasty body eager to debate problems and policies, will reach decisions. Meanwhile, it is essential that members make known their views through the Newsletter and elsewhere.

The Council took an important step at its September meeting to associate itself with those groups in and out of Congress that are concerned with the present legal arrangements for the Nixon tapes and other presidential documents. The executive director, as he reports in this issue, has moved vigorously to make clear that the AHA is eager to do everything in its power to help resolve the issues. Let us, in addition, press forward at full speed to seek funds for a professional examination of all the problems involved, perhaps in cooperation with the Organization of American Historians and the Society of American Archivists. Fortunately the report commissioned by the AHA in 1967 and prepared by H. G. Jones will provide an excellent basis.[1]

What more could and should be done? We cannot assume that historians, much less the general public, are necessarily familiar with all the complicated issues involved. Richard W. Leopold, chairman of the committee which performed yeoman service in connection with the charges against the Roosevelt Library, discovered in 1970 that "there was an enormous amount of ignorance among the profession regarding presidential papers." Would it not be useful, therefore, to encourage a national debate on such questions as:

What kinds of historical documentation are we talking about?

Oliver Wendell Holmes entitled his presidential address to the Society of American Archivists in 1959: "Public Papers--Who Knows What They Are?"[2] Dr. Holmes concluded that no one has the answer yet, urged more research on the meaning of the adjective "public," and conjectured that the concept of "public records" was expanded during the days when the United States was being established as a nation where the people were sovereign. He even suggested that this new concept may have been exported to Europe and "may have been responsible in part for the wholly new attitude toward archives displayed by the Revolutionary leaders, who, in establishing the National Archives of France, decreed that the records belong to the people."[3]

But what records are to be included? Is it possible to distinguish, for example, between the personal or party files of a president and those official papers that obviously belong to the nation? Perhaps we should not try to separate them. Professor Leopold believes that we should aim at establishing "the principle that presidents will deposit

1. Houston G. Jones, The Records of a Nation, Their Management, Preservation and Use (New York, 1969).
2. Printed in The American Archivist, 23, (1960), 3-26.
3. Ibid., 23-24.

their papers in a public archive, and hope that each one will refrain from trying to separate his private papers from his public ones."[4]

Is the 1955 Act of Congress establishing presidential libraries adequate today?

This act does not specifically declare that presidents own their papers, but the implication is there. Should there not be a definite decision on this basic point, after due debate and deliberation? Should not improvements be considered in the administration of presidential libraries that would still preserve the impressive benefits of the present system?

Has not the time arrived to make another attempt to establish the National Archives as a national cultural institution as independent as the Library of Congress?

The AHA, through its leaders such as John Franklin Jameson and Waldo G. Leland, was largely responsible, after a long campaign, for the establishment of the National Archives, and in more recent years Julian Boyd struggled to have this great repository made independent of politics. Yet today we find the National Archives is still administratively subject to the General Services Administration. Should we not object today as the future Archivist of the United States Robert H. Bahmer did in 1949 "to having records and archives grouped with office desks, lamps, rugs, and other items of supply as though there is one fraternity of interest or identity in the administration of the one with the other."[5] The bill (S.4016) introduced by Senator Nelson, with the support of such powerful figures as Senators Ervin, Muskie, Percy, Ribicoff, and Stevenson would place the Nixon tapes in the hands of the GSA administrator, a political appointee in one of the most political agencies in Washington. Moreover, this official, not the archivist of the United States, would have the authority to determine what were "reasonable regulations" for access to the tapes. No matter what law Congress passes on the tapes or other presidential documentation, if its administration is turned over to a political official concerned with routine administrative matters, historians and the public might be seriously hampered in their access to public records. Is this not a fundamental flaw?

The present GSA administrator, Arthur F. Sampson, was the official who signed the agreement on the Nixon tapes and papers that has been so widely and so properly criticized.

Who is to decide?

The numerous bills being put in the congressional hopper suggest that Congress believes it has power in the disposal of presidential papers. But the Jones report states: "It is clear that the national legislature cannot regulate the actions of the constitutionally independent Chief Executive in respect to the records of his office."[6] But neither does the report conclude that

> presidential records are the private property of the incumbent whether in or out of office. On the contrary, it would seem that

4. The quotations from Professor Leopold come from his letter to me dated November 4, 1974, and are reproduced with his permission.
5. As quoted in Jones, The Records of a Nation, 40.
6. Ibid., 161.

> if any proposition collides with constitutional principles it is that the President should be exempted from the legal obligation that rests upon all other officials in government to protect and refrain from appropriating to personal use records produced or received in custody by virtue of the exercise of a public office. To assume otherwise would be to vest in the highest officer of the land, or in his heirs or descendants, the right to sell, to destroy, to disclose, to refuse to disclose, or otherwise to dispose of documents of the highest official nature involving information that, if prematurely or irresponsibly revealed, could not only wreck private lives but also vitally endanger the security of the nation.[7]

We are--or we should be--on the verge of a historic decision on what constitutes public records and on access to them for historical purposes. Can we not all agree that the custody and use of these materials are matters of such importance to the people of the United States that the decision should be taken only after detailed study and national debate? Should we not determine to bring these issues to the attention of President Ford in 1975, and to invite every historical society in the nation to join with us?

---

7. *Ibid.*, 161-162.

PART IX

A BIBLIOGRAPHICAL NOTE AND INDEX

A BIBLIOGRAPHICAL NOTE

Most of the articles published in this volume are related to other writings of mine in other places. Here is a selection of such items, which often shed additional light on some aspects of the topic under discussion.

A BIBLIOGRAPHICAL NOTE

I. The Spanish Struggle for Justice in the Conquest of America

"Pope Paul III and the American Indians", Harvard Theological Review, XXX (1937), 65-102.

"A aplicacão do requerimiento na América Espanhola", Revista do Brasil, anno 1, 3ª phase, no. 3 (Rio de Janeiro, 1938), 321-248.

"Las Leyes de Burgos de 1512 y 1513", Anuario de historia argentina, 1942 (Buenos Aires, 1943), 33-56.

"The Colonization of the New World with Labourers (1521)", Bulletin of Spanish Studies, XXIV (Liverpool, 1947), 102-107.

La lucha por la justicia en la conquista de América (Buenos Aires: Editorial Sudamericana, 1949), 571 pp.

The Sturggle for Justice in the Spanish Conquest of America (Philadelphia: University of Pennsylvania Press, 1949), 217 pp.

"La aportación de Fray Juan de Zumárraga a la cultura mexicana", Cuadernos americanos, año 8, no. 4 (Mexico City, 1949), 163-171.

"'A Deadly Enemy of the Indians': The Royal Historian Gonzalo Fernández de Oviedo y Valdés", in Homenaje al Profesor Guillermo Feliú Cruz (Santiago de Chile: Editorial Andrés Bello, 1973), 523-536.

II. Bartolomé de Las Casas

Las teorías politicas de Bartolomé de Las Casas (Buenos Aires: Instituto de Investigaciones Históricas de la Universidad Nacional, 1935), 65 pp.

Ed., with Agustín Millares Carlo, Cuerpo de documentos inéditos del siglo XVI sobre los derechos de España en las Indias y las Filipinas (Mexico: Fonde de Cultura Económica, 1943), 364 pp.

Bartolomé de Las Casas: An Interpretation of his Life and Writings (The Hague: Martinus Nijhoff, 1951), 102 pp.

Bartolomé de Las Casas, Historian. (Gainesville: University of Florida Press, 1952), 125 pp.

Bartolomé de Las Casas, Bookman, Scholar and Propagandist (Philadelphia: University of Pennsylvania Press, 1952), 119 pp.

"What Still Needs to be Done on the Life and Works of Bartolomé de Las Casas (1474-1566)", Estudios Hispánicos. Homenaje a Archer M. Huntington (Wellesley, Mass., 1952), 229-232.

"Bartolomé de Las Casas and the Spanish Empire in America: Four Centuries of Misunderstanding", Proceedings of the American Philosophical Society, 97, No. 1 (Philadelphia, 1953), 26-30.

Ed., with Manuel Giménez Fernández, Bartolomé de Las Casas, 1474-1566. Bibliografía crítica y cuerpo de materiales para el estudio de su vida, escritos, actuación y polémicas que suscitaron durante cuatro siglos. (Santiago: Fondo Histórico y Bibliográfico José Toribio Medina, 1953), 394 pp.

"Was Las Casas a Scholar?", Miscelánea de estudios dedicados a Fernando Ortiz, II (Havana, 1956), 785-788.

Aristotle and the American Indians (London: Hollis and Carter, 1959), 164 pp.

Estudios sobre Fray Bartolomé de Las Casas y sobre la lucha por la justicia en la conquista española de América (Caracas: Universidad Central de Venezuela, 1968), 428 pp.
All Mankind Is One. A Study of the Disputation Between Bartolomé de Las Casas and Juan Ginés de Sepúlveda on the Religious and Intellectual Capacity of the American Indians (DeKalb: Northern Illinois University Press, 1974), 205 pp.

III. The Villa Imperial de Potosí

The Imperial City of Potosí: An Unwritten Chapter in the History of Spanish America (The Hague: Martinus Nijhoff, 1956), 60 pp.
"The 1608 Fiestas in Potosí", Boletín del Instituto Riva-Agüero, No. 3 (Lima, 1957), 107-128.
Ed., Luis Capoche: Relación general de la Villa Imperial de Potosí (Madrid: Biblioteca de Autores Españoles, 1959), tomo CXXII, 221 pp.
"Um misterio bibliográfico: A 'Historia de Potosí' de Antonio de Acosta", Revista portuguesa de história, VIII (Coimbra, 1961), 285-290.
"Pedro Peralta de Barnuevo y Bartolomé Arzáns de Orsúa y Vela", Revista histórica, XXVII (Lima, 1965), 70-81.
Ed., with Gunnar Mendoza, Historia de la Villa Imperial de Potosí por Bartolomé Arzáns de Orsúa y Vela, 3 vols. (Providence, R.I.: Brown University Press, 1965), 407, 501, 556 pp.
Bartolomé Arzáns de Orsúa y Vela's History of Potosí (Providence, R.I.: Brown University Press, 1965), 81 pp.

IV. Spanish Viceroys in Mexico and Peru

"Viceroy Francisco de Toledo and the Just Titles of Spain to the Inca Empire", The Americas, III (Academy of American Franciscan History, Washington, D.C., 1946), 3-19.
Ed., con la colaboración de Celso Rodríguez, Los virreyes españoles en América durante el gobierno durante la Casa de Austria. México, Vol. I (Madrid: Biblioteca de Autores Españoles, 1976), tomo CCLXXIII.
Ed., con la colaboración de Celso Rodríguez, Guía de las fuentes en el Archivo General de Indias para el estudio de la administración virreinal española en México y el Perú, 3 vols. (Cologne, 1977), Lateinamerikanische Forschungen, 7-9. Institute of Iberoamerican Studies, University of Cologne.

V. Teaching and Teachers

Ed., Readings in Latin American History. Selected Articles from The Hispanic American Historical Review, 2 vols. (New York: Thomas Y. Crowell, 1966), 336, 311 pp.
Modern Latin America. Continent in Ferment, 2 vols., revised and enlarged. (Princeton: Van Nostrand Co., 1967), 256, 250 pp.
Contemporary Latin America: A Short History (Princeton: Van Nostrand Co., 1968), 532 pp.
"The Quiet Revolution", The History Teacher, II (University of Notre Dame, 1969), 14-17.

"The Coming Revolution in the Teaching of Latin American History", *Social Studies*, III, No. 6 (1970), 608-612.

Ed., *The History of Latin American Civilization: Sources and Interpretations*, 2 vols. Revised ed. (Boston: Little, Brown & Co., 1973), 555, 672 pp.

Ed., *Latin America. A Historical Reader* (Boston: Little, Brown & Co., 1974), 671 pp.

VI. Other Topics in Latin American History

"Dos Palabras on Antonio de Ulloa and the Noticias Secretas", *The Hispanic American Historical Review*, XVI (1936), 479-514.

"Gilberto Freyre: Vida y obra. Bibliografía--antología", *Revista hispánica moderna*, año V (New York, 1939), No. 2, 97-119.

"A Biblioteca do Congresso de Washington e suas relacões culturais com São Paulo", *Vida intelectual nos Estados Unidos*, I (São Paulo, 1941), 1-8.

"The Latin American Bibliographical Activities of the Library of Congress, with Hints for Future Developments in this Field", *College and Research Libraries* (June, 1942), 235-240.

"The Development of Latin American Studies in the United States, 1939-1945", *The Americas*, IV (Academy of American Franciscan History, Washington, D.C., 1947), 32-64.

"¿Cómo debe estudiar la historia del derecho indiano?", *Homenaje para Jorge Basadre* (Lima, 1977).

VIII. Contemporary Affairs

"Latin America: Soil for Democracy?", *Harpers* (June, 1941), 46-57.

"A Goose on the Ramparts", *Survey Graphic*, XXX (New York), 142, 203-206.

Is the Good Neighbor Policy a Success? (Washington, D.C.: Government Printing Office, 1945), The American Historical Association, for the War Department. GI Roundtable Series. 46 pp.

"Friendship Now with Latin America", *The Virginia Quarterly Review*, XXII (Charlottesville, 1946), 498-518.

"Good Neighbor Realism", *The Virginia Quarterly Review*, XXIV (Charlottesville, 1948), 294-297.

With Kate Gilbert Hanke, "The Past Is Prologue", *The Junior Historian*, XIII (Texas State Historical Association, Austin, 1952), No. 3.

"Typologies of Academic Pollution in the Good Neighborhood", *Latin American Studies Association Newsletter*, III, No. 3 (1972), 39-43.

INDEX